Leadership

Ninth Edition

To Madison, Isla, Sullivan, and Edison

Sara Miller McCune founded SAGE Publishing in 1965 to support the dissemination of usable knowledge and educate a global community. SAGE publishes more than 1000 journals and over 600 new books each year, spanning a wide range of subject areas. Our growing selection of library products includes archives, data, case studies and video. SAGE remains majority owned by our founder and after her lifetime will become owned by a charitable trust that secures the company's continued independence.

Los Angeles | London | New Delhi | Singapore | Washington DC | Melbourne

Leadership
Theory and Practice

Ninth Edition

Peter G. Northouse

Western Michigan University

Los Angeles | London | New Delhi
Singapore | Washington DC | Melbourne

FOR INFORMATION:

SAGE Publications, Inc.
2455 Teller Road
Thousand Oaks, California 91320
E-mail: order@sagepub.com

SAGE Publications Ltd.
1 Oliver's Yard
55 City Road
London EC1Y 1SP
United Kingdom

SAGE Publications India Pvt. Ltd.
B 1/I 1 Mohan Cooperative Industrial Area
Mathura Road, New Delhi 110 044
India

SAGE Publications Asia-Pacific Pte. Ltd.
18 Cross Street #10-10/11/12
China Square Central
Singapore 048423

Acquisitions Editor: Maggie Stanley
Content Development Editor: Lauren Gobell
Editorial Assistant: Sarah Wilson
Production Editor: Tracy Buyan
Copy Editor: Melinda Masson
Typesetter: C&M Digitals (P) Ltd.
Proofreader: Jennifer Grubba
Indexer: Integra
Cover Designer: Gail Buschman
Marketing Manager: Jennifer Jones

Printed in Canada

Library of Congress Cataloging-in-Publication Data

Names: Northouse, Peter Guy, author.

Title: Leadership : theory and practice / Peter G. Northouse, Western Michigan University.

Description: Ninth Edition. | Thousand Oaks : SAGE Publishing, 2021. | Revised edition of the author's Leadership, [2019] | Includes bibliographical references and index.

Identifiers: LCCN 2020045038 | ISBN 9781544397566 (paperback) | ISBN 9781071836149 | 9781071834466 (epub) | ISBN 9781071834473 (epub) | ISBN 9781071834480 (pdf)

Subjects: LCSH: Leadership. | Leadership—Case studies.

Classification: LCC HM1261 .N67 2021 | DDC 303.3/4—dc23
LC record available at https://lccn.loc.gov/2020045038

This book is printed on acid-free paper.

21 22 23 24 25 10 9 8 7 6 5 4 3 2 1

Brief Contents

Detailed Contents

Preface

As this ninth edition of *Leadership: Theory and Practice* goes to press, the number of confirmed deaths worldwide from the COVID-19 pandemic is over 1 million. The horrific nature of this pandemic has challenged societies on a global scale and highlights for all of us the importance of understanding how leadership works and the value of leadership in times of crisis. To that end, this edition is written with the objective of bridging the gap between the often-simplistic popular approaches to leadership and the more abstract theoretical approaches. Like the previous editions, this edition reviews and analyzes a selected number of leadership theories, giving special attention to how each theoretical approach can be applied in real-world organizations. In essence, my purpose is to explore how leadership theory can inform and direct the way leadership is practiced.

NEW TO THIS EDITION

First and foremost, this edition includes a new chapter on *inclusive leadership*, which examines the nature of inclusive leadership, its underpinnings, and how it functions. Authored by two scholars in the areas of diversity and inclusion, Donna Chrobot-Mason and Quinetta Roberson, the chapter presents definitions, a model, and the latest research and applications of this emerging approach to leadership. Underscored in the chapter is how inclusion is an integration of two factors: (1) an individual's connectedness to others and (2) a person's uniqueness. Finally, this new chapter provides case studies and leadership instruments to explore how to practice inclusive leadership in a variety of contexts.

In addition to the discussion of inclusive leadership in Chapter 12, this edition includes an expanded analysis of leadership and morality—the "Hitler Question." It discusses the perplexing question of whether the process of leadership is inherently a *moral process* that is concerned with the common good or whether it is a *neutral process* that is not dependent on promoting the common good.

Another new feature in this edition is the inclusion of a real-world case study in each chapter. Because it is important to acknowledge and see real leaders exhibiting the behaviors and concepts behind the leadership approaches discussed in the text, the third case study in each chapter profiles a leader that epitomizes the chapter's concepts. These new real-world case studies include profiles from across the globe including a mental health program utilizing grandmothers in Africa, an Italian energy company, and New Zealand prime minister Jacinda Ardern.

In addition, there are profiles of leaders responding to crisis including closing a college and battling COVID-19 on a U.S. aircraft carrier.

This edition retains many special features from previous editions but has been updated to include new research findings, figures and tables, and everyday applications for many leadership topics including leader–member exchange theory, transformational and authentic leadership, team leadership, the labyrinth of women's leadership, and historical definitions of leadership. In addition, it includes an expanded look at the relationship between emotional intelligence and leadership. The format of this edition parallels the format used in earlier editions. As with previous editions, the overall goal of *Leadership: Theory and Practice* is to advance our understanding of the many different approaches to leadership and ways to practice it more effectively.

SPECIAL FEATURES

Although this text presents and analyzes a wide range of leadership research, every attempt has been made to present the material in a clear, concise, and interesting manner. Reviewers of the book have consistently commented that clarity is one of its major strengths. In addition to the writing style, several other features of the book help make it user-friendly.

- Each chapter follows the same format: It is structured to include first theory and then practice.

- Every chapter contains a discussion of the strengths and criticisms of the approach under consideration, and assists readers in determining the relative merits of each approach.

- Each chapter includes an application section that discusses the practical aspects of the approach and how it could be used in today's organizational settings.

- Three case studies are provided in each chapter to illustrate common leadership issues and dilemmas. Thought-provoking questions follow each case study, helping readers to interpret the case.

- A questionnaire is provided in each of the chapters to help readers apply the approach to their own leadership style or setting.

- Figures and tables illustrate the content of the theory and make the ideas more meaningful.

Through these special features, every effort has been made to make this text substantive, understandable, and practical.

AUDIENCE

This book provides both an in-depth presentation of leadership theory and a discussion of how it applies to real-life situations. Thus, it is intended for undergraduate and graduate classes in management, leadership studies, business, educational leadership, public administration, nursing and allied health, social work, criminal justice, industrial and organizational psychology, communication, religion, agricultural education, political and military science, and training and development. It can also be utilized outside of academia by small and large companies, as well as federal government agencies, to aid in developing the learner's leadership skills. It is particularly well suited as a supplementary text for core organizational behavior courses or as an overview text within MBA curricula. This book would also be useful as a text in student activities, continuing education, in-service training, and other leadership-development programs.

TEACHING RESOURCES

This text includes an array of instructor teaching materials designed to save you time and to help you keep students engaged. To learn more, visit **sagepub.com** or contact your SAGE representative at **sagepub.com/findmyrep**.

Acknowledgments

Many people directly or indirectly contributed to the development of the ninth edition of *Leadership: Theory and Practice*. First, I would like to acknowledge my editor, Maggie Stanley, and her talented team at SAGE Publications (Lauren Gobell and Sarah Wilson), who have contributed in so many different ways to the quality and success of this book. For their very capable work during the production phase, I would like to thank the copy editor, Melinda Masson, and the project editor, Tracy Buyan. In her own unique way, each of these people made valuable contributions to the ninth edition.

I would like to thank the following reviewers for their valuable contributions to the development of this manuscript:

Sidney R. Castle, *National University*

Jason Headrick, *Texas Tech University*

Michelle Jefferson, *Rutgers, The State University of New Jersey*

Gary F. Kohut, *The University of North Carolina at Charlotte*

R. Jeffery Maxfield, *Utah Valley University*

Daniel F. Nehring, *Morehead State University*

Michael Pace, *Texas A&M University*

Heather I. Scott, *Kennesaw State University*

Charlotte Silvers, *Texas Tech University*

Elena Svetieva, *University of Colorado Colorado Springs*

Mark Vrooman, *Utica College*

Isaac Wanasika, *University of Northern Colorado*

Rosie Watwood, *Concordia University Texas*

I would like to thank the following reviewers for their valuable contributions to the development of the eighth-edition manuscript:

Sandra Arumugam-Osburn, *St. Louis Community College–Forest Park*

Rob Elkington, *University of Ontario Institute of Technology*

Abimbola Farinde, *Columbia Southern University*

Belinda S. Han, *Utah Valley University*

Deborah A. Johnson-Blake, *Liberty University*

Benjamin Kutsyuruba, *Queen's University*

Chenwei Liao, *Michigan State University*

Heather J. Mashburn, *Appalachian State University*

Comfort Okpala, *North Carolina A&T State University*

Ric Rohm, *Southeastern University*

Patricia Dillon Sobczak, *Virginia Commonwealth University*

Victor S. Sohmen, *Drexel University*

Brigitte Steinheider, *University of Oklahoma-Tulsa*

Robert Waris, *University of Missouri–Kansas City*

Sandi Zeljko, *Lake-Sumter State College*

Mary Zonsius, *Rush University*

I would like to thank the following reviewers for their valuable contributions to the development of the seventh-edition manuscript:

Hamid Akbari, *Winona State University*

Meera Alagaraja, *University of Louisville*

Mel Albin, *Excelsior College*

Thomas Batsching, *Reutlingen University*

Cheryl Beeler, *Angelo State University*

Julie Bjorkman, *Benedictine University*

Mark D. Bowman, *Methodist University*

Dianne Burns, *University of Manchester*

Eric Buschlen, *Central Michigan University*

Steven Bryant, *Drury University*

Daniel Calhoun, *Georgia Southern University*

David Conrad, *Augsburg College*

Joyce Cousins, *Royal College of Surgeons in Ireland*

Denise Danna, *LSUHSC School of Nursing*

S. Todd Deal, *Georgia Southern University*

Caroline S. Fulmer, *University of Alabama*

Brad Gatlin, *John Brown University*

Greig A. Gjerdalen, *Capilano University*

Andrew Gonzales, *University of California, Irvine*

Decker B. Hains, *Western Michigan University*

Amanda Hasty, *University of Colorado-Denver*

Carl Holschen, *Missouri Baptist University*

Kiran Ismail, *St. John's University*

Irma Jones, *University of Texas at Brownsville*

Michele D. Kegley, *University of Cincinnati, Blue Ash College*

Jeanea M. Lambeth, *Pittsburg State University*

David Lees, *University of Derby*

David S. McClain, *University of Hawaii at Manoa*

Carol McMillan, *New School University*

Richard Milter, *Johns Hopkins University*

Christopher Neck, *Arizona State University–Tempe*

Keeok Park, *University of La Verne*

Richard Parkman, *University of Plymouth*

Lori M. Pindar, *Clemson University*

Chaminda S. Prelis, *University of Dubuque*

Casey Rae, *George Fox University*

Noel Ronan, *Waterford Institute of Technology*

Louis Rubino, *California State University, Northridge*

Shadia Sachedina, *Baruch College (School of Public Affairs)*

Harriet L. Schwartz, *Carlow University*

Kelli K. Smith, *University of Nebraska-Lincoln*

David Swenson, *The College of St. Scholastica*

Danny L. Talbot, *Washington State University*

Robert L. Taylor, *University of Louisville*

Precious Taylor-Clifton, *Cambridge College*

John Tummons, *University of Missouri*

Kristi Tyran, *Western Washington University*

Tamara Von George, *Granite State College*

Natalie Walker, *Seminole State College*

William Welch, *Bowie State University*

David E. Williams, *Texas Tech University*

Tony Wohlers, *Cameron University*

Sharon A. Wulf, *Worcester Polytechnic Institute School of Business*

Alec Zama, *Grand View University*

Xia Zhao, *California State University, Dominguez Hills*

In addition, I would like to thank, for their exceptional work on the leadership profile tool and the ancillaries, Isolde Anderson (Hope College), John Baker (Western Kentucky University), and Eric Buschlen.

A very special acknowledgment goes to Laurel Northouse who has been my number-one critic and supporter from the inception of the book in 1990 to the present. In addition, I am especially grateful to Marie Lee for her exceptional editing and guidance throughout this project. For her comprehensive literature reviews and chapter updates, I would like to thank Terri Scandura.

For his review of and comments on the morality and leadership section, I am indebted to Joseph Curtin (Northeastern University). I would like to thank Kate McCain (University of Nebraska–Lincoln) and Jason Headrick (University of Nebraska–Lincoln) for their contributions to the adaptive leadership chapter, John Baker for his contributions to the team leadership chapter, Jenny Steiner for her case study on adaptive leadership, Jeff Brink for sharing his story about transformational leadership, and Kassandra Gutierrez for her case study on authentic leadership. In addition, I would like to acknowledge Barbara Russell (Chemeketa Community College) for her research and writing of many of the new real-world case studies.

Finally, I would like to thank the many undergraduate and graduate students whom I have taught through the years. Their ongoing feedback has helped clarify my thinking about leadership and encouraged me to make plain the practical implications of leadership theories.

About the Author

Peter G. Northouse, PhD, is Professor Emeritus of Communication in the School of Communication at Western Michigan University. *Leadership: Theory and Practice* is the best-selling academic textbook on leadership in the world and has been translated into 16 languages. In addition to authoring publications in professional journals, he is the author of *Introduction to Leadership: Concepts and Practice* (now in its fifth edition) and co-author of *Leadership Case Studies in Education* (now in its third edition) and *Health Communication: Strategies for Health Professionals* (now in its third edition). His scholarly and curricular interests include models of leadership, leadership assessment, ethical leadership, and leadership and group dynamics. For more than 30 years, he has taught undergraduate and graduate courses in leadership, interpersonal communication, and organizational communication on both the undergraduate and graduate levels. Currently, he is a consultant and lecturer on trends in leadership research, leadership development, and leadership education. He holds a doctorate in speech communication from the University of Denver, and master's and bachelor's degrees in communication education from Michigan State University.

About the Contributors

Donna Chrobot-Mason, PhD, is an associate professor and director of the Center for Organizational Leadership at the University of Cincinnati (UC). She is director of UC Women Lead, a 10-month executive leadership program for high-potential women at UC. Her research and consulting work has spanned two decades and centers on leadership across differences and strategies for creating organizations that support diversity, equity, and inclusion and foster intergroup collaboration. She has published nearly 40 articles and scholarly works in journals such as the *Journal of Management*, *The Leadership Quarterly*, *Journal of Organizational Behavior*, and *Group and Organization Management*. She has served on the editorial review board for the *Journal of Management*, *Personnel Psychology*, and the *Journal of Business and Psychology*. Her book (co-authored with Chris Ernst), *Boundary Spanning Leadership: Six Practices for Solving Problems, Driving Innovation, and Transforming Organizations*, was published by McGraw-Hill Professional in 2010. Dr. Chrobot-Mason has been invited to address numerous audiences including the Brookings Institute, Federal Bureau of Investigation, Environmental Protection Agency, Internal Revenue Service, Catholic Health Partners, and the International Leadership Association. She has consulted with numerous organizations including Briggs and Stratton, Dayton Public Schools, Boehringer-Ingelheim, Emory University, Milacron, and Forest City Enterprises. She holds a PhD and master's degree in applied psychology from the University of Georgia.

Crystal L. Hoyt is a professor and associate dean for academic affairs, and holds the Thorsness Endowed Chair in Ethical Leadership at the Jepson School of Leadership Studies at the University of Richmond. Her research explores the role of belief systems, such as mindsets, self-efficacy, stereotypes, and political ideologies, in a range of social issues including stigma and discrimination, ethical failures in leadership, leadership and educational achievement gaps, public health, and wealth inequality. Dr. Hoyt's research appears in journals such as *Psychological Science, Journal of Experimental and Social Psychology, Personality and Social Psychology Bulletin, Group Processes & Intergroup Relations*, and *The Leadership Quarterly*. She has published over 70 journal articles and book chapters and has co-edited three books. Dr. Hoyt is an associate editor at the *Journal of Experimental Psychology: General*, is on the editorial boards at *Leadership Quarterly* and *Sex Roles*, and has served as a reviewer for over 45 journals.

Susan E. Kogler Hill (PhD, University of Denver, 1974) is Professor Emeritus and former chair of the School of Communication at Cleveland State University. Her research and consulting have been in the areas of interpersonal and organizational communication. She specializes in group leadership, teamwork, empowerment, and mentoring. She is author of a text titled *Improving Interpersonal Competence*. In addition, she has written book chapters and published articles in many professional journals.

Quinetta Roberson, PhD, is the John A. Hannah Distinguished Professor of Management and Psychology at Michigan State University. Prior to her current position, she was an Endowed Chair at Villanova University and a tenured professor at Cornell University. She has been a visiting scholar at universities on six continents and has more than 20 years of global experience in teaching courses, facilitating workshops, and advising organizations on diversity and inclusion, leadership, and talent management. Dr. Roberson has published over 40 scholarly journal articles and book chapters and edited a *Handbook of Diversity in the Workplace* (2013). Her research and consulting work focus on developing organizational capability and enhancing effectiveness through the strategic management of people, particularly diverse work teams, and is informed by her background in finance, having worked as a financial analyst and small business development consultant prior to obtaining her doctorate. She earned her PhD in organizational behavior from the University of Maryland and holds undergraduate and graduate degrees in finance.

Stefanie Simon is an assistant professor in the Department of Psychology at Siena College. She earned her PhD in social psychology from Tulane University and was the Robert A. Oden Jr. Postdoctoral Fellow for Innovation in the Liberal Arts at Carleton College before joining the faculty at Siena. Her research centers on the psychology of diversity, with a focus on prejudice, discrimination, and leadership. In her work, she focuses on the perspective of the *target* of prejudice and discrimination, as well as the perspective of the *perpetrator* of prejudice and discrimination. She is particularly interested in how leaders of diverse groups can promote positive intergroup relations and reduce inequality in society. She has published articles in various psychology and leadership journals including *The Leadership Quarterly*, *Group Processes & Intergroup Relations*, *Social Psychological and Personality Science*, and *Sex Roles*.

Introduction

Leadership is a highly sought-after and highly valued commodity. In the 25 years since the first edition of this book was published, the public has become increasingly captivated by the idea of leadership. People continue to ask themselves and others what makes good leaders. As individuals, they seek more information on how to become effective leaders. As a result, bookstore shelves are filled with popular books about leaders and how to be a leader. Many people believe that leadership is a way to improve their personal, social, and professional lives. Corporations seek those with leadership ability because they believe these individuals bring special assets to their organizations and, ultimately, improve the bottom line. Academic institutions throughout the country have responded by offering programs in leadership studies, including at the master's and doctoral levels.

In addition, leadership has gained the attention of researchers worldwide. Leadership research is increasing dramatically, and findings underscore that there is a wide variety of different theoretical approaches to explain the complexities of the leadership process (e.g., Bass, 2008; Bryman, 1992; Bryman, Collinson, Grint, Jackson, & Uhl-Bien, 2011; Day & Antonakis, 2012; Dinh et al., 2014; J. Gardner, 1990; W. Gardner et al., 2020; Hickman, 2016; Mumford, 2006; Rost, 1991). Some researchers conceptualize leadership as a trait or as a behavior, whereas others view leadership from an information-processing perspective or relational standpoint.

Leadership has been studied using both qualitative and quantitative methods in many contexts, including small groups, therapeutic groups, and large organizations. In recent years, this research has included experiments designed to explain how leadership influences follower attitudes and performance (Podsakoff & Podsakoff, 2019) in hopes of increasing the practical usefulness of leadership research.

Collectively, the research findings on leadership provide a picture of a process that is far more sophisticated and complex than the often-simplistic view presented in some of the popular books on leadership.

This book treats leadership as a complex process having multiple dimensions. Based on the research literature, this text provides an in-depth description and application of many different approaches to leadership. Our emphasis is on how theory can inform the practice of leadership. In this book, we describe each theory and then explain how the theory can be used in real situations.

LEADERSHIP DEFINED

There are many ways to finish the sentence "Leadership is . . ." In fact, as Stogdill (1974, p. 7) pointed out in a review of leadership research, there are almost as many different definitions of *leadership* as there are people who have tried to define it. It is much like the words *democracy, love,* and *peace*. Although each of us intuitively knows what we mean by such words, the words can have different meanings for different people. As Box 1.1 shows, scholars and practitioners have attempted to define leadership for more than a century without universal consensus.

Box 1.1

The Evolution of Leadership Definitions

While many have a gut-level grasp of what leadership is, putting a definition to the term has proved to be a challenging endeavor for scholars and practitioners alike. More than a century has lapsed since leadership became a topic of academic introspection, and definitions have evolved continuously during that period. These definitions have been influenced by many factors, from world affairs and politics to the perspectives of the discipline in which the topic is being studied. In a seminal work, Rost (1991) analyzed materials written from 1900 to 1990, finding more than 200 different definitions for leadership. His analysis provides a succinct history of how leadership has been defined through the last century:

1900–1929

Definitions of leadership appearing in the first three decades of the 20th century emphasized control and centralization of power with a common theme of domination. For example, at a conference on leadership in 1927, leadership was defined as "the ability to impress the will of the leader on those led and [to] induce obedience, respect, loyalty, and cooperation" (Moore, 1927, p. 124).

1930s

In the 1930s, traits became the focus of defining leadership, with an emerging view of leadership as influence rather than domination. Leadership was also identified as the interaction of an individual's specific personality traits with those of a group; it was noted that while the attitudes and activities of the many may be changed by the one, the many may also influence a leader.

1940s

The group approach came into the forefront in the 1940s with leadership being defined as the behavior of an individual while involved in directing group activities (Hemphill, 1949). At the same time, leadership by persuasion was distinguished from "drivership" or leadership by coercion (Copeland, 1942).

1950s

Three themes dominated leadership definitions during the 1950s:

- *continuance of group theory*, which framed leadership as what leaders do in groups;
- *leadership as a relationship that develops shared goals*, which defined leadership based on behavior of the leader; and
- *effectiveness*, in which leadership was defined by the ability to influence overall group effectiveness.

1960s

Although a tumultuous time for world affairs, the 1960s saw harmony among leadership scholars. The prevailing definition of leadership as *behavior* that influences people toward shared goals was underscored by Seeman (1960), who described leadership as "acts by persons which influence other persons in a shared direction" (p. 53).

1970s

In the 1970s, the group focus gave way to the organizational behavior approach, where leadership became viewed as "initiating and maintaining groups or organizations to accomplish group or organizational goals" (Rost, 1991, p. 59). Burns's (1978) definition, however, was the most important concept of leadership to emerge: "Leadership is the reciprocal process of mobilizing by persons with certain motives and values, various economic,

(Continued)

(Continued)

political, and other resources, in a context of competition and conflict, in order to realize goals independently or mutually held by both leaders and followers" (p. 425).

1980s

The 1980s exploded with scholarly and popular works on the nature of leadership, bringing the topic to the apex of the academic and public consciousness. As a result, the number of definitions for leadership became a prolific stew with several persevering themes:

- *Do as the leader wishes.* Leadership definitions still predominantly delivered the message that leadership is getting followers to do what the leader wants done.
- *Influence.* Probably the most often used word in leadership definitions of the 1980s, *influence* was examined from every angle. To distinguish leadership from management, however, scholars insisted that leadership is *noncoercive* influence.
- *Traits.* Spurred by the national best seller *In Search of Excellence* (Peters & Waterman, 1982), the leadership-as-excellence movement brought leader traits back to the spotlight. As a result, many people's understanding of leadership is based on a trait orientation.
- *Transformation.* Burns (1978) is credited for initiating a movement defining leadership as a transformational process, stating that leadership occurs "when one or more persons engage with others in such a way that leaders and followers raise one another to higher levels of motivation and morality" (p. 83).

1990s

While debate continued through the 1990s as to whether leadership and management were separate processes, research emphasized the *process* of leadership with the focus shifting to followers. Several approaches emerged that examine how leaders influence a group of individuals to achieve a common goal, placing particular attention on the role of followers in the leadership process. Among these leadership approaches were

- *servant leadership*, which puts the leader in the role of a servant who utilizes "caring principles" focusing on followers' needs to help followers become more autonomous, knowledgeable, and like servants themselves (Graham, 1991);

- *followership*, which puts a spotlight on followers and the role they play in the leadership process (Hollander, 1992); and
- *adaptive leadership*, in which leaders encourage followers to adapt by confronting and solving problems, challenges, and changes (Heifetz, 1994).

The 21st Century

The turn of the 21st century brought the emergence of moral approaches to leadership, with authentic and ethical leadership gaining interest from researchers and executives. These new approaches also include leader humility and spirituality. Leadership theory and research also highlighted communication between leaders and followers, and as organizational populations became increasingly diverse, inclusive leadership was introduced. Among these approaches were

- *authentic leadership*, in which the authenticity of leaders and their leadership is emphasized (George, 2003);
- *ethical leadership*, which draws attention to the appropriate conduct of leaders in their personal actions and interpersonal relationships, and the promotion of such conduct to followers (Brown, Treviño, & Harrison, 2005);
- *spiritual leadership*, which focuses on leadership that utilizes values and sense of calling and membership to motivate followers (Fry, 2003);
- *discursive leadership*, which posits that leadership is created not so much through leader traits, skills, and behaviors, but through communication practices that are negotiated between leader and follower (Aritz, Walker, Cardon, & Zhang, 2017; Fairhurst, 2007);
- *humble leadership*, in which leaders' humility allows them to show followers how to grow as a result of work (Owens & Hekman, 2012); and
- *inclusive leadership*, which focuses on diversity and leader behaviors that facilitate followers' feeling of belongingness to the group while maintaining their individuality (Shore, Cleveland, & Sanchez, 2018).

After decades of dissonance, leadership scholars agree on one thing: They can't come up with a common definition for leadership. Because of such factors as growing global influences and generational differences, leadership will continue to have different meanings for different people. The bottom line is that leadership is a complex concept for which a determined definition may long be in flux.

Ways of Conceptualizing Leadership

In the past 60 years, as many as 65 different classification systems have been developed to define the dimensions of leadership (Fleishman et al., 1991). One such classification system, directly related to our discussion, is the scheme proposed by Bass (2008, pp. 11–20). He suggested that some definitions view leadership as the *focus of group processes.* From this perspective, the leader is at the center of group change and activity and embodies the will of the group. Another set of definitions conceptualizes leadership from a *personality perspective,* which suggests that leadership is a combination of special traits or characteristics that some individuals possess. These traits enable those individuals to induce others to accomplish tasks. Other approaches to leadership define it as an *act* or a *behavior*—the things leaders do to bring about change in a group.

In addition, some define leadership in terms of the *power relationship* that exists between leaders and followers. From this viewpoint, leaders have power that they wield to effect change in others. Others view leadership as a *transformational process* that moves followers to accomplish more than is usually expected of them. Finally, some scholars address leadership from a *skills perspective.* This viewpoint stresses the capabilities (knowledge and skills) that make effective leadership possible.

Definition and Components

Despite the multitude of ways in which leadership has been conceptualized, the following components can be identified as central to the phenomenon: (a) Leadership is a process, (b) leadership involves influence, (c) leadership occurs in groups, and (d) leadership involves common goals. Based on these components, the following definition of leadership is used in this text:

> *Leadership* is a process whereby an individual influences a group of individuals to achieve a common goal.

Defining leadership as a *process* means that it is not a trait or characteristic that resides in the leader, but rather a transactional event that occurs between the leader and the followers. *Process* implies that a leader affects and is affected by followers. It emphasizes that leadership is not a linear, one-way event, but rather an interactive event. When leadership is defined in this manner, it becomes available to everyone. It is not restricted to the formally designated leader in a group.

Leadership involves *influence*. It is concerned with how the leader affects followers and the communication that occurs between leaders and followers (Ruben & Gigliotti, 2017). Influence is the sine qua non of leadership. Without influence, leadership does not exist.

Leadership occurs in *groups*. Groups are the context in which leadership takes place. Leadership involves influencing a group of individuals who have a common purpose. This can be a small task group, a community group, or a large group encompassing an entire organization. Leadership is about one individual influencing a group of others to accomplish common goals. Others (a group) are required for leadership to occur. Leadership training programs that teach people to lead themselves are not considered a part of leadership within the definition that is set forth in this discussion.

Leadership includes attention to *common goals*. Leaders direct their energies toward individuals who are trying to achieve something together. By *common*, we mean that the leaders and followers have a mutual purpose. Attention to common goals gives leadership an ethical overtone because it stresses the need for leaders to work with followers to achieve selected goals. Stressing mutuality lessens the possibility that leaders might act toward followers in ways that are forced or unethical. It also increases the possibility that leaders and followers will work together toward a common good (Rost, 1991).

Throughout this text, the people who engage in leadership will be called *leaders*, and those toward whom leadership is directed will be called *followers*. Both leaders and followers are involved together in the leadership process. Leaders need followers, and followers need leaders (Burns, 1978; Heller & Van Til, 1983; Hollander, 1992; Jago, 1982). An extended discussion of followership is provided in Chapter 12. Although leaders and followers are closely linked, it is the leader who often initiates the relationship, creates the communication linkages, and carries the burden for maintaining the relationship.

In our discussion of leaders and followers, attention will be directed toward follower issues as well as leader issues. Leaders have an ethical responsibility to attend to the needs and concerns of followers. As Burns (1978) pointed out, discussions of leadership sometimes are viewed as elitist because of the implied power and importance often ascribed to leaders in the leader–follower relationship. Leaders are not above or better than followers. Leaders and followers must be understood in relation to each other (Hollander, 1992) and collectively (Burns, 1978). They are in the leadership relationship together—and are two sides of the same coin (Rost, 1991).

LEADERSHIP DESCRIBED

In addition to definitional issues, it is important to discuss several other questions pertaining to the nature of leadership. In the following section, we will address questions such as how leadership as a trait differs from leadership as a process; how appointed leadership differs from emergent leadership; and how the concepts of power, coercion, morality, and management interact with leadership.

Trait Versus Process Leadership

We have all heard statements such as "He is born to be a leader" or "She is a natural leader." These statements are commonly expressed by people who take a trait perspective toward leadership. The trait perspective suggests that certain individuals have special innate or inborn characteristics or qualities that make them leaders, and that it is these qualities that differentiate them from nonleaders. Some of the personal qualities used to identify leaders include unique physical factors (e.g., height), personality features (e.g., extraversion), and other characteristics (e.g., intelligence and fluency; Bryman, 1992). In Chapter 2, we will discuss a large body of research that has examined these personal qualities.

To describe leadership as a trait is quite different from describing it as a process (Figure 1.1). The trait viewpoint conceptualizes leadership as a property or set of properties possessed in varying degrees by different people (Jago, 1982). This suggests that it resides *in* select people and restricts leadership to those who are believed to have special, usually inborn, talents.

The process viewpoint suggests that leadership is a phenomenon that resides in the context of the interactions between leaders and followers and makes leadership available to everyone. As a process, leadership can be observed in leader behaviors (Jago, 1982) and can be learned. The process definition of leadership is consistent with the definition of leadership that we have set forth in this chapter.

Assigned Versus Emergent Leadership

Some people are leaders because of their formal position in an organization, whereas others are leaders because of the way other group members respond to them. These two common forms of leadership are called *assigned leadership* and *emergent leadership*. Leadership that is based on occupying a position in an

FIGURE 1.1 The Different Views of Leadership

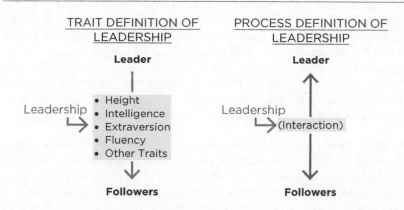

Source: Adapted from A Force for Change: How Leadership Differs From Management (pp. 3–8), by J. P. Kotter, 1990, New York, NY: Free Press.

organization is assigned leadership. Team leaders, plant managers, department heads, directors, and administrators are all examples of assigned leaders.

Yet the person assigned to a leadership position does not always become the real leader in a particular setting. When others perceive an individual as the most influential member of a group or an organization, regardless of the individual's title, the person is exhibiting emergent leadership. The individual acquires emergent leadership through other people in the organization who support and accept that individual's behavior. This type of leadership is not assigned by position; rather, it emerges over a period through communication. Some of the positive communication behaviors that account for successful leader emergence include *being verbally involved, being informed, seeking others' opinions, initiating new ideas,* and *being firm but not rigid* (Ellis & Fisher, 1994).

Researchers have found that, in addition to communication behaviors, personality plays a role in leadership emergence. For example, Smith and Foti (1998) found that certain personality traits were related to leadership emergence in a sample of 160 male college students. The individuals who were more dominant, more intelligent, and more confident about their own performance (general self-efficacy) were more likely to be identified as leaders by other members of their task group. Although it is uncertain whether these findings apply to women as well, Smith and Foti suggested that these three traits could be used to identify individuals perceived to be emergent leaders.

Leadership emergence may also be affected by gender-biased perceptions. In a study of 40 mixed-sex college groups, Watson and Hoffman (2004) found that women who were urged to persuade their task groups to adopt high-quality decisions succeeded with the same frequency as men with identical instructions. Although women were equally influential leaders in their groups, they were rated significantly lower than comparable men were on leadership. Furthermore, these influential women were also rated as significantly less likable than comparably influential men were. Another study found that men who spoke up to promote new ideas in teams were granted higher status compared to women who did so (McClean, Martin, Emich, & Woodruff, 2018). These results suggest that there continue to be barriers to women's emergence as leaders in some settings.

A unique perspective on leadership emergence is provided by social identity theory (Hogg, 2001). From this perspective, leadership emergence is the degree to which a person fits with the identity of the group as a whole. As groups develop over time, a group prototype also develops. Individuals emerge as leaders in the group when they become most like the group prototype. Being similar to the prototype makes leaders attractive to the group and gives them influence with the group.

The leadership approaches we discuss in the subsequent chapters of this book apply equally to assigned leadership and emergent leadership. When a person is engaged in leadership, that person is a leader, whether leadership was assigned or emerged. This book focuses on the leadership process that occurs when any individual is engaged in influencing other group members in their efforts to reach a common goal.

Leadership and Power

The concept of power is related to leadership because it is part of the influence process. Power is the capacity or potential to influence. People have power when they have the ability to affect others' beliefs, attitudes, and courses of action. Judges, doctors, coaches, and teachers are all examples of people who have the potential to influence us. When they do, they are using their power, the resource they draw on to effect change in us.

Although there are no explicit theories in the research literature about power and leadership, power is a concept that people often associate with leadership. It is common for people to view leaders (both good and bad) and people in positions of leadership as individuals who wield power over others, and as a result, power is often thought of as synonymous with leadership. In addition, people are often intrigued by how leaders use their power. Understanding how power is used in leadership is instrumental as well in understanding the dark side of leadership, where leaders use their leadership to achieve their own personal ends and lead in toxic and destructive ways (Krasikova, Green, & LeBreton, 2013). Studying how famous leaders, such as Adolf Hitler or Alexander the Great, use power to effect change in others is titillating to many people because it underscores that power can indeed effectuate change and maybe if they had power they too could effectuate change.

In her 2012 book *The End of Leadership*, Kellerman argues there has been a shift in leadership power during the last 40 years. Power used to be the domain of leaders, but that is diminishing and shifting to followers. Changes in culture have meant followers demand more from leaders, and leaders have responded. Access to technology has empowered followers, given them access to huge amounts of information, and made leaders more transparent. The result is a decline in respect for leaders and leaders' legitimate power. In effect, followers have used information power to level the playing field. Power is no longer synonymous with leadership, and in the social contract between leaders and followers, leaders wield less power, according to Kellerman. For example, Posner (2015) examined volunteer leaders, such as those who sit on boards for nonprofit organizations, and found that while these individuals did not have positional authority in the organization, they were able to influence leadership. Volunteer leaders engaged more frequently in leadership behaviors than did paid leaders.

TABLE 1.1 Six Bases of Power

Referent Power	Based on followers' identification and liking for the leader. A teacher who is adored by students has referent power.
Expert Power	Based on followers' perceptions of the leader's competence. A tour guide who is knowledgeable about a foreign country has expert power.
Legitimate Power	Associated with having status or formal job authority. A judge who administers sentences in the courtroom exhibits legitimate power.
Reward Power	Derived from having the capacity to provide rewards to others. A supervisor who compliments employees who work hard is using reward power.
Coercive Power	Derived from having the capacity to penalize or punish others. A coach who sits players on the bench for being late to practice is using coercive power.
Information Power	Derived from possessing knowledge that others want or need. A boss who has information regarding new criteria to decide employee promotion eligibility has information power.

Sources: Adapted from "The Bases of Social Power," by J. R. French Jr. and B. Raven, 1962, in D. Cartwright (Ed.), *Group Dynamics: Research and Theory* (pp. 259–269), New York, NY: Harper & Row; and "Social Influence and Power," by B. H. Raven, 1965, in I. D. Steiner & M. Fishbein (Eds.), *Current Studies in Social Psychology* (pp. 371–382), New York, NY: Holt, Rinehart, & Winston.

In college courses today, the most widely cited research on power is French and Raven's (1959) work on the bases of social power. In their work, they conceptualized power from the framework of a dyadic relationship that included both the person influencing and the person being influenced. French and Raven identified five common and important bases of power—*referent, expert, legitimate, reward,* and *coercive*—and Raven (1965) identified a sixth, *information* power (Table 1.1). Each of these bases of power increases a leader's capacity to influence the attitudes, values, or behaviors of others.

In organizations, there are two major kinds of power: position power and personal power. *Position power,* which includes legitimate, reward, coercive, and information power (Table 1.2), is the power a person derives from a particular office or rank in a formal organizational system. It is the influence capacity a leader derives from having higher status than the followers have. Position power allows leaders to attain central roles in organizations; for example, vice presidents and department heads have more power than staff personnel do because of the positions they hold in the organization. In addition, leaders' informal networks bring them greater social power, which separates leaders from nonleaders (Chiu, Balkundi, & Weinberg, 2017).

Personal power is the influence capacity a leader derives from being seen by followers as likable and knowledgeable. When leaders act in ways that are important to followers, it gives leaders power. For example, some managers have power because their followers consider them to be good role models. Others have power because their followers view them as highly competent or considerate. In both cases, these managers' power is ascribed to them by others, based on how they are seen in their relationships with others. Personal power includes referent and expert power (Table 1.2).

In discussions of leadership, it is not unusual for leaders to be described as wielders of power, as individuals who dominate others. In these instances, power is

TABLE 1.2 Types and Bases of Power

Position Power	Personal Power
Legitimate	Referent
Reward	Expert
Coercive	
Information	

Source: Adapted from *A Force for Change: How Leadership Differs From Management* (pp. 3–8), by J. P. Kotter, 1990, New York, NY: Free Press.

conceptualized as a tool that leaders use to achieve their own ends. Contrary to this view of power, Burns (1978) emphasized power from a relationship standpoint. For Burns, power is not an entity that leaders use over others to achieve their own ends; instead, power occurs in relationships. It should be used by leaders and followers to promote their collective goals.

In this text, our discussions of leadership treat power as a relational concern for both leaders and followers. We pay attention to how leaders work with followers to reach common goals.

Leadership and Coercion

Coercive power is one of the specific kinds of power available to leaders. Coercion involves the use of force to effect change. *To coerce* means to influence others to do something against their will and may include manipulating penalties and rewards in their work environment. Coercion often involves the use of threats, punishment, and negative reward schedules and is most often seen as a characteristic of the dark side of leadership. Classic examples of coercive leaders are Adolf Hitler in Germany, the Taliban leaders in Afghanistan, Jim Jones in Guyana, and Philippine president Rodrigo Duterte, each of whom used power and restraint to force followers to engage in extreme behaviors. At an extreme, coercion combines with other bullying and tyrannical behaviors known as abusive supervision (Tepper, 2007).

It is important to distinguish between coercion and leadership because it allows us to separate out from our examples of leadership the behaviors of individuals such as Hitler, the Taliban, and Jones. In our discussions of leadership, coercive people are not used as models of ideal leadership. Our definition suggests that leadership is reserved for those who influence a group of individuals toward a common goal. Leaders who use coercion are interested in their own goals and seldom are interested in the wants and needs of followers. Using coercion runs counter to working *with* followers to achieve a common goal.

Leadership and Morality

In considering the relationship of leadership and morality, let's start with a simple question: Do you agree or disagree with the following statement:

Hitler's rule in Germany could be considered a good example of leadership.

Throughout the United States and around the world, in classroom discussions of leadership, the question about whether or not Adolf Hitler was a "great" leader inevitably comes up. Your response to this statement is intended to bring out whether your conceptualization of leadership includes a moral dimension or if you think that leadership is a neutral concept that treats leadership as amoral.

If you answered *agree* to the statement, you probably come down on the side of thinking the phenomenon of leadership is neutral, or amoral. You might think it is obvious that Hitler *was* a leader because he was very charismatic and persuasive and his actions had a huge impact on Germany and the world. On the other hand, if you answered *disagree*, you most likely do not think of Hitler's leadership as being in any way positive and that the notion of Hitler as a model of leadership is repugnant because you reserve the concept of leadership for nondestructive leaders who create change for the common good. That is, you believe leadership cannot be divorced from values; it is a moral phenomenon and has a moral component.

For as long as leadership has been studied, the debate of whether or not leadership has a moral dimension has been a focus of leadership scholars. It is an important debate because it gets at the core of what we think the phenomenon of leadership actually entails. How we define leadership is central to how we talk about leadership, how we develop the components of leadership, how we research it, and how we teach it.

There are two consistent trains of thought regarding the relationship of leadership and morality: Either leadership is a *neutral process* that *is not* guided or dependent on a value system that advances the common good, or leadership is a *moral process* that *is* guided and dependent on values promotive of the common good.

Leadership Is a Neutral Process

It is common for people to think of leadership as a neutral concept—one that is not tied to morality. From this perspective, leadership can be used for good ends or bad, and can be employed both by individuals who have worthy intentions and by those who do not. For example, moral leaders like Mother Teresa, Nelson Mandela, and Martin Luther King Jr. used leadership for good. On the other hand, Adolf Hitler, Pol Pot, and Idi Amin used leadership destructively. Common to all of these examples is that these leaders used leadership to influence followers to move toward and accomplish certain goals. The only difference is that some leaders used leadership in laudatory ways while others used leadership in highly destructive ways.

A classic historical example of treating leadership as an amoral concept can be found in Niccolò Machiavelli's *The Prince* (c. 1505; Nederman, 2019). In this book, Machiavelli philosophizes that moral values need not play a role in decision making; instead, leaders should concentrate on using power to achieve their goals. Their focus should be on the ends, or consequences, of their leadership and need not be about the means. Machiavelli endorsed leaders' use of fear and deception, if necessary, to accomplish tasks; he was concerned with the pragmatics of what leaders do and not the rightness or wrongness of a leader's actions (Nederman, 2019).

There are an abundance of definitions of leadership, and most of these treat the concept of morality in a neutral fashion (e.g., Rost's 1991 analysis of 221 definitions of leadership). These definitions do not require that leadership result in only positive outcomes. To use a specific example, Padilla (2013) defines leadership as "an organized group process with associated goals resulting in a set of outcomes" (p. 12), which involves a leader, followers, and contexts. From his perspective, leadership is value-neutral and can be used for constructive or destructive ends. Padilla argues that Hitler should be considered a leader even though the outcome of his leadership was horrendously destructive.

Leadership Is a Moral Process

In contrast to describing leadership as a neutral process, some in the field of leadership argue (as we do in this chapter) that leadership has a value dimension—it is about influencing others to make changes *to achieve a common good*. From this perspective, Hitler, who thwarted the common good, *cannot* be considered a "great" leader.

One of the first scholars to conceptualize leadership as a moral process was James MacGregor Burns in his book *Leadership* (1978). For Burns, leadership is about raising the motivations and moral levels of followers. He argued it is the responsibility of a leader to help followers assess their own values and needs in order to raise them to a higher level of functioning, to a level that will stress values such as liberty, justice, and equality (Ciulla, 2014). Burns (2003) argued that values are central to what leaders do.

Expanding on Burns, Bass (1985) developed a model of leadership (see Chapter 8, "Transformational Leadership") that delineated transforming leadership, a kind of leadership that affects the level of values of followers. Because it is difficult to use the term *transformational leadership* when describing a leader such as Adolf Hitler, the term *pseudotransformational leadership* was coined by Bass to refer to leaders who focus on their own personal goals over the common good and are self-consumed, exploitive, and power-oriented, with warped moral values (Bass & Riggio, 2006; Bass & Steidlmeier, 1999). In contrast to pseudotransformational leadership, "real" or "ideal" transformational leadership is described as socialized leadership—leadership that is concerned with the collective good. Socialized leaders transcend their own interests for the sake of others (Howell & Avolio, 1993).

Additionally, morals have a central role in two established leadership theories, *authentic leadership* and *servant leadership*. Authentic leadership (see Chapter 9) is an extension of transformational leadership, stressing that leaders do what is "right" and "good" for their followers and society. They understand their own values, place followers' needs above their own, and work with followers to align their interests in order to create a greater common good. Similarly, servant leadership has a strong moral dimension. It makes altruism the central component of the leadership process and frames leadership around the principle of caring for others. Within this paradigm, leaders are urged to *not* dominate, direct, or control others; they are urged to give up control rather than seek control.

Referring back to the question about whether you agree or disagree that Hitler is an example of leadership, your answer has to be predicated on what you think leadership is. If you think leadership is a neutral process that does not have a moral requirement, then Hitler is an example of leadership. On the other hand, if you think leadership includes ethical considerations such as elevating the morals, values, and goals of followers to make more principled judgments (Burns, 1978), then Hitler is not an example of leadership. In this view, he was nothing more than a despotic, Machiavellian autocrat and an evil dictator responsible for the imprisonment, abuse, and execution of millions of innocent people and the unprovoked origin of World War II—the deadliest armed conflict in history.

Leadership and Management

Leadership is a process that is similar to management in many ways. Leadership involves influence, as does management. Leadership entails working with people, which management entails as well. Leadership is concerned with effective goal accomplishment, and so is management. In general, many of the functions of management are activities that are consistent with the definition of leadership we set forth at the beginning of this chapter.

But leadership is also different from management. Whereas the study of leadership can be traced back to Aristotle, management emerged around the turn of the 20th century with the advent of our industrialized society. Management was created as a way to reduce chaos in organizations, to make them run more effectively and efficiently. The primary functions of management, as first identified by Fayol (1916), were planning, organizing, staffing, and controlling. These functions are still representative of the field of management today.

In a book that compared the functions of management with the functions of leadership, Kotter (1990) argued that they are quite dissimilar (Figure 1.2). The overriding function of management is to provide order and consistency to organizations, whereas the primary function of leadership is to produce change and movement. Management is about seeking order and stability; leadership is about seeking adaptive and constructive change.

As illustrated in Figure 1.2, the major activities of management are played out differently than the activities of leadership. Although they are different in scope, Kotter (1990, pp. 7–8) contended that both management and leadership are essential if an organization is to prosper. For example, if an organization has strong management without leadership, the outcome can be stifling and bureaucratic. Conversely, if an organization has strong leadership without management,

FIGURE 1.2 Functions of Management and Leadership

Management Produces Order and Consistency	Leadership Produces Change and Movement
Planning and Budgeting	Establishing Direction
Establish agendas	Create a vision
Set timetables	Clarify the big picture
Allocate resources	Set strategies
Organizing and Staffing	Aligning People
Provide structure	Communicate goals
Make job placements	Seek commitment
Establish rules and procedures	Build teams and coalitions
Controlling and Problem Solving	Motivating and Inspiring
Develop incentives	Inspire and energize
Generate creative solutions	Empower followers
Take corrective action	Satisfy unmet needs

Source: Adapted from *A Force for Change: How Leadership Differs From Management* (pp. 3–8), by J. P. Kotter, 1990, New York, NY: Free Press.

the outcome can be meaningless or misdirected change for change's sake. To be effective, organizations need to nourish both competent management and skilled leadership.

Many scholars, in addition to Kotter (1990), argue that leadership and management are distinct constructs. For example, Bennis and Nanus (2007) maintained that there is a significant difference between the two. *To manage* means to accomplish activities and master routines, whereas *to lead* means to influence others and create visions for change. Bennis and Nanus made the distinction very clear in their frequently quoted sentence, "Managers are people who do things right and leaders are people who do the right thing" (p. 221).

Rost (1991) has also been a proponent of distinguishing between leadership and management. He contended that leadership is a multidirectional influence relationship and management is a unidirectional authority relationship. Whereas leadership is concerned with the process of developing mutual purposes, management is directed toward coordinating activities to get a job done. Leaders and followers work together to create real change, whereas managers and subordinates join forces to sell goods and services (Rost, 1991, pp. 149–152).

In a recent study, Simonet and Tett (2012) explored how best to conceptualize leadership and management by having 43 experts identify the overlap and differences between leadership and management in regard to 63 different competencies. They found a large number of competencies (22) descriptive of both leadership and management (e.g., productivity, customer focus, professionalism, and goal setting), but they also found several unique descriptors for each. Specifically, they found leadership was distinguished by motivating intrinsically, creative thinking, strategic planning, tolerance of ambiguity, and being able to read people, and management was distinguished by rule orientation, short-term planning, motivating extrinsically, orderliness, safety concerns, and timeliness.

Approaching the issue from a narrower viewpoint, Zaleznik (1977) went so far as to argue that leaders and managers themselves are distinct, and that they are basically different types of people. He contended that managers are reactive and prefer to work with people to solve problems but do so with low emotional involvement. They act to limit choices. Zaleznik suggested that leaders, on the other hand, are emotionally active and involved. They seek to shape ideas instead of responding to them and act to expand the available options to solve long-standing problems. Leaders change the way people think about what is possible.

Although there are clear differences between management and leadership, the two constructs overlap. When managers are involved in influencing a group to meet its goals, they are involved in leadership. When leaders are involved in planning, organizing, staffing, and controlling, they are involved in management. Both processes involve influencing a group of individuals toward goal attainment. For purposes of our discussion in this book, we focus on the leadership process. In our examples and case studies, we treat the roles of managers and leaders similarly and do not emphasize the differences between them.

PLAN OF THE BOOK

This book is user-friendly. It is based on substantive theories but is written to emphasize practice and application. Each chapter in the book follows the same format. The first section of each chapter briefly describes the leadership approach and discusses various research studies applicable to the approach. The second section of each chapter evaluates the approach and how it works, highlighting its strengths and criticisms. Special attention is given to how the approach contributes or fails to contribute to an overall understanding of the leadership process. Finally, beginning with Chapter 2, each chapter has an application section with case studies and a leadership questionnaire that measures the reader's leadership style to prompt discussion of how the approach can be applied in ongoing organizations. Each chapter ends with a summary and references.

CASE STUDY

Case 1.1 is provided to illustrate different dimensions of leadership as well as allow you to examine your own perspective on what defines a leader and leadership. At the end of the case, you will find questions that will help in analyzing the case.

Case 1.1 OPEN MOUTH . . .

When asked by a sports editor for the *Lanthorn*, Grand Valley State University's student publication, what three historical figures he would most like to have dinner with, Morris Berger, the newly announced offensive coordinator for the GVSU Lakers football team, responded Adolf Hitler, John F. Kennedy, and Christopher Columbus.

"This is probably not going to get a good review," he said, "but I'm going to say Adolf Hitler. It was obviously very sad and he had bad motives, but the way he was able to lead was second-to-none. How he rallied a group and a following, I want to know how he did that. Bad intentions of course, but you can't deny he wasn't a great leader" (Voss, 2020).

When the article ran, it caused a stir. Shortly after, the writer, Kellen Voss, was asked by someone in the university's athletics department to alter the online story to remove those comments. The *Lanthorn* initially complied, but then changed course and added the full interview back in. Once the *Lanthorn* republished the quote, the story went viral. It was covered in the *Washington Post*, on ESPN, and in *Sports Illustrated* and even ended up in the monologue of *The Tonight Show Starring Jimmy Fallon* (Boatner, 2020).

In addition to public dismay, GVSU's Hillel chapter, a Jewish campus organization, spoke out strongly against Coach Berger after his comments were made public. "It is unfortunate to see a member of our Grand Valley community glorify the Holocaust, a period that brought such destruction and travesty to the world," the group posted to its Facebook page. "We appreciate the university's swift response and we will continue to partner with them to educate our campus community and provide a safe and inclusive environment for all students" (Colf, 2020).

Seven days after the article appeared, GVSU announced that Coach Berger, who had been suspended by the university, had resigned.

(Continued)

(Continued)

Matt Mitchell, the team's head coach, gave a statement: "Nothing in our background and reference checks revealed anything that would have suggested the unfortunate controversy that has unfolded," Coach Mitchell said. "This has been a difficult time for everyone. I accepted Coach Berger's resignation in an effort for him to move on and for us to focus on the team and our 2020 season" (Wallner, 2020).

In another statement, Coach Berger said he was disappointed to leave, but added, "I do not want to be a distraction to these kids, this great university, or Coach Mitchell as they begin preparations for the upcoming season" (Wallner, 2020).

Coach Berger also issued a more personal apology in a Twitter post:

I failed myself, my parents, and this university—the answer
I attempted to give does not align with the values instilled
in me by my parents, nor [does it] represent what I stand for
or believe in—I mishandled the answer, and fell way short of
the mark.

For the last 11-years, I worked tirelessly for each and every opportunity and was excited to be a Laker.

Throughout my life, I have taken great pride in that responsibility—as a teacher, mentor, coach, role-model, and member of the community.

It is my hope that you will consider accepting my apology.

I recognize that I cannot undo the hurt and the embarrassment I have caused.

But I *can control* the way I choose to positively learn from my mistake moving forward—as I work to regain the trust and respect of everyone that I have let down. (Berger, 2020)

A few weeks later, GVSU announced that it would increase its curriculum around the Holocaust and Native American history. "We will use this moment to work diligently toward institutional systemic change that creates a healthier campus climate for all," the university's president, Philomena Mantella, said (Colf, 2020).

Questions

1. Who are the leaders in this situation? How would you describe their actions as leaders based on the definition of leadership in this chapter?

2. Do you think it was wrong for Coach Berger to cite Hitler as a "great leader"?

3. What is your reaction to Coach Berger resigning one week after signing a contract to coach at GVSU?

4. Based on our discussion of morality and leadership in this chapter, would you say Coach Berger's comments are based on leadership as a neutral process or on leadership as a process that has a moral dimension? Why?

5. What does the university's response suggest regarding how the university views leadership?

6. If you were the president of the university and you were asked to define leadership, how would you define it?

7. Bobby Knight was a coach who was known to use questionable leadership tactics. Do you think Coach Berger would have been safe to ask Coach Knight to dinner? Why?

LEADERSHIP INSTRUMENT

The meaning of leadership is complex and includes many dimensions. For some people, leadership is a *trait* or an *ability*, for others it is a *skill* or a *behavior*, and for still others it is a *relationship* or a *process*. In reality, leadership probably includes components of all of these dimensions. Each dimension explains a facet of leadership.

Which dimension seems closest to how you think of leadership? How would you define leadership? Answers to these questions are important because *how you think* about leadership will strongly influence *how you practice* leadership. In this section, the Conceptualizing Leadership Questionnaire is provided as an example of a measure that can be used to assess how you define and view leadership.

Conceptualizing Leadership Questionnaire

Purpose: To identify how you view leadership and to explore your perceptions of different aspects of leadership

Instructions: Using the scale below, indicate the extent to which you agree or disagree with the following statements about leadership.

Key: 1 = Strongly   2 = Disagree   3 = Neutral   4 = Agree   5 = Strongly
       disagree   agree

1. When I think of leadership, I think of a person with special personality traits.   1 2 3 4 5

2. Much like playing the piano or tennis, leadership is a learned ability.   1 2 3 4 5

3. Leadership requires knowledge and know-how.   1 2 3 4 5

4. Leadership is about what people do rather than who they are.   1 2 3 4 5

5. Followers can influence the leadership process as much as leaders.   1 2 3 4 5

6. Leadership is about the process of influencing others.   1 2 3 4 5

7. Some people are born to be leaders.   1 2 3 4 5

8. Some people have the natural ability to be leaders.   1 2 3 4 5

9. The key to successful leadership is having the right skills.   1 2 3 4 5

10. Leadership is best described by what leaders do.   1 2 3 4 5

11. Leaders and followers share in the leadership process.   1 2 3 4 5

12. Leadership is a series of actions directed toward positive ends.   1 2 3 4 5

13. A person needs to have certain traits to be an effective leader.   1 2 3 4 5

14. Everyone has the capacity to be a leader.   1 2 3 4 5

15. Effective leaders are competent in their roles.   1 2 3 4 5

16. The essence of leadership is performing tasks and dealing with people.   1 2 3 4 5

17. Leadership is about the common purposes of leaders and followers.   1 2 3 4 5

18. Leadership does not rely on the leader alone but is a process involving the leader, followers, and the situation.   1 2 3 4 5

19. People become great leaders because of their traits.   1 2 3 4 5

20. People can develop the ability to lead.   1 2 3 4 5

21. Effective leaders have competence and knowledge.   1 2 3 4 5

(Continued)

(Continued)

22. Leadership is about how leaders work with people to accomplish goals.　　　1 2 3 4 5

23. Effective leadership is best explained by the leader–follower relationship.　　　1 2 3 4 5

24. Leaders influence and are influenced by followers.　　　1 2 3 4 5

Scoring

1. Sum scores on items 1, 7, 13, and 19 (trait emphasis)

2. Sum scores on items 2, 8, 14, and 20 (ability emphasis)

3. Sum scores on items 3, 9, 15, and 21 (skill emphasis)

4. Sum scores on items 4, 10, 16, and 22 (behavior emphasis)

5. Sum scores on items 5, 11, 17, and 23 (relationship emphasis)

6. Sum scores on items 6, 12, 18, and 24 (process emphasis)

Total Scores

1. Trait emphasis: _____

2. Ability emphasis: _____

3. Skill emphasis: _____

4. Behavior emphasis: _____

5. Relationship emphasis: _____

6. Process emphasis: _____

Scoring Interpretation

The scores you received on this questionnaire provide information about how you define and view leadership. The emphasis you give to the various dimensions of leadership has implications for how you approach the leadership process. For example, if your highest score is for *trait emphasis*, it suggests that you emphasize the role of the leader and the leader's special gifts in the leadership process. However, if your highest score is for *relationship emphasis*, it indicates that you think leadership is centered on the communication between leaders and followers, rather than on the unique qualities of the leader. By comparing your scores, you can gain an understanding of the aspects of leadership that you find most important and least important. The way you think about leadership will influence how you practice leadership.

SUMMARY

Leadership is a topic with universal appeal; in the popular press and academic research literature, much has been written about leadership. Despite the abundance of writing on the topic, leadership has presented a major challenge to practitioners and researchers interested in understanding the nature of leadership. It is a highly valued phenomenon that is very complex.

Through the years, leadership has been defined and conceptualized in many ways. The component common to nearly all classifications is that leadership is an influence process that assists groups of individuals toward goal attainment. Specifically, in this book leadership is defined as a process whereby an individual influences a group of individuals to achieve a common goal.

Because both leaders and followers are part of the leadership process, it is important to address issues that confront followers as well as issues that confront leaders. Leaders and followers should be understood in relation to each other.

In prior research, many studies have focused on leadership as a trait. The trait perspective suggests that certain people in our society have special inborn qualities that make them leaders. This view restricts leadership to those who are believed to have special characteristics. In contrast, the approach in this text suggests that leadership is a process that can be learned, and that it is available to everyone.

Two common forms of leadership are *assigned* and *emergent*. *Assigned leadership* is based on a formal title or position in an organization. *Emergent leadership* results from what one does and how one acquires support from followers. Leadership, as a process, applies to individuals in both assigned roles and emergent roles.

Related to leadership is the concept of power, the potential to influence. There are two major kinds of power: position and personal. Position power, which is much like assigned leadership, is the power an individual derives from having a title in a formal organizational system. It includes legitimate, reward, information, and coercive power. Personal power comes from followers and includes referent and expert power. Followers give it to leaders because followers believe leaders have something of value. Treating power as a shared resource is important because it de-emphasizes the idea that leaders are power wielders.

While coercion has been a common power brought to bear by many individuals in charge, it should not be viewed as ideal leadership. Our definition of leadership stresses *using influence* to bring individuals toward a common goal, while coercion involves the use of threats and punishment to *induce change* in followers for the sake of the leaders. Coercion runs counter to leadership because it does not treat leadership as a process that emphasizes working *with* followers to achieve shared objectives.

There are two trains of thought regarding leadership and morality. Some argue that leadership is a *neutral process* that can be used by leaders for good and bad ends and treats Hitler as an example of strong leadership. Others contend that leadership is a *moral process* that involves influencing others to achieve a common good. From this perspective Hitler would not be an example of leadership.

Leadership and management are different concepts that overlap. They are different in that management traditionally focuses on the activities of planning, organizing, staffing, and controlling, whereas leadership emphasizes the general influence process. According to some researchers, management is concerned with creating order and stability, whereas leadership is about adaptation and constructive change. Other researchers go so far as to argue that managers and leaders are different types of people, with managers being more reactive and less emotionally involved and leaders being more proactive and more emotionally involved. The overlap between leadership and management is centered on how both involve influencing a group of individuals in goal attainment.

In this book, we discuss leadership as a complex process. Based on the research literature, we describe selected approaches to leadership and assess how they can be used to improve leadership in real situations.

Trait Approach

2

DESCRIPTION

Of interest to scholars throughout the 20th century, the trait approach was one of the first systematic attempts to study leadership. In the early 20th century, leadership traits were studied to determine what made certain people great leaders. The theories that were developed were called "great man" theories because they focused on identifying the innate qualities and characteristics possessed by great social, political, and military leaders (e.g., Catherine the Great, Mohandas Gandhi, Indira Gandhi, Abraham Lincoln, Joan of Arc, and Napoleon Bonaparte). It was believed that people were born with these traits, and that only the "great" people possessed them. During this time, research concentrated on determining the specific traits that clearly differentiated leaders from followers (Bass, 2008; Jago, 1982).

In the mid-20th century, the trait approach was challenged by research that questioned the universality of leadership traits. In a major review, Stogdill (1948) suggested that no consistent set of traits differentiated leaders from nonleaders across a variety of situations. An individual with leadership traits who was a leader in one situation might not be a leader in another situation. Rather than being a quality that individuals possess, leadership was reconceptualized as a relationship between people in a social situation. Personal factors related to leadership continued to be important, but researchers contended that these factors were to be considered as relative to the requirements of the situation.

The trait approach has generated much interest among researchers for its explanation of how traits influence leadership (Bryman, 1992). For example, Kirkpatrick and Locke (1991) went so far as to claim that effective leaders are actually distinct types of people. Lord, DeVader, and Alliger (1986) found that traits were strongly associated with individuals' perceptions of leadership. More recently, Dinh and Lord (2012) examined the relationship between leadership effectiveness and followers' perception of leadership traits.

The trait approach has earned new interest through the current emphasis given by many researchers to visionary and charismatic leadership (see Bass, 2008; Bennis & Nanus, 2007; Jacquart & Antonakis, 2015; Nadler & Tushman, 2012; Zaccaro, 2007; Zaleznik, 1977). Charismatic leadership catapulted to the forefront of public attention with the 2008 election of the United States' first African American president, Barack Obama, who is perceived by many to be charismatic, among many other attributes. In a study to determine what distinguishes charismatic leaders from others, Jung and Sosik (2006) found that charismatic leaders consistently possess traits of self-monitoring, engagement in impression management, motivation to attain social power, and motivation to attain self-actualization. In short, the trait approach is alive and well. It began with an emphasis on identifying the qualities of great persons, shifted to include the impact of situations on leadership, and, currently, has shifted back to reemphasize the critical role of traits in effective leadership.

When discussing the trait approach, it is important to define what is meant by traits. Traits refer to a set of distinctive characteristics, qualities, or attributes that describe a person. They are inherent and relatively unchanging over time. Taken together, traits are the internal factors that comprise our personality and make us unique. Because traits are derived from our personality and are fundamentally fixed, this chapter will not emphasize how people can use this approach to develop or change their leadership. Instead, the focus of the chapter will be on identifying leaders' traits and overall role of traits in leadership.

While research on traits spanned the entire 20th century, a good overview of the approach is found in two surveys completed by Stogdill (1948, 1974). In his first survey, Stogdill analyzed and synthesized more than 124 trait studies conducted between 1904 and 1947. In his second study, he analyzed another 163 studies completed between 1948 and 1970. By taking a closer look at each of these reviews, we can obtain a clearer picture of how individuals' traits contribute to the leadership process.

Stogdill's first survey identified a group of important leadership traits that were related to how individuals in various groups became leaders. His results showed that an average individual in a leadership role is different from an average group member with regard to the following eight traits: intelligence, alertness, insight, responsibility, initiative, persistence, self-confidence, and sociability.

The findings of Stogdill's first survey also indicated that an individual does not become a leader solely because that individual possesses certain traits. Rather, the traits that leaders possess must be relevant to situations in which the leader is functioning. As stated earlier, leaders in one situation may not necessarily be leaders in another situation. Findings showed that leadership was not a passive state but resulted from a working relationship between the leader and other group members. This research marked the beginning of a new approach to leadership research that focused on leadership behaviors and leadership situations.

Stogdill's second survey, published in 1974, analyzed 163 new studies and compared the findings of these studies to the findings he had reported in his first survey. The second survey was more balanced in its description of the role of traits and leadership. Whereas the first survey implied that leadership is determined principally by situational factors and not traits, the second survey argued more moderately that both traits and situational factors were determinants of leadership. In essence, the second survey validated the original trait idea that a leader's characteristics are indeed a part of leadership.

Similar to the first survey, Stogdill's second survey identified traits that were positively associated with leadership. The list included the following 10 characteristics:

1. Drive for responsibility and task completion

2. Vigor and persistence in pursuit of goals

3. Risk-taking and originality in problem solving

4. Drive to exercise initiative in social situations

5. Self-confidence and sense of personal identity

6. Willingness to accept consequences of decision and action

7. Readiness to absorb interpersonal stress

8. Willingness to tolerate frustration and delay

9. Ability to influence other people's behavior

10. Capacity to structure social interaction systems to the purpose at hand

Mann (1959) conducted a similar study that examined more than 1,400 findings regarding traits and leadership in small groups, but he placed less emphasis on how situational factors influenced leadership. Although tentative in his conclusions, Mann suggested that certain traits could be used to distinguish leaders from nonleaders. His results identified leaders as strong in the following six traits: intelligence, masculinity, adjustment, dominance, extraversion, and conservatism.

Lord et al. (1986) reassessed Mann's (1959) findings using a more sophisticated procedure called meta-analysis and found that intelligence, masculinity, and dominance were significantly related to how individuals perceived leaders.

From their findings, the authors argued strongly that traits could be used to make discriminations consistently across situations between leaders and nonleaders.

Both of these studies were conducted during periods in American history where male leadership was prevalent in most aspects of business and society. In Chapter 15, we explore more contemporary research regarding the role of gender in leadership, and we look at whether traits such as masculinity and dominance still bear out as important factors in distinguishing between leaders and nonleaders.

Yet another review argued for the importance of leadership traits: Kirkpatrick and Locke (1991, p. 59) contended that "it is unequivocally clear that leaders are not like other people." From a qualitative synthesis of earlier research, Kirkpatrick and Locke postulated that leaders differ from nonleaders on six traits: drive, motivation, integrity, confidence, cognitive ability, and task knowledge. According to these writers, individuals can be born with these traits, they can learn them, or both. It is these six traits that make up the "right stuff" for leaders. Kirkpatrick and Locke asserted that leadership traits make some people different from others, and this difference should be recognized as an important part of the leadership process.

In the 1990s, researchers began to investigate the leadership traits associated with "social intelligence," which is characterized as the ability to understand one's own and others' feelings, behaviors, and thoughts and act appropriately (Marlowe, 1986). Zaccaro (2002) defined social intelligence as having such capacities as social awareness, social acumen, self-monitoring, and the ability to select and enact the best response given the contingencies of the situation and social environment. A number of empirical studies showed these capacities to be a key trait for effective leaders. Zaccaro, Kemp, and Bader (2017) included such social abilities in the categories of leadership traits they outlined as important leadership attributes (Table 2.1).

Table 2.1 provides a summary of the traits and characteristics that were identified by researchers from the trait approach. It illustrates clearly the breadth of traits related to leadership. Table 2.1 also shows how difficult it is to select certain traits as definitive leadership traits; some of the traits appear in several of the survey studies, whereas others appear in only one or two studies. Regardless of the lack of precision in Table 2.1, however, it represents a general convergence of research regarding which traits are leadership traits.

Over the past 10 years, interest in leader traits has experienced a renaissance. Zaccaro, Green, Dubrow, and Kolze (2018) found that basic personality traits and capacities contribute to who emerges as a leader and one's effectiveness as a leader.

What, then, can be said about trait research? What has a century of research on the trait approach given us that is useful? The answer is an extended list of traits

TABLE 2.1 Studies of Leadership Traits and Characteristics

Stogdill (1948)	Mann (1959)	Stogdill (1974)	Lord, DeVader, and Alliger (1986)	Kirkpatrick and Locke (1991)	Zaccaro, Kemp, and Bader (2017)
intelligence	intelligence	achievement	intelligence	drive	cognitive ability
alertness	masculinity	persistence	masculinity	motivation	extraversion
insight	adjustment	insight	dominance	integrity	conscientiousness
responsibility	dominance	initiative		confidence	emotional stability
initiative	extraversion	self-confidence		cognitive ability	openness
persistence	conservatism	responsibility		task knowledge	agreeableness
self-confidence		cooperativeness			motivation
sociability		tolerance			social intelligence
		influence			self-monitoring
		sociability			emotional intelligence
					problem solving

Sources: Adapted from "The Bases of Social Power," by J. R. P. French Jr. and B. Raven, 1962, in D. Cartwright (Ed.), *Group Dynamics: Research and Theory* (pp. 259–269). New York, NY: Harper and Row; Zaccaro, Kemp, & Bader (2004).

that individuals might hope to possess or wish to cultivate if they want to be perceived by others as leaders. Some of the traits that are central to this list include intelligence, self-confidence, determination, integrity, and sociability (Table 2.2).

TABLE 2.2 Major Leadership Traits

• Intelligence	• Integrity
• Self-confidence	• Sociability
• Determination	

Intelligence

Intelligence or intellectual ability is positively related to leadership (Sternberg, 2004). Based on their analysis of a series of recent studies on intelligence and various indices of leadership, Zaccaro et al. (2017) found support for the finding that leaders tend to have higher intelligence than nonleaders. Having strong verbal, perceptual, and reasoning abilities appears to make one a better leader (Jacquart & Antonakis, 2015). Although it is good to be bright, if the leader's IQ is very different from that of the followers, it can have a counterproductive impact on leadership. Leaders with higher abilities may have difficulty communicating with followers because they are preoccupied or because their ideas are too advanced for their followers to accept.

In a study of the relationship between intelligence and perceived leadership in midlevel leaders from multinational companies, Antonakis, House, and Simonton (2017) found that the optimal IQ for perceived leadership appeared to be just over one standard deviation above the mean IQ of the group membership. Their study found a curvilinear relationship between IQ and perceived leadership—that is, as IQ increased, so did perceived leadership to a point, and then the IQ had a negative impact on leadership. Stated another way, it is good for leaders to be intelligent, but if their intelligence scores become too high, the benefits appear to taper off and can become negative.

An example of a leader for whom intelligence was a key trait was Steve Jobs, founder and CEO of Apple, who died in 2011. Jobs once said, "I have this really incredible product inside me and I have to get it out" (Sculley, 2011, p. 27). Those visionary products, first the Apple II and Macintosh computers and then the iMac, iPod, iPhone, and iPad, revolutionized the personal computer and electronic device industry, changing the way people play and work.

In the next chapter of this text, which addresses leadership from a skills perspective, intelligence is identified as a trait that significantly contributes to a leader's acquisition of complex problem-solving skills and social judgment skills.

Intelligence is described as having a positive impact on an individual's capacity for effective leadership.

Self-Confidence

Self-confidence is another trait that helps one to be a leader. Self-confidence is the ability to be certain about one's competencies and skills. It includes a sense of self-esteem and self-assurance and the belief that one can make a difference. Leadership involves influencing others, and self-confidence allows leaders to feel assured that their attempts to influence others are appropriate and right.

Again, Steve Jobs is a good example of a self-confident leader. When Jobs described the devices he wanted to create, many people said they weren't possible. But Jobs never doubted his products would change the world, and despite resistance, he did things the way he thought best. "Jobs was one of those CEOs who ran the company like he wanted to. He believed he knew more about it than anyone else, and he probably did," said a colleague (Stone, 2011, p. 40).

Determination

Many leaders also exhibit determination. Determination is the desire to get the job done and includes characteristics such as initiative, persistence, dominance, and drive. People with determination are willing to assert themselves, are proactive, and have the capacity to persevere in the face of obstacles. Being determined includes showing dominance at times and in situations where followers need to be directed. Duckworth, Peterson, Matthews, and Kelly (2007) expanded the concept of determination and conducted research on "grit," which measures the degree of perseverance toward goal attainment. Leaders with grit recover quickly from setbacks, not letting obstacles impede their success (Duckworth et al., 2007).

Dr. Paul Farmer has shown determination in his efforts to secure health care and eradicate tuberculosis for the very poor of Haiti and other third world countries. He began his efforts as a recent college graduate, traveling and working in Cange, Haiti. While there, he was accepted to Harvard Medical School. Knowing that his work in Haiti was invaluable to his training, he managed to do both: spending months traveling back and forth between Haiti and Cambridge, Massachusetts, for school. His first effort in Cange was to establish a one-room clinic where he treated "all comers" and trained local health care workers. Farmer found that there was more to providing health care than just dispensing medicine: He secured donations to build schools, houses, and communal sanitation and water facilities in the region. He spearheaded vaccinations of all the children in the area, dramatically reducing malnutrition and infant mortality. To keep working in Haiti, he returned to America and founded Partners In Health, a charitable foundation that raises money to fund these efforts. Since its founding, PIH not only has succeeded in improving the health of many communities in Haiti but now has projects in Haiti, Lesotho, Malawi, Peru, Russia, Rwanda, and the United States, and supports other projects in Mexico and Guatemala (Kidder, 2004; Partners In Health, 2017; see also Case 10.1, page 272).

Integrity

Integrity, another of the important leadership traits, is the quality of honesty and trustworthiness. People who adhere to a strong set of principles and take responsibility for their actions are exhibiting integrity. Leaders with integrity inspire confidence in others because they can be trusted to do what they say they are going to do. They are loyal, dependable, and not deceptive. Basically, integrity makes a leader believable and worthy of our trust.

In our society, integrity has received a great deal of attention in recent years. For example, as a result of two situations—the position taken by President George W. Bush regarding Iraq's alleged weapons of mass destruction and the impeachment proceedings during the Bill Clinton presidency—people are demanding more honesty of their public officials. Similarly, scandals in the corporate world (e.g., Enron and WorldCom) have led people to become skeptical of leaders who are not highly ethical. In the educational arena, new K–12 curricula are being developed to teach character, values, and ethical leadership. (For instance, see the Character Counts! program developed by the Josephson Institute of Ethics in California at www.charactercounts.org, and the Pillars of Leadership program taught at the J. W. Fanning Institute for Leadership Development in Georgia at www.fanning.uga.edu.) In short, society is demanding greater integrity of character in its leaders.

Sociability

A final trait that is important for leaders is sociability. Sociability is a leader's inclination to seek out pleasant social relationships. Leaders who show sociability are friendly, outgoing, courteous, tactful, and diplomatic. They are sensitive to others' needs and show concern for others' well-being. Social leaders have good interpersonal skills and create cooperative relationships with their followers.

An example of a leader with great sociability skills is Michael Hughes, a university president. Hughes prefers to walk to all his meetings because it gets him out on campus where he greets students, staff, and faculty. He has lunch in the dorm cafeterias or student union and will often ask a table of strangers if he can sit with them. Students rate him as very approachable, while faculty say he has an open-door policy. In addition, he takes time to write personal notes to faculty, staff, and students to congratulate them on their successes.

Although our discussion of leadership traits has focused on five major traits (i.e., intelligence, self-confidence, determination, integrity, and sociability), this list is not all-inclusive. While other traits indicated in Table 2.1 are associated with effective leadership, the five traits we have identified contribute substantially to one's capacity to be a leader.

Until recently, most reviews of leadership traits have been qualitative. In addition, they have lacked a common organizing framework. However, the research described in the following section provides a quantitative assessment of leadership traits that is conceptually framed around the five-factor model of personality. It describes how five major personality traits are related to leadership.

Five-Factor Personality Model and Leadership

Over the past 25 years, a consensus has emerged among researchers regarding the basic factors that make up what we call personality (Goldberg, 1990; McCrae & Costa, 1987). These factors, commonly called the *Big Five*, are neuroticism, extraversion (surgency), openness (intellect), agreeableness, and conscientiousness (dependability) (Table 2.3).

To assess the links between the Big Five and leadership, Judge, Bono, Ilies, and Gerhardt (2002) conducted a major meta-analysis of 78 leadership and personality studies published between 1967 and 1998. In general, Judge et al. found a strong relationship between the Big Five traits and leadership. It appears that having certain personality traits is associated with being an effective leader.

Specifically, in their study, *extraversion* was the factor most strongly associated with leadership. It is the most important trait of effective leaders. Extraversion was followed, in order, by *conscientiousness, openness,* and *low neuroticism.* The last

TABLE 2.3 Big Five Personality Factors

Neuroticism	The tendency to be depressed, anxious, insecure, vulnerable, and hostile
Extraversion	The tendency to be sociable and assertive and to have positive energy
Openness	The tendency to be informed, creative, insightful, and curious
Agreeableness	The tendency to be accepting, conforming, trusting, and nurturing
Conscientiousness	The tendency to be thorough, organized, controlled, dependable, and decisive

Source: Goldberg, L. R. (1990). An alternative "description of personality": The Big-Five factor structure. *Journal of Personality and Social Psychology, 59,* 1216-1229.

factor, *agreeableness*, was found to be only weakly associated with leadership. In a more recent study, Sacket and Walmsley (2014) found that *conscientiousness* had the highest correlation with overall job performance, task performance, organizational citizenship behavior, and counterproductive work behavior (negative correlation). It was found to be the most frequently assessed trait in job interviews for a variety of occupations.

Strengths and Leadership

Very closely related to the traits approach is the more contemporary emphasis on strengths and leadership. The idea behind strengths leadership is that everyone has talents in which they excel or thrive and leaders are able to recognize and capitalize on not only their own strengths but those of their followers as well. A strength is defined as an attribute or quality of an individual that accounts for successful performance. Strength researchers (Buckingham & Clifton, 2001; Rath, 2007) suggest that strengths are the ability to consistently demonstrate exceptional work.

The seminal research in this area has been undertaken by the Gallup organization, which has spent more than 40 years identifying and assessing individual strengths or "themes of human talent" and designing and publishing the StrengthsFinder profile, now called CliftonStrengths assessment, an online assessment of people's talents and potential strengths. Talents are similar to personality traits—they are relatively stable, fixed characteristics that are not easily changed. From talents, strengths emerge. Strengths are derived from having certain talents and then further developing those talents by gaining additional knowledge, skills, and practice (Rath, 2007).

In the strengths perspective, extraordinary individuals are "distinguished less by their impressive 'raw power' than by their ability to identify their strengths and then exploit them" (Gardner, 1997, p. 15). MacKie (2016) suggests that our leadership capability is enhanced when we are able to discover our fully utilized strengths, underutilized strengths, and weaknesses.

Strengths have also been of interest to researchers in the field of positive psychology who look at the best aspects in people, rather than their weaknesses. Most notably from this area of study, Peterson and Seligman (2004) developed an inventory of character strengths called the Values In Action Classification (see Table 2.4).

Based on this classification, an individual's strengths can be measured using the VIA Character Strengths Survey, which includes 24 strengths organized under six basic virtues. This survey identifies individuals' top five character strengths as well as a rank order of their scores on all 24 character strengths. It takes about 30 minutes to complete and is available free at www.viacharacter.org.

TABLE 2.4 VIA Classification of Character Strengths and Virtues

Classification	Strengths
WISDOM & KNOWLEDGE *Cognitive Strengths*	1. Creativity 2. Curiosity 3. Open-mindedness 4. Love of learning 5. Perspective
COURAGE *Emotional Strengths*	6. Authenticity 7. Bravery 8. Perseverance 9. Zest
HUMANITY *Interpersonal Strengths*	10. Kindness 11. Love 12. Social intelligence
JUSTICE *Civic Strengths*	13. Fairness 14. Leadership 15. Teamwork
TEMPERANCE *Strengths Over Excess*	16. Forgiveness 17. Modesty 18. Prudence 19. Self-regulation
TRANSCENDENCE *Strengths About Meaning*	20. Appreciation of beauty and excellence 21. Gratitude 22. Hope 23. Humor 24. Religiousness

Source: Adapted from *A Primer in Positive Psychology*, by Christopher Peterson, 2006, pp. 142–146.

In recent years, there has been an increased interest in studying the way character strengths can be utilized to improve leaders and leadership in organizations. For example, Sosik, Chun, Ete, Arenas, and Scherer (2019) studied the character strengths of a sample of more than 200 U.S. Air Force officers and found that character strengths played a pivotal role in fostering leader performance and psychological flourishing. When leaders demonstrate high self-control along with high levels of honesty/humility, empathy, and moral courage, it appears to benefit their ethical leadership, psychological functioning, and role performance. In another study, Sosik, Gentry, and Chun (2012) assessed data for 191 top-level U.S. executives of for-profit and nonprofit organizations and found that the character strengths of integrity, bravery, and social intelligence were positively related to executive leader performance. In addition, they found integrity contributed the most to explaining the differences in executive performance. These studies, as well as others, underscore the importance of understanding character strengths and the role they play in leadership.

Emotional Intelligence

Another way of assessing the impact of traits on leadership is through the concept of emotional intelligence, which emerged in the 1990s as an important area of study in psychology. It has been widely studied by researchers and has captured the attention of many practitioners (Caruso & Wolfe, 2004; Goleman, 1995, 1998; Mayer & Salovey, 1995, 1997; Mayer, Salovey, & Caruso, 2000; Shankman & Allen, 2015).

As the two words suggest, emotional intelligence has to do with our emotions (affective domain) and thinking (cognitive domain) and the interplay between the two. Whereas *intelligence* is concerned with our ability to learn *information* and apply it to life tasks, *emotional intelligence* is concerned with our ability to understand *emotions* and apply this understanding to life's tasks. Specifically, *emotional intelligence* can be defined as the ability to perceive and express emotions, to use emotions to facilitate thinking, to understand and reason with emotions, and to effectively manage emotions within oneself and in relationships with others (Mayer, Salovey, & Caruso, 2000).

There are different ways to measure emotional intelligence. One scale is the Mayer-Salovey-Caruso Emotional Intelligence Test (MSCEIT; Mayer, Caruso, & Salovey, 2000). The MSCEIT measures emotional intelligence as a set of mental abilities, including the abilities to perceive, facilitate, understand, and manage emotion. In general, the MSCEIT appears to have acceptable content validity and reliability (Boyatzis, 2019); however, a review of research on emotional intelligence found that the emotional intelligence levels in people assessed using this measure seem to be declining over time. Some posit that this may be due to initial studies of emotional intelligence overstating the findings (Gong & Jiao, 2019).

Goleman (1995, 1998) takes a broader approach to emotional intelligence, suggesting that it consists of a set of personal and social competencies. Personal competence consists of self-awareness, confidence, self-regulation, conscientiousness, and motivation. Social competence consists of empathy and social skills such as communication and conflict management.

Shankman and Allen (2015) developed a practice-oriented model of emotionally intelligent leadership, which suggests that leaders must be conscious of three fundamental facets of leadership: context, self, and others. In the model, emotionally intelligent leaders are defined by 21 capacities to which a leader should pay attention, including group savvy, optimism, initiative, and teamwork.

Unlike other traits we've discussed in this chapter, there is evidence that emotional intelligence is not a fixed characteristic; it can be improved through training that focuses on enabling leaders to label their emotions and then regulate them (Ashkanasy, Dasborough, & Ascough, 2009). One experiment compared leaders who received training to those who received no training (a control group). Those in the trained group exhibited improved emotional intelligence competencies and significantly improved outcomes: lower stress, higher morale, and improved civility (Slaski & Cartwright, 2003). Likewise, a meta-analysis of 58 studies of emotional intelligence training that included control groups showed a moderate positive effect for the training (Mattingly & Kraiger, 2019).

Goleman and Boyatzis (2017) articulated four broad aspects of emotional intelligence: Self-awareness, self-management, social awareness, and relationship management. They suggest that individuals can improve their emotional intelligence by engaging in a combination of personal reflection and seeking feedback to the following questions:

What are the differences between how you see yourself and how others see you? This can help you to understand how your self-perception might differ from your reputation.

What matters to you? The areas of your emotional intelligence that you want to improve on should reflect the feedback you've gotten as well as your personal aspirations.

What changes will you make to achieve these goals? Identify specific actions to take to improve.

Many organizations also see emotional intelligence as a trait that can be changed and have adopted emotional intelligence training as part of their leadership development. For example, FedEx's Global Leadership Institute has an emotional intelligence training program for new managers that challenges these leaders to focus on the following every day at work:

Know yourself—increase self-awareness of emotions and reactions

Choose yourself—shift from unconscious reactions to intentional responses

Give yourself—align moment-to-moment decisions with a larger sense of purpose

A key principle of the training is that "emotions drive people, [and] people drive performance." FedEx has tracked the improvements in managers' emotional intelligence and reported an 8% to 11% increase in competencies due to the training—a statistically significant difference (Freedman, 2014).

In addition, the U.S. Army developed a brief internet-based training program for enhancing emotional intelligence. Because military personnel serve under dangerous and emotionally stressful conditions, the training was designed to help reduce the development of depression, anxiety, and/or posttraumatic stress disorder (PTSD). The training helped service members strengthen their emotional flexibility, adaptability, and coping by improving the ability to understand and control their emotions (Killgore, 2017).

There is a debate in the field regarding how big a role emotional intelligence plays in helping people be successful in life. Some researchers, such as Goleman (1995), suggested that emotional intelligence plays a major role in whether people are successful at school, home, and work. Others, such as Mayer, Salovey, and Caruso (2000) and Antonakis (2009), made softer claims for the significance of emotional intelligence in meeting life's challenges. A major review of leadership research identifies "emotions in leadership" as a general category but does not specifically mention emotional intelligence (Dinh et al., 2014). It appears that emotional intelligence is not considered mainstream in leadership research. At the same time, Kotsou, Mikolajczak, Heeren, Grégoire, and Leys (2019) determined that the studies that have been done on the efficacy of emotional intelligence training have not included follow-up research to determine the long-term effects of such training.

A review of the literature by Ashkanasy and Daus (2002) summarizes what we can safely conclude: Emotional intelligence is distinct from, but positively related to, other intelligences (such as IQ). It is an individual difference; some people have more emotional intelligence than others. Emotional intelligence develops over a person's lifetime and can be improved with training. Finally, it involves abilities to effectively identify and perceive emotion and the skills to understand and manage emotions.

In summary, emotional intelligence appears to play a role in the leadership process. The underlying premise suggested by the emotional intelligence framework is that people who are more sensitive to their emotions and the impact of their emotions on others will be leaders who are more effective. As more research is conducted on emotional intelligence, the intricacies of how emotional intelligence relates to leadership will be better understood.

HOW DOES THE TRAIT APPROACH WORK?

The trait approach is very different from the other approaches discussed in subsequent chapters because it focuses exclusively on the leader, not on the followers or the situation. This makes the trait approach theoretically more straightforward than other approaches. In essence, the trait approach is concerned with what traits leaders exhibit and who has these traits.

The trait approach does not lay out a set of hypotheses or principles about what kind of leader is needed in a certain situation or what a leader should do, given a particular set of circumstances. Instead, this approach emphasizes that having a leader with a certain set of traits is crucial to having effective leadership. It is the leader and the leader's traits that are central to the leadership process.

The trait approach suggests that organizations will work better if the people in managerial positions have designated leadership profiles. To find the right people, it is common for organizations to use trait assessment instruments. The assumption behind these procedures is that selecting the right people will increase organizational effectiveness. Organizations can specify the characteristics or traits that are important to them for particular positions and then use trait assessment measures to determine whether an individual fits their needs.

The trait approach is also used for personal awareness and development. By analyzing their own traits, managers can gain an idea of their strengths and weaknesses and can get a feel for how others in the organization see them. A trait assessment can help managers determine whether they have the qualities to move up or to move to other positions in the company.

A trait assessment gives individuals a clearer picture of who they are as leaders and how they fit into the organizational hierarchy. In areas where their traits are lacking, leaders can try to make changes in what they do or where they work to increase their traits' potential impact.

Near the end of the chapter, a leadership instrument is provided that you can use to assess your leadership traits. This instrument is typical of the kind of assessments that companies use to evaluate individuals' leadership potential. As you will discover by completing this instrument, trait measures are a good way to assess your own characteristics.

STRENGTHS

The trait approach has several identifiable strengths. First, the trait approach is intuitively appealing. It fits clearly with our notion that leaders are the individuals who are out front and leading the way in our society. The image in the popular press and community at large is that leaders are a special kind of people—people with gifts who can do extraordinary things. The trait approach is consistent with this perception because it is built on the premise that leaders are different, and their difference resides in the special traits they possess. People have a need to see their leaders as gifted people, and the trait approach fulfills this need.

A second strength of the trait approach is that it has a century of research to back it up. No other theory can boast of the breadth and depth of studies conducted on the trait approach. The strength and longevity of this line of research give the trait approach a measure of credibility that other approaches lack. Out of this abundance of research has emerged a body of data that points to the important role of various traits in the leadership process.

Another strength, more conceptual in nature, results from the way the trait approach highlights the leader component in the leadership process. Leadership is composed of leaders, followers, and situations, but the trait approach is devoted to only the first of these—leaders. Although this is also a potential weakness, by focusing exclusively on the role of the leader in leadership the trait approach has been able to provide us with a deeper and more intricate understanding of how the leader and the leader's traits are related to the leadership process.

The trait approach has given us some benchmarks for what we need to look for if we want to be leaders. It identifies what traits we should have and whether the traits we do have are the best traits for leadership. Based on the findings of this approach, trait assessment procedures can be used to offer invaluable information to supervisors and managers about their strengths and weaknesses and ways to improve their overall leadership effectiveness.

Last, the trait approach helps organizations identify leaders and select individuals for leadership training programs. Organizations often use a battery of personality tests when selecting and placing people within their organizations. For example, conscientiousness, extraversion, and openness to experience are effective traits for sales positions (Frieder, Wang, & Oh, 2018). Personality traits can be used to screen employees, once hired, who will benefit most from leadership training. For example, one study found that extraversion, agreeableness, intellectual curiosity, and emotional stability were positively related to both self-ratings and director ratings of leader development in a training program (Blair, Palmieri, & Paz-Aparicio, 2018). Thus, traits offer a way to predict who will succeed in certain positions and who is best suited to leadership development.

CRITICISMS

In addition to its strengths, the trait approach has several weaknesses. First and foremost is the failure of the trait approach to delimit a definitive list of leadership traits. Although an enormous number of studies have been conducted over the past 100 years, the findings from these studies have been ambiguous and uncertain at times. Furthermore, the list of traits that has emerged appears endless. This is obvious from Table 2.1, which lists a multitude of traits. In fact, these are only a sample of the many leadership traits that were studied.

Another criticism is that the trait approach has failed to take situations into account. As Stogdill (1948) pointed out more than 70 years ago, it is difficult to isolate a set of traits that are characteristic of leaders without also factoring situational effects into the equation. People who possess certain traits that make them leaders in one situation may not be leaders in another situation. Some people may have the traits that help them emerge as leaders but not the traits that allow them to maintain their leadership over time. In other words, the situation influences leadership.

Leader traits also may interact with the situation in that certain traits may predispose a person to assume leadership roles in organizations. For example, leaders with higher openness to experience may thrive in the innovative, energetic environment of a high-technology start-up company, but once that company is established and running on a routine, they may begin to feel stagnant, negatively affecting their performance. Yet, research on traits has not incorporated the situation (Zaccaro et al., 2018), including such factors as the leader–member relationship, team characteristics, or organizational culture that enhance or constrain the influence of traits on performance.

A third criticism, derived from the prior two criticisms, is that this approach has resulted in highly subjective determinations of the most important leadership traits. Because the findings on traits have been so extensive and broad, there has been much subjective interpretation of the meaning of the data. This subjectivity is readily apparent in the many self-help, practice-oriented management books. For example, one author might identify ambition and creativity as crucial leadership traits; another might identify empathy and calmness. In both cases, it is the author's subjective experience and observations that are the basis for the identified leadership traits. These books may be helpful to readers because they identify and describe important leadership traits, but the methods used to generate these lists of traits are weak. To respond to people's need for a set of definitive traits of leaders, authors have set forth lists of traits, even if the origins of these lists are not grounded in strong, reliable research.

Research on traits can also be criticized for failing to look at traits in relationship to leadership outcomes. This research has emphasized the identification of traits but has not addressed how leadership traits affect group members and their work. In trying to ascertain universal leadership traits, researchers have focused on the link between specific traits and leader emergence, but they have not tried to link leader traits with other outcomes such as productivity or employee satisfaction. For example, trait research does not provide data on whether leaders who have high intelligence and strong integrity have better results than leaders without these traits. The trait approach is weak in describing how leaders' traits affect the outcomes of groups and teams in organizational settings.

A final criticism of the trait approach is that, other than for emotional intelligence, its usefulness for leadership training and development is limited. Even if definitive traits could be identified, teaching leaders to improve these traits is not an easy process because traits are not easily changed. For example, it is not reasonable to send managers to a training program to raise their IQ or to train them to become extraverted. While there is some evidence that the trait of emotional intelligence may be improved with training, it is unclear whether these effects are long lasting. The point is that traits are largely fixed psychological structures, and this limits the value of teaching and leadership training.

APPLICATION

Despite its shortcomings, the trait approach provides valuable information about leadership. It can be applied by individuals at all levels and in all types of organizations. Although the trait approach does not provide a definitive set of traits, it does provide direction regarding which traits are good to have if one aspires to a leadership position. By taking trait assessments and other similar questionnaires, people can gain insight into whether they have certain traits deemed important for leadership, and they can pinpoint their strengths and weaknesses with regard to leadership.

As we discussed previously, managers can use information from the trait approach to assess where they stand in their organization and what they need to do to strengthen their position. Trait information can suggest areas in which their personal characteristics are very beneficial to the company and areas in which they may want to get more training to enhance their overall approach. Using trait information, managers can develop a deeper understanding of who they are and how they will affect others in the organization.

CASE STUDIES

In this section, three case studies (Cases 2.1, 2.2, and 2.3) are provided to illustrate the trait approach and to help you understand how the trait approach can be used in making decisions in organizational settings. The settings of the cases are diverse—directing research and development at a large snack food company, being head of recruitment for a large bank, and a profile of entrepreneur Elon Musk—but all of the cases deal with trait leadership. At the end of each case, you will find questions that will help in analyzing the cases.

Case 2.1 CHOOSING A NEW DIRECTOR OF RESEARCH

Sandra Coke is vice president for research and development at Great Lakes Foods (GLF), a large snack food company that has approximately 1,000 employees. As a result of a recent reorganization, Sandra must choose the new director of research. The director will report directly to Sandra and will be responsible for developing and testing new products. The research division of GLF employs about 200 people. The choice of directors is important because Sandra is receiving pressure from the president and board of GLF to improve the company's overall growth and productivity.

Sandra has identified three candidates for the position. Each candidate is at the same managerial level. She is having difficulty choosing one of them because each has very strong credentials. Alexa Smith is a longtime employee of GLF who started part-time in the mailroom while in high school. After finishing school, Alexa worked in as many as 10 different positions throughout the company to become manager of new product marketing. Performance reviews of Alexa's work have repeatedly described her as being very creative and insightful. In her tenure at GLF, Alexa has developed and brought to market four new product lines. Alexa is also known throughout GLF as being very persistent about her work: When she starts a project, she stays with it until it is finished. It is probably this quality that accounts for the success of each of the four new products with which she has been involved.

A second candidate for the new position is Kelsey Metts, who has been with GLF for five years and is manager of quality control for established products. Kelsey has a reputation for being very bright. Before joining GLF, she received her MBA at Harvard, graduating at the top of her class. People talk about Kelsey as the kind of person who will be president of her own company someday. Kelsey is also very personable. On all her performance reviews, she received extra-high scores on sociability and human relations. There isn't a supervisor in the company who doesn't have positive things to say about how comfortable it is to work

(Continued)

(Continued)

with Kelsey. Since joining GLF, Kelsey has been instrumental in bringing two new product lines to market.

Thomas Santiago, the third candidate, has been with GLF for 10 years and is often consulted by upper management regarding strategic planning and corporate direction setting. Thomas has been very involved in establishing the vision for GLF and is a company person all the way. He believes in the values of GLF, and actively promotes its mission. The two qualities that stand out above the rest in Thomas's performance reviews are his honesty and integrity. Employees who have worked under his supervision consistently report that they feel they can trust Thomas to be fair and consistent. Thomas is highly respected at GLF. In his tenure at the company, Thomas has been involved in some capacity with the development of three new product lines.

The challenge confronting Sandra is to choose the best person for the newly established director's position. Because of the pressure she feels from upper management, Sandra knows she must select the best leader for the new position.

Questions

1. Based on the information provided about the trait approach in Tables 2.1 and 2.2, if you were Sandra, whom would you select?

2. In what ways is the trait approach helpful in this type of selection?

3. In what ways are the weaknesses of the trait approach highlighted in this case?

Case 2.2   RECRUITING FOR THE BANK

Pat is the assistant director of human resources in charge of recruitment for Central Bank, a large, full-service banking institution. One of Pat's major responsibilities each spring is to visit as many college campuses as he can to interview graduating seniors for credit analyst positions in the commercial lending area at Central Bank. Although the number varies, he usually ends up hiring about 20 new people, most of whom come from the same schools, year after year.

Pat has been doing recruitment for the bank for more than 10 years, and he enjoys it very much. However, for the upcoming spring he is feeling increased pressure from management to be particularly discriminating about whom he recommends hiring. Management is concerned about the retention rate at the bank because in recent years as many as 25% of the new hires have left. Departures after the first year have meant lost training dollars and strain on the staff who remain. Although management understands that some new hires always leave, the executives are not comfortable with the present rate, and they have begun to question the recruitment and hiring procedures.

The bank wants to hire people who can be groomed for higher-level leadership positions. Although certain competencies are required of entry-level credit analysts, the bank is equally interested in skills that will allow individuals to advance to upper management positions as their careers progress.

In the recruitment process, Pat always looks for several characteristics. First, applicants need to have strong interpersonal skills, they need to be confident, and they need to show poise and initiative. Next, because banking involves fiduciary responsibilities, applicants need to have proper ethics, including a strong sense of the importance of confidentiality. In addition, to do the work in the bank, they need to have strong analytical and technical skills, and experience in working with computers. Last, applicants need to exhibit a good work ethic, and they need to show commitment and a willingness to do their job even in difficult circumstances.

Pat is fairly certain that he has been selecting the right people to be leaders at Central Bank, yet upper management is telling him to reassess his hiring criteria. Although he feels that he has been doing the right thing, he is starting to question himself and his recruitment practices.

Questions

1. Based on ideas described in the trait approach, do you think Pat is looking for the right characteristics in the people he hires?

2. Could it be that the retention problem raised by upper management is unrelated to Pat's recruitment criteria?

3. If you were Pat, would you change your approach to recruiting?

Case 2.3   ELON MUSK

When he was 12, Elon Musk created and sold his first product. That video game, *Blastar*, was the start of Musk's meteoric entrepreneurial career, which has seen him take on everything from electric cars to space travel to alternative energy.

Musk grew up in South Africa, the son of an engineer and a Canadian model. In grade school Musk was introverted and often bullied, but at 15 he learned how to defend himself with karate and wrestling. He moved to Canada at 17 to

(Continued)

(Continued)

attend university and three years later left Canada to attend the University of Pennsylvania where he earned degrees in economics and physics. In 1995, only two days into a PhD program in energy physics at Stanford, Musk dropped out to launch his first company, Zip2, with his brother Kimbal. An online city guide, Zip2 provided content for websites of both the *New York Times* and the *Chicago Tribune*. Four years later, Compaq Computer Corporation bought Zip2 for $307 million.

The Musk brothers then founded X.com, an online financial services/payments company, which became PayPal. Three years later, eBay acquired PayPal for $1.5 billion.

Now a billionaire, Musk started Space Exploration Technologies Corporation, or SpaceX, in 2002 with the intention of building reusable spacecraft for commercial space travel. A year after launching SpaceX, Musk became the cofounder, CEO, and product architect at Tesla Motors, dedicated to producing affordable, mass-market electric cars as well as battery products and solar roofs. He also launched several other side projects, including establishment of The Boring Company devoted to boring and building underground tunnels to reduce street traffic, becoming cochair of the nonprofit research organization OpenAI with the mission of advancing digital intelligence to benefit humanity, and development of the Hyperloop to create a more expedient form of transportation between cities.

But unlike his earlier ventures, both SpaceX and Tesla had considerable challenges. In 2008, Musk was nearly out of money after SpaceX's Falcon 1 rocket, of which he was the chief designer, suffered three failed launches before it finally had a successful one. Meanwhile, Tesla was hitting speed bump after speed bump in the development of its vehicles, hemorrhaging money, and losing investor confidence as well as orders from customers who were unhappy with the long wait time to get their vehicles.

Musk faced these challenges the way he did as a bullied school kid: head on. "Leaders are . . . expected to work harder than those who report to them and always make sure that their needs are taken care of before yours, thus leading by example," he said (Jackson, 2017).

At SpaceX, Musk continued to innovate, and the company accomplished a stunning number of achievements including successfully having rockets land safely back on earth after launches, transporting supplies to the International Space Station, and developing a rocket that could carry heavier payloads. By 2019, SpaceX had 6,000-plus contracts, worth $12 billion, with NASA and other commercial satellite companies. The company, which says its ultimate mission is to foster interplanetary life, is planning a cargo mission to Mars in 2022 (Space Exploration Technologies Corp., 2020).

Many credit SpaceX's success to the unified culture at the company created by its fairly flat organizational structure and the fact that, despite its growth, the company still maintains a start-up mentality and feel.

"It's an incredible place to work," said one engineer. "There's a great sense of connectedness between everyone. Everyone's got the same goal in mind. Everyone's working super hard to deliver a product successfully. It's amazing when it all culminates in launch" (*Mind & Machine*, 2017).

Dolly Singh, the former head of human resources at SpaceX, said, "The thing that makes Elon Elon is his ability to make people believe in his vision" (Snow, 2015). Jim Cantrell, SpaceX's first engineer, added, "He is the smartest guy I've ever met, period. I know that sounds overblown. But I've met plenty of smart people, and I don't say that lightly. He's absolutely, frickin' amazing. I don't even think he sleeps" (Feloni, 2014).

But to turn Tesla around, Musk had to roll up his shirtsleeves. The company, which was four years behind on the production of its Model 3, was under severe public scrutiny from investors and industry analysts. After missing one deadline after another, Musk restructured the organization in April 2018 and took over as the head of engineering to personally oversee efforts in that division. In a 2018 Twitter post, Musk said that to meet production goals, it was time to "divide & conquer, so I'm back to sleeping at factory." By the end of June 2018, Tesla had met its goal of producing 5,000 Model 3 cars per week, while churning out another 2,000 Model S sedans and Model X SUVs (Sage & Rodriguez, 2018).

Musk has been described as an unconventional leader, even by Silicon Valley standards. He is a prolific tweeter in which he comments on everything from building cyborg dragons, to jokes about bankruptcy, to mixing Ambien with red wine (Davies, 2018). He has graced magazine covers and goes on talk shows and appeared on animated television shows *The Simpsons* and *South Park*. His peculiar sense of humor was on dramatic display when he launched his own red Tesla Roadster sports car into space atop the first SpaceX Falcon Heavy rocket. At the same time, some of his behavioral quirks have also become liabilities.

In a public earnings call with investors and financial analysts, Musk attacked two analysts for asking what he called "bonehead" and "dry" questions that he refused to answer, resulting in Tesla's stock value plunging 10% (Davies, 2018). When his efforts to assist in the rescue of 12 young soccer players and their coach from a flooded cave in Thailand were criticized as self-aggrandizing rather than serious, Musk responded with a tweet calling one of the divers involved in the rescue "pedo guy," insinuating he was a child molester (Levin, 2018).

In August 2018, Musk wrote on Twitter that he was considering taking Tesla private and that he had the necessary funding "secured" to do so. As a result,

(Continued)

(Continued)

Tesla's stock price immediately shot up, gaining the attention of the Securities and Exchange Commission (SEC), which investigated and ultimately fined Musk $20 million. Less than two weeks after that episode, Musk gave an emotional interview with the *New York Times*, in which he alternately laughed and cried in a display that left many questioning his mental state and sent Tesla investors into sell mode with their stock (Crum, 2018).

Not long after that interview, Musk changed his mind and said Tesla would remain a public company. He followed that decision with an appearance on the *Joe Rogan Experience* podcast during which he smoked what was said to be a marijuana-laced cigarette (Davies, 2018).

"The reason Elon seems to attract drama is that he is so transparent, so open, in a way that can come back to bite him," his brother and Tesla board member Kimbal Musk told the *New York Times*. "He doesn't know how to do it differently. It's just who he is" (Gelles, 2018).

After all of the drama in 2018, there were many concerns about where Tesla would go in 2019. The answer? Tesla ended 2019 on a high note, with a record stock price topping out at more than $400 per share.

"It's been quite the turnaround for Musk since his 'funding secured' tweet debacle of last year," one analyst noted. "Tesla's stock has been one of the top performers of the second-half of the year and Musk is proof that you can take on the SEC, smoke weed on podcasts, call people pedo guy and still run a $70 billion company" (Crum, 2018).

Questions

1. How does Musk exhibit each of the major leadership traits (Table 2.2)? Which of these traits do you believe he is the strongest in? Is there one where he is weak?

2. Describe how Musk has exhibited each of the Big Five personality factors. Which of these factors do you think has the most correlation with Musk's success as a leader?

3. Shankman and Allen (2015) suggest that an emotionally intelligent leader is conscious of context, self, and others. How would you characterize Musk's emotional intelligence using these three facets?

4. If you were asked to design a leadership training program based on the trait approach, how could you incorporate the story of Elon Musk and his leadership? Around which of his traits would you structure your training? Are some of his leadership traits more teachable than others? Discuss.

LEADERSHIP INSTRUMENT

Organizations use a wide variety of questionnaires to measure individuals' traits. In many organizations, it is common practice to use standard trait measures such as the Minnesota Multiphasic Personality Inventory or the Myers-Briggs Type Indicator. These measures provide valuable information to the individual and the organization about the individual's unique attributes for leadership and where the individual could best serve the organization.

In this section, the Leadership Trait Questionnaire (LTQ) is provided as an example of a measure that can be used to assess your personal leadership characteristics. The LTQ quantifies the perceptions of the individual leader and selected observers, such as followers or peers. It measures an individual's traits and points respondents to the areas in which they may have special strengths or weaknesses.

By taking the LTQ, you can gain an understanding of how trait measures are used for leadership assessment. You can also assess your own leadership traits.

Leadership Trait Questionnaire (LTQ)

Purpose: The purpose of this questionnaire is to measure personal characteristics of leadership and to gain an understanding of how traits are used in leadership assessment.

Instructions: Using the following scale, indicate the degree to which you agree or disagree with each of the 14 statements when viewing yourself as a leader. After you complete this questionnaire, it should be completed by five people you know (e.g., roommates, coworkers, relatives, friends) to show how they view you as a leader.

Key: 1 = Strongly disagree   2 = Disagree   3 = Neutral   4 = Agree   5 = Strongly agree

1.	**Articulate**: Communicates effectively with others	1 2 3 4 5
2.	**Perceptive**: Is discerning and insightful	1 2 3 4 5
3.	**Self-confident**: Believes in oneself and one's ability	1 2 3 4 5
4.	**Self-assured**: Is secure with oneself, free of doubts	1 2 3 4 5
5.	**Persistent**: Stays fixed on the goals, despite interference	1 2 3 4 5
6.	**Determined**: Takes a firm stand, acts with certainty	1 2 3 4 5
7.	**Trustworthy**: Is authentic and inspires confidence	1 2 3 4 5
8.	**Dependable**: Is consistent and reliable	1 2 3 4 5
9.	**Friendly**: Shows kindness and warmth	1 2 3 4 5
10.	**Outgoing**: Talks freely, gets along well with others	1 2 3 4 5
11.	**Conscientious**: Is thorough, organized, and controlled	1 2 3 4 5
12.	**Diligent**: Is persistent, hardworking	1 2 3 4 5
13.	**Sensitive**: Shows tolerance, is tactful and sympathetic	1 2 3 4 5
14.	**Empathic**: Understands others, identifies with others	1 2 3 4 5

Scoring

1. Enter the responses for Raters 1, 2, 3, 4, and 5 in the appropriate columns as shown in Example 2.1. The example provides hypothetical ratings to help explain how the questionnaire can be used.

2. For each of the 14 items, compute the average for the five raters and place that number in the "average rating" column.

3. Place your own scores in the "self-rating" column.

EXAMPLE 2.1 Leadership Traits Questionnaire Ratings

	Rater 1	Rater 2	Rater 3	Rater 4	Rater 5	Average rating	Self-rating
1. Articulate	4	4	3	2	4	3.4	4
2. Perceptive	2	5	3	4	4	3.6	5
3. Self-confident	4	4	5	5	4	4.4	4
4. Self-assured	5	5	5	5	5	5	5
5. Persistent	4	4	3	3	3	3.4	3
6. Determined	4	4	4	4	4	4	4
7. Trustworthy	5	5	5	5	5	5	5
8. Dependable	4	5	4	5	4	4.4	4
9. Friendly	5	5	5	5	5	5	5
10. Outgoing	5	4	5	4	5	4.6	4
11. Conscientious	2	3	2	3	3	2.6	4
12. Diligent	3	3	3	3	3	3	4
13. Sensitive	4	4	5	5	5	4.6	3
14. Empathic	5	5	4	5	4	4.6	3

Scoring Interpretation

The scores you received on the LTQ provide information about how you see your-self as a leader and how others see you as a leader. There are no "perfect" scores for this questionnaire. The purpose of the instrument is to provide a way to assess your strengths and weaknesses. This assessment can help you understand your assets as well as areas in which you may seek to improve. The chart allows you to see where your perceptions are the same as those of others and where they differ.

The example ratings show how the leader self-rated higher than the observers did on the characteristic *articulate*. On the second characteristic, *perceptive*, the leader self-rated substantially higher than others. On the *self-confident* characteristic, the leader self-rated quite close to others' ratings but lower.

A low or moderate self-rating (3 or below) on a trait may indicate that you have had little opportunity to develop this part of your personality or that your current work or school setting does not require you to exercise this trait. A high score (4 or above) suggests you are aware of this trait and use it often. How similar or dissimilar your self-ratings are from others' ratings may be affected by whom you chose to evaluate you, how long these people have known you, and the contexts in which they have observed your behavior.

SUMMARY

The trait approach has its roots in leadership theory that suggested that certain people were born with special traits that made them great leaders. Because it was believed that leaders and nonleaders could be differentiated by a universal set of traits, throughout the 20th century researchers were challenged to identify the definitive traits of leaders.

Around the mid-20th century, several major studies questioned the basic premise that a unique set of traits defined leadership. As a result, attention shifted to incorporating the impact of situations and of followers on leadership. Researchers began to study the interactions between leaders and their context instead of focusing only on leaders' traits. More recently, there have been signs that trait research has come full circle, with a renewed interest in focusing directly on the critical traits of leaders.

From the multitude of studies conducted through the years on personal characteristics, it is clear that many traits contribute to leadership. Some of the important traits that are consistently identified in many of these studies are intelligence, self-confidence, determination, integrity, and sociability. In addition, researchers have found a strong relationship between leadership and the traits described by the *five-factor personality model*. *Extraversion* was the trait most strongly associated with leadership, followed by *conscientiousness, openness, low neuroticism*, and *agreeableness*. *Conscientiousness* was found to have the highest correlation with overall job performance, task performance, organizational citizenship behavior, and counterproductive work behavior (negative correlation) and to be the most frequently assessed trait in job interviews for a variety of occupations.

Another recent line of research has focused on *emotional intelligence* and its relationship to leadership. This research suggests that leaders who are sensitive to their emotions and to the impact of their emotions on others may be leaders who are more effective.

On a practical level, the trait approach is concerned with which traits leaders exhibit and who has these traits. Organizations use personality assessment instruments to identify how individuals will fit within their organizations. The trait approach is also used for personal awareness and development because it allows managers to analyze their strengths and weaknesses to gain a clearer understanding of how they should try to change to enhance their leadership.

There are several advantages to viewing leadership from the trait approach. First, it is intuitively appealing because it fits clearly into the popular idea that leaders are special people who are out front, leading the way in society. Second, a great deal of research validates the basis of this perspective. Third, by focusing exclusively on the leader, the trait approach provides an in-depth understanding of the leader component in the leadership process. Last, it has provided some benchmarks against which individuals can evaluate their own personal leadership attributes.

On the negative side, the trait approach has failed to provide a definitive list of leadership traits. In analyzing the traits of leaders, the approach has failed to take into account the impact of situations. In addition, the approach has resulted in subjective lists of the most important leadership traits, which are not necessarily grounded in strong, reliable research.

Furthermore, the trait approach has not adequately linked the traits of leaders with other outcomes such as group and team performance, which makes this approach not particularly useful for training and development for leadership because individuals' personal attributes are largely stable and fixed, and their traits are not amenable to change. While there is some evidence that the trait of emotional intelligence may be improved with training, follow-up studies have not been conducted to determine the long-term effects of such training.

3 Skills Approach

DESCRIPTION

Like the trait approach discussed in Chapter 2, the skills approach takes a leader-centered perspective on leadership. However, in the skills approach we shift our thinking from focusing exclusively on traits to an emphasis on skills and abilities that can be learned and developed. Although personality and behavior certainly play a role in leadership, the skills approach emphasizes the capabilities, knowledge, and skills that are needed for effective leadership.

Researchers have studied leadership skills directly or indirectly for a number of years (see Bass, 2008, pp. 97–109). However, the impetus for research on skills was a classic article published by Katz in the *Harvard Business Review* in 1955, titled "Skills of an Effective Administrator." Katz's article appeared at a time when researchers were trying to identify a definitive set of leadership traits. Katz's approach was an attempt to transcend the trait problem by addressing leadership as a set of developable *skills*. More recently, a revitalized interest in the skills approach has emerged. Beginning in the early 1990s, a multitude of studies have been published that contend that a leader's effectiveness depends on the leader's ability to solve complex organizational problems. This research has resulted in a comprehensive skill-based model of leadership that was advanced by M. Mumford and his colleagues (M. Mumford, Zaccaro, Harding, Jacobs, & Fleishman, 2000; Yammarino, 2000).

In this chapter, our discussion of the skills approach is divided into two parts. First, we discuss the general ideas set forth by Katz regarding three basic administrative skills: technical, human, and conceptual. Second, we discuss the recent work of Mumford and colleagues that has resulted in a skills-based model of organizational leadership.

Three-Skill Approach

Based on field research in administration and his own firsthand observations of executives in the workplace, Katz (1955, p. 34) suggested that effective administration (i.e., leadership) depends on three basic personal skills: technical, human, and conceptual. Katz argued that these skills are quite different from traits or qualities of leaders. *Skills* are what leaders *can accomplish*, whereas *traits* are who leaders *are* (i.e., their innate characteristics). Leadership skills are defined in this chapter as the ability to use one's knowledge and competencies to accomplish a set of goals or objectives. This chapter shows that these leadership skills can be acquired and leaders can be trained to develop them.

Technical Skills

Technical skills are knowledge about and proficiency in a specific type of work or activity. They include competencies in a specialized area, analytical ability, and the ability to use appropriate tools and techniques (Katz, 1955). For example, in a computer software company, technical skills might include knowing software language and programming, the company's software products, and how to make these products function for clients. Similarly, in an accounting firm, technical skills might include understanding and having the ability to apply generally accepted accounting principles to a client's audit. In both of these examples, technical skills involve a hands-on activity with a basic product or process within an organization. Technical skills play an essential role in producing the actual products a company is designed to produce.

As illustrated in Figure 3.1, technical skills are most important at lower and middle levels of management and less important in upper management. For leaders at the highest level, such as CEOs, presidents, and senior officers, technical competencies are not as essential. Individuals at the top level depend on skilled followers to handle technical issues of the physical operation.

Human Skills

Human skills are knowledge about and ability to work with *people*. They are quite different from technical skills, which have to do with working with *things* (Katz, 1955). Human skills are "people skills." They are the abilities that help a leader to work effectively with followers, peers, and superiors to accomplish the organization's goals. Human skills allow a leader to assist group members in working cooperatively as a group to achieve common goals. For Katz, it means being aware of one's own perspective on issues and, at the same time, being aware of the perspective of others. Leaders with human skills adapt their own ideas to those of others. Furthermore, they create an atmosphere of trust where followers can feel comfortable and secure and where they can feel encouraged to become involved in the planning of things that will affect them. Being a leader with human skills means being sensitive to the needs and motivations of others and considering others' needs in one's decision making. In short, human skills are the capacity to get along with others as you go about your work.

FIGURE 3.1 Management Skills Necessary at Various Levels of an
Organization

SKILLS NEEDED

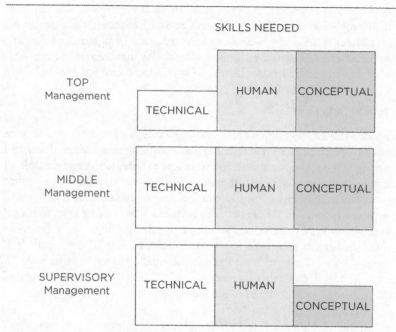

Source: Adapted from "Skills of an Effective Administrator," by R. L. Katz, 1955, *Harvard Business Review*, 33(1), pp. 33–42.

Figure 3.1 shows that human skills are important in all three levels of management. Although managers at lower levels may communicate with a far greater number of followers, human skills are equally important at middle and upper levels.

Conceptual Skills

Broadly speaking, conceptual skills are the ability to work with ideas and concepts. Whereas technical skills deal with *things* and human skills deal with *people*, conceptual skills involve the ability to work with *ideas*. A leader with conceptual skills is comfortable talking about the ideas that shape an organization and the intricacies involved. They are good at putting the organization's goals into words and can understand and express the economic principles that affect the organization. A leader with conceptual skills works easily with abstractions and hypothetical notions.

Conceptual skills are central to creating a vision and strategic plan for an organization. For example, it would take conceptual skills for a CEO in a struggling manufacturing company to articulate a vision for a line of new products that would steer the company into profitability. Similarly, it would take conceptual skills for the director of a nonprofit health organization to create a strategic plan to compete successfully with for-profit health organizations in a market with scarce resources. The point of these examples is that conceptual skills have to do with the mental work of shaping the meaning of organizational or policy issues—understanding what an organization stands for and where it is or should be going.

As shown in Figure 3.1, conceptual skills are most important at the top management levels. In fact, when upper-level managers do not have strong conceptual skills, they can jeopardize the whole organization. Conceptual skills are also important in middle management; as we move down to lower management levels, conceptual skills become less important.

Summary of the Three-Skill Approach

To summarize, the three-skill approach includes technical, human, and conceptual skills. It is important for leaders to have all three skills; depending on where they are in the management structure, however, some skills are more important than others.

Katz's work in the mid-1950s set the stage for conceptualizing leadership in terms of skills, but it was not until the mid-1990s that an empirically based skills approach received recognition in leadership research. In the next section, the comprehensive skill-based model of leadership is presented.

Skills Model

Beginning in the early 1990s, a group of researchers, with funding from the U.S. Army and Department of Defense, set out to test and develop a comprehensive theory of leadership based on problem-solving skills in organizations. The studies were conducted over a number of years using a sample of more than 1,800 Army officers, representing six grade levels, from second lieutenant to colonel. The project used a variety of new measures and tools to assess the skills of these officers, their experiences, and the situations in which they worked.

The researchers' main goal was to explain the underlying elements of effective performance. They addressed questions such as these: What accounts for why some leaders are good problem solvers and others are not? What specific skills do high-performing leaders exhibit? How do leaders' individual characteristics, career experiences, and environmental influences affect their job performance? As a whole, researchers wanted to identify the leadership factors that create exemplary job performance in an actual organization.

Based on the extensive findings from the project, M. Mumford and colleagues formulated a skill-based model of leadership (Figure 3.2). The model is characterized as a *capability* model because it examines the relationship between a leader's knowledge and skills (i.e., capabilities) and the leader's performance (M. Mumford, Zaccaro, Harding, et al., 2000, p. 12). Leadership capabilities can be developed over time through education and experience. Unlike the "great man" approach (discussed in Chapter 2 of this text), which implies that leadership is reserved for only the gifted few, the skills approach suggests that many people have the potential for leadership. If people are capable of learning from their experiences, they can acquire leadership skills. The skills approach can also be distinguished from the leadership approaches, discussed in subsequent chapters, that focus on behavioral patterns of leaders (e.g., the style approach, leader–member exchange theory, and transformational leadership). Rather than emphasizing *what leaders do*, the skills approach frames leadership as *the capabilities (knowledge and skills) that make effective leadership possible* (M. Mumford, Zaccaro, Harding, et al., 2000, p. 12).

The skill-based model of M. Mumford's group has five components: competencies, individual attributes, career experiences, environmental influences, and leadership outcomes (performance and problem solving) (Figure 3.2).

FIGURE 3.2 Influence of Leader Characteristics on Leader Performance

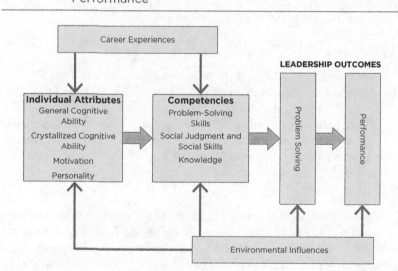

Source: Adapted from "Leadership Skills for a Changing World: Solving Complex Social Problems," by M. D. Mumford, S. J. Zaccaro, F. D. Harding, T. O. Jacobs, and E. A. Fleishman, *The Leadership Quarterly*, 11(1), p. 23. Copyright 2000 by Elsevier.

Individual Attributes

The leftmost box in Figure 3.2 identifies four individual attributes that have an impact on leadership skills and knowledge: general cognitive ability, crystallized cognitive ability, motivation, and personality. These attributes play important roles in the skills model. Complex problem solving is a very difficult process and becomes more difficult as people move up in an organization. These attributes support people as they apply their leadership competencies.

General Cognitive Ability. General cognitive ability can be thought of as a person's intelligence. It includes perceptual processing, information processing, general reasoning skills, creative and divergent thinking capacities, and memory skills. General cognitive ability is linked to biology, not to experience.

General cognitive ability is sometimes described as fluid intelligence, a type of intelligence that usually grows and expands up through early adulthood and then declines with age. In the skills model, intelligence is described as having a positive impact on the leader's acquisition of complex problem-solving skills and the leader's knowledge.

Crystallized Cognitive Ability. Crystallized cognitive ability is intellectual ability that is learned or acquired over time. It is the store of knowledge we acquire through experience. We learn and increase our capacities over a lifetime, increasing our leadership potential (e.g., problem-solving skills, conceptual ability, and social judgment skills). In normally functioning adults, this type of cognitive ability grows continuously and typically does not fall off in adulthood. It includes being able to comprehend complex information and learn new skills and information, as well as being able to communicate to others in oral and written forms (Connelly et al., 2000, p. 71). Stated another way, crystallized cognitive ability is *acquired intelligence*: the ideas and mental abilities people learn through experience. Because it stays fairly stable over time, this type of intelligence is not diminished as people get older (Rose & Gordon, 2015).

Motivation. Motivation is listed as the third attribute in the model. While Kerns (2015) identified three categories of motivations (self-interest, career considerations, and higher purposes) that propel leaders, the skills model takes a different approach, instead suggesting there are three aspects of motivation—*willingness, dominance,* and *social good*—that are essential to developing leadership skills (M. Mumford, Zaccaro, Harding, et al., 2000, p. 22).

First, leaders must be *willing* to tackle complex organizational problems. This first step is critical. For leadership to occur, a person must want to lead. Second, leaders must be willing to express *dominance*—to exert their influence, as we discussed in Chapter 2. In influencing others, the leader must take on the responsibility of dominance because the influence component of leadership is inextricably bound to dominance. Third, leaders must be committed to the *social good* of the organization. *Social good* is a broad term that can refer to a host of outcomes. However, in the skills model it refers to the leader's willingness to take on the responsibility of trying to advance the overall human good and value of the organization. Taken together, these three aspects of motivation (willingness, dominance, and social good) prepare people to become leaders.

Personality. Personality is the fourth individual attribute in the skills model. Placed where it is in the model, this attribute reminds us that our personality has an impact on the development of our leadership skills. For example, openness, tolerance for ambiguity, and curiosity may affect a leader's motivation to try to solve some organizational problems. Or, in conflict situations, traits such as confidence and adaptability may be beneficial to a leader's performance. The skills model hypothesizes that any personality characteristic that helps people to cope with complex organizational situations probably is related to leader performance (M. Mumford, Zaccaro, Harding, et al., 2000).

Competencies

As can be observed in Figure 3.2, problem-solving skills, social judgment skills, and knowledge are at the heart of the skills model. These three competencies are the key factors that account for effective performance (M. Mumford et al., 2012).

Problem-Solving Skills. What are problem-solving skills? According to M. Mumford, Zaccaro, Harding, and colleagues (2000), problem-solving skills are a leader's creative ability to solve new and unusual, ill-defined organizational problems. The skills include being able to define significant problems, gather problem information, formulate new understandings about the problem, and generate prototype plans for problem solutions. M. Mumford, Todd, Higgs, and McIntosh (2017, p. 28) identified nine key problem-solving skills leaders employ to address problems:

1. *Problem definition*, the ability to define noteworthy issues or significant problems affecting the organization

2. *Cause/goal analysis*, the ability to analyze the causes and goals relevant to addressing problems

3. *Constraint analysis*, the ability to identify the constraints, or limiting factors, influencing any problem solution

4. *Planning*, the ability to formulate plans, mental simulations, and actions arising from cause/goal and constraint analysis

5. *Forecasting*, the ability to anticipate the implications of executing the plans

6. *Creative thinking*, the ability to develop alternative approaches and new ideas for addressing potential pitfalls of a plan identified in forecasting

7. *Idea evaluation*, the ability to evaluate these alternative approaches' viability in executing the plan

8. *Wisdom*, the ability to evaluate the appropriateness of these alternative approaches within the context, or setting, in which the leader acts

9. *Sensemaking/visioning*, the ability to articulate a vision that will help followers understand, make sense of, and act on the problem

Figure 3.3 shows the relationship between these different skills as a developing process, where employment of one skill can lead to development of the next.

FIGURE 3.3 Hypothetical Relationships Between Problem-Solving Skills

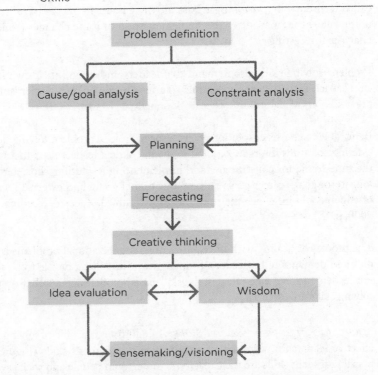

Source: Reprinted from "Cognitive Skills and Leadership Performance: The Nine Critical Skills," by M. D. Mumford, E. M. Todd, C. Higgs, and T. McIntosh, *The Leadership Quarterly, 28*(1), p. 28. Copyright 2017 by Elsevier.

To clarify how these problem-solving skills work in conjunction with one another, consider the following hypothetical situation. Imagine that you are the director of human resources for a medium-sized company and you have been informed by the president that you must develop a plan to reduce the company's health care costs. In deciding what you will do, you demonstrate problem-solving skills in the following ways. First, you identify the full ramifications for employees of changing their health insurance coverage (problem definition; forecasting). What is the impact going to be (cause/goal analysis)? Second, you gather information about how benefits can be scaled back (constraint analysis). What other companies have attempted a similar change, and what were their results (forecasting)? Third, you find a way to teach and inform the employees about the needed change (planning; creative thinking). How can you frame the change in such a way that it is clearly understood (planning; creative thinking; wisdom)? Fourth, you create possible scenarios for how the changes will be instituted (forecasting; idea evaluation). How will the plan be described? Fifth, you look closely at the solution itself (idea evaluation). How will implementing this change affect the company's mission and your own career (sensemaking; visioning)? Last, are there issues in the organization (e.g., union rules) that may affect the implementation of these changes (constraint analysis; forecasting)?

Problem-solving skills also demand that leaders understand their own leadership capacities as they apply possible solutions to the unique problems in their organization (M. Mumford, Zaccaro, Connelly, & Marks, 2000).

Being able to construct solutions plays a special role in problem solving. In considering solutions to organizational problems, skilled leaders need to attend to the time frame for constructing and implementing a solution, short-term and long-term goals, career goals and organizational goals, and external issues, all of which could influence the solution (M. Mumford, Zaccaro, Harding, et al., 2000, p. 15).

The process of dealing with novel, ill-defined organizational problems is complex and demanding for leaders. In many ways, it is like a puzzle to be solved. For leaders to solve such puzzles, the skill-based model suggests that problem-solving skills are essential.

Social Judgment and Social Skills. In addition to problem-solving skills, effective leadership performance requires social judgment skills (Figure 3.2). Social judgment skills are the capacity to understand people and social systems (Zaccaro, Mumford, Connelly, Marks, & Gilbert, 2000, p. 46). They enable leaders to *work with others* to solve problems and to marshal support to implement change within an organization. Social judgment skills are the people skills that are necessary to solve unique organizational problems.

Conceptually, social judgment skills are like Katz's (1955) early work on the role of human skills in management. In contrast to Katz's work, Mumford and colleagues have delineated social judgment skills into the following: perspective taking, social perceptiveness, behavioral flexibility, and social performance.

Perspective taking means understanding the attitudes that *others* have toward a particular problem or solution. It is empathy applied to problem solving. Perspective taking means being sensitive to other people's perspectives and goals—being able to understand their point of view on different issues. Included in perspective taking is knowing how different constituencies in an organization view a problem and possible solutions (Gasiorek & Ebesu Hubbard, 2017). According to Zaccaro, Gilbert, Thor, and Mumford (1991), perspective-taking skills can be likened to *social intelligence*. These skills are concerned with knowledge about people, the social fabric of organizations, and the interrelatedness of each of them.

Social perceptiveness is insight and awareness into how others in the organization function. What is important to others? What motivates them? What problems do they face, and how do they react to change? Social perceptiveness means understanding the unique needs, goals, and demands of different organizational constituencies (Zaccaro et al., 1991). A leader with social perceptiveness has a keen sense of how followers will respond to any proposed change in the organization. In a sense, you could say it allows the leader to know the pulse of followers on any issue at any time.

In addition to understanding others accurately, social judgment skills involve reacting to others with flexibility. *Behavioral flexibility* is the capacity to change and adapt one's behavior in light of understanding others' perspectives in the organization. Being flexible means one is not locked into a singular approach to a problem. One is not dogmatic but rather maintains an openness and willingness to change. As the circumstances of a situation change, a flexible leader changes to meet the new demands.

Social performance includes a wide range of leadership competencies. Based on an understanding of followers' perspectives, leaders need to be able to communicate their own vision to others. Skill in persuasion and communicating change is essential to do this. When there is resistance to change or interpersonal conflict about change, leaders need to function as mediators. To this end, skill in conflict resolution is an important aspect of social performance competency. In addition, social performance sometimes requires that leaders coach followers, giving them direction and support as they move toward selected organizational goals. In all, social performance includes many related skills that may come under the umbrella of communication.

To review, social judgment skills are about being sensitive to how your ideas fit in with others. Can you understand others' perspectives and their unique needs and motivations? Are you flexible, and can you adapt your own ideas to those of others? Can you work with others even when there is resistance and conflict? Social judgment skills are the people skills needed to advance change in an organization.

Knowledge. As shown in the model (Figure 3.2), the third aspect of competencies is knowledge. Knowledge is inextricably related to the application and implementation of problem-solving skills in organizations. It directly influences a leader's capacity to define complex organizational problems and to attempt to solve them (M. Mumford, Zaccaro, Harding, et al., 2000). *Knowledge* is the accumulation of information and the mental structures used to organize that information. Such a mental structure is called a *schema* (a summary, a diagrammatic representation, or an outline). Knowledge results from having developed an assortment of complex schemata for learning and organizing data.

For example, all of us take various kinds of facts and information into our minds. As we organize that information into categories or schemata, the information becomes more meaningful. Knowledge emerges from the facts *and* the organizational structures we apply to them. People with a lot of knowledge have more complex organizing structures than those with less knowledge. These knowledgeable people are called *experts.*

Consider the following baseball example. A baseball expert knows a lot of facts about the game; the expert knows the rules, strategies, equipment, players, and much, much more. The expert's knowledge about baseball includes the facts, but it also includes the complex mental structures used in organizing and structuring those facts. This person knows not only the season and lifetime statistics for each player, but also each player's quirks and injuries, the personality of the manager, the strengths and weaknesses of available substitutes, and so on. The expert comprehends the complexities and nuances of baseball, and thus knows the game. The same is true for leadership in organizations. Leaders with knowledge know much about the products, the tasks, the people, the organization, and all the different ways these elements are related to each other. A knowledgeable leader has many mental structures with which to organize the facts of organizational life.

Knowledge has a positive impact on how leaders engage in problem solving. It is knowledge and expertise that make it possible for people to think about complex system issues and identify possible strategies for appropriate change. Furthermore, this capacity allows people to use prior cases and incidents to plan for needed change. It is knowledge that allows people to use the past to constructively confront the future.

To summarize, the skills model consists of three competencies: problem-solving skills, social judgment skills, and knowledge. Collectively, these three components are positively related to effective leadership performance (Figure 3.2).

Influences on Skills Development

As you can see in Figure 3.2, the skills model identifies two influences that are related to the leader's attributes and competencies and leadership outcomes: career experiences and environmental influences.

Career Experiences. The skills model suggests that the *career experiences* (represented in Figure 3.2 as the topmost box) acquired in the course of leaders' careers influence their development of knowledge and skills for solving complex problems. M. Mumford, Zaccaro, Harding, and colleagues (2000, p. 24) pointed out that leaders can be helped through challenging job assignments, mentoring, appropriate training, and hands-on experience in solving new and unusual problems. In addition, the authors think that career experiences can positively affect the individual attributes of leaders. For example, certain on-the-job assignments could enhance a leader's motivation or intellectual ability.

In the first section of this chapter, we discussed Katz's (1955) work, which notes that conceptual skills are essential for upper-level administrators. This is consistent with M. Mumford, Zaccaro, Harding, and colleagues' (2000) skills model, which contends that leaders develop competencies over time. Career experiences help leaders to improve their skills and knowledge over time. Leaders learn and develop higher levels of conceptual capacity if, as they ascend the organizational hierarchy, the kinds of problems they confront are progressively more complex and longer term (M. Mumford, Zaccaro, Connelly, et al., 2000). Similarly, upper-level leaders, as opposed to first-line supervisors, develop new competencies because they are required to address problems that are more novel, are more poorly defined, and demand more human interaction. As these people move through their careers, higher levels of problem-solving and social judgment skills become increasingly important (M. Mumford & Connelly, 1991).

So the skills and knowledge of leaders are shaped by their career experiences as they address increasingly complex problems in the organization. This notion of developing leadership skills is unique and quite different from other leadership perspectives. If we say, "Leaders are shaped by their experiences," then it means leaders are not born to be leaders (M. Mumford, Zaccaro, Harding, et al., 2000). Leaders can develop their abilities through experience, according to the skills model.

Environmental Influences. Another important component of the skills model is environmental influences, which is illustrated at the bottom of Figure 3.2. Environmental influences represent factors that lie outside the leader's competencies, characteristics, and experiences. These environmental influences can be *internal* and *external*.

Internal environmental influences include such factors as technology, facilities, expertise of followers, and communication. For example, an aging factory lacking in high-speed technology could have a major impact on the nature of problem-solving activities. Another example might be the skill levels of followers: If a leader's followers are highly competent, they will definitely improve the group's problem solving and performance. Similarly, if a task is particularly complex or a group's communication poor, the leader's performance will be affected.

External environmental influences, including economic, political, and social issues, as well as natural disasters, can provide unique challenges to leaders. How U.S. public schools responded to the COVID-19 pandemic is a good recent example of this. As stay-at-home restrictions were enacted, most public schools closed months before the school year would have ended. A majority of these schools were unprepared to switch to online learning. Many districts faced an additional barrier in delivery of online learning due to access: 17% of U.S. students did not have computers in the home, and 18% of students lacked access to high-speed internet (Melia, Amy, & Fenn, 2019).

School leaders across the country scrambled to come up with solutions, including working with local governments and nonprofits to find ways to establish internet hotspots in neighborhoods and to secure and distribute devices to students so they could access online learning. In addition, because most teachers had never actually engaged in online teaching, they were untrained and struggled and underperformed. Others, however, found that having to teach online serendipitously improved their teaching performance. School leaders nationwide had to respond to the very unique challenges posed by an external force completely beyond their control and did so with varying degrees of success.

The skills model does not provide an inventory of specific environmental influences. Instead, it acknowledges the existence of these factors and recognizes that they are indeed influences that can affect a leader's performance, but not usually under the control of the leader.

Leadership Outcomes

In the right-hand boxes in Figure 3.2, effective problem solving and performance are the outcomes of leadership. These outcomes are strongly influenced by the leader's competencies (i.e., problem-solving skills, social judgment skills, and knowledge). When leaders exhibit these competencies, they increase their chances of problem solving and overall performance.

Effective Problem Solving. As we discussed earlier, the skills model is a *capability model*, designed to explain why some leaders are good problem solvers and others are not. Problem solving is the keystone in the skills approach. In the model (Figure 3.2), problem-solving skills, as competencies, lead to effective problem solving as a leadership outcome. The criteria for good problem solving are determined by the originality and the quality of expressed solutions to problems. Good problem solving involves creating solutions that are logical, effective, and unique, and that go beyond given information (Zaccaro et al., 2000).

Performance. In the model, performance outcomes reflect how well individual leaders have done their job. To measure performance, standard external criteria are used. If a leader has done well and been successful, the leader's evaluations will be positive. Leaders who are effective receive good annual performance reviews, get merit raises, and are recognized by superiors and followers as competent leaders. In the end, performance is the degree to which a leader has successfully performed the assigned duties.

Taken together, effective problem solving and performance are the outcomes used to assess leadership effectiveness in the skills model. Furthermore, good problem solving and good performance go hand in hand.

Summary of the Skills Model

In summary, the skills model frames leadership by describing five components of leader performance. At the heart of the model are three competencies: *problem-solving skills, social judgment skills*, and *knowledge*. These three competencies are the central determinants of effective problem solving and performance, although individual attributes, career experiences, and environmental influences all have impacts on leader competencies. Through job experience and training, leaders can become better problem solvers and more effective leaders.

HOW DOES THE SKILLS APPROACH WORK?

The skills approach is primarily descriptive: It *describes* leadership from a skills perspective. Rather than providing prescriptions for success in leadership, the skills approach provides a structure for understanding the nature of effective leadership. In the previous sections, we discussed the skills perspective based on the work of Katz (1955) and M. Mumford, Zaccaro, Harding, and colleagues (2000). What does each of these bodies of work suggest about the structure and functions of leadership?

The three-skill approach of Katz suggests that the importance of certain leadership skills varies depending on where leaders are in a management hierarchy. For leaders operating at lower levels of management, technical and human skills are most important. When leaders move into middle management, it becomes important that they have all three skills: technical, human, and conceptual. At the upper management levels, it is paramount for leaders to exhibit conceptual and human skills.

This approach was reinforced in a 2007 study that examined the skills needed by executives at different levels of management. The researchers used a four-skill model, similar to Katz's approach, to assess cognitive skills, interpersonal skills, business skills, and strategic skills of 1,000 managers at the junior, middle, and senior levels of an organization. The results showed that interpersonal and cognitive skills were required more than business and strategic skills for those on the lower levels of management. As one climbed the career ladder, however, the execution of higher levels of all four of these leadership skills became necessary (T. Mumford, Campion, & Morgeson, 2007).

In their skills model, M. Mumford, Zaccaro, Harding, and colleagues (2000) provided a more complex picture of how skills relate to the manifestation of effective leadership. Their skills model contends that leadership outcomes are the direct result of a leader's competencies in problem-solving skills, social judgment skills, and knowledge. Each of these competencies includes a large repertoire of abilities, and each can be learned and developed. In addition, the model illustrates how individual attributes such as general cognitive ability, crystallized cognitive ability, motivation, and personality influence the leader's competencies. And finally, the model describes how career experiences and environmental influences play a direct or indirect role in leadership performance.

The skills approach works by providing a *map* for how to reach effective leadership in an organization: Leaders need to have problem-solving skills, social judgment skills, and knowledge. Workers can improve their capabilities in these areas through training and experience. Although individual leaders' personal attributes affect their skills, it is a leader's *skills* themselves that are most important in addressing organizational problems.

STRENGTHS

In several ways, the skills approach contributes positively to our understanding about leadership. First, it is a leader-centered model that stresses the importance of developing particular leadership skills. It is the first approach to conceptualize and create a structure of the process of leadership around *skills*. Whereas the early research on skills highlighted the importance of skills and the value of skills across different management levels, the later work placed learned skills at the center of effective leadership performance at *all* management levels. The skills approach also supports succession planning in organizations by ensuring that there is a pool of potential managers ready to assume leadership at the next level (Griffith, Baur, & Buckley, 2019).

Second, the skills approach is intuitively appealing. To describe leadership in terms of skills makes leadership available to everyone. Unlike personality traits, skills are competencies that people can learn or develop. It is like playing a sport such as tennis or golf. Even without natural ability in these sports, people can improve their games with practice and instruction. The same is true with leadership. When leadership is framed as a set of skills, it becomes a process that people can study and practice to become better at performing their jobs.

An example of how individuals can improve their leadership skills is evident in game-based learning (GBL), which has been applied to developing leadership skills in recent years. Through GBL, individuals work toward a goal, choosing actions and experiencing the consequences of those actions in a risk-free setting. Through experimentation, participants learn and practice the right way to do things. In one study, a leadership game was found to improve motivation, facilitation, coaching, mindset changing, and communication (Sousa & Rocha, 2019) in participants. GBL also gives individuals at all levels in an organization access to training for leadership positions.

Third, the skills approach provides an expansive view of leadership that incorporates a wide variety of components, including problem-solving skills, social judgment skills, knowledge, individual attributes, career experiences, and environmental influences. Each of these components can further be subdivided into several subcomponents. The result is a picture of leadership that encompasses a multitude of factors. Because it includes so many variables, the skills approach captures many of the intricacies and complexities of leadership not found in other models.

Last, the skills approach provides a structure that is very consistent with the curricula of most leadership education programs. Leadership development was estimated to be a $14 billion industry in the United States (Gurdjian, Halbeisen, & Lane, 2014), and leadership education programs throughout the country have traditionally taught classes in creative problem solving, conflict resolution, listening, and teamwork, to name a few. The content of these classes closely mirrors many of the components in the skills model. Clearly, the skills approach provides a structure that helps to frame the curricula of leadership education and development programs.

CRITICISMS

Like all other approaches to leadership, the skills approach has certain weaknesses. First, the breadth of the skills approach seems to extend beyond the boundaries of leadership. For example, by including motivation, critical thinking, personality, and conflict resolution, the skills approach addresses more than just leadership. Another example of the model's breadth is its inclusion of two types of intelligence (i.e., general cognitive ability and crystallized cognitive ability). Although both areas are studied widely in the field of cognitive psychology, they are seldom addressed in leadership research. By including so many components, the skills model of M. Mumford and others becomes more general and less precise in explaining leadership performance.

Second, related to the first criticism, the skills model is weak in predictive value. It does not explain specifically how variations in social judgment skills and problem-solving skills affect performance. The model suggests that these components are related, but it does not describe with any precision just how that works. In short, the model can be faulted because it does not explain *how* skills lead to effective leadership performance. Despite the billions of dollars spent on leadership training, the overall effectiveness of these programs has not been clearly substantiated (Kellerman, 2012). In addition, the ability of leaders to transfer skills training to the job may be limited by the followers, the situation, or the organizational culture.

The final criticism of the skills approach is that it may not be suitably or appropriately applied to other contexts of leadership. The skills model was constructed by using a large sample of military personnel and observing their performance in the armed services. This represents a highly structured, hierarchical organizational culture where the variance in leader behavior is restricted. This raises an obvious question: Can the results be generalized to other populations or organizational settings? Although some research suggests that these military findings can be generalized to other groups (M. Mumford, Zaccaro, Connelly, et al., 2000), more research is needed to address this criticism.

APPLICATION

Despite its appeal to theorists and academics, the skills approach has not been widely used in applied leadership settings. For example, there are no training packages designed specifically to teach people leadership skills from this approach. Although many programs have been designed to teach leadership skills from a general self-help orientation, few of these programs are based on the conceptual frameworks set forth in this chapter.

Despite the lack of formal training programs, the skills approach offers valuable information about leadership. The approach provides a way to delineate the skills of the leader, and leaders at all levels in an organization can use it. In addition, this approach helps us to identify our strengths and weaknesses in regard to these technical, human, and conceptual skills. By taking a skills inventory such as the one provided at the end of this chapter, people can gain further insight into their own leadership competencies. Their scores allow them to learn about areas in which they may want to seek further training to enhance their overall contributions to their organization.

From a wider perspective, the skills approach may be used in the future as a template for the design of extensive leadership development programs. This approach provides the evidence for teaching leaders the important aspects of listening, creative problem solving, conflict resolution skills, and much more.

CASE STUDIES

The following three case studies (Cases 3.1, 3.2, and 3.3) describe leadership situations that can be analyzed and evaluated from the skills perspective. The first case involves the principal investigator of a federally funded research grant. In the second case, we learn about how the owner of an Italian restaurant has created his own recipe for success. The third case profiles Kenyan teacher Peter Tabichi and his work to improve not only his students' lives, but their community as well.

As you read each case, try to apply the principles of the skills approach to the leaders and their situations. At the end of each case are questions that will assist you in analyzing the case.

Case 3.1 A STRAINED RESEARCH TEAM

Dr. Adam Wood is the principal investigator on a three-year, $1 million federally funded research grant to study health education programs for older populations, called the Elder Care Project. Unlike previous projects, in which Dr. Wood worked alone or with one or two other investigators, on this project Dr. Wood has 11 colleagues. His project team is made up of two co-investigators (with PhDs), four intervention staff (with MAs), and five general staff members (with BAs). One year into the project, it has become apparent to Dr. Wood and the team that the project is underbudgeted and has too few resources. Team members are spending 20%–30% more time on the project than has been budgeted to pay them. Regardless of the resource strain, all team members are committed to the project; they believe in its goals and the importance of its outcomes. Dr. Wood is known throughout the country as the foremost scholar in this area of health education research. He is often asked to serve on national review and advisory boards. His publication record is second to none. In addition, his colleagues in the university know Dr. Wood as a very competent researcher. People come to Dr. Wood for advice on research design and methodology questions. They also come to him for questions about theoretical formulations. He has a reputation as someone who can see the big picture on research projects.

Despite his research competence, there are problems on Dr. Wood's research team. Dr. Wood worries there is a great deal of work to be done but that the members of the team are not devoting sufficient time to the Elder Care Project. He is frustrated because many of the day-to-day research tasks of the project are falling into his lap. He enters a research meeting, throws his notebook down on the table, and says, "I wish I'd never taken this project on. It's taking way too much of my time. The rest of you aren't pulling your fair share."

(Continued)

(Continued)

Team members feel exasperated at Dr. Wood's comments. Although they respect his competence, they find his leadership style frustrating. His negative comments at staff meetings are having a demoralizing effect on the research team. Despite their hard work and devotion to the project, Dr. Wood seldom compliments or praises their efforts. Team members believe that they have spent more time than anticipated on the project and have received less pay or credit than expected. The project is sucking away a lot of staff energy, yet Dr. Wood does not seem to understand the pressures confronting his staff.

The research staff is starting to feel burned out, but members realize they need to keep trying because they are under time constraints from the federal government to do the work promised. The team needs to develop a pamphlet for the participants in the Elder Care Project, but the pamphlet costs are significantly more than budgeted in the grant. Dr. Wood has been very adept at finding out where they might find small pockets of money to help cover those costs.

Although team members are pleased that he is able to obtain the money, they are sure he will use this as just another example of how he was the one doing most of the work on the project.

Questions

1. Based on the skills approach, how would you assess Dr. Wood's leadership and his relationship to the members of the Elder Care Project team? Will the project be successful?

2. Does Dr. Wood have the skills necessary to be an effective leader of this research team?

3. The skills model describes three important competencies for leaders: problem-solving skills, social judgment skills, and knowledge. If you were to coach Dr. Wood using this model, what competencies would you address with him? What changes would you suggest that he make in his leadership?

Case 3.2 ANDY'S RECIPE

Andy Garafallo owns an Italian restaurant that sits in the middle of a cornfield near a large midwestern city. On the restaurant's far wall is an elaborate mural of the canals of Venice. A gondola hangs on the opposite wall, up by the ceiling. Along another wall is a row of real potted lemon trees. "My ancestors are from Sicily," says Andy. "In fact, I can remember seeing my grandfather take a bite out of a lemon, just like the ones hanging on those trees."

Andy is very confident about his approach to this restaurant, and he should be, because the restaurant is celebrating its 25th anniversary. "I'm darned sure of what I want to do. I'm not trying different fads to get people to come here. People come here because they know they will get great food. They also want to support someone with whom they can connect. This is my approach. Nothing more, nothing less." Although other restaurants have folded, Andy seems to have found a recipe for success.

Since opening his restaurant, Andy has had a number of managers. Currently, he has three: Kelly, Danielle, and Patrick. Kelly is a kitchen (food prep) manager who is known as very honest and dependable. She loves her work, and is efficient, good with ordering, and good with preparation. Andy really likes Kelly but is frustrated with her because she has such difficulty getting along with the sales-people, delivery people, and waitstaff.

Danielle, who works out front in the restaurant, has been with Andy the longest, six years. Danielle likes working at Garafallo's—she lives and breathes the place. She fully buys into Andy's approach of putting customers first. In fact, Andy says she has a knack for knowing what customers need even before they ask. Although she is very hospitable, Andy says she is lousy with numbers. She just doesn't seem to catch on to that side of the business.

Patrick, who has been with Andy for four years, usually works out front but can work in the kitchen as well. Although Patrick has a strong work ethic and is great with numbers, he is weak on the people side. For some reason, Patrick treats customers as if they are faceless, coming across as very unemotional. In addition, Patrick tends to approach problems with an either–or perspective. This has got-ten him into trouble on more than one occasion. Andy wishes that Patrick would learn to lighten up. "He's a good manager, but he needs to recognize that some things just aren't that important," says Andy.

Andy's approach to his managers is that of a teacher and coach. He is always trying to help them improve. He sees part of his responsibility as teaching them every aspect of the restaurant business. Andy's stated goal is that he wants his managers to be "A" players when they leave his business to take on jobs else-where. Helping people to become the best they can be is Andy's goal for his restaurant employees.

Although Andy works 12 hours a day, he spends little time analyzing the numbers. He does not think about ways to improve his profit margin by cutting corners, raising an item price here, or cutting quality there. Andy says, "It's like this: The other night I got a call from someone who said they wanted to come in with a group and wondered if they could bring along a cake. I said 'yes' with one stipulation. . . . I get a piece! Well, the people came and spent a lot of money. Then they told me that they had actually wanted to go to another restaurant, but the other place would not allow them to bring in their own cake." Andy believes very strongly in his approach. "You get business by being what you should be."

(Continued)

(Continued)

Compared with other restaurants, his restaurant is doing quite well. Although many places are happy to net 5%–7% profit, Andy's Italian restaurant nets 30% profit, year in and year out.

Questions

1. What accounts for Andy's success in the restaurant business?

2. From a skills perspective, how would you describe the three managers, Kelly, Danielle, and Patrick? What does each of them need to do to improve their skills?

3. How would you describe Andy's competencies? Does Andy's leadership suggest that one does not need all three skills to be effective?

Case 3.3 2019 GLOBAL TEACHER OF THE YEAR: PETER TABICHI

How does one take nearly 500 secondary math and science students at a school in an impoverished, remote part of Kenya with only one computer, a poor internet connection, and a student–teacher ratio of 58:1 and turn them into motivated, successful students and award-winning scientists?

That's the question many have been asking Peter Tabichi, a math and science teacher at Keriko Mixed Day Secondary School in Pwani village, who was named the Varkey Foundation's 2019 Global Teacher of the Year after being chosen from more than 10,000 nominations from 179 countries.

For Peter, who is a friar in the Franciscan Brotherhood, teaching starts with understanding his students, their cultures, and the challenges they face. Keriko is a government-run school in a part of Kenya frequently stricken with drought and famine, and Peter's students come from poor families who barely eke out a living farming the land. A third of the school's students are orphans or have only one parent and have lives marked by drug abuse, teenage pregnancies, early school dropout, young marriages, and suicide.

The fifth of eight children, Peter understands his students' hardships. Peter's father was a teacher and his mother a farmer. "We lived in a mud house, and we ate maize and vegetables grown in the garden," he says. His mother died when he was 11, and his youngest sibling just 1. "After that, I had to go to the school where my father taught, and that was a 7-kilometer walk each way," he says. "It was hard, but I knew I was lucky to be getting an education. My father took out loan after loan to put us through school" (Moorhead, 2019).

Peter went on to university to become a teacher and began his teaching career in a private school, and while he felt he was making a difference for his students, he wanted to do more. "I felt that the surrounding communities, they also needed my help. I said, 'Let me stretch and extend the same love to the surrounding community'" (Talking Education, 2019).

"I felt increasingly inspired by the life of St. Francis of Assisi. His humility and simplicity appealed to me," he says. Peter took his vows to become a Franciscan in 2018. "It's a challenging life, but I knew it was the right path for me. There are big commitments to make, but this life brings me much happiness" (Moorhead, 2019).

Coming to Keriko, Peter began by giving away 80% of his income every year to provide the school's students with books and uniforms because many of the students' families could not afford to do so. Peter also saw that his students were "not able to concentrate mainly because they are not able to get enough meals at home" (Talking Education, 2019). To battle this food insecurity, he used his knowledge of science and farming to teach members of the community sustainable agriculture including ways of growing vegetables that use a very small portion of land and water. "Teaching the members of the community new ways of farming is a matter of life and death," he says (Talking Education, 2019).

Part of his efforts in the community also involved convincing families and community members of the value of education. He would personally visit families whose children were at risk of dropping out of school and try to change the minds of those who expected their daughters to get married at an early age, encouraging the families to instead keep their girls in school (Zaki, 2019).

In the classroom, Peter saw that he needed to do more for his students than impart the basics of math and science. For many of his students, success in school was about instilling them with confidence. "It is all about having confidence in the student. Every child has potential, a gift or a talent. I try to engage students in various activities and mentor them. It is not a matter of telling them 'do this' and then walking away. You need to work with them closely" (Wodon, 2019).

To help build his students' self-esteem, Peter started a series of school societies, notably the Talent Nurturing Club. "Everyone had something they were good at, and then they started to believe in themselves, and they started to do better at everything" (Moorhead, 2019).

Another pivotal group Peter formed was the Peace Club. Because the school's students are a mix of genders and come from several different tribes and villages, there was the potential for students to form groups and for conflict to occur between the groups. Members of the Peace Club engage in activities like debating, tree planting, and sports where they have to work together. "They see that they can achieve as a group, not only as individuals. They see themselves

(Continued)

(Continued)

as people who are united. This also helps them do well in the classroom because they are able to work as a team," Peter explains (Wodon, 2019).

Peter also expanded the school's Science Club, an effort that has been so successful that 60% of the club's research projects qualify for national competitions. At the 2018 Kenya Science and Engineering Fair, Keriko students showcased a device they invented to help people with vision and hearing impairments to measure objects. The club's math and science team qualified to participate at the Intel-sponsored International Science and Engineering Fair in 2019. Another group of students was recognized by the Royal Society of Chemistry for their work in harnessing local plant life to generate electricity.

Despite the school only having one computer, limited internet access, and no library or labs, Peter has been able to incorporate information technology into 80% of his lessons. He visits internet cafés to download online content to be used offline in class, which he pays for out of his own pocket. He and his colleagues also visit struggling students' homes on the weekends to provide one-on-one tutoring and meet their families to identify the challenges they face.

In just three years, Peter has dramatically improved his pupils' achievement and self-esteem. The school's enrollment has doubled, girls' achievement has been boosted, and discipline cases have fallen from 30 per week to 3. In 2017, only 16 out of Keriko's 59 graduating students went on to college; in 2018, 26 did (Wodon, 2019).

A colleague describes Peter as dedicated, passionate, and humble. "Bro Tabichi's belief in his students has made our poorly equipped school perform well in national science competitions. . . . He became our role model" (Matara & Njeru, 2019).

"The fact that many students have varying needs, has taught me to be creative in using the best approaches while teaching them. They want to feel recognized, loved, appreciated and respected. They have taught me that for them to realize their dreams, you need to work with them closely with a lot of resilience, patience and dedication" (Koigi, 2019).

Questions

1. Applying the Katz three-skills approach, describe Peter Tabichi's technical, human, and conceptual skills. Which of these three skills is most important to Tabichi's success as a leader?

2. How would you describe Peter's competencies?

3. Describe how you believe Peter's career experiences and environmental influences have shaped his leadership skills.

4. Describe some of the problem-solving skills Peter has exhibited. How have his competencies and individual attributes contributed to his problem solving?

LEADERSHIP INSTRUMENT

Many questionnaires assess an individual's skills for leadership. A quick search of the internet provides a host of these questionnaires. Almost all of them are designed to be used in training and development to give people a feel for their leadership abilities. Surveys have been used for years to help people understand and improve their leadership style, but most questionnaires are not used in research because they have not been tested for reliability and validity. Nevertheless, they are useful as self-help instruments because they provide specific information to people about their leadership skills.

In this chapter, we present a comprehensive skills model that is based on many empirical studies of leaders' skills. Although the questionnaires used in these studies are highly reliable and are valid instruments, they are not suitable for our more pragmatic discussion of leadership in this text. In essence, they are too complex and involved. For example, M. Mumford, Zaccaro, Harding, and colleagues (2000) used measures that included open-ended responses and very sophisticated scoring procedures. Though critically important for validating the model, these complicated measures are less valuable as self-instruction questionnaires.

A skills inventory is provided in the next section to assist you in understanding how leadership skills are measured and what your own skills might be. Your scores on the inventory will give you a sense of your own leadership competencies. You may be strong in all three skills, or you may be stronger in some skills than in others. The questionnaire will give you a sense of your own skills profile. If you are stronger in one skill and weaker in another, this may help you determine where you want to improve in the future.

Skills Inventory

Purpose: The purpose of this questionnaire is to determine your leadership strengths and weaknesses.

Instructions: Read each item carefully and decide whether the item describes you as a person. Indicate your response to each item by selecting one of the five options to the right of each item.

Key: 1 = Not true   2 = Seldom   3 = Occasionally   4 = Somewhat   5 = Very
                              true   true   true   true

1.	I enjoy getting into the details of how things work.	1	2	3	4	5
2.	As a rule, adapting ideas to people's needs is easy for me.	1	2	3	4	5
3.	I enjoy working with abstract ideas.	1	2	3	4	5
4.	Technical things fascinate me.	1	2	3	4	5
5.	Being able to understand others is the most important part of my work.	1	2	3	4	5
6.	Seeing the big picture comes easy for me.	1	2	3	4	5
7.	One of my skills is being good at making things work.	1	2	3	4	5
8.	My main concern is to have a supportive communication climate.	1	2	3	4	5
9.	I am intrigued by complex organizational problems.	1	2	3	4	5
10.	Following directions and filling out forms comes easily for me.	1	2	3	4	5
11.	Understanding the social fabric of the organization is important to me.	1	2	3	4	5
12.	I would enjoy working out strategies for my organization's growth.	1	2	3	4	5
13.	I am good at completing the things I've been assigned to do.	1	2	3	4	5
14.	Getting all parties to work together is a challenge I enjoy.	1	2	3	4	5
15.	Creating a mission statement is rewarding work.	1	2	3	4	5
16.	I understand how to do the basic things required of me.	1	2	3	4	5
17.	I am concerned with how my decisions affect the lives of others.	1	2	3	4	5
18.	Thinking about organizational values and philosophy appeals to me.	1	2	3	4	5

Scoring

The skills inventory is designed to measure three broad types of leadership skills: technical, human, and conceptual. Score the questionnaire by doing the following. First, sum the responses on items 1, 4, 7, 10, 13, and 16. This is your technical skill score. Second, sum the responses on items 2, 5, 8, 11, 14, and 17. This is your human skill score. Third, sum the responses on items 3, 6, 9, 12, 15, and 18. This is your conceptual skill score.

Total scores: Technical skill _____ Human skill _____ Conceptual skill _____

Scoring Interpretation

For each category:

23–30 High Range

14–22 Moderate Range

6–13 Low Range

The scores you received on the skills inventory provide information about your leadership skills in three areas. By comparing the differences between your scores, you can determine where you have leadership strengths and where you have leadership weaknesses. Your scores also point toward the level of management for which you might be most suited.

SUMMARY

The skills approach is a leader-centered perspective that emphasizes the competencies of leaders. It is best represented in the early work of Katz (1955) on the *three-skill approach* and the more recent work of M. Mumford and his colleagues (M. Mumford, Zaccaro, Harding, et al., 2000), who initiated the development of a comprehensive *skills model of leadership.*

In the three-skill approach, effective leadership depends on three basic personal skills: technical, human, and conceptual. Although all three skills are important for leaders, the importance of each skill varies between management levels. At lower management levels, technical and human skills are most important. For middle managers, the three different skills are equally important. At upper management levels, conceptual and human skills are most important, and technical skills become less important. Leaders are more effective when their skills match their management level.

In the 1990s, the skills model was developed to explain the capabilities (knowledge and skills) that make effective leadership possible. Far more complex than Katz's paradigm, this model delineated five components of effective leader performance: competencies, individual attributes, career experiences, environmental influences, and leadership outcomes. The leader competencies at the heart of the model are problem-solving skills, social judgment skills, and knowledge. These competencies are directly affected by the leader's individual attributes, which include general cognitive ability, crystallized cognitive ability, motivation, and personality. Individual leaders' competencies are also affected by their career experiences and the environment. The model postulates that effective problem solving and performance can be explained by a leader's basic competencies and that these competencies are in turn affected by the leader's attributes, experience, and environment.

There are several strengths in conceptualizing leadership from a skills perspective. First, it is a leader-centered model that stresses the importance of the leader's abilities, and it places learned skills at the center of effective leadership performance. Second, the skills approach describes leadership in such a way that makes it available to everyone. Skills are competencies that we all can learn to develop and improve. Third, the skills approach provides a sophisticated map that explains how effective leadership performance can be achieved. Based on the model, researchers can develop complex plans for studying the leadership process. Last, this approach provides a structure for leadership education and development programs that include creative problem solving, conflict resolution, listening, and teamwork.

In addition to the positive features, there are some negative aspects to the skills approach. First, the breadth of the model seems to extend beyond the boundaries of leadership, including, for example, conflict management, critical thinking, motivation theory, and personality theory. Second, the skills model is weak in predictive value. It does not explain how a person's competencies lead to effective leadership performance.

Third, the skills model is weak in general application because it was constructed using data only from military personnel. Until the model has been tested with other populations, such as small and large organizations and businesses, its basic tenets must still be questioned.

4 Behavioral Approach

DESCRIPTION

The behavioral approach emphasizes the behavior of the leader. This distinguishes it from the trait approach (Chapter 2), which emphasizes the personality characteristics of the leader, and the skills approach (Chapter 3), which emphasizes the leader's capabilities. The behavioral approach focuses exclusively on what leaders do and how they act. In shifting the study of leadership to leader behaviors, the behavioral approach expanded the research of leadership to include the actions of leaders toward followers in various contexts.

Researchers studying the behavioral approach determined that leadership is composed of two general kinds of behaviors: *task behaviors* and *relationship behaviors*. Task behaviors facilitate goal accomplishment: They help group members to achieve their objectives. Relationship behaviors help followers feel comfortable with themselves, with each other, and with the situation in which they find themselves. The central purpose of the behavioral approach is to explain how leaders combine these two kinds of behaviors to influence followers in their efforts to reach a goal.

Many studies have been conducted to investigate the behavioral approach. Some of the first studies to be done were conducted at The Ohio State University in the late 1940s, based on the findings of Stogdill's (1948) work, which pointed to the importance of considering more than leaders' traits in leadership research. At about the same time, another group of researchers at the University of Michigan was conducting a series of studies that explored how leadership functioned in small groups. A third line of research was begun by Blake and Mouton in the early 1960s; it explored how managers used task and relationship behaviors in the organizational setting.

Although many research studies could be categorized under the heading of the behavioral approach, the Ohio State studies, the Michigan studies, and the studies by Blake and Mouton (1964, 1978, 1985) are strongly representative of the ideas in this approach. By looking closely at each of these groups of studies, we can draw a clearer picture of the underpinnings and implications of the behavioral approach.

Task and Relationship Behaviors

The essence of leadership behavior has two dimensions—task behaviors and relationship behaviors. There are leadership situations and challenges that call for strong task behavior, while others demand strong relationship behavior, but some degree of each is required in every situation. At the same time, because of personality and life experiences, leaders bring to every situation their own unique tendencies to be either more task oriented or more relationship oriented, or some unique blend of the two. On the surface, this may seem incidental or ho-hum, but in regard to leader effectiveness, the utilization of both of these behaviors is absolutely pivotal to success or failure.

Task Orientation

Simply put, task-oriented people are doers, and task leadership behaviors facilitate goal accomplishment. Researchers have labeled these behaviors differently, but they are always about task accomplishment. Task leadership considers the elements involved in task accomplishment from organizing work and defining roles to determining policies and procedures to facilitate production.

Relationship Orientation

Relationship-oriented people differ from task-oriented people in that they are not as goal directed in their leadership behavior; they are more interested in connecting with others. Relationship-oriented leadership behaviors focus on the well-being of followers, how they relate to each other, and the atmosphere in which they work. Relationship leadership explores the human aspects of leadership from building camaraderie, respect, trust, and regard between leaders and followers to valuing followers' uniqueness and attending to their personal needs.

Task and relationship leadership behaviors are inextricably tied together, and the behavioral approach looks at how leaders engage in both of these behaviors and the extent to which situational factors affect these behaviors.

Historical Background of the Behavioral Approach

The Ohio State Studies

A group of researchers at Ohio State believed that the results of studying leadership as a personality trait seemed fruitless and decided to analyze how individuals *acted* when they were leading a group or an organization. This analysis was conducted by having followers complete questionnaires about their leaders. On the questionnaires, followers had to identify the number of times their leaders engaged in certain types of behaviors.

The original questionnaire used in these studies was constructed from a list of more than 1,800 items describing different aspects of leader behavior. From this long list of items, a questionnaire composed of 150 questions was formulated; it was called the Leader Behavior Description Questionnaire (LBDQ; Hemphill & Coons, 1957). The LBDQ was given to hundreds of people in educational, military, and industrial settings, and the results showed that certain clusters of behaviors were typical of leaders. Six years later, Stogdill (1963) published a shortened version of the LBDQ. The new form, which was called the LBDQ-XII, became the most widely used instrument in leadership research. A questionnaire similar to the LBDQ, which you can use to assess your own leadership behavior, appears later in this chapter.

Researchers found that followers' responses on the questionnaire clustered around two general types of leader behaviors: *initiating structure* and *consideration* (Stogdill, 1974). Initiating structure behaviors are essentially task behaviors, including such acts as organizing work, giving structure to the work context, defining role responsibilities, and scheduling work activities. Consideration behaviors are essentially relationship behaviors and include building camaraderie, respect, trust, and liking between leaders and followers.

The two types of behaviors identified by the LBDQ-XII represent the core of the behavioral approach and are central to what leaders do: Leaders provide structure for followers, and they nurture them. The Ohio State studies viewed these two behaviors as distinct and independent. They were thought of not as two points along a single continuum, but as two different continua. For example, a leader can be high in initiating structure and high or low in task behavior. Similarly, a leader can be low in setting structure and low or high in consideration behavior. The degree to which leaders exhibit one behavior is not related to the degree to which they exhibit the other behavior.

Many studies have been done to determine which leadership behavior is most effective in a particular situation. In some contexts, high consideration has been found to be most effective, but in other situations, high initiating structure is most effective. Some research has shown that being high in both behaviors is the best form of leadership. Determining how a leader optimally mixes task and relationship behaviors has been the central task for researchers from the behavioral approach. The path–goal approach, which is discussed in Chapter 6, exemplifies a leadership theory that attempts to explain how leaders should integrate consideration and structure into their behaviors.

The University of Michigan Studies

While researchers at Ohio State were developing the LBDQ, researchers at the University of Michigan were also exploring leadership behavior, giving special attention to the impact of leaders' behaviors on the performance of small groups (Cartwright & Zander, 1970; Katz & Kahn, 1951; Likert, 1961, 1967).

The program of research at Michigan identified two types of leadership behaviors: *employee orientation* and *production orientation*. Employee orientation is the behavior of leaders who approach followers with a strong human relations emphasis. They take an interest in workers as human beings, value their individuality, and give special attention to their personal needs (Bowers & Seashore, 1966). Employee orientation is very similar to the cluster of behaviors identified as consideration in the Ohio State studies.

Production orientation consists of leadership behaviors that stress the technical and production aspects of a job. From this orientation, workers are viewed as a means for getting work accomplished (Bowers & Seashore, 1966). Production orientation parallels the initiating structure cluster found in the Ohio State studies.

Unlike the Ohio State researchers, the Michigan researchers, in their initial studies, conceptualized employee and production orientations as opposite ends of a single continuum. This suggested that leaders who were oriented toward production were less oriented toward employees, and those who were employee oriented were less production oriented. As more studies were completed, however, the researchers reconceptualized the two constructs, as in the Ohio State studies, as two independent leadership orientations (Kahn, 1956). When the two behaviors are treated as independent orientations, leaders are seen as being able to be oriented toward both production and employees at the same time.

In the 1950s and 1960s, a multitude of studies were conducted by researchers from both Ohio State and the University of Michigan to determine how leaders could best combine their task and relationship behaviors to maximize the impact of these behaviors on the satisfaction and performance of followers. In essence, the researchers were looking for a universal theory of leadership that would explain leadership effectiveness in every situation. The results that emerged from this large body of literature were contradictory and unclear (Yukl, 2003). Although some of the findings pointed to the value of a leader being both highly task oriented and highly relationship oriented in all situations (Misumi, 1985), the preponderance of research in this area was inconclusive.

Blake and Mouton's Managerial (Leadership) Grid

Perhaps the best-known model of managerial behavior is the Managerial Grid®, which first appeared in the early 1960s and has been refined and revised several times (Blake & McCanse, 1991; Blake & Mouton, 1964, 1978, 1985). It is a model that has been used extensively in organizational training and development. The Managerial Grid, which has been renamed the Leadership Grid®, was designed to explain how leaders help organizations to reach their purposes through two factors: *concern for production* and *concern for people*. Although these factors are described as leadership orientations in the model, they closely parallel the task and relationship leadership behaviors we discuss throughout this chapter.

Concern for production refers to how a leader is concerned with achieving organizational tasks. It involves a wide range of activities, including attention to policy decisions, new product development, process issues, workload, and sales volume, to name a few. Not limited to an organization's manufactured product or service, concern for production can refer to whatever the organization is seeking to accomplish (Blake & Mouton, 1964).

Concern for people refers to how a leader attends to the people in the organization who are trying to achieve its goals. This concern includes building organizational commitment and trust, promoting the personal worth of followers, providing good working conditions, maintaining a fair salary structure, and promoting good social relations (Blake & Mouton, 1964).

The Leadership (Managerial) Grid joins concern for production and concern for people in a model that has two intersecting axes (Figure 4.1). The horizontal axis represents the leader's concern for results, and the vertical axis represents the leader's concern for people. Each of the axes is drawn as a 9-point scale on which a score of 1 represents *minimum concern* and 9 represents *maximum concern*. By plotting scores from each of the axes, various leadership styles can be illustrated. The Leadership Grid portrays five major leadership styles: authority–compliance management (9,1), country-club management (1,9), impoverished management (1,1), middle-of-the-road management (5,5), and team management (9,9).

Authority-Compliance Management (9,1). The 9,1 style of leadership places heavy emphasis on task and job requirements, and less emphasis on people, except to the extent that people are tools for getting the job done. Communicating with followers is not emphasized except for the purpose of giving instructions about the task. This style is result driven, and people are regarded as tools to that end. The 9,1 leader is often seen as controlling, demanding, hard driving, and overpowering.

Country-Club Management (1,9). The 1,9 style represents a low concern for task accomplishment coupled with a high concern for interpersonal relationships. De-emphasizing production, 1,9 leaders stress the attitudes and feelings of people, making sure the personal and social needs of followers are met. They try to create a positive climate by being agreeable, eager to help, comforting, and uncontroversial.

Impoverished Management (1,1). The 1,1 style is representative of a leader who is unconcerned with both the task and interpersonal relationships. This type of leader goes through the motions of being a leader but acts uninvolved and withdrawn. The 1,1 leader often has little contact with followers and could be described as indifferent, noncommittal, resigned, and apathetic.

FIGURE 4.1 The Leadership Grid

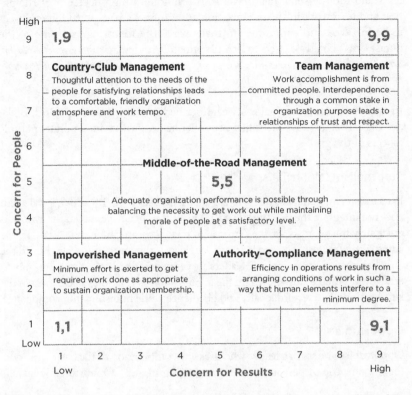

Middle-of-the-Road Management (5,5). The 5,5 style describes leaders who are compromisers, who have an intermediate concern for the task and an intermediate concern for the people who do the task. They find a balance between taking people into account and still emphasizing the work requirements. Their compromising style gives up some of the push for production and some of the attention to employee needs. To arrive at an equilibrium, the 5,5 leader avoids conflict and emphasizes moderate levels of production and interpersonal relationships. This type of leader often is described as one who is expedient, prefers the middle ground, soft-pedals disagreement, and swallows convictions in the interest of "progress."

Team Management (9,9). The 9,9 style places a strong emphasis on both tasks and interpersonal relationships. It promotes a high degree of participation and teamwork in the organization and satisfies a basic need in employees to be involved and committed to their work. The following are some of the phrases that could be used to describe the 9,9 leader: *stimulates participation, acts determined, gets issues into the open, makes priorities clear, follows through, behaves open-mindedly,* and *enjoys working.*

In addition to the five major styles described in the Leadership Grid, Blake and his colleagues have identified two other behaviors that incorporate multiple aspects of the grid.

Paternalism/Maternalism

Paternalism/maternalism refers to a leader who uses both 1,9 and 9,1 styles but does not integrate the two (Figure 4.2). This is the "benevolent dictator" who acts graciously but does so for the purpose of goal accomplishment. In essence, the paternalistic/maternalistic style treats people as if they were dissociated from the task. Paternalistic/maternalistic leaders are often described as "fatherly" or "motherly" toward their followers, regard the organization as a "family," make most of the key decisions, and reward loyalty and obedience while punishing noncompliance.

Opportunism

Opportunism refers to a leader who uses any combination of the basic five styles for the purpose of personal advancement (Figure 4.3). Opportunistic leaders

FIGURE 4.2 Paternalism/Maternalism

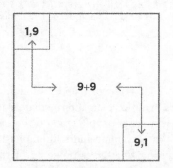

Source: The Leadership Grid© figure, Paternalism figure, and Opportunism figure from *Leadership Dilemmas—Grid Solutions,* by Robert R. Blake and Anne Adams McCanse. (Formerly the Managerial Grid by Robert R. Blake and Jane S. Mouton.) Houston, TX: Gulf Publishing Company (Grid figure: p. 29, Paternalism figure: p. 30, Opportunism figure: p. 31). Copyright 1991 by Scientific Methods, Inc. Reproduced by permission of the owners.

FIGURE 4.3 Opportunism

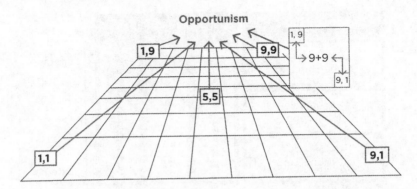

will adapt and shift their leadership behavior to gain personal advantage, putting self-interest ahead of other priorities. Both the performance and the effort of the leader are to realize personal gain. Some phrases used to describe this leadership behavior include *ruthless*, *cunning*, and *self-motivated*, while some could argue that these types of leaders are *adaptable* and *strategic*.

Blake and Mouton (1985) indicated that people usually have a dominant grid style (which they use in most situations) and a backup style. The backup style is what the leader reverts to when under pressure, when the usual way of accomplishing things does not work.

In summary, the Leadership Grid is an example of a practical model of leadership that is based on the two major leadership behaviors: task and relationship. It closely parallels the ideas and findings that emerged in the Ohio State and University of Michigan studies. It is used in consulting for organizational development throughout the world.

Recent Studies

More recently, Behrendt, Matz, and Göritz (2017) have created a leadership behavior model that reflects the evolving demands of organizational environments. The Integrated Model of Leadership Behavior (IMoLB; Figure 4.4), which is based on a multitude of studies on leader behavior, builds on the heuristic taxonomy of leader behavior developed by Yukl (2012). The IMoLB relates

FIGURE 4.4 Integrated Model of Leadership Behavior (IMoLB)

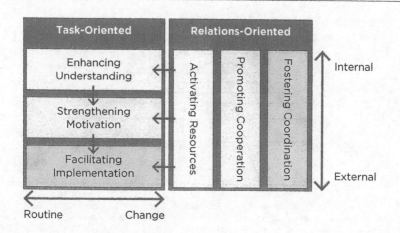

Source: Behrendt, P., Matz, S., & Göritz, A. S. (2017). An integrative model of leadership behavior. *The Leadership Quarterly, 28*(1), 229–244.

task-oriented behavior to organizational change demands through envisioning change, innovation, and encouraging learning. Relations-oriented behavior relates to influencing followers to meet the external demands of networking, monitoring the environment, and mobilizing resources to respond to them.

Still in the early stages of its development, this model has not been measured or tested at the time of this printing, but still offers a relevant look at the relationship of leadership behaviors in the context of modern organizational environments.

HOW DOES THE BEHAVIORAL APPROACH WORK?

Unlike many of the other approaches discussed in the book, the behavioral approach is not a refined theory that provides a neatly organized set of prescriptions for effective leadership behavior. Rather, the behavioral approach provides a framework for assessing leadership in a broad way, as behavior with a task and relationship dimension. The behavioral approach works not by telling leaders how to behave, but by describing the major components of their behavior.

The behavioral approach reminds leaders that their actions toward others occur on a task level and a relationship level. In some situations leaders need to be more task oriented, whereas in others they need to be more relationship oriented. Similarly, some followers need leaders who provide a lot of direction, whereas others need leaders who can show them a great deal of nurturance and support. And in some cases, a leader must combine both approaches (Casimir & Ng, 2010).

An example may help explain how the behavioral approach works. Imagine two college classrooms on the first day of class and two professors with entirely different styles. Professor Smith comes to class, introduces herself, takes attendance, goes over the syllabus, explains the first assignment, and dismisses the class. Professor Jones comes to class and, after introducing herself and handing out the syllabus, tries to help the students to get to know one another by having each of the students describe a little about themselves, their majors, and their favorite nonacademic activities. The leadership behaviors of Professors Smith and Jones are quite different. The preponderance of what Professor Smith does could be labeled task behavior, and the majority of what Professor Jones does could be labeled relationship behavior. The behavioral approach provides a way to inform the professors about the differences in their behaviors. Depending on the response of the students to their leadership behaviors, the professors may want to change their behavior to improve their teaching on the first day of class.

Overall, the behavioral approach offers a means of assessing in a general way the behaviors of leaders. It reminds leaders that their impact on others occurs through the tasks they perform as well as in the relationships they create.

STRENGTHS

The behavioral approach makes several positive contributions to our understanding of the leadership process. First, the behavioral approach marked a major shift in the general focus of leadership research. Before the inception of this approach, researchers treated leadership exclusively as a trait (see Chapter 2). The behavioral approach broadened the scope of leadership research to include the behaviors of leaders and what they do in various situations. No longer was the focus of leadership on the personal characteristics of leaders: It was expanded to include what leaders did and how they acted. The early research examined a broad set of leader behaviors (over 1,800) and distilled these down to two dimensions— consideration and initiation structure. These two behaviors—caring for others and goal attainment—are the two fundamental aspects of human behavior in groups, whether they be tribes, families, or work teams.

Second, a wide range of studies on leadership behavior validates and gives credibility to the basic tenets of the approach. First formulated and reported by researchers from The Ohio State University and the University of Michigan, and subsequently reported in the works of Blake and Mouton (1964, 1978, 1985); Blake and McCanse (1991); Judge, Piccolo, and Ilies (2004); and Littrell (2013), the behavioral approach is substantiated by a multitude of research studies that offer a viable approach to understanding the leadership process. An extensive meta-analysis of the LBDQ-XII developed by the Ohio State studies has been carried out by Judge et al. (2004), who found that all the survey instruments had significant predictive validity for leader success (Littrell, 2013). The Managerial Grid, which translates the research into categories that can be easily understood, is a popular leadership approach among managers.

Third, on a conceptual level, researchers of the behavioral approach have ascertained that a leader's style consists primarily of two major types of behaviors: task and relationship. The significance of this idea is not to be understated. Whenever leadership occurs, the leader is acting out both task and relationship behaviors; the key to being an effective leader often rests on how the leader balances these two behaviors. Together they form the core of the leadership process. Blake and Mouton defended 9,9 leadership, refuting what they called "situationalism" (see the next chapter), arguing that concerns for people and production reflect the situational context in organizations (Cai, Fink, & Walker, 2019).

Fourth, the behavioral approach is heuristic. It provides us with a broad conceptual map that is worthwhile to use in our attempts to understand the complexities of leadership. Leaders can learn a lot about themselves and how they come across to others by trying to see their behaviors in light of the task and relationship dimensions. Based on the behavioral approach, leaders can assess their actions and determine how they may want to change to improve their leadership behaviors. Unlike with most traits, leaders can learn to lead through leadership training.

CRITICISMS

Along with its strengths, the behavioral approach has several weaknesses. First, the research on the behavioral approach has not adequately shown how leaders' behaviors are associated with performance outcomes (Bryman, 1992; Yukl, 2003). Researchers have not been able to establish a consistent link between task and relationship behaviors and outcomes such as morale, job satisfaction, and productivity. According to Yukl (2003, p. 75), the "results from this massive research effort have been mostly contradictory and inconclusive." He further pointed out that the only strong finding about leadership behaviors is that leaders who are considerate have followers who are more satisfied.

In addition, leader behavior questionnaires are typically completed by followers, and their perceptions of leadership may differ from actual leader behavior (Dinh et al., 2014). Follower perceptions of their leaders may be biased due to overly positive attributions resulting in overestimation of a leader's effects (Behrendt et al., 2017). In other words, if a leader is considerate, then followers may overestimate that leader's task behavior because they like the leader.

Another criticism is that this approach has failed to find a universal style of leadership that could be effective in almost every situation. The overarching goal for researchers studying the behavioral approach appeared to be the identification of a universal set of leadership behaviors that would consistently result in effective outcomes. Because of inconsistencies in the research findings, this goal was never reached. Similar to the trait approach, which was unable to identify the definitive personal characteristics of leaders, the behavioral approach has been unable to identify the universal behaviors that are associated with effective leadership.

The difficulty in identifying a universal style may be due to the impact of contextual factors. For example, research by Martin, Rowlinson, Fellows, and Liu (2012) found that there is a strong situational element that impacts whether one leadership behavior or another is more effective. In their research on leadership style and cross-functional teams, they found that different leadership behaviors may be needed depending on team goals. They noted that managers of projects that span organizational, national, and ethnic boundaries (cross-functional teams) must "juggle between both task and person-oriented leadership when involved in managing problem solving teams across boundaries" (p. 19).

Leader effectiveness also may be influenced by characteristics of the leaders, the followers, and the situation, and the behavioral approach lacks attention to the possible interactions among these elements. For example, highly skilled followers who have a strong reward system make it easier for a leader to succeed. These leaders' effectiveness may be due more to the attributes of their followers who are rewarded for using their skills at work.

Another criticism of the behavioral approach is that it implies that the most effective leadership style is the high–high style (i.e., high task and high relationship). Although some researchers (e.g., Blake & McCanse, 1991; Misumi, 1985) suggested that high–high managers are most effective, that may not be the case in all situations. In fact, the full range of research findings provides only limited support for a universal high–high style (Yukl, 2003). In a thought-provoking article on popular leadership styles, Andersen (2009) argues that in modern business the high-task-leadership orientation is essential to be successful.

Certain situations may require different leadership styles; some may be complex and require high-task behavior, and others may be simple and require supportive behavior. At this point in the development of research on the behavioral approach, it remains unclear whether the high–high style is the best style of leadership.

A final criticism is that most of the research undertaken on the behavioral approach has come from a U.S.-centric perspective, reflecting the norms and values of U.S. culture. More recently, a small number of studies applying behavioral leadership concepts to non-U.S. contexts have been undertaken, and results show that different cultures prefer different leadership styles than those often espoused or favored by current U.S. management practice (Begum & Mujtaba, 2016; Engle, Elahee, & Tatoglu, 2013; Iguisi, 2014; Martin et al., 2012). For example, the paternalistic leadership style of benevolence plus authority is effective in Turkey, China, and India (Pellegrini & Scandura, 2008).

APPLICATION

The behavioral approach can be applied easily in ongoing leadership settings. At all levels in all types of organizations, managers are continually engaged in task and relationship behaviors. By assessing their own behaviors, managers can determine how they are coming across to others and how they could change their behaviors to be more effective. In essence, the behavioral approach provides a mirror for managers that is helpful in answering the frequently asked question, "How am I doing as a leader?"

Many leadership training and development programs throughout the country are structured along the lines of the behavioral approach. Almost all are designed similarly and include giving managers questionnaires that assess in some way their task and relationship behaviors toward followers. Participants use these assessments to improve their overall leadership behavior.

An example of a training and development program that deals exclusively with leader behaviors is Blake and Mouton's Leadership Grid (formerly Managerial Grid) seminar. Grid seminars are about increasing productivity, improving morale, and gaining employee commitment. They are offered by Grid International, an international organization development company (www.gridinternational.com). At grid seminars, self-assessments, small-group experiences, and candid critiques allow managers to learn how to define effective leadership, how to manage for optimal results, and how to identify and change ineffective leadership behaviors. The conceptual framework around which the grid seminars are structured is the behavioral approach to leadership.

In short, the behavioral approach applies to nearly everything a leader does. It is an approach that is used as a model by many training and development companies to teach managers how to improve their effectiveness and organizational productivity.

CASE STUDIES

In this section, you will find three case studies (Cases 4.1, 4.2, and 4.3) that describe the leadership behaviors of three different managers, each of whom is working in a different organizational setting. The first case is about a maintenance director in a large hospital, the second is concerned with the director of marketing and communications at a college, and the third is about the leadership behind a nationally recognized cheer team. At the end of each case are questions that will help you to analyze the case from the perspective of the behavioral approach.

Case 4.1 A DRILL SERGEANT AT FIRST

Mark is the head of the painting department in a large hospital; 20 union employees report to him. Before coming on board at the hospital, he had worked as an independent contractor. At the hospital, he took a position that was newly created because the hospital believed change was needed in how painting services were provided.

Upon beginning his job, Mark did a four-month analysis of the direct and indirect costs of painting services. His findings supported the perceptions of his administrators that painting services were inefficient and costly. As a result, Mark completely reorganized the department, designed a new scheduling procedure, and redefined the expected standards of performance.

Mark says that when he started out in his new job, he was "all task," like a drill sergeant who didn't seek any input from his soldiers. From Mark's point of view, the hospital environment did not leave much room for errors, so he needed to be strict about getting painters to do a good job within the constraints of the hospital environment.

As time went along, Mark relaxed his style and was less demanding. He delegated some responsibilities to two crew leaders who reported to him, but he always stayed in close touch with each of the employees. On a weekly basis, Mark was known to take small groups of workers to the local sports bar for burgers on the house. He loved to banter with the employees and could take it as well as dish it out.

Mark is very proud of his department. He says he always wanted to be a coach, and that's how he feels about running his department. He enjoys working with people; in particular, he says he likes to see the glint in their eyes when they realize that they've done a good job and they have done it on their own.

(Continued)

(Continued)

Because of Mark's leadership, the painting department has improved substantially and is now seen by workers in other departments as the most productive department in hospital maintenance. Painting services received a customer rating of 92%, which is the highest of any service in the hospital.

Questions

1. From the behavioral perspective, how would you describe Mark's leadership?

2. How did his behavior change over time?

3. In general, do you think he is more task oriented or more relationship oriented?

4. What score do you think he would get on Blake and Mouton's grid?

Case 4.2 WE ARE FAMILY

Betsy has been hired as the director of marketing and communications for a medium-sized college in the Midwest. With a long history of success as a marketing and public relations professional, she was the unanimous choice of the hiring committee. Betsy is excited to be working for Marianne, the vice president of college advancement, who comes from a similar background to Betsy's. In a meeting with Marianne, Betsy is told the college needs an aggressive plan to revamp and energize the school's marketing and communications efforts. Betsy and Marianne seem in perfect sync with the direction they believe is right for the college's program. Marianne also explains that she has established a departmental culture of teamwork and empowerment and that she is a strong advocate of being a mentor to her team members rather than a manager.

Betsy has four direct reports: two writers, Bridget and Suzanne, who are in their 20s; and Carol and Francine, graphic designers who are in their 50s. In her first month, Betsy puts together a meeting with her direct reports to develop a new communications plan for the college, presenting the desired goals to the team and asking for their ideas on initiatives and improvements to meet those goals. Bridget and Suzanne provide little in the way of suggested changes, with Bridget asking pointedly, "Why do we need to change anything?"

In her weekly meeting with the vice president, Betsy talks about the resistance to change she encountered from the team. Marianne nods, saying she heard some of the team members' concerns when she went to lunch with them earlier in the week. When Betsy looks surprised, Marianne gives her a knowing smile. "We are like a family here; we have close relationships outside of work. I go to lunch or the movies with Suzanne and Bridget at least once a week. But don't worry; I am only a sounding board for them, and encourage them to come to you to resolve their issues. They know you are their boss."

But they don't come to Betsy. Soon, Bridget stops coming to work at 8 a.m., showing up at 10 a.m. daily. As a result, she misses the weekly planning meetings. When Betsy approaches her about it, Bridget tells her, "It's OK with Marianne; she says as long as I am using the time to exercise and improve my health she supports it."

Betsy meets with Suzanne to implement some changes to Suzanne's pet project, the internal newsletter. Suzanne gets defensive, accusing Betsy of insulting her work. Later, Betsy watches Suzanne and Marianne leave the office together for lunch. A few hours later, Marianne comes into Betsy's office and tells her, "Go easy on the newsletter changes. Suzanne is an insecure person, and she is feeling criticized and put down by you right now."

Betsy's relationship with the other two staff members is better. Neither seems to have the close contact with Marianne that the younger team members have. They seem enthusiastic and supportive of the new direction Betsy wants to take the program in.

As the weeks go by, Marianne begins having regular "Mentor Meetings" with Bridget and Suzanne, going to lunch with them at least twice a week. After watching the three walk out together one day, Francine asks Betsy if it troubles her. Betsy replies calmly, "It is part of Marianne's mentoring program."

Francine rolls her eyes and says, "Marianne's not mentoring anyone; she just wants someone to go to lunch with every day."

After four months on the job, Betsy goes to Marianne and outlines the challenges that the vice president's close relationships with Bridget and Suzanne have presented to the progress of the marketing and communications program. She asks her directly, "Please stop."

Marianne gives her the knowing smile again. "I see a lot of potential in Bridget and Suzanne and want to help foster that," she explains. "They are still young in their careers, and my relationship with them is important because I can provide the mentoring and guidance to develop their abilities."

"But it's creating problems between them and me," Betsy points out. "I can't manage them if they can circumvent me every time they disagree with me. We aren't getting any work done. You and I have to be on the same team."

Marianne shakes her head. "The problem is that we have very different leadership styles. I like to empower people, and you like to boss them around."

(Continued)

(Continued)

Questions

1. Marianne and Betsy do indeed have different leadership styles. What style would you ascribe to Betsy? To Marianne?

2. Does Betsy need to change her leadership style to improve the situation with Bridget and Suzanne? Does Marianne need to change her style of leadership?

3. How can Marianne and Betsy work together?

Case 4.3 *CHEER* COACH MONICA ALDAMA

In January 2020, the world was introduced to the Navarro College cheer team and its coach of 25 years, Monica Aldama, through the Netflix docuseries *Cheer*.

The six-hour series followed the 40-member team from the small Texas community college as it prepared over a period of four months for the penultimate event of its season, the 2019 National Cheerleaders Association championships in Daytona Beach, Florida. At that meet, Navarro College would be seeking its 14th title in 19 years.

College-level competitive cheer is an exceedingly difficult and dangerous sport. With stunts including lifts, tumbling, towering pyramids, and basket tosses where a "flyer" is thrown high in the air, does several twists and turns, and is caught in the arms of the "bases" below, the risk of catastrophic injury is second only to football according to the National Center for Catastrophic Sport Injury Research (NCCSIR; Greenspan, 2020). This risk is apparent in the show as team member after team member is dropped, falls, or is injured while performing stunts. Concussions, fractured ribs, ankle injuries, and twisted, swollen limbs are the norm. And this is just at team practices.

For the 40 cheerleaders, it's all about "making mat"—securing one of the 20 spots on the team to compete at the national championships. For Coach Aldama, it is about creating and executing a two-minute, 15-second performance with breathtaking stunts that will result in the highest score possible to secure the team's legacy.

Coach Aldama records all the practice sessions on her tablet, watching the videos over and over to determine if the choreography needs to be altered and to monitor how each of the athletes is performing. She also consults with her two assistant coaches, Andy Cosferent and Kāpena Kea, about changes to make to the routine, which athletes to push, and which to cut.

As a leader, Coach Aldama sets high expectations for her team regarding their personal conduct, class attendance, and the effort and work they put into practice. She clearly articulates that accountability is her number-one criterion. When students don't meet expectations, there are consequences. The whole team will be required to run laps if one student sloughs off class. Team members are often roommates, and Coach Aldama says that, "whereas before they might just walk out and go to class and let their roommates stay in bed, now they're going to make sure that that person is up. And they do get mad if someone's not there yet. When class is about to start, they'll start texting them" (Zakin & Weisberg, 2020).

"That's just a big thing for me—self accountability. If you have a responsibility, you show up for it. If it's class, you show up for it. If it's practice, you show up for it. If it's a job, you show up for it. If you made the commitment to do it, you show up," she says (Zakin & Weisberg, 2020).

Athlete T. T. Barker gets a painful lesson in this when he arrives at practice with a back injury from competing with another, noncollegiate team after Coach Aldama advised him not to. Coach Aldama doesn't cut T. T. any slack, and he continues to practice, repeatedly hoisting flyers overhead, wincing and grunting in pain until he finally drops to the mat, crying.

Coach Aldama, who has a bachelor's degree in finance and an MBA, says she first approached coaching the team from a business perspective. "I was like, okay, what's the ultimate goal? To win?" she says. "I started from there and worked backwards (asking) what I need to do to win. And it was very black and white. 'There's a score sheet. I need to get a score. How am I gonna get this score?'

"I really started there, but then quickly realized, 'Oh, there's a whole 'nother part of coaching that has nothing to do with the score sheet. And it's these kids that are bickering or they broke up with their boyfriend or you know, okay, now I have to be a psychologist. I have to be an advisor, I have to be a counselor, I have to be a mother" (Zakin & Weisberg, 2020).

Many of the team members come from difficult life circumstances, and a place on the team is a ticket out of trouble and hardship. One of those is Morgan Simianer, who lived with an older brother in a Wyoming trailer after her biological parents abandoned them both at an early age. Morgan has an unwavering drive to succeed and to please her coach.

"Not everyone in the world has a strong mother figure in their lives . . . Monica has filled the gap [that was] created by what I didn't have. I didn't have anyone to go prom shopping with or talk about my boyfriend. I think because of that, I am even more appreciative of her and what we share. I feel like her kid," she says. "I really idolize her. Monica has changed my life in so many ways and truly helped me become a better version of myself" (Bennett, 2020).

(Continued)

(Continued)

That devotion is evident in episode five of the show when Morgan goes to the emergency room between practices for excruciating rib pain caused by "ribiosis," what team members call the damage to flyers' ribs caused by repeatedly falling from great heights into the arms of bases. At the ER, Morgan refuses treatment because the muscle relaxers she's prescribed would keep her from participating in that afternoon's practice, and—despite a warning that more stress on her ribs could damage her organs or kill her—she leaves and returns to the gym. "If Monica says full-out, I'm going full-out," she says (Whiteley, 2020).

Navarro College is located in Corsicana, a small town in a rural, conservative part of Texas. Several of the male athletes on the team are gay, and despite her Christian faith, Coach Aldama says she "will fight tooth and nail to protect my boys."

"I get upset when I see the world being so harsh and not understanding. I am not a very political person at all. I would say I'm smack in the middle: I've got some of the very conservative, some very liberal . . . I think everyone needs to be open to learning about different people's lifestyles and not be so closed-minded," she says (Silman, 2020).

Nurturing aside, Coach Aldama ultimately makes the very hard decision of selecting the athletes who will "make mat" and, even if they are chosen for mat, replacing the athletes if they aren't cutting it. She has also kicked key members off the team for rule infractions.

"I try to separate the coaching part and the nurturing part. Sometimes I'll have to 'mat-talk' myself to separate the feelings of 'I'm going to break this kid's heart because I'm not going to put them on mat.' I love this kid more than anything and I know what they've overcome," she says. "But you know that they don't have the skills that this other person does and that's where it really pulls at your heartstrings and that's where I have to be, like, 'Come on, Monica, you can do this. It's fine. Just separate it. Just separate it. Just separate it.' And I do. I always try to still circle back around and make sure they know 'You're still good, you're still good enough. It's just that you know right now it's not your time'" (Zakin & Weisberg, 2020).

When one team member didn't make mat, he was encouraged by his teammates to ask the coach why. He resisted, saying he thought it would be disrespectful to question her. When he finally did ask, she told him "he was not putting himself out there."

"I'm very honest with them. I will let them know, pull them to the side and tell them, 'I feel like maybe you don't want it as badly as someone else or you don't have that fight in you. Which makes me worried about are you going to have that fight when it's go-time.' I know I'm very honest because how are they going to know?" (Zakin & Weisberg, 2020).

As a result, the team member put in twice the amount of effort and adjusted his contributions in practice and ultimately made mat.

Coach Aldama appears patient, calm, and composed, even in crisis. In the national competition, one of the team members, Austin Bayles, was injured, and a replacement had to be made. The person replacing Austin had to learn his new role in mere minutes.

"When we were at finals and Austin got hurt, I was proud of myself because I literally went into focus mode. And although I was terrified, I couldn't even go there because I was so focused on what we needed to do to fix it in a very short time span," she says. "I definitely have always told myself no matter what I'm feeling inside, I can't let the team know. Because cheerleading is a very mental game. We can do all this work preparing mentally, but if they see me looking terrified or scared or losing it, all that work we've done could go down the drain" (Silman, 2020).

"I'm very competitive and I want to be successful, but I also want to be that person that leads by example. I really set a high standard for myself," Coach Aldama says (Church, 2020).

Questions

1. How would you describe Coach Aldama's leadership behavior in terms of initiating structure and consideration? Is she more task oriented or relationship oriented?

2. Where on the Blake and Mouton Leadership Grid would you place Coach Aldama? Defend your answer.

3. How would you describe Coach Aldama's leadership behavior in terms of paternalism/maternalism?

4. Do you think the leadership behavior of opportunism could apply to Coach Aldama? Explain your answer.

LEADERSHIP INSTRUMENT

Researchers and practitioners alike have used many different instruments to assess the behaviors of leaders. The two most commonly used measures have been the LBDQ (Stogdill, 1963) and the Leadership Grid (Blake & McCanse, 1991). Both of these measures provide information about the degree to which a leader acts task directed or people directed. The LBDQ was designed primarily for research and has been used extensively since the 1960s. The Leadership Grid was designed primarily for training and development; it continues to be used today for training managers and supervisors in the leadership process.

To assist you in developing a better understanding of how leadership behaviors are measured and what your own behavior might be, a leadership behavior questionnaire is included in this section. This questionnaire is made up of 20 items that assess two orientations: *task* and *relationship*. By scoring the Leadership Behavior Questionnaire, you can obtain a general profile of your leadership behavior.

Leadership Behavior Questionnaire

Purpose: The purpose of this questionnaire is to assess your task and relationship orientations as a leader.

Instructions: Read each item carefully and think about how often you engage in the described behavior. Indicate your response to each item by selecting one of the five options to the right of each item.

Key: 1 = Never   2 = Seldom   3 = Occasionally   4 = Often   5 = Always

1.	Tells group members what they are supposed to do.	1 2 3 4 5
2.	Acts friendly with members of the group.	1 2 3 4 5
3.	Sets standards of performance for group members.	1 2 3 4 5
4.	Helps others in the group feel comfortable.	1 2 3 4 5
5.	Makes suggestions about how to solve problems.	1 2 3 4 5
6.	Responds favorably to suggestions made by others.	1 2 3 4 5
7.	Makes their perspective clear to others.	1 2 3 4 5
8.	Treats others fairly.	1 2 3 4 5
9.	Develops a plan of action for the group.	1 2 3 4 5
10.	Behaves in a predictable manner toward group members.	1 2 3 4 5
11.	Defines role responsibilities for each group member.	1 2 3 4 5
12.	Communicates actively with group members.	1 2 3 4 5
13.	Clarifies their own role within the group.	1 2 3 4 5
14.	Shows concern for the well-being of others.	1 2 3 4 5
15.	Provides a plan for how the work is to be done.	1 2 3 4 5
16.	Shows flexibility in making decisions.	1 2 3 4 5
17.	Provides criteria for what is expected of the group.	1 2 3 4 5
18.	Discloses thoughts and feelings to group members.	1 2 3 4 5
19.	Encourages group members to do high-quality work.	1 2 3 4 5
20.	Helps group members get along with each other.	1 2 3 4 5

Scoring

The Leadership Behavior Questionnaire is designed to measure two major types of leadership behaviors: task and relationship. Score the questionnaire by doing the following: First, sum the responses on the odd-numbered items. This is your task score. Second, sum the responses on the even-numbered items. This is your relationship score.

Total scores: Task _____ Relationship _____

(Continued)

(Continued)

Scoring Interpretation

For each category:

40–50 High range

30–39 Moderate range

10–29 Low range

The score you receive for task refers to the degree to which you help others by defining their roles and letting them know what is expected of them. This factor describes your tendencies to be task directed toward others when you are in a leadership position. The score you receive for relationship is a measure of the degree to which you try to make followers feel comfortable with themselves, each other, and the group itself. It represents a measure of how people oriented you are.

Your results on the Leadership Behavior Questionnaire give you data about your task orientation and people orientation. What do your scores suggest about your leadership style? Are you more likely to lead with an emphasis on task or with an emphasis on relationship? As you interpret your responses to the Leadership Behavior Questionnaire, ask yourself if there are ways you could change your behavior to shift the emphasis you give to tasks and relationships. To gain more information about your style, you may want to have four or five of your coworkers or classmates fill out the questionnaire based on their perceptions of you as a leader. This will give you additional data to compare and contrast to your own scores about yourself.

SUMMARY

The behavioral approach is strikingly different from the trait and skills approaches to leadership because the behavioral approach focuses on what leaders do rather than who leaders are. It suggests that leaders engage in two primary types of behaviors: task behaviors and relationship behaviors. How leaders combine these two types of behaviors to influence others is the central focus of the behavioral approach.

The behavioral approach originated from three different lines of research: the Ohio State studies, the University of Michigan studies, and the work of Blake and Mouton on the Managerial Grid (now known as the Leadership Grid).

Researchers at Ohio State developed a leadership questionnaire called the Leader Behavior Description Questionnaire (LBDQ), which identified *initiation of structure* and *consideration* as the core leadership behaviors. The Michigan studies provided similar findings but called the leader behaviors *production orientation* and *employee orientation*.

Using the Ohio State and Michigan studies as a basis, much research has been carried out to find the best way for leaders to combine task and relationship behaviors. The goal has been to find a universal set of leadership behaviors capable of explaining leadership effectiveness in every situation. The results from these efforts have not been conclusive, however. Researchers have had difficulty identifying one best style of leadership.

Blake and Mouton developed a practical model for training managers that described leadership behaviors along a grid with two axes: concern for results and concern for people. How leaders combine these orientations results in five major leadership styles: authority–compliance management (9,1), country-club management (1,9), impoverished management (1,1), middle-of-the-road management (5,5), and team management (9,9).

The behavioral approach has several strengths and weaknesses. On the positive side, it has broadened the scope of leadership research to include the study of the behaviors of leaders rather than only their personal traits or characteristics. Second, it is a reliable approach because it is supported by a wide range of studies. Third, the behavioral approach is valuable because it underscores the importance of the two core dimensions of leadership behavior: task and relationship. Fourth, it has heuristic value in that it provides us with a broad conceptual map that is useful in gaining an understanding of our own leadership behaviors. On the negative side, researchers have not been able to associate the behaviors of leaders (task and relationship) with outcomes such as morale, job satisfaction, and productivity. In addition, researchers from the behavioral approach have not been able to identify a universal set of leadership behaviors that would consistently result in effective leadership. Furthermore, the behavioral approach implies but fails to support fully the idea that the most effective leadership style is a high–high style (i.e., high task and high relationship). Last, the approach is United States–centric and may not easily generalize to other cultures.

Overall, the behavioral approach is not a refined theory that provides a neatly organized set of prescriptions for effective leadership behavior. Rather, the behavioral approach provides a valuable framework for assessing leadership in a broad way as assessing behavior with task and relationship dimensions. Finally, the behavioral approach reminds leaders that their impact on others occurs along both dimensions.

Situational Approach

DESCRIPTION

One of the more widely recognized approaches to leadership is the situational approach, which was developed by Hersey and Blanchard (1969a) based on Reddin's (1967) 3-D management style theory. The situational approach has been refined and revised several times since its inception (see Blanchard, 1985; Blanchard, Zigarmi, & Nelson, 1993; Blanchard, Zigarmi, & Zigarmi, 2013; Hersey & Blanchard, 1977, 1988), and it has been used extensively in organizational leadership training and development.

As its name implies, the situational approach focuses on leadership in situations. The premise of the theory is that different situations demand different kinds of leadership. From this perspective, effective leadership requires that people adapt their style to the demands of different situations.

The situational approach is illustrated in the model developed by Blanchard and his colleagues (Blanchard et al., 1993; Blanchard et al., 2013), called SLII® (Figure 5.1). The SLII® model, which is Blanchard's situational approach to effective leadership, is an extension and refinement of the original model developed by Hersey and Blanchard (1969a). This chapter focuses on the SLII® model.

Blanchard's model stresses that leadership is composed of both a directive and a supportive dimension, and that each has to be applied appropriately in a given situation. To determine what is needed in a particular situation, leaders must evaluate their followers and assess how competent and committed the followers are to perform a given goal. Based on the assumption that followers' skills and motivation vary over time, Blanchard's SLII® suggests that leaders should change the degree to which they are directive or supportive to meet the changing needs of followers.

In brief, the essence of Blanchard's SLII® approach demands that leaders match their style to the competence and commitment of their followers. Effective leaders are those who can recognize what followers need and then adapt their style to meet those needs.

The dynamics of this approach are clearly illustrated in the SLII® model, which comprises two major components: *leadership style* and *development level of followers.*

Leadership Style

Leadership style consists of the behavior pattern of a person who attempts to influence others. It includes both *directive behaviors* and *supportive behaviors.* Directive behaviors help individuals and group members accomplish goals by giving directions, establishing goals and methods of evaluation, setting timelines, defining roles, and showing how the goals are to be achieved. Directive behaviors clarify, often with one-way communication, what is to be done, how it is to be done, and who is responsible for doing it. Supportive behaviors help individuals and group members feel comfortable about themselves, their coworkers, and the situation. Supportive behaviors involve two-way communication and responses that show social and emotional support to others. Examples of supportive behaviors include asking for input, solving problems, praising others, sharing information about oneself, and listening. Supportive behaviors are mostly job related.

Leadership styles can be classified further into four distinct categories of directive and supportive behaviors (Figure 5.1). The first style (S1) is a *high directive–low supportive* style, which is also called a *directing* style. In this approach, the leader focuses communication on goal achievement, and spends a smaller amount of time using supportive behaviors. Using this style, a leader gives instructions about what and how goals are to be achieved by the followers and then supervises them carefully.

The second style (S2) is called a *coaching* approach and is a *high directive–high supportive* style. In this approach, the leader focuses communication on both achieving goals and meeting followers' socioemotional needs. The coaching style requires that leaders involve themselves with followers by giving encouragement and soliciting follower input. However, coaching is an extension of S1 in that it still requires that the leader make the final decision on the *what* and *how* of goal accomplishment.

The third style (S3) is a *supporting* approach that requires that the leader take a *high supportive–low directive* style. In this approach, the leader does not focus exclusively on goals but uses supportive behaviors that bring out followers' skills around the goal to be accomplished. The supportive style includes listening, praising others, asking for input, and giving feedback. A leader using this style gives followers control of day-to-day decisions but remains available to facilitate problem solving. An S3 leader is quick to give recognition and social support to followers.

FIGURE 5.1 SLII® Model

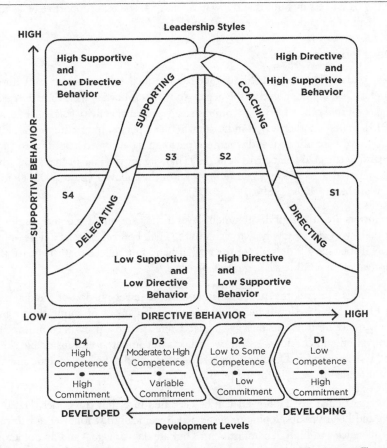

Source: From *Leadership and the One Minute Manager: Increasing Effectiveness Through Situational Leadership® II*, by K. Blanchard, P. Zigarmi, and D. Zigarmi, 2013, New York, NY: William Morrow. Used with permission. This model cannot be used without the expressed, written consent of The Ken Blanchard Companies. To learn more, visit www.kenblanchard.com

Last, the fourth style (S4) is called the *low supportive–low directive* style, or a *delegating* approach. In this approach, the leader offers less goal input and social support, facilitating followers' confidence and motivation in reference to the goal. The delegative leader lessens involvement in planning, control of details, and goal clarification. After the group agrees on what to do, this style lets followers take responsibility for getting the job done the way they see fit. A leader using S4 gives control to followers and refrains from intervening with unnecessary social support.

The SLII® model (Figure 5.1) illustrates how directive and supportive leadership behaviors combine for each of the four different leadership styles. As shown by the arrows on the bottom and left side of the model, directive behaviors are high in the S1 and S2 quadrants and low in S3 and S4, whereas supportive behaviors are high in S2 and S3 and low in S1 and S4.

Development Level

A second major part of the SLII® model concerns the development level of followers. Development level is the degree to which followers have the *competence* and *commitment* necessary to accomplish a given goal or activity (Blanchard et al., 2013). Stated another way, it indicates whether a person has mastered the skills to achieve a specific goal and whether a person has developed a positive attitude regarding the goal (Blanchard et al., 1993). In earlier versions of the model, this was referred to as the *readiness* or *maturity* of the follower (Bass, 2008; Hersey & Blanchard, 1969a, 1969b, 1977, 1996).

Followers are at a high development level if they are interested and confident in their work and know how to achieve the goal. Followers are at a developing level if they have little skill for the goal at hand but believe that they have the motivation or confidence to get the job done.

The levels of development are illustrated in the lower portion of the diagram in Figure 5.1. The levels describe various combinations of commitment and competence for followers on a given goal. There are two aspects of commitment: motivation and confidence; and two aspects of competence: transferable skills and task knowledge. Development levels are intended to be goal specific and are not intended to be used for the purpose of labeling followers.

On a particular goal, followers can be classified into four categories: D1, D2, D3, and D4, from developing to developed. Specifically, D1 followers are low in competence and high in commitment. They are new to a goal and do not know exactly how to do it, but they are excited about the challenge of it. D2 followers are described as having some competence but low commitment. They have started to learn a job, but they also have lost some of their initial confidence about the job. D3 represents followers who have moderate to high competence but may have variable commitment. They have essentially developed the skills for the job, but they are uncertain as to whether they can accomplish the goal by themselves. Finally, D4 followers are the highest in development, having both a high degree of competence and a high degree of commitment to getting the job done. They have the transferable skills and task knowledge to do the job and the confidence and motivation to get it done.

HOW DOES SLII® WORK?

SLII® is constructed around the idea that followers move forward and backward along the developmental continuum, which represents the relative competence and commitment of followers. For leaders to be effective, it is essential that they determine where followers are on the developmental continuum and adapt their leadership styles to directly match their followers' development levels.

In a given situation, the first task for leaders is to determine the nature of the situation. Questions such as the following must be addressed: What goal are followers being asked to achieve? How complex is the goal? Are the followers sufficiently skilled to accomplish the goal? Do they have the desire to complete the job once they start it? Answers to these questions will help leaders to identify correctly the specific development level at which their followers are functioning. For example, new followers who are very excited but lack understanding of job requirements would be identified as D1-level followers. Conversely, seasoned followers with proven abilities and great devotion to an organization would be identified as functioning at the D4 level.

Having identified the correct development level, the second task for leaders is to adapt their style to the prescribed leadership style represented in the SLII® model. There is a one-to-one relationship between the development level of followers (D1, D2, etc.) and the leader's style (S1, S2, etc.). For example, if followers are at the first level of development, D1, the leader needs to adopt a high directive–low supportive leadership style (S1, or directing). If followers are more advanced and at the second development level, D2, the leader needs to adopt a high directive–high supportive leadership style (S2, or coaching). For each level of development, there is a specific style of leadership that the leader should adopt.

An example of this would be Rene Martinez, who owns a house painting business. Rene specializes in restoration of old homes and over 30 years has acquired extensive knowledge of the specialized abilities required including understanding old construction, painting materials and techniques, plaster repair, carpentry, and window glazing. Rene has three employees: Ashley, who has worked for him for seven years and whom he trained from the beginning of her career; Levi, who worked for a commercial painter for four years before being hired by Rene two years ago; and Anton, who is just starting out.

Because of Ashley's years of experience and training, Rene would classify her as primarily D3. She is very competent, but still seeks Rene's insight on some tasks. She is completely comfortable prepping surfaces for painting and directing the others but has some reluctance to taking on jobs that involve carpentry. Depending on the work he assigns Ashley, Rene moves between S3 (supporting) and S4 (delegating) leadership behaviors.

When it comes to painting, Levi is a developed follower needing little direction or support from Rene. But Levi has to be trained in many other aspects of home restoration, making him a D1 or D2 in those skills. Levi is a quick learner, and Rene finds he only needs to be shown or told how to do something once before he is able to complete it easily. In most situations, Rene uses an S2 (coaching) leadership behavior with Levi. If the goal is more complicated and requires detailed training, Rene moves back into the S1 (directing) behavior with Levi.

Anton is completely new to this field, developing his skills but at the D1 level. What he lacks in experience he more than makes up for in energy. He is always willing to jump in and do whatever he's asked to do. He is not as careful as he needs to be, however, often neglecting the proper prepping techniques and cleanup about which Rene is a stickler. Rene finds that not only he, but also Ashley, uses an S1 (directing) behavior with Anton. Because Levi is also fairly new, he finds it difficult to be directive with Anton, but likes to give him help when he seems unsure of himself, falling into the S3 (supporting) behavior.

This example illustrates how followers can move back and forth along the development continuum, requiring leaders to be flexible in their leadership behavior. Followers may move from one development level to another rather quickly over a short period (e.g., a day or a week), or more slowly on goals that proceed over much longer periods of time (e.g., a month). Leaders cannot use the same style in all contexts; rather, they need to adapt their style to followers and their unique situations. Unlike the trait approach, which emphasizes that leaders have a fixed style, SLII® demands that leaders demonstrate a high degree of flexibility.

With the growing cross-cultural and technical influences on our society, it appears that the need for leaders to be flexible in their leadership style is increasingly important. Recent studies have examined the situational approach to leadership in different cultural and workplace contexts. In a study of the situational approach and air traffic control employees, Arvidsson, Johansson, Ek, and Akselsson (2007) assessed leaders in different contexts and found that the leader's style should change in different group and individual situations. In addition, they found that the most frequently used leadership style was high supportive–low directive and the most seldom-used style was high directive–low supportive. In another study, Larsson and Vinberg (2010), using a case study approach, found that successful leaders use a relation orientation as a base but include along with it a structure orientation and a change orientation.

STRENGTHS

The SLII® approach to leadership has several strengths, particularly for practitioners. The first strength is that it has a history of usefulness in the marketplace. SLII® is well known and frequently used for training leaders within organizations. Hersey and Blanchard (1993) reported that it has been a factor in training programs of more than 400 of the Fortune 500 companies. It is perceived by corporations as offering a useful model for training people to become effective leaders.

A second strength of the approach is its practicality. SLII® is easy to understand, intuitively sensible, and easily applied in a variety of settings. Whereas some leadership approaches provide complex and sophisticated ways to assess your own leadership behavior (e.g., the decision-making approach in Vroom & Yetton, 1973), SLII® provides a straightforward approach that is easily used. Because it is described at a level that is easily grasped, the ideas behind the approach are quickly acquired. Managers can relate to the description of followers as combinations of competence and commitment. In addition, the principles suggested by this approach are easy to apply across a variety of settings, including work, school, and family.

Closely akin to the strength of practicality is a third strength: It has prescriptive value. Whereas many theories of leadership are descriptive in nature, the SLII® approach is prescriptive. It tells you what you should and should not do in various contexts. For example, if your followers are very low in competence, the approach prescribes a directing style for you as the leader. On the other hand, if your followers appear to be competent but lack confidence, SLII® suggests that you lead with a supporting style. These prescriptions provide leaders with a valuable set of guidelines that can facilitate and enhance leadership. For example, in a recent study, Meirovich and Gu (2015) reported that the closer a leader's style is to the prescribed style, the better the performance and satisfaction of the employees. A computer simulation found that when leaders adapted their style to follower readiness over time, the followers' performance improved (Bosse, Duell, Memon, Treur, & van der Wal, 2017).

A fourth strength of the situational approach to leadership is that it emphasizes leader flexibility (Graeff, 1983; Yukl, 1989). This approach was one of the first contingency theories of leadership, which stated that leader effectiveness depends on situational factors. The approach stresses that leaders need to find out about their followers' needs and then adapt their leadership style accordingly. Leaders cannot lead using a single style: They must be willing to change their style to meet the requirements of the situation. This approach recognizes that followers act differently when working toward different goals, and that they may act differently during different stages of achieving the same goal. Effective leaders are those who can change their own style based on the goal requirements and the followers' needs, even in the middle of a project. For example, Zigarmi and Roberts (2017) reported that when followers perceive a fit between the leader's behavior and their own needs, it is positively related to job affect, trust, and favorable work intentions. In retrospect, the focus of the theory on followers was many years ahead since there has been a recent emphasis on "followership" in leadership theory and research.

Finally, the SLII® reminds us to treat each follower differently based on the goal at hand and to seek opportunities to help followers learn new skills and become more confident in their work (Fernandez & Vecchio, 1997; Yukl, 1998). Overall, this approach underscores that followers have unique needs and deserve our help in trying to become better at doing their work. The focus on the commitment and competence of followers allows leaders to assess follower performance and influence them through style and behavior (Cote, 2017).

CRITICISMS

Despite its history of use in leadership training and development, SLII® has several limitations. The following criticisms point out several weaknesses in this approach and help to provide a more balanced picture of the general utility of this approach in studying and practicing leadership.

The first criticism of this approach is that only a few research studies have been conducted to justify the assumptions and propositions set forth by the approach. Although many doctoral dissertations address dimensions of the situational approach to leadership, most of these research studies have not been published. The lack of a strong body of research on this approach raises questions about the theoretical basis for it (Fernandez & Vecchio, 1997; Graeff, 1997; Meirovich & Gu, 2015; Vecchio & Boatwright, 2002; Vecchio, Bullis, & Brazil, 2006). Can we be sure it is a valid approach? Is it certain that this approach does indeed improve performance? Does this approach compare favorably with other leadership approaches in its impact on followers? It is difficult to give firm answers to these questions when the testing of this approach has not resulted in a significant amount of published research findings.

A second criticism of SLII® concerns the ambiguous conceptualization in the model of followers' development levels. The authors of the model do not make clear how commitment is combined with competence to form four distinct levels of development (Graeff, 1997; Yukl, 1989). In one of the earliest versions of the model, Hersey and Blanchard (1969b) defined the four levels of commitment (maturity) as unwilling and unable (Level 1), willing and unable (Level 2), unwilling and able (Level 3), and willing and able (Level 4). In a more recent version, represented by the SLII® model, development level is described as high commitment and low competence in D1, low commitment and some competence in D2, variable commitment and high competence in D3, and high commitment and high competence in D4.

The authors of SLII® do not explain the theoretical basis for these changes in the composition of each of the development levels. Furthermore, they do not explain how competence and commitment are weighted across different development levels. As pointed out by Blanchard et al. (1993), there is a need for further research to establish how competence and commitment are conceptualized for each development level.

Closely related to the general criticism of ambiguity about followers' development levels is a concern with how commitment itself is conceptualized in the model.

For example, Graeff (1997) suggested the conceptualization is very unclear. Blanchard et al. (2013) stated that followers' commitment is composed of confidence and motivation, but it is not clear how confidence and motivation combine to define commitment. According to the SLII® model, commitment starts out high in D1, moves down in D2, becomes variable in D3, and rises again in D4. Intuitively, it appears more logical to describe follower commitment as existing on a continuum moving from low to moderate to high. Rather than viewing commitment and competence as having varying levels, the range of scores is cut, and followers are classified into categories. For example, a follower may be very close to the cutoff for having high commitment but is placed into the low category.

The argument provided by Blanchard et al. (1993) for how commitment varies in the SLII® model is that followers usually start out motivated and eager to learn, and then they may become discouraged and disillusioned. Next, they may begin to lack confidence or motivation, or both, and, last, they become highly confident and motivated. But why is this so? Why do followers who learn a task become less committed? Why is there a decrease in commitment at D2 and D3? Without more research to substantiate the way follower commitment is conceptualized, this dimension of SLII® remains unclear.

Some clarification of the ambiguity surrounding development levels is suggested by Thompson and Glasø (2015), who found that the predictions of the earlier model of the situational approach to leadership were more likely to hold true when the leaders' ratings and followers' ratings of competence and commitment are congruent. They stressed the importance of finding mutual agreement between leaders and followers on these ratings. These findings were replicated and extended by the authors (Thompson & Glasø, 2018). Again, the research showed that the principles underlying the situational approach are supported when leaders' ratings and followers' ratings of competence and commitment are in agreement. In comparing the two perspectives, there is no support for using followers' self-ratings of competence and commitment to predict performance. However, the leader's ratings appear to be more useful for determining the right type of direction to give followers.

A fourth criticism of the SLII® model has to do with how the model matches leader style with follower development levels—the prescriptions of the model. To determine the validity of the prescriptions suggested by the Hersey and Blanchard approach, Vecchio (1987) conducted a study of more than 300 high school teachers and their principals. He found that newly hired teachers were more satisfied and performed better under principals who had highly structured leadership styles, but that the performance of more experienced and mature teachers was unrelated to the style their principals exhibited.

Vecchio and his colleagues replicated this study twice: first in 1997, using university employees (Fernandez & Vecchio, 1997), and most recently in 2006, studying more than 800 U.S. Military Academy cadets (Vecchio et al., 2006). Both studies failed to find strong evidence to support the basic prescriptions suggested in the situational approach.

To further test the assumptions and validity of the situational approach, Thompson and Vecchio (2009) analyzed the original and revised versions of the model using data collected from 357 banking employees and 80 supervisors. They found no clear empirical support for the model in any of its versions. At best, they found some evidence to support leaders being more directive with newer employees and being more supportive and less directive as employees become more senior. Also, Meirovich and Gu (2015) found evidence that followers with more experience indicated a more positive response to autonomy and participation, a finding supporting the importance of leaders being less directive with experienced employees. There is also research evidence that shows that the directive style is being used less frequently, regardless of the readiness levels of followers (Zigarmi & Roberts, 2017). This may be due to a shift in organizational cultures toward empowering followers rather than "micromanaging" them.

A fifth criticism of SLII® is that it fails to account for how certain demographic characteristics (e.g., education, experience, age, and gender) influence the leader–follower prescriptions of the model. For example, a study conducted by Vecchio and Boatwright (2002) showed that level of education and job experience were inversely related to directive leadership and were not related to supportive leadership. In other words, followers with more education and more work experience desired less structure. An interesting finding is that age was positively related to desire for structure: The older followers desired more structure than the younger followers did. In addition, their findings indicated that female and male followers had different preferences for styles of leadership. Female followers expressed a stronger preference for supportive leadership, whereas male followers had a stronger desire for directive leadership. These findings indicate that demographic characteristics may affect followers' preferences for a particular leadership style. However, these characteristics are not considered in the situational approach.

SLII® can also be criticized from a practical standpoint because it does not fully address the issue of one-to-one versus group leadership in an organizational setting. The developers of the theory did not specify whether the theory operates at the individual, dyadic, or group level of analysis, and the sparse empirical research does not consider levels (Yammarino, Dionne, Chun, & Dansereau, 2005). For example, should leaders with a group of 20 followers lead by matching their style to the overall development level of the group or to the development level of individual members of the group? Carew, Parisi-Carew, and Blanchard (1990) suggested that groups go through development stages that are similar to individuals', and that therefore leaders should try to match their styles to the group's development level. However, if the leaders match their style to the mean development level of a group, how will this affect the individuals whose development levels are quite different from those of their colleagues? Existing research on SLII® does not answer this question. More research is needed to explain how leaders can adapt their styles simultaneously to the development levels of individual group members and to the group as a whole.

A final criticism of SLII® can be directed at the leadership questionnaires that accompany the model. Questionnaires on SLII® typically ask respondents to analyze various work situations and select the best leadership style for each situation. The questionnaires are constructed to force respondents to describe leadership style in terms of four specific parameters (i.e., directing, coaching, supporting, and delegating) rather than in terms of other leadership behaviors. Because the best answers available to respondents have been predetermined, the questionnaires are biased in favor of the situational approach (Graeff, 1983; Yukl, 1989).

APPLICATION

SLII® is frequently used by trainers and practitioners because it is an approach that is easy to conceptualize and apply. The straightforward nature of SLII® makes it practical for managers to use.

The principles of this approach can be applied at many different levels in an organization—from how a CEO of a large corporation works with a board of directors to how a crew chief in an assembly plant leads a small group of production workers. Middle managers can use SLII® to direct staff meetings, and heads of departments can use this approach in planning structural changes within an organization. There is no shortage of opportunities for using SLII®.

SLII® applies during the initial stages of a project, when idea formation is important, and during the various subsequent phases of a project, when implementation issues are important. The fluid nature of SLII® makes it ideal for applying to followers as they move forward or go backward (regress) on various projects. Because SLII® stresses adapting to followers, it is ideal for use with followers whose commitment and competence change over the course of a project.

Given the breadth of Blanchard's SLII® model, it is applicable in almost any type of organization, at any level, for nearly all types of goals. It is an encompassing model with a wide range of applications.

CASE STUDIES

To see how SLII® can be applied in different organizational settings, you may want to assess Cases 5.1, 5.2, and 5.3. The first case looks at a leader coaching runners at differing levels who hope to complete the New York City Marathon. The second case is concerned with problems of training new DJs at a campus radio station. The third explores two Chinese philosophies of leadership—Confucianism and Daoism—and how these philosophies contrast and affect leadership in the workplace. For each of these cases, ask yourself what you would do if you found yourself in a similar situation. At the end of each case, there are questions that will help you analyze the context from the perspective of the situational approach.

Case 5.1 MARATHON RUNNERS AT DIFFERENT LEVELS

David Abruzzo is the newly elected president of the Metrocity Striders Track Club (MSTC). One of his duties is to serve as the coach for runners who hope to complete the New York City Marathon. Because Abruzzo has run many marathons and ultramarathons successfully, he feels quite comfortable assuming the role and responsibilities of coach for the marathon runners.

The training period for runners intending to run New York is 16 weeks. During the first couple of weeks of training, Abruzzo was pleased with the progress of the runners and had little difficulty in his role as coach. However, when the runners reached Week 8, the halfway mark, some things began to occur that raised questions in Abruzzo's mind regarding how best to help his runners. The issues of concern seemed quite different from those that Abruzzo had expected to hear from runners in a marathon training program. All in all, the runners and their concerns could be divided into three different groups.

One group of runners, most of whom had never run a marathon, peppered the coach with all kinds of questions. They were very concerned about how to do the marathon and whether they had the ability to complete such a challenging event successfully. They asked questions about how far to run in training, what to eat, how much to drink, and what kind of shoes to wear. One runner wanted to know what to eat the night before the marathon, and another wanted to know whether it was likely that he would pass out when he crossed the finish line. For Abruzzo the questions were never-ending and rather basic. He wanted to treat the runners like informed adults, but they seemed to be acting immature, and rather childish.

The second group of runners, all of whom had finished the New York City Marathon in the previous year, seemed most concerned about the effects of training on their running. For example, they wanted to know precisely how their per-week running mileage related to their possible marathon finishing time. Would running long practice runs help them through the wall at the 20-mile mark? Would taking a rest day during training actually help their overall conditioning? Basically, the runners in this group seemed to want assurances from Abruzzo that they were training in the right way for New York. For Abruzzo, talking to this group was easy because he enjoyed giving them encouragement and motivational pep talks.

A third group was made up of seasoned runners, most of whom had run several marathons and many of whom had finished in the top 10 of their respective age divisions. Sometimes they complained of feeling flat and acted a bit moody and down about training. Even though they had confidence in their ability to compete and finish well, they lacked an element of excitement about running in the New York event. The occasional questions they raised usually concerned such things as whether their overall training strategy was appropriate or whether their training would help them in other races besides the New York City Marathon. Because of his running experience, Abruzzo liked to offer running tips to this group. However, when he did, he felt like the runners ignored and discounted his suggestions. He was concerned that they might not appreciate him or his coaching.

Questions

1. Based on the principles of the SLII® model (Figure 5.1), how would you describe the runners in Group 1? What kind of leadership do they want from Abruzzo, and what kind of leadership does he seem prepared to give them?

2. How would you describe the fit between the runners in Group 2 and Abruzzo's coaching style? Discuss.

3. The experienced runners in Group 3 appear to be a challenge to Abruzzo. Using SLII®, explain why he appears ineffective with this group.

4. If you were helping Abruzzo with his coaching, how would you describe his strengths and weaknesses? What suggestions would you make to him about how to improve?

Case 5.2 GETTING THE MESSAGE ACROSS

Ann Caldera is the program director of a college campus radio station (WCBA) that is supported by the university. WCBA has a long history and is viewed favorably by students, faculty, the board of trustees, and the people in the community.

Caldera does not have a problem getting students to work at WCBA. In fact, it is one of the most sought-after university-related activities. The few students who are accepted to work at WCBA are always highly motivated because they

(Continued)

(Continued)

value the opportunity to get hands-on media experience. In addition, those who are accepted tend to be highly confident (sometimes naïvely so) of their own radio ability. Despite their eagerness, most of them lack a full understanding of the legal responsibilities of being on the air.

One of the biggest problems that confronts Caldera every semester is how to train new students to follow the rules and procedures of WCBA when they are doing on-air announcing for news, sports, music, and other radio programs. It seems as if every semester numerous incidents arise in which an announcer violates in no small way the Federal Communications Commission (FCC) rules for appropriate airtime communication. For example, rumor has it that one year a first-year student disc jockey on the evening shift announced that a new band was playing in town, the cover was $10, and everyone should go to hear the group. Making an announcement such as this is a clear violation of FCC rules: It is illegal.

Caldera is frustrated with her predicament but cannot seem to figure out why it keeps occurring. She puts a lot of time and effort into helping new DJs, but they just do not seem to get the message that working at WCBA is a serious job and that obeying the FCC rules is an absolute necessity. Caldera wonders whether her leadership style is missing the mark.

Each semester, Caldera gives the students a very complete handout on policies and procedures. In addition, she tries to get to know each of the new students personally. Because she wants everybody to be happy at WCBA, she tries very hard to build a relational climate at the station. Repeatedly, students say that Caldera is the nicest adviser on campus. Because she recognizes the quality of her students, Caldera mostly lets them do what they want at the station.

Questions

1. What's the problem at WCBA?

2. Using SLII® as a basis, what would you advise Caldera to do differently at the station?

3. Based on SLII®, what creative schemes could Caldera use to reduce FCC infractions at WCBA?

Case 5.3 PHILOSOPHIES OF CHINESE LEADERSHIP

Before reading this case study, access and listen to the 2019 TED Talk by management consultant Fang Ruan here:
www.ted.com/talks/fang_ruan_management_lessons_from_chinese_business_ and_philosophy#t-153758. *Transcripts are also available on the site.*

In China, the business leadership landscape has long been guided by the ancient philosophical teachings of Confucius, which encourage authority, seniority, and obedience (Confucianism). For a nation, this is a time-tested formula to ensure order and harmony. For a company, this ensures precise execution on a large scale. But as business environments constantly change with internet and technology disrupting traditional industries and millennials becoming a major workforce, new ways of management are emerging within China.

Management consultant Fang Ruan says she sees many Chinese entrepreneurs leaning toward a more dynamic leadership style based on the philosophy of another revered, ancient Chinese thought leader, Lao-tzu (Laozi), known as Daoism. To understand these differences between the two, it's important to understand the underlying tenets of each of the philosophies.

Confucianism

Although sometimes referred to as a religion, Confucianism is more a habit of thought, a life philosophy. China's dominant social and political value system for over 1,000 years, Confucianism is based on the concepts of "respect for family, hard work and education" and "emphasizes social order and an active life" (Min-Huei, 2016).

Confucianism is built on the tenet that proper human relationships are essential to a well-functioning society. Four traits of Confucian ideology that have remained constant are

- socialization within the family unit in such a way as to promote sobriety, education, the acquisition of skills, and seriousness about tasks, job, family, and obligations;
- a tendency to help the group (however it might be identified);
- a sense of hierarchy and of its naturalness and rightness; and
- a sense of complementarity in relationships, which, combined with the sense of hierarchy, enhances perceptions of fairness and equity in institutions (Huang, 2000).

The Confucian hierarchical order is considered to lend stability and order; by understanding, honoring, and maintaining their place in society, followers can achieve harmony.

In the workplace, the hierarchical structure of Confucianism plays a pertinent role in the functioning of organizations. The characteristics of loyalty, obedience, respect, and service are expected of subordinates, and wisdom, moral purity, and leadership are expected of superiors (Huang, 2000). The patriarchal nature of Chinese culture is in direct relationship to Confucius's teachings, which advocate

(Continued)

(Continued)

an authoritative and patriarchal ruler. This authoritarian culture has developed a superior–subordinate bureaucracy where the paramount leader is the center of power (Huang, 2000). This perspective lends itself to elitist and patriarchal organizations where everyone knows their place and does not stray from the established boundaries.

Chinese communication styles are indirect, and that applies to those in leadership positions, as well. Wang (2018) notes that "the wise Confucian is expected to listen in silence." It's not that Chinese employees are unwilling to share information; rather, they must be prompted if one wants details. This becomes particularly complicated when the exchange involves criticism or a discussion of problems. To prevent a loss of face, or *mianzi* (MY-ann-ZEE), which is showing respect to others according to their status and reputation in society, such discussions are often held in private (Wang, 2018).

Yi-Hui Huang (2000) summarizes classic Confucianism dogma this way: "All will be right with the world if everyone conscientiously performs one's assigned role" (p. 227).

Daoism

Daoism (also referred to as Taoism) is the less rigid and more simplistic sibling of Confucianism and arose in the same period, known as the Hundred Schools of Thought.

Daoism originated with Chinese philosopher Laozi (also referred to as Lao-tzu), who was born in 604 BCE in central China. Laozi was the Keeper of Royal Archives for the Zhou dynasty until 516 BCE when he left the post to travel. He was inspired to write down his teachings in a book, which would become known as the *Dao De Jing* (aka the *Tao Te Ching*) or "The Way."

Like Confucianism, harmony is the backbone of the Daoist perspective, but with a key difference: Humans must be in harmony not only with each other but also with the natural flow of life, letting things take their natural course. Natural ways were considered better than imposed ways by Laozi. Allowing things to evolve in accordance with natural law is the cornerstone of Daoism. Where Confucianism focuses on creating social harmony, the goal of the Dao is to achieve balance.

The Dao is more dynamic and fluid, recognizing the need to navigate the *duality* of life—the Yin and the Yang—principles of life that are both complementing and opposing, such as dark and light, stillness and movement, sun and moon.

The metaphor of water is often used in Daoism. Water is seen to be powerful, yet altruistic, as it serves others. It is modest, flexible, and humble, because by its nature it seeks out the lowest place. Lee, Han, Byron, and Fan (2008) noted that "we human beings, especially leaders, should learn from water because water always remains in the lowest position and never competes with other things. Instead, water is very helpful and beneficial to all things."

The rivers and seas lead the hundred streams.

Because they are skillful at staying low.

Thus, they are able to lead the hundred streams. (Laozi, Chapter 66) (Lee et al., 2008, p. 91)

Laozi viewed leaders as being servants *and* followers. "The more one serves, the more one leads. Leadership, first, means follower-ship or service-ship just like water. Second, leadership means non-intrusiveness or non-interference" (Lee et al., 2008, p. 91).

Among other tenets, individuals who follow the Dao

- exert minimal influence on the lives of followers;
- encourage followers to take ownership of tasks;
- employ "soft tactics," such as persuasion, empowerment, modeling, teamwork, collaboration, and service;
- demonstrate creativity and flexibility;
- promote harmony with nature and others;
- reject the trappings of status and promote equality; and
- give to and serve others (Johnson, 1999).

Simplicity of life and respect for its natural flow epitomize a Daoist's life view.

Questions

1. Where on the SLII® model would you generally classify a leader who strictly leans toward Confucianism? Where would you classify a follower in an environment that strictly adheres to the Confucianist philosophy? Explain your reasoning.

2. Where on the SLII® model would you generally classify a leader who models the Daoist philosophy? Where would you classify a follower in an environment that follows Daoist principles? Explain your reasoning.

   In Fang Ruan's TED Talk, she discusses companies that have achieved notable success as they adopted more Daoist leadership philosophies. The following questions relate to those companies:

(Continued)

(Continued)

3. Raun discusses the situation of the founder of Ping An who, desiring to steer innovation, found it difficult to adopt Daoism-based philosophical changes due to the size and complexity of the business.

   a. From the perspective of the SLII® model, how does an organization's size and complexity relate to the effectiveness of each of the leadership styles represented in Figure 5.1?

   b. What about the development levels of the followers? How does size and complexity affect the needed directive behavior of leaders?

4. Which of these two philosophies most reflects your own? How does your own philosophical perspective affect your expression of the four styles of leadership?

— *Barbara Russell, MBA, BSCS, BBA, Chemeketa Community College*

LEADERSHIP INSTRUMENT

Although over the years different versions of instruments have been developed to measure SLII®, nearly all of them are constructed similarly. As a rule, the SLII® provides 20 work-related situations and asks respondents to select their preferred style for each situation from four alternatives. The situations and styles are written to directly represent the leadership styles of the four quadrants in the model. Questionnaire responses are scored to give respondents information about their primary and secondary leadership styles, their flexibility, and their leadership effectiveness.

The brief questionnaire provided in this section illustrates how the SLII® measures leadership style in the situational approach. For each situation on the questionnaire, you are asked to identify the development level of the followers in the situation and then select one of the four response alternatives that indicate the style of leadership you would use in that situation.

Expanded versions of the brief questionnaire give respondents an overall profile of their leadership style. By analyzing the alternatives a respondent makes on the questionnaire, one can determine that respondent's primary and secondary leadership styles. By analyzing the range of choices a respondent makes, one can determine that respondent's leadership flexibility. Leadership effectiveness and diagnostic ability can be measured by analyzing the number of times the respondent made accurate assessments of a preferred leadership style.

In addition to these self-scored questionnaires, SLII® uses similar forms to tap the concurrent perceptions that bosses, associates, and followers have of a person's leadership style. These questionnaires give respondents a wide range of feedback on their leadership styles and the opportunity to compare their own views of leadership with the way others view them in a leadership role.

SLII® Questionnaire: Sample Items

Purpose: The purpose of this questionnaire is to explore how different styles of leadership in the situational approach are used depending on the development level of the followers.

Instructions: Look at the following four leadership situations, from Blanchard, Zigarmi, and Zigarmi (1992), and indicate which SLII® leadership style is needed in each situation provided in the answer options beneath each statement.

Situation	A	B	C	D

1. Because of budget restrictions imposed on your   A B C D
   department, it is necessary to consolidate. You are
   thinking of asking a highly capable and experienced
   member of your department to take charge of the
   consolidation. This person has worked in all areas of
   your department and has the trust and respect of
   most of the staff. She is very willing to help with the
   consolidation.

   A. Assign the project to her and let her determine how
      to accomplish it.

   B. Assign the task to her, indicate to her precisely what
      must be done, and supervise her work closely.

   C. Assign the task to her and provide support and
      encouragement as needed.

   D. Assign the task to her and indicate to her precisely
      what must be done but make sure you incorporate
      her suggestions.

2. You have recently been made a department head of the   A B C D
   new regional office. In getting to know your departmental
   staff, you have noticed that one of your inexperienced
   employees is not following through on assigned tasks.
   She is enthusiastic about her new job and wants to get
   ahead in the organization.

   A. Discuss the lack of follow-through with her and
      explain the alternative ways this problem can be
      solved.

   B. Specify what she must do to complete the tasks but
      incorporate any suggestions she may have.

   C. Define the steps necessary for her to complete
      the assigned tasks and monitor her performance
      frequently.

   D. Let her know about the lack of follow-through and
      give her more time to improve her performance.

3. Because of a new and very important unit project, for the   A   B   C   D
past three months you have made sure that your staff
members understood their responsibilities and expected
level of performance, and you have supervised them
closely. Due to some recent project setbacks, your staff
members have become somewhat discouraged. Their
morale has dropped, and so has their performance.

    A. Continue to direct and closely supervise their
performance.

    B. Give the group members more time to overcome the
setbacks but occasionally check their progress.

    C. Continue to define group activities but involve
the group members more in decision making and
incorporate their ideas.

    D. Participate in the group members' problem-solving
activities and encourage and support their efforts to
overcome the project setbacks.

4. As a director of the sales department, you have asked   A   B   C   D
a member of your staff to take charge of a new sales
campaign. You have worked with this person on other
sales campaigns, and you know he has the job knowledge
and experience to be successful at new assignments.
However, he seems a little unsure about his ability to do
the job.

    A. Assign the new sales campaign to him and let him
function on his own.

    B. Set goals and objectives for this new assignment
but consider his suggestions and involve him in
decision making.

    C. Listen to his concerns but assure him he can do the
job and support his efforts.

    D. Tell him exactly what the new campaign involves
and what you expect of him, and supervise his
performance closely.

Source: Adapted from *Game Plan for Leadership and the One Minute Manager* (Figure 5.20,
Learning Activity, p. 5), by K. Blanchard, P. Zigarmi, and D. Zigarmi, 1992, Escondido, CA:
Blanchard Training and Development (phone 760-489-5005). Used with permission.

Scoring Interpretation

A short discussion of the correct answers to the brief questionnaire will help to
explain the nature of SLII® questionnaires.

Situation 1 in the brief questionnaire describes a common problem faced by
organizations during downsizing: the need to consolidate. In this particular

(Continued)

situation, the leader has identified a person who appears to be highly competent, experienced, and motivated to direct the downsizing project. According to the SLII® model, this person is at Development Level 4, which calls for a delegative approach. Of the four response alternatives, it is the (A) response, "Assign the project to her and let her determine how to accomplish it," that best represents delegating (S4): low supportive–low directive leadership.

Situation 2 describes a problem familiar to leaders at all levels in nearly all organizations: lack of follow-through by an enthusiastic follower. In the given example, the follower falls in Development Level 1 because she lacks the experience to do the job even though she is highly motivated to succeed. The SLII® approach prescribes directing (S1) leadership for this type of follower. She needs to be told when and how to do her specific job. After she is given directions, her performance should be supervised closely. The correct response is (C), "Define the steps necessary to complete the assigned tasks and monitor her performance frequently."

Situation 3 describes a very different circumstance. In this situation, the followers seem to have developed some experience and an understanding of what is required of them, but they have lost some of their motivation to complete the goal. Their performance and commitment have stalled because of recent setbacks, even though the leader has been directing them closely. According to SLII®, the correct response for the leader is to shift to a more supportive coaching style (S2) of leadership. The action response that reflects coaching is (C), "Continue to define group activities but involve the group members more in decision making and incorporate their ideas."

Situation 4 describes some of the concerns that arise for a director attempting to identify the correct person to head a new sales campaign. The person identified for the position obviously has the skills necessary to do a good job with the new sales campaign, but he appears apprehensive about his own abilities. In this context, SLII® suggests that the director should use a supportive style (S3), which is consistent with leading followers who are competent but lacking a certain degree of confidence. A supportive style is represented by action response (C), "Listen to his concerns but assure him he can do the job and support his efforts."

SUMMARY

SLII® is a prescriptive approach to leadership that suggests how leaders can become effective in many different types of organizational settings involving a wide variety of organizational goals. This approach provides a model that suggests to leaders how they should behave based on the demands of a particular situation.

The SLII® model classifies leadership into four styles: S1 is high directive–low supportive, S2 is high directive–high supportive, S3 is low directive–high supportive, and S4 is low directive–low supportive. The model describes how each of the four leadership styles applies to followers who work at different levels of development, from D1 (low in competence and high in commitment), to D2 (low to some competence and low in commitment), to D3 (moderately competent but lacking commitment), to D4 (a great deal of competence and a high degree of commitment).

Effective leadership occurs when the leader can accurately diagnose the development level of followers in a goal situation and then exhibit the prescribed leadership style that matches that situation.

Leadership is measured in this approach with questionnaires that ask respondents to assess a series of work-related situations. The questionnaires provide information about the leader's diagnostic ability, flexibility, and effectiveness. They are useful in helping leaders to learn about how they can change their leadership style to become more effective across different situations.

There are four major strengths to the situational approach. First, it is recognized by many as a standard for training leaders. Second, it is a practical approach, which is easily understood and easily applied. Third, this approach sets forth a clear set of prescriptions for how leaders should act if they want to enhance their leadership effectiveness. Fourth, the situational approach recognizes and stresses that there is not one best style of leadership; instead, leaders need to be flexible and adapt their style to the requirements of the situation.

Criticisms of the situational approach suggest that it also has limitations. Unlike many other leadership theories, this approach does not have a strong body of research findings to justify and support the theoretical underpinnings on which it stands. As a result, there is ambiguity regarding how the approach conceptualizes certain aspects of leadership. It is not clear in explaining how followers move from developing levels to developed levels, nor is it clear on how commitment changes over time for followers. Without the basic research findings, the validity of the basic prescriptions for matching leaders' styles to followers' development levels must be questioned. In addition, the model does not address how demographic characteristics affect followers' preferences for leadership. Finally, the model does not provide guidelines for how leaders should adapt their style to groups as opposed to one-to-one contexts.

6   Path–Goal Theory

DESCRIPTION

Path–goal theory discusses how leaders motivate followers to accomplish designated goals. Drawing heavily from research on what motivates followers, path–goal theory first appeared in the leadership literature in the early 1970s in the works of Evans (1970), House (1971), House and Dessler (1974), and House and Mitchell (1974). The stated goal of this theory is to enhance follower performance and follower satisfaction by focusing on follower motivation and the nature of the work tasks. At its inception, path–goal theory was incredibly innovative in the sense that it shifted attention to follower needs and motivations, and away from the predominant focus on tasks and relationships.

In contrast to the situational approach, which suggests that a leader must adapt to the development level of followers (see Chapter 5), path–goal theory emphasizes the relationship between the leader's style and the characteristics of the followers and the organizational setting. For the leader, the imperative is to use a leadership style that best meets followers' motivational needs. This is done by choosing behaviors that complement or supplement what is missing in the work setting. Leaders try to enhance followers' goal attainment by providing information or rewards in the work environment (Indvik, 1986); leaders provide followers with the elements they think followers need to reach their goals. According to House (1996), the heart of path–goal theory suggests that for leaders to be effective they must "engage in behaviors that complement subordinates' environments and abilities in a manner that compensates for deficiencies and is instrumental to subordinate satisfaction and individual and work unit performance" (p. 335). Put simply, path–goal theory puts much of the onus on leaders in terms of designing and facilitating a healthy and productive work environment to propel followers toward success.

According to House and Mitchell (1974), leadership generates motivation when it increases the number and kinds of payoffs that followers receive from their work. Leadership also motivates when it makes the path to the goal clear and easy to travel through coaching and direction, removing obstacles and roadblocks to attaining the goal, and making the work itself more personally satisfying (Figure 6.1). For example, even in professions where employees are presumed to be self-motivated such as in technical industries, leaders can greatly enhance follower motivation, engagement, satisfaction, performance, and intent to stay (Stumpf, Tymon, Ehr, & vanDam, 2016). Relatedly, research (Asamani, Naab, & Ansah Ofei, 2016) indicates that follower satisfaction and intent to leave are greatly impacted by a leader's communicative style. In other words, employing path–goal theory in terms of leader behavior and the needs of followers and the tasks they have to do could hold substantial implications for organizations that seek to enhance follower engagement and motivation while also decreasing turnover.

In brief, path–goal theory is designed to explain how leaders can help followers along the path to their goals by selecting specific behaviors that are best suited to followers' needs and to the situation in which followers are working. By choosing the appropriate behaviors, leaders increase followers' expectations for success and satisfaction.

Within path–goal theory, motivation is conceptualized from the perspective of the expectancy theory of motivation (Vroom, 1964). The underlying assumption of expectancy theory is that followers will be motivated if they think they are capable of performing their work, if they believe their efforts will result in a certain outcome, and if they believe that the payoffs for doing their work are worthwhile. Motivation rests with individuals and the choices they make about how a given behavior matches up with a given result. The challenge for a leader using ideas from expectancy theory is to understand fully the goals of each follower and the rewards associated with the goals. Followers want to feel efficacious, like they can accomplish what they set out to do. But they also want

FIGURE 6.1 The Basic Idea Behind Path–Goal Theory

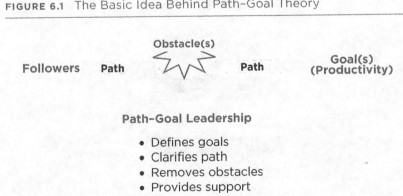

to know that they will be rewarded if they can accomplish their work. A leader needs to find out what is rewarding to followers about their work and then make those rewards available to them when they accomplish the requirements of their work. Expectancy theory is about the goals that followers choose and how leaders help them and reward them for meeting those goals.

Conceptually, path–goal theory is complex, and it is useful to break it down into smaller units so we can better understand the complexities of this approach.

Figure 6.2 illustrates the different components of path–goal theory, including leader behaviors, follower characteristics, task characteristics, and motivation. Path–goal theory suggests that each type of leader behavior has a different kind of impact on followers' motivation. Whether a particular leader behavior is motivating to followers is contingent on the followers' characteristics and the characteristics of the task.

Leader Behaviors

Since its inception, path–goal leadership has undergone numerous iterations and revisions (i.e., House, 1971, 1996; House & Mitchell, 1974) that have increased the number of contingencies associated with the theory. However, for our purposes, we will discuss only the primary four leadership behaviors identified as part of path–goal theory—*directive, supportive, participative,* and *achievement oriented* (House & Mitchell, 1974, p. 83). These four leader behaviors are not only foundational to understanding how path–goal theory works but are still more commonly used by researchers in contemporary studies of the path–goal leadership approach (e.g., Asamani et al., 2016).

FIGURE 6.2   Major Components of Path–Goal Theory

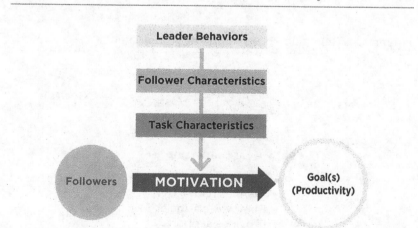

Directive Leadership

Directive leadership is similar to the "initiating structure" concept described in the Ohio State studies (Halpin & Winer, 1957), discussed in Chapter 4, and the "telling" style described in the situational leadership approach (Hersey & Blanchard, 1969), the subject of Chapter 5. It characterizes a leader who gives followers instructions about their task, including what is expected of them, how it is to be done, and the timeline for when it should be completed. It is thought that by being provided with explicit expectations and removing ambiguity, followers will have the clarity needed to focus on their jobs. A directive leader sets clear standards of performance and makes the rules and regulations clear to followers.

A good example of a directive leader is Professor Smith, discussed in Chapter 4 (page 93), an instructor who, at the beginning of a term, provides a syllabus to students that outlines what will be studied in the course, what chapters in a text to read, deadlines for assignments, and when tests will be administered. Often these syllabi will also outline grading policies so students know what scores are required to earn certain grades.

Supportive Leadership

Supportive leadership resembles the "consideration" behavior construct identified by the Ohio State studies (Hemphill & Coons, 1957; Stogdill, 1963). Supportive leadership consists of being friendly and approachable as a leader and includes attending to the well-being and human needs of followers. Leaders using supportive behaviors go out of their way to make work pleasant for followers, which, in turn, provides followers with the confidence necessary to succeed (House, 1971). In addition, supportive leaders treat followers as equals and give them respect for their status.

To understand the supportive leader role, consider the example of a coordinator of volunteers assigned to clean up trash and litter after an outdoor music festival. The task itself is not especially pleasant, especially in the hot sun, but the coordinator makes sure there are cool beverages and snacks for the volunteers, as well as a meal at the conclusion of their work. To give them extra incentive, he has developed a game of "trash bingo" in which volunteers have to find an array of items, such as caps to specific beverage bottles or pieces of trash in different colors, to win prizes. As the volunteers work, he walks among them, pulling a wagon filled with cold drinks, snacks, extra trash bags, sunscreen, and other necessities, which he offers them while asking each of them how they are doing and if they need anything.

Participative Leadership

Participative leadership consists of inviting followers to share in the decision making. A participative leader consults with followers, obtains their ideas and opinions, and integrates their suggestions into the decisions about how the group or organization will proceed. This particular leadership style may also result in increased group performance through member participation and dedication to shared group goals.

An example of a participative leader is the owner and chef of a fine dining restaurant that became very popular shortly after its opening. To deal with the "growing pains" of this quick success, she has regular weekly meetings with her staff to talk about what is working and what's not and how to improve processes. She looks to the servers to tell her about menu items that should be changed and has the kitchen staff discuss how changes to the menu can be implemented. At the same time, they all discuss plans to scale up the restaurant's capacity to lower the wait times for customers, without sacrificing quality.

Achievement-Oriented Leadership

Achievement-oriented leadership is characterized by a leader who challenges followers to perform work at the highest level possible. This leader establishes a high standard of excellence for followers and seeks continuous improvement. In addition to bringing significant expectations for followers, achievement-oriented leaders show a high degree of confidence that followers are capable of establishing and accomplishing challenging goals.

The captain of a firefighting crew that deals with wildfires is an example of an achievement-oriented leader. The goal for the crew is to contain the fire while saving property and people. The captain rigorously trains his crew members in the months before wildfire season, running them through countless drills that practice safety and firefighting methods so that they can perform at their highest level in the face of danger. For each drill, the captain grades crew members on a scale from 1 to 10. Those crew members who score the highest on the drills receive a special award at the end of training.

House and Mitchell (1974) suggested that leaders might exhibit any or all of these styles with various followers and in different situations. Path–goal theory is not a trait approach that locks leaders into only one kind of leadership. Leaders should adapt their styles to the situation or to the motivational needs of their followers. For example, if followers need participative leadership at one point in a task and directive leadership at another, leaders can change their style as needed. Different situations may call for different types of leadership behavior. Furthermore, there may be instances when it is appropriate for a leader to use more than one style at the same time.

In addition to leader behaviors, Figure 6.2 illustrates two other major components of path–goal theory: follower characteristics and task characteristics. Each of these two sets of characteristics influences the way leaders' behaviors affect follower motivation. In other words, the impact of leadership is *contingent* on the characteristics of both followers and their task.

Follower Characteristics

Follower characteristics determine how a leader's behavior is interpreted by followers in a given work context. Researchers have focused on followers' *needs for affiliation, preferences for structure, desires for control,* and *self-perceived level of task ability.* These characteristics and many others determine the degree to which followers find the behavior of a leader an immediate source of satisfaction or instrumental to some future satisfaction. As we discuss these follower characteristics, it is helpful to relate them to the characteristics exhibited by the athletes and coach of the Navarro College cheerleading team (Case Study 4.3). College-level competitive cheer is physically demanding and dangerous, and the coach of this 40-member team knows that each athlete has different follower characteristics that she must respond to in order to keep the individual athletes motivated to put in the hard work and practice required for the team to win at the national competition.

Path–goal theory predicts that followers who have strong *needs for affiliation* prefer supportive leadership because friendly and concerned leadership is a source of satisfaction. For many of the Navarro College cheer team's athletes, having been chosen by Coach Monica Aldama to be part of this elite squad makes them feel special and talented. The coach continues to foster those feelings in them by verbally recognizing her team members' hard work at practices and by attending to them individually when they need support.

For followers who are dogmatic and authoritarian and have to work in uncertain situations, path–goal theory suggests directive leadership because task clarity satisfies their *preferences for structure.* Directive leadership helps these followers by clarifying the path to the goal, making it less ambiguous. The authoritarian type of follower feels more comfortable when the leader provides a greater sense of certainty in the work setting. By establishing a mandatory, consistent team practice schedule and policies regarding the athletes' class attendance, practices, and personal conduct, Coach Aldama provides a very clear structure for her athletes. They know what is expected of them and what the consequences are if those expectations are not met.

Followers' *desires for control* have received special attention in path–goal research through studies of a personality construct locus of control that can be subdivided into internal and external dimensions. Followers with an *internal locus of control* believe that they are in charge of the events that occur in their life, whereas those with an *external locus of control* believe that chance, fate, or outside forces determine life events. Path–goal theory suggests that for followers with an internal locus of control participative leadership is most satisfying because it allows them to feel in charge of their work and to be an integral part of decision making. For followers with an external locus of control, path–goal theory suggests that directive leadership is best because it parallels followers' feelings that outside forces control their circumstances. On the Navarro College cheer team, Coach Aldama's assistant coach exhibits his internal locus of control in directing practices and also in participating with Coach Aldama regarding who will make the final cut for the team. On the other hand, for those athletes who have an external locus of control, Coach Aldama has to be very directive and tell them exactly what she needs from them.

Another way in which leadership affects follower motivation is the followers' *self-perceived level of task ability* to perform a specific task. As followers' perceptions of their abilities and competence go up, the need for directive leadership goes down. In effect, directive leadership becomes redundant and perhaps excessively controlling when followers feel competent to complete their own work. Through grueling, two-a-day practices, the cheer team's athletes become stronger and more competent performing the stunts, tumbling, and moves of the routine. As they do, their coach is able to pull back from directing them on their performance, instead focusing on the details that will enhance the team's routine. Athletes who do not gain confidence in their own abilities to be able to perform without direction will not make the cut for the 20-person competition squad.

Task Characteristics

In addition to follower characteristics, task characteristics have a major impact on the way a leader's behavior influences followers' motivation (Figure 6.2). Task characteristics include the *design of the followers' task*, the *formal authority system* of the organization, and the *primary work group of followers*. Collectively, these characteristics in themselves can provide motivation for followers. When a situation provides a clearly structured task, strong group norms, and an established authority system, followers will find the paths to desired goals apparent and will not need a leader to clarify goals or coach them in how to reach these goals. Followers will feel as if they can accomplish their work and that their work is of value. Leadership in these types of contexts could be seen as unnecessary, un-empathic, and excessively controlling.

In some situations, however, the *design of the task* characteristics may call for leadership involvement. Tasks that are unclear and ambiguous call for leadership input that provides structure. In addition, highly repetitive tasks call for leadership that gives support to maintain followers' motivation. In work settings where the *formal authority system* is weak, leadership becomes a tool that helps followers by making the rules and work requirements clear. In contexts where the *primary work group* norms are weak or nonsupportive, leadership assists in building cohesiveness and role responsibility.

A special focus of path–goal theory is helping followers overcome obstacles. Obstacles could be just about anything in the work setting that gets in the way of followers. Specifically, obstacles create excessive uncertainties, frustrations, or threats for followers. In these settings, path–goal theory suggests that it is the leader's responsibility to help followers by removing these obstacles or helping followers to navigate around them. Helping followers around these obstacles will increase followers' expectations that they can complete the task and increase their sense of job satisfaction. In coaching the Navarro cheer team, Coach Aldama sometimes finds elements of the routines that have been developed for her team to be too challenging for her athletes to accomplish. As a leader she will try to solve these issues by reworking the routine's elements and guiding the athletes on skills to help them master these elements.

As we mentioned earlier in the chapter, path–goal theory has undergone many revisions. In 1996, House published a reformulated path–goal theory that extends his original work to include eight classes of leadership behaviors. Besides the four leadership behaviors discussed previously in this chapter—(a) directive, (b) supportive, (c) participative, and (d) achievement-oriented behavior—the new theory adds (e) work facilitation, (f) group-oriented decision process, (g) work-group representation and networking, and (h) value-based leadership behavior. The essence of the new theory is the same as the original: To be effective, leaders need to help followers by giving them what is missing in their environment and by helping them compensate for deficiencies in their abilities.

HOW DOES PATH-GOAL THEORY WORK?

Path–goal theory is an approach to leadership that is not only theoretically complex, but also pragmatic. It provides a set of assumptions about how various leadership styles interact with characteristics of both followers and the work setting to affect the motivation of followers. In practice, the theory provides direction about how leaders can help followers to accomplish their work in a satisfactory manner. Table 6.1 illustrates how leadership behaviors are related to follower and task characteristics in path–goal theory.

Theoretically, the path–goal approach suggests that leaders need to choose a leadership style that best fits the needs of followers and the work they are doing. The theory predicts that a *directive style* of leadership is best in situations in which followers are dogmatic and authoritarian, the task demands are ambiguous, the organizational rules are unclear, and the task is complex. In these situations, directive leadership complements the work by providing guidance and psychological structure for followers (House & Mitchell, 1974, p. 90).

For tasks that are structured, unsatisfying, or frustrating, path–goal theory suggests that leaders should use a *supportive style*. The supportive style provides

TABLE 6.1 Path–Goal Theory: How It Works

Leadership Behavior	Follower Characteristics	Task Characteristics
Directive Leadership Provides structure	Dogmatic Authoritarian	Ambiguous Unclear rules Complex
Supportive Leadership Provides nurturance	Unsatisfied Need for affiliation Need for human touch	Repetitive Unchallenging Mundane
Participative Leadership Provides involvement	Autonomous Need for control Need for clarity	Ambiguous Unclear Unstructured
Achievement-Oriented Leadership Provides challenges	High expectations Need to excel	Ambiguous Challenging Complex

what is missing by nurturing followers when they are engaged in tasks that are repetitive and unchallenging. Supportive leadership offers a sense of human touch for followers engaged in mundane, mechanized activity.

Participative leadership is considered best when a task is ambiguous: Participation gives greater clarity to how certain paths lead to certain goals, and helps followers learn what leads to what (House & Mitchell, 1974, p. 92). In addition, participative leadership has a positive impact when followers are autonomous and have a strong need for control because this kind of follower responds favorably to being involved in decision making and in the structuring of work.

Furthermore, path–goal theory predicts that *achievement-oriented leadership* is most effective in settings in which followers are required to perform ambiguous tasks. In settings such as these, leaders who challenge and set high standards for followers raise followers' confidence that they have the ability to reach their goals. In effect, achievement-oriented leadership helps followers feel that their efforts will result in effective performance. In settings where the task is more structured and less ambiguous, however, achievement-oriented leadership appears to be unrelated to followers' expectations about their work efforts.

Pragmatically, path–goal theory is straightforward. An effective leader has to attend to the needs of followers. The leader should help followers to define their goals and the paths they want to take in reaching those goals. When obstacles arise, the leader needs to help followers confront them. This may mean helping a follower around the obstacle, or it may mean removing an obstacle. The leader's job is to help followers reach their goals by directing, guiding, and coaching them along the way.

STRENGTHS

Path–goal theory has several positive features. First, path–goal theory provides a useful theoretical framework for understanding how various leadership behaviors affect followers' satisfaction and work performance. It was one of the first theories to specify conceptually distinct varieties of leadership (e.g., directive, supportive, participative, achievement oriented), expanding the focus of prior research, which dealt exclusively with task- and relationship-oriented behaviors (Jermier, 1996). The path–goal approach was also one of the first situational contingency theories of leadership to explain how task and follower characteristics affect the impact of leadership on follower performance. The framework provided in path–goal theory informs leaders about how to choose an appropriate leadership style based on the various demands of the task and the type of followers being asked to do the task. Additionally, later iterations of the theory offer suggestions for how to motivate work groups for increased collaboration and enhanced performance.

A second positive feature of path–goal theory is that it attempts to integrate the motivation principles of expectancy theory into a theory of leadership. This makes path–goal theory unique because no other leadership approach deals directly with motivation in this way. Path–goal theory forces us continually to ask questions such as these about follower motivation: How can I motivate followers to feel that they can do the work? How can I help them feel that if they successfully do their work, they will be rewarded? What can I do to improve the payoffs that followers expect from their work? Understanding the processes and dynamics behind motivation is critical in any organization (Kanfer, Frese, & Johnson, 2017), and path–goal theory is designed to keep those questions that address issues of motivation at the forefront of the leader's mind.

Path–goal's third strength, and perhaps its greatest, is that the theory provides a model that in certain ways is very practical. The representation of the model (Figure 6.1) underscores and highlights the important ways leaders help followers. It shouts out for leaders to clarify the paths to the goals and remove or help followers around the obstacles to the goals. In its simplest form, the theory reminds leaders that the overarching purpose of leadership is to guide and coach followers as they move along the path to achieve a goal. The theory includes characteristics of both the followers and the situation and is more comprehensive than prior contingency theories.

CRITICISMS

Although path–goal theory has various strengths, it also has several identifiable weaknesses. First, path–goal theory is so complex and incorporates so many different aspects of leadership and related contingencies that interpreting the theory can be confusing. For example, path–goal theory makes predictions about which of the different leadership styles is appropriate for tasks with different degrees of structure, for goals with different levels of clarity, for followers at different levels of ability, and for organizations with different degrees of formal authority. To say the least, it is a daunting task to incorporate all these factors simultaneously into one's selection of a preferred leadership style. Because the scope of path–goal theory is so broad and encompasses so many different interrelated sets of assumptions, it is difficult to use this theory fully in trying to improve the leadership process in a given organizational context. The theory also includes follower characteristics that include personality traits. Due to the complexity of the theory, there has not been a complete empirical test of its propositions.

A second limitation of path–goal theory is that it has received only partial support from the many empirical research studies that have been conducted to test its validity (House & Mitchell, 1974; Indvik, 1986; C. Schriesheim, Castro, Zhou, & DeChurch, 2006; C. Schriesheim & Kerr, 1977; J. Schriesheim & Schriesheim, 1980; Stinson & Johnson, 1975; Wofford & Liska, 1993). For example, some research supports the prediction that leader directiveness is positively related to follower satisfaction when tasks are ambiguous, but other research has failed to confirm this relationship. Furthermore, not all aspects of the theory have been given equal attention. A great deal of research has been designed to study directive and supportive leadership, but fewer studies address the other articulated leadership behaviors. The claims of path–goal theory remain tentative because the research findings to date do not provide a full and consistent picture of the basic assumptions and corollaries of path–goal theory (Evans, 1996; Jermier, 1996; C. Schriesheim & Neider, 1996). There also is some confusion in the literature due to several iterations of path–goal theory and House's (1996) version having not been tested (Turner, Baker, & Kellner, 2018).

A third and more recent criticism is that the theory does not account for gender differences in how leadership is enacted or perceived (Mendez & Busenbark, 2015). Research has been done on the impact of gender on directive, supportive, and participative leadership but has not been integrated into path–goal theory. For example, Eagly and Johnson (1990) conducted a meta-analysis comparing leadership styles and found that women are more participative, while men are more directive. Other research has found that directive leadership by women is viewed negatively, regardless of whether path–goal theory prescribes it. Female leaders who show direction are negatively perceived compared to male leaders who demonstrate the same behavior (Eagly, Makhijani, & Klonsky, 1992), particularly in "masculine" jobs (Heilman, Wallen, Fuchs, & Tamkins, 2004). Race has also shown to be a factor—Black women and Asian women are perceived negatively when they show directive behavior (Rosette, Koval, Ma, & Livingston, 2016).

Another criticism of path–goal theory is that it fails to explain adequately the relationship between leadership behavior and follower motivation. Path–goal theory is unique in that it incorporates the tenets of expectancy theory; however, it does not go far enough in explicating how leadership is related to these tenets. The principles of expectancy theory suggest that followers will be motivated if they feel competent and trust that their efforts will get results, but path–goal theory does not describe how a leader could use various styles directly to help followers feel competent or assured of success. For example, path–goal theory does not explain how directive leadership during ambiguous tasks increases follower motivation. Similarly, it does not explain how supportive leadership during tedious work relates to follower motivation. The result is that practitioners are left with an inadequate understanding of how their leadership will affect followers' expectations about their work.

In addition, path–goal theory presumes that leaders possess the advanced communication skills necessary to swiftly jockey between the various leadership behaviors to effectively interact with followers in all given situations. Without constant feedback from followers, the shifting of leader behavior among directive, supportive, participative, and achievement-oriented behaviors may be viewed as inconsistent and confusing by followers.

A final criticism that can be made of path–goal theory concerns a practical outcome of the theory. Path–goal theory suggests that it is important for leaders to provide coaching, guidance, and direction for followers; to help followers define and clarify goals; and to help followers around obstacles as they attempt to reach their goals. Therefore, it is a "leader-centric" approach. As such, others have criticized the theory for relying on leader behavior as the primary means to motivate followers (Cote, 2017). In effect, this approach treats leadership as a one-way event: The leader affects the follower. The potential difficulty in this type of "helping" leadership is that followers may easily become dependent on the leader to accomplish their work. Path–goal theory places a great deal of responsibility on leaders and much less on followers. Over time, this kind of leadership could be counterproductive because it promotes dependency and fails to recognize the full abilities of followers.

APPLICATION

Path–goal theory is not an approach to leadership for which many management training programs have been developed. You will not find many seminars with titles such as "Improving Your Path–Goal Leadership" or "Assessing Your Skills in Path–Goal Leadership," either. Nevertheless, path–goal theory does offer significant insights that can be applied in ongoing settings to improve one's leadership.

Path–goal theory provides a set of general recommendations based on the characteristics of followers and tasks for how leaders should act in various situations if they want to be effective. It informs us about when to emphasize certain leader behaviors including clarifying goal behavior, lending support, and enhancing group decision-making processes, among others (House, 1996). For instance, the theory suggests that leaders should be directive when tasks are complex and that leaders should give support when tasks are dull. Similarly, it suggests that leaders should be participative when followers need control and that leaders should be achievement oriented when followers need to excel. In a general way, path–goal theory offers leaders a road map that gives directions about ways to improve follower satisfaction and performance.

The principles of path–goal theory can be used by leaders at all levels in the organization and for all types of tasks. To apply path–goal theory, a leader must carefully assess the followers and their tasks, and then choose an appropriate leadership style to match those characteristics. If followers are feeling insecure about doing a task, the leader needs to adopt a style that builds follower confidence. For example, in a university setting where junior faculty members feel apprehensive about their teaching and research, a department chair should give supportive leadership. By giving care and support, the chair helps the junior faculty members gain a sense of confidence about their ability to perform the work (Bess & Goldman, 2001). If followers are uncertain whether their efforts will result in reaching their goals, the leader needs to prove to them that their efforts will be rewarded. As discussed earlier in the chapter, *path–goal theory is useful because it continually reminds leaders that their central purpose is to help followers define their goals and then to help followers reach their goals in the most efficient manner.*

CASE STUDIES

The following case studies (Cases 6.1, 6.2, and 6.3) provide descriptions of various situations in which a leader is attempting to apply path–goal theory. The first case looks at the leadership of three managers at a manufacturing company. The second case is from the academic perspective of teaching orchestra students. The final case profiles football coach P. J. Fleck and how his unique leadership rejuvenated two floundering college teams. As you read the cases, try to apply the principles of path–goal theory to determine the degree to which you think the leaders in the cases have done a good job based on this theory.

Case 6.1 THREE SHIFTS, THREE SUPERVISORS

Brako is a small manufacturing company that produces parts for the automobile industry. The company has several patents on parts that fit in the brake assembly of nearly all domestic and foreign cars. Each year, the company produces 3 million parts that it ships to assembly plants throughout the world. To produce the parts, Brako runs three shifts with about 40 workers on each shift.

The supervisors for the three shifts (Art, Bob, and Carol) are experienced employees, and each has been with the company for more than 20 years. The supervisors appear satisfied with their work and have reported no major difficulty in supervising employees at Brako.

Art supervises the first shift. Employees describe him as being a very hands-on type of leader. He gets very involved in the day-to-day operations of the facility. Workers joke that Art knows to the milligram the amount of raw materials the company has on hand at any given time. Art often can be found walking through the plant and reminding people of the correct procedures to follow in doing their work. Even for those working on the production line, Art always has some directions and reminders.

Workers on the first shift have few negative comments to make about Art's leadership. However, they are negative about many other aspects of their work. Most of the work on this shift is very straightforward and repetitive; as a result, it is monotonous. The rules for working on the production line or in the packaging area are all clearly spelled out and require no independent decision making on the part of workers. Workers simply need to show up and go through the motions. On lunch breaks, workers often are heard complaining about how bored they are doing the same old thing over and over. Workers do not criticize Art, but they do not think he really understands their situation.

(Continued)

(Continued)

Bob supervises the second shift. He really enjoys working at Brako and wants all the workers on the afternoon shift to enjoy their work as well. Bob is a people-oriented supervisor whom workers describe as very genuine and caring. Hardly a day goes by that Bob does not post a message about someone's birthday or someone's personal accomplishment. Bob works hard at creating camaraderie, including sponsoring a company softball team, taking people out to lunch, and having people over to his house for social events.

Despite Bob's personableness, absenteeism and turnover are highest on the second shift. The second shift is responsible for setting up the machines and equipment when changes are made from making one part to making another. In addition, the second shift is responsible for the complex computer programs that monitor the machines. Workers on the second shift take a lot of heat from others at Brako for not doing a good job.

Workers on the second shift feel pressure because it is not always easy to figure out how to do their tasks. Each setup is different and entails different procedures. Although the computer is extremely helpful when it is calibrated appropriately to the task, it can be extremely problematic when the software it uses is off the mark. Workers have complained to Bob and upper management many times about the difficulty of their jobs.

Carol supervises the third shift. Her style is different from that of the others at Brako. Carol routinely has meetings, which she labels troubleshooting sessions, for the purpose of identifying problems workers are experiencing. Any time there is a glitch on the production line, Carol wants to know about it so she can help workers find a solution. If workers cannot do a particular job, she shows them how. For those who are uncertain of their competencies, Carol gives reassurance. Carol tries to spend time with each worker and help the workers focus on their personal goals. In addition, she stresses company goals and the rewards that are available if workers are able to make the grade.

People on the third shift like to work for Carol. They find she is good at helping them do their job. They say she has a wonderful knack for making everything fall into place. When there are problems, she addresses them. When workers feel down, she builds them up. Carol was described by one worker as an interesting mixture of part parent, part coach, and part manufacturing expert. Upper management at Brako is pleased with Carol's leadership, but they have experienced problems repeatedly when workers from Carol's shift have been rotated to other shifts at Brako.

Questions

1. Based on the principles of path–goal theory, describe why Art and Bob appear to be less effective than Carol.

2. How does the leadership of each of the three supervisors affect the motivation of their respective followers?

3. If you were consulting with Brako about leadership, what changes and recommendations would you make regarding the supervision of Art, Bob, and Carol?

Case 6.2 PLAYING IN THE ORCHESTRA

Martina Bates is the newly hired orchestra teacher at Middletown School District in rural Sparta, Kansas. After graduating from the Juilliard School of Music, Bates had intended to play violin professionally, but when no jobs became available, she accepted an offer to teach orchestra in her hometown, believing it would be a good place to hone her skills until a professional position became available.

Being the orchestra instructor at Middletown is challenging because it involves teaching music classes, directing the high school orchestra, and directing both the middle school and grade school orchestra programs. When classes started, Bates hit the ground running and found she liked teaching, and was exhilarated by her work with students. After her first year, however, she is having misgivings about her decision to teach. Most of all, she is feeling troubled by how different students are in each of the three programs, and how her leadership does not seem to be effective with all the students.

Running the elementary orchestra program is demanding, but fun. A lot of parents want their children to play an instrument, so the turnout for orchestra is really strong, and it is the largest of the three Middletown programs. Many students have never held an instrument before, so teaching them is quite a challenge. Learning to make the cornet sound like a cornet or moving the bow so a cello sounds like a cello is a huge undertaking. Whether it is drums, bass viol, clarinet, or saxophone, Bates patiently shows the kids how to play and consistently compliments them every small step of the way. First and foremost, she wants all of her learners to feel like they can "do it." She instructs her students with great detail about how to hold the instruments, position their tongues, and read notes. They respond well to Bates's kindness and forbearance, and the parents are thrilled. The orchestra's spring concert had many wild sounds but was also wildly successful, with excited children and happy parents.

The middle school orchestra is somewhat smaller in size and presents different challenges for Bates. The students in this orchestra are starting to sound good on their instruments and are willing to play together as a group, but some of them are becoming disinterested and want to quit. Bates uses a different style of leadership with the middle schoolers, stressing practice and challenging students

(Continued)

(Continued)

to improve their skills. At this level, students are placed in "chairs" for each instrument. The best players sit in the first chair, the next best are second chair, and so on down to the last chair. Each week, the students engage in "challenges" for the chairs. If students practice hard and improve, they can advance to a higher chair; students who don't practice can slip down to a lower chair. Bates puts up charts to track students' practice hours, and when they reach established goals, they can choose a reward from "the grab bag of goodies," which has candy, trinkets, and gift cards. Never knowing what their prize will be motivates the students, especially as they all want to get the gift cards. Although some kids avoid practice because they find it tedious and boring, many enjoy it because it improves their performance, to say nothing about the chance to get a prize. The spring concert for this group is Bates's favorite, because the sounds are better and the students are interested in playing well.

Middletown's high school orchestra is actually very small, which is surprising to Bates. Why does she have nearly a hundred kids in the elementary orchestra and less than half that number in the high school program? She likes teaching the high school students, but they do not seem excited about playing. Because she is highly trained herself, Bates likes to show students advanced techniques and give them challenging music to play. She spends hours listening to each student play, providing individualized feedback that, unfortunately in many cases, doesn't seem to have any impact on the students. For example, Chris Trotter, who plays third-chair trumpet, is considering dropping orchestra to go out for cross-country. Similarly, Lisa Weiss, who is first-chair flute, seems bored and may quit the orchestra to get a part-time job. Bates is frustrated and baffled; why would these students want to quit? They are pretty good musicians, and most of them are willing to practice. The students have such wonderful potential but don't seem to want to use it. Students profess to liking Bates, but many of them just don't seem to want to be in the orchestra.

Questions

1. Path–goal leadership is about how leaders can help followers reach their goals. Generally, what are the goals for the students in each of the different orchestras? What obstacles do they face? In what way does Bates help them address obstacles and reach their goals?

2. Based on the principles of expectancy theory described in the chapter, why is Bates effective with the elementary and middle school orchestras? Why do both of these groups seem motivated to play for her? In what ways did she change her leadership style for the middle schoolers?

3. Bates's competencies as a musician do not seem to help her with the students who are becoming disinterested in orchestra. Why? Using ideas

from expectancy theory, what would you advise her to do to improve her leadership with the high school orchestra?

4. Achievement-oriented leadership is one of the possible behaviors of path–goal leadership. For which of the three orchestras do you think this style would be most effective? Discuss.

Case 6.3 ROW THE BOAT

When P. J. Fleck was a wide receivers' coach for the Rutgers University football team, he told the team's then offensive coordinator, Kirk Ciarrocca, that his goal was to become the youngest head football coach of a college team (Mattingly, 2017a).

Just two years later, at the age of 32, he was named the head coach of the Western Michigan University (WMU) Broncos, making him the youngest coach of a NCAA Division I Football Bowl Subdivision team. When Coach Fleck took over the Broncos team, it had a 22–27 record. Four years later, the team was 13–1, became the Mid-American Conference (MAC) champion for the first time in 28 years, and earned a trip to the 2017 Cotton Bowl.

Coach Fleck then took the top coaching job at the University of Minnesota, a Big Ten school that hadn't seen a championship season in 50 years. In just three seasons, he built another floundering team into a formidable one. In 2019, the Golden Gophers finished the season 10–2. They also tied for the Big Ten West title, the first time the team had won a share of a division title since the Big Ten began divisional play. Minnesota defeated No. 9 Auburn in the 2020 Outback Bowl for its 11th win, the team's most since 1904.

The thing about being a successful football coach is that your success is based on how your players perform. Coach Fleck could only achieve his goals by setting goals for his players and then leading his players in achieving those. He boils down the ability to turn around a program into three pieces: the right people, cultural consistency, and the value of long-term vision over short-term desires (Giambalvo, 2019).

One of Coach Fleck's first actions as coach at WMU was to rescind all the scholarship offers to incoming players who had verbally committed to attend the university in Kalamazoo, under the previous coach. The scholarship withdrawals occurred just weeks before the national signing day and left players unable to arrange other Division I scholarships as slots were already filled at other schools. Despite the bad press and the hit to his reputation that resulted, Coach Fleck said his decision to start recruiting fresh was for the good of the program because recruits "commit to the coaching staff" (Ambrogi, 2013).

(Continued)

(Continued)

"He built Western Michigan by building it with better players," said *Sports Illustrated* writer Andy Staples (Mattingly, 2017b). By the next year, Coach Fleck had one of the highest-ranked recruiting classes in the MAC conference, and he continued that streak for the next three years.

When he began his tenure at WMU, Coach Fleck was clear that he was creating a culture for the program that emphasized athletes' growth in four areas: "academically, athletically, socially and spiritually."

He established a team mantra, which also became the team's rallying cry: Row the Boat. It came from the tragedy of losing his second son, Colt, to a heart condition just days after he was born in 2011. But it was more than a mantra; it was a mindset.

Coach Fleck explained the phrase, saying, "It's very simple when you break it down. There are three parts to rowing the boat. There is the oar, which is the energy behind rowing the boat. There is the boat, which is the actual sacrifice, either our team or the administration or the boosters or the audience or whoever is willing to sacrifice for this program. There is also the compass. Every single person that comes in contact with our football program, fans or not, they are all going for one common goal and that is success" (Drew, 2013).

Holding onto that mindset became important after his first season at WMU, when the team went 1–11. Coach Fleck, along with his rallying cry of Row the Boat, which was emblazoned on billboards, T-shirts, and posters in bars and restaurants across Kalamazoo, became an object of ridicule among fans, the media, and rivals, who happily flouted broken oars at away games. But he made it clear to his team that Row the Boat was for times of adversity.

"It's very easy to row the boat in times of triumph and success in calm seas, but when you're in the middle of the night, and there are really big storms and there are really big waves, and it's cold, and it's dark, and you can't see, you have to continue to keep your oar in the water. That's what it's for. It's not for the really amazing times. It's for when you get really tough times and you're tested," he said (Nothaft, 2017).

"And at one point, he was the only one who believed in it," said WMU running back Jarvion Franklin. "His voice never wavered. People were screaming at him and he stayed true to himself and his beliefs" (Markgraff, 2018).

Despite the team's deplorable record, Coach Fleck's energy and charisma was enough to help him draw top-level players to WMU, and the coach preached patience.

"When you take over a program, all 125 players have to adapt to your culture," he said. "I think it takes two or three years when you first get into a program," he said. "There's a new personality, and it takes two or three years until everyone begins wearing that personality. Once you start getting into year three and year four, it's really just incoming freshmen that are adapting" (Markgraff, 2018).

That culture made his players focus on more than athletics. Coach Fleck stressed that he was preparing the players for life after college. He wanted them to have the tools to be successful and overcome adversity in whatever life threw at them.

"Coaching is way different in 2018 than it was in 2008," he said. "All areas of the student-athletes' lives are affected by everything they do in college. I have to teach these four areas more than I ever have before" (Markgraff, 2018).

In the team's meeting room, a large sign detailed how to improve "academically, athletically, socially and spiritually." Under spirituality, it read, "connect with three new people."

"Stepping outside your comfort zone in all four areas helps you change the narrative of whatever that narrative is," said Coach Fleck. "We are here to change that by our actions every day of doing the right things. You should never be a better football player than you are a person" (Greder, 2017).

The winning record was one indication Coach Fleck was achieving what he set out to. Another was that by 2017, the WMU Broncos football team had the highest grade point average in the conference. Another indication was how the players' own outlooks had changed.

"It's not just about football or not just about the program, it's about life," WMU defensive lineman Keion Adams said. "It's about never giving up. The boat is sacrifice and the oar is the compass and direction you set for yourself. It's guided me through my life and made me the person that I am today" (Nichols, 2016).

Coach Fleck's success at WMU meant bigger football programs would be calling, and within months of the team's Cotton Bowl experience, it was announced that he would leave WMU to coach football at the University of Minnesota. Once in the Twin Cities, Coach Fleck immediately began to instill the same culture he created at WMU with his new team, building camaraderie, teaching life lessons, and developing a multilevel leadership committee of players. He was insistent that players assume leadership roles and consistently model the desired culture of the team, often repeating, "Bad teams, nobody leads. Average teams, coaches lead. Elite teams, players lead."

Once again, Coach Fleck knew it would take a couple of years before his culture became ingrained in his players. But with time, consistency, and a focus on cultural values, he produced "mature players who are ready to lead" (Markgraff, 2018).

"We define maturity as, 'When doing what you have to do becomes doing what you want to do,'" he said. "If our guys don't know what they have to do because it's a new program, that takes a couple of years for this maturity to take place.

(Continued)

(Continued)

Once the expectations are laid out for them, they know what they 'have to do.' Once they want to do it, they also know every reason why they want to do it. That shows a very mature football team. That's when you start seeing players lead elite football teams" (Markgraff, 2018).

"Everything's connected," Coach Fleck told ESPN. "How we live our life is going to be how we play. It sounds like a lot of slogans and all this other stuff. It's really not. It's very well connected, it's very organized, it's a very detailed culture, there's a standard, and that standard can't be compromised in any area of your life" (Rittenberg, 2019).

Questions

1. The focus of path–goal theory is for leaders to enhance follower performance by focusing on follower motivation and the nature of work tasks. Describe how Coach Fleck achieved this through (a) follower motivation and (b) work tasks.

2. Describe Coach Fleck in terms of the four path–goal leader behaviors— directive, supportive, participative, and achievement oriented.

3. Regarding the follower characteristics outlined in the chapter, how did Coach Fleck address followers' (a) needs for affiliation, (b) preferences for structure, (c) desires for control, and (d) self-perceived level of task ability?

4. Path–goal leadership and expectancy theory are about how leaders can help followers reach their goals. Were the goals the players were working toward their own or Coach Fleck's?

5. Explain Coach Fleck's leadership in terms of expectancy theory.

LEADERSHIP INSTRUMENT

Because the path–goal theory was developed as a complex set of theoretical assumptions to direct researchers in developing new leadership theory, it has used many different instruments to measure the leadership process. The Path–Goal Leadership Questionnaire has been useful in measuring and learning about important aspects of path–goal leadership (Indvik, 1985, 1988) and is still used in contemporary research (Asamani et al., 2016). This questionnaire provides information for respondents on the four leadership behaviors: directive, supportive, participative, and achievement oriented. Respondents' scores on each of the different styles provide them with information on their strong and weak styles and the relative importance they place on each of the styles.

To understand the path–goal questionnaire better, it may be useful to analyze a hypothetical set of scores. For example, hypothesize that your scores on the questionnaire were 29 for directive, which is high; 22 for supportive, which is moderate; 21 for participative, which is moderate; and 25 for achievement oriented, which is moderate. These scores suggest that you are a leader who is typically more directive than most other leaders, and quite similar to other leaders in the degree to which you are supportive, participative, and achievement oriented.

According to the principles of path–goal theory, if your scores matched these hypothetical scores, you would be effective in situations where the tasks and procedures are unclear and your followers have a need for certainty. You would be less effective in work settings that are structured and unchallenging. In addition, you would be moderately effective in ambiguous situations with followers who want control. Last, you would do fairly well in uncertain situations where you could set high standards, challenge followers to meet these standards, and help them feel confident in their abilities.

In addition to the Path–Goal Leadership Questionnaire, leadership researchers have commonly used multiple instruments to study path–goal theory, including measures of task structure, locus of control, follower expectancies, and follower satisfaction. Although the primary use of these instruments has been for theory building, many of the instruments offer valuable information related to practical leadership issues.

Path–Goal Leadership Questionnaire

Purpose: The purpose of this questionnaire is to identify your path–goal styles of leadership and examine how your use of each style relates to other styles of leadership.

Instructions: This questionnaire contains questions about different styles of path–goal leadership. Indicate how often each statement is true of your own behavior.

Key: 1 = Never   2 = Hardly ever   3 = Seldom   4 = Occasionally   5 = Often
6 = Usually   7 = Always

1.	I let followers know what is expected of them.	1 2 3 4 5 6 7
2.	I maintain a friendly working relationship with followers.	1 2 3 4 5 6 7
3.	I consult with followers when facing a problem.	1 2 3 4 5 6 7
4.	I listen receptively to followers' ideas and suggestions.	1 2 3 4 5 6 7
5.	I inform followers about what needs to be done and how it needs to be done.	1 2 3 4 5 6 7
6.	I let followers know that I expect them to perform at their highest level.	1 2 3 4 5 6 7
7.	I act without consulting my followers.	1 2 3 4 5 6 7
8.	I do little things to make it pleasant to be a member of the group.	1 2 3 4 5 6 7
9.	I ask followers to follow standard rules and regulations.	1 2 3 4 5 6 7
10.	I set goals for followers' performance that are quite challenging.	1 2 3 4 5 6 7
11.	I say things that hurt followers' personal feelings.	1 2 3 4 5 6 7
12.	I ask for suggestions from followers concerning how to carry out assignments.	1 2 3 4 5 6 7
13.	I encourage continual improvement in followers' performance.	1 2 3 4 5 6 7
14.	I explain the level of performance that is expected of followers.	1 2 3 4 5 6 7
15.	I help followers overcome problems that stop them from carrying out their tasks.	1 2 3 4 5 6 7
16.	I show that I have doubts about followers' ability to meet most objectives.	1 2 3 4 5 6 7
17.	I ask followers for suggestions on what assignments should be made.	1 2 3 4 5 6 7

18. I give vague explanations of what is expected of followers on the job.   1 2 3 4 5 6 7

19. I consistently set challenging goals for followers to attain.   1 2 3 4 5 6 7

20. I behave in a manner that is thoughtful of followers' personal needs.   1 2 3 4 5 6 7

Scoring

1. Reverse the scores for Items 7, 11, 16, and 18.

2. Directive style: Sum of scores on Items 1, 5, 9, 14, and 18.

3. Supportive style: Sum of scores on Items 2, 8, 11, 15, and 20.

4. Participative style: Sum of scores on Items 3, 4, 7, 12, and 17.

5. Achievement-oriented style: Sum of scores on Items 6, 10, 13, 16, and 19.

Scoring Interpretation

For each style, scores 17 and below are considered low, a moderate score is between 18 and 28, and scores 29 and above are considered high.

The scores you received on the Path–Goal Leadership Questionnaire provide information about which styles of leadership you use most often and which you use less often. In addition, you can use these scores to assess your use of each style relative to your use of the other styles.

Sources: Adapted from *A Path-Goal Theory Investigation of Superior-Subordinate Relationships*, by J. Indvik, unpublished doctoral dissertation, University of Wisconsin-Madison, 1985; and from Indvik (1988). Based on the work of House and Dessler (1974) and House (1977) cited in Fulk and Wendler (1982).

SUMMARY

Path–goal theory was developed to explain how leaders motivate followers to be productive and satisfied with their work. It is a contingency approach to leadership because effectiveness depends on the fit between the leader's behavior and the characteristics of followers and the task.

The basic principles of path–goal theory are derived from expectancy theory, which suggests that followers will be motivated if they feel competent, if they think their efforts will be rewarded, and if they find the payoff for their work valuable. A leader can help followers by selecting a style of leadership (directive, supportive, participative, or achievement oriented) that provides what is missing for followers in a particular work setting. In simple terms, it is the leader's responsibility to help followers reach their goals by directing, guiding, and coaching them along the way.

Path–goal theory offers a large set of predictions for how a leader's style interacts with followers' needs and the nature of the task. Among other things, it predicts that directive leadership is effective with ambiguous tasks, that supportive leadership is effective for repetitive tasks, that participative leadership is effective when tasks are unclear and followers are autonomous, and that achievement-oriented leadership is effective for challenging tasks.

Path–goal theory has three major strengths. First, it provides a theoretical framework that is useful for understanding how various styles of leadership affect the productivity and satisfaction of followers. Second, path–goal theory is unique in that it integrates the motivation principles of expectancy theory into a theory of leadership. Third, it provides a practical model that underscores the important ways in which leaders help followers.

On the negative side, several criticisms can be leveled at path–goal theory. First, the scope of path–goal theory encompasses so many interrelated sets of assumptions that it is hard to use this theory in a given organizational setting. Second, research findings to date do not support a full and consistent picture of the claims of the theory. Third, path–goal theory does not account for gender differences in how leadership is enacted or perceived. Fourth, path–goal theory does not show in a clear way how leader behaviors directly affect follower motivation levels. Also, the theory assumes that leaders have the skills to allow them to switch between various leadership behaviors needed by differing followers, and it assumes that leader behavior is the primary means to motivate followers. Last, path–goal theory is predominantly leader oriented and fails to recognize the interactional nature of leadership. It does not promote follower involvement in the leadership process.

Leader–Member Exchange Theory

DESCRIPTION

Most of the leadership theories discussed thus far in this book have emphasized leadership from the point of view of the leader (e.g., trait approach, skills approach, and behavioral approach) or the follower and the context (e.g., situational approach and path–goal theory). Leader–member exchange (LMX) theory takes still another approach and conceptualizes leadership as a process that is centered on the *interactions* between leaders and followers. As Figure 7.1 illustrates, LMX theory makes the *dyadic relationship* between leaders and followers the focal point of the leadership process.

FIGURE 7.1 Dimensions of Leadership

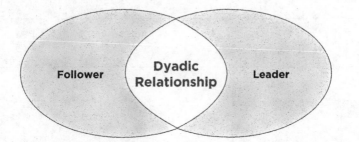

Source: Reprinted from *The Leadership Quarterly,* 6(2), G. B. Graen & M. Uhl-Bien, "Relationship-Based Approach to Leadership: Development of Leader–Member Exchange (LMX) Theory of Leadership Over 25 Years: Applying a Multi-Level, Multi-Domain Perspective," pp. 219–247, Copyright (1995), with permission from Elsevier.

Note: LMX theory was first described 28 years ago in the works of Dansereau, Graen, and Haga (1975), Graen (1976), and Graen and Cashman (1975). Since it first appeared, it has undergone several revisions, and it continues to be of interest to researchers who study the leadership process.

Before LMX theory, researchers treated leadership as something leaders did toward followers in a collective way, as a group, using an average leadership style. LMX theory challenged this assumption and directed researchers' attention to the differences that might exist between the leader and each of the leader's followers.

Early Studies

In the first studies of exchange theory, which was then called vertical dyad linkage (VDL) theory, researchers focused on the nature of the *vertical linkages* leaders formed with each of their followers (Figure 7.2). A leader's relationship to the work unit as a whole was viewed as a series of vertical dyads (Figure 7.3).

FIGURE 7.2 The Vertical Dyad

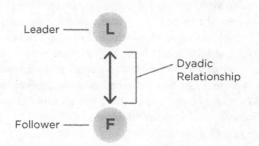

Note: The leader (L) forms an individualized working relationship with each follower (F). The exchanges (both content and process) between the leader and the follower define their dyadic relationship.

FIGURE 7.3 Vertical Dyads

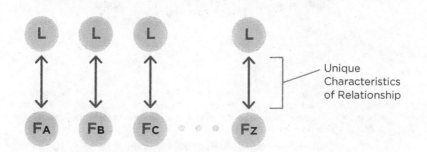

Note: The leader (L) forms special relationships with all followers (F). Each of these relationships is special and has unique characteristics.

In assessing the characteristics of these vertical dyads, researchers found two general types of linkages (or relationships): those that were based on expanded and negotiated role responsibilities (extra-roles), which were called the *in-group*, and those that were based on the formal employment contract (defined roles), which were called the *out-group* (Figure 7.4).

Within an organizational work unit, followers become a part of the in-group or the out-group based on how well they work with the leader and how well the leader works with them. Personality and other personal characteristics are related to this process (Dansereau, Graen, & Haga, 1975; Maslyn, Schyns, & Farmer, 2017; Randolph-Seng et al., 2016). In addition, membership in one group or the other is based on how followers involve themselves in expanding their role responsibilities with the leader (Graen, 1976). Followers who are interested in negotiating with the leader what they are willing to do for the group can become a part of the in-group. These negotiations involve exchanges in which followers do certain activities that go beyond their formal job descriptions, and the leader, in turn, does more for these followers. If followers are not interested in taking on new and different job responsibilities, they become a part of the out-group.

Followers in the in-group receive more information, influence, confidence, and concern from their leaders than do out-group followers (Dansereau et al., 1975). In addition, they are more dependable, more highly involved, and more communicative than out-group followers (Dansereau et al., 1975). Whereas in-group members do extra things for the leader and the leader does the same for them, followers in the out-group are less compatible with the leader and usually just

FIGURE 7.4 In-Groups and Out-Groups

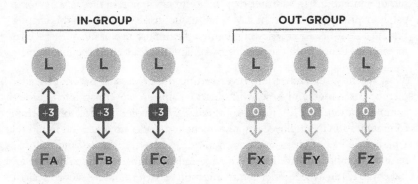

Note: A leader (L) and followers (F) form unique relationships. Relationships within the in-group are marked by mutual trust, respect, liking, and reciprocal influence. Relationships within the out-group are marked by formal communication based on job descriptions. Plus-3 is a high-quality relationship, and zero is a stranger.

come to work, do their job, and go home. Not to say that out-group members are poor performers. Poor performers are a third group that must be managed differently due to the need for performance monitoring and documentation. Out-group members perform to the specifications of their job description, but they don't go above and beyond that to help the leader and the work group.

Later Studies

After the first set of studies, there was a shift in the focus of LMX theory. Whereas the initial studies of this theory addressed primarily the nature of the differences between in-groups and out-groups, a subsequent line of research addressed how LMX theory was related to organizational effectiveness.

Specifically, these studies focus on how the quality of leader–member exchanges was related to positive outcomes for leaders, followers, groups, and the organization in general (Graen & Uhl-Bien, 1995).

Researchers found that high-quality leader–member exchanges produced less employee turnover, more positive performance evaluations, higher frequency of promotions, greater organizational commitment, more desirable work assignments, better job attitudes, more attention and support from the leader, greater participation, and faster career progress over 25 years (Buch, Kuvaas, Dysvik, & Schyns, 2014; Graen & Uhl-Bien, 1995; Liden, Wayne, & Stilwell, 1993; Malik, Wan, Ahmad, Naseem, & Rehman, 2015).

In a meta-analysis of 164 LMX studies, Gerstner and Day (1997) found that leader–member exchange was consistently related to member job performance, satisfaction (overall and supervisory), commitment, role conflict and clarity, and turnover intentions. In addition, they found strong support in these studies for the psychometric properties of the LMX-7 Questionnaire (included in this chapter). For purposes of research, they highlighted the importance of measuring leader–member exchange from the perspective of both the leader and the follower.

Most recently, researchers are investigating the processual nature of leader–member exchange and how work relationships are co-constructed through communication. N. Hill, Kang, and Seo (2014) studied the role of electronic communication in employee empowerment and work outcomes and found that a higher degree of electronic communication between leaders and followers resulted in more positive leader–member relationships. Omilion-Hodges and Baker (2017) analyzed leader communication behaviors and developed scales to assess how these behaviors can affect the growth or stagnation of leader–member relationships.

Based on a review of 130 studies of LMX research conducted since 2002, Anand, Hu, Liden, and Vidyarthi (2011) found that interest in studying leader–member exchange has not diminished. A large majority of these studies (70%) examined the antecedents (e.g., Maslyn et al., 2017) and outcomes of leader–member exchange. The research trends show increased attention to the context surrounding LMX relationships (e.g., group dynamics), analyzing leader–member exchange from individual and group levels, and studying leader–member exchange with non-U.S. samples (Malik et al., 2015) or racially diverse dyads (Randolph-Seng et al., 2016).

For example, using a sample of employees in a variety of jobs in Israeli organizations, Atwater and Carmeli (2009) examined the connection between employees' perceptions of leader–member exchange and their energy and creativity at work. They found that perceived high-quality leader–member exchange was positively related to feelings of energy in employees, which, in turn, was related to greater involvement in creative work. LMX theory was not directly associated with creativity, but it served as a mechanism to nurture people's feelings, which then enhanced their creativity.

Ilies, Nahrgang, and Morgeson (2007) did a meta-analysis of 51 research studies that examined the relationship between leader–member exchange and employee citizenship behaviors. Citizenship behaviors are discretionary employee behaviors that go beyond the prescribed role, job description, or reward system (Katz, 1964; Organ, 1988). They found a positive relationship between the quality of leader–member relationships and citizenship behaviors. In other words, followers who had higher-quality relationships with their leaders were more likely to engage in more discretionary (positive "payback") behaviors that benefited the leader and the organization.

Researchers have also studied how LMX theory is related to empowerment (Malik et al., 2015). Harris, Wheeler, and Kacmar (2009) explored how empowerment moderates the impact of leader–member exchange on job outcomes such as job satisfaction, turnover, job performance, and organizational citizenship behaviors. Based on two samples of college alumni, they found that empowerment and leader–member exchange quality had a slight synergistic effect on job outcomes. The quality of leader–member exchange mattered most for employees who felt little empowerment. For these employees, high-quality leader–member exchange appeared to compensate for the drawbacks of not being empowered. Volmer, Spurk, and Niessen (2012) investigated the role of job autonomy in the relationship between leader–member exchange and creativity of followers. Their study of a high-technology firm found that greater autonomy increased the positive relationship between leader–member exchange and creativity at work.

Finally, a meta-analysis conducted by Martin, Guillaume, Thomas, Lee, and Epitropaki (2016) supported LMX predictions regarding job performance. There was a positive relationship between LMX and task performance as well as citizenship performance, while a negative relationship existed between LMX and counterproductive performance. Of particular importance in this study, it was found that LMX was positively related to objective task performance (actual performance measurements, not ratings by supervisors). This study also found that trust, motivation, empowerment, and job satisfaction explain the effects of LMX on job performance with trust in the leader having the largest effect.

In essence, these findings clearly illustrate that organizations stand to gain much from having leaders who can create good working relationships. When leaders and followers have good exchanges, they feel better and accomplish more, and the organization prospers.

Leadership Development

Research into LMX theory has also focused on how exchanges between leaders and followers can be used for leadership development (Graen & Uhl-Bien, 1991). Leadership development emphasizes that leaders should develop high-quality exchanges with all of their followers rather than just a few. It attempts to make all followers feel as if they are a part of the in-group and, by so doing, avoids the inequities and negative implications of being in an out-group. In general, leadership development promotes partnerships in which the leader tries to build effective dyads with all followers in the work unit (Graen & Uhl-Bien, 1995). In addition, LMX theory suggests that leaders can create networks of partnerships throughout the organization, which will benefit the organization's goals and the leader's own career progress. Herman and Troth's (2013) findings regarding the emotional experiences described by followers in high- and low-quality LMX relationships align with the assertion that positive relationships benefit organizational and personal leader goals.

Graen and Uhl-Bien (1991) suggested that high-quality leader–member relationships develop progressively over time in three phases: (1) the stranger phase, (2) the acquaintance phase, and (3) the mature partnership phase (Table 7.1). During Phase 1, the stranger phase, the interactions in the leader–follower dyad generally are rule bound, relying heavily on contractual relationships. Leaders and followers relate to each other within prescribed organizational roles. They have lower-quality exchanges, similar to those of out-group members discussed earlier in the chapter. The follower complies with the formal leader, who has hierarchical status for the purpose of achieving the economic rewards the leader controls. The motives of the follower during the stranger phase are directed toward self-interest rather than toward the good of the group (Graen & Uhl-Bien, 1995).

While early descriptions of the LMX development process focused on the leader initiating the development process, followers have been shown to have an influence on how the LMX process unfolds as well. Xu, Loi, Cai, and Liden (2019) found that follower proactivity positively influenced LMX development.

TABLE 7.1 Phases in Leadership Development

	Phase 1 Stranger	Phase 2 Acquaintance	Phase 3 Mature Partnership
Roles	Scripted	Tested	Negotiated
Influences	One way	Mixed	Reciprocal
Exchanges	Low quality	Medium quality	High quality
Interests	Self	Self and other	Group

Time

→

Source: Adapted from "Relationship-Based Approach to Leadership: Development of Leader–Member Exchange (LMX) Theory of Leadership Over 25 Years: Applying a Multi-Level, Multi-Domain Perspective," by G. B. Graen and M. Uhl-Bien, *The Leadership Quarterly,* 6(2), pp. 219–247. Copyright 1995 by Elsevier. Reprinted with permission.

They found that take-charge followers whose efforts and actions make the leader's work more effective and whom the leader recognizes can subsequently develop high-quality LMX relationships with leaders. This is particularly true for followers who work for leaders with high achievement goals, so it is pre-scribed that LMX training include sensitizing leaders to appreciate followers' proactive attempts to build the relationship.

Phase 2, the acquaintance phase, begins with an offer by the leader or the fol-lower for improved career-oriented social exchanges, which involve sharing more resources and personal or work-related information. It is a testing period for both the leader and the follower to assess whether the follower is interested in taking on more roles and responsibilities and to assess whether the leader is willing to provide new challenges for the follower. During this time, dyads shift away from interactions that are governed strictly by job descriptions and defined roles and move toward new ways of relating. As measured by LMX theory, it could be said that the quality of their exchanges has improved to medium quality. Successful dyads in the acquaintance phase begin to develop greater trust and respect for each other. They also tend to focus less on their own self-interests and more on the purposes and goals of the group.

Phase 3, mature partnership, is marked by high-quality leader–member exchanges. People who have progressed to this stage in their relationships experience a high degree of mutual trust, respect, and obligation toward each other. In addition, during Phase 3, members may depend on each other for favors and special assistance. For example, leaders may rely on followers to do extra assignments, and followers may rely on leaders for needed support or encouragement. They have tested their relationship and found that they can depend on each other. In mature partnerships, there is a high degree of reciprocity between leaders and followers: Each affects and is affected by the other. For example, in a study of 75 bank managers and 58 engineering managers, Schriesheim, Castro, Zhou, and Yammarino (2001) found that good leader–member relations were more egalitarian and that influence and control were more evenly balanced between the supervisor and the follower.

In a study of leader–member relationship development, Nahrgang, Morgeson, and Ilies (2009) found that leaders look for followers who exhibit enthusiasm, participation, gregariousness, and extraversion. In contrast, followers look for leaders who are pleasant, trusting, cooperative, and agreeable. Leader extraversion did not influence relationship quality for the followers, and follower agreeableness did not influence relationship quality for the leaders. A key predictor of relationship quality for both leaders and followers over time was both leader and follower performance. Kelley (2014) investigated the ways leaders use narrative story lines to determine how leaders identify trustworthy, indeterminate, and untrustworthy followers. Others have suggested the importance of looking at the social interaction (Sheer, 2014) or cooperative communication between leaders and followers (Bakar & Sheer, 2013) as a means to predict and explore relationship quality. It has also been suggested that exploring the use of traditional relationship-building and maintenance techniques such as conflict management, shared tasks, and positivity in leader–member relationships can shed light on how leader and follower behaviors impact the quality of these relationships (Madlock & Booth-Butterfield, 2012; Omilion-Hodges, Ptacek, & Zerilli, 2015).

The point is that leaders and followers are tied together in productive ways that go well beyond a traditional hierarchically defined work relationship. They develop extremely effective ways of relating that produce positive outcomes for themselves and the organization. In effect, partnerships are transformational in that they assist leaders and followers in moving beyond their own self-interests to accomplish the greater good of the team and organization (see Chapter 8).

Emotions and LMX Development

Recently, Cropanzano, Dasborough, and Weiss (2017) have suggested that emotions play a critical role in the development of high-quality leader–member relationships. To explain the role of emotions in LMX, they constructed a model that complements the original phases suggested by Graen and Uhl-Bien as described in Table 7.1.

As illustrated in Table 7.2, Cropanzano et al. (2017) suggest that leaders and followers experience different emotional, or affective, processes as they progress through three stages—role taking, role making, and role routinization—in LMX development.

TABLE 7.2 Affective Processes and LMX Development

	STAGE I Role Taking	STAGE II Role Making	STAGE III Role Routinization
LMX Development	Leader initiates possibility of LMX relationship	Series of dyadic affective events shapes LMX quality	Stable relationship disrupted by LMX differentiation
Key Affective Process	Leader emotional expressions are affective events	Leader and members share affect (entrainment)	LMX relationship can change based on LMX differentiation
Level	Individual	Dyadic	Group

Source: Adapted from Cropanzano, R., Dasborough, M. T., & Weiss, H. M. (2017). Affective events and the development of leader–member exchange. *Academy of Management Review, 42*(2), 233–258.

Role Taking. In the first stage, the leader initiates a relationship, and cues are taken directly from the leader regarding the development of a higher-quality relationship based on interpersonal liking. In this stage, the leader's emotions are pivotal in the initiation and development of the LMX relationship.

Role Making. As depicted in Figure 7.5, through interactions that occur during the second stage, leaders' and members' emotional states become entrained, or synchronized. Leaders and followers begin sharing emotional affect at similar times, and leaders' and members' emotions become "contagious."

Role Routinization. During the third stage, LMX relationships have been formed and maintained, but can change based on *LMX differentiation*, or the emotional responses of other organizational members to the distribution of LMX relationships within the group. For example, the emergence of in-groups and out-groups may engender emotions of anger and/or contempt.

The benefits for employees who develop high-quality leader–member relationships include preferential treatment, increased job-related communication, ample access to supervisors, and increased performance-related feedback (Harris et al., 2009). The disadvantages for those with low-quality leader–member relationships include limited trust and support from supervisors and few benefits outside the employment contract (Harris et al., 2009). To evaluate leader–member exchanges, researchers typically use a brief questionnaire that asks

FIGURE 7.5 Stage II of LMX Development

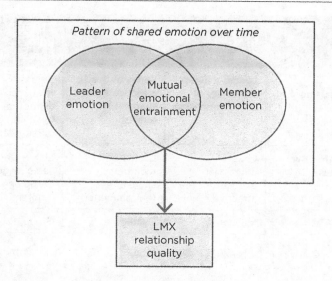

Source: Adapted from Cropanzano, R., Dasborough, M. T., & Weiss, H. M. (2017). Affective events and the development of leader–member exchange. *Academy of Management Review,* *42*(2), 233–258.

leaders and followers to report on the effectiveness of their working relationships. The questionnaire assesses the degree to which respondents express respect, trust, and obligation in their exchanges with others. At the end of this chapter, a version of the LMX questionnaire is provided for you to take for the purpose of analyzing some of your own leader–member relationships.

HOW DOES LMX THEORY WORK?

LMX theory works in two ways: It describes leadership, and it prescribes leadership. In both instances, the central concept is the dyadic relationship that leaders form with each of their followers. Descriptively, LMX theory suggests that it is important to recognize the existence of in-groups and out-groups within a group or an organization.

The differences in how goals are accomplished by in-groups and out-groups are substantial. Working with an in-group allows leaders to accomplish more work in a more effective manner than they can accomplish working without one. In-group members are willing to do more than is required in their job description and look for innovative ways to advance the group's goals. In response to their extra effort and devotion, leaders give them more responsibilities and more opportunities. Leaders also give in-group members more of their time and support.

Out-group members act quite differently than in-group members. Rather than trying to do extra work, out-group members operate strictly within their prescribed organizational roles. They do what is required of them but nothing more. Leaders treat out-group members fairly and according to the formal contract, but they do not give them special attention. For their efforts, out-group members receive the standard benefits as defined in the job description.

Prescriptively, LMX theory suggests that leaders should create a special relationship with all followers, similar to the relationships described as in-group relationships. Leaders should offer each follower the opportunity to take on new roles and responsibilities. Furthermore, leaders should nurture high-quality exchanges with their followers. Herman and Troth (2013) found that high-quality exchanges are described by followers as mentoring, respectful, and based on good communication.

A longitudinal study examining episodes in which leaders and members exchanged resources found that when more resources were given than taken, the other party, whether leader or follower, felt obligated to reciprocate (Liao, Liu, Li, & Song, 2019). In other words, if a leader gives more to a follower, it creates a "contribution surplus," which results in that member's subsequent reciprocation. Over time, these resource contribution surpluses increased work engagement immediately following the exchange episode and the resource contribution of the member in the next episode. Also, a member's obligation to reciprocate is related to the importance a member attaches to the leader–member relationship (Lee, Thomas, Martin, Guillaume, & Marstand, 2019).

In that regard, rather than focusing on differences between in-group and out-group members, the leadership development model suggests that leaders should look for ways to build trust and respect with all of their followers, thus making the entire work unit an in-group. Technology can lend a hand in that endeavor as N. Hill et al. (2014) found that electronic communication mediates the LMX relationship and can have a positive impact, thus broadening avenues for developing good communication and positive relationships across organizations— even those where workers are dispersed and work primarily online. In addition, leaders should look beyond their own work unit and create high-quality partnerships with people throughout the organization.

Whether descriptive or prescriptive, LMX theory works by focusing our attention on the unique relationships that leaders can create with individual followers. When these relationships are of high quality, the goals of the leader, the followers, and the organization are all advanced.

STRENGTHS

LMX theory makes several positive contributions to our understanding of the leadership process. First, it is a strong descriptive theory. Intuitively, it makes sense to describe work units in terms of those who contribute more and those who contribute less (or the bare minimum) to the organization. Anyone who has ever worked in an organization has felt the presence of in-groups and out-groups. Despite the potential harm of out-groups, we all know that leaders have special relationships with certain people who do more and get more. We may not like this because it seems unfair, but it is a reality, and the LMX theory has accurately described this situation. LMX theory validates our experience of how people within organizations relate to each other and the leader. Some contribute more and receive more; others contribute less and get less.

Second, LMX theory is unique in that it is the only leadership approach that makes the concept of the dyadic relationship the centerpiece of the leadership process. Other approaches emphasize the characteristics of leaders, followers, contexts, or a combination of these, but none of them addresses the specific relationships between the leader and each follower. LMX theory underscores that effective leadership is contingent on effective leader–member exchanges. This is underlined in the work of Gottfredson and Aguinis (2017), who conducted meta-analytic studies on the centrality of LMX in understanding the relationship between leader behaviors and job performance. Their results showed that LMX was a consistent explanation for why leadership behaviors affect follower performance.

Third, LMX theory is noteworthy because it directs our attention to the importance of communication in leadership. The high-quality exchanges advocated in LMX theory are inextricably bound to effective communication. Communication is the vehicle through which leaders and followers create, nurture, and sustain useful exchanges. Effective leadership occurs when the communication of leaders and followers is characterized by mutual trust, respect, and commitment.

Fourth, LMX theory provides an important alert for leaders. It warns leaders to avoid letting their conscious or unconscious biases influence who is invited into the in-group (e.g., biases regarding race, gender, ethnicity, religion, or age; see Randolph-Seng et al., 2016). The principles outlined in LMX theory serve as a good reminder for leaders to be fair and equal in how they approach each of their followers.

Fifth, LMX has proven to be a cross-cultural concept and has been studied in many cultures. Rockstuhl, Dulebohn, Ang, and Shore (2012) examined the role of the national culture of 23 countries as a moderator of LMX and found that national culture does not affect the relationship of LMX with followers' task performance, organizational commitment, and transformational leadership. While the study findings suggested that members' responses to LMX in Asian contexts may also be influenced by collective interests and role-based obligations, LMX appears to be universal.

Finally, a large body of research substantiates how the practice of LMX theory is related to positive organizational outcomes. In a review of this research, Graen and Uhl-Bien (1995) pointed out that leader–member exchange is related to performance, organizational commitment, job climate, innovation, organizational citizenship behavior, empowerment, procedural and distributive justice, career progress, and many other important organizational variables. By linking the use of LMX theory to real outcomes, researchers have been able to validate the theory and increase its practical value.

CRITICISMS

LMX theory also has some limitations. First, leader–member exchange in its initial formulation (VDL theory) runs counter to the basic human value of fairness. Throughout our lives, beginning when we are very young, we are taught to try to get along with everyone and to treat everyone equally. We have been taught that it is wrong to form in-groups or cliques because they are harmful to those who cannot be a part of them. Because LMX theory divides the work unit into two groups and one group receives special attention, it gives the appearance of discrimination against the out-group.

Our culture is replete with examples of people of different genders, ages, cultures, and abilities who have experienced discrimination. Although LMX theory was not designed to do so, it supports the development of privileged groups in the organizations. In so doing, it appears unfair and discriminatory. Furthermore, as reported by McClane (1991), the existence of in-groups and out-groups may have undesirable effects on the group as a whole. The creation of in-groups and out-groups within a work group can cause members to engage in social comparisons that invoke perceptions of injustice (Matta & Van Dyne, 2020). This influences emotions that affect how team members interact with one another. For example, out-group members may engage in less organizational citizenship and helping behaviors for others on their team if they feel there is injustice.

Whether LMX theory actually creates inequalities is questionable (cf. Harter & Evanecky, 2002; Scandura, 1999). If a leader does not intentionally keep out-group members "out," and if they are free to become members of the in-group, then LMX theory may not create inequalities. However, the theory does not elaborate on strategies for how one gains access to the in-group if one chooses to do so.

Furthermore, LMX theory does not address other fairness issues, such as followers' perceptions of the fairness of pay increases and promotion opportunities (distributive justice), decision-making rules (procedural justice), or communication of issues within the organization (interactional justice) (Scandura, 1999). There is a need for further research on how these types of fairness issues affect the development and maintenance of LMX relationships.

A second criticism of LMX theory is that the basic ideas of the theory are not fully developed. For example, the theory does not fully explain how high-quality leader–member exchanges are created (Anand et al., 2011). In the early studies, it was implied that they were formed when a leader found certain followers more compatible in regard to personality, interpersonal skills, or job competencies, but these studies never described the relative importance of these factors or how this process worked (Yukl, 1994). Research has suggested that leaders should work to create high-quality exchanges with all followers, but the guidelines for how this is done are not clearly spelled out. Fairhurst and Uhl-Bien (2012) have done research into the construction of the LMX relationship, but more work needs to be done to substantiate and clarify guidelines. For example, the model of leadership development highlights the importance of role making, incremental influence, and type of reciprocity (Table 7.1), but it does not explain how these concepts function to build mature partnerships. Similarly, the model strongly promotes building trust, respect, and obligation in leader–follower relationships, but it does not describe the means by which these factors are developed in relationships.

Some researchers challenge the idea that LMX is an exchange theory. Bernerth, Armenakis, Feild, Giles, and Walker (2007) state that "the theoretical underpinning of [LMX] is not based on the conceptualization of social exchange defined by Blau (1964), but rather a role-making model of negotiation between subordinates and supervisors" (p. 983). Thus, LMX may be grounded better in role theory than exchange theory, but this needs clarification.

Based on an examination of 147 studies of leader–member exchange, Schriesheim, Castro, and Cogliser (1999) concluded that improved theorization about leader–member exchange and its basic processes is needed. Similarly, in a review of the research on relational leadership, Uhl-Bien, Maslyn, and Ospina (2012) point to the need for further understanding of how high- and low-quality relationships develop in leader–member exchange. Although many studies have been conducted on leader–member exchange, these studies have not resulted in a clear, refined set of definitions, concepts, and propositions about the theory. While LMX researchers publish in the most reputable journals, there is little agreement on how to define LMX (Gottfredson, Wright, & Heaphy, 2020).

A third criticism of the theory is that researchers have not adequately explained the contextual factors that may have an impact on LMX relationships (Anand et al., 2011). Since leader–member exchange is often studied in isolation, researchers have not examined the potential impact of other variables on LMX dyads. For example, workplace norms and other organizational culture variables are likely to influence leader–member exchange. There is a need to explore how the surrounding constellations of social networks influence specific LMX relationships and the individuals in those relationships.

Finally, questions have been raised about the measurement of leader–member exchanges in LMX theory (Graen & Uhl-Bien, 1995; Schriesheim et al., 1999; Schriesheim et al., 2001). For example, no empirical studies have used dyadic measures to analyze the LMX process (Schriesheim et al., 2001). In addition, leader–member exchanges have been measured with different versions of leader–member exchange scales and with different levels of analysis, so the results are not always directly comparable. A recent review reported that the most commonly used measure of LMX is the LMX-7 developed by Graen and his colleagues, which is used in 66% of empirical studies of LMX. The second-most-common measure is the LMX-MDM (multidimensional measure) developed by Liden and Maslyn (1998), which is used in 11% of studies (Gottfredson et al., 2020). The remainder is a variety of different measures presented over the years, and there is not enough data to fully assess those. Even the content validity and dimensionality of the LMX-7 and LMX-MDM scales have been questioned (Graen & Uhl-Bien, 1995; Schriesheim et al., 2001).

APPLICATION

Although LMX theory has not been packaged in a way to be used in standard management training and development programs, it offers many insights that leaders could use to improve their own leadership behavior. Foremost, LMX theory directs leaders to assess their leadership from a relationship perspective. This assessment will sensitize leaders to how in-groups and out-groups develop within their own organization. In addition, LMX theory suggests ways in which leaders can improve their organization by building strong leader–member exchanges with all of their followers.

The ideas set forth in LMX theory can be used by leaders at all levels within an organization. A CEO selects vice presidents and develops dyadic relationships with them. Vice presidents lead their own units, with their own dyadic relationships with followers. These paired relationships between leader and follower repeat down each level of an organizational chart.

On a lower level, LMX theory could be used to explain how line managers in a manufacturing plant develop high-quality relationships with workers to accomplish the production quotas of their work unit. The ideas presented in LMX theory are applicable throughout organizations, not just at the highest levels.

In addition, the ideas of LMX theory can be used to explain how individuals create leadership networks throughout an organization to help them accomplish work more effectively (Graen & Scandura, 1987). A person with a network of high-quality partnerships can call on many people to help solve problems and advance the goals of the organization. Sparrowe and Liden (2005) tested the LMX network approach and found that LMX networks predicted the amount of influence the organization members enjoyed, and this was a function of how central their leaders were in the network. When leaders are well connected in organizational networks, sharing ties in the LMX network is beneficial to members.

LMX theory can also be applied in different types of organizations. It applies in volunteer settings as well as traditional business, education, and government settings. Imagine a community leader who heads a volunteer program that assists older adults. To run the program effectively, the leader depends on a few of the volunteers who are more dependable and committed than the rest of the volunteers. This process of working closely with a small cadre of trusted volunteers is explained by the principles of LMX theory. Similarly, a manager in a traditional business setting might use certain individuals to achieve a major change in the company's policies and procedures. The way the manager goes about this process is explicated in LMX theory.

In summary, LMX theory tells leaders to be aware of how they relate to their followers. It tells leaders to be sensitive to whether some followers receive special attention and some followers do not. In addition, it tells leaders to be fair to all followers and allow each of them to become as involved in the work of the unit as they want to be. LMX theory tells leaders to be respectful and to build trusting relationships with all of their followers, recognizing that each follower is unique and wants to relate to leadership in a special way.

CASE STUDIES

In the following section, three case studies (Cases 7.1, 7.2, and 7.3) are presented to clarify how LMX theory can be applied to various group settings. The first case is about the creative director who oversees several account teams at an advertising agency. The second is about a production manager at a mortgage company who works hard to be fair with her large team of employees. The third case profiles leadership behind the creative work at Pixar Animation Studios. After each case, there are questions that will help you analyze it, using the ideas from LMX theory.

Case 7.1   HIS TEAM GETS THE BEST ASSIGNMENTS

Carly Peters directs the creative department of the advertising agency of Mills, Smith, & Peters. The agency has about 100 employees, 20 of whom work for Carly in the creative department. Typically, the agency maintains 10 major accounts and a number of smaller accounts. It has a reputation for being one of the best advertising and public relations agencies in the country.

In the creative department, there are four major account teams. Each is led by an associate creative director, who reports directly to Carly. In addition, each team has a copywriter, an art director, and a production artist. These four account teams are headed by Jack, Terri, Julie, and Sarah.

Jack and his team get along really well with Carly, and they have done excellent work for their clients at the agency. Of all the teams, Jack's team is the most creative and talented and the most willing to go the extra mile for Carly. As a result, when Carly has to showcase accounts to upper management, she often uses the work of Jack's team. Jack and his team members are comfortable confiding in Carly and she in them. Carly is not afraid to allocate extra resources to Jack's team or to give them free rein on their accounts because they always come through for her.

Terri's team also performs well for the agency, but Terri is unhappy with how Carly treats her team. She thinks that Carly is not fair because she favors Jack's team. For example, Terri's team was counseled out of pursuing an ad campaign because the campaign was too risky, whereas Jack's group was praised for developing a very provocative campaign. Terri believes that Jack's team is Carly's pet: His team gets the best assignments, accounts, and budgets. Terri finds it hard to hold back the animosity she feels toward Carly.

(Continued)

(Continued)

Like Terri, Julie is concerned that her team is not in the inner circle, close to Carly. She has noticed repeatedly that Carly favors the other teams. For example, whenever additional people are assigned to team projects, it is always the other teams who get the best writers and art directors. Julie is mystified as to why Carly doesn't notice her team or try to help her team members with their work. She believes Carly undervalues her team because Julie knows the quality of her team's work is indisputable.

Although Sarah agrees with some of Terri's and Julie's observations about Carly, she does not feel any antagonism about Carly's leadership. Sarah has worked for the agency for nearly 10 years, and nothing seems to bother her. Her account teams have never been earthshaking, but they have never been problematic either. Sarah views her team members and their work more as a nuts-and-bolts operation in which the team is given an assignment and carries it out. Being in Carly's inner circle would entail putting in extra time in the evening or on weekends and would create more headaches for Sarah. Therefore, Sarah is happy with her role as it is, and she has little interest in trying to change the way the department works.

Questions

1. Based on the principles of LMX theory, what observations would you make about Carly's leadership at Mills, Smith, & Peters?

2. Are there an in-group and an out-group, and if so, which are they?

3. In what way are Carly's relationships with the four groups productive or counterproductive to the overall goals of the agency?

4. Do you think Carly should change her approach toward the associate directors? If so, what should she do differently?

Case 7.2   WORKING HARD AT BEING FAIR

City Mortgage is a medium-sized mortgage company that employs about 25 people. Jenny Hernandez, who has been with the company for 10 years, is the production manager, overseeing its day-to-day operations.

Reporting to Jenny are loan originators (salespeople), closing officers, mortgage underwriters, and processing and shipping personnel. Jenny is proud of the company and knows she has contributed substantially to its steady growth and expansion.

The climate at City Mortgage is very positive. People like to come to work because the office environment is comfortable. They respect each other at the company and show tolerance for those who are different from themselves.

Whereas at many mortgage companies it is common for resentments to build between people who earn different incomes, this is not the case at City Mortgage.

Jenny's leadership has been instrumental in shaping the success of City Mortgage. Her philosophy stresses listening to employees and then determining how each employee can best contribute to the mission of the company. She makes a point of helping individual employees explore their own talents, and challenges each one to try new things.

At the annual holiday party, Jenny devised an interesting event that symbolizes her leadership style. She bought a large piece of colorful glass and had it cut into 25 pieces and handed out one piece to each person. Then she asked the employees to come forward one by one with the piece of glass and briefly state what they liked about City Mortgage and how they had contributed to the company in the past year. After the statements were made, the pieces of glass were formed into a cut-glass window that hangs in the front lobby of the office. The glass is a reminder of how individual employees contribute their uniqueness to the overall purpose of the company.

Another characteristic of Jenny's style is her fairness. She does not want to give anyone the impression that certain people have the inside track, and she goes to great lengths to prevent this from happening. For example, she avoids social lunches because she thinks they foster the perception of favoritism. Similarly, even though her best friend is one of the loan originators, she is seldom seen talking with her, and if she is, it is always about business matters.

Jenny also applies her fairness principle to how information is shared in the office. She does not want anyone to feel "out of the loop," so she tries very hard to keep her employees informed on all the matters that could affect them. Much of this she does through her open-door office policy. Jenny does not have a special group of employees with whom she confides her concerns; rather, she shares openly with each of them.

Jenny is very committed to her work at City Mortgage. She works long hours and carries a beeper on the weekend. At this point in her career, her only concern is that she could be burning out.

Questions

1. Based on the LMX model, how would you describe Jenny's leadership?

2. How do you think the employees at City Mortgage respond to Jenny?

3. If you were asked to follow in Jenny's footsteps, do you think you could or would want to manage City Mortgage with a similar style?

(Continued)

Harvard management professor Linda Hill led a team of researchers on a decade-long study of exceptional leaders of innovation. The team studied a select group of 16 men and women from a variety of industries around the world, observing the leaders in action, on-site in their own environments, and interacting directly with them. What the team discovered may seem counterintuitive to the way many people perceive that successful innovative organizations operate; in her words, "Leading innovation is not about creating a vision, and inspiring others to execute it" (L. Hill, 2014).

So how do highly successful companies that innovate again and again do it? Ed Catmull, CEO of Pixar Animation Studios, exemplifies Professor Hill's findings. Pixar, known for its highly innovative computer-generated imagery (CGI) feature films like *Toy Story, Ratatouille, The Incredibles, Finding Nemo, Cars,* and *Coco,* to name just a few, took 20 years to create its first full-length film, *Toy Story,* which was released in 1995. By the end of 2020, the company had generated 23 feature films with an additional 4 more planned.

Noting that it takes approximately 250 people four to five years to make one of these animated films with story lines that evolve as the making of the movie progresses, Professor Hill (2014) emphasizes that "innovation is not about solo genius, it's about collective genius."

Innovation is the result of trial and error, subject to mistakes and even failures. The "heart of innovation is a paradox. You have to unleash the talents and passions of many people and you have to harness them into a work that is actually useful. Innovation is a journey. It's a type of collaborative problem solving, usually among people who have different expertise and different points of view" (L. Hill, 2014).

That Pixar employs this philosophy was evident in an article CEO Catmull wrote for *Harvard Business Review.* "You get great creative people, you bet big on them, you give them enormous leeway and support, and you provide them with an environment in which they can get honest feedback from everyone" (Catmull, 2008).

Providing support without undermining authority is encouraged at all levels of the organization, and there are essentially two leaders for each production—a director and a producer. The executive management communicates that operational decisions are left to the film's leaders without second-guessing or micromanaging from the top.

Successful leaders at Pixar "must have a unifying vision—one that will give coherence to the thousands of ideas that go into a movie—and they must be able to turn that vision into clear directives that the staff can implement. They must set people up for success by giving them all the information they need to do the job right without telling them how to do it. Each person on a film should be given creative ownership of even the smallest task" (Catmull, 2008).

For example, an animator drew an arched eyebrow on a character to show the character's mischievous side, only to have his animation cut because it was viewed as not representative of the character. Two weeks later, it was added back by the director. "Because that animator was allowed to share what we referred to as his slice of genius, he was able to help that director reconceive the character in a subtle but important way that really improved the story," said Professor Hill (2014).

Hill's research team found that innovative organizations have three common capabilities: creative abrasion, creative agility, and creative resolution.

Creative abrasion centers on the concept that a portfolio of ideas is percolated through a process of "debate and discourse," which amplifies differences rather than minimizes them. Unlike brainstorming, where people suspend their judgment, creative abrasion results in heated but constructive arguments to develop a set of alternatives. Through this process, people and organizations learn how to inquire, how to actively listen, and how to advocate for their points of view.

Pixar's "Creative Brain Trust" is an example of its approach to creative abrasion. The Creative Brain Trust consists of several accomplished filmmakers, and if a film runs into problems during production, the director is encouraged to solicit advice from this group. Because the Creative Brain Trust members can give "unvarnished expert opinions" and the director has the freedom to ask for and consider the advice, the "problem-solving powers of this group are immense and inspirational to watch" (Catmull, 2008).

Creative agility is the ability to test and refine the portfolio of ideas where participants learn through experimenting irrespective of the outcome. "Experiments are usually about learning. When you get a negative outcome, you're still really learning something that you need to know" (L. Hill, 2014).

Pixar's use of "dailies"—daily reviews giving feedback in a positive way— exemplifies creative agility. The team members working on the film review each other's work in progress, in its incomplete state, with the opportunity to comment and provide feedback. The intention of these reviews is to circumvent the natural desire to develop a project to a certain level of perfection before sharing it with the team.

Creative resolution involves injecting integrated decision making into the process to bring together opposing ideas and "reconfigure them in new combinations to produce a solution that is new and useful" (L. Hill, 2014).

(Continued)

(Continued)

"Innovative organizations never go along to get along. They don't compromise. They don't let one group or one individual dominate, even if it's the boss, even if it's the expert," Professor Hill explained. "Instead, they have developed a rather patient and more inclusive decision-making process that allows for both/and solutions to arise and not simply either/or solutions" (L. Hill, 2014).

At Pixar, everyone must have the freedom to communicate with anyone, and it must be safe for everyone to offer ideas. This means that managers learn "that they don't always have to be the first to know about something going on in their realm" and that "the most efficient way to deal with numerous problems is to trust people to work out the difficulties directly with each other without having to check for permission" (Catmull, 2008).

To maximize opportunity for interactions among its employees, Pixar's building has a large, central atrium housing the cafeteria, all meeting rooms, bathrooms, and mailboxes. Everyone in the company has a plethora of reasons to pass through this space several times a day, and "it's hard to describe just how valuable the resulting chance encounters are" (L. Hill, 2014).

"They understand that innovation takes a village. The leaders focus on building a sense of community and building those three capabilities. How do they define leadership? They say leadership is about creating a world to which people want to belong. What kind of world do people want to belong in at Pixar? A world where you're living at the frontier. What do they focus their time on? Not on creating a vision. Instead they spend their time thinking about, 'How do we design a studio that has the sensibility of a public square so that people will interact? Let's put in a policy that anyone, no matter what their level or role, is allowed to give notes to the director about how they feel about a particular film. What can we do to make sure that all the disruptors, all the minority voices in this organization, speak up and are heard? And, finally, let's bestow credit in a very generous way'" (L. Hill, 2014).

To emphasize her point, she notes that the credits of a Pixar movie even include the names of babies born to team members during production.

Questions

1. As noted in the chapter, the early research of LMX focused on the concepts of in-groups and out-groups.

    a. How do you think this applies to Pixar's approach to leading the large teams required for the making of its feature films?

    b. From what you have gleaned about Pixar, do you feel that team members have a strong sense of a division between in-groups and out-groups? Why or why not?

c. Do you think that most members of Pixar's teams feel they are part of the in-group?

d. Do you think the "creative abrasion" discussed in the case is something that is a product of an in-group mentality? Why or why not?

e. What about those who might perceive themselves in the out-group—would *creative abrasion* be possible or productive? Why or why not?

2. Later LMX studies focused on the leader–member exchanges. Given what you know about the work environment, how would you rank the quality of the leader–member exchange at Pixar? Why?

3. Do you think the individual Pixar team members feel a sense of empowerment?

a. How might the idea of *creative agility* discussed in the case fit into a feeling of empowerment by employees?

b. What about the idea of *creative resolution*?

4. In looking at the phases of leadership development discussed in the text, in what phase do you think a highly innovative company, like Pixar, would fall? Why?

5. Does Pixar's culture allow for the stages of affective processes in LMX development—*role taking*, *role making*, and *role routinization*—to occur? Explain your answer.

—*Barbara Russell, MBA, BSCS, BBA, Chemeketa Community College*

LEADERSHIP INSTRUMENT

Researchers have used many different questionnaires to study LMX theory. All of them have been designed to measure the quality of the working relationship between leaders and followers. We have chosen to include in this chapter the LMX-7, a seven-item questionnaire that provides a reliable and valid measure of the quality of leader–member exchanges (Graen & Uhl-Bien, 1995).

The LMX-7 is designed to measure three dimensions of leader–member relationships: respect, trust, and obligation. It assesses the degree to which leaders and followers have mutual respect for each other's capabilities, feel a deepening sense of reciprocal trust, and have a strong sense of obligation to one another. Taken together, these dimensions are the ingredients of strong partnerships.

LMX-7 Questionnaire

Purpose: The purpose of this questionnaire is to provide you with a fuller understanding of how LMX theory works.

Instructions: This questionnaire contains items that ask you to describe your relationship with either your leader or one of your followers. For each of the items, indicate the degree to which you think the item is true for you by selecting one of the responses that appear below the item.

Key: 1 = Strongly   2 = Disagree   3 = Neutral   4 = Agree   5 = Strongly
      Disagree   Agree

1. I know where I stand with my leader (follower) . . . [and]   1 2 3 4 5
   usually know how satisfied my leader (follower) is with
   what I do.

2. My leader (follower) understands my job problems and   1 2 3 4 5
   needs.

3. My leader (follower) recognizes my potential.   1 2 3 4 5

4. Regardless of how much formal authority my leader   1 2 3 4 5
   (follower) has built into their position, my leader
   (follower) will use their power to help me solve problems
   in my work.

5. Again, regardless of the amount of formal authority my   1 2 3 4 5
   leader (follower) has, they would "bail me out" at their
   expense.

6. I have enough confidence in my leader (follower) that   1 2 3 4 5
   I would defend and justify their decision if they were not
   present to do so.

7. I have an extremely effective working relationship with my   1 2 3 4 5
   leader (follower).

By completing the LMX-7, you can gain a fuller understanding of how LMX theory works. The score you obtain on the questionnaire reflects the quality of your leader–member relationships and indicates the degree to which your relationships are characteristic of partnerships, as described in the LMX model.

You can complete the questionnaire both as a leader and as a follower. In the leader role, you would complete the questionnaire multiple times, assessing the quality of the relationships you have with each of your followers. In the follower role, you would complete the questionnaire based on the leaders to whom you report.

(Continued)

(Continued)

Scoring Interpretation

Although the LMX-7 is most commonly used by researchers to explore theoretical questions, you can also use it to analyze your own leadership style. You can interpret your LMX-7 scores using the following guidelines: high = 25–35, moderate = 20–24, low = 7–19. Scores in the upper ranges indicate stronger, higher-quality leader–member exchanges (e.g., in-group members), whereas scores in the lower ranges indicate exchanges of lesser quality (e.g., out-group members).

Source: Reprinted from *The Leadership Quarterly*, 6(2), G. B. Graen and M. Uhl-Bien, "Relationship-Based Approach to Leadership: Development of Leader–Member Exchange (LMX) Theory of Leadership Over 25 Years: Applying a Multi-Level, Multi-Domain Perspective," pp. 219–247. Copyright (1995) with permission from Elsevier.

SUMMARY

Since it first appeared more than 30 years ago under the title "vertical dyad linkage (VDL) theory," leader–member exchange theory has been and continues to be a much-studied approach to leadership. LMX theory addresses leadership as a process centered on the interactions between leaders and followers. It makes the leader–member relationship the pivotal concept in the leadership process.

In the early studies of LMX theory, a leader's relationship to the overall work unit was viewed as a series of vertical dyads, categorized as being of two different types: Leader–member dyads based on expanded role relationships were called the leader's in-group, and those based on formal job descriptions were called the leader's out-group. According to LMX theory, followers become in-group members based on how well they get along with the leader and whether they are willing to expand their role responsibilities. Followers who maintain only formal hierarchical relationships with their leader are out-group members. Whereas in-group members receive extra influence, opportunities, and rewards, out-group members receive standard job benefits.

Subsequent studies of LMX theory were directed toward how leader–member exchanges affect organizational performance. Researchers found that high-quality exchanges between leaders and followers produced multiple positive outcomes (e.g., less employee turnover, greater organizational commitment, and more promotions). In general, researchers determined that good leader–member exchanges result in followers feeling better, accomplishing more, and helping the organization prosper.

A select body of LMX research focuses on leadership development, which emphasizes that leaders should try to develop high-quality exchanges with all of their followers. Leadership develops over time and includes a stranger phase, an acquaintance phase, and a mature partnership phase. By taking on and fulfilling new role responsibilities, followers move through these three phases to develop mature partnerships with their leaders. These partnerships, which are marked by a high degree of mutual trust, respect, and obligation, have positive payoffs for the individuals themselves, and help the organization run more effectively.

More recently, LMX research has explored the role of emotions, or affective states, in the development of high-quality relationships between leaders and members. The development of these relationships progresses through three affective processes—role taking, role making, and role routinization—that reflect the growing emotional interactions between leaders and members.

There are several positive features to LMX theory. First, LMX theory is a strong descriptive approach that explains how leaders use some followers (in-group members) more than others (out-group members) to accomplish organizational goals effectively. Second, LMX theory is unique in that, unlike other approaches, it makes the leader–member relationship the focal point of the leadership process. Related to this focus, LMX theory is noteworthy because it directs our attention to the importance of effective communication in leader–member relationships. In addition, it reminds us to be evenhanded in how we relate to our followers. Another strength of LMX theory is its universality and that its concepts are the same across different national cultures. Finally, LMX theory is supported by a multitude of studies that link high-quality leader–member exchanges to positive organizational outcomes.

There are also negative features in LMX theory. First, the early formulation of LMX theory (VDL theory) runs counter to our principles of fairness and justice in the workplace by suggesting that some members of the work unit receive special attention and others do not. The perceived inequalities created by the use of in-groups can have a devastating impact on the feelings, attitudes, and behavior of out-group members. Second, LMX theory emphasizes the importance of leader–member exchanges but fails to explain the intricacies of how one goes about creating high-quality exchanges. Although the model promotes building trust, respect, and commitment in relationships, it does not fully explicate how this takes place. While many studies have been conducted on LMX, they have not resulted in a clear, refined set of definitions, concepts, and propositions about the theory. In addition, there is some debate about whether LMX is based on social exchange theory or whether it fits better in role theory. Third, researchers have not adequately explained the contextual factors that influence LMX relationships. Finally, there are questions about whether the measurement procedures used in LMX research are adequate to fully capture the complexities of the leader–member exchange process.

Transformational Leadership

DESCRIPTION

As one of the current and most popular approaches to leadership, the transformational leadership approach has been the focus of much research since the 1980s. As its name implies, transformational leadership is a process that changes and transforms people. It is concerned with emotions, values, ethics, standards, and long-term goals. It includes assessing followers' motives, satisfying their needs, and treating them as full human beings. Transformational leadership involves an exceptional form of influence that moves followers to accomplish more than what is usually expected of them. It is a process that often incorporates charismatic and visionary leadership.

Transformational leadership is part of the "New Leadership" paradigm (Bryman, 1992), which gives more attention to the charismatic and affective elements of leadership. In a content analysis of articles published in *The Leadership Quarterly*, Lowe and Gardner (2001) found that one third of the research was about transformational or charismatic leadership. That interest has continued into the new millennium; in a follow-up review of leadership research, Dinh et al. (2014) found that interest in transformational leadership was sustained from 2000 to 2012. Similarly, Antonakis (2012) found that the number of papers and citations in the field has grown at an increasing rate, not only in traditional areas like management and social psychology, but in other disciplines such as nursing, education, and industrial engineering. Bass and Riggio (2006) suggested that transformational leadership's popularity might be due to its emphasis on intrinsic motivation and follower development, which fits the needs of today's work groups, who want to be inspired and empowered to succeed in times of uncertainty. Clearly, many scholars are studying transformational leadership, and it occupies a central place in leadership research. However, others (i.e., Andersen, 2015; Anderson, Baur, Griffith, & Buckley, 2017) have suggested that the interest in transformational leadership may be exaggerated and that this approach to leading may be less significant as millennials continue to flood into the workplace.

An encompassing approach, transformational leadership can be used to describe a wide range of leadership, from very specific attempts to influence followers on a one-to-one level, to very broad attempts to influence whole organizations and even entire cultures. Although the transformational leader plays a pivotal role in precipitating change, followers and leaders are inextricably bound together in the transformation process. In fact, transformational leadership focuses so heavily on the relationship between leader and follower that some (Andersen, 2015) have suggested that this bias may limit explanations for transformational leadership on organizational effectiveness.

Transformational Leadership Defined

The emergence of *transformational leadership* as an important approach to leadership began with a classic work by political sociologist James MacGregor Burns titled *Leadership* (1978). In his work, Burns attempted to link the roles of leadership and followership. He wrote of leaders as people who tap the motives of followers in order to better reach the goals of leaders and followers (p. 18). For Burns, leadership is quite different from power because it is inseparable from followers' needs.

Transformational Versus Transactional Leadership. Burns distinguished between two types of leadership: *transactional* and *transformational.* Transactional leadership refers to the bulk of leadership models, which focus on the exchanges that occur between leaders and their followers. Politicians who win votes by promising "no new taxes" are demonstrating transactional leadership. Similarly, managers who offer promotions to employees who surpass their goals are exhibiting transactional leadership. In the classroom, teachers are being transactional when they give students a grade for work completed. The exchange dimension of transactional leadership is very common and can be observed at many levels throughout all types of organizations. While exchanges or transactions between leader and member are a natural component of employment contracts, research suggests that employees do not necessarily perceive transactional leaders as those most capable of creating trusting, mutually beneficial leader–member relationships (Notgrass, 2014). Instead, employees prefer managers to perform transformational leadership behaviors such as encouraging creativity, recognizing accomplishments, building trust, and inspiring a collective vision (Notgrass, 2014).

In contrast to transactional leadership, transformational leadership is the process whereby a person engages with others and creates a connection that raises the level of motivation and morality in both the leader and the follower. This type of leader is attentive to the needs and motives of followers and tries to help followers reach their fullest potential. Burns points to Mohandas Gandhi as a classic example of transformational leadership. Gandhi raised the hopes and demands of millions of his people and, in the process, was changed himself.

Another good example of transformational leadership can be observed in the efforts of Swedish teenager Greta Thunberg, who raised awareness around the world regarding global climate change. Thunberg began her activism by sitting outside the Swedish parliament every school day, holding a sign reading *Skolstrejk för klimatet* ("School strike for climate"). This inspired an international movement, and Thunberg spoke in public and to political leaders and assemblies, where she criticized world leaders for their failure to sufficiently address the climate crisis.

In the organizational world, an example of transformational leadership would be a manager who attempts to change a company's corporate values to reflect a more humane standard of fairness and justice. In the process, both the manager and the followers may emerge with a stronger and higher set of moral values. In fact, Mason, Griffin, and Parker (2014) demonstrated that through transformational leadership training, leaders were able to enhance their self-efficacy, positive affect, and ability to consider multiple perspectives. Their findings suggest that transformational leadership can result in positive psychological gains for both leader and follower.

Pseudotransformational Leadership. Because the conceptualization of transformational leadership set forth by Burns (1978) includes raising the level of morality in others, it is difficult to use this term when describing a leader such as Adolf Hitler, who was transforming but in a negative way. To deal with this problem, Bass (1998) coined the term *pseudotransformational leadership*. This term refers to leaders who are self-consumed, exploitive, and power oriented, with warped moral values (Bass & Riggio, 2006). Pseudotransformational leadership is considered *personalized leadership*, which focuses on the leader's own interests rather than on the interests of others (Bass & Steidlmeier, 1999). Authentic transformational leadership is *socialized leadership*, which is concerned with the collective good. Socialized transformational leaders transcend their own interests for the sake of others (Howell & Avolio, 1993).

In a series of four experimental studies, Christie, Barling, and Turner (2011) set forth a preliminary model of pseudotransformational leadership that reflected four components of transformational leadership discussed later in this chapter: *idealized influence, inspirational motivation, intellectual stimulation,* and *individualized consideration.* This model helps to clarify the meaning of pseudotransformational leadership. It suggests that pseudotransformational leadership is inspired leadership that is self-serving, is unwilling to encourage independent thought in followers, and exhibits little general caring for others. Pseudotransformational leaders have strong inspirational talent and appeal but are manipulative and dominant and direct followers toward the leader's values. This type of leadership is threatening to the welfare of followers because it ignores the common good.

To sort out the complexities related to the "moral uplifting" component of authentic transformational leadership, Zhu, Avolio, Riggio, and Sosik (2011) proposed a theoretical model examining how authentic transformational leadership influences the ethics of individual followers and groups. The authors hypothesize that authentic transformational leadership positively affects followers' moral identities and moral emotions (e.g., empathy and guilt) and this, in turn, leads to moral decision making and moral action by the followers. Furthermore, the authors theorize that authentic transformational leadership is positively associated with group ethical climate, decision making, and moral action. In the future, research is needed to test the validity of the assumptions laid out in this model.

Transformational Leadership and Charisma

At about the same time Burns's book was published, House (1976) published a theory of charismatic leadership. Since its publication, charismatic leadership has received a great deal of attention by researchers (e.g., Conger, 1999; Hunt & Conger, 1999). It is often described in ways that make it similar to, if not synonymous with, transformational leadership.

The word *charisma* was first used to describe a special gift that certain individuals possess that gives them the capacity to do extraordinary things. Weber (1947) provided the most well-known definition of charisma as a special personality characteristic that gives a person superhuman or exceptional powers and is reserved for a few, is of divine origin, and results in the person being treated as a leader. Despite Weber's emphasis on charisma as a personality characteristic, he also recognized the important role played by followers in validating charisma in these leaders (Bryman, 1992; House, 1976).

In his theory of charismatic leadership, House suggested that charismatic leaders act in unique ways that have specific charismatic effects on their followers (Table 8.1). For House, the personality characteristics of a charismatic leader include being dominant, having a strong desire to influence others, being self-confident, and having a strong sense of one's own moral values.

In addition to displaying certain personality characteristics, charismatic leaders demonstrate specific types of behaviors. First, they are strong role models for the beliefs and values they want their followers to adopt. For example, Gandhi advocated nonviolence and was an exemplary role model of civil disobedience. Second, charismatic leaders appear competent to followers. Third, they articulate ideological goals that have moral overtones. Martin Luther King Jr.'s famous "I Have a Dream" speech is an example of this type of charismatic behavior.

Fourth, charismatic leaders communicate high expectations for followers, and they exhibit confidence in followers' abilities to meet these expectations.

TABLE 8.1 Personality Characteristics, Behaviors, and Effects on Followers of Charismatic Leadership

Personality Characteristics	Behaviors	Effects on Followers
Dominant	Sets strong role model	Trust in leader's ideology
Desire to influence	Shows competence	Belief similarity between leader and follower
Self-confident	Articulates goals	Unquestioning acceptance
Strong moral values	Communicates high expectations	Affection toward leader
	Expresses confidence	Obedience
	Arouses motives	Identification with leader
		Emotional involvement
		Heightened goals
		Increased confidence

The impact of this behavior is to increase followers' sense of competence and self-efficacy (Avolio & Gibbons, 1988), which in turn improves their performance.

Fifth, charismatic leaders arouse task-relevant motives in followers that may include affiliation, power, or esteem. For example, former U.S. president John F. Kennedy appealed to the human values of the American people when he stated, "Ask not what your country can do for you; ask what you can do for your country." Within the organizational context, charismatic CEOs may motivate members of their organization by modeling and fostering a transformational leadership climate (Boehm, Dwertmann, Bruch, & Shamir, 2015), which may result in increases in employee identification with their organization and in overall organizational performance.

According to House's charismatic theory, several effects are the direct result of charismatic leadership. They include follower trust in the leader's ideology, similarity between the followers' beliefs and the leader's beliefs, unquestioning acceptance of the leader, expression of affection toward the leader, follower obedience, identification with the leader, emotional involvement in the leader's goals, heightened goals for followers, and increased follower confidence in goal achievement. Consistent with Weber, House contends that these charismatic effects are more likely to occur in contexts in which followers feel distress because in stressful situations followers look to leaders to deliver them from their difficulties.

House's charismatic theory has been extended and revised through the years (see Conger, 1999; Conger & Kanungo, 1998). One major revision to the theory was made by Shamir, House, and Arthur (1993). They postulated that charismatic leadership transforms followers' self-concepts and tries to link the identity of followers to the collective identity of the organization. Charismatic leaders forge this link by emphasizing the intrinsic rewards of work and de-emphasizing the extrinsic rewards. The hope is that followers will view work as an expression of themselves. Throughout the process, leaders express high expectations for followers and help them gain a sense of confidence and self-efficacy.

In summary, charismatic leadership works because it ties followers and their self-concepts to the organizational identity.

A Model of Transformational Leadership

In the mid-1980s, Bass (1985) provided a more expanded and refined version of transformational leadership that was based on, but not fully consistent with, the prior works of Burns (1978) and House (1976). In his approach, Bass extended Burns's work by giving more attention to followers' rather than leaders' needs, by suggesting that transformational leadership could apply to situations in which the outcomes were not positive, and by describing transactional and transformational leadership as a single continuum (Figure 8.1) rather than mutually independent continua (Yammarino, 1993). Bass gave more attention to the emotional elements and origins of charisma, suggesting that charisma is a necessary but not sufficient condition for transformational leadership (Yammarino, 1993).

Bass (1985, p. 20) argued that transformational leadership motivates followers to do more than expected by (a) raising followers' levels of consciousness about the importance and value of specified and idealized goals, (b) getting followers to transcend their own self-interest for the sake of the team or organization, and (c) moving followers to address higher-level needs. An elaboration of the

FIGURE 8.1 Leadership Continuum From Transformational to Laissez-Faire Leadership

Transformational Leadership	Transactional Leadership	Laissez-Faire Leadership
•	•	•

TABLE 8.2 Leadership Factors

Transformational Leadership	Transactional Leadership	Laissez-Faire Leadership
Factor 1 Idealized influence Charisma	**Factor 5** Contingent reward Constructive transactions	**Factor 7** Laissez-faire Nontransactional
Factor 2 Inspirational motivation	**Factor 6** Management by exception Active and passive Corrective transactions	
Factor 3 Intellectual stimulation		
Factor 4 Individualized consideration		

dynamics of the transformation process is provided in his model of transformational and transactional leadership (Bass, 1985, 1990; Bass & Avolio, 1993, 1994). Additional clarification of the model is provided by Avolio in his book *Full Leadership Development: Building the Vital Forces in Organizations* (1999).

As can be seen in Table 8.2, the model of transformational and transactional leadership incorporates seven different factors. These factors are also illustrated in the Full Range of Leadership model, which is provided in Figure 8.2 on page 192. A discussion of each of these seven factors will help to clarify Bass's model. This discussion will be divided into three parts: transformational factors (4), transactional factors (2), and the nonleadership, nontransactional factor (1).

Transformational Leadership Factors

Transformational leadership is concerned with improving the performance of followers and developing followers to their fullest potential (Avolio, 1999; Bass & Avolio, 1990a). People who exhibit transformational leadership often have a strong set of internal values and ideals, and they are effective at motivating followers to act in ways that support the greater good rather than their own self-interests (Kuhnert, 1994). Individuals' intentions to lead in a transformational manner appear related to effective transformational leadership behaviors (Gilbert, Horsman, & Kelloway, 2016).

FIGURE 8.2 Full Range of Leadership Model

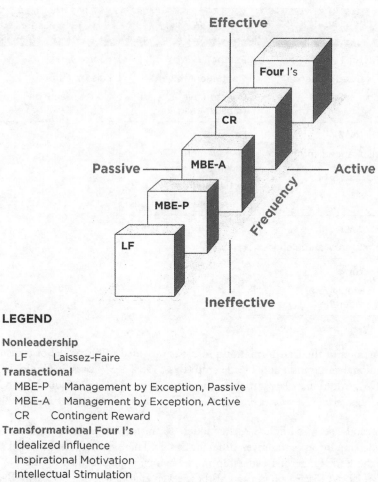

LEGEND

Nonleadership
LF   Laissez-Faire
Transactional
MBE-P   Management by Exception, Passive
MBE-A   Management by Exception, Active
CR   Contingent Reward
Transformational Four I's
Idealized Influence
Inspirational Motivation
Intellectual Stimulation
Individualized Consideration

Idealized Influence. Factor 1 is called *charisma* or *idealized influence.* It is the emotional component of leadership (Antonakis, 2012). Idealized influence describes leaders who act as strong role models for followers; followers identify with these leaders and want very much to emulate them. These leaders usually have very high standards of moral and ethical conduct and can be counted on to do the right thing. They are deeply respected by followers, who usually place a great deal of trust in them. They provide followers with a vision and a sense of mission.

The idealized influence factor is measured on two components: an *attributional component* that refers to the attributions of leaders made by followers based on perceptions they have of their leaders, and a *behavioral component* that refers to followers' observations of leader behavior.

In essence, the charisma factor describes people who are special and who make others want to follow the vision they put forward. A person whose leadership exemplifies the charisma factor is Nelson Mandela, the first Black president of South Africa. Mandela is viewed as a leader with high moral standards and a vision for South Africa that resulted in monumental change in how the people of South Africa would be governed. His charismatic qualities and the people's response to them transformed an entire nation.

Inspirational Motivation. Factor 2 is called *inspiration* or *inspirational motivation.* This factor is descriptive of leaders who communicate high expectations to followers, inspiring them through motivation to become committed to and a part of the shared vision in the organization. In practice, leaders use symbols and emotional appeals to focus group members' efforts to achieve more than they would in their own self-interest. Team spirit is enhanced by this type of leadership. An example of this factor would be a sales manager who motivates members of the sales force to excel in their work through encouraging words and pep talks that clearly communicate the integral role they play in the future growth of the company.

Intellectual Stimulation. Factor 3 is *intellectual stimulation.* It includes leadership that stimulates followers to be creative and innovative and to challenge their own beliefs and values as well as those of the leader and the organization.

This type of leadership supports followers as they try new approaches and develop innovative ways of dealing with organizational issues. It encourages followers to think things out on their own and engage in careful problem solving. An example of this type of leadership is a plant manager who promotes workers' individual efforts to develop unique ways to solve problems that have caused slowdowns in production.

Individualized Consideration. Factor 4 of transformational leadership is called *individualized consideration.* This factor is representative of leaders who provide a supportive climate in which they listen carefully to the individual needs of followers. Leaders act as coaches and advisers while trying to assist followers in becoming fully actualized. These leaders may use delegation to help followers grow through personal challenges. An example of this type of leadership is a manager who spends time treating each employee in a caring and unique way. To some employees, the leader may give strong affiliation; to others, the leader may give specific directives with a high degree of structure.

In essence, transformational leadership produces greater effects than transactional leadership (Figure 8.3). Whereas transactional leadership results in expected outcomes, transformational leadership results in performance that goes well beyond what is expected. In a meta-analysis of 39 studies in the transformational literature, for example, Lowe, Kroeck, and Sivasubramaniam (1996) found that people who exhibited transformational leadership were perceived to be more effective leaders with better work outcomes than those who exhibited only transactional leadership. These findings were true for higher- and lower-level leaders, and for leaders in both public and private settings.

Transformational leadership has an additive effect; it moves followers to accomplish more than what is usually expected of them. They become motivated to transcend their own self-interests for the good of the group or organization (Bass & Avolio, 1990a). In fact, transformational leaders are most likely to have a positive impact on followers when followers identify with or find meaning in their work (Mohammed, Fernando, & Caputi, 2013).

In a study of 220 employees at a large public transport company in Germany, Rowold and Heinitz (2007) found that transformational leadership augmented the impact of transactional leadership on employees' performance and company profit. In addition, they found that transformational leadership and charismatic leadership were overlapping but unique constructs, and that both were different from transactional leadership.

Similarly, Nemanich and Keller (2007) examined the impact of transformational leadership on 447 employees from a large multinational firm who were

FIGURE 8.3 The Additive Effect of Transformational Leadership

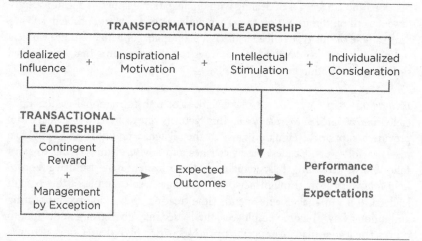

going through a merger and being integrated into a new organization. They found that transformational leadership behaviors such as idealized influence, inspirational motivation, individualized consideration, and intellectual stimulation were positively related to acquisition acceptance, job satisfaction, and performance.

Tims, Bakker, and Xanthopoulou (2011) examined the relationship between transformational leadership and work engagement in 42 employees and their supervisors in two different organizations in the Netherlands. Findings revealed that employees became more engaged in their work (i.e., vigor, dedication, and absorption) when their supervisors were able to boost employees' optimism through a transformational leadership style. These findings underscore the important role played by personal characteristics (i.e., optimism) in the transformational-leadership-performance process. Similarly, Hamstra, Van Yperen, Wisse, and Sassenberg (2014) found that transformational leaders were more likely than transactional leaders to promote achievement of followers' mastery goals. This suggests that transformational leaders may be especially effective in environments where followers need to focus on learning, development, and mastering job-related tasks rather than a more competitive or performance-based work context. Transformational leaders can propel followers to even greater levels of success when they have a high-quality relationship based on trust, loyalty, and mutual respect (Notgrass, 2014).

Transactional Leadership Factors

Transactional leadership differs from transformational leadership in that the transactional leader does not individualize the needs of followers or focus on their personal development. Transactional leaders exchange things of value with followers to advance their own and their followers' agendas (Kuhnert, 1994). Transactional leaders are influential because it is in the best interest of followers for them to do what the leader wants (Kuhnert & Lewis, 1987).

Contingent Reward. Factor 5, *contingent reward*, is the first of two transactional leadership factors (Figure 8.3). It is an exchange process between leaders and followers in which effort by followers is exchanged for specified rewards. With this kind of leadership, the leader tries to obtain agreement from followers on what must be done and what the payoffs will be for the people doing it. An example of this type of *constructive transaction* is a parent who negotiates with a child about how much time the child can spend playing video games after doing homework assignments. Another example often occurs in the academic setting: A dean negotiates with a college professor about the number and quality of published works the professor needs to have written in order to receive tenure and promotion. Notgrass (2014) found that contingent rewards, or the leader's use of clarifying or supporting achievement behaviors, are most effective when followers feel that they have a high-quality relationship with their leader.

Management by Exception. Factor 6 is called *management by exception*. It is leadership that involves corrective criticism, negative feedback, and negative reinforcement. Management by exception takes two forms: *active and passive.* A leader using the active form of management by exception watches followers closely for mistakes or rule violations and then takes *corrective action.* An example of active management by exception can be illustrated in the leadership of a sales supervisor who daily monitors how employees approach customers. The supervisor quickly corrects salespeople who are slow to approach customers in the prescribed manner. A leader using the passive form intervenes only after standards have not been met or problems have arisen. An example of passive management by exception is illustrated in the leadership of a supervisor who gives employees poor performance evaluations without ever talking with them about their prior work performance. In essence, both the active and passive management types use more negative reinforcement patterns than the positive reinforcement pattern described in Factor 5 under contingent reward.

Nonleadership Factor

In the model, the nonleadership factor diverges farther from transactional leadership and represents behaviors that are nontransactional.

Laissez-Faire. Factor 7 describes leadership that falls at the far-right side of the transactional–transformational leadership continuum (Figure 8.1). This factor represents the absence of leadership. As the French phrase implies, the *laissez-faire* leader takes a "hands-off, let-things-ride" (*nontransactional*) approach. This leader abdicates responsibility, delays decisions, gives no feedback, and makes little effort to help followers satisfy their needs. There is no exchange with followers or attempt to help them grow. An example of a laissez-faire leader is the president of a small manufacturing firm who calls no meetings with plant supervisors, has no long-range plan for the firm, acts detached, and makes little contact with employees. While laissez-faire leadership has traditionally been viewed negatively, recent research (Yang, 2015) argues that laissez-faire leadership may not be the absence of leadership, but instead may be a strategic behavioral choice by the leader to acknowledge and defer to followers' abilities, decrease their dependency, and increase their self-determination, self-competence, and autonomy. In this case, the leader would be strategically performing laissez-faire leadership by empowering followers to lead.

Interestingly, research does indicate that leaders may be most effective when they combine transformational leadership behaviors with elements of laissez-faire and transactional leadership (Antonakis & House, 2014). This reiterates what most of the leadership theories in this book suggest: All approaches to leadership have strengths and weaknesses, and because leading effectively means consistently surveying follower, task, and environmental needs and pressures, oftentimes the best approach is a combination of leadership approaches.

Transformational Leadership Measurements

The popularity of transformational leadership has resulted in researchers developing a number of assessments to measure its characteristics and efficacy. The Multifactor Leadership Questionnaire (MLQ) was one of the earliest and most widely used assessments of transformational leadership. The MLQ was developed by Bass (1985), based on a series of interviews he and his associates conducted with 70 senior executives in South Africa. These executives were asked to recall leaders who had raised their awareness to broader goals, moved them to higher motives, or inspired them to put others' interests ahead of their own. The executives were then asked to describe how these leaders behaved—what they did to effect change. From these descriptions and from numerous other interviews with both junior and senior executives, Bass constructed the questions that make up the MLQ. The questions measure followers' perceptions of a leader's behavior for each of the factors in the Full Range of Leadership model (Figure 8.2).

Antonakis, Avolio, and Sivasubramaniam (2003) assessed the psychometric properties of the MLQ using a business sample of more than 3,000 raters and found strong support for the validity of the MLQ. They found that the MLQ (Form 5X) clearly distinguished nine factors in the Full Range of Leadership model. Similarly, Hinkin and Schriesheim (2008) examined the empirical properties of the transactional and the nonleadership factors on the MLQ and identified several ways to use the questionnaire to generate more reliable and valid results. Since the MLQ was first designed, it has gone through many revisions, and it continues to be refined to strengthen its reliability and validity.

Based on a summary analysis of a series of studies that used the MLQ to predict how transformational leadership relates to outcomes such as effectiveness, Bryman (1992) and Bass and Avolio (1994) have suggested that the charisma and motivation factors on the MLQ are the most likely to be related to positive effects. Individualized consideration, intellectual stimulation, and contingent reward are the next most important factors. Management by exception in its passive form has been found to be somewhat related to outcomes, and in its active form it has been found to be negatively related to outcomes. Generally, laissez-faire leadership has been found to be negatively related to outcomes such as effectiveness and satisfaction in organizations.

Other Transformational Perspectives

In addition to Bass's (1985, 1990; Bass & Avolio, 1994) work, two other lines of research have contributed in unique ways to our understanding of the nature of transformational leadership. They are the research of Bennis and Nanus (1985, 2007) and the work of Kouzes and Posner (2002, 2017a). These scholars used similar qualitative research methods. They identified a number of middle- or senior-level leaders and conducted interviews with them, using open-ended, semi-structured questionnaires. From this information, they constructed their models of leadership.

Bennis and Nanus

Bennis and Nanus (2007) asked 90 leaders basic questions such as "What are your strengths and weaknesses?" "What past events most influenced your leadership approach?" and "What were the critical points in your career?" From the answers leaders provided to these questions, Bennis and Nanus identified four common strategies used by leaders in transforming organizations.

First, transforming leaders had a clear *vision* of the future state of their organizations. It was an image of an attractive, realistic, and believable future (Bennis & Nanus, 2007, p. 89). The vision usually was simple, understandable, beneficial, and energy creating. The compelling nature of the vision touched the experiences of followers and pulled them into supporting the organization. When an organization has a clear vision, it is easier for people within the organization to learn how they fit in with the overall direction of the organization and even the society in general. It empowers them because they feel they are a significant dimension of a worthwhile enterprise (pp. 90–91). Bennis and Nanus found that, to be successful, the vision had to grow out of the needs of the entire organization and to be claimed by those within it. Although leaders play a large role in articulating the vision, the emergence of the vision originates from both the leaders and the followers.

Second, transforming leaders were *social architects* for their organizations. This means they created a shape or form for the shared meanings people maintained within their organizations. These leaders communicated a direction that transformed their organization's values and norms. In many cases, these leaders were able to mobilize people to accept a new group identity or a new philosophy for their organizations.

A good example of a transforming leader with a clear vision and who is a social architect for his organization is college football coach P. J. Fleck, who is highlighted in Case 6.3 on page 149. First as the coach at Western Michigan University and then at the University of Minnesota, Coach Fleck created a culture for these programs that emphasized athletes' growth in four areas: academic, athletic, social, and spiritual. He was insistent that players assume leadership roles and consistently model the desired culture of the team. Coach Fleck would often repeat, "Bad teams, nobody leads. Average teams, coaches lead. Elite teams, players lead."

The third strategy identified by Bennis and Nanus was that transforming leaders created *trust* in their organizations by making their own positions clearly known and then standing by them. Trust has to do with being predictable or reliable, even in situations that are uncertain. In organizations, leaders built trust by articulating a direction and then consistently implementing the direction even though the vision may have involved a high degree of uncertainty. Bennis and Nanus (2007) found that when leaders established trust in an organization, it gave the organization a sense of integrity analogous to a healthy identity (p. 48).

Fourth, transforming leaders used *creative deployment of self* through positive self-regard. Leaders knew their strengths and weaknesses, and they emphasized their strengths rather than dwelled on their weaknesses. Based on an awareness of their own competence, effective leaders were able to immerse themselves in their tasks and the overarching goals of their organizations. They were able to fuse a sense of self with the work at hand. Bennis and Nanus also found that positive self-regard in leaders had a reciprocal impact on followers, creating in them feelings of confidence and high expectations. In addition, leaders in the study were committed to learning and relearning, so in their organizations there was consistent emphasis on education.

Bennis and Nanus (2007) proposed that transformational leaders "move organizations from current to future states, create visions of potential opportunities for organizations, instill within employees [a] commitment to change and instill new cultures and strategies in organizations that mobilize and focus energy and resources" (p. 19).

Kouzes and Posner

Kouzes and Posner (2002, 2017a) developed their model by interviewing leaders about leadership. They interviewed more than 1,300 middle- and senior-level managers in private and public sector organizations and asked them to describe their "personal best" experiences as leaders. Based on a content analysis of these descriptions, Kouzes and Posner constructed a model of leadership.

The Kouzes and Posner model consists of five fundamental *practices* that enable leaders to get extraordinary things accomplished: model the way, inspire a shared vision, challenge the process, enable others to act, and encourage the heart. For each of the five practices of exemplary leadership, Kouzes and Posner also have identified two commitments that serve as strategies for practicing exemplary leadership.

Model the Way. To model the way, leaders need to be clear about their own values and philosophy. They need to find their own voice and express it to others. Exemplary leaders set a personal example for others by their own behaviors.

They also follow through on their promises and commitments and affirm the common values they share with others.

Inspire a Shared Vision. Effective leaders create compelling visions that can guide people's behavior. They are able to visualize positive outcomes in the future and communicate them to others. Leaders also listen to the dreams of others and show them how their dreams can be realized. Through inspiring visions, leaders challenge others to transcend the status quo to do something for others.

Challenge the Process. Challenging the process means being willing to change the status quo and step into the unknown. It includes being willing to innovate, grow, and improve. Exemplary leaders are like pioneers: They want to experiment and try new things. They are willing to take risks to make things better. When exemplary leaders take risks, they do it one step at a time, learning from their mistakes as they go.

Enable Others to Act. Outstanding leaders are effective at working with people. They build trust with others and promote collaboration. Teamwork and cooperation are highly valued by these leaders. They listen closely to diverse points of view and treat others with dignity and respect. They also allow others to make choices, and they support the decisions that others make. In short, they create environments where people can feel good about their work and how it contributes to the greater community.

Interestingly, research indicates that women tend to display transformational leadership through more enabling behaviors whereas men tend to enact more challenging behavior (Brandt & Laiho, 2013).

Encourage the Heart. Leaders encourage the heart by rewarding others for their accomplishments. It is natural for people to want support and recognition. Effective leaders are attentive to this need and are willing to give praise to workers for jobs well done. They use authentic celebrations and rituals to show appreciation and encouragement to others. The outcome of this kind of support is greater collective identity and community spirit.

A later study by Caza and Posner (2019) found that the characteristic of "grit," or perseverance, was related to some aspects of transformational leadership. High-grit leaders engaged in more frequent role modeling and innovating behaviors, but less inspiring behavior.

Overall, the Kouzes and Posner model emphasizes behaviors and has a prescriptive quality: It recommends what people need to do to become effective leaders. Kouzes and Posner (2002, p. 13) stressed that the five practices of exemplary leadership are available to everyone and are not reserved for those with "special" ability. The model is not about personality: It is about practice.

For this reason, Kouzes and Posner (2017b) fundamentally disagree with the trait approach to leadership, described in Chapter 2, that views leadership as preordained or reserved for a special few leaders who are charismatic.

> Leadership is not a gene. Neither is it a trait. There is just no hard evidence to suggest that leadership is imprinted in the DNA of some people and not others. One of the competencies you have is the ability to look ahead. The capacity to imagine the future is a fundamental defining characteristic of human beings, separating *Homo sapiens* from other species. (p. 30)

To help leaders identify and measure the behaviors described in their model, Kouzes and Posner developed the Leadership Practices Inventory (LPI). The LPI is a 360-degree leadership assessment tool that consists of 30 questions that assess individual leadership competencies. It has been widely used in leadership training and development. A review of the measurement properties of the LPI, based on answers from 2.8 million respondents, found the measure had good reliability and consistency across samples and populations and that the underlying five-factor structure has been sustained across a variety of studies and settings. Finally, scores from the LPI are positively related to employee engagement and perceptions of leader effectiveness (Posner, 2016).

HOW DOES THE TRANSFORMATIONAL LEADERSHIP APPROACH WORK?

The transformational approach to leadership is a broad-based perspective that encompasses many facets and dimensions of the leadership process. In general, it describes how leaders can initiate, develop, and carry out significant changes in organizations. Although not definitive, the steps followed by transformational leaders usually take the following form.

Transformational leaders set out to empower followers and nurture them in change. They attempt to raise the consciousness in individuals and to get them to transcend their own self-interests for the sake of others. For example, Jung, Chow, and Wu (2003) studied upper-level leadership in 32 Taiwanese companies and found that transformational leadership was directly related to organizational innovation. Transformational leadership created a culture in which employees felt empowered and encouraged to freely discuss and try new things.

To create change, transformational leaders become strong role models for their followers. They have a highly developed set of moral values and a self-determined sense of identity (Avolio & Gibbons, 1988). They are confident, competent, and articulate, and they express strong ideals.

They listen to followers and are tolerant of opposing viewpoints. A spirit of cooperation often develops between these leaders and their followers. Followers want to emulate transformational leaders because they learn to trust them and believe in the ideas for which they stand.

It is common for transformational leaders to create a vision. The vision emerges from the collective interests of various individuals and units in an organization. The vision is a focal point for transformational leadership. It gives the leader and the organization a conceptual map for where the organization is headed; it gives meaning and clarifies the organization's identity. Furthermore, the vision gives followers a sense of identity within the organization and also a sense of self-efficacy (Shamir et al., 1993).

The transformational approach also requires that leaders become social architects. This means that they make clear the emerging values and norms of the organization. They involve themselves in the culture of the organization and help shape its meaning. People need to know their roles and understand how they contribute to the greater purposes of the organization. Transformational leaders are out front in interpreting and shaping for organizations the shared meanings that exist within them. As Mason et al. (2014) pointed out, enacting transformational behaviors changes leaders too, not just followers.

Throughout the process, transformational leaders are effective at working with people. They build trust and foster collaboration with others. Transformational leaders encourage others and celebrate their accomplishments. In the end, transformational leadership results in people feeling better about themselves and their contributions to the greater common good.

Many of us have had transformational leaders in our lives. We tend to remember them as very special. They had an impact on who we are and what we have become. Transformational leaders were the people who trusted us and allowed us the space to experiment and grow. As described so poignantly in Box 8.1, transformational leaders are leaders who raise us up to be better people.

Box 8.1

A Letter to Coach Z

The following letter was sent by a former student to his high school coach who was in the final stages of dying of cancer. While a student, Jeff was the runner-up to the state singles tennis title and went on to play No. 1 singles at a major university for four years where he was a two-time Mid-American Conference champion. He gave permission to publish this letter.

Dear Coach Z,

I wanted to write you a letter to express my sincere gratitude for the role you have played in my personal and professional development. I suspect you are aware of this fact, but my high school years were very challenging for me socially. My small stature and size brought tremendous teasing and shaming that profoundly affected my sense of self-esteem and self-worth. I found myself with very few friends and I experienced a deep loneliness and a strong desire to "escape" times of social interaction such as the noon hour. There was a strong culture of clique formation at our high school and I did not belong.

It was at these times that I would retreat to the safety of your office and the comfort of your friendship. This truly meant the world to me and was critical to my survival. As a 40-year old now, it blows my mind that you, then in your mid-50s, befriended me and cared for me. Even though your time was limited, you were so gracious to frequently offer me your undivided attention. I am convinced that I could not have become the person I am today without your influence in my life.

You have always believed in me and made me feel like I could do something exceptional. You always encouraged me and pushed me to dig deeper, work harder, and give it my all. You trained me in the areas of honesty, integrity, teamwork, and commitment. The lessons you've taught me have formed me and stayed with me throughout my life. Your influence has led me to achieve things in life that few would have thought possible.

It is my hope that this letter will honor you and that God will refresh and prosper you all the remaining days of your life.

Gratefully Yours,

Jeff

—Courtesy of Jeff Brink

STRENGTHS

In its present stage of development, the transformational approach has several strengths. First, transformational leadership has been widely researched from many different perspectives, including a series of qualitative studies of prominent leaders and CEOs in large, well-known organizations. It has also been the focal point for a large body of leadership research since its introduction in the 1970s. For example, content analysis of all the articles published in *The Leadership Quarterly* from 1990 to 2000 showed that 34% of the articles were about transformational or charismatic leadership (Lowe & Gardner, 2001). In an updated review examining the period from 2000 to 2012, 39% of the articles published in 10 top-tier academic journals were about transformational or charismatic leadership (Dinh et al., 2014). In addition, qualitative research on transformational leadership, which has appeared in highly popular mass-market leadership books, has provided rich descriptions of the qualities and characteristics of transformational leaders.

Second, transformational leadership has intuitive appeal. The transformational perspective describes how the leader is out front advocating change for others; this concept is consistent with society's popular notion of what leadership means. People are attracted to transformational leadership because it makes sense to them. It is appealing that a leader will provide a vision for the future. Transformational leaders are "movers and shakers" that get an organization moving when change is needed by getting followers to face the future and achieve results through their influence (Nicholls, 1988).

Third, transformational leadership treats leadership as a process that occurs between followers and leaders. One of the components of transformational leadership is individualized consideration (Bass, 1985). Because this process incorporates both the followers' and the leader's needs, leadership is not the sole responsibility of a leader but rather emerges from the interplay between leaders and followers. The needs of others are central to the transformational leader. As a result, followers gain a more prominent position in the leadership process because their attributions are instrumental in the evolving transformational process (Bryman, 1992, p. 176).

Fourth, the transformational approach provides a broader view of leadership that augments other leadership models. Many leadership models focus primarily on how leaders exchange rewards for achieved goals—the transactional process. The transformational approach provides an expanded picture of leadership that includes not only the exchange of rewards, but also leaders' attention to the needs and growth of followers (Avolio, 1999; Bass, 1985). Contingent rewards and transformational behaviors combine to explain employee job satisfaction (Puni, Mohammed, & Asamoah, 2018). In other words, followers respond to both transactional and transformational behaviors, which are encompassed in the Full Range of Leadership model (Figure 8.2) that provides a comprehensive view of leadership.

Fifth, transformational leadership places a strong emphasis on followers' needs, values, and morals. Burns (1978) suggested that transformational leadership involves attempts by leaders to move people to higher standards of moral responsibility. It includes motivating followers to transcend their own self-interests for the good of the team, organization, or community (Howell & Avolio, 1993; Shamir et al., 1993). Transformational leadership is fundamentally morally uplifting (Avolio, 1999). This emphasis sets the transformational approach apart from all other approaches to leadership because it suggests that leadership has a moral dimension. Therefore, the coercive uses of power by people such as Hitler, cult leader David Koresh, and Philippine president Rodrigo Duterte can be disregarded as models of leadership.

Finally, there is substantial evidence that transformational leadership is an effective form of leadership (Yukl, 1999). In a critique of transformational and charismatic leadership, Yukl reported that in studies using the MLQ to appraise leaders, transformational leadership was positively related to follower satisfaction, motivation, and performance. Furthermore, in studies that used interviews and observations, transformational leadership was shown to be effective in a variety of different situations. At the same time, transformational leadership has also been demonstrated to contribute to the leader's personal growth (Notgrass, 2014).

CRITICISMS

Transformational leadership has several weaknesses. One criticism is that it lacks conceptual clarity. Because it covers such a wide range of activities and characteristics—creating a vision, motivating, being a change agent, building trust, giving nurturance, and acting as a social architect, to name a few—it is difficult to define exactly the parameters of transformational leadership. Knippenberg and Sitkin (2013) critically reviewed the transformational leadership research and found the following weaknesses: lack of a clear conceptual definition, failure to outline a well-defined causal model that accounts for the unique effects of theoretical dimensions, and the confounding of the conceptualization and operationalization—a disconnect between the theory and how it is measured. For example, research by Tracey and Hinkin (1998) has shown substantial overlap between each of the Four Is (idealized influence, inspirational motivation, intellectual stimulation, and individualized consideration), suggesting that the dimensions are not clearly delimited.

Furthermore, the parameters of transformational leadership often overlap with similar conceptualizations of leadership. Bryman (1992), for example, pointed out that transformational and charismatic leadership often are treated synonymously, even though in some models of leadership (e.g., Bass, 1985) charisma is only one component of transformational leadership. Others have questioned whether the four dimensions of transformational leadership (i.e., the Four Is) are the reasons for transformational leadership or if they are simply descriptions of transformational leadership (e.g., Andersen, 2015; Tourish, 2013). At present, researchers are not sure if these dimensions predict transformational leadership or just help to explain the presence of transformational leadership.

In addition, Andersen (2015) suggested that transformational leadership was created to be used within social and political contexts—not in corporations. However, many researchers have been using the theory to explore managerial rather than political leadership.

Another criticism revolves around how transformational leadership is measured. Researchers typically have used some version of the MLQ to measure transformational leadership. However, some studies have challenged the validity of the MLQ. In some versions of the MLQ, the four factors of transformational leadership (the Four Is) correlate highly with each other, which means they are not distinct factors (Tejeda, Scandura, & Pillai, 2001). In addition, some of the transformational factors correlate with the transactional and laissez-faire factors, which means they may not be unique to the transformational model (Tejeda et al., 2001). It has also been suggested that transformational leadership could be better measured and understood through a narrative perspective (Andersen, 2015; Tengblad, 2012). Reviews of research on transformational leadership reveal that the factor structure does not replicate across studies (Knippenberg & Sitkin, 2013).

A third criticism is that transformational leadership treats leadership as a personality trait or personal predisposition rather than a behavior that people can learn (Bryman, 1992, pp. 100–102). If it is a trait, training people in this approach becomes more problematic because it is difficult to teach people how to change their traits. Even though many scholars, including Weber, House, and Bass, emphasized that transformational leadership is concerned with leader behaviors, such as how leaders involve themselves with followers, there is an inclination to see this approach from a trait perspective. Perhaps this problem is exacerbated because the word *transformational* creates images of one person being the most active component in the leadership process. For example, even though "creating a vision" involves follower input, there is a tendency to see transformational leaders as visionaries. There is also a tendency to see transformational leaders as people who have special qualities that *transform* others. These images accentuate a trait characterization of transformational leadership.

Fourth, researchers have not established that transformational leaders are actually able to transform individuals and organizations (Antonakis, 2012). There is evidence that indicates that transformational leadership is associated with positive outcomes, such as organizational effectiveness; however, studies have not yet clearly established a causal link between transformational leaders and changes in followers or organizations. However, there may be a glimmer of hope in this regard as Arthur and Hardy (2014) were able to use an experimental design to evaluate the effectiveness of a transformational leadership intervention in remediating poor performance in an organization. This provides initial evidence that transformational leadership behaviors may result in some expected positive changes.

A fifth criticism some have made is that transformational leadership is elitist and antidemocratic (Avolio, 1999; Bass & Avolio, 1993). Transformational leaders often play a direct role in creating changes, establishing a vision, and advocating new directions. This gives the strong impression that the leaders are acting independently of followers or putting themselves above the followers' needs. Although this criticism of elitism has been refuted by Bass and Avolio (1993) and Avolio (1999), who contended that transformational leaders can be directive and participative as well as democratic and authoritarian, the substance of the criticism raises valid questions about transformational leadership. The transformational leadership approach has focused predominantly on leaders at the top echelons of organizations. However, some research suggests that transformational leadership can occur at all levels of the organization (Lovelace, Neely, Allen, & Hunter, 2019).

Related to this criticism, some have argued that transformational leadership suffers from a "heroic leadership" bias (Yukl, 1999). Transformational leadership stresses that it is the *leader* who moves *followers* to do exceptional things. By focusing primarily on the leader, researchers have failed to give attention to shared leadership or reciprocal influence. Followers can influence leaders just as leaders can influence followers. More attention should be directed toward how leaders can encourage followers to challenge the leader's vision and share in the leadership process.

Another criticism of transformational leadership is that it has the potential to be abused. Transformational leadership is concerned with changing people's values and moving them to a new vision. But who is to determine whether the new directions are good and more affirming? Who decides that a new vision is a better vision? If the values to which leaders are moving their followers are not better, and if the set of human values is not more redeeming, then the leadership must be challenged. However, the dynamics of how followers challenge leaders or respond to their visions are not fully understood. There is a need to understand how transformational leaders affect followers psychologically and how leaders respond to followers' reactions. In fact, Burns (1978) argued that understanding this area (i.e., charisma and follower worship) is one of the central problems in leadership studies today (Bailey & Axelrod, 2001). The charismatic nature of transformational leadership presents significant risks for organizations because it can be used for destructive purposes (Conger, 1999; Howell & Avolio, 1993). A meta-analysis of psychopathic tendencies and transformational leadership showed that psychopathic people are somewhat more likely to emerge as leaders, but they are viewed as less effective leaders. Further, this study found that women are penalized for displaying psychopathic tendencies but that men may be rewarded for similar behaviors (Landay, Harms, & Credé, 2019).

History is full of examples of charismatic individuals who used coercive power to lead people to evil ends. For this reason, transformational leadership puts a burden on individuals and organizations to be aware of how they are being influenced and in what directions they are being asked to go. Christie et al. (2011) warn that astute followers need to be vigilant and pay careful attention to the vision of their leader, whether the vision is collective or self-focused, whether the leader is tolerant or intolerant of opposing viewpoints, and whether or not the leader is caring of followers. The potential for abuse of transformational leadership is mitigated when followers are aware and engaged in how they are being led.

Another criticism of the transformational leadership approach is that it may not be viewed as effective in all national cultures. Despite prior claims that transformational leadership is universal (Bass, 1997), this is not supported by data. A meta-analysis of more than 57,000 employees in 34 countries found that the value of transformational leadership behaviors may be limited in developed economies such as Western Europe and North America, while transformational leadership is most effective in Africa, the Middle East, South America, and parts of Southeast Asia (Credé, Jong, & Harms, 2019).

A final potential weakness of transformational leadership is the fact that it may not be well received by millennials (Anderson et al., 2017). As millennials continue to replace baby boomers in the workforce, organizations are recognizing that they are having to modify previous ways of doing things to meet millennials' needs. Transformational leadership is one such example. Drawing from the individualistic orientation of many millennials, Anderson and colleagues predict that transformational leaders may be less effective because this cohort may be less willing to collaborate with others to achieve common goals. Relatedly, today's transformational leaders communicate in a way to encourage followers to prioritize organizational and task needs and goals over individual interests (Anderson et al., 2017). However, it is predicted that this will be met with resistance as millennials have expressed a greater desire for work–life balance and want to "work to live" rather than "live to work" (Ng, Schweitzer, & Lyons, 2010). Finally, it has been suggested that because millennials expect frequent promotions and value extrinsic rewards, two of the fundamental components of transformational leadership—idealized influence and inspirational motivation—may be ineffective (Anderson et al., 2017).

APPLICATION

Rather than being a model that tells leaders what to do, transformational leadership provides a broad set of generalizations of what is typical of leaders who are transforming or who work in transforming contexts. Unlike other leadership approaches, such as the situational approach (discussed in Chapter 5), transformational leadership does not provide a clearly defined set of assumptions about how leaders should act in a particular situation to be successful. Rather, it provides a general way of thinking about leadership that emphasizes ideals, inspiration, innovations, and individual concerns. Transformational leadership requires that leaders be aware of how their own behavior relates to the needs of their followers and the changing dynamics within their organizations.

Bass and Avolio (1990a) suggested that transformational leadership can be taught to people at all levels in an organization and that it can positively affect a firm's performance. It can be used in recruitment, selection and promotion, and training and development. It can also be used in improving team development, decision-making groups, quality initiatives, and reorganizations (Bass & Avolio, 1994).

Programs designed to develop transformational leadership usually require that leaders or their associates take the MLQ (Bass & Avolio, 1990b) or a similar questionnaire to determine the leader's particular strengths and weaknesses in transformational leadership. These assessments help leaders pinpoint areas in which they could improve their leadership. For example, leaders might learn that it would be beneficial if they were more confident in expressing their goals, that they need to spend more time nurturing followers, or that they need to be more tolerant of opposing viewpoints. Such transformational leadership measures can be springboards to helping leaders improve a whole series of their leadership attributes.

One particular aspect of transformational leadership that has been given special emphasis in training programs is the process of building a vision. For example, it has become quite common for training programs to have leaders write elaborate statements that describe their own five-year career plans and their perceptions of the future directions for their organizations. Working with leaders on vision statements is one way to help them enhance their transformational leadership behavior. Another important aspect of training is teaching leaders to exhibit greater individual consideration and promote intellectual stimulation for their followers. Lowe et al. (1996) found that this is particularly valuable for lower-level leaders in organizations.

The desire to provide effective training in how to be more successful in demonstrating transactional and transformational leadership resulted in the development of a guide by Sosik and Jung (2010). This comprehensive, evidence-based approach includes self-assessments, 360-degree feedback, and leadership development planning. Their work serves as a thorough training guide that explains how, when, and why the full range of leadership behaviors work.

Overall, transformational leadership provides leaders with information about a full range of their behaviors, from nontransactional to transactional to transformational. In the next section, we provide some actual leadership examples to which the principles of transformational leadership can be applied.

CASE STUDIES

In the following section, three brief case studies (Cases 8.1, 8.2, and 8.3) from very different contexts are provided. Each case describes a situation in which transformational leadership is present to some degree. The first case looks at the efforts of a new CEO to transform the traditional culture of aircraft equipment manufacturing company. The second case comes from the perspective of a college professor and archaeologist who leads student groups on digs in the Middle East. The final case profiles the Friendship Bench project that trains grandmothers to help tackle depression in Zimbabwe. The questions at the end of each case point to some of the unique issues surrounding the use of transformational leadership in ongoing organizations.

Case 8.1 THE VISION FAILED

High Tech Engineering (HTE) is a 50-year-old family-owned manufacturing company with 250 employees that produces small parts for the aircraft industry. The president of HTE is Harold Barelli, who came to the company from a smaller business with strong credentials as a leader in advanced aircraft technology. Before Barelli, the only other president of HTE was the founder and owner of the company. The organizational structure at HTE was very traditional, and it was supported by a very rich organizational culture.

As the new president, Barelli sincerely wanted to transform HTE. He wanted to prove that new technologies and advanced management techniques could make HTE one of the best manufacturing companies in the country. To that end, Barelli created a vision statement that was displayed throughout the company. The two-page statement, which had a strong democratic tone, described the overall purposes, directions, and values of the company.

During the first three years of Barelli's tenure as president, several major reorganizations took place at the company. These were designed by Barelli and a select few of his senior managers. The intention of each reorganization was to implement advanced organizational structures to bolster the declared HTE vision.

Yet the major outcome of each of the changes was to dilute the leadership and create a feeling of instability among the employees. Most of the changes were made from the top down, with little input from lower or middle management. Some of the changes gave employees more control in circumstances where they needed less, whereas other changes limited employee input in contexts where employees should have been given more input. There were some situations in which individual workers reported to three different bosses, and other situations in which one manager had far too many workers to oversee. Rather than feeling comfortable in their various roles at HTE, employees began to feel uncertain about their responsibilities and how they contributed to stated goals of the company. The overall effect of the reorganizations was a precipitous drop in worker morale and production.

In the midst of all the changes, the vision that Barelli had for the company was lost. The instability that employees felt made it difficult for them to support the company's vision. People at HTE complained that although mission statements were displayed throughout the company, no one understood in which direction they were going.

To the employees at HTE, Barelli was an enigma. HTE was an American company that produced U.S. products, but Barelli drove a foreign car. Barelli claimed to be democratic in his style of leadership, but he was arbitrary in how he treated people. He acted in a nondirective style toward some people, and he showed arbitrary control toward others. He wanted to be seen as a hands-on manager, but he delegated operational control of the company to others while he focused on external customer relations and matters of the board of directors.

At times Barelli appeared to be insensitive to employees' concerns. He wanted HTE to be an environment in which everyone could feel empowered, but he often failed to listen closely to what employees were saying.

He seldom engaged in open, two-way communication. HTE had a long, rich history with many unique stories, but the employees felt that Barelli either misunderstood or did not care about that history.

Four years after arriving at HTE, Barelli stepped down as president after his operations officer ran the company into a large debt and cash-flow crisis. His dream of building HTE into a world-class manufacturing company was never realized.

Questions

1. If you were consulting with the HTE board of directors soon after Barelli started making changes, what would you advise them regarding Barelli's leadership from a transformational perspective?

2. Did Barelli have a clear vision for HTE? Was he able to implement it?

3. How effective was Barelli as a change agent and social architect for HTE?

4. What would you advise Barelli to do differently if he had the chance to return as president of HTE?

Every year, Dr. Cook, a college professor, leads a group of 25 college students to the Middle East on an archaeological dig that usually lasts about eight weeks. The participants, who come from big and small colleges throughout the country, usually have little prior knowledge or background in what takes place during an excavation. Dr. Cook enjoys leading these expeditions because he likes teaching students about archaeology and because the outcomes of the digs actually advance his own scholarly work.

While planning for his annual summer excavation, Dr. Cook told the following story:

This summer will be interesting because I have 10 people returning from last year. Last year was quite a dig. During the first couple of weeks everything was very disjointed. Team members seemed unmotivated and tired. In fact, there was one time early on when it seemed as if nearly half the students were either physically ill or mentally exhausted. Students seemed lost and uncertain about the meaning of the entire project.

For example, it is our tradition to get up every morning at 4:30 a.m. to depart for the excavation site at 5:00 a.m. However, during the first weeks of the dig, few people were ever ready on time, even after several reminders.

Every year it takes some time for people to learn where they fit with each other and with the purposes of the dig. The students all come from such different backgrounds. Some are from small, private, religious schools, and others are from large state universities. Each comes with a different agenda, different skills, and different work habits. One person may be a good photographer, another a good artist, and another a good surveyor. It is my job to complete the excavation with the resources available to us.

At the end of Week 2, I called a meeting to assess how things were going. We talked about a lot of things including personal things, how our work was progressing, and what we needed to change. The students seemed to appreciate the chance to talk at this meeting. Each of them described their special circumstances and hopes for the summer.

I told the students several stories about past digs; some were humorous, and others highlighted accomplishments. I shared my particular interests in this project and how I thought we as a group could accomplish the work that needed to be done at this important historical site. In particular, I stressed two points: (a) that they shared the responsibility for the successful outcome of the venture, and (b) that they had independent authority to design, schedule, and carry out the details of their respective assignments, with the director and other senior staff available at all times as advisers and resource persons. In regard to the departure time issue, I told the participants that the standard departure time on digs was 5:00 a.m.

Well, shortly after our meeting I observed a real shift in the group attitude and atmosphere. People seemed to become more involved in the work, there was less sickness, and there was more camaraderie. All assignments were completed without constant prodding and in a spirit of mutual support. Each morning at 5:00 a.m. everyone was ready to go.

I find that each year my groups are different. It's almost as if each of them has a unique personality. Perhaps that is why I find it so challenging. I try to listen to the students and use their particular strengths. It really is quite amazing how these students can develop in eight weeks. They really become good at archaeology, and they accomplish a great deal.

This coming year will again be different because of the 10 returning "veterans."

Questions

1. How is this an example of transformational leadership?

2. Where are Dr. Cook's strengths on the Full Range of Leadership model (Figure 8.2)?

3. What is the vision Dr. Cook has for the archaeology excavations?

Case 8.3 GRANDMOTHERS AND BENCHES

The invitation of a park bench and the compassion of a grandmother are saving lives in Zimbabwe.

Zimbabwe, an African nation of more than 16 million people, had only 12 psychiatrists available to meet the mental health needs of the entire country. Dr. Dixon Chibanda is one of them (Chibanda, 2017c; Nuwer, 2018).

After losing a young patient he had treated for depression to suicide because she and her mother could not afford the $15 bus fare to come to his office for treatment, Dr. Chibanda realized that the traditional delivery of mental health care—offering services in a facility and waiting for patients to come to him—would not work in his country. After much soul searching and consideration of the effectiveness of his role as a psychiatrist in Zimbabwe, Dr. Chibanda had an epiphany.

Suicide is not unusual when it comes to mental health concerns. According to the World Health Organization (WHO), suicide is the leading cause of death of those ages 15 to 29 worldwide. Globally, more than 300 million people suffer from depression, according to the WHO. Depression is the world's leading cause of disability and contributes to 800,000 suicides per year, the majority of which occur in developing countries (Nuwer, 2018).

(Continued)

(Continued)

Depression, often the result of loneliness, abuse, conflict, and violence, is a treatable mental illness. But treatment needs to be available and affordable, which are large concerns for a country like Zimbabwe with extremely limited resources.

In 2006, Dr. Chibanda began leading a team of Zimbabwean researchers in testing new ways of addressing anxiety and depression disorders and making treatment accessible to those who need it (Chibanda, 2017a). With no money or facilities available, he accessed the most abundant and reliable resource he could think of: grandmothers. Thus, the Friendship Bench approach was conceived.

The Friendship Bench involves the engagement and training of laypeople—grandmothers, to be precise—from local communities, as well as the integration of digital technologies.

Why grandmothers? Grandmothers are often a trusted, cultural cornerstone in Zimbabwean communities. "It suddenly dawned on me that actually, one of the most reliable resources we have in Africa are grandmothers. Yes, grandmothers. And I thought, grandmothers are in every community. There are hundreds of them" (Chibanda, 2017c).

In addition, Dr. Chibanda realized that grandmothers, unlike many younger workers, were more likely to stay in place and not leave the communities to seek other opportunities. Furthermore, many grandmothers were already doing community work, and association with this program would reinforce their role in the community.

"When we started, we didn't know what the core competencies were . . . Later we discovered that our lay therapists needed strong listening skills, an ability to convey empathy and an ability to reflect—all skills the grandmothers had and could develop further" (WHO, 2018, p. 377).

Training these community counselors involved the application of basic cognitive therapy (often referred to as "talk therapy") concepts. The grandmothers were taught to adopt a nonjudgmental and practical approach, allowing the clients to discuss their challenges and talk through possible solutions. Dr. Chibanda's strategy was to "empower them [the grandmothers] with the skills to provide behavior activation, [and] activity scheduling; and support them using digital technology. You know, mobile phone technology. Pretty much everyone in Africa has a mobile phone today" (Chibanda, 2017c).

The program launched in 2007, and Dr. Chibanda spent the first four years of the program working with 14 grandmothers and his colleague, Petra Mesu, to develop a "culturally appropriate and evidence-based intervention they could deliver" (WHO, 2018, p. 377). Together, they developed a therapy focused on problem solving that incorporated the native Shona language and familiar, local cultural concepts.

The first step of the program is screening, which is done at a health facility. Using a locally developed diagnosis tool called the Shona Symptom Questionnaire, clients are evaluated as to whether they are suffering from mental illness and what form of mental illness. If it is found that they are, then they are referred to the Friendship Bench where they meet with one of the trained community counselors (the grandmothers). The Friendship Bench is a literal wooden park bench, initially located in discreet areas around the health facility, where patient and grandmother (counselor) can openly discuss a patient's concerns in a comfortable setting. Due to the growing acceptance of the program, these benches are now more publicly visible.

As part of their training, counselors are taught to use language and terms familiar to their clients such as *kuvhura pfungwa* ("opening the mind"), *kusimudzira* ("uplifting"), and *kusimbisa* ("to strengthen"). Many of the clients suffer with depression, which is commonly referred to as *kufungisisa* ("thinking too much") in the Shona language.

"They provide six sessions of individual problem-solving therapy to each patient and refer those at risk of suicide to their immediate supervisors. The first session takes an hour or more, during which the grandmother listens, establishes a rapport with the client, and takes notes. Their notes are reviewed regularly by the team, together with the grandmothers, particularly during debrief sessions. The sessions are recorded for their supervisors to monitor," said Dr. Chibanda. "Afterwards, the grandmother reflects on what the client said and decides what needs to be done with the other grandmothers. Subsequent sessions with the client can be quite short, 20–30 minutes, because the client has an understanding of what to focus on" (WHO, 2018, p. 377).

Technology plays an important role in the program. To store patient data, the team uses a secure platform combined with cloud computing. "Each patient receives text messages between sessions to encourage their problem-solving efforts. When a client does not turn up for a session on the bench, we call them and if there is no response, the grandmother and a health professional visit the client's home," Dr. Chibanda said (WHO, 2018, p. 377).

Dedicated to the success of the program, Dr. Chibanda ran the initial pilot in Mbare, using his own salary to pay for supplies and space rental for the training. The program would eventually receive funding from the National Healthcare Trust, Zimbabwe and other organizations.

Some of the grandmothers are paid, receiving an allowance from their city's health department. During the clinical trials, funding was available, but once those trials concluded, that funding dried up and Dr. Chibanda was concerned the grandmothers might cease working. To his surprise, they did not. When he and his colleagues looked into why, they found the grandmothers exhibited negative

(Continued)

(Continued)

mental health conditions of their own, and the team hypothesized that perhaps the work the grandmothers were doing helped them as well, enabling them to expand their own well-being and resilience to adversity.

Dr. Chibanda's own mother came up with the income-generating model for the grandmothers. "After finishing sessions on the bench, the grandmothers sit in a circle and share the challenges they face with their colleagues, while crocheting bags with recycled plastic to sell. Now, after completing therapy, the grandmothers give their patients further support and show them how to make the bags. So, this is a forum for problem solving and income generation" (WHO, 2018, p. 377).

The success of the program speaks for itself. In 2017, the program had been scaled into more than 70 communities, with "hundreds of grandmothers" providing mental health services in those communities. More than 30,000 people have received treatment on the Friendship Bench. "Our results—this was a clinical trial—in fact, this clinical trial showed that grandmothers were more effective at treating depression than doctors" (Chibanda, 2017c).

"When we compared the Friendship Bench approach to standard care, plus information, education, and support on common mental disorders, we found that after nine months the Friendship Bench patients had a significantly lower risk of symptoms than the standard of care group," Dr. Chibanda said (WHO, 2018, p. 377).

Not surprisingly, Chibanda sees the potential in expanding the program globally. Even in developed countries, the availability of mental health professionals is rapidly declining, with waiting times to receive care increasing to dangerous levels. "In the United Kingdom, thousands of people attempt suicide while waiting, sometimes for months, on the National Health Service list to see a psychologist. Similarly, long waiting lists have been reported in the United States" (Chibanda, 2017b).

Dr. Chibanda notes that today there are more than 600 million people worldwide who are above 65, with this number expected to expand to 1.5 billion people by the year 2050. He envisions "a global network of grandmothers in every city in the world who are trained in evidence-based talk therapy, supported through digital platforms, networked. And they will make a difference in communities. They will reduce the treatment gap for mental, neurological and substance-use disorders" (Chibanda, 2017c).

The realization of this vision has already begun. The program has expanded to rural areas in Zimbabwe and is developing a component for adolescents. The Friendship Bench approach is being implemented in Malawi with plans for it to be used in Zanzibar, United Republic of Tanzania. Its use is even being explored in the United States, Canada, Australia, and New Zealand (WHO, 2018, p. 377).

Questions

1. Based on the definition of transformational leadership in this chapter:

   a. What aspects of the implementation of the Friendship Bench and the effectiveness of the grandmothers do you see as related to the transformational leadership processes? Explain why.

   b. Are there aspects of this process outlined in this case study that you would classify as transactional leadership? Why?

2. Charisma and its relationship to transformational leadership was discussed at length and outlined in Table 8.1. View Dr. Dixon Chibanda's 2017 TED Talk at www.ted.com/talks/dixon_chibanda_why_i_train_grandmothers_to_treat_depression and respond to the following:

   a. Do you perceive Dr. Chibanda to be a charismatic leader? Why or why not?

   b. What about the grandmothers? What characteristics of charismatic leadership, if any, would you ascribe to them? Explain your answer.

   c. Bass suggested that "charisma is a necessary but not sufficient condition for transformational leadership." Based on the elements of this case study, would you agree or disagree? Why?

3. How do each of the leadership factors of idealized influence, intellectual stimulation, and individualized consideration relate to this case?

4. Bennis and Nanus expanded on the transformational perspective by identifying four common strategies for transformational leaders. Discuss how each of these relates to Dr. Chibanda and the grandmothers:

   a. Clear vision

   b. Social architect

   c. Creation of trust

   d. Creative deployment of self

5. Kouzes and Posner identified five fundamental practices of transformational leaders. Discuss how these apply to this case:

   a. Model the way

   b. Inspire a shared vision

   c. Challenge the process

   d. Enable others to act

   e. Encourage the heart

6. The chapter lists seven criticisms of the transformational leadership model. Select three of these and address them with respect to this case.

LEADERSHIP INSTRUMENT

The Transformational Leadership Inventory developed by Podsakoff, MacKenzie, Moorman, and Fetter (1990) provides a measure of transactional and transformational leadership. The purpose of this questionnaire is to determine which style of leadership you tend to use, transformational or transactional. If you have held leadership positions in the past, you might have some idea which style you tend to use. Even if you have no leadership experience, this self-assessment can provide a starting point for you to determine which style you are more likely to use.

Transformational Leadership Inventory

Purpose: The purpose of this questionnaire is to determine which style of leadership you intend to use, transformational or transactional.

Instructions: To respond to the following questions, consider a time when you have been a leader of a group. Read each of the following statements and select the response that best describes your leadership behavior as a member of this group.

Key: 1 = Strongly   2 = Disagree   3 = Neutral   4 = Agree   5 = Strongly
            disagree   agree

1. I have a clear understanding of where my group is going.   1 2 3 4 5
2. I always give others positive feedback when they perform well. 1 2 3 4 5
3. I paint an interesting picture of the future for our group.   1 2 3 4 5
4. I give special recognition to group members when their work   1 2 3 4 5
   is very good.
5. I am always seeking new opportunities for the group.   1 2 3 4 5
6. I commend others when they do a better than average job.   1 2 3 4 5
7. I inspire others with my plans for the future.   1 2 3 4 5
8. I frequently acknowledge others' good performance.   1 2 3 4 5

Scoring and Interpretation

Write the number you selected for each question in the blanks in the following box.

Transformational Leadership	Transactional Leadership
1. _____	2. _____
3. _____	4. _____
5. _____	6. _____
7. _____	8. _____
Total: _____	Total: _____

Transformational Leadership (Identifying and Articulating a Vision): Identifying new opportunities for a leader's unit/division/company, and developing, articulating, and inspiring others with a vision of the future.

Transactional Leadership (Contingent Reward): Promising or delivering rewards to followers, contingent on their performance.

Your scores for each dimension (transformational or transactional) can range from 4 to 20. In general, scores from 4 to 12 represent lower levels of your preference for the leadership style, and scores above 12 indicate higher levels of your preference for the leadership style.

Source: Adapted from Podsakoff, P. M., MacKenzie, S. B., Moorman, R. H., & Fetter, R. (1990). Transformational leader behaviors and their effects on followers' trust in leader, satisfaction, and organizational citizenship behaviors. *The Leadership Quarterly, 1*(2), 107–142.

SUMMARY

One of the most encompassing approaches to leadership—transformational leadership—is concerned with the process of how certain leaders are able to inspire followers to accomplish great things. This approach stresses that leaders need to understand and adapt to the needs and motives of followers. Transformational leaders are recognized as change agents who are good role models, who can create and articulate a clear vision for an organization, who empower followers to meet higher standards, who act in ways that make others want to trust them, and who give meaning to organizational life.

Transformational leadership emerged from and is rooted in the writings of Burns (1978) and Bass (1985). The works of Bennis and Nanus (1985, 2007) and Kouzes and Posner (2002, 2017a) are also representative of transformational leadership. Qualitative studies provided additional perspectives on transformational leadership and served as guides for practicing managers.

There are several positive features of the transformational approach, including that it is a popular model that has received a lot of attention by researchers, it has strong intuitive appeal, it emphasizes the importance of followers in the leadership process, it goes beyond traditional transactional models and broadens leadership to include the growth of followers, and it places strong emphasis on morals and values. Transformational leadership has also proven to be an effective form of leadership that is positively related to follower satisfaction, motivation, and performance.

Balancing against the positive features of transformational leadership are several weaknesses. These include that the approach lacks conceptual clarity and a well-defined causal model; it is based on the MLQ, which has been challenged by some research; it creates a framework that implies that transformational leadership has a trait-like quality; it is sometimes seen as elitist and undemocratic; it suffers from a "heroic leadership" bias; and it has the potential to be used counterproductively in negative ways by leaders. Finally, transformational leadership may not be viewed as an effective leadership approach in all national cultures and among millennials. Despite the weaknesses, transformational leadership appears to be a valuable and widely used approach.

Authentic Leadership

DESCRIPTION

Authentic leadership represents one of the newer areas of leadership research. It focuses on whether leadership is genuine and "real." As the title of this approach implies, authentic leadership is about the authenticity of leaders and their leadership. Unlike many of the theories that we have discussed in this book, authentic leadership is still in the formative phase of development. As a result, authentic leadership needs to be considered more tentatively: It is likely to change as new research about the theory is published.

In recent times, upheavals in society have energized a tremendous demand for authentic leadership. The destruction on 9/11, corporate scandals at companies like WorldCom and Enron, deliberate misinformation and claims of "fake news," and civil unrest resulting from incidents of racial injustice have all created anxiety and uncertainty. People feel apprehensive and insecure about what is going on around them, and as a result, they long for bona fide leadership they can trust and for leaders who are honest and good. People's demands for trustworthy leadership make the study of authentic leadership timely and worthwhile.

In addition to the public's interest, authentic leadership has been intriguing to researchers: It was identified earlier in transformational leadership research but never fully articulated (Bass, 1990; Bass & Steidlmeier, 1999; Burns, 1978; Howell & Avolio, 1993). Furthermore, practitioners had developed approaches to authentic leadership that were not evidence based and so needed further clarification and testing. In attempts to more fully explore authentic leadership, researchers set out to identify the parameters of authentic leadership and more clearly conceptualize it, efforts that continue today.

Authentic Leadership Defined

On the surface, authentic leadership appears easy to define. In actuality, it is a complex process that is difficult to characterize. Among leadership scholars, there is no single accepted definition of authentic leadership. Instead, there are multiple definitions, each written from a different viewpoint and with a different emphasis (Chan, 2005).

One of those viewpoints is the *intrapersonal* perspective, which focuses closely on the leader and what goes on within the leader. It incorporates the leader's self-knowledge, self-regulation, and self-concept. In their description of the intrapersonal approach, Shamir and Eilam (2005) suggest that authentic leaders exhibit genuine leadership, lead from conviction, and are originals. This perspective emphasizes the life experiences of a leader and the meaning one attaches to those experiences as being critical to the development of the authentic leader.

A second way of defining authentic leadership is as an *interpersonal* process. This perspective outlines authentic leadership as relational, created by leaders and followers together (Eagly, 2005). It results not from the leader's efforts alone, but also from the response of followers. Authenticity emerges from the interactions between leaders and followers. It is a reciprocal process because leaders affect followers and followers affect leaders.

Finally, authentic leadership can be defined from a *developmental* perspective, which is exemplified in the work of Avolio and his associates (Avolio & Gardner, 2005; Gardner, Avolio, & Walumbwa, 2005b; Walumbwa, Avolio, Gardner, Wernsing, & Peterson, 2008). This perspective, which underpins the approaches to authentic leadership discussed in the following section, views authentic leadership as something that can be nurtured in a leader, rather than as a fixed trait. Authentic leadership develops in people over a lifetime and can be triggered by critical life events, such as a severe illness or a new career.

Taking a developmental approach, Walumbwa et al. (2008) conceptualized authentic leadership as a pattern of leader behavior that develops from, and is grounded in, the leader's positive psychological qualities and strong ethics. They suggest that authentic leadership is composed of four distinct but related components: self-awareness, internalized moral perspective, balanced processing, and relational transparency (Avolio, Walumbwa, & Weber, 2009). Over a lifetime, authentic leaders learn and develop each of these four types of behavior.

Approaches to Authentic Leadership

Formulations about authentic leadership can be differentiated into two areas: (1) the practical approach, which evolved from real-life examples as well as the training and development literature; and (2) the theoretical approach, which is based on findings from social science research. Both approaches offer interesting insights about the complex process of authentic leadership.

Practical Approach

Books and programs about authentic leadership are popular today; people are interested in the basics of this type of leadership. Specifically, they want to know the "how to" steps to become an authentic leader. In this section, we discuss Bill George's (2003) authentic leadership approach.

Bill George's Authentic Leadership Approach. The authentic leadership approach developed by George (2003; George & Sims, 2007) focuses on the characteristics of authentic leaders. George describes, in a practical way, the essential qualities of authentic leadership and how individuals can develop these qualities if they want to become authentic leaders.

Based on his experience as a corporate executive and through interviews with a diverse sample of 125 successful leaders, George found that authentic leaders have a genuine desire to serve others, they know themselves, and they feel free to lead from their core values. Specifically, authentic leaders demonstrate five basic characteristics: (1) They have a strong sense of purpose, (2) they have strong values about the right thing to do, (3) they establish trusting relationships with others, (4) they demonstrate self-discipline and act on their values, and (5) they are sensitive and empathetic to the plight of others (George, 2003).

Figure 9.1 illustrates five dimensions of authentic leadership identified by George: purpose, values, relationships, self-discipline, and heart. The figure also illustrates each of the related characteristics—passion, behavior, connectedness, consistency, and compassion—that individuals need to develop to become authentic leaders.

In his interviews, George found that authentic leaders have a real sense of *purpose.* They know what they are about and where they are going. In addition to knowing their purpose, authentic leaders are inspired and intrinsically motivated about their goals. They are *passionate* individuals who have a deep-seated interest in what they are doing and truly care about their work.

A good example of an authentic leader who exhibited passion about his goals was Terry Fox, a cancer survivor, whose right leg was amputated above the knee after a malignant tumor was discovered. Using a customized leg prosthesis, Terry attempted to run across Canada, from the Atlantic to the Pacific, to raise awareness and money for cancer research. Although he died before he finished his run, his courage and passion affected the lives of millions of people. He also accomplished his goals to increase cancer awareness and to raise money for cancer research. Today, the Terry Fox Foundation is going strong and has raised more than $800 million (Canadian) for cancer research (www.terryfox.org). Of the dimensions and characteristics in Figure 9.1, Terry Fox clearly demonstrated purpose and passion in his leadership.

FIGURE 9.1 Authentic Leadership Characteristics

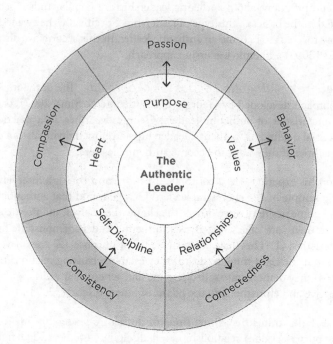

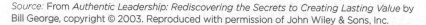

Authentic leaders understand their own *values* and *behave* toward others based on these values. Stated another way, George suggests that authentic leaders know their "True North." They have a clear idea of who they are, where they are going, and what the right thing is to do. When tested in difficult situations, authentic leaders do not compromise their values, but rather use those situations to strengthen their values.

An example of a leader with a strong set of values is Nobel Peace Prize laureate Nelson Mandela. Mandela was a deeply moral man with a strong conscience. While fighting to abolish apartheid in South Africa, he was unyielding in his pursuit of justice and equality for all. When he was in prison and was offered early release in exchange for denouncing his viewpoint, he chose to remain incarcerated rather than compromise his position. Nelson Mandela knew who he was at his core. He knew his values, and his leadership reflected those values.

A third characteristic of authentic leadership in the George approach is strong *relationships*. Authentic leaders have the capacity to open themselves up and establish a *connection* with others. They are willing to share their own story with others and listen to others' stories. Through mutual disclosure, leaders and followers develop a sense of trust and closeness.

George argued that people today want to have access to their leaders and want their leaders to be open with them. In a sense, people are asking leaders to soften the boundary around their leadership role and to be more transparent. People want to have a trusting relationship with their leaders. In exchange, people are willing to give leaders greater loyalty and commitment.

As we discussed in Chapter 7 (leader–member exchange theory), effective leader–follower relationships are marked by high-quality communication in which leaders and followers demonstrate a high degree of mutual trust, respect, and obligation toward each other. Leaders and followers are tied together in productive ways that go beyond the stereotypical leader–follower relationship. This results in strong leader–member relationships, greater understanding, and higher productivity.

Self-discipline is another dimension of authentic leadership and is the quality that helps leaders to reach their goals. Self-discipline gives leaders focus and determination. When leaders establish objectives and standards of excellence, self-discipline helps them to reach these goals and to keep everyone accountable. Furthermore, self-discipline gives authentic leaders the energy to carry out their work in accordance with their values.

Like long-distance runners, authentic leaders with self-discipline are able to stay focused on their goals. They are able to listen to their inner compass and can discipline themselves to move forward, even in challenging circumstances. In stressful times, self-discipline allows authentic leaders to remain cool, calm, and *consistent*. Because disciplined leaders are predictable in their behavior, other people know what to expect and find it easier to communicate with them. When the leader is self-directed and "on course," it gives other people a sense of security.

Last, the George approach identifies *compassion* and *heart* as important aspects of authentic leadership. Compassion refers to being sensitive to the plight of others, opening one's self to others, and being willing to help them. George (2003, p. 40) argued that as leaders develop compassion, they learn to be authentic. Leaders can develop compassion by getting to know others' life stories, doing community service projects, being involved with other racial or ethnic groups, or traveling to developing countries (George, 2003). These activities increase the leader's sensitivity to other cultures, backgrounds, and living situations.

In summary, George's authentic leadership approach highlights five important features of authentic leaders. Collectively, these features provide a practical picture of what people need to do to become authentic in their leadership. Authentic leadership is a lifelong developmental process, which is formed and informed by each individual's life story.

Theoretical Approach

Although still in its initial stages of development, a theory of authentic leadership is emerging in social science literature (see Kumar, 2014; Leroy, Anseel, Gardner, & Sels, 2015; Peus, Wescher, Streicher, Braun, & Frey, 2012). In this section, we identify the basic components of authentic leadership and describe how these components are related to one another.

Background to the Theoretical Approach. Although people's interest in "authenticity" is probably timeless, research on authentic leadership is rather recent. Luthans and Avolio (2003) published one of the first articles on the topic, focusing on authentic leadership development and positive organizational scholarship. Initial writing on authentic leadership gave rise to a leadership summit at the University of Nebraska. This summit was sponsored by the Gallup Leadership Institute and focused on the nature of authentic leadership and its development. From the summit, two sets of publications emerged: (1) a special issue of *The Leadership Quarterly* in the summer of 2005, and (2) *Monographs in Leadership and Management*, titled "Authentic Leadership Theory and Process: Origins, Effects and Development," also published in 2005.

Interest in authentic leadership increased following 9/11, a time in which there was a great deal of societal upheaval and instability in the United States. The attacks of 9/11, widespread corporate corruption, and a troubled economy all created a sense of uncertainty and anxiety in people about leadership. Widespread unethical and ineffective leadership necessitated the need for more humane, constructive leadership that served the common good (Fry & Whittington, 2005; Luthans & Avolio, 2003).

In addition, researchers felt the need to extend the work of Bass (1990) and Bass and Steidlmeier (1999) regarding the meaning of authentic transformational leadership. There was a need to operationalize the meaning of authentic leadership and create a theoretical framework to explain it. To develop a theory of authentic leadership, researchers drew from the fields of leadership, positive organizational scholarship, and ethics (Cooper, Scandura, & Schriesheim, 2005; Gardner et al., 2005b).

A major challenge confronting researchers in developing a theory was to define the construct and identify its characteristics. As we discussed earlier in the chapter, authentic leadership has been defined in multiple ways, with each definition emphasizing a different aspect of the process. For this chapter, we have selected the definition set forth by Walumbwa et al. (2008), who defined authentic leadership as

> a pattern of leader behavior that draws upon and promotes both positive psychological capacities and a positive ethical climate, to foster greater self-awareness, an internalized moral perspective, balanced processing of information, and relational transparency on the part of leaders working with followers, fostering positive self-development. (p. 94)

Although complex, this definition captures the current thinking of scholars regarding the phenomenon of authentic leadership and how it works.

Different models have been developed to illustrate the process of authentic leadership. Gardner et al. (2005b) created a model that frames authentic leadership around the developmental processes of leader and follower self-awareness and self-regulation. Ilies, Morgeson, and Nahrgang (2005) constructed a multicomponent model that discusses the impact of authenticity on leaders' and followers' happiness and well-being. In contrast, Luthans and Avolio (2003) formulated a model that explains authentic leadership as a developmental process. In this chapter, we will present a basic model of authentic leadership derived from the research literature that focuses on the core components of authentic leadership. Our discussion will examine authentic leadership as a process.

Components of Authentic Leadership. In an effort to further our understanding of authentic leadership, Walumbwa and associates (2008) conducted a comprehensive review of the literature and interviewed groups of content experts in the field to determine what components constituted authentic leadership and to develop a valid measure of this construct. Their research identified four components: self-awareness, internalized moral perspective, balanced processing, and relational transparency (Figure 9.2). Together, these four components form the foundation for a theory of authentic leadership.

Self-awareness refers to the personal insights of the leader. It is not an end in itself but a process in which individuals understand themselves, including their strengths and weaknesses, and the impact they have on others. Self-awareness includes reflecting on your core values, identity, emotions, motives, and goals, and coming to grips with who you really are at the deepest level. In addition, it includes being aware of and trusting your own feelings (Kernis, 2003). A meta-analysis including 11 studies and more than 3,500 respondents found that emotional intelligence is significantly and positively related to authentic leadership

FIGURE 9.2 Authentic Leadership

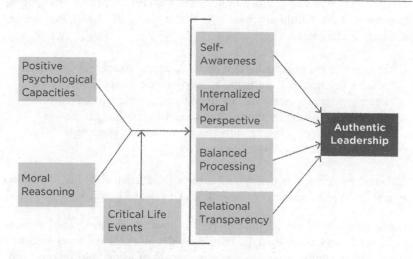

(Miao, Humphrey, & Qian, 2018). Leaders with high emotional intelligence are more self-aware and able to benefit from reflection on their past experiences to improve their authenticity.

When leaders know themselves and have a clear sense of who they are and what they stand for, they have a strong anchor for their decisions and actions (Gardner et al., 2005b). Other people see leaders who have greater self-awareness as more authentic. More recently, research has shown that self-knowledge and self-consistency also have a positive impact on followers' satisfaction with leaders, organizational commitment, and perceived team effectiveness (Leroy et al., 2015; Peus et al., 2012).

Internalized moral perspective refers to a self-regulatory process whereby individuals use their internal moral standards and values to guide their behavior rather than allow outside pressures to control them (e.g., group or societal pressure). It is a self-regulatory process because people have control over the extent to which they allow others to influence them. Others see leaders with an internalized moral perspective as authentic because their actions are consistent with their expressed beliefs and morals.

Balanced processing is also a self-regulatory behavior. Although not completely clear from its title, it refers to an individual's ability to analyze information objectively and explore other people's opinions before making a decision. It also means avoiding favoritism about certain issues and remaining unbiased. Balanced processing includes soliciting viewpoints from those who disagree with you and fully considering their positions before taking your own action. Leaders with balanced processing are seen as authentic because they are open about their own perspectives but are also objective in considering others' perspectives.

Relational transparency refers to being open and honest in presenting one's true self to others. It is self-regulating because individuals can control their transparency with others. Relational transparency occurs when individuals share their core feelings, motives, and inclinations with others in an appropriate manner (Kernis, 2003). It includes the individuals showing both positive and negative aspects of themselves to others. In short, relational transparency is about communicating openly and being real in relationships with others.

Factors That Influence Authentic Leadership. There are other factors such as positive psychological capacities, moral reasoning, and critical life events that influence authentic leadership (Figure 9.2). Individuals perceive the critical events that occur in their lives according to their capacities for confidence, hope, optimism, and resilience and for moral reasoning, which is related to how they cultivate the qualities needed to be authentic leaders.

The four key *positive psychological capacities* that have an impact on authentic leadership—confidence, hope, optimism, and resilience—have been drawn from the fields of positive psychology and positive organizational behavior (Table 9.1; Luthans & Avolio, 2003). Positive attributes predispose or enhance a leader's capacity to develop the components of authentic leadership discussed in the previous section. Each of these attributes has a trait-like and a state-like quality. They are believed to be malleable and can be enhanced with training.

Confidence refers to having self-efficacy—the belief that one has the ability to successfully accomplish a specified task. Leaders who have confidence are more likely to be motivated to succeed, to be persistent when obstacles arise, and to welcome a challenge (Bandura, 1997; Luthans & Avolio, 2003). *Hope* is a positive motivational state based on willpower and goal planning (Luthans & Avolio, 2003). Authentic leaders with hope have goals they know can be accomplished; their hope inspires followers to trust them and believe in their goals. *Optimism* refers to the cognitive process of viewing situations from a positive light and having favorable expectations about the future. Leaders with optimism are positive about their capabilities and the outcomes they can achieve. They approach life with a sense of abundance rather than scarcity (Covey, 1990). *Resilience* is

TABLE 9.1 Related Positive Psychological Capacities

• Confidence	• Optimism
• Hope	• Resilience

Source: Luthans, F., & Avolio, B. J. (2003). Authentic leadership development. In K. S. Cameron, J. E. Dutton, & R. E. Quinn (Eds.), *Positive organizational scholarship* (pp. 241-258). San Francisco: Berrett-Koehler.

the capacity to recover from and adjust to adverse situations. It includes the ability to positively adapt to hardships and suffering. During difficult times, resilient people are able to bounce back from challenging situations and feel strengthened and more resourceful as a result of them (Sutcliffe & Vogus, 2003).

Moral reasoning is another factor that can influence authentic leadership (Figure 9.2). It is the capacity to make ethical decisions about issues of right or wrong and good or bad. Developing the capacity for moral reasoning is a lifelong process. Higher levels of moral reasoning make it possible for the authentic leader to make decisions that transcend individual differences and align individuals toward a common goal. They enable leaders to be selfless and make judgments that serve the greater good of the group, organization, or community. Moral reasoning capacity also enables authentic leaders to use this ability to promote justice and achieve what is right for a community. An extended discussion of how moral reasoning develops is provided in Chapter 13.

Critical life events are major events that shape people's lives, and therefore also shape individuals' development as authentic leaders (Figure 9.2). The events can be positive, like receiving an unexpected promotion, having a child, or reading an important book; or they can be negative, like being diagnosed with cancer, getting a negative year-end employment evaluation, or experiencing the death of a loved one. Critical life events act as catalysts for change. Shamir and Eilam (2005) argued that authentic leadership rests heavily on the insights people attach to their life experiences. Authentic leaders often express their genuine emotions and values through telling stories about their pasts—particularly stories that are sensitive, negative, and even embarrassing (Lemoine, Hartnell, & Leroy, 2019). When leaders tell their life stories, they gain greater self-knowledge, more clarity about who they are, and a better understanding of their role. By understanding their own life experiences, leaders become more authentic.

Critical life events also stimulate growth in individuals and help them become stronger leaders (Luthans & Avolio, 2003). For example, Howard Schultz (founder and chairman emeritus of Starbucks) tells a story about when he was little: His father, who was a delivery driver, fell and was hurt on the job but did not have health insurance or workers' compensation. Seeing the problems that resulted from his father's difficulties, when Schultz built Starbucks he provided comprehensive health insurance for employees who worked as few as 20 hours a week. Schultz's style of leadership was triggered by his childhood experience ("Howard Schultz," 2008).

Authentic leadership is a unique approach to understanding leadership due to its focus on leaders' self-concept and their corresponding self-expression (Lemoine et al., 2019). As such, authentic leadership is consistent with the movement of positive organizational behavior with its emphasis on an individual's personal experiences, traits, and development to enhance organizational performance (Yavuz, 2020).

As the theory of authentic leadership develops further, other antecedent factors that influence the process may be identified. To date, however, it is positive psychological capacities, moral reasoning, and critical life events that have been identified as factors that are influential in a person's ability to become an authentic leader.

HOW DOES AUTHENTIC LEADERSHIP WORK?

In this chapter, we have discussed authentic leadership from a practical and theoretical perspective. Both perspectives describe authentic leadership as a process that develops in leaders over time; however, each perspective provides a different description for how authentic leadership works.

The practical approach provides prescriptions for how to be authentic and how to develop authentic leadership. For example, the George approach focuses on five characteristics leaders should develop to become authentic leaders. More specifically, George (2003) advocates that leaders become more *purposeful, value centered, relational, self-disciplined*, and *compassionate*. The essence of authentic leadership is being a leader who strongly demonstrates these five qualities.

Rather than simple prescriptions, the theoretical approach describes what authentic leadership is and what accounts for it. From this perspective, authentic leadership works because leaders demonstrate *self-awareness*, an *internalized moral perspective, balanced processing*, and *relational transparency*. Leaders develop these attributes through a lifelong process that is often influenced by critical life events. In addition, the literature suggests that positive psychological capacities and moral reasoning have a significant impact on authentic leaders.

Authentic leadership is a complex process that emphasizes the development of qualities that help leaders to be perceived as trustworthy and believable by their followers. The job of authentic leaders is to learn to develop these qualities and apply them to the common good as they serve others.

Throughout this chapter, we have focused on the *development* of authentic leadership in the leader. Recent research has focused on the *effects* of authentic leadership on followers, and the impact of followers on authentic leadership development. Xu, Zhao, Li, and Lin (2017) and Semedo, Coelho, and Ribeiro (2016) not only found that authentic leadership correlates directly to followers who thrive at work, but also found a positive relationship between employee creativity and authentic leadership. Rego, Sousa, Marques, and Pina e Cunha (2014) found similar results regarding creativity, and also found positive relationships between authentic leadership and employees' hope. Stander, Beer, and Stander (2015) found that authentic leadership led significantly to optimism and trust, and that those qualities led directly to stronger work engagement. Finally, research has shown that the four key positive psychological attributes that have an impact on authentic leadership—confidence, hope, optimism, and resilience—explain why authentic leaders may have followers who are more proactive. Authentic leadership is related to the psychological state of followers and indirectly influences them to invest in their work, maintain passion for what they do, and solve problems proactively (Hu et al., 2018).

Furthermore, Wang, Sui, Luthans, Wang, and Wu (2014) directly investigated, and positively correlated, the impact of authentic leadership on follower performance. Azanza, Moriano, Molero, and Lévy Mangin (2015) extended the findings of positive relationships between authentic leadership and work engagement to also include employee satisfaction and intent to stay while Kumar (2014) studied the effects of authentic leadership on followers' psychological ownership of their organizations. Wei, Li, Zhang, and Liu (2018) report that authentic leadership increases followers' task performance and organizational citizenship behavior. This effect is enhanced by followers' views of the leader's competence and their own work engagement.

Finally, Lyubovnikova, Legood, Turner, and Mamakouka (2017) found that authentic leadership was effective in directing teams. Because authentic leaders encourage team members to reflect on team goals and strategies and openly communicate about them, these followers often exhibit more flexibility and higher performance.

STRENGTHS

Authentic leadership has several strengths. First, it fulfills an expressed need for trustworthy leadership in society. During the past 20 years, failures in public and private leadership have created distrust in people. Authentic leadership helps to fill a void and provides an answer to people who are searching for good and sound leadership in an uncertain world. When a leader is authentic, it gives followers a clear picture of who the leader is and how the leader will act. It informs their understanding of the leader and whether or not they can depend on this person's leadership.

Second, authentic leadership provides broad guidelines for individuals who want to become authentic leaders. Both the practical and theoretical approaches clearly point to what leaders should do to become authentic leaders. Social science literature emphasizes that to be authentic it is important for leaders to have self-awareness, an internalized moral perspective, balanced processing, and relational transparency. Taken together, these approaches provide a map for becoming an authentic leader.

Third, similar to transformational, inclusive, and servant leadership, authentic leadership has an explicit moral dimension. Underlying both the practical and theoretical approaches is the idea that authenticity requires leaders to do what is "right" and "good" for their followers and society. Authentic leaders understand their own values, place followers' needs above their own, and work with followers to align their interests to create a greater common good. Steffens, Mols, Haslam, and Okimoto (2016) found that when a leader champions the collective good, followers are more inspired, and the leader's authenticity is enhanced.

Authentic leadership emphasizes that authentic values and behaviors can be developed in leaders over time. Authentic leadership is not an attribute that only some people exhibit: Everyone can develop authenticity and learn to be more authentic. For example, leaders can learn to become more aware and transparent, or they can learn to be more relational and other-directed. Leaders can also develop moral reasoning capacities. Furthermore, Luthans and Avolio (2003) contended that leaders can learn to develop positive psychological capacities such as confidence, hope, optimism, and resilience, and can use these to create a positive organizational climate. There are many ways that leaders can learn to become authentic leaders over a lifetime.

Finally, authentic leadership can be measured using the Authentic Leadership Questionnaire (ALQ). The ALQ is a validated, theory-based instrument comprising 16 items that measure four factors of authentic leadership (Avolio et al., 2009; Walumbwa et al., 2008). Nearly a decade after its development, Avolio, Wernsing, and Gardner (2018) reexamined the ALQ and concluded that the four-factor structure of the measure (self-awareness, internalized moral perspective, balanced processing, and relational transparency) is supported using recently developed statistical techniques. As research moves forward in refining authentic leadership theory, it is valuable to have an established instrument of this construct that is based in theory and can be used to measure authentic leadership in future research.

CRITICISMS

Despite increased research on authentic leadership, a number of questions still need to be addressed about the theory. First, the concepts and ideas presented in George's practical approach are not fully substantiated. While the practical approach is interesting and offers insight on authentic leadership, it is not built on a broad empirical base, nor has it been tested for validity. Because of its reliance on a leader's personal experiences, the authentic leadership approach can make it difficult to predict the course of action an authentic leader will take. Without research support, the ideas set forth in the practical approach should be treated cautiously as explanations of the authentic leadership process.

Second, the moral component of authentic leadership is not fully explained. Whereas authentic leadership implies that leaders are motivated by higher-order end values such as justice and community, the way that these values function to influence authentic leadership is not clear. Authentic leaders judge what is moral based on personal experience and not societal norms. This raises a number of questions. For example, how are a leader's values related to a leader's self-awareness? Or, what is the path or underlying process through which moral values affect other components of authentic leadership? In its present form, authentic leadership does not offer thorough answers to these questions.

Third, researchers have questioned whether positive psychological capacities should be included as components of authentic leadership. Although there is an interest in the social sciences to study positive human potential and the best of the human condition (Cameron, Dutton, & Quinn, 2003), the rationale for including positive psychological capacities as an inherent part of authentic leadership has not been clearly explained by researchers. In addition, some have argued that the inclusion of positive leader capacities in authentic leadership broadens the construct of authentic leadership too much and makes it difficult to measure (Cooper et al., 2005). In a review of the authentic leadership theory and research, Alvesson and Einola (2019) concluded that the foundations of the theory are too shaky for the theory to have inspired the popularity it has among scholars and that the promise offered by consultants and inspirational talks are not well grounded in research evidence. It is fair to say that at this point in the development of research on authentic leadership, the role of positive psychological capacities in authentic leadership theory needs further clarification.

In addition, new research is required to determine if the millennial generation can be effectively led by authentic leaders. This generation's individualism, commitment to work–life balance, and subsequent preference for extrinsic rewards have been identified by Anderson, Baur, Griffith, and Buckley (2017) as potential stumbling points for effectively leading millennials as followers using the model of authentic leadership.

Finally, it is not clear how authentic leadership results in positive organizational outcomes. Given that it is a relatively new area of research, it is not unexpected that there are few data on outcomes. Research has begun to come out on organizational outcomes (see Azanza et al., 2015; Gatling, Kang, & Kim, 2016; Rego, Sousa, Marques, & Pina e Cunha, 2012; Semedo et al., 2016; Xu et al., 2017), but more data are necessary to substantiate the value of the theory. In addition, Hoch, Bommer, Dulebohn, and Wu (2018) questioned the degree to which authentic leadership contributes to explaining differences in follower performance and work attitudes. They conducted a meta-analysis and found that authentic leadership failed to explain significant incremental variance in these outcomes over and above transformational leadership, leaving the authors to conclude that the authentic leadership approach's utility is low. Although authentic leadership is intuitively appealing on the surface, questions remain about whether this approach is effective, in what contexts it is effective, and whether authentic leadership results in productive outcomes. In some contexts, authenticity may be counterproductive. For example, in some organizations, expressing what one really thinks might be risky and lead to being fired or marginalized by one's boss and/or coworkers (Alvesson & Einola, 2019).

Relatedly, it is also not clear in the research whether authentic leadership is sufficient to achieve organizational goals. For example, can an authentic leader who is disorganized and lacking in technical competence be an effective leader? Authenticity is important and valuable to good leadership, but how authenticity relates to effective leadership is unknown. Sidani and Rowe (2018) reconceptualized authentic leadership as a process of followers legitimizing a leader's authenticity based on moral judgments. They provide the example of former U.S. president Donald Trump, whose followers view him as having self-awareness and relational transparency (Mintz, 2015). These followers share Trump's value system and believe that he is genuine, and while those with a different value system may disagree, his influence lies in the followers who make his behavior legitimate. Clearly, future research should be conducted to explore how follower perceptions of authentic leadership translate into the attainment of organizational outcomes.

APPLICATION

Because authentic leadership is still in the early phase of its development, there has been little research on strategies that people can use to develop or enhance authentic leadership behaviors. While there are prescriptions set forth in the practical approach, there is little evidence-based research on whether these prescriptions or how-to strategies actually increase authentic leadership behavior.

In spite of the lack of intervention research, there are common themes from the authentic leadership literature that may be applicable to organizational or practice settings. One theme common to all of the formulations of authentic leadership is that people have the capacity to learn to be authentic leaders. In their original work on authentic leadership, Luthans and Avolio (2003) constructed a model of authentic leadership development. Conceptualizing it as a lifelong learning process, they argued that authentic leadership is a process that can be developed over time. This suggests that human resource departments may be able to foster authentic leadership behaviors in employees who move into leadership positions.

Another theme that can be applied to organizations is the overriding goal of authentic leaders to try to do the "right" thing, to be honest with themselves and others, and to work for the common good. Authentic leadership can have a positive impact in organizations. For example, Cianci, Hannah, Roberts, and Tsakumis (2014) investigated the impact of authentic leadership on followers' morality. Based on the responses of 118 MBA students, they found that authentic leaders significantly inhibited followers from making unethical choices in the face of temptation. Authentic leadership appears to be a critical contextual factor that morally strengthens followers. Cianci et al. suggest that the four components of authentic leadership (i.e., self-awareness, internalized moral perspective, balanced processing, and relational transparency) should be developed in organizational leadership to increase ethical organizational behavior.

Last, authentic leadership is shaped and reformed by critical life events that act as triggers to growth and greater authenticity. Being sensitive to these events and using them as springboards to growth may be relevant to many people who are interested in becoming leaders who are more authentic. Avolio and Wernsing (2008) describe the importance of trigger events as a way to enhance self-awareness. Self-awareness means asking questions: When am I showing my best? When am I being my true self? How can I improve? Such questions are asked as part of training programs in authentic leadership that increase self-awareness. Reflecting on trigger events encourages leaders to consider the meaning and implications of the event for their leadership style.

CASE STUDIES

The following section provides three case studies (Cases 9.1, 9.2, and 9.3) of individuals who demonstrate authentic leadership. The first case is about Sally Helgesen, author of *The Female Advantage: Women's Ways of Leadership* (1990). The second case is about Kassandra Gutierrez, a preschool teacher whose life story is inextricably connected to her teaching. The final case profiles Dr. Brené Brown, a best-selling author and speaker who has a large following around her study of difficult topics including shame, vulnerability, courage, and empathy. At the end of each case study, questions are provided to help you analyze the case using ideas from authentic leadership.

Case 9.1 AM I REALLY A LEADER?

Sally Helgesen was born in the small Midwest town of Saint Cloud, Minnesota. Her mother was a housewife who later taught English, and her father taught speech as a college professor. After attending a local state college, where she majored in English and comparative religion, Helgesen spread her wings and moved to New York, inspired by the classic film *Breakfast at Tiffany's.*

Helgesen found work as a writer, first in advertising and then as an assistant to a columnist at the then-influential *Village Voice*. She contributed freelance articles to magazines such as *Harper's, Glamour, Vogue, Fortune,* and *Inside Sports.* She also returned to school, completing a degree in classics at Hunter College and taking language courses at the city graduate center in preparation for a PhD in comparative religion. She envisioned herself as a college professor, but also enjoyed freelancing. She felt a strong dichotomy within her, part quiet scholar and part footloose dreamer. The conflict bothered her, and she wondered how she would resolve it. Choosing to be a writer—actually declaring herself to be one—seemed scary, grandiose, and fraudulent.

Then one day, while walking on a New York side street in the rain, Helgesen saw an adventuresome black cat running beside her. It reminded her of Holly Golightly's cat in *Breakfast at Tiffany's,* an emblem in the movie for Holly's dreamy temperament and rootlessness. It made her realize how much the freedom and independence offered by her "temporary" career as a writer suited her temperament. Helgesen told the cat she was a writer—she'd never been able to say the words before—and decided she was going to commit to full-time writing, at least for a time. When she saw the opportunity to cover a prominent murder trial in Fort Worth, Texas, she took it.

(Continued)

(Continued)

While covering the trial, Helgesen became intrigued with the culture of Texas, and decided she wanted to write a book on the role of independent oil producers in shaping the region. Doing so required a huge expenditure of time and money, and for almost a year Helgesen lived out of the trunk of her car, staying with friends in remote regions all over Texas. It was lonely and hard and exhilarating, but Helgesen was determined to see the project through. When the book, *Wildcatters* (1981), was published, it achieved little recognition, but Helgesen felt an enormous increase in confidence and commitment as a result of having finished the book. It strengthened her conviction that, for better or worse, she was a writer.

Helgesen moved back to New York and continued to write articles and search around for another book. She also began writing speeches for the CEO at a Fortune 500 company. She loved the work, and particularly enjoyed being an observer of office politics, even though she did not perceive herself to be a part of them. Helgesen viewed her role as being an "outsider looking in," an observer of the culture. She sometimes felt like an actor in a play about an office, but this detachment made her feel professional rather than fraudulent.

As a speechwriter, Helgesen spent a lot of time interviewing people in the companies she worked for. Doing so made her realize that men and women often approach their work in fundamentally different ways. She also became convinced that many of the skills and attitudes women brought to their work were increasingly appropriate for the ways in which organizations were changing, and that women had certain advantages as a result. She also noticed that the unique perspectives of women were seldom valued by CEOs or other organizational leaders, who could have benefited if they had better understood and been more attentive to what women had to offer.

These observations inspired Helgesen to write another book. In 1988, she signed a contract with a major publisher to write a book on what women had to contribute to organizations. Until then, almost everything written about women at work focused on how they needed to change and adapt. Helgesen felt strongly that if women were encouraged to emphasize the negative, they would miss a historic opportunity to help lead organizations in a time of change. The time was right for this message, and *The Female Advantage: Women's Ways of Leadership* (1990) became very successful, topping a number of best-seller charts and remaining steadily in print for nearly 20 years. The book's prominence resulted in numerous speaking and consulting opportunities, and Helgesen began traveling the world delivering seminars and working with a variety of clients.

This acclaim and visibility was somewhat daunting to Helgesen. While she recognized the value of her book, she also knew that she was not a social scientist with a body of theoretical data on women's issues. She saw herself as an author rather than an expert, and the old questions about fraudulence that she had dealt with in her early years in New York began to reassert themselves in a different form. Was she really being authentic? Could she take on the mantle of leadership and all it entailed? In short, she wondered if she could be the leader that people seemed to expect.

The path Helgesen took to answer these questions was simply to present herself for who she was. She was Sally Helgesen, an outsider looking in, a skilled and imaginative observer of current issues. For Helgesen, the path to leadership did not manifest itself in a step-by-step process. Helgesen's leadership began with her own journey of finding herself and accepting her personal authenticity. Through this self-awareness, she grew to trust her own expertise as a writer with a keen eye for current trends in organizational life.

Helgesen continues to be an internationally recognized consultant and speaker on contemporary issues and has published five books. She remains uncertain about whether she will finish her degree in comparative religion and become a college professor, but always keeps in mind the career of I. F. Stone, an influential political writer in the 1950s and 1960s who went back to school and got an advanced degree in classics at the age of 75.

Questions

1. Learning about one's self is an essential step in becoming an authentic leader. What role did self-awareness play in Sally Helgesen's story of leadership?

2. How would you describe the authenticity of Sally Helgesen's leadership?

3. At the end of the case, Sally Helgesen is described as taking on the "mantle of leadership." Was this important for her leadership? How is taking on the mantle of leadership related to a leader's authenticity? Do all leaders reach a point in their careers where embracing the leadership role is essential?

Case 9.2 KASSY'S STORY

Kassandra Gutierrez is a preschool teacher at Living Stones Academy, a private faith-based (Christian) school in Michigan serving a diverse student population in preschool through sixth grade. Forty-four percent are students of color, while nearly 60 percent come from lower socioeconomic status households. Gutierrez recently shared her story about being yourself with the school community:

As a child, it was a challenge for me to find a sense of community. I felt a lack of belonging growing up with my peers because of the difference in my ethnic background, socioeconomic status, and family dynamics.

(Continued)

(Continued)

I am Mexican-American; my dad was born in Oaxaca, Mexico, one of nine children. He came to the United States at 16 to find work to support his family after his father passed away.

My mom, who is white, was raised in Mentone, California, with a mom and step-dad, dad and step-mom, sister, and two half-brothers; you could say I understand "complicated" when it comes to family dynamics.

Growing up as a biracial child, I felt empowered by the fact that I was able to embrace two different cultures. Unfortunately, I felt others around me did not embrace this aspect of me. I often felt overwhelmed and torn between my two identities.

My father's family members would call me "gringa" and "weda" because I had a white mom who didn't cook mole or menudo, I didn't speak Spanish to my parents, and there was a perception that I had money because I went to a private Christian school.

There were many days I would walk onto that school's campus and feel utterly alone among my peers. I was appreciative of having the opportunity to go to a private school, but something didn't feel right. There was a lack of diversity and cultural awareness around me. I didn't see myself represented in the textbooks or within the school's staff and student body. From kindergarten to 8th grade, I didn't have a single teacher that was a person of color. There were two other Mexican-Americans in my classes; but even then, I felt different from them because of my lower socioeconomic status.

My dad started his own landscaping business and early in the morning he would pull up to school in his work truck to drop me off. I felt embarrassed because my classmates would always tease me about his business. All they saw was a Mexican man working a stereotypical job. But I saw a hardworking man who came to the U.S. for a better life, learned English, and started his own business. When my mom would pick me up from school, my classmates made comments and asked questions about her being white and me having dark skin. Sometimes we received curious stares as to why we looked so different. It was exhausting having to explain my family dynamics so many times.

I was bullied quite often. I was called a lot of racial slurs on the playground and was excluded from playing games because of my ethnic background. At home, when I would tell my mom about these experiences or ask questions, she didn't provide support and encouragement in embracing my two cultures or help as I tried to understand why I felt so different from others.

Sadly, those same racial slurs I heard on the playground were being used by my mom towards my dad. My parents had a toxic marriage and they would fight with each other daily. During these arguments, my mom would use hateful and racially derogatory language towards my dad. That kind of hate was not easy to listen to or watch as a child. Why my mother would express that hatred towards a part of who I am was very confusing to me. Also, my father's family would express their dislike about my mom being white. These conflicts between my parents and their families, along with hearing racial slurs towards myself, led me to question my own identity and have thoughts of how easy it would be if I were just white.

So, I grew up as the little Mexican girl who doubted herself everywhere she went. At school, she felt like an outcast because she didn't have white skin or light eyes like many of her teachers and classmates. At home, she doubted herself among her family members who looked like her but had their own stereotypes for her.

Where did I belong? I felt voiceless against those who would tell me who I was or what I should be based on stereotypes they held.

Providing Space for Others

When I look back on my experiences—as a child that was searching for belonging, it is essential for me now as an educator to create an environment that is welcoming, safe, and a place to feel embraced. My classroom is a space where families, children, and I can be vulnerable and transparent to build relationships. There have been children in my class who have experienced hard challenges and trauma, whether it's separation from their parents, conflicts in their households, and insecurities within themselves.

Because of the challenges in my childhood, I can relate to and have conversations with my students. There have been moments where I've embraced a child who was in tears because of the trauma they experienced. It reminds me that there's a reason for the challenges we may face and how God will use them to strengthen us and the relationships we have with one another.

I had a student who was dealing with trauma at home. She was asked questions from other curious 5-year-olds about why her skin was so dark. I could tell she felt insecure about the differences in her appearance from the other children. To ensure a safe community in the classroom, I did not ignore the situation but made it a priority to address it. Through the help of my colleagues, books about diversity, and honest conversations, I made sure to remind her of how God created his daughter in His image. It was a time I could remind all my children the beauty of how God created us to look, speak, and think differently, but all in his image.

Being Authentic and Promoting Authenticity

Belonging is not only essential to my class but in every classroom, preschool through 6th grade at school where I teach. The environment our staff has created

(Continued)

(Continued)

is radically inclusive. There is a deep commitment to teaching students to embrace all cultural, economic, and racial diversities.

We welcome children will all kinds of needs, circumstances, and learning abilities. We are intentional with giving every child, from preschool to 6th grade, a time to use their voice. Time from the academic curriculum is set aside to provide a space for these children to share while teaching the importance of listening. We practice proactive circles to check in on our students and talk about the praises in their lives with their peers and teachers. We also encourage working through hardships they may have with one another through the practice of restorative circles. Proactive and restorative circles have become a part of the daily routine to teach social skills and problem-solving while building a positive classroom community.

Our staff is also intentional about building trustworthy relationships with their students and their colleagues. One day, a student came to school with her hair down naturally after having her hair in braids the week before. She was feeling insecure because her peers had noticed a difference and were asking questions. This student talked to her teacher about her feelings towards her hair and how others were responding. Her teacher encouraged her through her feelings but took it one step further to ensure that this student felt empowered. After talking with her student, she asked a colleague, who is a person of color, to have a one-on-one conversation with the student because she knew her colleague could relate.

Once the student was able to connect with the teacher, the student's confidence increased—not only was she able to connect with someone who looked like her, but she felt supported by not just one teacher, but two.

As a teacher here at this school, I no longer question my own belonging. I bring a feeling of belonging to work with me every day and use it to help my students and colleagues feel the same.

—Reprinted with permission of Kassandra Gutierrez.

Questions

1. In the chapter, Bill George's approach to authentic leadership suggests that truly authentic leaders exhibit passion, strong values, connectedness, consistency, and compassion. In what way has Gutierrez shown these qualities? Which characteristics are most representative of Gutierrez? Discuss.

2. The Model of Authentic Leadership (Figure 9.2) posits that critical life events shape an individual's development as an authentic leader. In what way do you think this has been true for Gutierrez?

3. When leaders tell their life stories, they gain greater self-knowledge and a clearer picture of who they are and their role. Do you think telling her story has been helpful to Gutierrez and the school community? If you were Gutierrez, would you have shared your story so openly? What are the implications for a leader when sharing personal stories with the public? Discuss.

4. As illustrated in Figure 9.2, authentic leaders use their internal moral perspective to guide their behavior and are motivated by higher-order values such as justice and community. Describe Gutierrez's moral perspective and the impact it has on her behavior as a leader. How does her moral perspective impact how she is viewed by others?

Case 9.3 THE ARENA OF AUTHENTICITY

Note: This case study provides insights into Dr. Brené Brown's personal history, her strengths, and the trajectory of her career. You might find it informative to also view her Netflix special, The Call to Courage, or her videos on TED.com, which can provide additional insight into her leadership behavior.

It is not the critic who counts. It is not the man who sits and points out how the doer of deeds could have done things better and how he falls and stumbles. The credit belongs to the man who is actually in the arena whose face is marred with dust and sweat and blood. . . . But when he's in the arena, at best, he wins, and at worst, he loses, but when he fails, when he loses, he does so daring greatly.

This passage, inspired by a speech by former U.S. president Theodore Roosevelt (Dalton, 2002) is one that Dr. Brené Brown teaches, preaches, and lives by.

The author of five number-one *New York Times* best-selling books who has become a world-renowned thought leader and sought-after speaker, Brown is more likely to bill herself as simply a "research professor." She is, in fact, a professor at the University of Houston with a $2 million endowed chair funded by the Huffington Foundation, but also an entrepreneur, CEO, mother, and wife who has built a very large following around the study of such difficult topics as shame, vulnerability, courage, and empathy.

Brown is a high-energy Harry Potter fan who prefers "shit kickers" (cowboy boots) or clogs and jeans to just about any form of business attire and doesn't hesitate to wear these even for her most visible engagements. She would be the first to say that authenticity and courage do not happen without vulnerability. In her words, "vulnerability is not a weakness . . . it is our most accurate measurement of courage—to be vulnerable, to let ourselves be seen, to be honest" (Brown, 2012).

(Continued)

(Continued)

Brown's research data, as well as her personal life experiences, clearly support what she says. The "man in the arena" quote, a rallying cry in many of her books, came to her at a particularly low point. She had recently delivered a TEDxHouston talk on the subject of vulnerability. Rather than deliver a comfortable academic talk complete with academic terminology and data, she opted instead to share a very personal story of her own challenges with vulnerability and an emotional breakdown she experienced when faced with the truth of her own data. That truth—that vulnerability, a topic she despised and personally avoided—and the courage to be imperfect were necessary ingredients to living what she coined as a "whole-hearted life." They could not be separated.

She had chosen research as her livelihood because, in her words, "the definition of research is . . . to study phenomena for the explicit reason to control and predict." But her research results challenged this premise. What she found was the way to live is with vulnerability and to stop controlling and predicting (Brown, 2010).

While the talk was well received, it left Brown feeling exposed and regretting sharing such a deeply personal and revealing story. She found some solace in convincing herself that the talk would likely only be watched by perhaps 500 or so local people. Instead, it went viral. The Power of Vulnerability has become one of the most accessed TED Talks with nearly 50 million views (TED, n.d.).

Instantly propelled into the public spotlight, her mortification was heightened by the anonymous ugly comments made about her on social media, which led her to seek comfort in a jar of peanut butter, binge-watching Downton Abbey, and not leaving her house for three days (Winfrey, 2013). Curious about the time period depicted in the show, Brown did a little research and happened upon Teddy Roosevelt's famous words. It became a turning point for her.

"The fear of shame, the fear of criticism, was so great in my life up until that point—I mean, just paralyzing—that I engineered smallness in my life. I did not take chances. I did not put myself out there. I mean, I just didn't. It wasn't worth it to me to step into my power and play big, because I didn't know if I could literally, physically withstand the criticism" (Efros, Findlay, Mussman, & Restrepo, 2019).

Interestingly, Brown wasn't a stranger to withstanding criticism and marching to the beat of her own drum. Her career was shaped by choices to remain true to her own path.

A fifth-generation Texan, Cassandra Brené Brown was a plucky, curious young girl who grew to be tenacious and outspoken with a quick and infectious wit. However, she spent most of her young adult life feeling like an outsider. This sense of not belonging followed her throughout her school years. In high school, she was not selected for the school's drill team (the Bearkadettes) despite her years of dance lessons, knowing the try-out routine by heart, and weighing six pounds under the required weight. She would later learn that, though she was considered a solid dancer, she just wasn't thought to be "Bearkadette material," leaving her heart broken and ashamed (Brown, 2017).

But these formative years shaped her later success. "I owed my career to not belonging. First as a child, then as a teenager. I found my primary coping mechanism for not belonging in studying people. I was a seeker of pattern and connection. I knew if I could recognize patterns in people's behaviors and connect those patterns to what people were feeling and doing, I could find my way," she said. "I used my pattern recognition skills to anticipate what people wanted, what they thought, or what they were doing. I learned how to say the right thing or show up the right way. I became an expert fitter-in, a chameleon" (Brown, 2017, p. 16).

After high school, Brown had unsettled years of rebellion, hitchhiking across Europe and working as a bartender and waitress, gaining a variety of life experiences. She returned to college and, at 29, graduated at the top of her class with a bachelor's degree in social work and went on to graduate school. Through her studies, Brown found a passion for social work and qualitative research. She became interested in and trained in a methodology known as grounded theory, which starts with a topic rather than a theory and, through the process of collecting and analyzing data based on discussions with the study participants, reveals patterns and theories. The grounded theory model fit Brown's gift for storytelling and her ability to connect patterns in her subjects through the listening and observation skills she developed as coping mechanisms in her teens.

"I fell in love with the richness and depth of qualitative research," she said. "Storytelling is my DNA, and I couldn't resist the idea of research as story-catching. Stories are data with a soul and no methodology honors that more than grounded theory" (Brown, 2019b).

Unfortunately, the grounded theory model is a departure from traditional academic research, which tends to place higher value on the cleaner, more measurable outcomes of quantitative research. Despite being discouraged by other academics and counseled to not use the methodology for her doctoral dissertation, Brown pushed forward. And like the research method she espouses, Brown allowed the stories emerging from the data to shape her explorations, and she began to study the emotion of shame.

"I didn't sign on to study shame—one of the most (if not the most) complex and multifaceted emotions that we experience. A topic that not only took me six years to understand, but an emotion that is so powerful that the mere mention of the word *shame* triggers discomfort and avoidance in people. I innocently started with an interest in learning more about the anatomy of connection," she says. "Because the research participants had the courage to share their stories,

(Continued)

(Continued)

experiences, and wisdom, I forged a path that defined my career and my life" (Brown, 2019b).

Those research participants, who often asked Brown to share her findings, inspired her to once again deviate from a traditional academic trajectory by publishing her work in more mainstream publications and journals rather than as peer-reviewed articles in academic journals. Soon her work became available for the masses and later became best-selling books.

Brown brings herself totally to every speaking engagement, despite efforts to temper the subject matter of her talks or her way of delivering them. She has been asked by some not to talk about uncomfortable things like shame and vulnerability, even though those are her areas of expertise. Religious groups have requested she not cuss, and business groups have asked she not use the word *God* in her talks. She has been asked to dress differently. But Brown says the only way she can be effective is by being completely herself, knowing that you can't impress on others the importance of vulnerability, and how it relates to courage, if you don't have the courage to be authentically yourself.

Being able to maintain this authenticity isn't an innate skill, Brown says, but requires using "shared language, skills, tools, and daily practices that can support us through the rumble." She defines "the rumble" as a discussion, conversation, or meeting defined by a commitment to such things as being vulnerable, sticking with the messiness of problem identification and problem solving, being fearless in "owning our parts," and "listening with the same passion with which we want to be heard" (Brown, 2019c).

"More than anything else, when someone says, 'Let's rumble,' it cues me to show up with an open heart and mind so we can serve the work and each other, not our egos" (Brown, 2019c).

The fearlessness of owning who you are and risking vulnerability to find the courage to bring yourself authentically into your work, your family, and your community is what Brown is all about. In living by the ideals she espouses to millions of followers, she has unwittingly achieved the true belonging that had eluded her. She encapsulates her philosophy with a simple observation: "True belonging doesn't require us to change who we are. It requires us to be who we are" (Brown, 2017, p. 40).

Questions

1. Do you find Brené Brown to be an authentic leader? Why or why not?

2. This chapter discusses three different perspectives—intrapersonal, interpersonal, and developmental—used to define authentic leadership. Discuss how these perspectives do or do not fit Brené Brown.

3. Discuss how each of the five dimensions of authentic leadership identified by George apply to Brené Brown:

   a. Purpose

   b. Values

   c. Relationships

   d. Self-discipline

   e. Heart

4. Discuss how each of the components of the theoretical approach apply to Brené Brown:

   a. Self-awareness

   b. Internalized moral perspective

   c. Balanced processing

   d. Relational transparency

5. This approach describes four key positive psychological attributes that impact authentic leadership. Discuss each in relationship to Brené Brown.

   a. Confidence

   b. Hope

   c. Optimism

   d. Resilience

6. Critical life events are a key component in the authentic leadership model (see Figure 9.2). What do you think are the critical events that shaped Brené Brown and who she has become?

—Barbara Russell, MBA, BSCS, BBA, Chemeketa Community College

LEADERSHIP INSTRUMENT

The Authentic Leadership Questionnaire (ALQ) was created by Walumbwa and associates (2008) to explore and validate the assumptions of authentic leadership. It is a 16-item instrument that measures four factors of authentic leadership: self-awareness, internalized moral perspective, balanced processing, and relational transparency. Based on samples in China, Kenya, and the United States, Walumbwa and associates validated the dimensions of the instrument and found it positively related to outcomes such as organizational citizenship, organizational commitment, and satisfaction with supervisor and performance. To obtain this instrument, contact Mind Garden Inc., in Menlo Park, California, or visit www.mindgarden.com.

In this section, we provide an authentic leadership self-assessment to help you determine your own level of authentic leadership. This questionnaire will help you understand how authentic leadership is measured and provide you with your own scores on items that characterize authentic leadership. The questionnaire includes 16 questions that assess the four major components of authentic leadership discussed earlier in this chapter: self-awareness, internalized moral perspective, balanced processing, and relational transparency. Your results on this self-assessment questionnaire will give you information about your level of authentic leadership on these underlying dimensions of authentic leadership. This questionnaire is intended for practical applications to help you understand the complexities of authentic leadership. It is not designed for research purposes.

Authentic Leadership Self-Assessment Questionnaire

Purpose: The purpose of this questionnaire is to assess facets of your authentic leadership.

Instructions: This questionnaire contains items about different dimensions of authentic leadership. There are no right or wrong responses, so please answer honestly. Use the following scale when responding to each statement by writing the number from the scale that you feel most accurately characterizes your response to the statement.

Key: 1 = Strongly   2 = Disagree   3 = Neutral   4 = Agree   5 = Strongly
         disagree   agree

1. I can list my three greatest weaknesses.   1 2 3 4 5

2. My actions reflect my core values.   1 2 3 4 5

3. I seek others' opinions before making up my own mind.   1 2 3 4 5

4. I openly share my feelings with others.   1 2 3 4 5

5. I can list my three greatest strengths.   1 2 3 4 5

6. I do not allow group pressure to control me.   1 2 3 4 5

7. I listen closely to the ideas of those who disagree with me.   1 2 3 4 5

8. I let others know who I truly am as a person.   1 2 3 4 5

9. I seek feedback as a way of understanding who I really am   1 2 3 4 5
    as a person.

10. Other people know where I stand on controversial issues.   1 2 3 4 5

11. I do not emphasize my own point of view at the expense   1 2 3 4 5
    of others.

12. I rarely present a "false" front to others.   1 2 3 4 5

13. I accept the feelings I have about myself.   1 2 3 4 5

14. My morals guide what I do as a leader.   1 2 3 4 5

15. I listen very carefully to the ideas of others before making   1 2 3 4 5
    decisions.

16. I admit my mistakes to others.   1 2 3 4 5

Scoring

1. Sum the responses on items 1, 5, 9, and 13 (self-awareness).

2. Sum the responses on items 2, 6, 10, and 14 (internalized moral perspective).

3. Sum the responses on items 3, 7, 11, and 15 (balanced processing).

4. Sum the responses on items 4, 8, 12, and 16 (relational transparency).

(Continued)

(Continued)

Total Scores

Self-Awareness: _____

Internalized Moral Perspective: _____

Balanced Processing: _____

Relational Transparency: _____

Scoring Interpretation

This self-assessment questionnaire is designed to measure your authentic leadership by assessing four components of the process: self-awareness, internalized moral perspective, balanced processing, and relational transparency. By comparing your scores on each of these components, you can determine which are your stronger and which are your weaker components in each category. You can interpret your authentic leadership scores using the following guideline: high = 16–20 and low = 15 and below. Scores in the upper range indicate stronger authentic leadership, whereas scores in the lower range indicate weaker authentic leadership.

SUMMARY

As a result of leadership failures in the public and private sectors, authentic leadership is emerging in response to societal demands for genuine, trustworthy, and good leadership. Authentic leadership describes leadership that is transparent, morally grounded, and responsive to people's needs and values. Even though research on authentic leadership is still in the early stages of development, the study of authentic leadership is timely and worthwhile, offering hope to people who long for true leadership.

Although there is no single accepted definition of authentic leadership, it can be conceptualized intrapersonally, interpersonally, and developmentally. The intrapersonal perspective focuses on the leader and the leader's knowledge, self-regulation, and self-concept. The interpersonal perspective claims that authentic leadership is a collective process, created by leaders and followers together. The developmental perspective emphasizes major components of authentic leadership that develop over a lifetime and are triggered by major life events.

The practical approach to authentic leadership provides basic "how to" steps to become an authentic leader. George's (2003) approach identifies five basic dimensions of authentic leadership and the corresponding behavioral characteristics individuals need to develop to become authentic leaders.

In the social science literature, a theoretical approach to authentic leadership is emerging. Drawing from the fields of leadership, positive organizational scholarship, and ethics, researchers have identified four major components of authentic leadership: self-awareness, internalized moral perspective, balanced processing, and relational transparency.

In addition, researchers have found that authentic leadership is influenced by a leader's positive psychological capacities, moral reasoning, and critical life events.

Authentic leadership has several positive features. First, it provides an answer to people who are searching for good and sound leadership in an uncertain world. Second, authentic leadership provides broad guidelines about how leaders can learn to become authentic. Third, it has an explicit moral dimension that asserts that leaders need to do what is "right" and "good" for their followers and society. Fourth, it is framed as a process that is developed by leaders over time rather than as a fixed trait. Last, authentic leadership can be measured with a theory-based instrument.

There are also negative features to authentic leadership. First, the ideas set forth in the practical approach need to be treated cautiously because they have not been fully substantiated by research. Second, the moral component of authentic leadership is not fully explained. For example, it does not describe how values such as justice and community are related to authentic leadership. Third, the rationale for including positive psychological capacities as an inherent part of a model of authentic leadership has not been fully explicated and remains as a shaky foundation for use of the theory by consultants and inspirational speakers. Fourth, there is evidence emerging that authentic leadership may be ineffective with the millennial generation. Finally, there is a lack of evidence regarding the effectiveness of authentic leadership and how it is related to positive organizational outcomes.

In summary, authentic leadership is a new and exciting area of research that holds a great deal of promise. As more research is conducted on authentic leadership, a clearer picture will emerge about the true nature of the process and the assumptions and principles that it encompasses.

Servant Leadership

DESCRIPTION

Servant leadership is a paradox—an approach to leadership that runs counter to common sense. Our everyday images of leadership do not coincide with leaders being servants. Leaders influence, and servants follow. How can leadership be both service *and* influence? How can a person be a leader *and* a servant at the same time? Although servant leadership seems contradictory and challenges our traditional beliefs about leadership, it is an approach that offers a unique perspective.

Servant leadership, which originated in the writings of Greenleaf (1970, 1972, 1977), has been of interest to leadership scholars for more than 40 years. Until recently, little empirical research on servant leadership has appeared in established peer-reviewed journals. Most of the academic and nonacademic writing on the topic has been prescriptive, focusing on how servant leadership should ideally be, rather than descriptive, focusing on what servant leadership actually is in practice (van Dierendonck, 2011). However, in the past 10 years, multiple publications have helped to clarify servant leadership and substantiate its basic assumptions.

Similar to earlier leadership theories discussed in this book (e.g., skills approach and behavioral approach), servant leadership is an approach focusing on leadership from the point of view of leaders and their behaviors. Servant leadership emphasizes that leaders be attentive to the concerns of their followers, empathize with them, and nurture them. Servant leaders put followers *first*, empower them, and help them develop their full personal capacities.

In addition, like the authentic leadership approach, which is discussed in Chapter 9, and ethical leadership, which is explored in Chapter 15, servant leadership is viewed as a "moral" form of leadership. Servant leaders are ethical and lead in ways that serve the greater good of the organization, community, and society at large. What sets servant leadership apart from other moral leadership approaches is its focus on serving these multiple stakeholders (Lemoine, Hartnell, & Leroy, 2019).

Servant Leadership Defined

What is servant leadership? Scholars have addressed this approach from many different perspectives resulting in a variety of definitions of servant leadership. Greenleaf (1970) provides the most frequently referenced definition:

> [Servant leadership] begins with the natural feeling that one wants to serve, to serve *first*. Then conscious choice brings one to aspire to lead.... The difference manifests itself in the care taken by the servant—first to make sure that other people's highest priority needs are being served. The best test ... is: do those served grow as persons; do they, *while being served*, become healthier, wiser, freer, more autonomous, more likely themselves to become servants? *And*, what is the effect on the least privileged in society; will they benefit, or, at least, will they not be further deprived? (p. 15)

Although complex, this definition sets forth the basic ideas of servant leadership that have been highlighted by current scholars. Servant leaders place the good of followers over their own self-interests and emphasize follower development (Hale & Fields, 2007). They demonstrate strong moral behavior toward followers (Graham, 1991; Walumbwa, Hartnell, & Oke, 2010), the organization, and other stakeholders (Ehrhart, 2004). Practicing servant leadership comes more naturally for some than for others, but everyone can learn to be a servant leader (Spears, 2010). Although servant leadership is sometimes treated by others as a trait, in our discussion servant leadership is viewed as a set of behaviors.

Historical Basis of Servant Leadership

Robert K. Greenleaf coined the term *servant leadership* and is the author of the seminal works on the subject. Greenleaf's persona and writings have significantly influenced how servant leadership has developed on the practical and theoretical level. He founded the Center for Applied Ethics in 1964, now the Greenleaf Center for Servant Leadership, which provides a clearinghouse and focal point for research and writing on servant leadership.

Greenleaf worked for 40 years at AT&T and, after retiring, began exploring how institutions function and how they could better serve society. He was intrigued by issues of power and authority and how individuals in organizations could creatively support each other. Decidedly against coercive leadership, Greenleaf advocated using communication to build consensus in groups.

Greenleaf credits his formulation of servant leadership to Hermann Hesse's (1956) novel *The Journey to the East*. It tells the story of a group of travelers on a mythical journey who are accompanied by a servant who does menial chores for the travelers but also sustains them with his spirits and song. The servant's presence has an extraordinary impact on the group. When the servant becomes lost and disappears from the group, the travelers fall into disarray and abandon the journey. Without the servant, they are unable to carry on. It was the servant who was ultimately leading the group, emerging as a leader through his selfless care of the travelers.

In addition to serving, Greenleaf states that a servant leader has a social responsibility to be concerned about those who are marginalized and those less privileged. If inequalities and social injustices exist, a servant leader tries to remove them (Graham, 1991). In becoming a servant leader, a leader uses less institutional power and control while shifting authority to those who are being led. Servant leadership values community because it provides a face-to-face opportunity for individuals to experience interdependence, respect, trust, and individual growth (Greenleaf, 1970).

Ten Characteristics of a Servant Leader

In an attempt to clarify servant leadership for practitioners, Spears (2002) identified 10 characteristics in Greenleaf's writings that are central to the development of servant leadership. Together, these characteristics comprise the first model or conceptualization of servant leadership.

1. *Listening.* Communication between leaders and followers is an interactive process that includes sending and receiving messages (i.e., talking and listening). Servant leaders communicate by listening first. They recognize that listening is a learned discipline that involves hearing and being receptive to what others have to say. Through listening, servant leaders acknowledge the viewpoint of followers and validate these perspectives.

2. *Empathy.* Empathy is "standing in the shoes" of another person and attempting to see the world from that person's point of view. Empathetic servant leaders demonstrate that they truly understand what followers are thinking and feeling. When a servant leader shows empathy, it is confirming and validating for the follower. It makes the follower feel unique.

3. *Healing.* To heal means to make whole. Servant leaders care about the personal well-being of their followers. They support followers by helping them overcome personal problems. Greenleaf argues that the process of healing is a two-way street—in helping followers become whole, servant leaders themselves are healed.

4. *Awareness.* For Greenleaf, awareness is a quality within servant leaders that makes them acutely attuned and receptive to their physical, social, and political environments. It includes understanding oneself and the impact one has on others. With awareness, servant leaders are able to step aside and view themselves and their own perspectives in the greater context of the situation.

5. *Persuasion.* Persuasion is clear and persistent communication that convinces others to change. As opposed to coercion, which utilizes positional authority to force compliance, persuasion creates change through the use of gentle nonjudgmental argument. According to Spears (2002), Greenleaf's emphasis on persuasion over coercion is perhaps related to his denominational affiliation with the Religious Society of Friends (Quakers).

6. *Conceptualization.* Conceptualization refers to an individual's ability to be a visionary for an organization, providing a clear sense of its goals and direction. This characteristic goes beyond day-to-day operational thinking to focus on the "big picture." Conceptualization also equips servant leaders to respond to complex organizational problems in creative ways, enabling them to deal with the intricacies of the organization in relationship to its long-term goals.

7. *Foresight.* Foresight encompasses a servant leader's ability to know the future. It is an ability to predict what is coming based on what is occurring in the present and what has happened in the past. For Greenleaf, foresight has an ethical dimension because he believes leaders should be held accountable for any failures to anticipate what reasonably could be foreseen and to act on that understanding.

8. *Stewardship.* Stewardship is about taking responsibility for the leadership role entrusted to the leader. Servant leaders accept the responsibility to carefully manage the people and organization they have been given to lead. In addition, they hold the organization in trust for the greater good of society.

9. *Commitment to the growth of people.* Greenleaf's conceptualization of servant leadership places a premium on treating each follower as a unique person with intrinsic value that goes beyond the individual's tangible contributions to the organization. Servant leaders are committed to helping each person in the organization grow personally and professionally. Commitment can take many forms, including providing followers with opportunities for career development, helping them develop new work skills, taking a personal interest in their ideas, and involving them in decision making (Spears, 2002).

10. *Building community.* Servant leadership fosters the development of community. A community is a collection of individuals who have shared interests and pursuits and feel a sense of unity and relatedness. Community allows followers to identify with something greater than themselves that they value. Servant leaders build community to provide a place where people can feel safe and connected with others, but are still allowed to express their own individuality.

These 10 characteristics of servant leadership represent Greenleaf's seminal work on the servant as leader. They provide a creative lens from which to view the complexities of servant leadership.

Building a Theory About Servant Leadership

For more than three decades after Greenleaf's original writings, servant leadership remained a set of loosely defined characteristics and normative principles. In this form it was widely accepted as a leadership approach, rather than a theory, that has strong heuristic and practical value. Praise for servant leadership came from a wide range of well-known leadership writers, including Bennis (2002), Blanchard and Hodges (2003), Covey (2002), DePree (2002), Senge (2002), and Wheatley (2002). At the same time, servant leadership was adopted as a guiding philosophy in many well-known organizations such as The Toro Company, Herman Miller, Synovus Financial Corporation, ServiceMaster, Men's Wearhouse, The Container Store, Southwest Airlines, and TDIndustries (Spears, 2002). Although novel and paradoxical, the basic ideas and prescriptions of servant leadership resonated with many as an ideal way to run an organization.

More recently, researchers have begun to examine the conceptual underpinnings of servant leadership in an effort to build a theory about it. This has resulted in a wide array of models that describe servant leadership that incorporate a multitude of variables. For example, Russell and Stone (2002) developed a practical model of servant leadership that contained 20 attributes, 9 functional characteristics (distinctive behaviors observed in the workplace), and 11 accompanying characteristics that augment these behaviors. Similarly, Patterson (2003) created a value-based model of servant leadership that distinguished 7 constructs that characterize the virtues and shape the behaviors of servant leaders.

Other conceptualizations of servant leadership have emerged from researchers' efforts to develop and validate instruments to measure the core dimensions of the servant leadership process. Table 10.1 provides a summary of some of these studies, illustrating clearly the extensiveness of characteristics related to servant leadership. This table demonstrates how servant leadership is treated as a trait phenomenon (e.g., courage, humility) in some studies while other researchers regard it as a behavioral process (e.g., serving and developing others).

Table 10.1 also exhibits the lack of agreement among researchers on what specific characteristics define servant leadership. While some of the studies include common characteristics, such as humility or empowerment, none of the studies conceptualize servant leadership in exactly the same way. Most recently, Coetzer, Bussin, and Geldenhuys (2017) analyzed the existing literature and created a framework that summarizes the functions of servant leadership to make it more practical in organizations. They highlight 8 servant leadership characteristics (authenticity, humility, integrity, listening, compassion, accountability, courage,

TABLE 10.1 Key Characteristics of Servant Leadership

Laub (1999)	Wong & Davey (2007)	Barbuto & Wheeler (2006)	Dennis & Bocarnea (2005)	Sendjaya, Sarros, & Santora (2008)	van Dierendonck & Nuijten (2011)
• Developing people	• Serving and developing others	• Altruistic calling	• Empowerment	• Transforming influence	• Empowerment
• Sharing leadership	• Consulting and involving others	• Emotional healing	• Trust	• Voluntary subordination	• Humility
• Displaying authenticity	• Humility and selflessness	• Persuasive mapping	• Humility	• Authentic self	• Standing back
• Valuing people	• Modeling integrity and authenticity	• Organizational stewardship	• Agapao love	• Transcendental spirituality	• Authenticity
• Providing leadership	• Inspiring and influencing others	• Wisdom	• Vision	• Covenantal relationship	• Forgiveness
• Building community				• Responsible morality	• Courage
					• Accountability
					• Stewardship

Source: Adapted from "Servant Leadership: A Review and Synthesis," by D. van Dierendonck, 2011, Journal of Management, 37(4), pp. 1228-1261.

and altruism) and 4 competencies, 10 measures, and 3 outcomes of servant leadership. Although scholars are not in agreement regarding the primary attributes of servant leadership, all these studies provide the groundwork necessary for the development of a refined model of servant leadership.

MODEL OF SERVANT LEADERSHIP

This chapter presents a servant leadership model based on Liden, Wayne, Zhao, and Henderson (2008) and Liden, Panaccio, Hu, and Meuser (2014) that has three main components: *antecedent conditions, servant leader behaviors*, and *outcomes* (Figure 10.1). The model is intended to clarify the phenomenon of servant leadership and provide a framework for understanding its complexities.

Antecedent Conditions

As shown on the left side of Figure 10.1, three antecedent, or existing, conditions have an impact on servant leadership: *context and culture, leader attributes*, and *follower receptivity*. These conditions are not inclusive of all the conditions that affect servant leadership, but do represent some factors likely to influence the leadership process.

FIGURE 10.1 Model of Servant Leadership

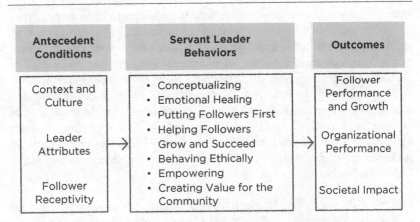

Antecedent Conditions	Servant Leader Behaviors	Outcomes
Context and Culture	• Conceptualizing • Emotional Healing • Putting Followers First	Follower Performance and Growth
Leader Attributes	• Helping Followers Grow and Succeed • Behaving Ethically • Empowering	Organizational Performance
Follower Receptivity	• Creating Value for the Community	Societal Impact

Sources: Adapted from Liden, R. C., Panaccio, A., Hu, J., & Meuser, J. D. (2014). Servant leadership: Antecedents, consequences, and contextual moderators. In D. V. Day (Ed.), *The Oxford handbook of leadership and organizations*. Oxford, UK: Oxford University Press; and van Dierendonck, D. (2011). Servant leadership: A review and syntheses. *Journal of Management, 37*(4), 1228–1261.

Context and Culture. Servant leadership does not occur in a vacuum but occurs within a given organizational context and a particular culture. The nature of each of these affects the way servant leadership is carried out. For example, in health care and nonprofit settings, the norm of caring is more prevalent, while for Wall Street corporations it is more common to have competition as an operative norm. Because the norms differ, the ways servant leadership is performed may vary.

Dimensions of culture (see Chapter 16, "Culture and Leadership") will also influence servant leadership. For example, in cultures where power distance is low (e.g., Nordic Europe) and power is shared equally among people at all levels of society, servant leadership may be more common. In cultures with low humane orientation (e.g., Germanic Europe), servant leadership may present more of a challenge. The point is that cultures influence the way servant leadership is able to be achieved.

Leader Attributes. As in any leadership situation, the qualities and disposition of the leader influence the servant leadership process. Individuals bring their own traits and ideas about leading to leadership situations. Some may feel a deep desire to serve or are strongly motivated to lead. Others may be driven by a sense of higher calling (Sendjaya, Sarros, & Santora, 2008). These dispositions shape how individuals demonstrate servant leadership. In addition, people differ in areas such as moral development, emotional intelligence, and self-determinedness, and these traits interact with their ability to engage in servant leadership.

Recent research has attempted to determine if specific leader traits are important to servant leadership. Emotional intelligence, or the leader's ability to monitor the feelings, beliefs, and internal states of the self and followers, has been identified as an important attribute for a leader implementing a servant leader ideology (Barbuto, Gottfredson, & Searle, 2014; Beck, 2014; Chiniara & Bentein, 2016). An empirical study by Hunter and colleagues (2013) concluded that "leaders scoring high in agreeableness and low in extraversion were more likely to be perceived as servant leaders by their followers" (p. 327). In addition, a study by Sousa and van Dierendonck (2017) determined that having humility can make servant leaders more impactful regardless of their hierarchical position in an organization.

Follower Receptivity. The receptivity of followers is a factor that appears to influence the impact of servant leadership on outcomes such as personal and organizational job performance. Follower receptivity concerns the question "Do all followers show a desire for servant leadership?" Research suggests the answer may be no. Some followers do not want to work with servant leaders. They equate servant leadership with micromanagement, and report that they do not want their leader to get to know them or try to help, develop, or guide them (Liden et al., 2008). Similarly, empirical studies have shown that when servant leadership was matched with followers who desired it, this type of leadership had a positive impact on performance and organizational citizenship behavior (Meuser, Liden, Wayne, & Henderson, 2011; Otero-Neira, Varela-Neira, & Bande, 2016; Ozyilmaz & Cicek, 2015). The opposite was seen when there was no match between servant leadership and the desire of followers for it. It appears that, for some followers, servant leadership has a positive impact and, for others, servant leadership is not effective. A recent experiment found that servant leadership benefits followers who have higher levels of self-interest. Followers who are inclined to care only about themselves were more likely to improve their helping behaviors after exposure to a manager who supports helping behaviors (Wu, Liden, Liao, & Wayne, 2020).

Servant Leader Behaviors

The middle component of Figure 10.1 identifies seven *servant leader behaviors* that are the core of the servant leadership process. These behaviors emerged from Liden et al.'s (2008) vigorous efforts to develop and validate a measure of servant leadership. The findings from their research provide evidence for the soundness of viewing servant leadership as a multidimensional process. Collectively, these behaviors are the central focus of servant leadership. Individually, each behavior makes a unique contribution.

Conceptualizing. Conceptualizing refers to the servant leader's thorough understanding of the organization—its purposes, complexities, and mission. This capacity allows servant leaders to think through multifaceted problems, to know if something is going wrong, and to address problems creatively in accordance with the overall goals of the organization.

For example, Kate Simpson, a senior nursing supervisor in the emergency room of a large hospital, uses conceptualizing to lead her department. She fully understands the mission of the hospital and, at the same time, knows how to effectively manage staff on a day-to-day basis. Her staff members say Simpson has a sixth sense about what is best for people. She is known for her wisdom in dealing with difficult patients and helping staff diagnose complex medical problems. Her abilities, competency, and value as a servant leader earned her the hospital's Caregiver of the Year Award.

Emotional Healing. Emotional healing involves being sensitive to the personal concerns and well-being of others. It includes recognizing others' problems and being willing to take the time to address them. Servant leaders who exhibit emotional healing make themselves available to others, stand by them, and provide them with support.

Emotional healing is apparent in the work of Father John, a much sought-after hospice priest on Chicago's South Side. Father John has a unique approach to hospice patients: He doesn't encourage, give advice, or read Scripture. Instead he simply listens to them. "When you face death, the only important thing in life is relationships," he said. "I practice the art of standing by. I think it is more important to come just to be there than to do anything else."

Putting Followers First. Putting others first is the sine qua non of servant leadership—the defining characteristic. It means using actions and words that clearly demonstrate to followers that their concerns are a priority, including placing followers' interests and success ahead of those of the leader. It may mean leaders break from their own tasks to assist followers with theirs.

Dr. Autumn Klein, a widely published health education professor at a major research university, is responsible for several ongoing large interdisciplinary public health studies. Although she is the principal investigator on these studies, when multiauthored articles are submitted for publication, Dr. Klein puts the names of other researchers before her own. She chooses to let others be recognized because she knows it will benefit them in their annual performance reviews. She puts the success of her colleagues ahead of her own interests.

Helping Followers Grow and Succeed. This behavior refers to knowing followers' professional or personal goals and helping them to accomplish those aspirations. Servant leaders make followers' career development a priority, including mentoring followers and providing them with support. At its core, helping followers grow and succeed is about aiding these individuals to become self-actualized, reaching their fullest human potential.

An example of how a leader helps others grow and succeed is Mr. Yon Kim, a high school orchestra teacher who consistently receives praise from parents for his outstanding work with students. Mr. Kim is a skilled violinist with high musical standards, but he does not let that get in the way of helping each student, from the most highly accomplished to the least capable. Students like Mr. Kim because he listens to them and treats them as adults. He gives feedback without being judgmental. Many of his former students have gone on to become music majors. They often visit Mr. Kim to let him know how important he was to them. Yon Kim is a servant leader who helps students grow through his teaching and guidance.

Behaving Ethically. Behaving ethically is doing the right thing in the right way. It is holding to strong ethical standards, including being open, honest, and fair with followers. Servant leaders do not compromise their ethical principles in order to achieve success.

An example of ethical behavior is how CEO Elizabeth Angliss responded when one of her employees brought her a copy of a leaked document from their company's chief competitor, outlining its plans to go after some of

Angliss's largest customers. Although she knew the document undoubtedly had valuable information, she shredded it instead of reading it. She then called the rival CEO and told him she had received the document and wanted him to be aware that he might have a security issue within his company. "I didn't know if what I received was real or not," she explains. "But it didn't matter. If it was the real thing, someone on his end did something wrong, and my company wasn't going to capitalize on that."

Empowering. Empowering refers to allowing followers the freedom to be independent, make decisions on their own, and be self-sufficient. It is a way for leaders to share power with followers by allowing them to have control. Empowerment builds followers' confidence in their own capacities to think and act on their own because they are given the freedom to handle difficult situations in the way they feel is best.

For example, a college professor teaching a large lecture class empowers two teaching assistants assigned to him by letting them set their own office hours, independently grade student papers, and practice teaching by giving one of the weekly class lectures. They become confident in their teaching abilities and bring new ideas to the professor to try in the classroom.

Creating Value for the Community. Servant leaders create value for the community by consciously and intentionally giving back to the community. They are involved in local activities and encourage followers to also volunteer for community service. Creating value for the community is one way for leaders to link the purposes and goals of an organization with the broader purposes of the community.

An example of creating value for the community can be seen in the leadership of Mercedes Urbanez, principal of Alger High School. Alger is an alternative high school in a midsize community with three other high schools. Urbanez's care and concern for students at Alger is remarkable. Ten percent of Alger's students have children, so the school provides on-site day care. Fifteen percent of the students are on probation, and Alger is often their last stop before dropping out and becoming further entangled with the criminal justice system. While the other schools in town foster competition and push Advanced Placement courses, Alger focuses on removing the barriers that keep its students from excelling and offers courses that provide what its students need, including multimedia skills, reading remediation, and parenting.

Under Urbanez, Alger High School is a model alternative school appreciated at every level in the community. Students, who have failed in other schools, find they have a safe place to go where they are accepted and adults try to help them solve their problems. Law enforcement supports the school's efforts to help these students get back into the mainstream of society and away from crime. The other high schools in the community know that Alger provides services they find difficult to provide. Urbanez serves those who are marginalized in the community, and the whole community reaps the benefits.

Different researchers have used the servant leadership behaviors as identified by Liden et al.'s (2008) work as well as the work of Page and Wong (2000), Sendjaya and Sarros (2002), Dennis and Bocarnea (2005), and Barbuto and Wheeler (2006) as the foundation to understand servant leadership and how it is established in an organization. For example, Winston and Fields (2015) developed and validated a scale that identifies 10 leader behaviors that are essential to developing servant leadership in an organization.

Outcomes

Although servant leadership focuses primarily on leader behaviors, it is also important to examine the potential outcomes of servant leadership. The outcomes of servant leadership are *follower performance and growth*, *organizational performance*, and *societal impact* (see Figure 10.1). As Greenleaf highlighted in his original work (1970), the central goal of servant leadership is to create healthy organizations that nurture individual growth, strengthen organizational performance, and, in the end, produce a positive impact on society.

Follower Performance and Growth. In the model of servant leadership, most of the servant leader behaviors focus directly on recognizing followers' contributions and helping them realize their human potential. The expected outcome for followers is greater self-actualization. That is, followers will realize their full capabilities when leaders nurture them, help them with their personal goals, and give them control.

Another outcome of servant leadership, suggested by Meuser et al. (2011), is that it will have a favorable impact on followers' in-role performance—the way followers do their assigned work. When servant leaders were matched with followers who were open to this type of leadership, the results were positive. Followers became more effective at accomplishing their jobs and fulfilling their job descriptions. For example, Bauer, Perrot, Liden, and Erdogan (2019) found that when servant leaders helped new employees "learn the ropes" in a new job, those employees' proactivity increased.

Another example is a study of servant leadership in a sales setting in Spain that found sales managers' servant leadership was directly related to salespeople's performance within the organization and indirectly related to salespeople's identification with the organization. In addition, it enhanced the salespeople's adaptability and proactivity by positively affecting their self-efficacy and intrinsic motivation (Bande, Fernández-Ferrín, Varela-Neira, & Otero-Neira, 2016; Otero-Neira et al., 2016). Hunter et al. (2013) found that servant leadership fosters a positive service climate, induces followers to help coworkers and sell products, and reduces turnover and disengagement behaviors. In addition, Chiniara and Bentein (2016) found that when servant leaders attended to followers' needs for autonomy, competence, and relatedness, it had a positive impact on followers' task performance and organizational citizenship behavior.

Finally, another expected result of servant leadership is that followers themselves may become servant leaders. Greenleaf's conceptualization of servant leadership hypothesizes that when followers receive care and empowerment from ethical leaders, they, in turn, will likely begin treating others in this way. Servant leadership would produce a ripple effect in which servant leaders create more servant leaders. For example, Hunter et al. (2013) report that employees who perceived their leaders as having servant qualities were more likely to help their coworkers with task and interpersonal matters, as well as less likely to disengage.

Organizational Performance. Initial research has shown that, in addition to positively affecting followers and their performance, servant leadership has an influence on organizational performance. Several studies have found a positive relationship between servant leadership and organizational citizenship behaviors, which are follower behaviors that go beyond the basic requirements of the follower's duties and help the overall functioning of the organization (Ehrhart, 2004; Liden et al., 2008; Neubert, Kacmar, Carlson, Chonko, & Roberts, 2008; Walumbwa et al., 2010).

Servant leadership also affects the way organizational teams function. Hu and Liden (2011) found that servant leadership enhanced team effectiveness by increasing the shared confidence among team members that they could be effective as a work group. Furthermore, their results showed that servant leadership contributed positively to team potency by enhancing group process and clarity. However, when servant leadership was absent, team potency decreased, despite clearer goals. In essence, it frustrates people to know exactly what the goal is, but not get the support needed to accomplish the goal.

While research on the organizational outcomes of servant leadership is in its initial stages, more and more studies are being undertaken to substantiate the direct and indirect ways that servant leadership is related to organizational performance.

Societal Impact. Another outcome expected of servant leadership is that it is likely to have a positive impact on society. Although societal impact is not commonly measured in studies of servant leadership, several examples of servant leadership's impact are highly visible. One example we are all familiar with is the work of Mother Teresa, whose years of service for those who are hungry, homeless, and rejected resulted in the creation of a new religious order, the Missionaries of Charity. This order now has more than 1 million workers in over 40 countries that operate hospitals, schools, and hospices for people living in poverty. Mother Teresa's servant leadership has had an extraordinary impact on society throughout the world.

In the business world, an example of the societal impact of servant leadership can be observed at Southwest Airlines (see Case 10.2). Leaders at Southwest instituted an "others first" organizational philosophy in the management of the company, which starts with how it treats its employees. This philosophy is adhered to by those employees who themselves become servant leaders in regards to the airline's customers. Because the company thrives, it impacts society by providing jobs in the communities it serves and, to a lesser extent, by providing the customers who rely on it with transportation.

In his conceptualization of servant leadership, Greenleaf did not frame the process as one that was intended to directly change society. Rather, he visualized leaders who become servants first and listen to others and help them grow. As a result, their organizations are healthier, ultimately benefiting society. In this way, the long-term outcomes of putting others first include positive social change and helping society flourish.

Summary of the Model of Servant Leadership

In summary, the model of servant leadership consists of three components: antecedent conditions, servant leader behaviors, and outcomes. The central focus of the model is the seven behaviors of leaders that foster servant leadership: conceptualizing, emotional healing, putting followers first, helping followers grow and succeed, behaving ethically, empowering, and creating value for the community. These behaviors are influenced by context and culture, the leader's attributes, and the followers' receptivity to this kind of leadership. When individuals engage in servant leadership, it is likely to improve outcomes at the individual, organizational, and societal levels.

HOW DOES SERVANT LEADERSHIP WORK?

The servant leadership approach works differently than many of the prior theories we have discussed in this book. For example, it is unlike the trait approach (Chapter 2), which emphasizes that leaders should have certain specific traits. It is also unlike path–goal theory (Chapter 6), which lays out principles regarding what style of leadership is needed in various situations. Instead, servant leadership focuses on the behaviors leaders should exhibit to put followers first and to support followers' personal development. It is concerned with how leaders treat followers and the outcomes that are likely to emerge.

So what is the mechanism that explains how servant leadership works? It begins when leaders commit themselves to putting their followers first, being honest with them, and treating them fairly. Servant leaders make it a priority to listen to their followers and develop strong long-term relationships with them. This allows leaders to understand the abilities, needs, and goals of followers, which, in turn, allows these followers to achieve their full potential. When many leaders in an organization adopt a servant leadership orientation, a culture of serving others within and outside the organization is created (Liden et al., 2008).

Servant leadership works best when leaders are altruistic and have a strong motivation and deep-seated interest in helping others. In addition, for successful servant leadership to occur, it is important that followers are open and receptive to servant leaders who want to empower them and help them grow.

It should be noted that in much of the writing on servant leadership there is an underlying philosophical position, originally set forth by Greenleaf (1970), that leaders should be altruistic and humanistic. Rather than using their power to dominate others, leaders should make every attempt to share their power and enable others to grow and become autonomous. Leadership framed from this perspective downplays competition in the organization and promotes egalitarianism.

Finally, in an ideal world, servant leadership results in community and societal change. Individuals within an organization who care for each other become committed to developing an organization that cares for the community. Organizations that adopt a servant leadership culture are committed to helping those in need who operate outside of the organization. Servant leadership extends to serving those who are marginalized in society (Graham, 1991). Case 10.1 in this chapter provides a striking example of how one servant leader's work led to positive outcomes for many throughout the world.

STRENGTHS

In its current stage of development, research on servant leadership has made several positive contributions to the field of leadership. First, while there are other leadership approaches such as transformational and authentic leadership that include an ethical dimension, servant leadership is unique in the way it makes altruism the central component of the leadership process. Servant leadership argues unabashedly that leaders should put followers first, share control with followers, and embrace their growth. It is the only leadership approach that frames the leadership process around the principle of caring for others.

In comparing servant leadership to transformational leadership, a meta-analysis found servant leadership was better at predicting employee performance and attitudes, showing promise as a stand-alone theory that can help leadership researchers and practitioners better explain employee performance and attitudes than other recent approaches (Hoch, Bommer, Dulebohn, & Wu, 2018). Servant leadership is recognized as a viable approach that makes a unique contribution to our understanding of the leadership process.

Third, servant leadership provides a counterintuitive and provocative approach to the use of influence, or power, in leadership. Nearly all other theories of leadership treat influence as a positive factor in the leadership process, but servant leadership does just the opposite. It argues that leaders should not dominate, direct, or control; rather, leaders should share control and influence. To give up control rather than seek control is the goal of servant leadership. Servant leadership is an influence process that does not incorporate influence in a traditional way. This difference has resulted in servant leadership being conceptually and empirically distinct from other leadership approaches, which are leader-centric rather than follower-centric.

Another key distinction in servant leadership research is the consideration of multiple stakeholders, including followers, organizations, customers, communities, and societies, and the outcomes that result. Most notably, followers are recognized as being served by the actions and decisions of leaders. Outcomes such as work–family balance have been linked to servant leadership (Wang, Kwan, & Zhou, 2017). Also, servant leaders create more awareness of spirituality at work (Williams, Randolph-Seng, Hayek, Haden, & Atinc, 2017). Studies have included customer service behaviors, such as putting the customer first, and customer-helping behaviors as outcome variables as well (Chen, Zhu, & Zhou, 2015). Stakeholders also extend beyond the organization's followers and customers to the broader community (Lemoine et al., 2019).

Fifth, rather than imply that servant leadership is a panacea, research on servant leadership has shown there are conditions under which servant leadership is not a preferred kind of leadership. Findings indicate that servant leadership may not be effective in contexts where followers are not open to being guided, supported, and empowered. Followers' readiness to receive servant leadership moderates the potential usefulness of leading from this approach (Liden et al., 2008). In addition, Sousa and van Dierendonck (2017) found that servant leadership may be more effective for those at higher ranks in the organization. When expressed by executive- and board-level leaders, the combination of humility and action predicts engagement. However, for managers at lower ranks, a focus on the actions relating to operations results in more engagement.

Finally, there are multiple ways to assess servant leadership. A review of servant leadership research identified 16 different measures of servant leadership (Eva, Robin, Sendjaya, van Dierendonck, & Liden, 2019). The measure we have selected to highlight at the end of this chapter—the Servant Leadership Questionnaire (SLQ)—was developed and validated by Liden et al. (2008). It is comprised of 28 items that identify 7 distinct dimensions of servant leadership. Studies show that the SLQ is unique and measures aspects of leadership that are different from those measured by the transformational and leader–member exchange theories (Liden et al., 2008; Schaubroeck, Lam, & Peng, 2011). While the SLQ has proved to be a suitable instrument for use in research on servant leadership, Liden and his colleagues have also validated a short 7-item measure of servant leadership (Liden et al., 2015).

CRITICISMS

In addition to the positive features of servant leadership, this approach has several limitations. First, the paradoxical nature of the title "servant leadership" creates semantic noise that diminishes the potential value of the approach. Because the name appears contradictory, servant leadership is prone to be perceived as fanciful or whimsical. In addition, being a servant leader implies following, and following is viewed as the opposite of leading. Although servant leadership incorporates influence, the mechanism of how influence functions as a part of servant leadership is not fully explicated in the approach.

Second, it is not clear how servant leadership leads to organizational change. For example, Newman, Schwarz, Cooper, and Sendjaya (2017) found that servant leadership was positively related to psychological empowerment, but it did not result in followers engaging in extra-role performance (organizational citizenship) above and beyond that accounted for by leader–member exchange (LMX). Similar findings were found for work engagement; LMX explained the influence of servant leadership (Bao, Li, & Zhao, 2018). Therefore, an explanatory mechanism for the relationship between servant leadership and outcomes may be the quality of the working relationship between leaders and followers. Followers view their servant leaders positively and respond with higher performance if they have a good relationship with those leaders.

Third, there is debate among servant leadership scholars regarding the core dimensions of the process. As illustrated in Table 10.1, servant leadership is hypothesized to include a multitude of abilities, traits, and behaviors. To date, researchers have been unable to reach consensus on a common definition or theoretical framework for servant leadership (van Dierendonck, 2011). Some conceptualizations of servant leadership included outcomes such as organizational citizenship behavior and even antecedents such as personality traits. Some authors defined servant leadership in terms of examples such as self-sacrifice. This resulted in definitions that were confusing to both scholars and leaders (Eva et al., 2019). Despite 20 years of research on servant leadership, questions remain regarding the robustness of its theoretical formulations.

Fourth, a large segment of the writing on servant leadership has a prescriptive overtone that implies that good leaders "put others first." While advocating an altruistic approach to leadership is commendable, it has a utopian ring because it conflicts with individual autonomy and other principles of leadership such as directing, concern for production, goal setting, and creating a vision (Gergen, 2006). Furthermore, along with the "value-push" prescriptive quality, there is a moralistic nature that surrounds servant leadership. For example, some literature characterizes servant leaders as courageous heroes who work for the common good (Gandolfi & Stone, 2018). This premise, that leadership is about serving a higher purpose, is not always seen by researchers as one of the central features of servant leadership.

Finally, it is unclear why "conceptualizing" is included as one of the servant leadership behaviors in the model of servant leadership (see Figure 10.1). Is conceptualizing actually a behavior, or is it a cognitive ability? Is it a skill? Furthermore, what is the rationale for identifying conceptualizing as a determinant of servant leadership? Being able to conceptualize is undoubtedly an important cognitive capacity in all kinds of leadership, but why is it a defining characteristic of servant leadership? In the revised 7-item SLQ developed by Liden et al. (2015), only one item to measure conceptual skills was retained. The authors note that the item for conceptualization was changed by adding the word *work-related* to more closely relate it to conceptual skills rather than an emotional or personal item. But no explanation was offered for why this apparent skill is included in the servant leadership concept. A clearer explanation for its central role in servant leadership needs to be addressed in future research.

APPLICATION

Servant leadership can be applied at all levels of management and in all types of organizations. Within a philosophical framework of caring for others, servant leadership sets forth a list of behaviors that individuals can engage in if they want to be servant leaders. Most of the prescribed behaviors of servant leadership are not esoteric; they are easily understood and generally applicable to a variety of leadership situations.

Unlike leader–member exchange theory (Chapter 7) or authentic leadership (Chapter 9), which are not widely used in training and development, servant leadership has been used extensively in a variety of organizations for more than 30 years. Many organizations in the Fortune 500 (e.g., Starbucks, AT&T, Southwest Airlines, and Vanguard Group) employ ideas from servant leadership. Training in servant leadership typically involves self-assessment exercises, educational sessions, and goal setting. The content of servant leadership is straightforward and accessible to followers at every level within the organization.

Liden et al. (2008) suggest that organizations that want to build a culture of servant leadership should be careful to select people who are interested in and capable of building long-term relationships with followers. Furthermore, because "behaving ethically" is positively related to job performance, organizations should focus on selecting people who have high integrity and strong ethics. In addition, organizations should develop training programs that spend time helping leaders develop their emotional intelligence, ethical decision making, and skills for empowering others. Behaviors such as these will help leaders nurture followers to their full potential.

Servant leadership is taught at many colleges and universities around the world and is the focus of numerous independent coaches, trainers, and consultants. In the United States, Gonzaga University and Regent University are recognized as prominent leaders in this area because of the academic attention they have given to servant leadership. Overall, the most recognized and comprehensive center for training in servant leadership is the Greenleaf Center for Servant Leadership (www.greenleaf.org).

In summary, servant leadership provides a philosophy and set of behaviors that individuals in the organizational setting can learn and develop. The following section features cases illustrating how servant leadership has been manifested in different ways.

CASE STUDIES

This section provides three case studies (Cases 10.1, 10.2, and 10.3) that illustrate different facets of servant leadership. The first case is about Dr. Paul Farmer and his efforts to stop disease in Haiti and other parts of the world. The second case is about the leaders of Southwest Airlines who created a servant leadership culture that permeates the company. The third case discusses the culture and leadership of Italian energy corporation Snam. At the end of each case, several questions are provided to help analyze the case from the perspective of servant leadership.

Case 10.1 GLOBAL HEALTH CARE

"Education wasn't what he wanted to perform on the world. . . . He was after transformation."

—Kidder (2003, p. 44)

When Paul Farmer graduated from Duke University at 22, he was unsure whether he wanted to be an anthropologist or a doctor. So he went to Haiti. As a student, Paul had become obsessed with the island nation after meeting many Haitians at local migrant camps. Paul was used to the grittier side of life; he had grown up in a family of eight that lived in a converted school bus and later on a houseboat moored in a bayou. But what he observed at the migrant camps and learned from his discussions with Haitian immigrants made his childhood seem idyllic.

In Haiti, he volunteered for a small charity called Eye Care Haiti, which conducted outreach clinics in rural areas. He was drawn in by the lives of the Haitian people and the deplorable conditions so many of them endured and determined to use his time there to learn everything he could about illness and disease afflicting people living in poverty. Before long, Paul realized that he had found his life's purpose: He'd be a doctor to people living in poverty, and he'd start in Haiti.

Paul entered Harvard University in 1984 and, for the first two years, traveled back and forth to Haiti where he conducted a health census in the village of Cange. During that time he conceived of a plan to fight disease in Haiti by developing a public health system that included vaccination programs and clean water and sanitation. The heart of this program, however, would be a cadre of people from the villages who were trained to administer medicines, teach health classes, treat minor ailments, and recognize the symptoms of grave illnesses such as HIV, tuberculosis, and malaria.

His vision became reality in 1987, thanks to a wealthy donor who gave $1 million to help Paul create Partners In Health (PIH). At first it wasn't much of an organization—no staff, a small advisory board, and three committed volunteers. But its work was impressive: PIH began building schools and clinics in and around Cange. Soon PIH established a training program for health outreach workers and organized a mobile unit to screen residents of area villages for preventable diseases.

In 1990, Paul finished his medical studies and became a fellow in infectious diseases at Brigham and Women's Hospital in Boston. He was able to remain in Haiti for most of each year, returning to Boston to work at Brigham for a few months at a time, sleeping in the basement of PIH headquarters.

It wasn't long before PIH's successes started gaining attention outside of Haiti. Because of its success treating the disease in Haiti, the World Health Organization appointed Paul and PIH staffer Jim Yong Kim to spearhead pilot treatment programs for multiple-drug-resistant tuberculosis (MDR-TB). Paul's attention was now diverted to the slums of Peru and Russia where cases of MDR-TB were on the rise. In Peru, Paul and PIH encountered barriers in treating MDR-TB that had nothing to do with the disease. They ran headlong into governmental resistance and had to battle to obtain expensive medications. Paul learned to gently navigate governmental obstacles, while the Bill & Melinda Gates Foundation stepped in with a $44.7 million grant to help fund the program.

In 2005, PIH turned its attention to another part of the world: Africa, the epicenter of the global AIDS pandemic. Beginning its efforts in Rwanda, where few people had been tested or were receiving treatment, PIH tested 30,000 people in eight months and enrolled nearly 700 in drug therapy to treat the disease. Soon, the organization expanded its efforts to the African nations of Lesotho and Malawi (Partners In Health, 2011).

But Paul's efforts weren't just in far-flung reaches of the world. From his work with patients at Brigham, Paul observed the needs of low-income communities in Boston. The Prevention and Access to Care and Treatment (PACT) project was created to offer drug therapy for HIV and diabetes for residents living in poverty of the Roxbury and Dorchester neighborhoods. PIH has since sent PACT project teams across the United States to provide support to other community health programs.

By 2020, PIH had grown to 18,000 employees working in health centers and hospitals in throughout the world, including the Dominican Republic, Peru, Mexico, Rwanda, Lesotho, Malawi, the Navajo Nation (U.S.), and Russia. Each year the organization increases the number of facilities and personnel that provide health care to those most in need around the world. Paul continues to travel around the world, monitoring programs and raising funds for PIH in addition to leading the Department of Global Health and Social Medicine at Harvard Medical School.

(Continued)

(Continued)

Questions

1. Would you characterize Paul Farmer as a servant leader? Explain your answer.

2. Putting others first is the essence of servant leadership. In what way does Paul Farmer put others first?

3. Another characteristic of a servant leader is getting followers to serve. Who are Paul Farmer's followers, and how did they become servants to his vision?

4. What role do you think Paul Farmer's childhood had in his development as a servant leader?

Case 10.2   SERVANT LEADERSHIP TAKES FLIGHT

A young mother traveling with a toddler on a long cross-country flight approached the flight attendant looking rather frantic. Because of weather and an hour-and-a-half wait on the runway to take off, the plane would arrive at its destination several hours late. The plane had made an intermediate stop in Denver to pick up passengers but not long enough for travelers to disembark. The mother told the attendant that with the delays and the long flight, her child had already eaten all the food she brought and if she didn't feed him soon he was bound to have a total meltdown. "Can I get off for five minutes just to run and get something for him to eat?" she pleaded.

"I have to recommend strongly that you stay on the plane," the attendant said, sternly. But then, with a smile, she added, "But I can get off. The plane won't leave without me. What can I get your son to eat?"

Turns out that flight attendant not only got the little boy a meal, but brought four other children on board meals as well. Anyone who has traveled in a plane with screaming children knows that this flight attendant not only took care of some hungry children and frantic parents, but also indirectly saw to the comfort of a planeload of other passengers.

This story doesn't surprise anyone familiar with Southwest Airlines. The airline's mission statement is posted every 3 feet at all Southwest locations: Follow the Golden Rule—treat people the way you want to be treated.

It's a philosophy that the company takes to heart, beginning with how it treats employees. Colleen Barrett, the president emeritus of Southwest Airlines, said the company's cofounder and her mentor, Herb Kelleher, was adamant that "a happy and motivated workforce will essentially extend that goodwill to Southwest's customers" (Knowledge@Wharton, 2008). If the airline took care of its employees, the employees would take care of the customers, and the shareholders would win, too.

From the first days of Southwest Airlines, Herb resisted establishing traditional hierarchies within the company. He focused on finding employees with substance, willing to say what they thought and committed to doing things differently. Described as "an egalitarian spirit," he employed a collaborative approach to management that involved his associates at every step.

Colleen, who went from working as Herb's legal secretary to being the president of the airline, is living proof of his philosophy. A woman with little money from rural Vermont who got the opportunity of a lifetime to work for Herb when he was still just a lawyer, she rose from his aide to become vice president of administration, then executive vice president of customers, and then president and chief operating officer in 2001 (which she stepped down from in 2008). She had no formal training in aviation, but that didn't matter. Herb "always treated me as a complete equal to him," she said.

It was Colleen who instituted the Golden Rule as the company motto and developed a model that focuses on employee satisfaction and issues first, followed by the needs of the passengers. The company hired employees for their touchy-feely attitudes and trained them for skill. Southwest Airlines developed a culture that celebrated and encouraged humor. The example of being themselves on the job started at the top with Herb and Colleen.

This attitude has paid off. Southwest Airlines posted a profit for 35 consecutive years and continues to make money while other airlines' profits are crashing. Colleen said the most important numbers on the balance sheet, however, are those that indicate how many millions of people have become frequent flyers of the airline, a number that grows every year.

Questions

1. What type of servant leader behaviors did Herb Kelleher exhibit in starting the airline? What about Colleen Barrett?

2. How do the leaders of Southwest Airlines serve others? What others are they serving?

3. Southwest Airlines emphasizes the Golden Rule. What role does the Golden Rule play in servant leadership? Is it always a part of servant leadership? Discuss.

4. Based on Figure 10.1, describe the outcomes of servant leadership at Southwest Airlines, and how follower receptivity may have influenced those outcomes.

Marco Alverà has found the secret ingredient in making a business be best. Fairness.

Marco is the CEO of Snam, an independent energy company based in Italy whose largest shareholder is a holding company controlled by the Italian state. Historically, Italy had been dependent on its neighbors to the north to supply the country with natural gas. Snam's mission has been to reverse the flow of natural gas, and it has succeeded. By "reducing bottlenecks" and "harmonizing prices in the European market," Snam has made Italy a natural gas hub in Europe and is now Europe's second-largest network operator in terms of extension of pipeline, providing gas to countries like Russia, Algeria, Libya, Norway, Holland, Austria, France, and the United Kingdom (Elliott, 2018).

Marco came to the energy industry from big banking—Goldman Sachs, to be specific—where competition created by big bonuses and large salaries was used to motivate people and cull the high performers from the low. He quickly realized that this motivational tool kit was effectively useless at Snam, which offered fixed salaries and lifelong jobs. How, then, to inspire 3,000 employees to strive for excellence and motivate them to bring their best to work every day?

To Marco's surprise, he found areas of unmitigated excellence in the company. Snam was beating its competition in tough and highly competitive business sectors like trading, project management, and exploration. "Our exploration team was finding more oil and gas than any other company in the world. It was a phenomenon," he said (Alverà, 2017). At first, Marco attributed this to luck, but when it continued to happen, he dug a little deeper to figure out why. The secret? Fairness.

Marco notes that unfairness is the "root cause of polarization" and "makes people defensive and disengaged" at work. Unfairness causes us pain. Fairness, on the other hand, brings us satisfaction. Behavioral research has shown that people sense fairness (or unfairness) even before they begin to analyze a situation and reach logical conclusions (Ronen, 2018).

Marco said Snam employees worked for a company where they didn't have to worry about short-term results or about being penalized for making mistakes. They knew they would be rewarded for their overall performance and not on individual success. "They knew they were valued for what they were trying to do, not the outcome. They were valued as human beings. They were part of a community. Whatever happened, the company would stand by them . . . These guys could be true to their purpose, which was finding oil and gas. They didn't have to worry about company politics or greed or fear. They could be good risk-takers . . . and they were excellent team workers. They could trust their colleagues. They didn't need to look behind their backs" (Alverà, 2017).

For example, Marco shared the story of his friend and employee who drilled seven dry wells at the cost of $1 billion to the company. Marco was worried for him, but his friend didn't seem to be concerned, and on the eighth drill he successfully found gas.

Giving employees the latitude to do what they did best was key. Having freedom to do what they feel is right is a motivator "in a way that no bonus can buy" that works at every level of the company, he said. For example, an employee asked Marco for the budget to build a cheese factory next to Snam's plant in a village in Ecuador.

"It didn't make any sense: no one ever built a cheese factory. But this is what the village wanted, because the milk they had would spoil before they could sell it, so that's what they needed. And so we built it" (Alverà, 2017).

This kind of culture comes from what Marco calls a "company psychoanalysis," a top-down analysis of every aspect of the company. "We went back to something that Aristotle said: 'A human being with a purpose is much more motivated' and that purpose is in the intersection of what someone is really good at doing, what his talents are and what the world needs. So we went through a long journey, a lot of introspective work, and we really came up with what our strengths were and what we think the world needs" (Alverà, 2017).

Marco and his team took a hard look at how decisions were made and how company resources were allocated. They scrutinized the existing processes, systems, and rules. From those analyses they removed anything that wasn't clear, wasn't rational, or limited the flow of information within the company. Company culture and how people were motivated were given the same type of evaluation.

To allow this to happen, Marco said he had to take himself "out of the equation" and "that means being aware of my own biases . . . to actively promote a culture of diversity of opinions and diversity of character" (UniBocconi, 2019).

Marco, who has degrees in philosophy and economics from the London School of Economics, found his philosophy background particularly useful. "It teaches you about having different opinions of the same topic . . . And I find that very helpful in negotiating and managing people to be able to look at different perspectives" (Alverà, 2017).

This process resulted in the company defining its purpose as "Energy to Inspire the World." "The purpose is on top, the purpose said, 'What you are for, why you exist,'" he said. "But it's not enough just to have a purpose. Then you need to have the mission, the vision, the strategy, the values, the competencies, so that it's an entire framework" (Alverà, 2017).

(Continued)

(Continued)

Marco said the definition of ideal fairness is "when you can fold down your antenna in your search for unfairness." He admits the last element of fairness is the hardest, because it is not something that is easily analyzed and requires something altogether different from the norm in the business world. "It's about what people's emotions are, what their needs are, what's going on in their private lives, what society needs" (Alverà, 2017).

This requires judgment and risk, he said.

"And if we turn on our hearts, that's the key to getting the real best out of people, because they can smell it if you care, and only when you really care will they leave their fears behind and bring their true selves to work" (Alverà, 2017).

Questions

1. The text suggests that for servant leadership to be effective, three antecedent (or existing) conditions must exist—context and culture, leader attributes, and follower receptivity. Discuss how each of these antecedents plays a role at Snam.

2. The servant leadership model identifies seven leader behaviors core to the servant leadership process. How do each of these relate to Marco Alverà and Snam? Which of these behaviors are most relevant to Marco's leadership success?

3. Servant leadership is unique in that it considers multiple stakeholders. Who are the stakeholders in this case? How do Marco Alverà and Snam exhibit consideration to these stakeholders?

4. The text identifies the potential outcomes of servant leadership as follower performance and growth, organizational performance, and societal impact. How is each of these outcomes evident in the approach Marco Alverà and Snam take toward leadership? Provide examples from the case to support your answers.

5. According to Greenleaf, the servant leader has a social responsibility to be concerned about those who are marginalized and those less privileged. If inequalities and social injustices exist, a servant leader tries to remove them.

   a. How would you apply this statement to Marco Alverà and his role as a servant leader?

   b. Do you view Marco Alverà as a servant leader? Why or why not?

   —Barbara Russell, MBA, BSCS, BBA, Chemeketa Community College

LEADERSHIP INSTRUMENT

Many questionnaires have been used to measure servant leadership (see Table 10.1). Because of its relevance to the content, the Servant Leadership Questionnaire (SLQ) by Liden et al. (2008) was chosen for inclusion in this chapter. It is a 28-item scale that measures 7 major dimensions of servant leadership: conceptualizing, emotional healing, putting followers first, helping followers grow and succeed, behaving ethically, empowering, and creating value for the community. Using exploratory and confirmatory factor analysis, Liden et al. established the multiple dimensions of this scale and described how it is uniquely different from other leadership measures. In addition, Liden et al. (2015) have developed and validated a 7-item scale that measures global servant leadership, which correlates strongly with the 28-item measure used in this section.

By completing the SLQ you will gain an understanding of how servant leadership is measured and explore where you stand on the different dimensions of servant leadership. Servant leadership is a complex process, and taking the SLQ is one way to discover the dynamics of how it works.

Servant Leadership Questionnaire

Purpose: The purpose of this questionnaire is to examine the servant leadership behaviors you exhibit.

Instructions: Have a friend, colleague, or classmate read each item carefully and use the following 7-point scale to indicate the extent to which they agree or disagree with the following statements as they pertain to your leadership. In these statements, "the leader" is referring to you in a leadership capacity.

Key: 1 = Strongly disagree   2 = Disagree   3 = Disagree somewhat
      4 = Undecided   5 = Agree somewhat   6 = Agree   7 = Strongly agree

1. Others would seek help from the leader if they had   1 2 3 4 5 6 7
    a personal problem.

2. The leader emphasizes the importance of giving   1 2 3 4 5 6 7
    back to the community.

3. The leader can tell if something work-related is   1 2 3 4 5 6 7
    going wrong.

4. The leader gives others the responsibility to make   1 2 3 4 5 6 7
    important decisions about their own jobs.

5. The leader makes others' career development   1 2 3 4 5 6 7
    a priority.

6. The leader cares more about others' success than   1 2 3 4 5 6 7
    their own.

7. The leader holds high ethical standards.   1 2 3 4 5 6 7

8. The leader cares about others' personal well-being.   1 2 3 4 5 6 7

9. The leader is always interested in helping people in   1 2 3 4 5 6 7
    the community.

10. The leader is able to think through complex problems.   1 2 3 4 5 6 7

11. The leader encourages others to handle important   1 2 3 4 5 6 7
    work decisions on their own.

12. The leader is interested in making sure others reach   1 2 3 4 5 6 7
    their career goals.

13. The leader puts others' best interests above their own.   1 2 3 4 5 6 7

14. The leader is always honest.   1 2 3 4 5 6 7

15. The leader takes time to talk to others on a   1 2 3 4 5 6 7
    personal level.

16. The leader is involved in community activities.   1 2 3 4 5 6 7

17. The leader has a thorough understanding of the   1 2 3 4 5 6 7
    organization and its goals.

18. The leader gives others the freedom to handle   1 2 3 4 5 6 7
    difficult situations in the way they feel(s) is best.

19. The leader provides others with work experiences that enable them to develop new skills. 1 2 3 4 5 6 7

20. The leader sacrifices their own interests to meet others' needs. 1 2 3 4 5 6 7

21. The leader would not compromise ethical principles in order to meet success. 1 2 3 4 5 6 7

22. The leader can recognize when others are feeling down without asking them. 1 2 3 4 5 6 7

23. The leader encourages others to volunteer in the community. 1 2 3 4 5 6 7

24. The leader can solve work problems with new or creative ideas. 1 2 3 4 5 6 7

25. If others need to make important decisions at work, they do not need to consult the leader. 1 2 3 4 5 6 7

26. The leader wants to know about others' career goals. 1 2 3 4 5 6 7

27. The leader does what they can to make others' jobs easier. 1 2 3 4 5 6 7

28. The leader values honesty more than profits. 1 2 3 4 5 6 7

Source: Adapted from *The Leadership Quarterly, 19,* by R. C. Liden, S. J. Wayne, H. Zhao, and D. Henderson, "Servant Leadership: Development of a Multidimensional Measure and Multi-Level Assessment," pp. 161–177, Copyright (2008).

Scoring

1. Add up the scores for 1, 8, 15, and 22. This is your score for emotional healing.

2. Add up the scores for 2, 9, 16, and 23. This is your score for creating value for the community.

3. Add up the scores for 3, 10, 17, and 24. This is your score for conceptual skills.

4. Add up the scores for 4, 11, 18, and 25. This is your score for empowering.

5. Add up the scores for 5, 12, 19, and 26. This is your score for helping followers grow and succeed.

6. Add up the scores for 6, 13, 20, and 27. This is your score for putting followers first.

7. Add up the scores for 7, 14, 21, and 28. This is your score for behaving ethically.

(Continued)

(Continued)

Scoring Interpretation

The scores you received on the SLQ indicate the degree to which you exhibit the seven behaviors characteristic of a servant leader. You can use the results to assess areas in which you have strong servant leadership behaviors and areas in which you may strive to improve. Based on the responses of the person who filled out this questionnaire on your leadership, the following scores for each category can be broken down as follows:

- *High range:* A score between 23 and 28 means others believe you strongly exhibit this servant leadership behavior.

- *Moderate range:* A score between 14 and 22 means others believe you tend to exhibit this behavior in an average way.

- *Low range:* A score between 4 and 13 means others believe you exhibit this leadership behavior below the average or expected degree.

SUMMARY

Originating in the seminal work of Greenleaf (1970), servant leadership is a paradoxical approach to leadership that challenges our traditional beliefs about leadership and influence. Servant leadership emphasizes that leaders should be attentive to the needs of followers, empower them, and help them develop their full human capacities.

Servant leaders make a conscious choice to *serve first*—to place the good of followers over the leaders' self-interests. They build strong relationships with others, are empathic and ethical, and lead in ways that serve the greater good of followers, the organization, the community, and society at large.

Based on an idea from Hermann Hesse's (1956) novel *The Journey to the East*, Greenleaf argued that the selfless servant in a group has an extraordinary impact on the other members. Servant leaders attend fully to the needs of followers, are concerned with those with less privilege, and aim to remove inequalities and social injustices. Because servant leaders shift authority to those who are being led, they exercise less institutional power and control.

Scholars have conceptualized servant leadership in multiple ways. According to Spears (2002), there are 10 major characteristics of servant leadership: listening, empathy, healing, awareness, persuasion, conceptualization, foresight, stewardship, commitment to the growth of people, and building community. Additional efforts by social science researchers to develop and validate measures of servant leadership have resulted in an extensive list of other servant leadership attributes (Coetzer et al., 2017; Winston & Fields, 2015).

Liden et al. (2014) created a promising model of servant leadership that has three main components: antecedent conditions, servant leader behaviors, and outcomes. *Antecedent conditions* that are likely to impact servant leaders include context and culture, leader attributes, and follower receptivity. Central to the servant leader process are the seven *servant leader behaviors:* conceptualizing, emotional healing, putting followers first, helping followers grow and succeed, behaving ethically, empowering, and creating value for the community. The *outcomes* of servant leadership are follower performance and growth, organizational performance, and societal impact.

Research on servant leadership has several strengths. First, it is unique because it makes altruism the main component of the leadership process. Second, it can be used to explain employee performance. Third, servant leadership provides a counterintuitive and provocative approach to the use of influence wherein leaders give up control rather than seek control. Fourth, rather than a panacea, research has shown that there are conditions under which servant leadership is not a preferred kind of leadership. Last, recent research has resulted in a sound measure of servant leadership (Servant Leadership Questionnaire) that identifies seven distinct dimensions of the process.

The servant leadership approach also has limitations. First, the paradoxical nature of the title "servant leadership" creates semantic noise that diminishes the potential value of the approach. Second, no consensus exists on a common theoretical framework for servant leadership. Third, servant leadership has a utopian ring that conflicts with traditional approaches to leadership. Last, it is not clear why "conceptualizing" is a defining characteristic of servant leadership.

Despite the limitations, servant leadership continues to be an engaging approach to leadership that holds much promise. As more research is done to test the substance and assumptions of servant leadership, a better understanding of the complexities of the process will emerge.

Adaptive Leadership

DESCRIPTION

As the name of the approach implies, adaptive leadership is about how leaders encourage people to adapt—to face and deal with problems, challenges, and changes. Adaptive leadership focuses on the *adaptations* required of people in response to changing environments. Simply stated, adaptive leaders prepare and encourage people to deal with change. Unlike the trait approach (Chapter 2) and authentic leadership (Chapter 9), which focus predominantly on the characteristics of the leader, adaptive leadership stresses the *behaviors of the leader* in relation to the *work of followers* in the *situations* in which they find themselves.

Since Heifetz first published *Leadership Without Easy Answers* (1994), the seminal book on adaptive leadership, this approach has occupied a unique place in the leadership literature. Adaptive leadership has been used effectively to explain how leaders encourage productive change across multiple levels, including self, organizational, community, and societal. However, most of the writing about adaptive leadership has been prescriptive and based on anecdotal and observational data rather than data derived from rigorous scientific inquiry. Scholars and practitioners have recognized the merits of the approach, but the theoretical underpinnings of adaptive leadership remain in the formative stages.

Development of the adaptive leadership framework emerged largely from the work of Heifetz and his associates (Heifetz, 1994; Heifetz, Grashow, & Linsky, 2009; Heifetz & Laurie, 1997; Heifetz & Linsky, 2002; Heifetz, Sinder, Jones, Hodge, & Rowley, 1991). From the beginning, they set out to create a different approach to leadership. Rather than seeing the leader as a savior who solves problems for people, they conceptualized the leader as one who plays the role of assisting people who need to confront tough problems (e.g., sexism in the workplace or pandemic-induced restrictions and social distancing requirements). An adaptive leader challenges others to face difficult situations, providing them with the space or opportunity they need to learn new ways of dealing with the inevitable changes in beliefs, attitudes, perceptions, and behaviors that they are likely to encounter in addressing real problems.

Adaptive Leadership Defined

Although people often think of adaptive leadership as being leader centered, it is actually more follower centered. It focuses primarily on how leaders help others do the work they need to do, to adapt to the challenges they face. Generally, adaptive leadership is concerned with how people change and adjust to new circumstances. In this chapter, we emphasize the process leaders use to encourage others to grapple with difficult problems.

In the leadership literature, Heifetz and his colleagues suggest that "adaptive leadership is the practice of mobilizing people to tackle tough challenges and thrive" (Heifetz et al., 2009, p. 14). In contrast to emphasizing the position or characteristics of the leader, this definition suggests that leadership is concerned with the *behaviors* of leaders. Adaptive leaders engage in activities that *mobilize, motivate, organize, orient, and focus the attention of others* (Heifetz, 1994). In addition, adaptive leadership is about helping others to explore and change their values. The goal of adaptive leadership is to encourage people to change and to learn new behaviors so that they may effectively meet their challenges and grow in the process. In short, adaptive leadership is the behavior of and the actions undertaken by leaders to encourage others to address and resolve changes that are central in their lives. To better understand how adaptive leadership works, Table 11.1 provides some examples of situations in which adaptive leadership would be an ideal form of leadership.

Conceptually, the process of adaptive leadership incorporates four different biases: systems, biological, service orientation, and psychotherapeutic (Heifetz, 1994). Taken together, these biases help explain and characterize the nature of adaptive leadership:

Systems Bias. The adaptive leadership approach assumes that many problems people face are actually embedded in complicated interactive systems (see Uhl-Bien, Marion, & McKelvey, 2007). Problems are viewed as complex and multifaceted, dynamic in that they can evolve and change, and connected to others in a web of relationships.

Biological Bias. Adaptive leadership recognizes that people develop and evolve as a result of having to adapt to both their internal cues/state and external environments. The ability to adapt allows people to thrive in new circumstances.

Service Orientation Bias. Similar to physicians, adaptive leaders use their expertise or authority *to serve* people by diagnosing their problems and helping them find solutions.

Psychotherapeutic Bias. The way clients address issues in psychotherapy is similar to how people accomplish adaptive work. Adaptive leaders understand that people need a supportive environment and adapt more successfully when they face difficult problems directly, learn to distinguish between fantasy and reality, resolve internal conflicts, and learn new attitudes and behaviors.

TABLE 11.1 Adaptive Leadership in Practice

Adaptive leaders *mobilize, motivate, organize, orient, and focus the attention of others* to address and resolve changes that are central in their lives. These are some examples of cases where adaptive leadership would be beneficial:

Student Organization

You are the president of Women in Business, a student organization at a large public university whose mission is to prepare women for successful careers in business. Some members have expressed that issues affecting transwomen should be discussed and explored; other group members are not interested in adding this to the focus of the group. As the president, you must guide the group to reach a resolution.

Company Merger

A midsize, family-owned paper company merges with another similar paper company. The merger creates tensions between the employees regarding job titles and duties, different wage schedules, overtime, and vacation pay. The new owners must bring these two groups of employees together to have the company function successfully.

Merit Pay

In an established engineering company, a small group of young, high-achieving engineers wants to change the way merit pay is given by removing seniority and years of service as part of the criteria. Long-time employees are resisting the change. The management must find a way to address this issue without alienating either group.

Health and Safety

You are mayor of a moderate-sized city that is home to a large prison where over 600 inmates have tested positive for COVID-19. The number of new cases in the city is rising sharply. Sheltering in place and wearing masks has been found to be the only way to curtail and control the virus's spread, but a large majority of city residents think the problem is the prison's and refuse to obey your recent orders to close all businesses in the city.

Source: Reprinted (adapted version) from *The Leadership Quarterly, 19,* R. C. Liden, S. J. Wayne, H. Zhao, and D. Henderson, "Servant Leadership: Development of a Multidimensional Measure and Multi-Level Assessment," pp. 161–177, Copyright (2008), with permission from Elsevier.

In addition to the way Heifetz and his colleagues defined adaptive leadership, it has been conceptualized as an element or subset of complexity leadership theory, a framework designed to explain leadership for organizations of the 21st century that concentrate on knowledge or information as a core commodity, rather than the production of goods as was prevalent in the industrial era (Uhl-Bien et al., 2007). Complexity leadership theory (which includes administrative, adaptive, and enabling leadership) focuses on strategies and behaviors that encourage learning, creativity, and adaptation in complex organizational systems.

Within this framework, adaptive leadership is described as a complex process that emerges to produce adaptive change in a social system. It originates in struggles or tensions among people over conflicting needs, ideas, and preferences. It is not conceptualized as a person or a specific act, but rather is defined as leadership that seeks to emerge from a system, or a "generative dynamic" (see Uhl-Bien et al., 2007, p. 299). Similarly, DeRue (2011) addresses adaptive leadership as a process where individuals engage in repeated leading–following interactions that evolve as group needs change, enabling groups to adapt and remain viable in dynamic contexts.

Adaptive leadership is a unique kind of leadership that focuses on the dynamics of mobilizing people to address change. In the next section, we describe the various components of adaptive leadership and discuss how each component contributes to the overall process of adaptive leadership.

A MODEL OF ADAPTIVE LEADERSHIP

Figure 11.1 offers a visual representation of the major components of adaptive leadership and how they fit together, including situational challenges, leader behaviors, and adaptive work. Heuristically, this model provides a basis for clarifying the process of adaptive leadership as well as generating empirical research to validate and refine the concepts and principles described by the model.

Situational Challenges

As illustrated on the left side of Figure 11.1, this practice of leadership requires that leaders address three kinds of situational challenges: those that are primarily *technical* in nature, those that have both a *technical and adaptive* dimension, and those that are primarily *adaptive* in nature. While addressing technical challenges is important, adaptive leadership is concerned with helping people address adaptive challenges.

Technical Challenges

Technical challenges are problems in the workplace, community, or self that are clearly defined, with known solutions that can be implemented through existing organizational procedures. They are problems that can be solved by experts or by those who have what Heifetz calls a "repertoire" of skills or procedures based on current know-how. For technical challenges, people look to the leader for a solution, and they accept the leader's authority to resolve the problem. For example, if employees at a tax accounting firm are frustrated about a newly adopted tax software program, the manager at the firm can assess the software issues, identify the weaknesses and problems with the software, contact the company that provided the software, and have the programs modified in accordance with the accountants' needs at the tax firm. In this example, the problem is identifiable,

FIGURE 11.1 Model of Adaptive Leadership

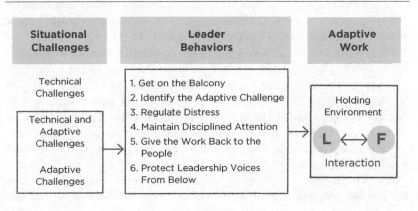

it has an achievable solution, and the manager at the tax firm has the authority to address the problem through the accepted structures and procedures of the organization. The employees accept that authority and look to the manager to solve the technical problem.

Technical and Adaptive Challenges

Some challenges have both a technical and adaptive dimension. In this case, the challenges are clearly defined but do not have distinct straightforward solutions within the existing organizational system. The responsibility of tackling this type of challenge is shared between the leader and the people. The leader may act as a resource for others and provide support, but the people need to do the work—they need to learn to change and adapt. For example, if an urban hospital with a traditional approach to care (i.e., providers are the experts, and patients are the visitors) wanted to establish a patient-centered culture, the goal could be clearly laid out. To reach the goal, the hospital leadership, through its hierarchical authority, could provide in-service training on how to involve patients in their own care. New rules could be designed to preserve patients' personal routines, give them access to their own records, and give them more control of their own treatment. However, the staff, doctors, patients, and family members would need to accept the proposed change and learn how to implement it. Making the hospital a model of patient-centered care would require a lot of work and adaptation on the part of many different people.

Adaptive Challenges

Central to the process of adaptive leadership are adaptive challenges, or problems that are not clear-cut or easy to identify. They cannot be solved solely by the leader's authority or expertise, or through the normal ways of doing things in the organization. Adaptive challenges require that leaders encourage others to define challenging situations and implement solutions. Not easy to tackle and often resisted, adaptive challenges are difficult because they usually require changes in people's priorities, beliefs, roles, and values. An example of adaptive challenges involves the problems and concerns a family confronts when placing a parent in hospice care. In a hospice, there is a great deal of uncertainty for patients and families about how and when the patient will die, and how to best comfort the patient during this time. While hospice workers can give support and informal feedback about the dying process, the patient and families have to come to grips with how they want to approach the patient's final days. What does the impending loss mean? How can they prepare for it? How will they cope with the loss going forward? In this context, those in the health care system act as leaders and mobilize the patient and family members to address the many questions and concerns that surround the death of the family member. How these hospice nurses, social workers, and staff communicate, demonstrate empathy, offer support, and so on is important in this process of helping families to confront the complexities and concerns of the impending loss.

Leader Behaviors

As shown in the middle of Figure 11.1, six leader behaviors, or activities, play a pivotal role in the process of adaptive leadership. Based on the work of Heifetz and his colleagues (Heifetz, 1994; Heifetz & Laurie, 1997), these behaviors are general prescriptions for leaders when helping others confront difficult challenges and the inevitable changes that accompany them. Although there is a general order as to which leader behavior comes first in the adaptive leadership process, many of these behaviors overlap with each other and should be demonstrated by leaders at the same time. Taken together, these leader behaviors suggest a kind of recipe for being an adaptive leader.

1. Get on the Balcony. A prerequisite for the other adaptive leader behaviors, "getting on the balcony" is a metaphor for stepping out of the fray and finding perspective in the midst of a challenging situation. It is an allusion to a dance floor and that one needs to be above the dancing to understand what's going on below. Being on the balcony enables the leader to see the big picture—what is really happening. On the balcony, the leader is momentarily away from the noise, activity, and chaos of a situation, and able to gain a clearer view of reality. This behavior allows the leader to identify value and power conflicts among people, ways they may be avoiding work, and other dysfunctional reactions to change (Heifetz & Laurie, 1997). Getting on the balcony can include such things as taking some quiet time, forming a group of unofficial advisers for alternative discussions about organizational issues, or simply attending meetings as an observer. In this model, the adaptive leader is urged to step away from the conflict in order to see it fully, but never to dissociate entirely from the conflict. Effective leaders are able to move back and forth as participants and observers between the struggles of their people and the intentions of the organization or community.

To understand what it means to stand on the balcony, imagine yourself as the principal of an elementary school. From the balcony, you see all the pieces that go into educating your students: federal and state requirements, teachers and staff, budgets, teacher evaluations, parents, and discipline, not to mention the children themselves. From above, you can see how these issues relate to and affect one another, and who is dancing with which partners, all while working toward the common goal of educating children.

As another example, imagine you are a chief union negotiator who, in the midst of difficult labor talks, steps away from the table for a moment to separate yourself from the emotion and intensity of the talks and reflect on their goals. Once you feel you again have a grasp of the issues at hand, you can dive directly back into negotiations.

In both of these examples, the leader takes time to see the big picture as an observer but also stays engaged as a participant with the challenges people are confronting.

2. Identify the Adaptive Challenge. In addition to getting on the balcony and observing the dynamics of the complex situations people face, leaders must analyze and diagnose these challenges. Central to this process is differentiating between technical and adaptive challenges. Failures in leadership often occur because leaders fail to diagnose challenges correctly. The adaptive leadership process suggests that leaders are most effective using adaptive leadership behaviors for adaptive challenges and technical leadership behaviors for technical challenges. Approaching challenges with the wrong style of leadership is maladaptive.

If challenges are technical in nature, leaders can fix the problem with their own expertise. For example, in a manufacturing environment, problems that arise in scheduling, product sales quotas, facility expansion, or raising the minimum wage are all problems that leaders can use their authority to resolve. However, it is essential that leaders also know when their authority is not sufficient or appropriate to address a particular challenge.

When people's beliefs, attitudes, and values are affected by a problem, leaders need to take an adaptive approach. Determining if the challenge is an adaptive one requires the leader to determine whether or not the challenge strikes at the core feelings and thoughts of others. Adaptive challenges are usually value laden and stir up people's emotions. Furthermore, if challenges are adaptive, they require that people learn new ways of coping. Take the manufacturing environment discussed earlier: If another company buys that manufacturing facility and the new owners implement production procedures and standards that the facility's workers are unfamiliar with, these changes will create adaptive challenges for the workers. Identifying adaptive challenges means leaders need to focus their attention on problems they cannot solve themselves and that demand collaboration between the leader and followers. For adaptive challenges, leaders make themselves available to support others as they do the work they need to do.

To more easily identify complex adaptive challenges and also distinguish them from technical challenges, there are four archetypes or basic patterns in need of adaptive change to consider (Heifetz et al., 2009).

Archetype 1: Gap Between Espoused Values and Behavior. This archetype is present when an organization espouses, or claims to adhere to, values that aren't in reality supported by its actions. For example, a company that promotes itself as a family-friendly place to work but does not have a flexible work policy, an extended maternity leave policy, or in-house childcare doesn't have behaviors that match the family-friendly image it promotes itself as having.

Archetype 2: Competing Commitments. When an organization has numerous commitments and some come into conflict with each other, this archetype is in play. For example, a health and fitness center wants to grow and expand its services but at the same time sees the best way to reduce costs is by trimming the number of trainers and staff it employs.

Archetype 3: Speaking the Unspeakable. The phrases "sacred cow" and "elephant in the room" are examples of this archetype; it occurs when there are radical ideas, unpopular issues, or conflicting perspectives that people don't dare address because of their sensitive or controversial nature. Speaking out about these is seen as "risky." Consider an organization with a well-liked, established owner who is perceived by the employees as "over the hill" and not in touch with the current business climate, but no one is willing to discuss the matter. It is easier to suffer the consequences of dated leadership than confront and risk angering the owner.

Archetype 4: Work Avoidance. This archetype represents a situation where people avoid addressing difficult issues by staying within their "comfort zone" or by using diversionary methods. For example, coworkers at a company refuse to confront or discuss a very skilled employee who is not participating in organizational planning because of serious concerns about institutional racism within the company. It is easier to continue to do the same things and avoid the concerns of the disgruntled employee. Another example is an ad agency that has a graphic designer who is not able to produce the quality of creative work needed, so, rather than address the problem directly, the agency assigns that designer menial jobs that are essentially busywork. It then hires a second graphic designer to do the more creative work despite the cost and the fact that the agency doesn't have enough work to justify two designers.

These four archetypes are representative of some of the common challenges that require adaptive change. Although they do not describe every possible type of adaptive change, they are useful as frames of reference when trying to identify adaptive challenges in a particular organizational setting.

3. Regulate Distress. A third behavior, or activity, important for adaptive leaders is to regulate distress. Psychologically, we all have a need for consistency—to keep our beliefs, attitudes, and values the same. In fact, it is quite natural for individuals to be more comfortable when things are predictable and their way of doing things stays the same. But adaptive challenges create the need to change, and the process of change creates uncertainty and distress for people. Feeling a certain level of distress during change is inevitable and even useful for most, but feeling too much distress is counterproductive and can be debilitating. The challenge for a leader is to help others recognize the need for change but not become overwhelmed by the need for the change itself. The adaptive leader needs to monitor the stress people are experiencing and keep it within a productive range, or regulate it. The model suggests three ways that leaders can maintain productive levels of stress.

Create a Holding Environment. This refers to establishing an atmosphere in which people can feel safe tackling difficult problems, but not so safe that they can avoid the problem. The idea of a holding environment has its roots in the field of psychotherapy where the counselor creates a therapeutic setting and uses effective communication and empathy to provide a sense of safety and protection for the client (Heifetz & Linsky, 2002; Modell, 1976; Winnicott, 1965). You can think of a holding environment in terms of children learning to swim—the instructor is within a watchful distance, but allows the children to do the hard work of overcoming their fears and learning to kick, breathe, and stroke in sync. A holding environment is a structural, procedural, or virtual space formed by cohesive relationships between people. It can be physical space, a shared language, common history, a deep trust in an institution and its authority, or a clear set of rules and processes that allow groups to function with safety. As illustrated in Figure 11.1, the holding environment represents the space where the work of adaptive leadership gets played out. Within the holding environment, adaptive leaders use their leverage to help people attend to the issues, to act as a reality test regarding information, to orchestrate conflicting perspectives, and to facilitate decision making (Heifetz, 1994, p. 113).

Creating a holding environment also allows a leader to regulate the pressures people face when confronting adaptive challenges. Heifetz often describes it as analogous to a pressure cooker, because initially a leader turns up the heat on the issues. This gets dialogue started and also allows some of the pressures from the issues to escape. If too much tension concerning issues is expressed, the holding environment can become too intense and ineffective for addressing problems. However, without the leader's initial catalyst, little dialogue will transpire.

Similar to labor negotiations in organizations, the holding environment is the place where all parties gather to begin talking to each other, define issues, and clarify competing interests and needs. If this discussion is too heated, negotiations reach a quick impasse. However, as negotiation develops, newer issues can be addressed. Over time, the holding environment provides the place where new contractual relationships can be agreed upon and enacted.

Provide Direction, Protection, Orientation, Conflict Management, and Productive Norms. This refers to specific ways leaders can help people manage the uncertainty and distress that accompany adaptive work. They are prescribed behaviors for adaptive leaders.

- *Providing direction* involves identifying the adaptive challenges that others face and then framing these so they can be addressed. In difficult situations, it is not uncommon for people to be unclear or confused about their goals. Sometimes the goal is unknown, sometimes it is obscure, and at other times it is entangled with competing goals. By providing direction, the leader helps people feel a sense of clarity, order, and certainty, reducing the stress people feel in uncertain situations.

- *Protection* refers to a leader's responsibility to manage the rate of adaptive change for people. It includes monitoring whether the change is too much or too fast for people. Furthermore, it requires monitoring external pressures people are experiencing and keeping these within a range they can tolerate.

- *Orientation* is the responsibility a leader has to orient people to new roles and responsibilities that may accompany adaptive change. When a change requires adopting new values and acting in accordance with those values, people may need to adopt entirely new roles within the organization. Orientation is the process of helping people to find their identity within a changing system.

- *Conflict management* refers to the leader's responsibility to handle conflict effectively. Conflict is inevitable in groups and organizations during adaptive challenges and presents an opportunity for people to learn and grow. Although conflict can be uncomfortable, it is not necessarily unhealthy, nor is it necessarily bad. The question is not "How can people avoid conflict and eliminate change?" but rather "How can people manage conflict and produce positive change?"

- Establishing *productive norms* is a responsibility of the adaptive leader. Norms are the rules of behavior that are established and shared by group members but are not easily changed. When norms are constructive, they have a positive influence on the progress of the group. However, when norms are unproductive and debilitating, they can impede the group. A leader should pay close attention to norms and challenge those that need to be changed and reinforce those that maximize the group's effectiveness and ability to adapt to change.

Collectively, these five prescribed behaviors provide a general blueprint for how adaptive leaders can mitigate the frustrations people feel during adaptive change. While not inclusive, they highlight some of the many important ways leaders can help people during the change process.

Regulating Personal Distress. This is another way leaders can maintain a productive level of stress during adaptive change. As we discussed previously, change and growth within an organization do not occur without uncertainty and stress. Because stress is inherent in change, adaptive leaders need to withstand the pressures from those who want to avoid change and keep things the same. While moderate amounts of tension are normal and necessary during change, too much or too little tension is unproductive. Leaders need to keep people focused on the hard work they need to do and the tension that accompanies that, while at the same time being sensitive to the very real frustrations and pain that people feel when doing adaptive work.

To help others through the adaptive process, adaptive leaders need to make sure their own ideas, opinions, and processes are well thought out. They must be strong and steady because people look to them and depend on them for support in situations that can be very trying and painful. Adaptive leaders need to be role models and exhibit confidence and the emotional capacity to handle conflict. This is not a stress-free role. Adaptive leaders need to be willing to experience the frustrations and pain that people feel during change but not to the extent that they lose their own sense of who they are as leaders.

An example of the demands of regulating personal distress can be seen in the leadership of a therapist who runs a support group for high school students with substance use disorders. In her role as a group facilitator, the therapist faces many challenges. She has to listen to students' stories and the challenges they face as they try to stay clean. She also has to push people to be honest about their successes and failures regarding drug use. She cannot push so hard, however, that group members feel threatened, stop communicating, or stop attending the group sessions. In the holding environment, she has to be able to show nurturance and support, but not enable destructive behavior. The pain and frustration people in treatment for addiction feel is tremendous, and the therapist has to be in touch with this pain without losing her role as a therapist. Hearing stories of recovery and failed recovery can be heartbreaking, while hearing success stories can be uplifting. Throughout all of this, the therapist needs to monitor herself closely and control her own anxieties regarding recovery. Group members look to the therapist for direction and support. They want the therapist to be strong, confident, and empathic. Regulating her own stress is essential in order to make herself fully available to students who are recovering from substance abuse disorders.

4. Maintain Disciplined Attention. The fourth leader behavior prescribed by the adaptive leadership process is to maintain disciplined attention. This means that the leader needs to encourage people to focus on the tough work they need to do. This does not come easily; people naturally do not want to confront change, particularly when it is related to changing their beliefs, values, or behaviors. It is common for all of us to resist change and strive for a sense of balance and equilibrium in our day-to-day experiences. People do not like things "out of sync," so when their sense of balance is disrupted by the need to change, it is natural for them to engage in avoidance behavior. This leader behavior is about helping people address change and not avoid it.

Avoidance behaviors can take many forms. People can ignore the problem, blame the problem on the authority, blame coworkers for the problem, attack those who want to address the problem, pretend the problem does not exist, or work hard in areas unrelated to the problem. No matter the form of avoidance, the leader's task is to mobilize and encourage people to drop their defenses and openly confront their problems. Adaptive leaders help people focus on issues. If some topics are deemed too "hot" in the organization, the leader should support people in getting these topics on the agenda for discussion. If some issues create deep divisions between people, the leader should provide a vessel of safety where competing sides can address the issues without feeling as if the organization will explode. If there is an "elephant in the room"—an issue that no one wants to address but is pivotal in making change—the leader needs to nudge people to talk about it. Whatever the situation, the adaptive leader gets people to focus, and to show disciplined attention to the work at hand.

An example of disciplined attention can be seen in how the director of a nursing home responds to the members of a family who are struggling with their decision to move their 80-year-old mother into nursing care. The mother has early signs of dementia, but has successfully lived alone since her husband died 10 years earlier. She prides herself on being able to cook, drive, and live independently. But her forgetfulness and physical problems are worrisome to her two adult children who are very concerned about their mother's health and safety. The children know their mother could benefit from nursing care, but they just cannot bring themselves to force their mother to move from her home to the care facility. They say things like "Mom just doesn't need it yet. We'll just take her car keys away. She is so much better than those people at the care facility. She won't survive in a new environment. She just won't be herself if she's not at their own home. We have the resources; we just don't need to put her in there yet." The director of the nursing home frequently hears the arguments expressed by the children, and his challenge is help them make the decision—a decision they are afraid of making and avoiding. He consistently gives a listening ear and sets up multiple appointments for the children to visit the care facility as well as meetings for the children to talk to staff members and other families who have parents at the facility. Throughout all of these sessions, the director emphasizes the importance of the children communicating their concerns. He lets them know that it is normal to not want to take a parent out of their own home, and to want to think of a parent as independent and whole. He lets them know that everyone has trouble accepting the failing health of a parent, and as difficult as this decision is, going into the nursing care facility is a good and reasonable decision because the parent will be safer, receive good care, and learn to thrive in her new home. In this example, the director is sensitive to the adaptive challenges the children face, and he makes a point of "standing by" and giving guidance and support. The director helps the children stay focused on the changes they need to make and mobilizes them to confront the decisions they need to make.

5. Give the Work Back to the People. People want leaders to provide some direction and structure to their work and want to feel secure in what they are doing; they also want to actively participate in problem solving. Too much leadership and authority can be debilitating to an organization, decrease people's confidence to solve problems on their own, and suppress their creative capacities. Overly directive leadership can result in people being dependent on their leaders and inhibit them from doing adaptive work. Even though it makes people feel comfortable and secure to have leaders tell them what to do, leaders need to learn ways to curtail their influence and shift problem solving back to the people involved.

Leaders need to be aware of and monitor the impact they have on others. Giving work back to the people requires leaders to be attentive to when they should drop back and let the people do the work that they need to do. This can be a fine line; leaders have to provide direction, but they also have to say, "This is your work—how do you think you want to handle it?" For adaptive leaders, giving work back to the people means empowering people to decide what to do in circumstances where they feel uncertain, expressing belief in their ability to solve their own problems, and encouraging them to think for themselves rather than doing that thinking for them.

Summerhill, the famous boarding school on the east coast of England, provides a good example of giving the work back to the people taking center stage. Summerhill is a self-governing, democratic school where adults and students have equal status. Summerhill's philosophy stresses that students have the freedom to take their own path in life and develop their own interests so long as it does not harm others. Classes are optional for students who have the freedom to choose what they do with their time. The schedules and rules of the school are established in weekly group meetings at which all participants have an equal vote. Summerhill's leaders give the work of learning back to the students. Instead of the teachers telling students what to study and learn, the students themselves make those decisions within a supportive environment. It is an unusual model of education and not without its problems, but it clearly demonstrates recognition of the need for students, and not their teachers, to identify and define their goals and take responsibility for meeting those goals.

6. *Protect Leadership Voices From Below.* This final leader behavior means that adaptive leaders have to be careful to listen and be open to the ideas of people who may be at the fringe, marginalized, or even deviant within the group or organization. This is a challenge because when the leader gives voice to an out-group member, it is upsetting to the social equilibrium of the group. To be open to the ideas of low-status individuals, who often may express themselves ineffectively, is also challenging because it is disruptive to the "normal" way of doing things. Too often, leaders find it convenient to ignore the dissident, nonconforming voices in an effort to maintain things as they are and keep things moving. Adaptive leaders should try to resist the tendency to minimize or shut down minority voices for the sake of the majority. To give voice to others requires that a leader relinquish some control, giving other individual members more control. This is why it is a challenging process.

Protecting voices from below puts low-status individuals on equal footing with other members of the group. It means the leader and the other people of the group give credence to the out-group members' ideas and actions. When out-group members have a voice, they know their interests are being recognized and that they can have an impact on the leader and the group. Giving them a voice allows low-status members to be more involved, independent, and responsible for their actions. It allows them to become more fully engaged in the adaptive work of the group, and they can feel like full members in the planning and decision making of the group.

Consider a college social work class in which students are required to do a service-learning project. For this project, one group chose to build a wheelchair ramp for an older woman in the community. In the initial stages of the project, morale in the group was down because one group member (Alissa) chose not to participate. Alissa said she was not comfortable using hand tools, and she chose not to do manual labor. The other team members, who had been doing a lot of planning for the project, wanted to proceed without her help. As a result, Alissa felt rejected and began to criticize the purpose of the project and the personalities of the other team members. At that point, one of the group's leaders decided to start listening to Alissa's concerns and learned that while Alissa could not work with her hands, she had two other talents: She was good with music, and she made wonderful lunches.

Once the leader found this out, things started to change. Alissa started to participate. During the construction of the ramp, Alissa kept up morale by playing each group member's and the older woman's favorite music while they worked on the ramp. In addition, Alissa made sandwiches and provided drinks that accommodated each of the group members' unique dietary interests. By the last day, Alissa felt so included by the group, and was praised for providing great food, that she joined in the manual labor and began raking up trash around the ramp site. Although Alissa's talents didn't tie in directly with constructing a ramp, she still contributed to building a successful team. Everybody was included and useful in a community-building project that could have turned sour if the leader had not given voice to Alissa's concerns and talents.

Adaptive Work

As represented on the right side of the model of adaptive leadership (Figure 11.1), *adaptive work* is the process toward which adaptive leaders direct their work. It is the focus and intended goal of adaptive leadership. Adaptive work develops from the communication processes that occur between the leader and followers but is primarily the work of followers. Ideally, it occurs within a holding environment where people can feel safe as they confront possible changes in their roles, priorities, and values.

The model illustrates that the *holding environment* is the place where adaptive work is conducted. It is a real or virtual space where people can address the adaptive challenges that confront them. Because the holding environment plays a critical role in the adaptive process, leaders direct considerable energy toward establishing and maintaining it.

While the term *followers* is used to depict individuals who are not the leader, it is important to note that throughout most of the writing on adaptive leadership, the term is avoided, due to its implication of a submissive role in relationship to the leader. In adaptive leadership, leaders do not use their authority to control others; rather, leaders *interact* with people to help them do adaptive work. *Followers* is used in the model simply to distinguish the specific individuals who are doing adaptive work.

An example of adaptive work can be seen at a fitness center where a fitness instructor is running a class for a group of individuals who have had heart problems and struggle with being overweight. The goal of the instructor is to provide a safe place where people can challenge themselves to do mundane training exercises that will help them to lose weight and reduce their risk for health problems. Because the people must change their lifestyles to live more healthfully, they must engage in adaptive work with the support of the fitness instructor. Another example where adaptive work can be observed is in a public elementary school where the principal is asking the teachers to adopt new Common Core standards but the teachers, who have a proven record of success using their own student-centered curriculum, are resisting. To help the teachers with the intended change, the principal sets up a series of 10 open faculty meetings where teachers are invited to freely discuss their concerns about the new policies. The meetings provide a holding environment where the teachers can confront their deeply held positions regarding the usefulness and efficacy of standardized testing and what it will mean for them to have to shift to Common Core standards. The principal's role is to communicate in ways that support the teachers in their adaptive work, and help shift values, beliefs, and perceptions to allow them to work effectively under the new system.

HOW DOES ADAPTIVE LEADERSHIP WORK?

Adaptive leadership is a complex process comprising multiple dimensions, including situational challenges, leader behaviors, and adaptive work. The overriding focus of the process is to engage individuals in doing adaptive work. This unique emphasis on mobilizing individuals (followers) to confront adaptive challenges makes adaptive leadership very different from other traditional leadership approaches that focus on leader traits (Chapter 2), skills (Chapter 3), behaviors (Chapter 4), and authenticity (Chapter 9). Adaptive leadership centers on the adaptations required of people in response to changing environments, and how leaders can support them during these changes.

As illustrated in Figure 11.2, the process of adaptive leadership works like this: First, the leader takes time to step back from a challenging situation to understand the complexities of the situation and obtain a fuller picture of the interpersonal dynamics occurring among the participants. Second, in any situation or context where people are experiencing change, the leader makes an initial assessment to determine if the change creates challenges that are technical or adaptive in nature. If the challenges are technical, the leader addresses the problems with authority and expertise or through the rules and procedures of the organization. If the challenges are adaptive, the leader engages in several specific leader behaviors to move the adaptive process forward.

While the recipe for adaptive leadership comprises many leader behaviors and activities, there is no particular order to the prescribed behaviors. Adaptive leadership incorporates many of these behaviors simultaneously, and interdependently, with some of them being more important at the beginning of a particular process and others at the end. Some important adaptive leader behaviors are regulating distress, creating a holding environment, providing direction, keeping people focused on important issues, empowering people, and giving voice to those who feel unrecognized or marginalized.

FIGURE 11.2   The Adaptive Leadership Process

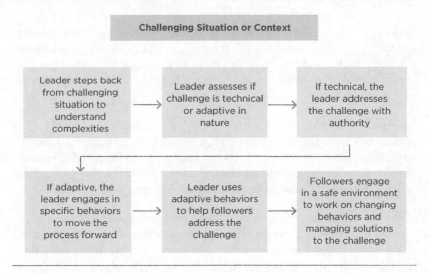

An example illustrating how the adaptive leadership process works can be seen in one university's handling of issues of freedom of speech on campus. Within the course of two years, the university had three separate incidents related to freedom of speech: college football players kneeling in protest to police violence toward people of color; an English Department lecturer harassing an undergraduate member of Turning Point USA, an organization that is considered to be politically conservative and far right; and an undergraduate student displaying White nationalist behavior.

The university's leaders approached these freedom of speech issues as adaptive challenges. First, they took the time to step back from each challenging situation to understand the complexities and obtain a fuller picture of the interpersonal dynamics occurring among the students and stakeholders involved (i.e., faculty, students, regents, parents, and political figures).

Second, the leaders made an initial assessment to determine if the challenges were technical or adaptive in nature. "Freedom of speech controversies are considered adaptive challenges because they tend to be unclear, require people to consider their values and beliefs, and [require people to] face resistance" (Sunderman, Headrick, & McCain, in press).

To confront each issue, the administration incorporated adaptive behaviors. The university's administration demonstrated the behavior of getting on the balcony by hosting forums with faculty and students to discuss their thoughts and feelings regarding freedom of speech issues. The forums allowed university leaders to regulate distress by creating a space for people on campus to process their emotions and fears.

Following the forums, the university conducted a system-wide survey regarding free speech and campus climate with the Gallup organization to gain perspective and better understand the challenges. After identifying the root issues, administrators decided to pursue a national search for a vice chancellor of diversity and inclusion.

These efforts to give the work back to the people allowed university leaders to empower and educate students, staff, and faculty to lead conversations and change. As universities make decisions in hopes of promoting civil discourse and positive campus culture, it becomes important to consider students' perspectives, which are often left out of conversations about free speech (Shapiro, 2018).

Complex campus issues that create disagreement and tension will undoubtedly continue to occur within colleges and universities and their surrounding communities. Adaptive leaders can aid institutions of higher education in doing the difficult and important work of taking perspective, empowering others on their campuses to bring change, and protecting campus voices (Sunderman et al., in press).

Finally, another example of adaptive leadership in action is in the work of Ramalingam, Wild, and Ferrari (2020), who describe the role of adaptive leadership in response to the coronavirus pandemic of 2019–2020. The outbreak created a worldwide need for adaptive leadership. Leaders at the federal, state, and local levels had to respond quickly to circumstances that changed every day. Decisions had to be made based on available data, which weren't always consistent, and information from many different spheres, including health care, natural resource management, military planning, international development, and humanitarian efforts. The collective ability to identify which interventions—or combination of interventions—might work best and why, as well as to understand the impacts of these interventions, was a major leadership challenge.

Overall, it is safe to say that adaptive leadership works because leaders are willing to engage in all of these behaviors with the intention of helping followers do adaptive work.

STRENGTHS

In its present stage of development, adaptive leadership has multiple strengths. First, in contrast to many other leadership theories, adaptive leadership takes a *process* approach to the study of leadership. Consistent with the process definition of leadership discussed in Chapter 1, adaptive leadership underscores that leadership is not a trait or characteristic of the leader, but rather a complex transactional event that occurs between leaders and followers in different situations. The process perspective highlights that leaders and followers mutually affect each other, making leadership an interactive activity that is not restricted to only a formally designated leader. This approach emphasizes that the phenomenon of leadership is a complex interactive process comprising multiple dimensions and activities. An adaptive leader addresses problems by engaging followers who are close to the problem in a system. These followers know the system because they exist within it every day and know what may or may not work. Follower participation is an important component of adaptive leadership as the approach recognizes that the leader does not have all the answers. The leader's role is one of facilitation rather than direction, and followers put processes in place to implement solutions (Nelson & Squires, 2017).

Second, adaptive leadership stands out because it is *follower centered*. Adaptive leaders mobilize people to engage in adaptive work. The adaptive approach to leadership is other directed, stressing follower involvement and follower growth. A primary obligation of adaptive leaders is to provide interventions to enable progress and regulate stress, and to create holding environments where others can learn, grow, and work on the changes that are needed. This approach encapsulates leadership as those behaviors and actions leaders need to engage in to give followers the greatest opportunity to do adaptive work.

Third, adaptive leadership is unique in how it directs authority to help followers *deal with conflicting values* that emerge in changing organizational environments and social contexts. Change and learning are inherent in organizational life, and adaptive leadership focuses specifically on helping followers to confront change and examine the emergence of new values that may accompany change. No other leadership approach holds as a central purpose to help followers confront their personal values and adjust these as needed in order for change and adaptation to occur.

From the perspective of Uhl-Bien and Arena (2018) and their work on complexity theory, the requirement for adaptive leadership often emerges from the tension between an organization's need to innovate and its need to produce. Innovative leaders propose new ideas that challenge the status quo and strain the current operating system. Resistance to change often occurs when followers realize that implementing these new ideas diverges from the current mission of the organization. It is this organizational resistance that adaptive leadership can address.

Another strength of adaptive leadership is that it provides a *prescriptive approach* to leadership that is useful and practical. In their writings, Heifetz and his colleagues identify many things leaders can do to facilitate adaptive leadership. The leader behaviors in Figure 11.1 are prescriptions for what an adaptive leader should do. For example, "get on the balcony," "regulate distress," and "give the work back to the people" are all prescriptive behaviors leaders can use to mobilize followers to do the work they need to do to adapt or change. In a general sense, even the model is prescriptive. It suggests that followers should learn to adapt and leaders should set up a context where this is most likely to occur. In short, adaptive leadership provides a recipe for what leaders and followers should do to facilitate adaptive change. It describes the kind of work (i.e., technical or adaptive) that followers should address and then the behaviors leaders should employ to help them accomplish this work.

Adaptive leadership's prescriptive nature is of value as organizations are faced with increasing levels of disruptive change that challenge organizational structures, and they must develop an adaptive response to address these challenges. Because adaptive leadership is not a "top-down" approach, new order emerges when networks of people, technology, information, and resources combine to solve problems (Uhl-Bien & Arena, 2017). With its emphasis on collaboration, adaptive leadership is especially applicable to complex organizational problems (Nelson & Squires, 2017).

Finally, adaptive leadership makes a unique contribution to the field of leadership studies by identifying the concept of *a holding environment* as an integral part of the leadership process. Few leadership theories discuss how leaders are responsible for creating a safe environment for followers to address difficult issues. The holding environment can be physical, virtual, or relational, but most important, it is an atmosphere where people feel safe tackling difficult issues. It is a place where leaders get a dialogue started, but do not let it become too heated or explosive. Although abstract, the concept of a holding environment can be easily visualized and is useful for anyone wanting to demonstrate adaptive leadership.

CRITICISMS

In addition to its strengths, adaptive leadership has several weaknesses. First, very little empirical research has been conducted to test the claims of adaptive leadership theory even though the conceptual framework for this approach was set forth more than 20 years ago in Heifetz's *Leadership Without Easy Answers* (1994). Originally intended as a practical framework for theory building, adaptive leadership is based on ideas and assumptions, but not on established research. Without evidence-based support for the tenets of the model, the ideas and principles set forth on adaptive leadership should be viewed cautiously. Recently, however, preliminary research that aims to provide an evidentiary basis for the basic assumptions and theoretical tenets of the model has begun to emerge (see Adams, Bailey, Anderson, & Galanos, 2013; Benzie, Pryce, & Smith, 2017; Corazzini et al., 2014; Gilbert, 2013; Hlalele, Manicom, Preece, & Tsotetsi, 2015; Klau & Hufnagel, 2016; Mugisha & Berg, 2017; Preece, 2016). Regarding measurement of adaptive leadership, some preliminary work on adaptive performance has been done that addresses solving problems creatively; dealing with uncertain or unpredictable work situations; learning new tasks, technologies, and procedures; and handling work stress (Marques-Quinteiro, Ramos-Villagrasa, Passos, & Curral, 2015).

Second, conceptualization of the process of adaptive leadership needs further refinement. Adaptive leadership was designed intentionally as a practical approach to leadership and is composed of a series of prescriptions for leaders to help people engage in adaptive work. However, the major factors in the adaptive process and the way these factors relate to one another to facilitate adaptive work are not clearly delineated. Figure 11.1 provides a "first attempt" at modeling the phenomenon of adaptive leadership, but much more needs to be done to clarify the essential factors in the model, the empirical relationships among these factors, and the process through which these factors lead to adaptive change within groups and organizations.

Third, adaptive leadership can be criticized for being too wide-ranging and abstract. For example, the approach suggests that leaders should "identify your loyalties," "mobilize the system," "name the default," "hold steady," "act politically," "anchor yourself," and many more behaviors that were not discussed in this chapter. Interpreting these prescriptions and their relationship to being an adaptive leader can be overwhelming because of the breadth and wide-ranging nature of these prescriptions. In addition, the recommended leader behaviors such as "give the work back to the people" often lack specificity and conceptual clarity. Without clear conceptualizations of recommended behaviors, it is difficult to know how to analyze these in research or implement them in practice. As a result, leaders may infer their own conceptualizations of these prescriptions, which may vary widely from what Heifetz and his colleagues intended.

Fourth, adaptive leadership can be uncomfortable for followers since it encourages conflict. Although the concept of a "holding environment" is central in the theory where it is safe to voice concerns and explore solutions, it is not clear how to keep the environment safe. Those who question the leadership may be penalized for their views. The theory needs to address how to guard against manipulation by an autocratic leader (Nelson & Squires, 2017).

Finally, from a theoretical perspective, the adaptive leadership framework hints at but does not directly explain how adaptive leadership incorporates a moral dimension. Adaptive leadership focuses on how people evolve and grow through change. It implies that the evolution of one's values leads to a greater common good, but the way the evolution of values leads to a greater common good is not fully explicated. It advocates mobilizing people to do adaptive work but does not elaborate or explain how doing adaptive work leads to socially useful outcomes. The model acknowledges the importance of promoting values such as equality, justice, and community, but the link between adaptive work and achieving those social values is not clear.

APPLICATION

How can adaptive leadership be applied to real-life situations? There are several ways. On an individual level, adaptive leadership provides a conceptual framework made up of a unique set of constructs that help us determine what type of challenges we face (e.g., *technical* versus *adaptive*) and strategies for managing them (e.g., *establishing a holding environment*). Individuals can easily integrate these constructs into their own practice of leadership. Furthermore, it is an approach to leadership that people can apply in a wide variety of settings, including family, school, work, community, and society.

On the organizational level, adaptive leadership can be used as a model to explain and address a variety of challenges that are ever present during change and growth. Consultants have applied adaptive leadership at all levels in many different kinds of organizations. In particular, it has been an approach to leadership of special interest to people in nonprofits, faith-based organizations, and health care.

At this point in the development of adaptive leadership, the context in which most of the research has been conducted is health care. For example, one group of researchers suggests that adaptive leadership can improve the practice of medicine (Thygeson, Morrissey, & Ulstad, 2010). They contend that health professionals who practice from an adaptive leadership perspective would view patients as complex adaptive systems who face both technical and adaptive challenges (Figure 11.3). Overall, they claim the adaptive leadership approach has promise to make health care more efficient, patient-centered, and sustainable.

FIGURE 11.3 Adaptive Leadership Framework Developed by Heifetz and Linsky

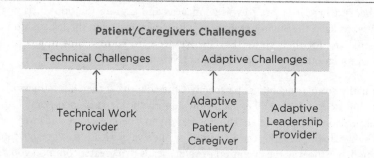

Sources: Adapted from "Finding Your Way Through EOL Challenges in the ICU Using Adaptive Leadership Behaviours: A Qualitative Descriptive Case Study," by J. A. Adams, D. E. Bailey Jr., R. A. Anderson, and M. Thygeson, 2013, *Intensive and Critical Care Nursing, 29*, pp. 329–336; and "Adaptive Leadership and the Practice of Medicine: A Complexity-Based Approach to Reframing the Doctor-Patient Relationship," by M. Thygeson, L. Morrissey, and V. Ulstad, 2010, *Journal of Evaluation in Clinical Practice, 16*, pp. 1009–1015.

Eubank, Geffken, Orzano, and Ricci (2012) used adaptive leadership as the overarching framework to guide the curriculum they developed for a family medicine residency program. They argue that if physicians practice the behaviors promoted in adaptive leadership (e.g., *get on the balcony*, *identify adaptive challenges*, or *regulate distress*), they can acquire the process skills that are necessary to implement and sustain true patient-centered care and healing relationships. Furthermore, to assist patients who are suffering, they contend that physicians need more than technical problem-solving competencies. Physicians also need adaptive skills that will enable them to help patients process and learn to live with the challenges resulting from changes in their health and well-being.

In two separate case studies, researchers found adaptive leadership could be used to help patients and family members confront health care challenges. Using the adaptive leadership framework, Adams, Bailey, Anderson, and Thygeson (2013) identified nurse and physician behaviors that can facilitate the transition from curative to palliative care by helping family members do the adaptive work of letting go. Similarly, Adams, Bailey, Anderson, and Galanos (2013) found adaptive leadership principles were useful in helping family members of patients in hospital intensive care units come to terms with loss and change, and make decisions consistent with the patient's goals.

In summary, there are many applications for adaptive leadership, on both the personal and organizational level, as well as in the research environment. While further research needs to be done to support the tenets of adaptive leadership, it is clearly a leadership approach that can be utilized in many settings.

CASE STUDIES

This section provides three case studies (Cases 11.1, 11.2, and 11.3) from very different contexts where adaptive leadership is present to a degree. The first case describes the challenges faced by two editors of a high school newspaper who wanted to write about lessening the stigma of mental illness. The second case is about how two co-captains tried to change the culture of their college Ultimate Frisbee team. The third case describes how the leadership of a financially struggling small college dealt with the possibility of having to close. At the end of each case, questions are provided to help you explore dimensions of adaptive leadership and how it can be utilized.

Case 11.1   SILENCE, STIGMA, AND MENTAL ILLNESS

Madeline Halpert and Eva Rosenfeld had three things in common: They were on the high school newspaper staff, they both suffered from depression, and until they shared their experiences with each other, both felt the isolation of the stigma that comes with suffering from mental illness.

The two student editors knew they were far from the only ones in their high school who experienced these challenges and, in a concerted effort to support others and lessen the stigma of mental illness, decided to write an in-depth feature on the topic for their student newspaper. Recent cases of school shootings had brought mental illness in teens to the forefront, and evidence shows that depression is a major cause of suicide in young people. Yet, the strong stigma that surrounds depression and mental illness often isolates those who suffer from it. The purpose of Eva and Madeline's feature was to open the dialogue and end the stigma. They interviewed a number of teens from schools in the surrounding area who agreed to use their real names and share their personal stories about mental illness, including depression, eating disorders, and homelessness. The student editors even obtained waivers from the subjects' parents giving them permission to use the stories. However, their stories never made it to print.

While they were putting the story together, their school's principal called them into her office and told them about a former college football player from the area who struggled with depression and would be willing to be interviewed. The editors declined, not wanting to replace the deeply personal articles about their peers with one from someone removed from the students. The principal then told them she wouldn't support printing the stories. She objected to the use of students' real names, saying she feared potential personal repercussions such as bullying or further mental health problems that publishing such an article could have for those students. District officials stood by the principal's decision to halt printing of the piece, saying it was the right one to protect the students featured in the article.

This move surprised the two student editors because they felt that their school had a very tolerant atmosphere, which included offering a depression awareness group. "We were surprised that the administration and the adults who advocated for mental health awareness were the ones standing in the way of it," they wrote. "By telling us that students could not talk openly about their struggles, they reinforced the very stigma we were trying to eliminate."

Instead, the two editors penned an op-ed piece, "Depressed, but Not Ashamed," which was published in the *New York Times*. The article discussed their dismay with having the articles halted by school administrators, an act that they believe further stigmatized those with mental illnesses.

"By interviewing these teenagers for our newspaper, we tried—and failed—to start small in the fight against stigma. Unfortunately, we've learned this won't be easy. It seems that those who are charged with advocating for our well-being aren't ready yet to let us have an open and honest dialogue about depression," they wrote.

The op-ed piece generated a response—and, interestingly, a dialogue—about the topic.

The two student editors were subsequently interviewed on the National Public Radio show *Weekend Edition* (2014). In that interview, the editors acknowledged that they had experienced mostly positive reactions to their piece, with more than 200 comments after the initial publication. Many of those comments said the article resonated with readers and gave them the courage to talk to someone about their struggles with mental illness in a way they hadn't before.

"And I think, most importantly, it's opening a dialogue," said one of the editors in the interview. "There were negative comments. There were positive comments. But the most important thing is that it's so amazing to see people discussing this and finally opening up about it."

Questions

1. How do you define the problem the editors were trying to address? Was this a *technical* or an *adaptive* challenge?

2. What is your reaction to what the principal did in this situation? How do you think what she did fits in with *providing direction, protection, orientation, conflict management, and productive norms*?

3. Describe the *holding environment* in this case. Was the holding environment sufficient to meet the adaptive challenges in this situation? How would you improve it?

4. Based on Figure 11.1, discuss who were the adaptive leaders in this case. Which of the leader behaviors (*get on the balcony, identify adaptive challenges, regulate distress*, etc.) did these leaders exhibit?

Dominic Santana is a serious Ultimate player. He became involved in the sport—which is a bit like soccer, only with a flying disc—in middle school and played competitively in high school. When he went to college at a small liberal arts school in the Pacific Northwest, he was excited to find the school had an Ultimate team. His excitement quickly turned to dismay when he found the team members were more interested in partying than playing.

Dominic remembers this about his first year on the team: "The team really had this sort of fraternity culture in that there was light hazing, drinking was a priority, and tournaments were about parties, not competition. The team threw a lot of parties and had this reputation for exclusivity." Even the team's name, Bacchus (the Roman god of wine and drunkenness), reflected this culture.

Dominic found a like-minded soul in his teammate Harrison, and together they sought to turn the team into a program that operated on a more competitive level. The two were chosen as co-captains and began to share their deeper knowledge of the sport with the team. They also communicated their aspirations for success. This flew in the face of some team members who were there for the parties. As one player put it, "Either you were down with it or you decided it was too intense and you left the club."

The two captains knew that the team's culture wasn't going to change just because they wanted it to. They also knew that they couldn't be captains, coach the team, and be players at the same time. They began taking a number of steps to help the team change its own culture.

First, they brought in Mario O'Brien, a well-known Ultimate coach, to help guide the team and teach the players skills and strategy. The team had had other coaches in the past, but none of those had the knowledge, experience, or reputation that O'Brien did.

"That really took some forethought," says a player, "to be able to step back and say, 'What does this team really need to become a strong program?' And then making a move to bring in someone of O'Brien's stature."

After a few weeks of practice with O'Brien, the captains and coach organized a team dinner. Before the dinner they asked each player to anonymously submit in writing what he thought of the team and what he wanted to see the team be. "There were no rules—just say what you need to say," says a player. Each submission was read aloud and discussed by team members.

"No one was put in the position of having to publicly speak out and be embarrassed in front of the others," says a player. "We came out of that meeting more together, more bonded as a team. We hashed out a lot of issues, and came to the realization that we were looking for the same goals. The process helped filter out those that weren't as committed to those goals, but not in a confrontational way."

The goals agreed to at that dinner meeting were for the team to do well enough at the sectional competition to obtain a berth at the national collegiate competition. But the team had a number of inexperienced players, which sometimes caused stress, frustration, and friction. The captains continued to have multiple meetings to talk about concerns, discussed the team's goals before and after each practice, and organized social events (with a minimum of drinking) where team members engaged in activities together other than playing Ultimate. More experienced players began mentoring the newer players to help improve their skills. Even Harrison, who was an exceptional offensive player, put himself on the defensive line to help improve those players' skills. While it wasn't optimum for his own enjoyment and playing abilities, he felt it was needed to help improve the team.

Bacchus reached its goals two years later; it came in second at sectionals and earned a spot in the national competition. After the team completed its last game at nationals, Dominic and Harrison gathered the team members together in a circle. "We accomplished something more than being here today," Dominic said. "We've become a family with goals, and with respect for one another and for our game. And that's a better victory than any other."

Questions

1. What changes were Dominic and Harrison trying to make? How did these changes affect the beliefs, attitudes, or values of the players?

2. Were the challenges the team faced technical, technical and adaptive, or adaptive? What examples can you give to explain your answer?

3. Citing examples, explain how the captains engaged in each of these adaptive leader behaviors: (1) *get on the balcony*, (2) *identify adaptive challenges*, (3) *regulate distress*, (4) *maintain disciplined attention*, (5) *give the work back to the people*, and (6) *protect leadership voices from below.*

4. Describe the holding environment that the co-captains created for the team. Do you think it was successful? Why or why not?

Case 11.3 AGONIZING OPTIONS FOR MARLBORO COLLEGE

To close or not to close? This is the question confronting many small colleges in the United States.

A number of factors have created these dire circumstances. First, student enrollment in higher education across the United States has declined due to a strong

(Continued)

(Continued)

economy (Nadworny & Larkin, 2019). Second, states are no longer funding higher education to help subsidize costs, so institutions are more reliant on the tuition dollars of enrolled students. As a result, tuition at private colleges increased by more than 29% from 2008 to 2018 (Hess, 2019). Third, the coronavirus pandemic in 2019–2020 resulted in increased online education offerings, making students second-guess the need for a residential, small-college experience. Finally, the number of high school graduates has plateaued, making the landscape for interested college applicants highly competitive.

These factors have resulted in sizeable drops in enrollment at many schools. Low enrollment means less revenue, and that decline has forced colleges to make difficult decisions, like choosing to cut staff and faculty to make up for budget deficits (Harlow, 2019) or simply making the choice to close their doors (Jaschik, 2019).

Marlboro College, a small liberal arts college in rural Vermont, recently faced the decision of whether or not it should continue to operate as an institution of higher education. Marlboro served a specific type of student—those who wanted to create their own academic plan, to graduate having written the equivalent of a master's thesis, and to have intentional interaction with faculty (ratio 7:1) (Zahneis, 2019). Was Marlboro's philosophy academic utopia or sadly doomed to fail? To the students who found Marlboro, it was an academic dream, but with the myriad of factors impacting its enrollment, staying open was becoming a harder reality.

Marlboro president Kevin F. F. Quigley wanted to explore options rather than simply closing. He cared deeply about Marlboro and did not want it to fail. To that end, he initiated a Strategic Options Task Force, comprised of the board chair, the president, four trustees, two faculty members, and one student, to review the options for Marlboro (Marlboro College, 2019). Among the questions the team investigated included these: Could the campus still operate, but as a branch campus of another institution? Would there be a way to ensure current students didn't have a break in their academic journey? How would a campus closure impact the small town (also called Marlboro) in which the college resides? What would happen to the history and values of the school? How would students, faculty, and alumni handle a change that would most certainly impact the identification they had with the school?

As the school entered the 2019–2020 academic year, it became clear that Marlboro, at best, could only remain open for a few more years (Audette, 2019b). In collaboration with the task force, President Quigley put out a call to other institutions to see if they wanted to partner with the college, ultimately talking to 10 (Audette, 2019a).

The task force narrowed the options, landing on the University of Bridgeport, the only partnership that would allow Marlboro to maintain its rural campus. Marlboro signed a letter of intent with Bridgeport, a vocationally oriented institution that focuses on science, technology, engineering, and mathematics and enrolls 5,000 students annually, in late July. But it was not to be. Negotiations between Marlboro and Bridgeport broke off in September 2019 (Zahneis, 2019).

Surprisingly, in November 2019, a new deal was reached. Marlboro and Emerson College in Boston announced that there would be a partnership between the two institutions (Zahneis, 2019). The agreement would wind down operations at Marlboro College at the end of the 2020 school year, with the opportunity for all remaining students to transfer to Emerson College in Boston to finish their studies with their current tuition packages. Emerson agreed to hire all Marlboro's tenure and tenure-track faculty and accept any current Marlboro student, honoring Marlboro's current tuition rate if the students did not change majors. All other positions at Marlboro would cease to exist at the end of the academic year. In this process, Emerson received a transfer of assets from Marlboro, including a $30 million endowment and $10 million in buildings. Emerson College indicated that the Marlboro campus would close, and that it had no interest in having a campus in Marlboro (Audette, 2019a).

Many were surprised by the announcement. President Quigley said negotiations with Emerson had been intentionally kept under wraps. "Since the collapse of the talks with Bridgeport in the middle of September, my community has really been on pins and needles, waiting for the shoe to drop," he said. "We changed how we talked about it on campus and who was involved in the process, so we had a tighter circle of people involved. There were really no updates to the community" (Zahneis, 2019).

The move created a mix of feelings among Marlboro's students and alumni. A previous Marlboro faculty member felt the situation was mishandled, saying, "All of this has taken place through secret negotiations. Nobody knew what was happening" (Zahneis, 2019). This sentiment was also expressed by the residents of the town of Marlboro, many of whom were employed by the college.

As soon as word became more public, one alumnus attempted to buy the institution with plans to have it run by alumni sharing (Zahneis, 2019). Through Facebook, a large following of alumni pledged to quit their jobs, take pay cuts, and help to rebuild their alma mater. They felt as though campus leadership did not think about all the alternatives to the campus closure. But, the agreement with Emerson was binding, and the university needed to move forward with the plan.

Many faculty and alumni were disheartened by the course of action, and to help ease fears, Marlboro students and faculty made a number of visits to Emerson (Marlboro College Board of Trustees, 2019) to ensure that the Emerson experience would fit with the Marlboro philosophy. Current students have expressed a sense of unity over the situation. One shared, "I'm pretty optimistic about the merger. We recognize that it's the best of a bad situation" (Zahneis, 2019).

(Continued)

(Continued)

At the same time, however, there was considerable concern by residents as to what would happen to the college's campus located in a prominent part of the town. To address that, Marlboro College established the Marlboro Campus Working Group, comprised of Marlboro alumni, trustees, staff, faculty, students, and a representative from the town of Marlboro, to seek proposals "for endeavors that would benefit the community and make productive use of the Marlboro campus" (Audette, 2020).

Questions

1. What were the competing commitments Marlboro's president was trying to navigate?

2. Would you describe the work of Marlboro's president as adaptive leadership? Why or why not?

3. Which of the following leader behaviors did the president utilize: (1) get on the balcony, (2) identify adaptive challenges, (3) regulate distress, (4) maintain disciplined attention, (5) give the work back to the people, (6) protect leadership voices from below? Provide an example of each.

4. Do you think there is a different course of action the college should take to resolve this challenge? Why or why not?

5. If you were the president of Marlboro College, how could you have created a *holding environment* for the students, faculty, and townspeople of Marlboro?

6. Adaptive leadership is about helping followers address value struggles. Who in the case is struggling, and what is their struggle?

—Jenny Steiner, PhD, University of Minnesota

LEADERSHIP INSTRUMENT

To assist you in understanding the process of adaptive leadership and what your own style might be, the Adaptive Leadership Questionnaire is included in this section. This questionnaire provides 360-degree, or multirater, feedback about your leadership. The Adaptive Leadership Questionnaire comprises 30 items that assess the six dimensions of adaptive leadership discussed earlier in this chapter: *get on the balcony, identify the adaptive challenge, regulate distress, maintain disciplined attention, give the work back to the people,* and *protect leadership voices from below.* The results you obtain on this questionnaire will provide you information on how others view you and how you view yourself on these six dimensions of adaptive leadership.

Adaptive leadership is a complex process, and taking this questionnaire will help you understand the theory of adaptive leadership as well as your own style of adaptive leadership.

Adaptive Leadership Questionnaire

Purpose: The purpose of this questionnaire is to identify your adaptive leadership strengths and weaknesses.

Instructions: This questionnaire contains items that assess different dimensions of adaptive leadership and will be completed by someone who knows you (coworkers, friends, members of a group you belong to).

1.   Have 1 individual fill out the assessment regarding your leadership

2.   Have the individual indicate the degree to which they agree with each of the 30 statements below regarding your leadership by selecting the number from the scale that they believe most accurately characterizes their response to the statement. There are no right or wrong responses.

Key: 1 = Strongly disagree   2 = Disagree   3 = Neutral   4 = Agree   5 = Strongly agree

1.   When difficulties emerge in our organization, this leader is good at stepping back and assessing the dynamics of the people involved. 1 2 3 4 5

2.   When events trigger strong emotional responses among employees, this leader uses their authority as a leader to resolve the problem. 1 2 3 4 5

3.   When people feel uncertain about organizational change, they trust that this leader will help them work through the difficulties. 1 2 3 4 5

4.   In complex situations, this leader gets people to focus on the issues they are trying to avoid. 1 2 3 4 5

5.   When employees are struggling with a decision, this leader tells them what they think they should do. 1 2 3 4 5

6.   During times of difficult change, this leader welcomes the thoughts of group members with low status. 1 2 3 4 5

7.   In difficult situations, this leader sometimes loses sight of the "big picture." 1 2 3 4 5

8.   When people are struggling with value questions, this leader reminds them to follow the organization's policies. 1 2 3 4 5

9.   When people begin to be disturbed by unresolved conflicts, this leader encourages them to address the issues. 1 2 3 4 5

10.   During organizational change, this leader challenges people to concentrate on the "hot" topics. 1 2 3 4 5

11.   When employees look to this leader for answers, they encourage them to think for themselves. 1 2 3 4 5

12. Listening to group members with radical ideas is valuable to this leader.   1 2 3 4 5

13. When this leader disagrees with someone, they have difficulty listening to what the person is really saying.   1 2 3 4 5

14. When others are struggling with intense conflicts, this leader steps in to resolve the differences.   1 2 3 4 5

15. This leader has the emotional capacity to comfort others as they work through intense issues.   1 2 3 4 5

16. When people try to avoid controversial organizational issues, this leader brings these conflicts into the open.   1 2 3 4 5

17. This leader encourages their employees to take initiative in defining and solving problems.   1 2 3 4 5

18. This leader is open to people who bring up unusual ideas that seem to hinder the progress of the group.   1 2 3 4 5

19. In challenging situations, this leader likes to observe the parties involved and assess what's really going on.   1 2 3 4 5

20. This leader encourages people to discuss the "elephant in the room."   1 2 3 4 5

21. People recognize that this leader has confidence to tackle challenging problems.   1 2 3 4 5

22. This leader thinks it is reasonable to let people avoid confronting difficult issues.   1 2 3 4 5

23. When people look to this leader to solve problems, they enjoy providing solutions.   1 2 3 4 5

24. This leader has an open ear for people who don't seem to fit in with the rest of the group.   1 2 3 4 5

25. In a difficult situation, this leader will step out of the dispute to gain perspective on it.   1 2 3 4 5

26. This leader thrives on helping people find new ways of coping with organizational problems.   1 2 3 4 5

27. People see this leader as someone who holds steady in the storm.   1 2 3 4 5

28. In an effort to keep things moving forward, this leader lets people avoid issues that are troublesome.   1 2 3 4 5

29. When people are uncertain about what to do, this leader empowers them to decide for themselves.   1 2 3 4 5

30. To restore equilibrium in the organization, this leader tries to neutralize comments of out-group members.   1 2 3 4 5

(Continued)

(Continued)

Scoring

Get on the Balcony—This score represents the degree to which you are able to step back and see the complexities and interrelated dimensions of a situation.

To arrive at this score:

Sum items 1, 19, and 25 and the reversed (R) score values for 7 and 13 (i.e., change 1 to 5, 2 to 4, 4 to 2, and 5 to 1, with 3 remaining unchanged).

_____ 1 _____ 7(R) _____ 13(R) _____ 19 _____ 25 _____ Total (Get on the Balcony)

Identify the Adaptive Challenge—This score represents the degree to which you recognize adaptive challenges and do not respond to these challenges with technical leadership.

To arrive at this score:

Sum items 20 and 26 and the reversed (R) score values for 2, 8, and 14 (i.e., change 1 to 5, 2 to 4, 4 to 2, and 5 to 1, with 3 remaining unchanged).

_____ 2(R) _____ 8(R) _____ 14(R) _____ 20 _____ 26 _____ Total (Identify the Adaptive Challenge)

Regulate Distress—This score represents the degree to which you provide a safe environment in which others can tackle difficult problems and to which you are seen as confident and calm in conflict situations.

To arrive at this score:

Sum items 3, 9, 15, 21, and 27.

_____ 3 _____ 9 _____ 15 _____ 21 _____ 27 _____ Total (Regulate Distress)

Maintain Disciplined Attention—This score represents the degree to which you get others to face challenging issues and not let them avoid difficult problems.

To arrive at this score:

Sum items 4, 10, and 26 and the reversed (R) score values for 22 and 28 (i.e., change 1 to 5, 2 to 4, 4 to 2, and 5 to 1, with 3 remaining unchanged).

_____ 4 _____ 10 _____ 16 _____ 22(R) _____ 28(R) _____ Total (Maintain Disciplined Attention)

Give the Work Back to the People—This score is the degree to which you empower others to think for themselves and solve their own problems.

To arrive at this score:

Sum items 11, 17, and 29 and the reversed (R) score values for 5 and 23 (i.e., change 1 to 5, 2 to 4, 4 to 2, and 5 to 1, with 3 remaining unchanged).

____ 5(R) ____ 11 ____ 17 ____ 23(R) ____ 29 ____ Total (Give the Work Back to the People)

Protect Leadership Voices From Below—This score represents the degree to which you are open and accepting of unusual or radical contributions from low-status group members.

To arrive at this score:

Sum items 6, 12, 18, and 24 and the reversed (R) score value for 30 (i.e., change 1 to 5, 2 to 4, 4 to 2, and 5 to 1, with 3 remaining unchanged).

____ 6 ____ 12 ____ 18 ____ 24 ____ 30(R) ____ Total (Protect Leadership Voices From Below)

Scoring Interpretation

- *High range*: A score between 21 and 25 means others find you are strongly inclined to exhibit this adaptive leadership behavior.

- *Moderately high range*: A score between 16 and 20 means others find you moderately exhibit this adaptive leadership behavior.

- *Moderate low range*: A score between 11 and 15 means others find you at times exhibit this adaptive leadership behavior.

- *Low range*: A score between 5 and 10 means others find you are seldom inclined to exhibit this adaptive leadership behavior.

This questionnaire measures adaptive leadership assessing six components of the process: get on the balcony, identify the adaptive challenge, regulate distress, maintain disciplined attention, give the work back to the people, and protect leadership voices from below. By completing the questionnaire yourself and comparing your scores on each of these components, you can determine which are your stronger and which are your weaker components in each category. There are no "perfect" scores for this questionnaire. While it is confirming when others see you in the same way as you see yourself, it is also beneficial to know when they see you differently. This assessment can help you understand those dimensions of your adaptive leadership that are strong and dimensions of your adaptive leadership you may seek to improve.

SUMMARY

Adaptive leadership is about helping people change and adjust to new situations. Originally formulated by Heifetz (1994), adaptive leadership conceptualizes the leader not as one who solves problems for people, but rather as one who encourages others to do the problem solving. Adaptive leadership occupies a unique place in the leadership literature. While the merits of the approach are well recognized, the theoretical conceptualizations of adaptive leadership remain in the formative stages.

While the name of this approach, adaptive leadership, makes one think it is concerned with how leaders adapt, it is actually more about the adaptations of followers. Adaptive leadership is defined as "the practice of mobilizing people to tackle tough challenges and thrive" (Heifetz et al., 2009, p. 14). Consistent with complexity theory, adaptive leadership is about leader behaviors that encourage learning, creativity, and adaptation by followers in complex situations.

This chapter offers a model of the major components of adaptive leadership and how they fit together, including *situational challenges, leader behaviors,* and *adaptive work* (Figure 11.1). Leaders confront three kinds of *situational challenges* (technical, technical and adaptive, and adaptive); adaptive leadership is concerned with helping people address adaptive challenges. The six *leader behaviors* that play a major role in the process are (1) *get on the balcony,* (2) *identify adaptive challenges,* (3) *regulate distress,* (4) *maintain disciplined attention,* (5) *give the work back to the people,* and (6) *protect leadership voices from below.* These six behaviors form a kind of recipe for being an adaptive leader. *Adaptive work* is the focus and goal of adaptive leadership. Central to adaptive work is awareness of the need for creating *a holding environment,* and skill in creating holding environments when needed. A holding environment is a space created and maintained by adaptive leaders where people can feel secure as they confront and resolve difficult life challenges.

Adaptive leadership has several strengths. First, adaptive leadership takes a unique approach that emphasizes that leadership is a complex interactive process comprising multiple dimensions and activities. Second, unlike most other leadership theories, adaptive leadership clearly describes leadership as actions the leaders undertake to afford followers the best opportunity to do adaptive work. Third, adaptive leadership is unique in describing how leaders can help people confront and adjust their values in order to adapt and thrive. Fourth, adaptive leadership provides a useful and practical set of prescriptions for leaders and followers to facilitate adaptive change. Last, adaptive leadership highlights the important role a holding environment plays in the leadership process.

The adaptive leadership process also has certain weaknesses. Foremost, there is very little empirical research to support the claims and tenets of adaptive leadership. Second, the conceptualizations of the process of adaptive leadership need further refinement. The major factors and how they fit together are not clearly delineated. Third, interpreting the prescriptions of adaptive leadership can become overwhelming because of the breadth and wide-ranging nature of these prescriptions. In addition, the abstract nature of the recommended leadership behaviors makes these behaviors difficult to analyze in research or implement in practice. Fourth, adaptive leadership does not explain how leaders can guarantee safe holding environments for followers who have to deal with the conflict inherent in the adaptive process. Finally, on a theoretical level, adaptive leadership acknowledges the moral dimension of leadership and the importance of change for the common good, but does not show how doing adaptive work leads to such socially useful outcomes.

Overall, adaptive leadership offers a unique prescriptive approach to leadership that is applicable in many situations. Going forward, more research is needed to clarify the conceptualizations of adaptive leadership and validate the assumptions and propositions regarding how it works.

Inclusive Leadership

Donna Chrobot-Mason and
Quinetta Roberson

DESCRIPTION

Although the term *inclusive leadership* is relatively new, scholars have been advising leaders for quite some time to be prepared to address the challenges of a more diverse workforce (Roberson, Ryan, & Ragins, 2017). A now famous report from 1987 titled *Workforce 2000* predicted that for organizations to remain competitive in the future, they must find ways to integrate and support women and people of color in the workplace (Johnston & Packer, 1987). Cox and Blake (1991) further reinforced the value of diversity in organizations, arguing that diversity can create a competitive advantage if managed effectively such that all employees are contributing to the best of their abilities and at their highest potential.

In the years following the *Workforce 2000* report, numerous scholarly and practitioner publications touted the need for effective diversity management (see Dass & Parker, 1999; Ivancevich & Gilbert, 2000; Kalev, Kelly, & Dobbin, 2006; Yang & Konrad, 2011). *Diversity management* incorporates programs and practices designed to "(a) improve interaction among diverse people; and (b) make this diversity a source of innovation and increased effectiveness rather than miscommunication, conflict, or obstacles to employees' performance, satisfaction, and advancement" (Hays-Thomas, 2017, p. 5). The concept and practice of diversity management has quickly evolved, and today researchers and practitioners emphasize inclusion and inclusive leadership as central elements of successful diversity management.

Initially, approaches to diversity management within research and practice included formalized human resource practices focused on improving opportunities for historically marginalized groups or organizational initiatives to promote and value all types of differences among employees (Linnehan & Konrad, 1999). While many organizations primarily approached diversity in terms of increasing the number of members of underrepresented groups within their workforces and maintaining legal compliance consistent with equal employment opportunity legislation (Thomas & Ely, 1996), more systemic approaches focused on leveraging the benefits of diverse knowledge, perspectives, and skills to facilitate organizational learning and growth were developed (Ely & Thomas, 2001). Such approaches were shown to require environments in which all employees feel valued, able to fully utilize their perspectives and talents, and that they have an opportunity to commit and contribute to organizational objectives (Davidson & Ferdman, 2002; Ely & Thomas, 2001). As such, they highlighted inclusion as critical to valuing and leveraging diversity in organizations (Mor Barak & Cherin, 1998).

Since the beginning of the millennium, the concept of inclusion has emerged as a key psychological construct for realizing the benefits that diversity can bring to the workplace. Ferdman (2014) contends that a focus on inclusion not only promotes the reduction of negative and problematic processes grounded in discrimination and oppression, but also fosters a positive vision of what might replace these undesired behaviors, policies, and systems. Despite this shift toward clarifying a vision of what the workplace should be like in order to fully engage a diverse workforce, scholarly contributions to the inclusion literature have largely progressed without a clear theoretical foundation and have primarily focused on construct definition. Additionally, strategies for creating more inclusive organizations, including the importance and role of leaders, have been largely missing from the literature.

What has become clearer over time is that the demand and need for inclusive leadership has come at a moment when leaders' plates are already full. Today's leaders are finding themselves responsible for guiding others in an increasingly global and complex marketplace, fulfilling the role of boundary spanner, linking and creating direction, alignment, and commitment across individuals, teams, and networks (Ernst & Chrobot-Mason, 2010). In addition, leaders are tasked with driving the transfer of knowledge and resources across organizations to enhance collaboration and support innovation (Corsaro, Ramos, Henneberg, & Naudé, 2012). As technological advances have made work less bound by geography and time and characterized by more diverse customers, suppliers, and employees, leaders play a critical role in facilitating coordination and learning across groups, organizations, and cultures (Arnett & Wittmann, 2014; Carter et al., 2020; Miles, Snow, Fjeldstad, Miles, & Lettl, 2010). Given the complexities and challenges that global markets, geographic dispersion, rapid advances in technology, the influence of social media, the rapid pace of change, and diversity bring, more is expected of leaders than ever before.

In today's multifaceted and multicultural organizational environment, leaders must be able to identify or create opportunities for growth and competitiveness. As such, they must be able to create environments in which differences are valued and can be incorporated into the main work of an organization to enhance strategies, processes, and overall effectiveness (Ernst & Chrobot-Mason, 2010; Ferdman, 2014; Thomas & Ely, 1996). While organizational policies and human resource practices may help create an infrastructure to foster this type of environment, leaders are the primary drivers of organizational culture. Accordingly, leaders who can create a sense of inclusion among followers and leverage the benefits of diversity are needed in organizations.

This chapter explores the nature of inclusive leadership, beginning by defining inclusion by drawing on both the diversity and the leadership literature. It will then examine an inclusive leadership model that describes the antecedent conditions, behaviors, and outcomes of inclusive leadership, followed by a discussion of how inclusive leadership works, its strengths and criticisms, and how it can be developed. Finally, case studies and a leadership instrument will provide an opportunity to evaluate inclusive leadership practices in a variety of contexts.

Inclusion Defined

To understand the role inclusion plays in diversity management, it makes sense to first explore what is meant by inclusion. More than a half-century ago, Schutz (1958) posited that inclusion (along with control and affection) is a basic human need that people experience in their interpersonal relationships. Schutz argued that people express their need to be included by how they communicate with others. He contends that people experience less anxiety if their need to be "in the group" matches the degree to which they want others to "include them." This suggests that it is beneficial for leaders to open their arms to include all followers, but not to the extent that the individual differences of others get smothered or lost in the process.

In the leadership literature, some researchers view inclusive leadership as a particular form of *relational leadership*, which focuses on the relationship between a leader and follower as the unit of analysis. From this perspective, inclusiveness is enacted and socially constructed through leader–follower interactions (Uhl-Bien, 2006). In effect, inclusive leadership is driven by the two-way influence process between leader and follower (Hollander, 2009). Rather than leaders directing followers, inclusive approaches establish norms of active consultation and participation, which drive shared decision making within a team or organization.

Despite its participative qualities, however, inclusive leadership differs from *participative leadership* (defined in Chapter 6, "Path–Goal Theory") in that it is applicable to situations in which members' statuses vary according to the degree to which they are considered insiders and incorporate behaviors to include those whose perspectives and opinions might otherwise be ignored. By inviting and appreciating the contributions of all individuals, an inclusive leadership approach helps people feel they are genuinely valued members of a team or organization (Tyler & Lind, 1992). Accordingly, inclusive leadership is fundamental to relational leadership, as it focuses on interpersonal relationships and drives followers' perceptions that leaders are fair, accountable, and attentive to their needs.

Given research that shows that individuals from a variety of social and cultural groups are often excluded from networks of information and opportunity in organizations (Ibarra, 1993; Pettigrew & Martin, 1989), inclusion has also been used to describe worker participation and empowerment. For example, Mor Barak and Cherin (1998) define inclusion as the extent to which individuals can access information and resources, are involved in groups, and have the ability to influence decision-making processes. Rather than emphasizing difference as an organizational commodity, inclusion is focused on the degree to which individuals feel they are a part of critical organizational processes (Roberson, 2006). While it encapsulates diversity in its various forms, including characteristics that are both observable and unobservable within a social system, and recognizes such diversity as a means for achieving collective goals, inclusion requires that all individuals feel able to fully and meaningfully contribute to shared goals regardless of group memberships and to do so without assimilating to established norms or relinquishing any part of their identity (Ferdman, 2014).

Brewer (1991) links inclusion to *optimal distinctiveness theory*. According to this theory, individuals strive to balance their basic human need to be part of larger social groups with their need to maintain a distinctive self-concept. People want to belong, feel accepted, and be connected to others, but not to the extent that they lose their sense of self as unique individuals. Inclusion means feeling like you are a full member of the group, but at the same time maintaining your own sense of self.

Following the theoretical tenets of optimal distinctiveness theory (Brewer, 1991), Shore and colleagues (2011) define inclusion as "the degree to which an employee perceives that he or she is an esteemed member of the work group through experiencing treatment that satisfies his or her needs for belongingness and uniqueness" (p. 1265). Further, they put forth an inclusion framework proposing that groups that allow members to feel like insiders while retaining their sense of uniqueness generate feelings of inclusion while providing opportunities for improved group outcomes. This framework, depicted in Table 12.1, illustrates how varying levels of *belongingness* (i.e., the desire to be included) interact with *uniqueness* (i.e., the desire to maintain one's own identity) and result in four outcomes: *exclusion, differentiation, assimilation,* and *inclusion.*

The upper left quadrant of Table 12.1 is *Exclusion*, which is characterized by low levels of both belongingness and uniqueness. Individuals in this quadrant feel excluded in their group or organization; they do not feel a part of the

TABLE 12.1 Inclusion: Combination of Uniqueness and Belongingness

	Low Belongingness	High Belongingness
Low Uniqueness	**Exclusion** Individuals are not treated as organizational insiders with unique value in the group, but there are other members or groups who are insiders.	**Assimilation** Individuals are treated as insiders in the group when they conform to organizational/dominant culture norms and downplay uniqueness.
High Uniqueness	**Differentiation** Individuals are not treated as organizational insiders in the group, but their unique characteristics are seen as valuable and required for group/organization success.	**Inclusion** Individuals are treated as insiders and allowed/encouraged to retain uniqueness within the group.

Source: Shore, L. M., Randel, A. E., Chung, B. G., Dean, M. A., Holcombe Ehrhard, K., & Singh, G. (2011). Inclusion and diversity in work groups: A review and model for future research. *Journal of Management, 37*(4), 1266.

environment, and they do not feel valued. Exclusion occurs when organizations fail to see and value the unique qualities of individual members and fail to accept them as organizational insiders. An example might be a young female vice president of a bank whose ideas are discounted by her male counterparts and who is seldom invited to corporate planning meetings. In effect, exclusion represents a complete failure to deal with matters of diversity.

The *Differentiation quadrant* (lower left), characterized by low belongingness but high uniqueness levels, describes individuals who feel unique and respected but who also feel left out and not a part of the in-group. Differentiation occurs when organizations accept and value the unique qualities of members who are different but do not treat these individuals as full members of the organization. For example, this might occur when a customer service center hires several Spanish-speaking representatives because the center is working with more Spanish-speaking customers. Yet, those representatives are not asked for their input on organizational issues, such as the scripting they use for complaint calls or process improvements. In terms of diversity, differentiation goes halfway—it recognizes differences among individuals, but does not fully accept them.

The *Assimilation quadrant* (upper right), characterized by high belongingness but low uniqueness levels, represents people who feel they are insiders and in the organizational in-group but whose unique characteristics are not really valued by the organization. An example of assimilation could be a Jewish college student who is accepted and involved in various student groups but is criticized for missing meetings scheduled on Jewish religious holidays. In effect, this student's religious background is not acknowledged by the other students, who expect the Jewish student to ignore that background and adopt dominant group norms. In terms of diversity, assimilation represents an attempt by organizations to open their arms and bring everyone in; however, the same organizations can be faulted for failing to acknowledge the uniqueness of their members—they accept different individuals, but do not fully value the unique perspectives and experiences they bring.

Finally, the *Inclusion quadrant* (lower right), characterized by high levels of both belongingness and uniqueness, describes individuals who feel they belong and are valued for their unique beliefs, attitudes, values, and background. This quadrant represents the optimal way to address diversity. It means, in short, accepting others and at the same time valuing them for who they are without requiring them to give up valued identities or cultural features (Ferdman, 1992). For example, inclusion occurs when a professor is informed that because a student who is hearing-impaired will be taking an online course next semester, the closed captioning and automatic transcript features on the teaching platform must be enabled. The professor makes these accommodations but also changes the syllabus to require all students to offer their comments and questions using the chat features. In doing so, the professor recognizes the student's disability and incorporates such differences into the norms for class participation so that all students can fully engage and interact in course discussions.

Conceptualizing inclusion as seen in Table 12.1 is useful for understanding ways to address inclusion because it illustrates an integration of two factors: (1) an individual's connectedness (i.e., belonging) to others and (2) a person's individuality (i.e., uniqueness). These factors combine to create a dynamic system that is prescribed by the values, policies, and practices of an organization and enacted by people at all levels, including supervisors and coworkers (Ferdman & Davidson, 2002). Still, because a leader's values, processes, and decisions influence member experiences within groups and organizations, research shows that leaders are essential to facilitating inclusion (Ferdman, 2014). As such, inclusive leaders are critical for creating and maintaining environments in which employees feel valued and are capable of fully utilizing their perspectives and talents to contribute to organizational objectives (Davidson & Ferdman, 2002; Ely & Thomas, 2001).

Despite being a relatively new construct in leadership studies, the literature provides strong rationale to suggest that inclusive leadership has three goals: (1) *to create a shared identity among group or organizational members such that everyone feels a sense of belonging*, (2) *to reduce status differences and ensure that each individual is treated with respect and concern*, and (3) *to facilitate the participation and involvement of all so that everyone has equal voice and input in making important decisions.*

A MODEL OF INCLUSIVE LEADERSHIP

In contrast to many of the leadership approaches covered in this book (e.g., leader–member exchange theory, transformational leadership, or servant leadership), inclusive leadership has not been extensively researched, nor has the research on inclusive leadership been clearly organized around a common theme or framework. This section presents a "working" theoretical model of inclusive leadership, outlining the factors that influence inclusive leader behaviors and the outcomes of such behaviors.

As illustrated in Figure 12.1, the process of inclusive leadership consists of three major components: *antecedent conditions*, *behaviors*, and *outcomes*. Each component has multiple subcomponents, which collectively capture and explain inclusive leadership.

Antecedent Conditions

The first component in the Model of Inclusive Leadership (Figure 12.1) is *antecedent conditions*, which are preceding factors that affect the development of and use of inclusive behaviors by leaders. As suggested by prior research, such factors may be *characteristics of the leader*, *group cognitions*, or *organizational policies and practices*.

Leader Characteristics

Randel et al. (2018) propose that a leader's *pro-diversity beliefs*—the degree to which a leader sees diversity in groups as beneficial and is able to recognize each person's differences as strengths—are influential to the leader's propensity to engage in inclusive leadership. For example, a CEO for a nonprofit that coordinates after-school programs for marginalized youth not only sees the value in having representatives of those marginalized communities on the organization's board of directors, but also recruits members with business, health care, and educational backgrounds to serve on the board but who aren't from the marginalized communities. The CEO believes differing perspectives can inform all members of the board and the organization, allowing for better decision making in regard to effective programming for youth.

FIGURE 12.1 Model of Inclusive Leadership

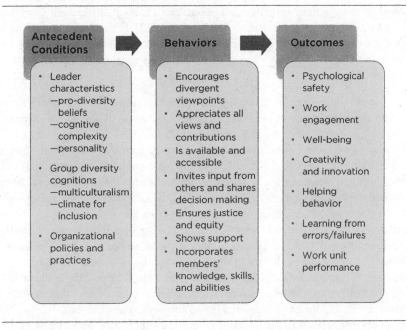

Randel et al. (2018) also suggest that a leader's *cognitive complexity*, or the capability for seeing and analyzing situations in different ways, enhances a leader's ability to recognize member differences as strengths as well as ways to incorporate them into work processes. For example, some leaders may see only one specific way to complete a task and perceive other approaches to be "wrong." In contrast, a leader with greater cognitive complexity is capable of seeing multiple "right" ways of approaching a task and encourages diverse approaches and ways of thinking.

Finally, *leader personality factors*, such as agreeableness and openness to experience, have also been shown to influence individuals' diversity orientation and, subsequently, their contextual performance as leaders (see Strauss & Connerley, 2003). While there are many individual differences that may influence a leader's style and behavior, those related to a leader's capacity for valuing individual identities and contributions within a group while simultaneously emphasizing the group's identity and goals will increase the likelihood that a leader will engage in inclusive leadership.

Group Diversity Cognitions

Research also suggests that *diversity cognitions within the group* may influence inclusive leadership. Individuals' beliefs in the value of diversity as well as their *multicultural beliefs* can positively influence their propensity to make use of diversity within groups and to enhance engagement of underrepresented groups (see van Knippenberg, Homan, & van Ginkel, 2013). For example, groups with positive diversity cognitions hold a collective view that differences in perspectives, experiences, values, and ways of working can enhance the overall performance of their group.

At the same time, *psychological climates*, or the perceptions of an organization's values and human resource policies and practices such as its climate for diversity (Kossek & Zonia, 1993) or climate for inclusion (Nishii, 2013), may also drive inclusive leadership. For instance, although an organization may have an explicit statement on its website stating that diversity is a corporate value, organizational members may perceive the climate quite differently such that there is a mismatch between stated and enacted values. However, when the organization not only has a policy against harassment but also enforces a zero-tolerance approach to harassment and terminates violators of such a policy, members perceive a strong positive diversity climate. Studies highlight the effects of such perceptions on behavioral intentions concerning diversity as well as behaviors to enhance the success of organizational diversity initiatives (see van Knippenberg et al., 2013). Although there may be other diversity-related beliefs and attitudes that influence leader behavior, those that support a leader's ability to recognize and incorporate diversity into a group or organization's work will enhance the leader's propensity for inclusive leadership.

Organizational Policies and Practices

A third antecedent condition, an *organization's policies and practices*, may also motivate inclusive leadership. Specifically, research suggests that certain groups of practices may facilitate the participation of all employees and leverage the effects of diversity in organizations. Roberson (2006) found diversity among all stakeholder groups, fair treatment initiatives, collaborative work arrangements, and conflict resolution processes to be supportive of inclusive organizational environments. Similarly, Nishii (2013) highlights the importance of fairly implemented employment practices and diversity-specific practices to eliminate bias as critical to establishing positive climates for diversity and inclusion. One example of this is ensuring that job applicants are interviewed by multiple interviewers and all applicants are asked the same set of questions that pertain directly to job duties. Standardizing task-based questions asked during an interview and using multiple interviewers are two hiring practices that help to eliminate bias during the interview process (Levashina, Hartwell, Morgeson, & Campion, 2014). While other policies and practices may capture the extent to which diversity is considered to be an important resource that should be utilized to enhance an organization's functioning, those that facilitate leaders' capacity for valuing and integrating diverse perspectives and approaches into organizations will be more likely to facilitate inclusive leadership.

Inclusive Leadership Behaviors

A second component of the Model of Inclusive Leadership (Figure 12.1) addresses specific behaviors by leaders that can facilitate inclusive leadership. Foundational research on inclusive leadership behaviors was developed by Edmondson (1996, 2003) and based on qualitative insights taken from the study of health care teams. Using data from operating room and intensive care unit teams, researchers explored leader approaches to creating *psychologically safe environments*, or cultures with a shared belief that members are safe to engage in interpersonal risk-taking and will not be subjected to negative repercussions, such as embarrassment or rejection, for speaking up within those teams (Edmondson, 1999). The findings showed that nurse managers and surgeon team leaders who acknowledged and proactively invited others' input, regardless of those individuals' professional roles or status relationships, helped team members to feel greater psychological safety (Edmondson, 1996, 2003).

Based on this evidence, Nembhard and Edmondson (2006) put forth the concept of *leader inclusiveness*, which represents behaviors engaged in by leaders to include opinions and contributions of those who might be otherwise excluded from certain deliberations and decisions. While considered to be related to participative decision making and effective facilitation of group processes, inclusive leadership is particularly relevant in situations characterized by status or power differences, which constrain the ability of some group members to express themselves and feel their contributions are valued. Therefore, inclusive leaders are characterized by behaviors that *encourage divergent viewpoints* and *genuinely appreciate the views and contributions* of all followers regardless of status or power.

Edmonson (2004) proposed additional inclusive leader behaviors for encouraging individuals to be themselves in their organizational environments and feel comfortable raising divergent viewpoints. First, she speculated that leaders who are *available and accessible* both physically and psychologically to followers may help to create a climate of approachability, which reduces barriers to voice and input. Second, she reasoned that because leaders model appropriate behavior within teams, *inviting input from others* and *sharing decision-making* responsibilities may help to create a climate of trust and learning.

Diversity researchers view inclusive leadership as behaviors that create the psychological experience of feeling included within a team or organization. Randel et al. (2018) describe a set of behaviors that facilitate individuals' perceptions of belonging to a group and of being valued for their uniqueness that can result in positive group outcomes. For example, inclusive leadership behaviors to *ensure the fair treatment of all group members, make everyone feel comfortable and supported*, and *share decision making* are considered to facilitate perceptions of belongingness. At the same time, leader behaviors to *solicit different perspectives and approaches* and *fully incorporate members' knowledge, skills, and abilities* into the group's work help to facilitate feelings of uniqueness.

Outcomes

As depicted in the Model of Inclusive Leadership (Figure 12.1), there are a number of positive organizational outcomes that result from the facilitation and implementation of inclusive leadership. Research suggests that leader inclusiveness makes others—particularly low-status individuals—feel supported and valued as members of a team (Nembhard & Edmondson, 2006). As such, *psychological safety* and *work engagement* tend to be higher in teams with inclusive leaders (Choi, Tran, & Park, 2015; Nembhard & Edmondson, 2006). Inclusive leadership is also positively related to employee *well-being*, including positive emotional states and quality relationships with others (Choi, Tran, & Kang, 2017).

Inclusive leadership has also been shown to have direct effects on follower *creativity and innovative work behavior* (Choi et al., 2017; Choi et al., 2015; Javed, Naqvi, Khan, Arjoon, & Tayyeb, 2017; Qi, Liu, Wei, & Hu, 2019). Leader openness to, and respect for, new ideas and feedback facilitates a supportive climate in which followers feel comfortable to offer alternative perspectives and to experiment. Subsequently, followers are more strongly motivated to engage in innovative activities. Similarly, leader inclusiveness has been shown to interact with psychological diversity climates, or individual perceptions of the degree to which an organization promotes and maintains a diversity-friendly environment, to positively influence followers' behavior (Randel, Dean, Ehrhart, Chung, & Shore, 2016). Leader inclusiveness within the context of a positive diversity climate was found to be related to follower *helping behaviors* directed at both the leader and other group members.

Feelings of psychological safety resulting from leader inclusiveness have been linked to followers *learning from errors and failures* (Hirak, Peng, Carmeli, & Schaubroeck, 2012; Ye, Wang, & Li, 2018). Inclusive behaviors help to create a safe work environment in which followers feel comfortable experimenting, examining the results of their actions, and developing improved work processes and approaches (Ye et al., 2018). Consequently, inclusive leadership has also been shown to positively impact *unit performance* (Hirak et al., 2012; Mitchell et al., 2015).

Overall, the Model of Inclusive Leadership (Figure 12.1) highlights factors that influence relevant behaviors and the resultant outcomes of such behavior. Based on extant research, it identifies leader, group, and organizational characteristics that may influence specific inclusive leadership behaviors. It also depicts the effects of these behaviors on a variety of follower outcomes, including positive emotional states, behaviors that enhance group functioning, and both individual and team performance.

HOW DOES INCLUSIVE LEADERSHIP WORK?

Although inclusive leadership theory and research derive from the leadership and diversity literatures, a few common elements have emerged from these literature streams that together illustrate how this approach to leadership works.

First, inclusive leadership incorporates a sense of *shared identity* among group members. According to leadership research, information regarding an individual's value to the group is communicated by the leader (Tyler & Lind, 1992), who is seen as a representative or prototype group member that establishes behaviors that group members should adopt. Accordingly, leader behaviors that invite and appreciate others' contributions help all members feel like they are part of the in-group, thereby facilitating a common identity within the group. Similarly, the diversity literature highlights the importance of satisfying individuals' belongingness needs in order for them to feel treated like insiders within groups and for leaders to act in an inclusive manner.

Inclusive leadership within the leadership and diversity literatures also incorporates behaviors to *reduce status differences* within groups. From a leadership perspective, inclusiveness involves behaviors to solicit and integrate viewpoints and opinions from those whose input into decision-making processes may not typically be valued. Further, it involves being approachable and reachable to all members of the group, which helps to reduce potential barriers to interaction and information exchange, particularly among those who might typically be considered outsiders. As such, inclusive leaders attempt to eradicate cliques and other status boundaries within the team. This reduction of status distinction is also an important component of inclusive leadership from a diversity management perspective. Inclusiveness encompasses actions to ensure equity and justice within the group, which reduces the likelihood of bias or differences in treatment based on a member's value to the team.

Existing theory and research also underscore the importance of follower *participation and involvement* in decision processes. Leadership researchers posit leader inclusiveness to be a relational approach that operates according to norms of input and shared decision making, even when members' contributions may be divergent from those of the leader or others on the team. Likewise, diversity researchers emphasize the importance of group members each having a sense of uniqueness, such that their distinct characteristics and contributions are considered to be valuable to the group's success. Yet, rather than simply acknowledging members' individuality, leader inclusiveness takes action to ensure that decision-making power is distributed across group members and members have a say in how the group's work is done.

STRENGTHS

In this chapter, we have outlined a working model of inclusive leadership drawing from literature in the areas of diversity, diversity management, inclusion, and inclusive leadership. The literature summarized in the present chapter has three strengths.

First, inclusive leadership emphasizes the involvement and engagement of everyone in the group. While certain group members may be more likely to perceive and experience exclusion (e.g., members of historically marginalized groups), the aim of inclusive leadership is to create an organizational environment in which *everyone* feels a sense of belonging while also feeling valued for their unique attributes.

Second, inclusive leadership is consistent with and enhances other relational leadership theories such as leader–member exchange and transformational leadership. Each of these theories places value on developing positive relationships with followers, recognizing each follower's unique strengths and interests, and fostering a positive and affirming organizational environment. Although the specific behaviors and expected outcomes of these relational leadership theories are different, valuing and developing relationships with followers are fundamentally at the core of all three.

Finally, inclusive leadership is a shared responsibility of everyone in the group. This is a strength for two reasons. First, it is consistent with emerging paradigms that define leadership as a socially constructed and shared phenomena. Second, it means that no single person is solely responsible for creating an inclusive environment; all organizational members play an important role in doing so. In other words, everyone both creates and benefits from inclusive leadership.

CRITICISMS

Despite an existing body of literature that provides insight into the core elements of inclusive leadership, there are several limitations to such insight. First, while researchers have attempted to conceptualize inclusive leadership, it has to some degree been used as an all-encompassing construct for any approach to leadership that incorporates behaviors to form quality-based interpersonal relationships with followers and to show appreciation and support for their efforts (Javed et al., 2017). As a result, findings regarding antecedents and outcomes of transformational, charismatic, participative, servant, ethical, and other forms of leadership have been confounded with those of inclusive leadership. Similarly, given its conceptual focus on high-quality relationships between leader and follower, inclusive leadership has also been used interchangeably with leader–member exchange (Nishii & Mayer, 2009).

Second, there are also challenges associated with the measurement of inclusive leadership. For example, some researchers have used measures for assessing leader inclusiveness that ask employees to provide such ratings for their direct manager, supervisor, or other organizational authority responsible for directing others' efforts (see Carmeli, Reiter-Palmon, & Ziv, 2010; Nembhard & Edmondson, 2006). The problem with this approach to measuring inclusive leadership is that it may not adequately capture variability in member experiences of inclusiveness or differences in the quality of relationships between the leader and individual members of the team. In other words, using this approach, leaders may be considered inclusive yet only rate highly on inclusive leadership measures for some members of their group. Thus, it is important to develop more nuanced and multifaceted ways to measure inclusive leadership than currently exist to capture the experiences and perceptions of everyone in the group.

Lastly, although prior research has identified core components of inclusive leadership, few studies to date have attempted to reconcile these components across the leadership and diversity literatures. We have attempted to do so in providing the Model of Inclusive Leadership (Figure 12.1), yet more research is needed to empirically examine the relationships between the antecedent conditions, leadership behaviors, and outcomes outlined in the model. Perhaps the greatest need is to determine the relative importance of key leadership behaviors in creating an inclusive environment. For example, some researchers emphasize the extent to which a leader invites and appreciates others as contributing members to the work product (see Nembhard & Edmondson, 2006) while others focus on a leader's invitation and openness, availability, and accessibility (see Carmeli et al., 2010). Still others emphasize actions to create a sense of belonging and uniqueness (see Randel et al., 2018). Though all of these leadership behaviors may play an important role in fostering inclusion, additional research is needed to link specific behaviors to outcomes.

APPLICATION

Because inclusive leadership is defined as a set of behaviors, it follows that inclusive leadership can be both learned and developed. However, there is limited insight into the specific skills and competencies that must be learned as well as the most effective strategies for developing into an inclusive leader. Booysen (2014) provides a helpful comparison of the differences between more traditional approaches to leadership and an inclusive approach to leadership. Her work highlights the fact that developing inclusive leaders requires a shift in the use of power deriving from position and control to a more distributed approach characterized by high levels of empowerment of followers. Rather than a conventional "direct, tell, and sell" approach to decision making, inclusive leaders elicit and facilitate dialogue. They view themselves as part of the collective and focus on fostering perceptions of "we and all" rather than a more traditional view of leadership as a formal position that considers "me, us, and them" and strives to achieve uniformity. Further, inclusive leaders strive to both pursue and value differences of followers, including capabilities, viewpoints, and opinions (Booysen, 2014). Learning to be a more inclusive leader requires a *change in mindset*, *a shift in values*, and *the adoption of a new style of interacting with others*.

The process of inclusive leadership development can be illustrated using the assessment-challenge-support (ACS) model (Van Velsor, McCauley, & Ruderman, 2010) developed by scholars at the Center for Creative Leadership based on decades of data collection to determine how leaders grow and develop leadership skills. The ACS model describes the three critical elements of leadership development—*assessment*, *challenge*, and *support*. Although the ACS model is based on research conducted on leader development experiences (Van Velsor et al., 2010), to our knowledge it has not yet been applied specifically to inclusive leadership. Thus, in the sections that follow, we consider each element of the ACS model in relation to inclusive leadership development and provide examples of each.

Assessment

The first step in leadership development work, *assessment*, involves an evaluation of strengths and opportunities for development as it relates to creating an inclusive organizational environment. This should involve understanding and reflection on one's identity, ethnocentrism, biases, stereotypes, prejudice, and privilege (Chrobot-Mason, Ruderman, & Nishii, 2013; Northouse, 2018, pp. 201–205; Wasserman, 2014). For instance, leaders should consider their memberships in dominant or majority groups as well as the nondominant, minority, or stigmatized groups to which they belong, as such reflection may provide insight into experiences of exclusion. Similarly, the identification of sources of advantage or circumstances in which leaders have benefited from their identity or group memberships may provide perspective on entitlement and privilege that exists in their organizations, and what needs to be done to create more inclusive environments in which all followers have access to key resources and opportunities for involvement and success.

One example of this type of identity work is illustrated by Ferdman and Morgan Roberts (2014). They present an activity in which participants list their multiple social identities (ethnicity, education, life experiences, birth order, nationality, professional affiliation, etc.). Participants then reflect on the impact of these identities by addressing questions such as "How/why are these identities important to you?" and "How do they or can they make a difference for you and others at your organization?"

Another useful activity for assessment is to complete a privilege worksheet. One such worksheet, the White Privilege Checklist, based on work by Peggy

McIntosh (1988; available at https://teacherworksheets.co.uk/sheets/privilege), focuses on white privilege and asks respondents to agree or disagree with a series of statements. For example, statements on the worksheet include "I can arrange to be in the company of people of my race most of the time" and "I am never asked to speak for all of the people of my racial group."

Some scholars and practitioners suggest that it is only by acknowledging and recognizing the biases, stereotypes, and privilege they have as a result of their upbringing, past experiences, media influence, societal values, and any number of other sources that people can mitigate the impact of such mindsets and enhance their interactions with others (Nkomo & Ariss, 2014; Offermann et al., 2014). Accordingly, many organizations offer diversity training sessions, workshops, and seminars to help leaders uncover their implicit biases and understand how such biases influence decision making (Church, Rotolo, Shull, & Tuller, 2014).

Other strategies for assessing leaders' mindsets related to diversity and inclusion are tools that measure personal attitudes and beliefs, such as the popular Implicit Association Test (https://implicit.harvard.edu/implicit/takeatest.html; Greenwald, McGhee, & Schwartz, 1998), or organizational support for diversity and practices that integrate diverse followers into the organizational environment (see Mor Barak, Cherin, & Berkman, 1998). Regardless of the tool, uncovering one's thoughts and assumptions about others and the value of their contributions to work processes and output can help leaders to better understand how and why they make decisions and take actions to do so more inclusively.

Challenge

While self-awareness of one's diversity-related attitudes and beliefs is important to becoming an inclusive leader, it is equally as important to understand one's level of behavioral skill. Thus, the next step in developing an inclusive leadership style and skill set is to identify one's gaps and developmental needs across various diversity and inclusion competency areas and then formulate an action plan to facilitate skill building. Consistent with the ACS model (Van Velsor et al., 2010), this behavioral feedback process illuminates *challenges* for leaders to overcome and enhances motivation to develop and strengthen skills needed to create inclusive organizational environments.

For example, as inclusive leadership involves strong communication skills, a leader should develop the capacity for listening to diverse viewpoints, diagnosing the core issues of a problem between individuals and groups, and serving as a boundary spanner or liaison to facilitate cross-group interactions. Accordingly, a leader may attempt to practice these skills during team meetings, such as seeking followers' opinions or inviting debate on a specific topic. Alternatively, if after determining that all team members' voices are not being heard in brainstorming sessions, a leader may try a nominal group technique, which encourages contributions from everyone and prioritizes ideas with input from the entire group (https://asq.org/quality-resources/nominal-group-technique).

In general, breaking with conventional leadership strategies will help leaders adapt their current approaches to create more diverse organizational environments and develop new capacities for inclusiveness. Seeking out such challenges often forces leaders outside their comfort zone; yet this is exactly what must happen for them to become more confident and capable of fostering inclusion.

Support

Because challenges push leaders to go beyond what they have been comfortable with in the past and try new approaches, they need *support* to successfully deal with such challenges. For inclusive leaders, this means having an infrastructure and relationships that help to reinforce behaviors learned, as suggested by the ACS model (Van Velsor et al., 2010). For example, colleagues, mentors, and significant others often serve as sounding boards for leaders, offering affirmations and feedback as leaders struggle through the challenges of being more inclusive and adopting new behaviors to lead inclusively. The organization itself may also play a significant role in offering support to leaders attempting to create a more inclusive environment by providing accountability structures, diversity councils or advisory boards, a diversity and inclusion mission statement and strategies, and zero-tolerance policies toward discrimination, which can all positively impact the climate for diversity (Roberson, King, & Hebl, 2020). Support may also come in the form of coaching and mentoring, which are often included as components of many leadership development programs to help leaders develop personal accountability for creating and promoting diverse and inclusive workplaces.

CASE STUDIES

The following case studies (Cases 12.1, 12.2, and 12.3) offer an opportunity to apply inclusive leadership concepts introduced in the chapter as well as inclusive behaviors identified in the Inclusive Leadership Reflection Instrument on page 346. The first case involves a situation where group members stereotype another member based on race, whereas the second case examines group members who seem to hold back from participating in group discussions. The final case is derived from an interview with the vice president for equity, inclusion, and community impact at the University of Cincinnati, Dr. Bleuzette Marshall, who found inclusive leadership critical in helping the institution to navigate a very difficult and traumatic time.

In addition to answering the discussion questions listed at the end of each case, determine the key issue presented in each case, the underlying causes of that issue, and possible solutions. Using this analysis, consider how you would address the identified issue as an inclusive leader and the actions you might take to create a more inclusive environment going forward.

Case 12.1 DIFFICULT DECISION

Sondra is the leader of a nonprofit organization with about 40 full- and part-time employees. She is proud of her organization and its very dedicated staff. Sondra has been with the organization for 10 years, having worked her way up through the ranks into the director role, a position she finds equally challenging and rewarding. She describes her leadership style as highly collaborative and empowering. Furthermore, Sondra views herself as a leader who values diversity and does all that she can to create an environment in which everyone feels comfortable and supported.

Antonio is a Hispanic male employee who has been with the organization just eight months but shows promise as a highly dedicated employee and future leader. However, he has missed the last three days of work, which seems to have caused some speculation among his coworkers about why he has been absent. While walking past a cubicle in the office building, Sondra overhears two of her direct reports (both white) talking about Antonio. One employee, Terry, says, "I heard that Antonio was undocumented, which wouldn't surprise me." The second employee, Pat, responds, saying, "Maybe he's been deported. Or maybe he just left town for fear that he would be deported." Surprised by what she overhears, Sondra decides to just keep walking by, as it seems no one noticed her.

(Continued)

(Continued)

However, when she returns to her desk, she lets out a sigh and looks out her window. She feels conflicted about what she should do. On the one hand, she considers doing nothing because Terry and Pat were only speaking to one another. On the other hand, she is concerned that other colleagues may be speculating about Antonio's absence as well and jumping to false conclusions since Sondra knows that Antonio has not been deported but instead is battling an illness. She decides to take a walk to try and clear her head so that she can decide what to do, if anything.

Questions

1. Why do you think Sondra is conflicted in this situation?

2. Do you believe Sondra has a responsibility, as an inclusive leader, to do something? Why or why not?

3. What inclusive leadership behaviors from the Model of Inclusive Leadership (Figure 12.1) could Sondra use to deal with this situation?

4. Why do you think Terry and Pat jumped to the conclusion that Antonio had been deported? What is your opinion about them discussing this with one another?

5. What do you think Sondra should do, if anything?

Case 12.2 THE EXTRAVERSION ADVANTAGE

Quinn is a midlevel manager who does his best to create an inclusive team environment. He leads a group of seven employees who are diverse along a variety of dimensions. Quinn feels that he does his best to create opportunities for everyone to speak up during their weekly team meetings. He frequently asks for input on issues and decisions and takes the first 5–10 minutes each week to ask his team members to share updates about their personal lives to build trust and comfort among his team members.

Recently, however, Quinn has started to become concerned that two team members are not sharing much during meetings. These team members, Brett and Alex, both come prepared and offer input whenever they are asked directly. In addition, Brett has been leading a project and has been sharing updates on project goals each week very effectively. Still, Quinn has noticed that Brett and Alex are often quiet during the times when the rest of the team engages in a discussion in which team members have very different opinions. Indeed, sometimes these discussions can get a bit heated when people feel passionate about something. Truth be told, Quinn is proud of this and feels like this is an indication that the team is deeply engaged in their work. The conversations are never disrespectful in Quinn's opinion, just naturally healthy task-related conflict that keeps the team energized.

Quinn decides to ask another team member, Shawn, who seems to have no trouble jumping into the conversations for thoughts on what could be done to better engage Brett and Alex in these debates. Shawn tells Quinn that some members of the team are just "quiet by nature" and could benefit from learning how to be more assertive during meetings. To help them do so, Shawn recommends enrolling Brett and Alex in a public-speaking or other type of communication skills training course.

Questions

1. What do you think is the underlying issue within this team?

2. Based on the leader behaviors identified in the Model of Inclusive Leadership (Figure 12.1), what should Quinn do to make team meetings more inclusive for everyone?

3. Since inclusion is the responsibility of everyone, not just the leader's, what can other team members do to help create a more inclusive team environment?

4. This particular case involves only male coworkers. In what ways might your answers change if Quinn were Lynn (a woman) or if Brett and Alex were women reporting to a male supervisor?

Case 12.3   INCLUSIVE LEADERSHIP DURING A CRISIS

On July 19, 2015, in Cincinnati, Ohio, Samuel DuBose, an unarmed Black man, was fatally shot by Ray Tensing, a University of Cincinnati police officer, during a traffic stop for a missing front license plate and a suspended driver's license. In response to the shooting, protestors took to the streets to demonstrate their anger, frustration, and pain. Protests were held both on campus and off campus and included students, faculty, staff, and community members. A student-led movement emerged called the Irate 8, which derived its name from the fact that only 8% of the University of Cincinnati student body was composed of Black students.

In a short period of time, support grew across the university and the broader community for the student-led activist movement. The students demanded to meet with university senior leaders and gave them a list of 10 demands. As vice president for equity, inclusion, and community impact at the University of Cincinnati, Dr. Bleuzette Marshall found herself at the center of this very difficult and traumatic time in the university's history.

(Continued)

(Continued)

Dr. Marshall describes her role during this time as one of healer and reconciler. "I worked with people so that they could express themselves about how they were thinking and feeling about the institution. It wasn't just about this particular incident. People were inflamed by the shooting, but other past experiences and practices fueled the anger they were feeling. And I took it," she said. "I did my best to respond to questions about what the university was doing or not doing, I stood outside among the demonstrators and listened, I worked with our president and vice presidents to consider what changes we could and could not make. I responded to the demands our students made to the university and communicated with them about our progress. It required a lot of time, patience, and listening to both what was said and not said—being able to read others' emotions was equally important" (Dr. Bleuzette Marshall, personal communication, July 1, 2020).

Multiple groups presented demands to Dr. Marshall's office, and one of the things she stressed was the need to be real and authentic in communicating with these various constituents. She met with leaders across the university including colleagues from the provost's, finance, human resources, investments, and admissions offices, as well as the campus police department. She met with various groups about the demands made by student and community activists to determine what the university's current practices were and what kinds of change were possible. She explained that it was important to not just take the list of demands and disappear, but to offer to involve those making the demands in the change process. She describes how the university practiced inclusive leadership by inviting others to engage in finding solutions.

To address the list of demands from the Irate 8 and practice inclusion, Dr. Marshall invited University of Cincinnati students to develop and offer recommendations for change to the university's administration. "We created committees of students to have them involved in working on the responses to these demands. For example, to recruit more Black students to the university, our students came up with the idea to partner with Cincinnati Public Schools to create an ambassador program. The goal was to have high school students serve as ambassadors in partnership with university students to educate neighboring high school students about the University of Cincinnati's application and admissions process and to get them excited about college from fellow students. I'll always remember their excitement going through the process of meeting with members of our admissions team, putting a proposal together, submitting the proposal to university administration, and then securing funding to run the program" (Dr. Bleuzette Marshall, personal communication, July 1, 2020).

In talking about lessons learned as a result of her experiences following the DuBose shooting, Dr. Marshall noted how important it is for leaders to be humble and always be open to learning. "I learned that when assuming a leadership role there is always going to be some type of challenge that I call the 'welcome to leadership moment,' because it comes unexpectedly and it is not at all clear what you should do. It's nothing that you could have ever planned for. The right answer is not written in any manual that you can simply look up to figure out how to navigate this challenge. Instead, you have to rely on your own sensibilities, your own strategic and creative thinking, and evolving skill set to be able to navigate" (Dr. Bleuzette Marshall, personal communication, July 1, 2020).

She shared another "welcome to leadership" moment involving a student group that staged a demonstration outside her office protesting the university's handling of sexual assault on campus. The group informed local media who were also present to film the group marching to the administration building with their mouths taped. Group members then proceeded to sit on the floor in a circle outside of Dr. Marshall's office.

"The first thing I did was take a deep breath when I heard the students were outside. I came out of my office and told them that I was ready to talk to them whenever they were ready to speak with me. They texted me to say they would be ready in 15 minutes. So I set my watch for 15 minutes, walked out, and immediately sat down in their circle to listen to their concerns and personal stories. Some concerns I could address right then and there, but some I could not, so I encouraged the students to schedule some time with me to deal with the lingering issues, which they did, and we worked together to implement changes" (Dr. Bleuzette Marshall, personal communication, July 1, 2020).

In her role as the vice president of equity, inclusion, and community impact at a large urban university with nearly 50,000 students and over 15,000 employees, Dr. Marshall says she continues to learn and grow her inclusive leadership skill set. She describes her leadership style as participatory, because she invites people who are important to the process and encourages them to stay involved. She is also boundary spanning in the sense that she works across campus to infuse inclusive practices in any and all areas of the university. Another example of how Dr. Marshall practices inclusive leadership is that she begins a meeting by asking everyone in the meeting to share something with the group such as a movie or book they recently enjoyed, or a favorite quote. The topic is not important; what is important is allowing everyone in the room to speak and share because the goal is to create a foundation in which everyone in the room has exercised their voice. She finds this simple practice can make a big difference as it tends to open up subsequent conversation and makes it easier for people to feel comfortable speaking up later in the meeting.

For aspiring inclusive leaders, Dr. Marshall recommends they first and foremost become good at self-reflection. She says it is important to spend time

(Continued)

(Continued)

understanding who you are as a person, what you appreciate about other people, what your shortcomings are, what you are doing to try to be a better person, how you do or do not connect with others, and what your hot buttons are and how to manage them. She also suggests that inclusive leaders must make a concerted effort to expand their circle of friends so they can be exposed to different ideas, opinions, and perspectives. Surrounding yourself with people who hold different opinions than you enhances your cognitive complexity and allows the opportunity to know yourself better by understanding how your upbringing and experiences differ from others. Finally, she encourages those attempting to be more inclusive to remember not to fight fire with fire, but instead fight fire with water. She has learned that during heated and difficult situations she continually reminds herself that in some way, shape, or form, those expressing their anger are frustrated and hurting, and they are coming to her and the university for relief.

"The only way I can really help is to know the full extent of what's going on—so if it means you need to fuss, then fuss; if it means you need to cuss, then cuss to get it out so that we can fully dissect what's going on. Only then can we determine what changes can be made" (Dr. Bleuzette Marshall, personal communication, July 1, 2020).

Questions

1. What inclusive leadership behaviors as identified in the Model of Inclusive Leadership (Figure 12.1) does Dr. Marshall exhibit in her role?

2. In what ways do you practice these inclusive leadership behaviors in your interactions with others? In what ways could you practice these behaviors in the future?

3. Active listening is an important theme in this case. Dr. Marshall mentions the importance of listening and learning from others multiple times. Why is it often difficult for us to really listen and understand others?

4. What one thing can you do moving forward to enhance your active listening skills?

LEADERSHIP INSTRUMENT

To measure inclusive leadership, researchers have primarily utilized the Inclusive Leadership Scale developed by Carmeli et al. (2010). This 9-item scale assesses leaders on the dimensions of availability, accessibility, and openness. More recently, Chung and colleagues (2020) developed a 10-item scale, structured around the dimensions of belonging and uniqueness, to assess perceptions of individuals' experiences within their immediate work environment that help them to feel included.

This section includes a self-assessment instrument to help you reflect on your own inclusive leadership. It is based on the most recent research as well as best practices from organizations engaged in diversity and inclusion efforts. The instrument provides a list of inclusive leadership behaviors in which you may (or may not) be engaging. Because inclusiveness may feel different in different situations, the instrument also highlights inclusive leadership behaviors in a variety of settings, including one-on-one meetings, team meetings, and mentoring sessions. Based on this assessment, leaders can learn more about inclusive behaviors that can be incorporated into their daily activities and interactions as well as recognize areas for future development.

Inclusive Leadership Reflection Instrument

Purpose: The purpose of this questionnaire is to reflect on your inclusive behaviors and challenge yourself to exhibit inclusive behaviors in your daily interactions.

Instructions: The following instrument is a checklist designed to encourage you to reflect on the inclusive behaviors you exhibit in a variety of settings: meeting one-on-one with individuals, facilitating a team meeting, participating in a team meeting, and mentoring someone less experienced. In each case, you are encouraged to place a check mark in the *Yes* column or *No* column.

Types of Interactions	Inclusive Leadership Behaviors	Yes	No
One-on-One	I begin our interaction by showing interest in the other person (e.g., asking questions, sharing something personal, and inviting the other person to share as well).		
	I make eye contact with the person.		
	I face the individual I am speaking with.		
	I put away all distractions such as my cell phone.		
	I eliminate physical or technological barriers between us, such as sitting behind my desk and/or keeping my camera off.		
	I ask open-ended questions to learn about the other person.		
	I regularly designate time for people to come and talk to me.		
	I treat each and every person with respect and dignity.		
	I recognize and reward employees/people according to their individual motivations.		
Teams (as leader)	I identify unique skill sets of team members.		
	I use the full range of talents on my team to achieve work objectives.		
	I ask everyone on the team for input and through different means (in person, via email, pulse checks, etc.).		

Types of Interactions	Inclusive Leadership Behaviors	Yes	No
Teams (as leader)	I ask everyone on the team what and how they want to contribute.		
	I configure project teams to include people who do not regularly interact with one another.		
	I provide different members of the team with leadership opportunities.		
	I seek feedback from others and make changes based on that feedback.		
Teams (as facilitator)	I prepare an agenda and send it out ahead of a meeting so that people can prepare and better participate.		
	I utilize a process in which everyone gives feedback and input at times (e.g., nominal group technique, round-robin discussion, online real-time data collection tools).		
	When possible, I ask team members to provide updates rather than being the only one to speak.		
	I adapt physical arrangements such as seating and/or technology that allows people to interact with one another.		
	When someone new joins the team or when a team is forming, I ask for everyone's preferred names, pronunciations, and pronouns.		
	I encourage conflicting views and/or dissension within team discussions.		
	I create "airtime" limits so that outspoken people do not dominate the conversation.		
Teams (as participant)	We rotate roles in team meetings each time (time keeper, note-taker, action item capturer, etc.).		
	If a colleague is interrupted by someone, I will say that I would like to hear the colleague finish the thought, prompting the group to go back to let that person finish speaking.		
	I come prepared to share my thoughts and ideas.		
	If a colleague has been silent during the meeting, I will encourage the colleague to share by saying something like "I would love to hear what you are thinking about this issue."		

(Continued)

(Continued)

Types of Interactions	Inclusive Leadership Behaviors	Yes	No
Mentor/ Protégé	I ask my protégé about preferred work style and communication cadence.		
	I discuss and develop a list of expectations with my protégé such that we are both able to clarify expectations of one another early in the relationship.		
	Rather than assume I know what is best, I start meetings with my protégé by asking how our time together can be most useful for the protégé.		

Scoring

1. There are 30 items contained in the Inclusive Leadership Reflection Instrument. First, count up the total number of check marks you placed in the *No* column.

   Total Score _____

2. Next, count up the number of check marks you placed in the *No* column for the various types of interactions:

   - One-on-one = 9 total _____
   - Teams (as leader) = 7 total _____
   - Teams (as facilitator) = 7 total _____
   - Teams (as participant) = 4 total _____
   - Mentor/Protégé = 3 total _____

Scoring Interpretation

Upon completion of this instrument, you will have identified inclusive leader behaviors you should continue to display as well as those you will want to consider using and developing in the future. To interpret your scores, we suggest you consider the following:

1. Examine the total number of check marks you placed in the *No* column.

   - A score of 0–9 indicates that you exemplify many behaviors of inclusive leaders. You may be able to thus serve as a role model to others and foster inclusive leadership in members of your team and in your colleagues at work.

   - A score of 10–19 suggests that you are working to become an inclusive leader. You are likely motivated to foster an inclusive organizational environment but have a somewhat limited number of tactics and strategies that you have utilized in the past. You may need to try out some additional inclusive leader behaviors and seek feedback from others to determine if what you are doing equates to others feeling more included in the organization.

- A score of 20–30 indicates that you either previously were not aware of the value of inclusive leadership or were not motivated to adapt a more inclusive approach to leadership. Hopefully, after reading this chapter, you better understand how and why inclusive leadership may create benefits for your team and the organization as a whole. Additionally, we hope that you are now motivated to try out various inclusive leadership behaviors described in the checklist and seek feedback from others to determine if what you are doing equates to others feeling more included in the organization.

2. Examine the number of check marks you placed in the *No* column for the various types of interactions. Circle the types of interactions with the most *No* check marks as follows. That is a good place to identify where and how you can make changes and challenge yourself to step outside of your comfort zone to become a more inclusive leader.

- One-on-one
- Teams (as leader)
- Teams (as facilitator)
- Teams (as participant)
- Mentor/Protégé

SUMMARY

The concept of inclusion has emerged as a key psychological construct for realizing the benefits that diversity can bring to the workplace. In today's multifaceted and multicultural business environment, leaders must be able to identify or create opportunities for growth and competitiveness. As such, they must be able to create environments in which differences are valued and can be incorporated into the main work of an organization to enhance strategies, processes, and overall effectiveness.

Inclusion requires the consideration of belongingness (i.e., the desire to be included) and the extent to which it interacts with uniqueness (i.e., the desire to maintain one's own identity). An inclusive organization is one in which members' perceptions of both belongingness and uniqueness are high. In this type of organization, individuals feel they belong and are valued for their unique beliefs, attitudes, values, and background. Inclusive leaders play a key role in creating such an organization as a result of their behavior toward others.

The Model of Inclusive Leadership (Figure 12.1) offered in this chapter highlights factors that influence relevant inclusive leader behaviors and the resultant outcomes of such behavior. It clarifies the importance of the leader, group, and organizational characteristics that influence the degree to which inclusive leadership behaviors are encouraged and practiced in the organization. It also depicts the effects of inclusive leadership behaviors on a variety of follower outcomes, including positive emotional states, behaviors that enhance group functioning, and both individual and team performance.

Based on inclusive leadership theory and research derived from the leadership and diversity literatures, common elements have emerged to illustrate how this approach to leadership works. First, inclusive leadership incorporates a sense of *shared identity* among group members. Second, inclusive leadership incorporates behaviors to *reduce status differences* within groups. Third, inclusive leaders foster employee *participation and involvement* in decision processes.

Existing research on inclusive leadership has several strengths. The first is that inclusive leadership emphasizes the involvement and engagement of everyone in the group. A second strength is inclusive leadership's focus on the relational aspects of leadership such as identifying the strengths and interests of each follower and fostering positive relationships with each follower. A third strength of inclusive leadership is that it frames inclusivity as a shared responsibility between leaders and followers and one that does not fall solely on the shoulders of an individual leader.

One criticism of inclusive leadership is that research on inclusive leadership has been confounded with other leadership theories and sets of behaviors.

Another criticism is that current methods of measuring inclusive leadership do so in an aggregate fashion such that individual differences in perceptions of inclusion may be lost. Thus, more nuanced and complex measurement strategies are needed in future research. Finally, existing research has not been able to clearly determine links between specific inclusive behaviors and outcomes. In other words, future research is needed to test the Model of Inclusive Leadership presented in Figure 12.1.

Because inclusive leadership is defined as a set of behaviors, it follows that inclusive leadership can be both learned and developed. Learning to be a more inclusive leader requires a *change in mindset, a shift in values,* and *the adoption of a new style of interacting with others.* Leaders who wish to develop a more inclusive style of leading should identify strengths and weaknesses through feedback and assessment tools, identify new and challenging experiences to strengthen their inclusive leadership skills, and seek support from others to stay motivated and positive in the face of change.

As the workforce is projected to become increasingly diverse and organizations continue to operate in fiercely competitive environments, inclusive leadership may be viewed as a strategy to ensure that the potential benefits of a diverse workforce are realized. That is, inclusive leaders play a critical role in creating environments in which different ideas, perspectives, experiences, and values are leveraged to foster greater creativity and innovation as well as more effective problem solving. A key takeaway from this chapter is that practicing inclusive leadership requires both a mindset and everyday behaviors to foster inclusion. An inclusive mindset means constantly being vigilant to recognize bias, discrimination, stereotyping, and exclusion in the words and actions of both oneself and others. Practicing inclusive behaviors means engaging in both proactive and reactive tactics to ensure that everyone feels like they are part of the group, that all members are treated with respect and fairness, and that everyone feels that they can participate fully.

Followership

DESCRIPTION

You cannot have leaders without followers. In the previous chapter, "Inclusive Leadership" (Chapter 12), we focused on inclusive leadership and how leaders can ensure that followers feel a part of the group. In this chapter, we shift the focus to *followers* and the central role *followers* play in the leadership process. The process of leading requires the process of following. Leaders and followers together create the leadership relationship, and without an understanding of the process of following, our understanding of leadership is incomplete (Shamir, 2007; Uhl-Bien, Riggio, Lowe, & Carsten, 2014).

For many people, being a follower and the process of followership have negative connotations. One reason is that people do not find followership as compelling as leadership. Leaders, rather than followers, have always taken center stage. For example, in school, children are taught early that it is better to be a leader than a follower. In athletics and sports, the praise for performance consistently goes to the leaders, not the team players. When people apply for jobs, they are asked to describe their leadership abilities, not their followership activities. Clearly, it is leadership skills that are applauded by society, not followership skills. It is just simply more intriguing to talk about how leaders use power than to talk about how followers respond to power.

While the interest in examining the active role of followers was first approached in the 1930s by Follett (1949), groundwork on follower research wasn't established until several decades later through the initial works of scholars such as Zaleznik (1965), Kelley (1988), Meindl (1990), and Chaleff (1995). Still, until recently, only a minimal number of studies have been published on followership. Traditionally, leadership research has focused on leaders' traits, roles, and behaviors because leaders are viewed as the causal agents for organizational change. At the same time, the impact of followers on organizational outcomes has not been generally addressed. Researchers often conceptualize leadership as a leader-centric process, emphasizing the role of the leader rather than the role of the follower. Furthermore, little research has conceptualized leadership as a *shared process* involving the interdependence between leaders and followers in a shared relationship. Even though followers share in the overall leadership process, the nature of their role has not been scrutinized. In effect, followership has rarely been studied as a central variable in the leadership process.

There are indications that this is beginning to change. In a 2017 *New York Times* article, Susan Cain (author of *Quiet: The Power of Introverts in a World That Can't Stop Talking* [2012]) decries the glorification of leadership skills in college admissions and curricula and argues that the world needs more followers. It needs team players, people called to service, and individuals committed to something outside of themselves. Followership is also receiving more attention now because of three major works devoted exclusively to the process of following: *The Art of Followership: How Great Followers Create Great Leaders and Organizations* by Riggio, Chaleff, and Lipman-Blumen (2008), *Followership: How Followers Are Creating Change and Changing Leaders* by Kellerman (2008); and *Followership: What Is It and Why Do People Follow?* by Lapierre and Carsten (2014). Collectively, these books have put the spotlight on followership and helped to establish it as a legitimate and significant area of study.

In this chapter, we examine followership and how it is related to the leadership process. First, we define followers and followership and discuss the implications of these definitions. Second, we discuss selected typologies of followership that illustrate different styles used by followers. Next, we explore a formal theory of followership that has been set forth by Uhl-Bien et al. (2014) and new perspectives on followership suggested by Carsten, Harms, and Uhl-Bien (2014). Last, we explore types of ineffective followership that contribute to destructive leadership.

Followership Defined

It is challenging to define *followership* because the term conjures up different meanings for people, and the idea of being a follower is positive for some and negative for others. For example, followership is seen as valuable in military situations when soldiers follow orders from a platoon leader to complete a mission, or when passengers boarding a plane follow the boarding agent's instructions. In contrast, however, followership is thought of negatively in such situations as when people follow a cult leader such as David Koresh of the Branch Davidians, or when members of a college fraternity take it upon themselves to conduct life-threatening hazing rituals with new members. Clearly, followership can be positive or negative, and it plays out differently in different settings.

What is followership? *Followership is a process whereby an individual or individuals accept the influence of others to accomplish a common goal.* Followership involves a power differential between the follower and the leader. Typically, followers comply with the directions and wishes of leaders—they defer to leaders' power.

Followership also has an ethical dimension. Like leadership, followership is not amoral; that is, it is not a process that is morally neutral. Followership carries with it a responsibility to consider the morality of one's actions and the rightness or wrongness of the outcomes of what one does as a follower. Followers and leaders work together to achieve common goals, and both share a moral obligation regarding those goals. There are ethical consequences to followership and to what followers do because the character and behavior of followers has an impact on leaders and on organizational outcomes.

Role-Based and Relational-Based Perspectives

Followership can be divided into two broad categories: *role-based* and *relational-based* (Uhl-Bien et al., 2014).

The *role-based* perspective focuses on followers in regard to the typical roles or behaviors they exhibit while occupying a formal or informal position within a hierarchical system. For example, in a staff planning meeting, some people are very helpful to the group because they bring energy and offer insightful suggestions regarding how the group might proceed. Their role as engaged followers, in this case, has a positive impact on the meeting and its outcomes. Emphasis in the role-based approach is on the roles and styles of followers and how their behaviors affect the leader and organizational outcomes.

The *relational-based* approach to followership is quite different from the role-based approach. To understand the relational-based approach it is helpful to understand social constructivism. Social constructivism is a sociological theory that argues that people create meaning about their reality as they interact with each other. For example, a fitness instructor and an individual in an exercise class negotiate with each other about the kind of influence the instructor will have and the amount of influence the individual will accept. From a social constructivist perspective, followership is *co-created* by the leader and follower in a given situation. The meaning of followership emerges from the communication between leaders and followers and stresses the interplay between following and leading. Rather than focusing on roles, it focuses on the interpersonal process and one person's attempt to influence and the other person's response to these influence attempts. Leadership occurs within the interpersonal context of people exerting influence and responding to those influence attempts. In the relational-based approach, followership is tied to interpersonal *behaviors* rather than to specific *roles* (Carsten, Uhl-Bien, West, Patera, & McGregor, 2010; DeRue & Ashford, 2010; Fairhurst & Uhl-Bien, 2012; Uhl-Bien et al., 2014).

Typologies of Followership

How can we describe followers' roles? Trying to do just that has been the primary focus of much of the existing followership research. As there are many types

TABLE 13.1 Typologies of Followership

Zaleznik (1965)	Kelley (1992)	Chaleff (1995)	Kellerman (2008)
Withdrawn	Alienated	Resource	Isolate
Masochistic	Passive	Individualist	Bystander
Compulsive	Conformist	Implementer	Participant
Impulsive	Pragmatist	Partner	Activist
	Exemplary		Diehard

Source: Adapted from "Conceptualizing followership: A review of the literature," by B. Crossman and J. Crossman, 2011, *Leadership, 7*(4), 481–497.

of leaders, so, too, are there many types of followers (Table 13.1). Grouping followers' roles into distinguishable categories to create an accurate classification system, or typology, of follower behaviors has been undertaken by several researchers. A typology enhances our understanding of the broader area of followership by breaking it down into smaller pieces. In this case, these pieces are different types of follower roles observed in various settings.

The Zaleznik Typology

The first typology of followers was provided by Zaleznik (1965) and was intended to help leaders understand followers and also to help followers understand and become leaders. In an article published in the *Harvard Business Review*, Zaleznik created a matrix that displayed followers' behaviors along two axes: dominance–submission and activity–passivity (Figure 13.1). The vertical axis represents a range of followers from those who want to control their leaders (i.e., be dominant) to those who want to be controlled by their leaders (i.e., be submissive). The horizontal axis represents a range of followers from those who want to initiate and be involved to those who sit back and withdraw. Based on the two axes, the model identifies four types of followers: *withdrawn* (submissive/passive), *masochistic* (submissive/active), *compulsive* (highly dominant/passive), and *impulsive* (highly dominant/active). Because Zaleznik was trained in psychoanalytic theory, these follower types are based on psychological concepts. Zaleznik was interested in explaining the communication breakdowns between authority figures and subordinates, in particular the dynamics of subordinacy conflicts. The follower types illustrated in Figure 13.1 exist as a result of followers' responses to inner tensions regarding authority. These tensions may be unconscious but can often come to the surface and influence the communication in leader–follower relationships.

FIGURE 13.1   Zaleznik Follower Typology

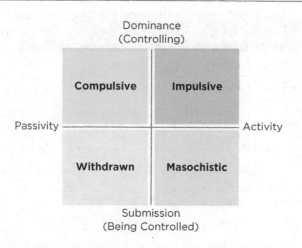

Dominance
(Controlling)

| Compulsive | Impulsive |

Passivity ———————————— Activity

| Withdrawn | Masochistic |

Submission
(Being Controlled)

Source: Zaleznik, A. (1965). The dynamics of subordinacy, *Harvard Business Review*, May-Jun.

The Kelley Typology

Kelley's (1992) typology (Figure 13.2) is currently the most recognized followership typology. Kelley believes followers are enormously valuable to organizations and that the power of followers often goes unrecognized. He stresses the importance of studying followers in the leadership process and gave impetus to the development of the field of followership. While Zaleznik (1965) focused on the personal aspects of followers, Kelley emphasizes the *motivations* of followers and follower behaviors. In his efforts to give followership equal billing to leadership, Kelley examined those aspects of followers that account for *exemplary followership*.

Kelley sorted followers' styles on two axes: independent critical thinking–dependent uncritical thinking and active–passive. These dimensions resulted in five follower role types:

- *passive followers* (sometimes pejoratively called "sheep"), who look to the leader for direction and motivation,

- *conformist followers*, who are "yes people"—always on the leader's side but still looking to the leader for direction and guidance,

- *alienated followers*, who think for themselves and exhibit a lot of negative energy,

FIGURE 13.2 Kelley Follower Typology

Independent, Critical Thinking

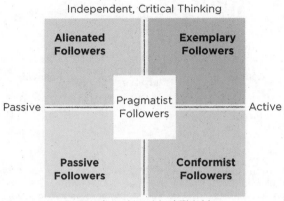

Dependent, Uncritical Thinking

Source: Based on excerpts from Kelley, Robert. E. (1992). *The Power of Followership: How to Create Leaders People Want to Follow and Followers Who Lead Themselves.* New York: Doubleday.

- *pragmatist followers,* who are "fence-sitters" who support the status quo but do not get on board until others do, and

- *exemplary followers* (sometimes called "star" followers), who are active and positive and offer independent constructive criticism.

Based on his observations, Kelley (1988, 2008) asserts that effective followers share the same indispensible qualities: (1) They self-manage and think for themselves, exercise control and independence, and work without supervision; (2) they show strong commitment to organizational goals (i.e., something outside themselves) as well as their own personal goals; (3) they build their competence and master job skills; and (4) they are credible, ethical, and courageous. Rather than framing followership in a negative light, Kelley underscores the positive dimensions of following.

The Chaleff Typology

Chaleff (1995, 2008, 2009) developed a typology to amplify the significance of the role of followers in the leadership process (Table 13.1). He developed his typology as a result of a defining moment in his formative years when he became aware of the horrors of the World War II Holocaust that killed more than 6 million European Jews. Chaleff felt a moral imperative to seek answers

FIGURE 13.3 Leader–Follower Interaction

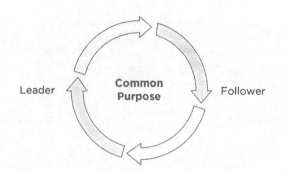

Source: Adapted from "Creating new ways of following" by I. Chaleff, in R. E. Riggio, I. Chaleff, and J. Lipman-Blumen (Eds.), *The Art of Followership: How Great Followers Create Great Leaders and Organizations* (p. 71), 2008. Permission conveyed through Copyright Clearance Center, Inc. Republished with permission of John Wiley & Sons.

as to why people followed German leader Adolf Hitler, a purveyor of hate and death. What could be done to prevent this from happening again? How could followers be emboldened to help leaders use their power appropriately and act to keep leaders from abusing their power?

Rather than *serving leaders*, Chaleff argues that followers *serve a common purpose along with leaders* (Figure 13.3) and that both leaders and followers work to achieve common outcomes. Chaleff states that followers need to take a more proactive role that brings it into parity with the leader's role. He sought to make followers more responsible, to change their own internal estimates of their abilities to influence others, and to help followers feel a greater sense of agency.

To achieve equal influence with leaders, Chaleff emphasizes that followers need to be *courageous*. His approach is a prescriptive one; that is, it advocates how followers *ought to* behave. According to Chaleff, followers need the courage to

a. assume responsibility for the common purpose,

b. support the leader and the organization,

c. constructively challenge the leader if the common purpose or integrity of the group is being threatened,

d. champion the need for change when necessary, and

e. take a moral stand that is different from the leader's to prevent ethical abuses.

FIGURE 13.4 Chaleff Follower Typology

High Support

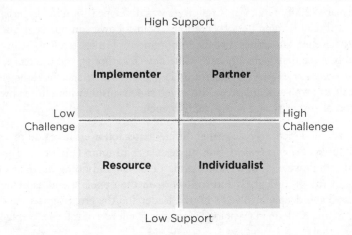

Low
Challenge

High
Challenge

Low Support

Source: Adapted from "Creating new ways of following" by I. Chaleff, in R. E. Riggio, I. Chaleff, and J. Lipman-Blumen (Eds.), *The Art of Followership: How Great Followers Create Great Leaders and Organizations* (p. 71), 2008; permission conveyed through Copyright Clearance Center, Inc. Republished with permission of John Wiley & Sons.

In short, Chaleff proposes that followers should be morally strong and work to do the right thing when facing the multiplicity of challenges that leaders place upon them.

Chaleff created a follower typology (Figure 13.4), which is constructed using two characteristics of courageous followership: *the courage to support* the leader (vertical axis) and the *courage to challenge* the leader's behavior and policies (horizontal axis). This typology differentiates four styles of followership:

1. *Resource* (lower left quadrant), which exhibits low support and low challenge. This describes those followers who do just enough to get by.

2. *Individualist* (lower right quadrant), which demonstrates low support and high challenge. Often marginalized by others, individualists speak up and let the leader know where they stand.

3. *Implementer* (upper left quadrant), which acts with high support and low challenge. Often valued by the leader, implementers are supportive and get the work done but, on the downside, fail to challenge the leader's goals and values.

4. *Partner* (upper right quadrant), which shows high support and high challenge. Followers who exhibit this style take responsibility for themselves and for the leader and fully support the leader but are always willing to challenge the leader when necessary.

The Kellerman Typology

Kellerman's (2008) typology of followers was developed from her experience as a political scientist and her observations about followers in different historical contexts. Kellerman argues that the importance of leaders tends to be overestimated because they generally have more power, authority, and influence, while the *importance of followers* is underestimated. From her perspective, followers are subordinates who are "unleaders," by which she means they have little power, no position of authority, and no special influence.

Kellerman designed a typology that differentiates followers in regard to a single attribute: *level of engagement*. She suggests a continuum (Figure 13.5), which describes followers on one end as being detached and doing nothing for the leader or the group's goals and followers on the opposite end as being very dedicated and deeply involved with the leader and the group's goals. As shown in the figure, Kellerman's typology identifies five levels of follower engagement and behaviors:

1. *Isolates* are completely unengaged. They are detached and do not care about their leaders. Isolates who do nothing actually strengthen the influence potential of a leader. For example, when an individual feels alienated from the political system and never votes, elected officials end up having more power and freedom to exert their will.

2. *Bystanders* are observers who do not participate. They are aware of the leader's intentions and actions but deliberately choose to not become involved. In a group situation, a bystander is one who listens to the discussion but, when it is time to make a decision, disengages and declares neutrality.

3. *Participants* are partially engaged individuals who are willing to take a stand on issues, either supporting or opposing the leader. For example,

FIGURE 13.5 Kellerman Follower Typology

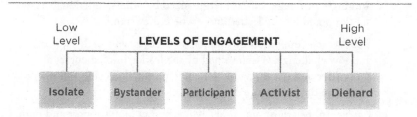

Source: From *Followership: How Followers Are Creating Change and Changing Leaders*, by Barbara Kellerman, 2008, Brighton, MA: Harvard Business Review Press.

participants would be the employees who challenge or support their leader regarding the fairness of their company's new overtime policy.

4. *Activists* feel strongly about the leader and the leader's policies and are determined to act on their own beliefs. They are change agents. For example, in 2020 after the death of George Floyd, an African American man, at the hands of a white Minneapolis, Minnesota, police officer, antiracism activists took to the streets in protest to demand change in police practices. Their protests inspired similar protests across the United States and abroad.

5. *Diehards* are engaged to the extreme. They are deeply committed to supporting the leader or opposing the leader. Diehards are totally dedicated to their cause, even willing to risk their lives for it. In a small-group setting, diehards are followers who are all-consumed with their own position within the group to the point of forcing the group members to do what they want them to do or forcing the group process to implode. For example, there have been U.S. representatives willing to force the government into economic calamity by refusing to vote to raise the country's debt ceiling in order to force their will on a particular issue, such as increased defense spending or funding for a roads project in their district.

What do these four typologies (i.e., Zaleznik, Kelley, Chaleff, and Kellerman) tell us about followers? What insights or conclusions are suggested by the typologies?

First, these typologies provide a starting point for research. The first step in building theory is to define the phenomenon under observation, and these typologies are that first step to identifying key followership variables. Second, these typologies highlight the multitude of different ways followers have been characterized, from alienated or masochistic to activist or individualist. Third, while the typologies do not differentiate a definitive list of follower types, there are some commonalities among them. Generally, the major followership types are active–engaged, independent–assertive, submissive–compliant, and supportive–conforming—or, as suggested by Carsten et al. (2014), passive followers, antiauthoritarian followers, and proactive followers.

Fourth, the typologies are important because they label individuals engaged in the leadership process. This labeling brings followers to the forefront and gives them more credence for their role in the leadership process. These descriptions can also assist leaders in effectively communicating with followers. By knowing that a follower adheres to a certain type of behavior, the leaders can adapt their style to optimally relate to the role the follower is playing.

Collectively, the typologies of followership provide a beginning point for theory building about followership. Building on these typologies, the next section discusses some of the first attempts to create a theory of followership.

THEORETICAL APPROACHES TO
FOLLOWERSHIP

What is the phenomenon of followership? Is there a theory that explains it? Uhl-Bien and her colleagues (2014) set out to answer those questions by systematically analyzing the existing followership literature and introducing a broad theory of followership. They state that followership comprises "characteristics, behaviors and processes of individuals acting in relation to leaders" (p. 96). In addition, they describe followership as a *relationally based process* that includes how followers and leaders interact to construct leadership and its outcomes (Uhl-Bien et al., 2014, p. 99).

Based on these definitions, Uhl-Bien et al. proposed a formal theory of followership. They first identified four constructs (i.e., components or attributes) and variables that comprise the process of followership as shown in Table 13.2.

Followership characteristics refer to the attributes of followers, such as the follower's traits (e.g., confidence), motivations, and the way an individual perceives what it means to be a follower.

Leadership characteristics refer to the attributes of the leader, such as the leader's power and/or willingness to empower others, the leader's perceptions of followers, and the leader's affect (i.e., the leader's positive or negative feelings toward

TABLE 13.2 Theoretical Constructs and Variables of Followership

Followership Characteristics	Leadership Characteristics	Followership and Leadership Behaviors	Followership Outcomes
Follower Traits	Leader Power	Followership Behaviors	Individual Follower Outcomes
Follower Motivation	Perceptions and Constructions	Leadership Behaviors	Individual Leader Outcomes
Follower Perceptions and Constructions	Leader Affect		Relationship Outcomes
			Leadership Process Outcomes

Source: From "Followership Theory: A Review and Research Agenda," by M. Uhl-Bien, R. R. Riggio, R. B. Lowe, and M. K. Carsten, *The Leadership Quarterly, 25*, p. 98. Copyright 2014 by Elsevier. Reprinted with permission.

followers). *Followership behaviors* are the behaviors of individuals who are in the follower role—that is, the extent to which they obey, defer, or resist the leader. *Leadership behaviors* are the behaviors of the individuals in the leadership role, such as how the leader influences followers to respond. Finally, *followership outcomes* are the results that occur based on the followership process. The outcomes can influence the individual follower, the leader, the relationship between the leader and the follower, and the leadership process. For example, how a leader reacts to a follower, whether a follower receives positive or negative reinforcement from a leader, and whether a follower advances the organizational goals all contribute to followership outcomes.

To explain the possible relationships between the variables and constructs identified in Table 13.2, the authors proposed two theoretical frameworks: *reversing the lens* (Figure 13.6) and *the leadership co-created process* (Figure 13.7).

Reversing the Lens

Reversing the lens is an approach to followership that addresses followers in a manner opposite of the way they have been studied in most prior leadership research. Rather than focusing on how *followers are affected by* leaders, it focuses on how *followers affect* leaders and organizational outcomes. Reversing the lens emphasizes that followers can be change agents. As illustrated in Figure 13.6, this approach addresses (1) the impact of followers' characteristics on followers' behavior, (2) the impact of followers' behavior on leaders' perceptions and behavior and the impact of the leaders' perceptions and behavior on followers' behaviors, and (3) the impact of both followers' behavior and leaders' perceptions and behavior on followership outcomes.

FIGURE 13.6 Reversing the Lens

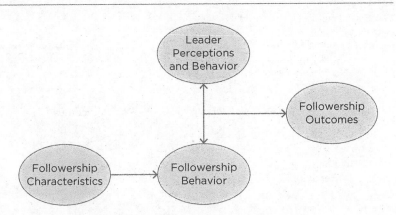

Source: From "Followership Theory: A Review and Research Agenda," by M. Uhl-Bien, R. R. Riggio, R. B. Lowe, and M. K. Carsten, *The Leadership Quarterly, 25*, p. 98. Copyright 2014 by Elsevier. Reprinted with permission.

A hypothetical example of how *reversing the lens* might work is the research a team is doing on employees and followership in a small, nonprofit organization. In this situation, researchers might be interested in how followers' personality traits (e.g., introversion–extraversion, dogmatism) relate to how they act at work—that is, their style and work behavior. Researchers might also examine how employees' behavior affects their supervisors' leadership behavior or how the follower–leader relationship affects organizational outcomes. These are just a sample of the research questions that could be addressed. However, notice that the overriding purpose and theme of the study is the *impact of followers on the followership process.*

The Leadership Co-Created Process

A second theoretical approach, *the leadership co-created process,* is shown in Figure 13.7. The name of this approach is almost a misnomer because it implies that it is about leadership rather than followership. However, that is not the case. *The leadership co-created process* conceptualizes followership as a give-and-take process where one individual's following behaviors interact with another individual's leading behaviors to create leadership and its resulting outcomes. This approach does not frame followership as role-based or as a lower rung on a hierarchical ladder; rather, it highlights how leadership is co-created through the combined act of leading and following.

Leading behaviors are influence attempts—that is, using power to have an impact on another. Following behaviors, on the other hand, involve granting power to

FIGURE 13.7 The Leadership Co-Created Process

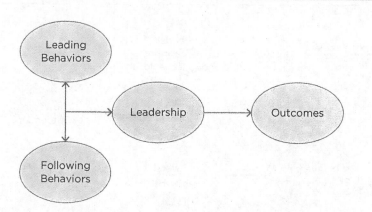

Source: Based on *The Allure of Toxic Leaders* by J. Lipman-Blumen, 2005, p. 29; permission conveyed through Copyright Clearance Center, Inc. Republished with permission of Oxford University Press.

another, complying, or challenging. Figure 13.7 illustrates that (1) followers and leaders have a mutual influence on each other; (2) leadership occurs as a result of their interaction (i.e., their leading and following); and (3) this resulting process affects outcomes.

The following example illustrates what followership would entail using the leadership co-created process framework in Figure 13.7. Terry Smith is a seasoned high school football coach who paints houses in the summer to supplement his income. One summer, Coach Smith invited one of his players, Jason Long, to work with him as a painter. Coach Smith and Jason worked well together, sharing painting responsibilities, and often finding innovative ways to accomplish their painting jobs more efficiently.

When the summer was over and football practice resumed, however, Coach Smith and Jason ran into problems. At practice, Jason called Coach Smith by his first name, joking with him about their painting jobs, and behaving as a peer rather than a team member. Although Coach Smith liked being on a first-name basis with Jason in the summer, he was concerned that other team members would also start calling him by his first name and he would lose their respect of him as the coach. Jason, on the other hand, felt good about his relationship with Coach Smith and the influence he had with him. He did not want to lose this, which would happen if he was forced to resume calling him Coach Smith, like the rest of the players.

To resolve their issues, Coach Smith and Jason discussed how they would address one another in a series of interactions and decided it was best for Jason to call Smith "Coach Smith" during the academic year to facilitate a positive working relationship between the coach and all of the team members.

In this example, the leadership co-created process can be seen in the different leading and following moves Smith and Jason made. For example, when Coach Smith asked Jason to join him to paint, he was asserting friendly influence which Jason accepted by agreeing to work with Smith. When Jason suggested more efficient methods of painting, Smith accepted the influence attempt and deferred to Jason's ideas. By calling each other by their first names while working together, both Jason and Smith assumed that leadership was being shared.

But, when football practice started in the fall and Jason continued to call Smith by his first name instead of "Coach Smith," it was apparent that for Coach Smith to retain his influence with the other players, Jason and Smith needed to reach an agreeable decision on "who was in charge" and "who was to follow." Together they decided what leadership (i.e., coaching) and followership meant in the different contexts. The result was better football practices because all players received what they perceived as equal treatment. In this situation, researchers studying followership would focus on the way Smith's and Jason's leading and following behaviors resulted in leadership that in turn resulted in effective or ineffective outcomes.

Because followership research is in the initial stages of development, the two frameworks—*reversing the lens* and *the leadership co-created process*—set forth by Uhl-Bien and her colleagues (2014) are initial attempts to create a theory of followership. The frameworks provide a way to conceptualize followership that is useful to researchers in generating further studies to explore the intricacies of followership such as the work we discuss in the next section.

New Perspectives on Followership

The research on followership is continuing to evolve and has resulted in a growing interest in the role followers have in organizations. Work by Carsten et al. (2014) not only helps organizations understand followers but also presents positive aspects of being a follower and suggests several practical perspectives on followership.

Perspective 1: Followers Get the Job Done

In the past, there has been what Meindl (1995) called a "romance of leadership," which emphasized the importance of leaders and leadership to the functioning of groups and organizations. There has been less recognition of the importance of followers to *getting the job done*. When viewed from a less leader-centric perspective, leadership can be seen as something that occurs among followers as a result of how they interpret leadership. This places less emphasis on the personality of the leader and more on followers' reactions to the leader. It shifts attention away from leaders as the causal agents of organizational change and focuses on how the behavior of followers affects organizational outcomes. Clearly, followers carry out the mission of the group and the organization; in short, they do the work. They are central to the life of the organization. Going forward, more attention needs to be given to the personalities, cognitive abilities, interpersonal skills, and problem-solving abilities of followers (Carsten et al., 2014).

Perspective 2: Followers Work in the Best Interest of the Organization's Mission

Although not true of all followers, proactive followers are committed to achieving the goals of the group or organization to which they belong. Rather than being passive and blindly obedient to the wishes of the *leader*, these followers report asserting themselves in ways that are in alignment with the goals of the *organization*. They put the organization's goals ahead of the leader's goals. The advantage of proactive followers is that they guard against leaders who act in self-serving or unethical ways. For example, if the president of the United States asked a cabinet member to do something that would personally benefit only the president, the cabinet member might refuse, arguing that what they were asked to do was not in the best interests of the country, which they ultimately serve. Followers act as a check and balance on a leader's power, protecting the organization against abuse of this power. Proactive followers keep the organization front and center.

Perspective 3: Followers Challenge Leaders

As illustrated in the typologies outlined earlier in the chapter, being engaged, active, and challenging are identifying characteristics of effective followers. But followers who challenge the leader can also help to make an organization run more effectively and successfully. When followers have knowledge about a process or procedure of which the leader is unaware, the followers become a strong asset both to the leader and to the organization. They become extra "eyes" to make sure the leader sees the organization from another angle. In addition, followers who are proactive and challenge the leader can keep the leader in sync with the overall mission of the organization.

In his work on a conceptual framework of "authentic followership," de Zilwa (2014) focuses on the relational interactions between leaders and followers and how authentic followership impacts leadership processes. De Zilwa argues that followership is proactive—followers make a conscious decision to follow a leader. This challenges the conventional view that a leader's influence is a one-way process. In being authentic, followers are assertive and offer independent, critical thought. Rather than blindly following a leader, authentic followers develop capacities for cooperation as they focus on organizational effectiveness. They are self-aware and know when to place the needs of others above their own, making the leader more effective.

To illustrate this point, consider what happened between Amy Malley, an upper-level college student, and her professor, Dr. Orville. After Dr. Orville posted the final grades for a capstone course that he taught, Amy came to see him in his office.

"I saw my posted grade, and I want you to know it is wrong," she said. "I know for certain I did very well on the exam and my grade for the course should be an A, but your posting indicates I got a B. Something is wrong with your calculations or the key for the exam."

Dr. Orville, who had taught for 25 years and never made an error in a student's grade, began to shrug off Amy's assertions and tell her she was wrong. She persisted and challenged Dr. Orville because she was confident that her exam grade was incorrect. After much discussion, Dr. Orville offered to let Amy see her exam and the scoring key. To his surprise, her answers were correct, but he had marked them wrong. Upon looking further into the matter, Dr. Orville became aware that he had wrongly scored all the students' exams because he had used the incorrect scoring key. Recognizing his error, Dr. Orville immediately changed

Amy's grade and recalculated the grades for the rest of the class. In this example, Amy's challenging of Dr. Orville's leadership resulted in positive outcomes for all the students and also for the leader.

Perspective 4: Followers Support the Leader

In addition to challenging a leader, it is equally important for followers to support the leader. To advance an organization's mission, it is valuable for leaders when followers validate and affirm the leaders' intentions. Consider what happens in a small-group setting when an individual member attempts to make a point or advance an idea. If someone in the group supports the individual, the group member's idea is heard and gains traction in the group, as does the group member. However, if individual members do not receive support from other group members, they tend to feel disconfirmed and question their role in the group.

For a leader, having a follower who supports you is like having a lieutenant. The lieutenant affirms the leader's ideas to others and in so doing gives the leader's ideas validity. This support strengthens a leader's position in the group and helps advance the leader's goals (Yelsma, 1999). We all need lieutenants, but leaders especially need lieutenants. Support from others is essential to advancing ideas with others. An example of how not having this support can affect outcomes can be seen in the leadership of Michigan governor Gretchen Whitmer during the COVID-19 crisis, when she gave a mandate to close down businesses in the entire state to slow the spread of the virus but could not muster enough support from the state legislature to keep the measure solidly in place. In this case, not having the support of others in a group was detrimental to the leader.

Perspective 5: Followers Learn From Leaders

A serendipitous outcome of being a follower is that in the process of following you learn about leading. Followership gives individuals the opportunity to view leadership from a position unencumbered from the burdens and responsibilities of being the leader. Followers get to observe what does or does not work for a leader; they can learn which leadership approaches or methods are effective or ineffective and apply this learning if they become leaders.

Consider the training that individuals undergo to become teachers. In most education programs, becoming certified as a teacher requires students to do "student teaching" or "supervised teaching," spending a semester working with a certified teacher in a classroom where actual teaching and learning are taking place. The student gets a chance to observe what teachers do and what teaching requires without the full responsibility of being in charge of the students and the educational outcomes. These student teachers have the opportunity to explore their own competencies and hone their teaching skills. From a followership perspective, the student is playing the follower role but in the process learns the leader role.

Followership and Destructive Leaders

Thus far in this chapter, we have focused on effective rather than ineffective followership. For example, we have discussed how followers provide valuable confirmation to leaders and help them accomplish organizational goals. But there is another side to followership in which followers can play unproductive, and even harmful, roles.

Some research suggests there is actually a "dark side" to followership. Schyns, Wisse, and Sanders (2019) found that followers who exhibit the "dark triad" of traits—narcissism, Machiavellianism, and psychopathy—are likely to have negative effects on fellow organization members and the organization as a whole. The authors identified "red flag" behaviors of dark triad followers such as taking credit for others' work, self-promotion, becoming aggressive after feedback, controlling others, manipulation, and bullying. When both leaders and followers have dark triad traits, the outcomes for the other group members and the organization may be even more negative.

Another way followers can have a debilitating impact is through their facilitation of toxic leadership. For example, when followers are passive or submissive, their inaction can contribute to unfettered leadership and unintentionally support toxic leaders. Furthermore, followers can create contexts that are unhealthy and make it possible for leaders who are not interested in the common good to thrive. When followers act in ways that contribute to the power of destructive leaders and their goals, it can have a debilitating impact on not just the group or organization they serve, but the followers as well.

In *The Allure of Toxic Leaders* (2005), Jean Lipman-Blumen explored toxic leadership from the perspective of followership. Toxic, or harmful, leaders are leaders who have dysfunctional personal characteristics and engage in numerous destructive behaviors. Yet, people follow them. There are many examples of such leaders in world history, among them Adolf Hitler, whose leadership led to the extermination of 6 million Jews in Europe; former Serbian and Yugoslavian president Slobodan Milošević, who ordered the genocide of thousands of Albanians and forced deportation of nearly a million, and Enron's Jeffrey Skilling and Kenneth Lay, whose conspiracy and fraud cost nearly 20,000 people their jobs and future retirement earnings.

Lipman-Blumen seeks to answer this question: Why do people follow bad leaders? She identifies a series of psychological factors on the part of followers that contribute to harmful leadership and explains why followers can be compliant even with highly destructive leaders. She also examines how some followers become "henchmen" for toxic leaders, helping and supporting the toxic leader in enacting a destructive agenda.

Her thesis is that unhealthy followership occurs as a result of people's needs to find safety, feel unique, and be included in community, and her work is useful for developing an understanding of why some followership is negative and has counterproductive outcomes.

Among the psychological factors of followers that can foster destructive leadership identified by Lipman-Blumen are our need for reassuring authority figures; our need for security and certainty; our need to feel chosen or special; our need for membership in the human community; our fear of ostracism, isolation, and social death; and our fear of powerlessness to challenge a bad leader (Table 13.3).

TABLE 13.3 Psychological Factors and Dysfunctional Leadership

1. Our need for reassuring authority figures

2. Our need for security and certainty

3. Our need to feel chosen or special

4. Our need for membership in the human community

5. Our fear of ostracism, isolation, and social death

6. Our fear of powerlessness to challenge a bad leader

Source: From "Followership Theory: A Review and Research Agenda," by M. Uhl-Bien, R. R. Riggio, R. B. Lowe, and M. K. Carsten, *The Leadership Quarterly, 25,* p. 98. Copyright 2014 by Elsevier. Reprinted with permission.

1. Our Need for Reassuring Authority Figures

As far back as psychoanalyst Sigmund Freud's research in the early 1900s, much has been written about how people deal with authority. When we are very young, we depend on our parents to guide and protect us; but as we mature, we learn to be our own compass/authority/person and make decisions without being dependent on others. However, even as adults, some people still have a high need for authority figures. They want their leaders to provide guidance and protection like their parents used to. This need can open the door for leaders who use followers for their own ends. When followers' needs for a reassuring authority figure are extremely strong, it makes them vulnerable to following abusive and destructive leaders. For example, a middle school student who plays an instrument may practice considerably more than is necessary just to obtain assurance from the teacher that they are good and worthwhile. In this example, the teacher could take advantage of this student's need for validation by having the student do more than is commonly required.

2. Our Need for Security and Certainty

The freedom many people experience when achieving adulthood can bring uncertainty and disruption to their lives. Psychologists who study people's belief systems have found that people have a need for consistency—to keep their beliefs and attitudes balanced. Our drive for certainty means we struggle in contexts where things are disrupted and we do not feel "in charge" of events. This uncertainty and insecurity creates stress from which we seek to find relief. It is in contexts like these that followers are susceptible to the lure of unethical leaders who have power. For example, think about migrant workers who come from Mexico to the United States to work on a large produce farm. The farmer they work for has promised good wages and a place to live. But upon arriving at the farm, the workers find they are required to work in the fields for up to 15 hours a day, seven days a week, and the housing provided is substandard. In addition, the farmer charges the workers a high rent for the housing, plus additional fees for providing drinking water in the fields. The workers, who are undocumented immigrants, put up with these conditions because they need the meager income they make and they know that if they complain, the farmer will report them to immigration authorities and they will be deported. The fragile security of working for the farmer outweighs the uncertainty of living in poverty in Mexico.

3. Our Need to Feel Chosen or Special

To explain the need to feel "chosen," Lipman-Blumen points to historic religious leaders, such as Moses and John Calvin, who emphasized to their people that there were "chosen ones" among them who were special and singled out by a higher authority. Being a part of "the chosen" means one has "truth" on one's side and those who are the "others" do not. Being chosen means protecting one's uniqueness and distinguishing oneself from others. While being chosen provides some comfort and even a feeling of immortality, it can motivate some to do battle with others. Being part of the chosen and feeling that they are "right" gives a sense of security to followers, but it does so at the expense of appreciating the humanity of "the others."

Consider, for example, those who adhere to a white supremacist ideology based on the belief that white people are "chosen" and superior to all other races and should have control over people of those other races. White supremacists oppose people of color and those members of non-Christian religions who they believe threaten the "purity" of the white race. Followers of white supremacy's belief in being somehow special reinforces their behaviors, which often involve treating others inhumanely.

4. Our Need for Membership in the Human Community

Psychologist William Schutz (1958) argued that one of humans' strongest interpersonal needs is to know whether they belong to the group. Are we "in" or "out"? Are we included with others and acknowledged as a member of the community or not?

When groups and organizations function positively, it is healthy for all group members, not detrimental. Group members feel accepted, comfortable, valued, and inspirited. But people's need to be members of the group can be exploited by destructive leaders who take advantage of individuals who are highly dependent on the group for their own personal meaning and purpose. Highly dependent followers may be willing to give up their individuality, beliefs, and integrity just to make sure they can retain their social belonging (Lipman-Blumen, 2005).

Consider the number of disturbing hazing incidents at fraternities or other groups on college campuses that have resulted in the injuries and deaths of new members (pledges) who are willing to endure dangerous rituals because of their high need to belong to the group. Followers can become vulnerable to bad leadership when they are unable to moderate their own personal need for belonging.

5. Our Fear of Ostracism, Isolation, and Social Death

When an individual becomes a part of and acquires full membership to a group, the individual typically learns and begins to practice the norms of the group. Surrounded by the group, followers become comfortable with the group's values, mission, and beliefs. In addition, followers begin to like being a group member and doing what group members do and find the inclusion and community of the group comforting.

But being a part of the group also has a downside. This inclusion and community makes it difficult for individuals to break out of the group or dissent if the group's mission or values run counter to their own. Pressure to conform to the group makes it challenging for individuals to disagree with the group or try to get the group to change. When followers act against group norms or bring attention to the negative aspects of what the group is doing (e.g., whistle-blowers), they run a high risk of becoming ostracized and isolated from the group.

For example, imagine being in a group of friends, and several members of your group have started to make fun of a young man in your class who is on the autism spectrum and often acts awkwardly in social situations. You dislike how they treat this young man and consider their behavior to be bullying. Do you speak up and tell them to stop, knowing that you might be ostracized by the rest of the group? Or do you "keep quiet" and maintain your relationships with your friends? Being an ethical follower carries with it the burden of acting out your individual values even when it can mean social death.

6. Our Fear of Powerlessness to Challenge a Bad Leader

Finally, followers may unintentionally enable destructive leaders because they feel helpless to change them. Once a part of a group, followers often feel pressure to conform to the norms of the group. They find that it is not easy to challenge the leader or go against the leader's plans for the group. Even when a leader acts inappropriately or treats others in harmful ways, it is hard for followers to muster the courage to address the leader's behavior. Groups provide security for followers, and the threat of losing this security can make it scary to challenge authority figures. To speak truth to power is a brave act, and followers often feel powerless to express themselves in the face of authority. Although being an accepted follower in a group carries with it many benefits, it does not always promote personal agency. After all, who would support you if you challenged the leader? For example, imagine what it would be like to be a gay employee in an organization whose leadership is openly prejudiced against individuals who identify as lesbian, gay, bisexual, or transgender. Would you be likely to express disapproval of the leadership and its policies?

The six psychological needs of followers outlined by Lipman-Blumen are essential to understanding the role of followers in fostering destructive leadership. When followers attempt to fulfill these needs, it can create contexts where unethical and destructive leaders are allowed to thrive.

HOW DOES FOLLOWERSHIP WORK?

Unlike established leadership theories such as leader–member exchange theory (Chapter 7) or transformational leadership (Chapter 8) for which there are formulated models, assumptions, and theorems, followership is an area of study still in its infancy. However, it does provide several "takeaways" that have valuable implications for practicing followership.

First, simply discussing followership forces us to elevate its importance and the value of followers. For many years, the role of leaders in the leadership process has been esteemed far above that of followers, as evidenced by the thousands of research studies that exist on leaders and leadership approaches and the very few that have been done on followership. Leadership has been idealized as a central component of organizational behavior. But by focusing on followership, we are forced to engage in a new way of thinking about those who do the work of leadership and to explore the merits of the people who do the work of followership. Leadership does not exist in a vacuum; it needs followers to be operationalized. Followership research highlights the essential role that followers fulfill in every aspect of organizational accomplishments. Why should we focus on followership? Because it is just as important as leadership.

Second, followership is about how individuals accept the influence of others to reach a common goal. It describes the characteristics and actions of people who have less power than the leader yet are critical components in the leadership process. The typologies of follower behaviors discussed in this chapter provide a criterion of what followers typically do in different situations when they are being influenced by a leader. Do they help the leader, or do they fight the leader? Do they make the organization run better or worse? Categorizations of followers are beneficial because they help us understand the way people act when occupying a follower role. To know that a person is a follower is useful, but to know if that follower is dependent-passive or proactive-antiauthoritarian is far more valuable. These categories provide information about how followers act and how a leader can respond accordingly. It also helps leaders know followers' attitudes toward work and the organization and how to best communicate with these followers.

Third, followership research provides a means of understanding why harmful leadership occurs and sometimes goes unrestrained. Followers are interdependent with leaders in the leadership process—each affects and is affected by the other. When leaders are abusive or unethical, it affects followers. But followers often feel restrained to respond. While they may want to respond to destructive leaders, followers will often become passive and inactive instead. This occurs because they fear losing the security provided by their membership in the group. By understanding their own feelings of powerlessness and need for security and community, followers can more easily identify and confront destructive leaders.

STRENGTHS

In this chapter, we trace the development of followership and how it has been conceptualized by researchers over the past 50 years. This research has several strengths.

First, it gives recognition to followership as an integral part of the leadership equation. While some earlier theories of leadership (e.g., implicit leadership theory [Lord & Maher, 1991] and social identity theory [Tajfel & Turner, 1986]) recognize followers as an element in the leadership process, the most recent literature suggests an approach to followership that elevates it considerably and gives it equal footing with leadership. Further underscoring the complexity and importance of followership, Popper (2014) suggests that followers' attraction to leaders emerges from one of three perspectives: (a) psychoanalytic, where the leader is seen as a protective figure; (b) cognitive-psychological, where the leader is seen as a suitable and psychologically convenient explanation for a complex reality; or (c) social-psychological, in which the leader is a kind of narrative imparting meaning to followers' social identity and sense of self-worth. This emphasis broadens our purview of leadership and suggests that followership will—and should—receive far more attention by researchers and practitioners in the future.

Second, a focus on followership forces a whole new way for people to think about leadership. While there are textbooks on leadership, such as Hughes, Ginnett, and Curphy's *Leadership: Enhancing the Lessons of Experience* (2014), that give special attention to followership, current followership research and literature go further and challenge us to take leadership off its pedestal and replace it with followership. It forces us to focus on followers rather than leaders. It looks to answer questions like these: What makes effective followership? How do followers affect group processes and influence goal accomplishment? How do followers influence leaders? For example, recent research by Carsten, Uhl-Bien, and Huang (2018) found that followers influence their leaders through less voice and upward delegation (for example, passing problems to a manager rather than solving the problem themselves). Leaders were less motivated, and less likely to contribute to goal attainment, when followers were passive and engaged in upward delegation. It makes sense that organizations should pay more attention to training followers, rather than just leaders, in how to work effectively together.

In addition, new followership literature invites us to view leadership as a co-constructed process in which followers and leaders share equally. Rather than focusing on the individuals with the power, our thinking needs to shift to embracing the individuals without the power and the relationship these people make with the leader. The study of followership reminds us that leadership is incomplete and cannot be understood without focusing on and understanding the role and dimensions of followers. For example, Pietraszewski (2019) describes how leadership and followership can solve the problem of coordination and cooperation toward goal attainment. He points out that no one follower has all the information needed to solve complex problems alone. Therefore, leaders and followers create a "social marketplace" where leaders propose alternatives, and leaders and followers choose their responses from among them. This marketplace operates on social information processing where leaders and followers propose and evaluate options.

Third, although in its infancy, followership research provides a set of basic prescriptions for what a follower should or should not do to be effective. These prescriptions provide a general blueprint of the types of behaviors that create effective followership. For example, effective followers balance their need for community with their need for self. They act in the best interests of the organization and challenge the leader when the leader's agenda is self-serving or unethical. Effective followers do not act antiauthoritarian, but collaborate to get the job done. Furthermore, they recognize powerlessness in themselves but do not let this keep them from challenging the leader when necessary. While the followership research has not yet produced elegant theories that explain the intricacies of how followership works, it does provide a set of ideas that have strong practical applications.

Furthermore, research on implicit followership theory suggests that leaders look for both attributes related to performance and attributes such as loyalty and being able to cooperate with others in their view of an "ideal" follower (Carsten et al., 2010). Sy (2010) found six factors constitute the ideal follower: industry, enthusiasm, good citizenship, conformity, insubordination, and incompetence. The first three were valued positively (i.e. followership prototype), and the latter three had negative values (i.e., followership antiprototype). This research also found that when followers fit the leader's implicit prototype for being a good follower, they reported that they liked the leader more and had higher relationship quality and trust. Alipour, Mohammed, and Martinez (2017) propose that timing plays an important role in understanding the effects of followership prototypes. Meeting a leader's expectations on deadlines, time perspective, preference for multitasking, and pacing style all could depend on whether the follower matches the leader's implicit follower prototype. A follower who is aware of and able to engage in behaviors that are consistent with a leader's ideal follower prototype may be more likely to meet the leader's time-related expectations, reducing coordination problems. Followers who perceive an alignment between their followership prototype and their actual behavior are more likely to view followership as part of their self-concept, claim to be a follower rather than a leader, and be more open to their leader's attempts to shape their social identity as a good follower (Epitropaki, Kark, Mainemelis, & Lord, 2017).

CRITICISMS

In addition to its strengths, the study of followership has certain limitations. First, the methodical research that has been conducted on the process of followership is in the nascent stage. The absence of advanced research makes it difficult to concretely conceptualize the nature of followership including what defines followers and how followers contribute to the leadership process. Without precise theories and models of followership, there can be no clear set of principles or practices about how followership works and the role it plays in groups, organizations, and the community.

Second, the current followership literature is primarily personal observations and anecdotal. For example, the typologies of followership styles discussed earlier in the chapter (i.e., Zaleznik, Kelley, Chaleff, and Kellerman) are useful category systems to differentiate between followers' styles, but the derivation of the typologies is simply the conjectures and hypotheses of a single author. While such descriptive research, including designing different typologies, is a traditional process in the initial phase of theory development, the value and power of our thinking on followership will not advance until followership is fully conceptualized and tested.

Third, the leader-centric orientation that exists in the world may be too ingrained for followership to blossom. For followership to succeed, it will need both leaders and followers to be strong in their roles; followers must serve the purpose of teaching the leader as well as learning from the leader (Chaleff, 1995). And in a leader-centric world, where followership's primary purpose is seen as important only to make leaders leaders (you can't be a leader if no one is following), this evolution may take a very long time to come about. There is a need for research that considers both leader and follower prototypes and how these expectations influence the leadership process and outcomes (Foti, Hansbrough, Epitropaki, & Coyle, 2017). Until we have more research that is dyadic, we will only understand parts of the dynamics that explain effective followership.

Fourth, research on followers has not fully addressed the question "Why follow?" Bastardoz and Van Vugt (2019) critiqued the followership literature from an evolutionary psychology perspective. They assert that followership is puzzling because there has been no explanation for why followers give up autonomy and put their own goals aside to follow leaders. From an evolutionary perspective, followership evolved to address problems in groups such as hunting, gathering, and peacekeeping. Those who do not have the ability to lead are more likely to become followers. Also, followership occurs because of the rewards followers receive from a leader, goal alignment, the challenges faced by the group, and the leader's style. The authors argue that evolutionary psychology offers a more robust explanation for followership than current theoretical approaches offered in the literature.

Fifth, there has been little research on when and/or how patterns of followership are beneficial or detrimental. Followership is not without risks. Qualitative research conducted by Benson, Hardy, and Eys (2016) found that leaders viewed followership as important because they rely on followers to offer alternative insights on and solutions to problems. However, they also expect followers to support leader directives. In some instances, follower attempts to influence their leaders were "at the wrong time and place" and viewed as disruptive by the leader. This research raises an important caveat for followers: While proactivity is important, followers must be aware and calibrate their influence attempts by taking the situational factors into account.

APPLICATION

"Follow the leader" is an expression familiar to many. Whether it was a way for teachers to avoid confusion and keep peace with their charges or a game played on the playground, "follow the leader" means people need to get in line behind the designated leader and do what the leader tells them to do. Following the leader is about the process of accepting the leader's authority and influence. More importantly, it is about deciding how to respond to what the leader says.

Followership research is about just that: understanding how and why followers respond to leaders. There are several applications of followership research.

First and foremost, the research underscores the importance of followership—it is *as important* as leadership. This chapter helps us understand the critical and complex role followers play in regard to leaders. It differentiates common roles followers play, from very active and positive to very inactive and negative.

When applied to real-life leadership situations, knowledge about followers and their roles and behaviors expands our understanding of the major components that contribute to group and organizational success.

In addition, the study of followership has implications for organizational training and development. Although followership is not currently recognized as a top topic in the training and development field, it is not difficult to see how workshops and training in followership could become very important to organizations in the near future. Learning about followership could help followers understand themselves, how they function, and how they can best contribute to the goals of the group or organization of which they are members. Clearly, there is demonstrable value in training programs on such topics as "Being an Effective Follower," "Dealing With Destructive Bosses," or "Accepting the Challenges of Followership." With the increased attention being given to followership research, it is expected that an increase in training programs on followership will result as well.

Furthermore, the information described in this chapter can help leaders to understand followers and how to most effectively work with them. So much of the current leadership literature is about the leader and the leader's behavior; however, this chapter shifts the attention to the follower and why followers act the way they do. Leaders can use this followership information to adjust their style to the needs of followers. For example, if the leader finds that followers are aggressive and disruptive, the information in this chapter suggests that they may have authority issues and are acting out because of their own needs for security. Or, some followers may be quiet and compliant, suggesting they need leadership that assures them that they are a part of the group and encourages them to participate more in the group process. Leaders have tried for years to treat followers as individuals with unique needs, but this chapter goes further and provides leaders with cues for action that are derived directly from the followership literature.

CASE STUDIES

The following three case studies (Cases 13.1, 13.2, and 13.3) present followership in three different contexts. The first case describes a home health care agency and the unique ways followers contribute to the work of the agency. The second case discusses a renowned rowing team and the way the followers worked together to create cohesiveness and a magical outcome. The last case examines the role of followership in the circumstances that brought down a well-regarded collegiate football program and the university's leadership. At the end of each case, there are questions that will help you to analyze the case utilizing the principles of followership discussed in the chapter.

Case 13.1 BLUEBIRD CARE

Robin Martin started Bluebird Care, an in-home health care agency, 20 years ago with a staff of 2 and 5 clients. The agency has grown to a staff of 25 serving 50 clients.

Robin started in elder care as an aide at a reputable assisted living facility. She liked caring for patients and was good at it. When she began running Bluebird Care, Robin knew all her staff members and their clients. But as the demand for in-home health care has increased, Bluebird Care has grown as well—hiring more staff and expanding its service area. For Robin, this means less time with the company's clients and more time managing her growing agency. She admits she feels as if she is losing her connections with her clients and staff.

When asked to describe a time when the agency was really running smoothly, Robin talks about when Bluebird Care had just 10 employees. "This was a good time for us. Everyone did what they were assigned and did not complain. No one called in sick; they were very dependable. But, it was different then because we all lived in the same area and I would see each of our employees every week. On Tuesdays they had to hand in their time sheets, and every other Thursday they stopped to pick up their paycheck. I enjoyed this."

Because the agency's service area is much larger now, encompassing many of the city's suburbs, Robin seldom sees her employees. Time sheets are emailed in by employees, and paychecks are sent through the mail or directly deposited into employees' bank accounts. Robin says, "Because they never see us, the staff feels like they can do what they want, and management has nothing to say about it. It's not the same as when we were smaller."

There is a core of agency staff that Robin does interact with nearly every day. Terry, a staff member who has been with Robin since the beginning, is Robin's go-to

(Continued)

(Continued)

person. "I trust her," Robin says. "When she says, 'Robin—we need to do it this way,' I do what she says. She is always right." Terry is very positive and promotive of the agency and complimentary of Robin. When other staff members challenge the rules or procedures of the agency, Terry is the person to whom Robin goes to for advice. But, Terry also challenges Robin to make Bluebird Care the best agency it can be.

Terry is a direct contrast to Belinda, another employee. A five-year staff member, Belinda is dogmatic and doesn't like change, yet frequently challenges Robin and the rules of the agency. Robin describes Belinda as "a bully" and not a team player. For example, Belinda and Robin had a conflict about a rule in the agency's procedural manual that requires staff to work every other weekend. Belinda argued that it was unfair to force staff members to work every other weekend and that other similar agencies don't have such policies. To prove her point, Belinda obtained a competing agency's manual that supported her position and showed it to Robin.

Robin, who does not like confrontation, was frustrated by Belinda's aggressive conflict style. Robin brought up the issue about weekends with Terry, and Terry supported her and the way the policy was written. In the end, Belinda did not get the policy changed, but both Belinda and Robin are sure there will be more conflicts to come.

Two other key staff members are Robin's son, Caleb, who hires and trains most of the employees, and her son-in-law, James, who answers the phone and does scheduling. Robin says as a manager James does his work in a quiet, respectful manner and seldom causes problems. In addition to handling all the hiring and training, Robin relies on Caleb to troubleshoot issues regarding client services. For both James and Caleb, the job can become stressful because it is their phones that ring when a staff member doesn't show up to a client's for work and they have to find someone to fill in.

Caleb also says he is working hard to instill a sense of cohesiveness among the agency's far-flung staff and to reduce turnover with their millennial-age staff members. Caleb says while the agency's growth is seen as positive, he worries that the caring philosophy his mother started the agency with is becoming lost.

Questions

1. Who are the followers at Bluebird Care?

2. In what way is followership related to the mission of the agency? Do Robin and her managers recognize the importance of followership? Explain.

3. Using the roles identified in Chaleff's follower typology (Figure 13.4), what roles do Terry, Belinda, Caleb, and James play at the agency?

4. Using the "reversing the lens" framework (Figure 13.6), explain how Caleb and James's characteristics contribute to the followership outcomes at Bluebird Care.

5. Terry and Robin have a unique relationship in that they both engage in leading and following. How do you think each of them views leadership and followership? Discuss.

6. If you were an organizational consultant, what would you suggest to Robin that could strengthen Bluebird Care? If you were a followership coach, how would you advise Robin?

Case 13.2 OLYMPIC ROWERS

In the 1930s, rowing was the most popular sport in the country. The sport not only was physically brutal, but required inexhaustible teamwork. In an eight-man rowing shell, each member of the team has a role to fulfill based on where he sits in the boat. The movements of each rower are precisely synchronized with the movements of the others in the boat. Every rower in the shell must perform flawlessly with each and every pull of the oar; if one member of the crew is off, the whole team is off. Any one rower's mistake can throw off the tempo for the boat's thrust and jeopardize the balance and success of the boat.

In the early 1930s, rowing was a sport dominated by elite East Coast universities like Cornell, Harvard, and Princeton. However, two West Coast teams, the University of California, Berkeley, and the University of Washington, had an intense rivalry not only with the crews from the East Coast but with one another as well. Al Ulbrickson, the varsity crew coach at the University of Washington, had watched jealously as the California team ascended to national prominence, representing the United States in the 1932 Olympics, and was determined that his University of Washington team would be the one to represent the United States at the 1936 Olympics in Berlin, Germany.

Ulbrickson's program had a number of talented rowers, including those who had rowed to win the national freshman championships in 1934. Unlike teams from the East Coast whose members' lives were often marked by privilege and wealth, many of the boys in the University of Washington program came from poor, working-class backgrounds. They were the sons of loggers, farmers, and fishermen, and gaining a spot on the rowing team would help pay for their college education. Over the summer break these same boys would work, often in dangerous and physically taxing jobs, so they could afford to return to college in the fall.

Finding the ideal makeup of members for a successful rowing team is a complex process. A great crew is a carefully balanced mix of rowers with different physical abilities and personalities. According to Brown (2013), "Good crews are blends of personalities: someone to lead the charge, someone to hold something in reserve, someone to pick a fight, someone to make peace, someone to think through,

(Continued)

(Continued)

someone to charge ahead without thinking. . . . Even after the right mixture is found, each oarsman must recognize their place in the fabric of the crew and accept the others as they are" (pp. 179–180).

To find that magic mix, Ulbrickson experimented with different combinations of rowers, putting individual rowers on different teams to see how they performed together. But it was more than just putting the right abilities together; it was finding the right chemistry. He finally did with a team of boys who "had been winnowed down by punishing competition, and in the winnowing a kind of common character had issued forth: they were all skilled, they were all tough, they were all fiercely determined, but they were also all good-hearted. Every one of them had come from humble origins or been humbled by the hard times in which they had grown up. . . . The challenges they had faced together had taught them humility—the need to subsume their individual egos for the sake of the boat as a whole—and humility was the common gateway through which they were able now to come together" (Brown, 2013, p. 241). One of those team members said when he stepped into the shell with his new teammates, he finally felt at home.

This Washington varsity team decimated the competition on the East and West Coasts, earning a spot on the U.S. Olympic team. At the Berlin Olympics, the team faced a number of challenges. One of their key oarsmen had fallen seriously ill on the transatlantic voyage to Germany and remained sick throughout the competition. There were distractions everywhere. But every time the American boys saw tension or nervousness in one another, they drew closer together as a group and talked earnestly and seriously to each other. They draped arms over one another's shoulders and talked through their race plan. "Each of them knew a defining moment in his life was nearly at hand and no one wanted to waste it. And none wanted to waste it for the others" (Brown, 2013, p. 326).

The team defeated England in its preliminary heat, and made it to the finals. But the odds were stacked against them: They were in the worst lane in the final race, which put them at a two-length disadvantage; they experienced a delayed start because their coxswain missed the signal that the race had begun; and their sick oarsman was barely conscious. But they came from behind and triumphed, winning Olympic gold.

As Brown (2013) points out, "No other sport demands and rewards the complete abandonment of the self the way that rowing does. Great crews may have men or women of exceptional talent or strength; they may have outstanding skills . . . but they have no stars. The team effort—the perfectly synchronized flow of muscle, oars, boat, and water . . . the single, whole, unified, and beautiful symphony that a crew in motion becomes—is all that matters. Not the individual, not the self" (pp. 177–178).

Questions

1. In what way is this case about followership? Who were the followers? Who were the leaders?

2. The coxswain is the crew member who sits in the stern facing the bow, steers the boat, and coordinates the power and rhythm of the rowers. In this case, is the coxswain's role more or less important than the roles of other crew members? Explain your answer.

3. Reversing the lens emphasizes that followers can be change agents—what was the impact of followers' characteristics on followers' behaviors in this case? What impact do you think Ulbrickson's perception and behaviors had on the rowers in his program?

4. How would you describe the impact of both followers and leaders on followership outcome?

5. In this case, the boys in the boat created a highly cohesive unit. Do you think highly effective followership always results in cohesiveness? Defend your answer.

Case 13.3 PENN STATE SEXUAL ABUSE SCANDAL

In the 46 years that Joe Paterno was head football coach of the Penn State Nittany Lions, he racked up 409 victories and was the most victorious football coach in the history of the National Collegiate Athletic Association. Paterno called his brand of coaching "The Grand Experiment" because he aimed to prove that football excellence and academic integrity could coexist. Imbuing his program with the motto "Success With Honor," Paterno was as interested in the moral character of his players as in their physical abilities, a fact borne out by the program's unusually high graduation rates (Mahler, 2011). Over four decades, a positive mythology enveloped the program, the university, and Paterno, instilling a fervent Penn State pride in students, faculty, staff, athletes, and fans across the globe, contributing to Penn State's reputation as one of the most highly regarded public universities in the United States.

But in 2011, a child sexual abuse scandal involving a former Penn State assistant football coach caused "The Grand Experiment" to tumble from its high perch, bringing down with it not only Coach Paterno, the university's athletic director Tim Curley, and the storied Penn State football program, but also the university's president, Graham B. Spanier.

The seeds of the scandal began in 1977 when Penn State's then defensive line coach Jerry Sandusky established a nonprofit organization called The Second

(Continued)

(Continued)

Mile that was described as a "group foster home devoted to helping troubled boys." Sandusky's position and association with Penn State gave the charity credibility, but The Second Mile ultimately proved to be a cover and conduit for Sandusky's sexual abuse of boys. It is alleged that through The Second Mile, Sandusky was able to identify and meet many of the young men who ultimately became his victims.

Fast-forward to more than 30 years later when, in 2008, the mother of a high school freshman reported to officials that her son was sexually abused by Sandusky. Sandusky had been retired from Penn State since 1999, but continued to coach as a volunteer, working with kids through his Second Mile charity. As a result of the call, the state's attorney general launched an investigation of Sandusky, and evidence was uncovered that this wasn't the first time Sandusky had been alleged of committing sexual abuse. Allegations of his abuse had been cropping up since the late 1990s.

In 1998, the mother of an 11-year-old boy called Penn State University police after she learned her son had showered naked with Sandusky in the campus's athletic locker room and that Sandusky touched the child inappropriately. At the time, Paterno, Curley, and Spanier, as well as Gary C. Schultz, senior vice president for finance and business, were all informed of the incident, and an investigation was conducted. Even though police talked with another boy who reported similar treatment, they opted to close the case. During an interview with university police and a representative from the Pennsylvania Department of Public Welfare (now known as Human Services), Sandusky said he would not shower with children again.

Two years later, in the fall of 2000, a janitor in Penn State's Lasch football building told a coworker and supervisor that he saw Sandusky engaged in sexual activity with a boy in the assistant coach's shower. Fearing for their jobs, neither the janitor nor his coworker filed a report; their supervisor did not file a report, either.

"They knew who Sandusky was," Special Investigative Counsel Louis J. Freeh later said after he completed an eight-month investigation of the scandal in 2012. "They said the university would circle around it. It was like going against the president of the United States. If that's the culture on the bottom, God help the culture at the top" (Wolverton, 2012).

In 2001, Penn State graduate assistant Mike McQueary witnessed Sandusky sexually assaulting a boy in the showers at the Lasch football building. McQueary visited Coach Paterno's home the next morning to tell the coach what he had witnessed. Paterno, in turn, reported the incident to Athletic Director Curley. It wasn't until 10 days later, however, that McQueary finally met with Curley and Schultz to describe what he saw.

Initially Curley, Schultz, and Spanier decided to report the incident to the Department of Public Welfare. However, two days later, Curley informed Schultz and Spanier that he had changed his mind after "talking it over with Joe" Paterno. They decided instead to offer Sandusky "professional help" and tell him to stop bringing guests to the locker room (Wolverton, 2012). No report was made to the police or the child protection agency. It was later found that in an email, Spanier told Curley he approved of the athletic director's decision not to report the incident, calling it a "humane and reasonable way to proceed" (Wolverton, 2012).

McQueary, meanwhile, continued to work at Penn State, being promoted to an assistant football coach's position. And over the next seven years, Sandusky reportedly kept meeting and sexually assaulting young boys.

When Sandusky was finally arrested and charged with 40 counts of sexual abuse in 2011, it was at the end of a three-year investigation launched by that mother's 2008 phone call. The investigation not only uncovered that Sandusky sexually abused eight boys over a 15-year period, but determined that university leaders, including Spanier and Schultz, knew about the coach's behavior and did not act. During testimony they gave during the attorney general's investigation, these same leaders denied knowing about the 1998 and 2001 incidents; but the investigation proved through emails and other documents that university leaders did not truthfully admit what they knew about these incidents and when they knew it. As a result, Curley and Schultz were charged with perjury and failure to report what they knew of the allegations.

While Spanier called Sandusky's behavior "troubling," he pledged his unconditional support for both Curley and Schultz, predicting they would be exonerated (Keller, 2012). Two days later, however, Paterno and Spanier were fired by the university's Board of Trustees, and the board hired Freeh to conduct an independent investigation of the scandal.

Eight months later, Freeh released a scathing 267-page report that detailed how and when university leaders knew about Sandusky's behavior and stated that they failed to report repeated allegations of child sexual abuse by Sandusky. The report stated that Spanier and Paterno displayed "a total disregard for the safety and welfare of children" and hid critical facts from authorities on the alleged abuses (Wolverton, 2012).

The investigation by Freeh found emails and other documents suggesting that Spanier, Paterno, Schultz, and Curley all knew for years about the sexual nature of the accusations against Sandusky and kept these allegations under wraps. The report stated that Paterno, especially, "was an integral part of the act to conceal" (Keller, 2012). Athletic Director Curley was described in the report as "someone who followed instruction regardless of the consequences and was 'loyal to a fault.'" One senior official called Curley Paterno's "errand boy." And finally, the investigation concluded that Spanier "failed in his duties as president" for "not promptly and fully advising the Board of Trustees about the 1998 and

(Continued)

(Continued)

2001 child-sexual abuse allegations against Sandusky and the subsequent grand jury investigation of him" (Keller, 2012).

But it wasn't just the university administrators who took fire. The report also cited the university's Board of Trustees for failing "to exercise its oversight," stating "the Board did not create a 'tone at the top' environment wherein Sandusky and other senior university officials believed they were accountable to it." Ultimately, Freeh's report concluded that the reputations of the university and its exalted football program were "more important to its leaders than the safety and welfare of young children" (Keller, 2012).

Joe Paterno died in January 2012. Six months later, Sandusky, the assistant coach he protected, was convicted of 45 counts of child sexual abuse and sentenced to 30 to 60 years in prison. Former Penn State officials Curley, Schultz, and Spanier were all sentenced to jail time for failing to alert authorities of the allegations against Sandusky, allowing him to continue molesting boys for years.

A month after Sandusky's conviction and 10 days after Freeh's report was released, a much-beloved 7-foot, 900-pound bronze statue of Paterno was removed from its pedestal outside Penn State's Beaver Stadium, providing symbolic evidence of the failure of Paterno's "Success With Honor" motto and the public's faith in Penn State's program.

Questions

1. How would you describe the followership at Penn State? Whom would you identify as the followers? Who are the leaders?

2. Using Kelley's typology, how would you describe the follower styles for Schultz and Curley? What about McQueary?

3. How did followers in this case act in ways that contribute to the power of destructive leaders and their goals? What was the debilitating impact their actions had on the organization?

4. Based on Lipman-Blumen's psychological factors that contribute to harmful leadership (Table 13.3), explain why those who could have reported Sandusky's behaviors chose not to.

5. Based on the outcome, where did Paterno's intentions go wrong? In what ways could followers have changed the moral climate at Penn State?

6. In the end, who carries the burden of responsibility regarding the failure of Paterno's program—the leaders or the followers? Defend your answer.

LEADERSHIP INSTRUMENT

As discussed earlier in this chapter, Kelley (1992) developed a typology that categorized followers into one of five styles (exemplary, alienated, conformist, passive, and pragmatist) based on two axes (independent thinking and active engagement). These different dimensions of followership became the basis for Kelley's Followership Questionnaire, a survey that allows followership style to be determined through an empirical approach, rather than through observation.

Followership Questionnaire

Purpose: The purpose of this questionnaire is to learn about your style as a follower.

Instructions: Think of a specific leader–follower situation where you were in the role of follower. For each statement, please use the following scale to indicate the extent to which the statement describes you and your behavior in this situation.

Key: 0 = Rarely   1 = Almost rarely   2 = Seldom   3 = Occasionally
      4 = More often than not   5 = Often   6 = Almost always

1. Does your work help you fulfill some societal goal or   0 1 2 3 4 5 6
    personal dream that is important to you?

2. Are your personal work goals aligned with the   0 1 2 3 4 5 6
    organization's priority goals?

3. Are you highly committed to and energized by your   0 1 2 3 4 5 6
    work and organization, giving them your best ideas
    and performance?

4. Does your enthusiasm also spread to and energize   0 1 2 3 4 5 6
    your coworkers?

5. Instead of waiting for or merely accepting what   0 1 2 3 4 5 6
    the leader tells you, do you personally identify
    which organizational activities are most critical for
    achieving the organization's priority goals?

6. Do you actively develop a distinctive competence   0 1 2 3 4 5 6
    in those critical activities so that you become more
    valuable to the leader and the organization?

7. When starting a new job or assignment, do you   0 1 2 3 4 5 6
    promptly build a record of successes in tasks that
    are important to the leader?

8. Can the leader give you a difficult assignment   0 1 2 3 4 5 6
    without the benefit of much supervision, knowing
    that you will meet your deadline with highest-quality
    work and that you will "fill in the cracks" if need be?

9. Do you take the initiative to seek out and   0 1 2 3 4 5 6
    successfully complete assignments that go above
    and beyond your job?

10. When you are not the leader of a group project, do   0 1 2 3 4 5 6
    you still contribute at a high level, often doing more
    than your share?

11. Do you independently think up and champion new   0 1 2 3 4 5 6
    ideas that will contribute significantly to the leader's
    or the organization's goals?

12. Do you try to solve the tough problems (technical or   0 1 2 3 4 5 6
    organizational), rather than look to the leader to do
    it for you?

13. Do you help out other coworkers, making them look good, even when you don't get any credit?   0 1 2 3 4 5 6

14. Do you help the leader or group see both the upside potential and downside risks of ideas or plans, playing the devil's advocate if need be?   0 1 2 3 4 5 6

15. Do you understand the leader's needs, goals, and constraints, and work hard to help meet them?   0 1 2 3 4 5 6

16. Do you actively and honestly own up to your strengths and weaknesses rather than put off evaluation?   0 1 2 3 4 5 6

17. Do you make a habit of internally questioning the wisdom of the leader's decision rather than just doing what you are told?   0 1 2 3 4 5 6

18. When the leader asks you to do something that runs contrary to your professional or personal preferences, do you say "no" rather than "yes"?   0 1 2 3 4 5 6

19. Do you act on your own ethical standards rather than the leader's or the group's standards?   0 1 2 3 4 5 6

20. Do you assert your views on important issues, even though it might mean conflict with your group or reprisals from the leader?   0 1 2 3 4 5 6

Source: Excerpts from Kelley, Robert E. (1992). *The Power of Followership: How to Create Leaders People Want to Follow and Followers Who Lead Themselves.* New York: Doubleday.

Scoring

The Followership Questionnaire measures your style as a follower based on two dimensions of followership: *independent thinking* and *active engagement*. Your responses indicate the degree to which you are an independent thinker and actively engaged in your follower role. Score the questionnaire by doing the following. Your scores will classify you as being primarily one of the five styles: exemplary, alienated, conformist, pragmatist, or passive.

1. Independent Thinking Score: Sum of questions 1, 5, 11, 12, 14, 16, 17, 18, 19, and 20

2. Active Engagement Score: Sum of questions 2, 3, 4, 6, 7, 8, 9, 10, 13, and 15

   - *Exemplary Followership Style:* If you scored high (above 40) on both independent thinking and active engagement, your followership style is categorized as exemplary.

   - *Alienated Followership Style:* If you scored high (above 40) on independent thinking and low (below 20) on active engagement, your followership style is categorized as alienated.

(Continued)

(Continued)

- *Conformist Followership Style:* If you scored low (below 20) on independent thinking and high (above 40) on active engagement, your followership style is categorized as conformist.
- *Pragmatist Followership Style:* If you scored in the middle range (from 20 to 40) on both independent thinking and active engagement, your followership style is categorized as pragmatist.
- *Passive Followership Style:* If you scored low (below 20) on both independent thinking and active engagement, your followership style is categorized as passive.

Followership Style	Independent Thinking Score	Active Engagement Score
EXEMPLARY	High	High
ALIENATED	High	Low
CONFORMIST	Low	High
PRAGMATIST	Middling	Middling
PASSIVE	Low	Low

Source: Adapted from Kelley, Robert E. (1992). *The Power of Followership: How to Create Leaders People Want to Follow and Followers Who Lead Themselves.* New York: Doubleday.

Scoring Interpretation

What do the different styles mean? How should you interpret your style? The followership styles characterize how you carry out the followership role, not who you are as a person. At any point in time, or under different circumstances, you may use one followership pattern rather than another.

Exemplary Follower

Exemplary followers score high in both independent thinking and active engagement. They exhibit independent, critical thinking, separate from the group or leader. They are actively engaged, using their talents for the benefit of the organization, even when confronted with bureaucracy or other noncontributing members. Up to 35% of people are categorized as exemplary followers.

Alienated Follower

Alienated followers score high in independent thinking but low in active engagement. This means that they think independently and critically, but are not active in carrying out the role of a follower. They might disengage from the group at times and may view themselves as victims who have received unfair treatment. Approximately 15%–25% of people are categorized as alienated followers.

Conformist Follower

Conformist followers often say "yes" when they really want to say "no." Low in independent thinking and high in active engagement, they willingly take orders and are eager to please others. They believe that the leader's position of power entitles the leader to followers' obedience. They do not question the social order and find comfort in structure. Approximately 20%–30% of people are categorized as conformist followers.

Pragmatist Follower

With independent thinking and active engagement styles that fall between high and low, pragmatic followers are most comfortable in the middle of the road and tend to adhere to a motto of "better safe than sorry." They will question a leader's decisions, but not too often or too openly. They perform required tasks, but seldom do more than is asked or expected. Approximately 25%–35% of people are categorized as pragmatist followers.

Passive Follower

With low independent thinking and low active engagement behaviors, passive followers are the opposite of exemplary followers, looking to the leader to do their thinking for them. They do not carry out their assignments with enthusiasm and lack initiative and a sense of responsibility. Approximately 5%–10% of people are categorized as passive followers.

Source: Excerpts from Kelley, Robert E. (1992). *The Power of Followership: How to Create Leaders People Want to Follow and Followers Who Lead Themselves*. New York: Doubleday.

SUMMARY

Leadership requires followership, and without understanding what the act of following entails, it is difficult to fully understand leaders and leadership. Therefore, the focus in this chapter is on followership and the central role followers play in the leadership process.

In recent years, followership has received increased attention as a legitimate and significant area of leadership study. Followership is defined as a process whereby an individual or individuals accept the influence of others to accomplish a common goal. It involves a power differential between the follower and the leader. From a social constructivist perspective, followership emerges from communication between leaders and followers and involves the relational process of people exerting influence and others responding to that influence.

Early research on followership resulted in a series of typologies that differentiate the roles followers can play. The primary types of follower roles identified are *active–engaged, independent–assertive, submissive–compliant*, and *supportive–conforming*.

The development of these typologies provides a starting point for building theory on followership. Based on a systematic analysis of the research literature, Uhl-Bien and her colleagues (2014) introduced a broad theory of followership comprising the characteristics, behaviors, and outcomes of followers and leaders acting in relation to each other. Furthermore, these researchers proposed two ways of theorizing about followership: (1) *reversing the lens*, which addresses followers in the opposite way they have been studied in most prior leadership research, and (2) *the leadership co-created process*, which conceptualizes followership as a give-and-take process in which individuals' following behaviors and leading behaviors interact with each other to create leadership and its resulting outcomes.

Work by Carsten and colleagues (2014) also advanced several positive facets of followership—*followers get the job done, work in the best interest of the organization's mission, challenge leaders, support the leader*, and *learn from leaders*.

In addition to having a positive impact, there is another, darker side to followership. Followers can play ineffective, and even harmful, roles. Lipman-Blumen (2005) identified a series of psychological factors of followers that contribute to harmful, dysfunctional leadership. These factors include people's *need for reassuring authority figures; need for security and certainty; need to feel chosen or special; need for membership in the human community; fear of ostracism, isolation, and social death;* and *fear of powerlessness to challenge a bad leader*. The emergence of these factors occurs as a result of people's needs to find safety to feel unique and to be included in community.

The existing followership literature has several strengths and certain limitations. On the positive side, the most recent literature gives recognition to followership as an integral part of the leadership equation and elevates it considerably, giving it equal footing with leadership. Second, it forces us to take leadership off its pedestal and replace it with followership. Third, it provides a useful set of basic prescriptions for what a follower should or should not do in order to be an effective follower.

On the negative side, very little methodical research has been conducted on the process of followership, which makes it difficult to theorize about followership's role in groups, organizations, and the community. Furthermore, the descriptive research that has been conducted on followership is primarily anecdotal and observational. Third, the world's pervasive emphasis on and glorification of leadership may be so ingrained that the study of followership will remain constrained and never flourish. Fourth, followership research has not fully addressed the question "Why follow?" Finally, there has been little research on when and/or how patterns of followership are beneficial or detrimental.

In summary, the demand in society for effective, principled followers is growing and along with it a strong need for research-based theories of the process of followership. Until more research is done on the intricacies of followership, our understanding of leadership will be incomplete.

14 Gender and Leadership

Stefanie Simon and Crystal L. Hoyt

DESCRIPTION

While academic researchers ignored issues related to gender and leadership until the 1970s (Chemers, 1997), the increasing numbers of women in leadership positions and women in academia brought about by dramatic changes in American society have fueled the now robust scholarly interest in the study of leadership and gender.

Scholars started out asking, "Can women lead?"—a question that is now moot. In addition to the increasing presence of women in corporate and political leadership roles, we can point to highly effective leaders who are women, including former prime minister Benazir Bhutto (Pakistan), former president Ellen Johnson Sirleaf (Liberia), and former prime minster Indira Gandhi (India), and current world leaders such as Chancellor Angela Merkel of Germany, Prime Minister Sanna Marin of Finland, and Prime Minister Jacinda Ardern of New Zealand (featured in Case Study 14.3). Beyond politics, there are many examples of highly effective female leaders including YouTube's CEO Susan Wojcicki, Anthem's CEO Gail Boudreaux, General Motors Company's CEO Mary Barra, retired four-star general Ann E. Dunwoody, and U.S. Supreme Court justices Elena Kagan, Sonia Sotomayor, and Ruth Bader Ginsburg.

The primary research questions now—"Do men and women lead differently?" and "Are men more effective leaders than women?"—are often subsumed under a larger question: "Why are women underrepresented in elite leadership roles?" This chapter explores empirical evidence related to these issues of gender and leadership by discussing the gender gap in leadership and prominent explanations for it, and by addressing approaches to promoting women in leadership.

The Glass Ceiling Turned Labyrinth

Evidence of the Leadership Labyrinth

Although the gender gap in leadership has improved significantly in recent decades, there is still a long way to go. Women now earn 57% of the bachelor's degrees, 60% of the master's degrees, and 53% of the doctoral degrees acquired each year in the United States (National Center for Education Statistics, 2018), and as of December 2019 (prior to the COVID-19 pandemic), women made up more than half of the U.S. labor force (50.03%; Kelly, 2020). However, women are still underrepresented in the upper echelons of America's corporations and political system. Women represent only 5.8% of S&P 500 CEOs and hold only 21.2% of S&P 500 board seats (Catalyst, 2020). On the political front, 2018 was a noteworthy year for women in U.S. politics, particularly for women of color in the House of Representatives (Warner, Ellmann, & Boesch, 2018). In addition, Senator Kamala Harris, a daughter of Indian and Jamaican immigrants, became the first woman of color selected as a U.S. vice presidential candidate on the Democratic Party ticket. However, women currently occupy just 127 of the 535 seats in the U.S. Congress (26% in the Senate and 23.2% in the House); women of color occupy 48 seats (Center for American Women and Politics, 2020a, 2020b). As of June 2020, the United States ranked 83 out of 193 countries in women's representation in national legislatures or parliaments (Inter-Parliamentary Union, 2020).

The invisible barrier preventing women from ascending into elite leadership positions was initially dubbed the *glass ceiling*, a term introduced into the American vernacular by two *Wall Street Journal* reporters in 1986 (Hymowitz & Schellhardt, 1986). Even in female-dominated occupations, women face the glass ceiling, whereas white men appear to ride a *glass escalator* to the top leadership positions (Maume, 1999; C. Williams, 1992, 1995). Eagly and Carli (2007) identified limitations with the glass ceiling metaphor, including that it implies that everyone has equal access to lower positions until all women hit this single, invisible, and impassable barrier. They put forward an alternative image: a leadership labyrinth, conveying the impression of a journey riddled with challenges all along the way—not just near the top—that can be and has been successfully navigated by women. Related, Facebook CEO Sheryl Sandberg proffered the metaphor of a jungle gym in her book *Lean In* (2013).

Understanding the Labyrinth

The gender gap in leadership is a global phenomenon whereby women are disproportionately concentrated in lower-level and lower-authority leadership positions compared to men (Powell & Graves, 2003). Discussions of women's underrepresentation in high-level leadership positions generally revolve around three types of explanations (Figure 14.1). The first set of explanations highlights differences in women's and men's investments in human capital. The next category of explanations considers gender differences between women and men. The final type of explanation focuses on prejudice and discrimination against female leaders.

Human Capital Differences. One prominent set of explanations for the labyrinth is that women have less human capital investment in education, training,

FIGURE 14.1   Understanding the Leadership Labyrinth

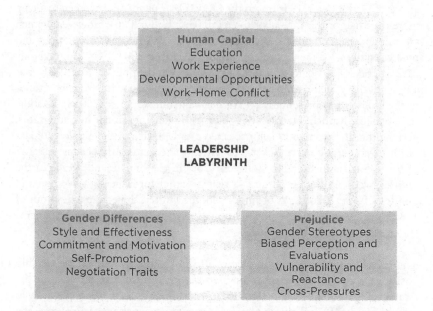

Human Capital
Education
Work Experience
Developmental Opportunities
Work–Home Conflict

LEADERSHIP
LABYRINTH

Gender Differences
Style and Effectiveness
Commitment and Motivation
Self-Promotion
Negotiation Traits

Prejudice
Gender Stereotypes
Biased Perception and Evaluations
Vulnerability and Reactance
Cross-Pressures

and work experience than men (Eagly & Carli, 2004, 2007). This supposed lack of human capital is said to result in a dearth of qualified women, sometimes called a "pipeline problem." However, a closer look at the numbers reveals that women are indeed in the pipeline, but that the pipeline is leaking. As already discussed, women are obtaining undergraduate degrees at a far higher rate than men, and women are earning professional and doctoral degrees at a rate greater or nearly equal to that of men, but women are still vastly underrepresented in top leadership positions. In the domain of law, women earn 50% of all law degrees and make up 46% of associates, but they make up only 22.7% of partners (American Bar Association, 2019). And even though women represent about 40% of those graduating with MBAs (Hess, 2019), their representation in the upper echelons of American business pales in comparison.

Women do have somewhat less work experience and employment continuity than men, driven largely by the disproportionate responsibility women assume for child rearing and domestic duties (Bowles & McGinn, 2005; Eagly & Carli, 2007). Although men's participation in domestic labor has increased in recent years (Galinsky, Aumann, & Bond, 2008), women continue to do the majority of the child care responsibilities and household chores (Belkin, 2008; Craig, 2006; Pailhe & Solaz, 2006). Furthermore, it appears that in times of crisis, working mothers are hit the hardest. During the COVID-19 pandemic, women were more likely to lose a job and take on extra domestic labor as schools and day cares closed around the nation (Cohen & Hsu, 2020). Economists have noted that this disruption to women's careers could set women back significantly as women who drop out of the workforce to take care of children have trouble reentering and making up for lost time (Cohen & Hsu, 2020).

In normal times, women must respond to work–home conflicts and do so in a variety of ways (Bowles & McGinn, 2005). Some women choose not to marry or have children, others choose to become "superwomen" and attempt to excel in every role, and others take leaves of absence, take sick days, or choose part-time employment to juggle these work–home conflicts (Hewlett, 2002; Nieva & Gutek, 1981). Antiquated workplace norms make it difficult for women to rise in the leadership ranks: Those who take advantage of workplace leave and flexibility programs are often marginalized, and those who take time off from their careers often find reentry difficult, returning at a lower level than the level they left (J. Williams, 2010). A related explanation for the leadership gap is that this culturally prescribed division of labor leads women to self-select to take themselves out of leadership tracks by choosing "mommy track" positions that do not funnel into leadership positions (Belkin, 2003); however, research does not support this argument (Eagly & Carli, 2004; J. Williams, 2010).

Despite their presence in the workforce, women have fewer developmental opportunities at work than do men. Many of these gender differences in developmental opportunities may be driven in part by the prejudice women experience in the domain of leadership. In addition to having fewer responsibilities in the same jobs as men, women are less likely to receive encouragement, be included in key networks, and receive formal job training than their male counterparts (Knoke & Ishio, 1998; Morrison & Von Glinow, 1990; Ohlott, Ruderman, & McCauley, 1994; Powell & Graves, 2003). One important developmental experience that affects career success is effective mentor relationships (Ensher & Murphy, 2005), and women confront greater barriers to establishing informal mentor relationships than men do (Powell & Graves, 2003). Additionally, women are disproportionately represented in business positions that are less visible, have less responsibility, and do not lead to top leadership positions (Bowles & McGinn, 2005).

Relatedly, when women are promoted to leadership positions, they may be more likely than men to be placed on a "glass cliff"—in other words, appointed to precarious leadership situations associated with greater risk and criticism (Mulcahy & Linehan, 2014; Ryan, Haslam, Hersby, & Bongiorno, 2011; for a recent meta-analysis, see Morgenroth, Kirby, Ryan, & Sudkämper, 2020). Ryan and Haslam (2005) first coined the term *glass cliff* based on a pattern of women being appointed to corporate boards of companies in the United Kingdom only after those companies were experiencing poor performance. Setting women up for failure by placing them in these precarious leadership positions can reaffirm preconceived notions that women are not effective leaders. However, women may be placed on a glass cliff at times because they are seen as being more fit to handle a crisis situation (Ryan et al., 2011; Ryan, Haslam, & Postmes, 2007).

Recent research has put this proposition to the test by comparing outcomes in U.S. states led by male versus female governors during the COVID-19 pandemic, a grave societal crisis. Using publicly available data on COVID-19 deaths in the United States, Sergent and Stajkovic (2020) found that states with female governors had fewer COVID-19 deaths compared to states with male governors, and female governors expressed more empathy and confidence in their briefings. While there are many reasons for differences in COVID-related deaths across the United States, these data suggest that female governors may have handled this particular crisis more effectively than male governors. A similar pattern of women's leadership effectiveness during COVID-19 seems to be appearing more globally. For example, Prime Minister Jacinda Ardern of New Zealand has been credited for leading her country effectively and quickly through the COVID-19 crisis (Cave, 2020).

In sum, there is scant support for the notions that women receive less education than men, that they quit their jobs more often than men, or that they opt out of the leadership track for the mommy track. There is support for the notion that women have less work experience and more career interruptions than men, largely because women assume significantly more domestic responsibility. Women receive less formal training and have fewer developmental opportunities at work than men, both of which likely are related to prejudice against female leaders. While women at times may be set up for leadership failure on a glass cliff, they may also be quite effective as leaders in crisis situations.

GENDER DIFFERENCES IN LEADERSHIP STYLES AND EFFECTIVENESS

Other arguments attempting to explain the leadership gap revolve around the notion that women are just different from men. This line of reasoning reflects more general views about a stark dichotomy between men and women in American society. While the term *gender* refers to the social meaning ascribed to biological sex categories (male and female), the perceived differences between men and women are often assumed to be natural consequences of innate differences (Eagly & Wood, 2013). One argument in this vein is that women's underrepresentation in elite leadership positions is a result of differences in leadership style and effectiveness.

Increasingly, writers in the mainstream press are asserting that there are indeed gender differences in leadership styles, and that women's leadership is more effective in contemporary society (Book, 2000; Helgesen, 1990; Rosener, 1995).

Rather than explaining the leadership gap, these assertions make the gap that much more perplexing. However, academic researchers have a greater diversity in their views; indeed, many argue that gender has little or no relationship to leadership style and effectiveness (Dobbins & Platz, 1986; Kaiser & Wallace, 2016; Powell, 1990; van Engen, van der Leeden, & Willemsen, 2001).

Meta-analyses of research examining style differences between women and men found that, contrary to stereotypic expectations, women were not found to lead in a more interpersonally oriented and less task-oriented manner than men in organizational studies. One robust gender difference found across settings is that women led in a more democratic, or participative, manner than men (Eagly & Johnson, 1990; van Engen & Willemsen, 2004). It is important to consider these results in conjunction with findings from a large-scale meta-analysis of the literature on evaluations of female and male leaders showing that women were devalued compared to men when they led in a masculine manner, when they occupied a typically masculine leadership role, and when the evaluators were men (Eagly, Makhijani, & Klonsky, 1992). These findings indicate that women's greater use of democratic style appears to be adaptive in that they are using the style that produces the most favorable evaluations.

More recent research has examined gender differences in transformational leadership (Bass, 1985; Burns, 1978; see Chapter 8). A meta-analysis by Eagly, Johannesen-Schmidt, and van Engen (2003) found small but robust differences between female and male leaders on these styles such that women's styles tend to be more transformational than men's, and that women tend to engage in more contingent reward behaviors than men. Although these styles predict effectiveness, recent findings suggest that the devaluation of female leaders by male subordinates has been shown to extend to female transformational leaders (Ayman, Korabik, & Morris, 2009).

Recent research also points to potential gender differences in leaders' values that may impact the way men and women lead (Eagly, 2013). For example, women tend to emphasize social values that promote others' welfare to a greater extent than men (S. Schwartz & Rubel, 2005), a difference that has been shown among CEOs and board members (Adams & Funk, 2012). This difference in emphasis on social values may influence leadership behaviors, such as company philanthropy (R. Williams, 2003) and corporate responsibility (Boulouta, 2012).

In addition to leadership style and leadership values, the relative effectiveness of male and female leaders has been assessed in a number of studies (Jacobson & Effertz, 1974; Tsui & Gutek, 1984). In a meta-analysis comparing the effectiveness of female and male leaders, men and women were equally effective leaders, overall, but there were gender differences such that women and men were more effective in leadership roles that were congruent with their gender (Eagly, Karau, & Makhijani, 1995). Thus, women were less effective to the extent that the leader role was masculinized. For example, women were less effective than men in military positions, but they were somewhat more effective than men in education, government, and social service organizations and substantially more effective than men in middle management positions where communal interpersonal skills are highly valued. In addition, women were less effective than men when they supervised a higher proportion of male subordinates or when a greater proportion of male raters assessed the leaders' performance.

In recent years, new research on leadership effectiveness that has come from analyzing 360 evaluations made by peers, bosses, and direct reports that rate a leader's overall effectiveness has shown that women are viewed as better leaders (Zenger & Folkman, 2012, 2019). These 360 evaluations judge competencies on 16 traits most important to leadership effectiveness, such as how good the leader is at taking initiative, developing others, and motivating others. At every level of leadership, women were rated by peers, bosses, direct reports, and other associates as better overall leaders than men, and this gap in effectiveness grew wider at higher leadership levels (Zenger & Folkman, 2012). In a recent replication of these findings, Zenger and Folkman's results (2019) again demonstrated a leadership competence advantage for women in leadership roles.

Beyond what a leader's peers think of women in leadership roles, social advocates often make a "business case" for increasing the representation of women on corporate boards of directors by claiming that it would positively affect financial outcomes for those organizations (Eagly, 2016). This research would suggest boards with women are more effective than boards that are made up of men only. While a bottom-line argument would provide a potentially convincing reason to increase gender diversity of board memberships, research has demonstrated that the effect of gender diversity of boards on an organization's financial outcomes is often nonexistent or very small (Eagly, 2016).

Boards that are comprised of more women, however, can have other positive consequences for organizations. An analysis of the S&P 500 companies from 2009 to 2013 demonstrates that gender pay disparities among top executives decreased when women served as the chair of the organization's compensation committee but did not decrease when women were added to boards in general (Cook, Ingersoll, & Glass, 2019). Fortune 500 companies with gender-diverse boards also tend to have stronger business and equity practices (Glass & Cook, 2018), offer more LGBT-friendly policies (Cook & Glass, 2016), and appoint women as CEOs (Cook & Glass, 2015). Thus, when looking beyond the effectiveness of a single leader to the effectiveness of a leading body, a gender-diverse board can at times result in more positive outcomes for an organization but not necessarily impact the bottom line.

Another oft-cited barrier to women's advancement is the presumed gender difference in commitment to employment and motivation to lead. However, research indicates that women show the same level of identification with and commitment to paid employment roles as men do, and both women and men view their roles as workers to be secondary to their roles as parents and partners (Bielby & Bielby, 1988; Thoits, 1992). Empirical research does indicate that women are less likely than men to promote themselves for leadership positions (Bowles & McGinn, 2005). For example, women are more likely to take on informal, as opposed to official, leadership roles, and use terms such as *facilitator* or *organizer* instead of *leader* (Andrews, 1992; Fletcher, 2001). A meta-analytic review of the research literature on leader emergence revealed that although women were less likely than men to emerge as group leaders, they were more likely to serve as social facilitators than men (Eagly & Karau, 1991).

Why are women less likely to emerge as leaders? Recent research suggests that it may be because women do not expect to have much influence in groups where the majority of the members are male. In a series of studies, Goodwin, Dodson, Chen, and Diekmann (2020) demonstrated that women expected to have a lower sense of power when applying for a majority-male leadership committee compared to a committee that is gender-balanced. This lower sense of power explained why women expressed a lower desire to lead and lower intentions to apply for a committee position compared to men.

Furthermore, men are more likely than women to ask for what they want (Babcock & Laschever, 2003). Reaching elite leadership positions is not done in a vacuum; people must negotiate with others to access the right positions, experiences, opportunities, resources, and assistance in both the professional and domestic spheres. Not only are women less likely to negotiate than men (Small, Gelfand, Babcock, & Gettman, 2007), but the negotiations needed to ascend the leadership hierarchy often are unstructured, ambiguous, and rife with gender triggers (factors that prompt gender-related behavioral responses)—exactly the type of situation that particularly disadvantages women (Bowles & McGinn, 2005).

This research must be interpreted in light of the social costs, or backlash, women experience when they promote themselves or are competent in positions of authority (Rudman & Glick, 2001). Women face significant gender biases and social disincentives when they self-promote and negotiate. Unlike men, for example, self-promoting women are seen as less socially attractive and less hirable (Rudman, 1998), and women face greater social costs for negotiating than men do (Amanatullah & Tinsley, 2013a, 2013b; Bowles, Babcock, & Lai, 2007).

In sum, empirical research supports small differences in leadership style and effectiveness between men and women. Women experience slight effectiveness disadvantages in masculine leader roles, whereas roles that are more feminine offer them some advantages. Additionally, women exceed men in the use of democratic or participatory styles, and they are more likely to use transformational leadership behaviors and contingent rewards, which are styles associated with contemporary notions of effective leadership. Women are no less effective at leading than men, and women are no less committed to their jobs or motivated for leadership roles than men. In fact, the research on leadership competencies seems to indicate a slight leadership competence advantage for women. However, women are less likely to self-promote and negotiate than men, and women may avoid leadership positions where the group membership is majority male. Furthermore, research shows a small gender difference such that women are more likely to focus on the welfare of others and ethical behavior.

Prejudice. One prominent explanation for the leadership gap revolves around gender biases stemming from stereotyped expectations that women take care and men take charge (Hoyt & Chemers, 2008). Stereotypes are cognitive shortcuts that influence the way people process information regarding groups and group members. People assign characteristics to groups, or individual members of groups, regardless of the actual variation in characteristics between the members (Hamilton, Stroessner, & Driscoll, 1994). Gender stereotypes are pervasive, well documented, and highly resistant to change (Dodge, Gilroy, & Fenzel, 1995; Heilman, 2001). Gender stereotypes both describe stereotypic beliefs about the attributes of women and men and prescribe how men and women ought to be (Burgess & Borgida, 1999; Glick & Fiske, 1999). Men are stereotyped with agentic characteristics such as confidence, assertiveness, independence, rationality, and decisiveness, whereas women are stereotyped with communal characteristics such as concern for others, sensitivity, warmth, helpfulness, and nurturance (Deaux & Kite, 1993; Heilman, 2001).

Gender stereotypes are easily and automatically activated, and they often lead to biased judgments (Fiske, 1998; Kunda & Spencer, 2003). In addition to facing gender-based prejudice, women of color often confront racial or ethnic prejudice (Bell & Nkomo, 2001). A vivid illustration of gender-based prejudice can be seen in the evaluation of men and women auditioning for symphony orchestras. In the 1970s and 1980s, male-dominated symphony orchestras made one simple change: All applicants were asked to audition while hidden behind a screen. This small change greatly increased the proportion of women in symphony orchestras (Goldin & Rouse, 2000). Merely seeing the applicant's gender evoked stereotype-based expectations in the judges' minds that resulted in a significant bias toward selecting men.

In leadership roles, gender stereotypes are particularly damaging for women because agentic, as opposed to communal, tendencies often are indispensable (Chemers & Murphy, 1995). According to role congruity theory, the agentic qualities thought necessary in the leadership role are incompatible with the predominantly communal qualities stereotypically associated with women, thus resulting in prejudice against female leaders (Eagly & Karau, 2002). Although the masculine construal of leadership has decreased somewhat over time, it remains pervasive and robust (Koenig, Eagly, Mitchell, & Ristikari, 2011). Thus, in the leadership role, women are confronted with cross-pressures: As leaders, they should be masculine and tough, but as women, they should not be "too manly." These opposing expectations for women often result in the perception that women are less qualified for elite leadership positions than men, and in harsh evaluations of effective female leaders for not being "female enough."

This prejudice against female leaders helps explain the numerous findings indicating less favorable attitudes toward female compared to male leaders, greater difficulty for women to attain top leadership roles, and greater difficulty for women to be viewed as effective in these roles (Eagly & Karau, 2002). The penalties for violating one's gender stereotypes are clearly illustrated in the classic 1989 Supreme Court case *Price Waterhouse v. Ann Hopkins*. Price Waterhouse told Hopkins that she would not make partner because she was too masculine, going as far as advising her to go to charm school, wear jewelry and makeup, and be less aggressive. In the end, the Supreme Court ruled that Price Waterhouse was discriminating based on gender stereotypes (Fiske, Bersoff, Borgida, Deaux, & Heilman, 1991). Gender bias was also evident in the media coverage of the 2008 U.S. presidential primaries involving Hillary Clinton. As Katie Couric noted after Clinton bowed out of contention, "One of the great lessons of that campaign is the continued and accepted role of sexism in American life, particularly the media . . . if Senator Obama had to confront the racist equivalent of an 'Iron My Shirt' poster at campaign rallies or a Hillary nutcracker sold at airports . . . the outrage would not be a footnote, it would be front page news" (Couric, 2008).

Gender biases can be particularly detrimental in the decision-making processes for selecting elite leaders, given that the generally unstructured nature of those decisions allows biased decisions without accountability (Powell & Graves, 2003). Not only are the decision makers influenced by the stereotypes that disadvantage women in the leadership role, but also they may succumb to homosocial reproduction, a tendency for a group to reproduce itself in its own image (Kanter, 1977). People prefer similar others and report the most positive decisions about and evaluations of people who are most like them, biases that can clearly disadvantage women when male leaders are looking for replacements. This seems to be particularly true for people who prefer group hierarchies in society (i.e., who are high in social dominance orientation) in that they show an even stronger preference for leaders who are white and male (Hoyt & Simon, 2016).

These stereotypic expectations not only affect others' perceptions and evaluations of female leaders, but also can directly affect the women themselves. Women who make up a very small minority of a male-dominated group are seen as tokens representing all women; they experience significant pressure as their highly visible performance is scrutinized, and they are perceived through gender-stereotyped lenses (Kanter, 1977). Women often are very aware of their gender and the accompanying stereotypes (Sekaquaptewa & Thompson, 2003). Research shows that women respond in one of two ways to the gender-based leadership stereotype: Either they demonstrate vulnerability by assimilating to the stereotype, or they react against it by engaging in stereotype-countering behaviors (Hoyt, 2010; Simon & Hoyt, 2013). Whether the threat of the gender–leader stereotype is met with vulnerability or reactance responses depends on factors such as the leader's self-efficacy, the explicitness of the stereotype, the type of task, the group sex-composition, and the power that the leader holds (Bergeron, Block, & Echtenkamp, 2006; Davies, Spencer, & Steele, 2005; Hoyt & Blascovich, 2007, 2010; Kray, Reb, Galinsky, & Thompson, 2004; Kray, Thompson, & Galinsky, 2001). Furthermore, although female leaders may demonstrate reactance to certain solitary gender stereotype threats, when such threats are combined, women are likely to demonstrate deleterious vulnerability responses (Hoyt, Johnson, Murphy, & Skinnell, 2010). In sum, substantial empirical evidence reveals that gender stereotypes can significantly alter the perception and evaluation of female leaders and directly affect women in or aspiring to leadership roles.

While most past research has focused on perceptions of white men and white women in leadership positions, recent research has begun to take an intersectional approach (Purdie-Vaughns & Eibach, 2008; Rosette, Koval, Ma, & Livingston, 2016) by investigating the experiences of people with multiple subordinate-group identities, such as women of color in leadership positions. Research in this area is limited, but suggests that Black women may experience bias in leadership positions differently than white women or Black men—sometimes gaining an advantage (e.g., Livingston, Rosette, & Washington, 2012) and sometimes experiencing a disadvantage (e.g., Rosette & Livingston, 2012). This remains an important area of research as women of color are entering new levels of leadership in society, such as Kamala Harris as the vice presidential running mate of Democratic presidential candidate Joe Biden in the 2020 election. Their experiences in elite leadership positions remain to be seen.

Navigating the Labyrinth

The number of women who successfully navigate the labyrinth is on the rise (Eagly & Carli, 2007). A confluence of factors contributes to this increase in effective female leaders (Figure 14.2). Changes in organizations are beginning to make it easier for women to reach top positions. The culture of many organizations is changing; gendered work assumptions such as the male model of work, the notion of uninterrupted full-time careers, and the separation of work and family are being challenged (Cooper & Lewis, 1999; J. Williams, 2010). Moreover, many organizations are valuing flexible workers and diversity in their top echelons. These organizations can augment women's career development by involving them in career development programs and formal networks and offering work–life support. In addition, assigning more women to high-visibility positions and developing effective and supportive mentoring relationships for women are key strategies for reducing the leadership gap (Bell & Nkomo, 2001; Ensher & Murphy, 2005; Ragins, Townsend, & Mattis, 1998).

FIGURE 14.2 Leadership Effectiveness

```
┌──────────────────────────┐        ┌──────────────────────────┐
│     Individual Level     │        │    Interpersonal Level   │
│ Promoting Effective Negotiations │  │ Decreasing Gender Stereotypes │
│ Use of Effective Leadership Styles │ │                          │
└──────────────────────────┘        └──────────────────────────┘

              PROMOTING
         LEADERSHIP EFFECTIVENESS

┌──────────────────────────┐        ┌──────────────────────────┐
│      Societal Level      │        │    Organizational Level  │
│ Gender Equity in Domestic Responsibilities │ │ Diversifying Leadership │
│                          │        │ Equity in Maternity/Paternity Leave │
└──────────────────────────┘        └──────────────────────────┘
```

As Gloria Steinem famously noted, "We've begun to raise daughters more like sons . . . but few have the courage to raise our sons more like our daughters." Increasing parity in the involvement of women and men in child care and housework will go a long way in reducing the leadership gap (Eagly & Carli, 2007). In balancing work and home life, an appealing approach for women is structural role redefinition (Hall, 1972). This approach involves negotiating with both family and colleagues to renegotiate role expectations both at work and at home. For example, at home women can negotiate workload between spouses, team up with friends and family members, and, if able, hire help when necessary (Bowles & McGinn, 2005). At work women can work for family-friendly reforms such as job-protected maternity leaves.

Beyond work–home issues, negotiations for valued positions, experiences, and resources are important social interactions on the road to top leadership positions. Thus, another approach to reducing the leadership gap is to enhance women's negotiation power and restructure negotiations to their advantage (Bowles & McGinn, 2005). For example, research has shown that the term *negotiation* is laden with gendered connotations, so one approach would be to reframe negotiation situations in nongendered terms such as "asking" situations.

Women who are aware of the labyrinth may circumvent barriers by starting their own ventures (Wirth, 2001). Women-owned businesses account for

39% of all privately owned firms, contribute 8% of employment, and make up 4.2% of revenues (National Association of Women Business Owners, 2020). Women's successful foray into entrepreneurship is working to change the face of business, and by extension leadership, as we know it.

Many of the impediments women face in the leadership domain stem from the incongruity between the female gender role and the leadership role. Women face a double standard in the leadership role; they must come across as extremely competent but also as appropriately "feminine," a set of standards men are not held to (Eagly & Carli, 2003). One way that women can increase their perceived warmth and their influence is by combining communal qualities such as warmth and friendliness with agentic qualities such as exceptional competence and assertiveness (Carli, 2001; Rudman & Glick, 2001). Additionally, the transformational leadership style discussed in Chapter 8 is particularly beneficial for women because it is not a markedly masculine style. This style encompasses traditionally feminine behaviors, such as being considerate and supportive, and is strongly associated with leadership effectiveness. Recent research suggests that blending individualized consideration with inspirational motivation is prudent for women seeking leadership advancement (Vinkenburg, van Engen, Eagly, & Johannesen-Schmidt, 2011). The incongruity between the leadership role and the female gender role does appear to be decreasing (Eagly & Carli, 2007). Recent research indicates that women have become significantly more masculine—for example, becoming more assertive and valuing leadership and power more as job attributes, without losing their femininity (Konrad, Ritchie, Lieb, & Corrigall, 2000; Twenge, 2001). In addition, evidence suggests that the leadership role is starting to be seen as less masculine and more androgynous (Koenig et al., 2011; Schein, 2001). Relatedly, people perceive heroes, a specific type of leader, as more androgynous than a typical leader (Hoyt, Allison, Barnowski, & Sultan, 2020), which may provide a different pathway for people to start identifying women as heroic leaders.

In sum, we likely will see more women in elite leadership roles with (1) changes in workplace norms and developmental opportunities for women; (2) greater gender equity in domestic responsibilities; (3) greater negotiation power of women, especially regarding the work–home balance; (4) effectiveness and predominance of women-owned businesses; and (5) changes in the incongruity between women and leadership.

STRENGTHS

Understanding the research into gender and leadership can help us promote more women into the upper echelons of leadership. Doing so will fulfill the promise of equal opportunity by allowing everyone the possibility of taking on leadership roles, from the boardroom to the Senate floor. This larger and more demographically diverse pool of candidates not only makes it easier to find talented people, but also facilitates greater levels of organizational success. Furthermore, promoting a richly diverse group of women into leadership roles will not only help make societal institutions, businesses, and governments more representative, but can also contribute to more ethical, productive, innovative, and financially successful organizations that demonstrate higher levels of collective intelligence and are less rife with conflict (Bernardi, Bosco, & Columb, 2009; Catalyst, 2004; Forsyth, 2010; Miller & Del Carmen Triana, 2009; Nielsen & Huse, 2010; Woolley, Chabris, Pentland, Hashmi, & Malone, 2010).

A consideration of the effects of gender on leadership has important implications for a comprehensive understanding of leadership. Contemporary approaches to gender and leadership involve questions that directly affect leadership success, such as style and effectiveness differences between men and women, and the varied barriers confronting women. Gender is integral to contemporary notions of effective leadership styles that have morphed from a traditional masculine, autocratic style to the more feminine or androgynous styles of democratic and transformational leadership. Developing a more androgynous conception of leadership will enhance leadership effectiveness by giving people the opportunity to engage in the best leadership practices, and not by restricting people to those behaviors that are most appropriate for their gender.

Research on gender and leadership is productive in both dispelling myths about the gender gap and shining a light on aspects of the gender barriers that are difficult to see and therefore are often overlooked. For example, gender biases generally are no longer overt but more often take the form of subtle and implicit preconceptions and institutionalized discrimination, making them particularly potent and pernicious. These biases have a detrimental impact on the perception and evaluation of women, and they limit the range of leadership behavior deemed appropriate for women. In addition, the mere awareness of these gender biases can be detrimental to women performing in leadership roles. The changes needed to overcome these problems within organizations and society can occur only when we are aware of these often subtle and disguised prejudices.

Understanding the many components of the labyrinth will give us the tools necessary to combat this inequality from many perspectives, including individual, interpersonal, organizational, and societal approaches. In addition, this research addresses larger, more significant considerations about gender and social systems. For example, it acknowledges the profound power division between men and women, and it opens up dialogue on structural questions such as the gendered division of work in society. By acknowledging and attempting to understand issues of gender and leadership, rather than ignoring them, we can help ensure that women have equal opportunity in attaining influential leadership positions, that organizations and constituents have access to the greatest talent pool when selecting leaders, and that there is greater gender diversity in the ranks of leadership, which has been linked to organizational success.

CRITICISMS

Issues of gender and leadership can be subsumed under a more general topic of leadership and diversity. This perspective involves an understanding of the impact of various demographic characteristics on leadership, including—but not limited to—gender, race, ethnicity, and sexual orientation (Chemers & Murphy, 1995; Hoyt & Chemers, 2008). However, unlike the research examining gender and leadership, research into racial-ethnic minority leaders is scant (Hoyt & Chemers, 2008). Although some of the issues surrounding people of color in leadership may bear similarities to those surrounding women (e.g., people of color also face negative stereotypes and resulting difficulties ascending the leadership hierarchy), the underlying dynamics and mechanisms are no doubt distinct (Gurin, 1985; Stangor, Lynch, Duan, & Glass, 1992). Leadership researchers should put a greater emphasis on understanding the role of race, ethnicity, sexual orientation, and other types of diversity, as well as important interactive effects between, for example, race and gender (Smith & Stewart, 1983), in leadership processes.

Much of the research examining gender in leadership has taken place in Western contexts; research on gender and leadership in other contexts is sparse. Because most of the findings regarding female leaders stem from the culturally defined role of women in society, many of the findings discussed in this chapter will not generalize well across cultures in which the roles of women and men differ. Therefore, we must realize the limited generalizability of the extant literature on gender and leadership, and researchers should expand their purview to address gender and leadership from a cross-cultural perspective. A final criticism concerns the dearth of essential, complementary research agendas on the domestic sphere. Research on gender and leadership focuses on decreasing the gender gap in leadership positions, thereby lessening gender segregation at work; however, the leadership gap will not be closed without a concurrent focus on closing the gender gap at home.

APPLICATION

Although the gender gap in influential leadership positions remains clearly visible, there is evidence that it is starting to close. Understanding the obstacles that make up the labyrinth and tactics to eradicate the inequality will make it easier for women to reach top positions. The labyrinth has many barriers, and the necessary changes occur at many levels, ranging from individual and interpersonal levels to organizational and societal levels. Prejudice plays an important role in the interpersonal and individual levels; the first step in dealing with these biases is to become aware of them in others and in ourselves. Women are faced with the problem of needing to bolster their leadership competence with appropriate "femaleness": Adopting behaviors such as individualized consideration and inspirational motivation is a promising approach to overcome these biased expectations. In addition, women's use of effective negotiation techniques can aid them in procuring the resources they need at work and at home to augment their leadership advancement.

Changes are also taking place at more macro-organizational and societal levels that will contribute to greater gender equality in leadership. For example, changes in organizational culture, women's career development, mentoring opportunities for women, and increased numbers of women in strategic positions will increase the presence of women in prominent leadership roles. At the societal level, structural changes regarding a more equitable distribution of child rearing and domestic duties are also contributing to the influx of women into elite positions.

CASE STUDIES

In the following section, three case studies (Cases 14.1, 14.2, and 14.3) are presented to provide practice in diagnosing and making recommendations on situations confronting female leaders in organizations. The first case is about a market analyst in a Wall Street firm, the second case is about a senior managing director at a manufacturing company, and the third case is about New Zealand prime minister Jacinda Ardern. After each case, questions are provided to assist your analysis of the case.

Case 14.1 THE "GLASS CEILING"

Lisa Weber never doubted that she would be a partner in her Wall Street firm. A graduate of a prestigious business school with a doctorate in economics, she had taught briefly at a major university. She was the first woman hired as a market analyst in her well-regarded firm. Within two years, she became one of four senior portfolio managers reporting directly to a senior partner. Her clients give her the highest commendations for her outstanding performance; over the past two years, she has brought in the largest number of new accounts to the firm.

Despite the admiration of her colleagues and their seeming acceptance of her, there is a disturbing, if flattering, aspect to her job. Most of her peers and some of the partners visit her office during the day to discuss in private her opinions on market performance and financial projections. She enjoys these private sessions but is dismayed that at the weekly staff meetings the CEO, Michael Breyer, usually says something like, "Okay, let's get started and bring Lisa up to date on some of the trouble spots." None of her peers or the partners mention that Lisa knows as much as they do about what's going on in the firm. She never protests this slight to her competence and knowledge of firm business, nor does she mention the almost-daily private meetings where her advice is sought. As the only woman on the executive level, she prefers to be considered a team player and one of the boys.

In the past year, one of her peers has been promoted to partner, although Lisa's performance clearly surpassed his, as measured by the success of her accounts and the amount of new business she brought to the firm. Having heard no mention of partnership for herself, she approached her boss, one of the partners, and asked about the path to a partnership. He replied, "You're doing great, Lisa, but professors do not partners make. What happens if you are a partner and you make a huge mistake? How would you take it? And what about our clients? There's never been a female partner in the 103 years of our firm."

Shortly thereafter, another woman, Pamela Tobias, was hired as a marketing analyst. Once, when the CEO saw Lisa and Pamela together, he called out to the men, "Hey, guys, two women in one room. That's scary."

During the next six months, Lisa meets several times with the CEO to make her case for a partnership on the basis of her performance. She finally realizes that there is no possibility of change in the foreseeable future and decides to leave and form her own investment firm.

—Adapted from Blank, R., & Slipp, S. (1994).
Voices of diversity. *New York, NY: AMACOM.*

Questions

1. What advancement barriers did Lisa encounter?

2. What should the firm's top executives, including Michael, have done differently to retain Lisa?

3. What type of organizational policies and opportunities might have benefited Lisa and Pamela?

4. What could the organization do to raise the gender consciousness of Michael and Lisa's male colleagues?

Case 14.2 PREGNANCY AS A BARRIER TO JOB STATUS

Marina Soslow is a senior managing director at a manufacturing company. She has worked at the company for 10 years, gradually working her way up to a responsible position. She would like to win promotion to a top executive position and has recently finished an MBA, which supplements her master's degree in chemical engineering.

Several months ago, she found out she was pregnant. She is reluctant to tell her boss, Roy Bond, the division head, because she knows several other women who were eased out of their positions before they gave birth or shortly thereafter.

After a meeting with Roy about a new product, Marina mentions her pregnancy and says that she plans to take a three-month leave of absence after her delivery. She begins describing the plans she has carefully worked out for distributing her work. Roy cuts her short and says, "I knew this was going to happen sooner or later; it always does." He said this as if a disaster were about to occur. "There's no point in talking about this now. We'll think about it later."

(Continued)

(Continued)

Marina can tell that he's very annoyed about what he thinks is going to happen. She can see his wheels spinning and worries about the implications for her. She thinks, "Doesn't Roy know about the Family and Medical Leave Act of 1993? Legally, this company has to guarantee my job, but I know he can make it very rough for me."

—Adapted from Blank, R., & Slipp, S. (1994).
Voices of diversity. New York, NY: AMACOM.

Questions

1. What advancement barriers is Marina encountering?

2. What should Roy have said when Marina told him she was pregnant?

3. What could Roy do to ensure that Marina's work will be covered during her absence and that taking this time off will not hurt her advancement?

4. What type of organizational changes could be made to benefit Marina and other pregnant women in this organization?

Case 14.3 JACINDA ARDERN, PRIME MINISTER OF NEW ZEALAND

On March 15, 2019, a shooter opened fire during Friday prayers at two Muslim mosques in Christchurch, New Zealand. More than 50 people were killed (including several children), a number that rivaled the island country's total murders for a year, and dozens more were wounded. Prior to the attack, the shooter penned a chilling 74-page manifesto, which was sent to the prime minister's office. He then livestreamed himself on Facebook as he stormed the Al Noor Mosque. The hate-based attacks left New Zealand, a country known for its low crime rates and reputation for welcoming immigrants, in a state of shock and grief.

The response by Prime Minister Jacinda Ardern, New Zealand's 39-year-old leader, was swift and unflinching. Avoiding divisive language, she instead united and galvanized a country in crisis. Speaking at a press conference, she reminded people of the importance of the diversity of their culture:

> *For many, New Zealand was their choice . . . The place they actively came to, and committed themselves to . . . where they were part of communities who they loved and who loved them. A place where they were free to practice their culture and their religion.*

For those of you who are watching at home tonight, and questioning how this could have happened here, we—New Zealand—we were not a target because we are a safe harbor for those who hate. We were not chosen for this act of violence because we condone racism. We were chosen for the very fact that we are none of these things. Because we represent diversity, kindness, compassion, a home for those who share our values, refuge for those who need it. . . .

We are a proud nation of more than 200 ethnicities, 160 languages. And amongst that diversity we share common values. And the one that we place the currency on right now—and tonight—is our compassion and support for the community of those directly affected by this tragedy. (Chandler, 2020)

In an address to Parliament a few days later, she stood firm, refusing to give the shooter the one thing she felt he desired: notoriety. After opening her address with the Arabic greeting *As-salamu alaykum* ("Peace be upon you"), she expounded, "He is a terrorist, he is a criminal, he is an extremist, but he will, when I speak, be nameless, and to others I implore you: Speak the names of those who were lost rather than the name of the man who took them. He may have sought notoriety but we in New Zealand will give him nothing—not even his name" (Hjelmgaard, 2019).

Focusing her efforts on honoring those who lost their lives and standing up to right-wing terrorism, Ardern vowed to cover funeral costs and provide financial assistance to grief-stricken families. Recognizing that gun control was a weak link in New Zealand, a land where gun ownership is widespread, she also pledged to take swift action on gun control. A month later, under her leadership, New Zealand's Parliament approved a ban on semiautomatic and military-style weapons, a feat that much larger countries struggling with long histories of mass shootings had yet to accomplish.

While Prime Minister Ardern was well supported in her efforts, her detractors were not quiet. The speed of the process was criticized, to which she countered, "You either believe that in New Zealand these weapons have a place or you do not. And if you believe, like us, that they do not, you should be able to agree that we can move swiftly. My view is that an argument about process is an argument to do nothing" (M. Schwartz, 2019).

Her resolute and expedient actions were only one element of Ardern's approach to leading her country through uncertainty, tragedy, and grief. She reached out directly to the communities most affected, visiting Christchurch the day after the shooting and taking with her the leaders of all New Zealand's political parties. She visited the mosques to mourn directly with the families, and personally met with, listened to, hugged, and consoled family and friends of those lost and injured

(Continued)

(Continued)

in the shooting. In a show of respect and empathy, she donned a black hijab, a traditional headscarf of the Muslim faith.

"The Prime Minister, when she came wearing her scarf, that was big for us," shared Dalia Mohamed, one of the many mourners who attended (Hjelmgaard, 2019).

Who Is Jacinda Ardern?

At 37, Jacinda Kate Laurell Ardern became the youngest prime minister (PM) of New Zealand since 1856 and only the third woman to hold the position. Her rise in New Zealand politics was termed the "most meteoric rise to power of any New Zealand PM" (Atkinson, 2018).

Ardern was born in 1980 in Hamilton, located in New Zealand's politically conservative Waikato Region. She was the second of two daughters and raised in the Mormon religion, a conservative faith that advocates for the traditional role of women within the family. She ultimately broke from the church over its prohibitive view on homosexuality and same-sex marriage (Wallenfeldt, 2020).

Ardern spent her early years in Murupara, a small, isolated town known as the center of Maori gang activity. Maori are the indigenous Polynesian people of New Zealand and comprise almost 15% of the country's population (New Zealand History, n.d.). Seeing "children without shoes on their feet or anything to eat for lunch" inspired her to enter politics (Jones, 2017).

At the age of 17, she deviated from her conservative roots and joined New Zealand's more liberal Labour Party. With the help of an aunt, she joined the reelection campaign of Harry Duynhoven, a Labour member of Parliament (MP). After receiving a bachelor's degree in communication studies from the University of Waikato in 2001, Ardern became a researcher for Labour MP Phil Goff, which led to a position on the staff of then prime minister Helen Clark. The second woman to hold New Zealand's highest office, Clark was Ardern's political hero and mentor (Wallenfeldt, 2020).

In 2005, Ardern left this position for an "overseas experience," a traditional rite of passage for New Zealand's middle- and upper-class youth involving an extended—usually working—trip to Britain. While many young New Zealanders often use this as a time to work menial jobs and tour the continent, Ardern instead secured a position in the cabinet office of British prime minister Tony Blair. As the associate director for Better Regulation Executive, she spent two and a half years working to improve the interactions between local authorities and small businesses. Her subsequent election as president of the International Union of Socialist Youth in 2007 further expanded her horizons, taking her to Algeria, China, India, Israel, Jordan, and Lebanon (Wallenfeldt, 2020).

Back in New Zealand, Ardern was selected for a Parliament seat as a list candidate and, at the age of 28, took her place as New Zealand's youngest member of the House of Representatives. Unafraid to speak her mind, in her first address to the House "she called for the introduction of compulsory instruction in the Maori language in New Zealand schools and she castigated the government for its 'shameful' response to climate change" (Wallenfeldt, 2020).

Because she was a rising political star, Ardern's age and physical attractiveness did not go unnoticed. In 2011, in what was dubbed by the press as the "Battle of the Babes," she ran for the seat representing Auckland Central that was held by another of New Zealand's young political women, Nikki Kaye of the National Party, who was five months older than Ardern. Ardern bristled at the media attention on her physical attractiveness, characterizing herself as an "acceptable nerd" with a "relentlessly positive" approach to life. Narrowly losing to Kaye by 717 votes, Ardern returned to Parliament again as a list candidate (Wallenfeldt, 2020).

Ardern spent the next few years fostering key relationships and beneficial assignments, being named the Labour Party's spokesperson for social development and for arts, culture and heritage, children, justice, and small business. In 2017, after a landslide win for a vacant parliamentary seat, she was unanimously elected as the Labour Party's deputy leader. But just weeks before the 2017 September general parliamentary election, the party's leader stepped down. Before he did, he convinced Ardern to take his place (reportedly, she refused seven times before agreeing). On August 1, Ardern found herself unanimously elected the Labour Party leader and the party's new candidate for prime minister.

Ardern's "charismatic optimism, strength, and down-to-earth charm quickly energized voters—especially women and the young" (Wallenfeldt, 2020). She campaigned for free university education, reductions in immigration, decriminalization of abortion, and the creation of new programs to alleviate poverty among children. More broadly, her platform included a "fairer deal" for the marginalized (Wallenfeldt, 2020).

Dubbed "Jacindamania," Ardern's public support rapidly escalated, and political experts began characterizing her as a "rock star" politician likening her to Canadian prime minister Justin Trudeau and former U.S. president Barack Obama.

If elected, she would be only the third female prime minister of New Zealand, a fact she did not shy away from in her campaign. When an interviewer asked her whether she planned to have children, she initially had no problem answering such a personal question. However, when another interviewer took the issue further by implying that employers had a right to know whether prospective female employees planned on taking time off from work to have children, she quickly clarified her previous response and the acceptability of such questions. "I decided to talk about it, it was my choice . . . but . . . it is totally unacceptable in 2017 to say that women should have to answer that question in the workplace. It is the woman's decision about when they choose to have children. It should not predetermine whether or not they are given a job or have job opportunities" (Wallenfeldt, 2020).

(Continued)

(Continued)

The election was held, but no party had enough votes to gain a majority. After weeks of negotiation and the subsequent tally of special votes (overseas votes), Ardern found out at the same time as the rest of her country that she would become its 40th prime minister. She was sworn in on October 26, 2017.

When she took office as the world's youngest world leader, she was 37, unmarried, and pregnant. She and her partner, Clarke Gayford, welcomed their first child in June 2018, making her only the second elected head of state in modern history to give birth while serving, as well as the first elected leader known to ever take maternity leave (Hjelmgaard, 2019).

She continued to make history when she brought her three-month-old daughter to a United Nations General Assembly meeting. In an interview with *The New Yorker*, Ardern and Gayford shared their perspectives on juggling family and professional responsibilities, with Gayford saying, "It was a no-brainer to say, 'Right, I'll take care of her, you take care of the country'" (Hollander, 2018).

"I don't want to ever give the impression that I'm some kind of Wonder Woman," Ardern added. "Or that women should be expected to do everything because I am. I'm not doing everything" (Hjelmgaard, 2019).

Less than a week after the Christchurch shootings, Ardern was extolled not only by the citizens of her own country but also by the international community for her decisive and compassionate response to her nation's shock and grief. Sheryl Sandberg, Facebook's chief operating officer, described Ardern as a "political prodigy" who was "changing the game" for women around the globe (Hjelmgaard, 2019). Later that year, Ardern was named by *Time* magazine as one of the world's 100 most influential people.

In the words of her mentor, former New Zealand prime minister Helen Clark, Ardern is a natural and empathetic communicator who doesn't preach at people, but instead signals that she's "standing with them."

"They may even think: 'Well, I don't quite understand why the government did that, but I know she's got our back.' There's a high level of trust and confidence in her because of that empathy" (Friedman, 2020).

Questions

1. In a *USA Today* article shortly after the mosque attacks in New Zealand, writer Neill Borowski (2019) profiled Ardern's accomplishments during the crisis, listing these four things to know about Ardern:
   - She's New Zealand's youngest leader in decades.
   - She refuses to the give the shooter notoriety.
   - She promised tougher gun laws.

- She's a mom.
  a. What do you see as the relevance of the last bullet point?
  b. Do you think if Ardern had been male and a father, this author would have found it equally as important to include that he was a father? Why or why not?

2. Human capital is the first element of the leadership labyrinth discussed in this chapter. Discuss how each of the four aspects of the human capital element relates to Ardern. How has she addressed the challenges of each?

3. The chapter describes the existence of "perceived" differences between men and women in how they lead, which, in the past, have been considered to be natural consequences of innate differences.
   a. Do you agree or disagree that these are innate to each gender? Why?
   b. What are some ways that Ardern leads that might be different from a male leader?
   c. What are some ways that Ardern leads that might be the same as a male leader?

4. This textbook has discussed several different leadership approaches (authentic, situational, leader–member exchange, transformational, etc.). Which of these approaches apply to Ardern's leadership? Explain why.

5. It is suggested in this chapter that women are more likely to serve as "social facilitators" than men. Do you feel this true of Ardern? If so, how has this served or not served her and her constituents?

6. Prejudice is one of the leading contributors to the leadership gap between men and women. Discuss how the four aspects of prejudice outlined in the leadership labyrinth may have influenced Ardern and her political career. What types of barriers and obstacles did they each present?

7. The book notes that "women face a double standard in the leadership role; they must come across as extremely competent but also as appropriately 'feminine,' a set of standards men are not held to" (Eagly & Carli, 2003). The burden to balance agentic qualities and communal qualities is greater for women than for men. How did Ardern experience this double standard?

—Barbara Russell, MBA, BSCS, BBA, Chemeketa Community College

LEADERSHIP INSTRUMENT

The Gender-Leader Bias Questionnaire was developed to measure implicit gender biases by examining the value people place on communal leadership characteristics and agentic leadership characteristics. Gender stereotypes of women as communal and men as agentic have been damaging to women in leadership due to the lower value placed on communal behaviors. This questionnaire will examine the gender-stereotypical associations that contribute to the bias against women as leaders. The items in this questionnaire were taken from the gender implicit association test (IAT) developed by Dasgupta and Asgari (2004) that examines the gender-stereotypical associations that contribute to the bias against women as leaders (Eagly & Karau, 2002).

Gender-Leader Bias Questionnaire

Purpose: The purpose of this questionnaire is to learn about gender biases and how to become aware of them in order to break harmful stereotypes.

Instructions: This questionnaire contains characteristics associated with communal and agentic behaviors. Indicate the degree to which you feel each characteristic is important for leadership using a scale from 1 (*not important*) to 5 (*very important*).

Key: 1 = Not   2 = Somewhat   3 = Neutral   4 = Important   5 = Very
       Important   Important   Important

1.	Supporter	1	2	3	4	5
2.	Leader	1	2	3	4	5
3.	Ambitious	1	2	3	4	5
4.	Determined	1	2	3	4	5
5.	Helpful	1	2	3	4	5
6.	Dynamic	1	2	3	4	5
7.	Understanding	1	2	3	4	5
8.	Compassionate	1	2	3	4	5
9.	Assertive	1	2	3	4	5
10.	Sympathetic	1	2	3	4	5
11.	Warm	1	2	3	4	5
12.	Kind	1	2	3	4	5
13.	Controlling	1	2	3	4	5
14.	Caring	1	2	3	4	5
15.	Independent	1	2	3	4	5
16.	Dominant	1	2	3	4	5

Scoring

The logic behind the questionnaire is that people tend to view communal characteristics, which are a stereotypically associated with women, as less important to leadership while they view agentic characteristics, which are stereotypically associated with men, as more important to leadership.

The sum of questions 1, 5, 7, 8, 10, 11, 12, and 14 makes up your communal characteristics score.

The sum of questions 2, 3, 4, 6, 9, 13, 15, and 16 makes up your agentic characteristics score.

(Continued)

(Continued)

Communal scores between 8 and 24 indicate a weak value of communal characteristics in leadership; scores between 25 and 32 indicate a neutral association; scores between 33 and 40 indicate a strong value of communal characteristics in leadership.

Agentic scores between 8 and 24 indicate a weak value of agentic characteristics in leadership; scores between 25 and 32 indicate a neutral association; scores between 33 and 40 indicate a strong value of agentic characteristics in leadership.

Scoring Interpretation

Many people are surprised to find out that they have a biased association favoring traditional leadership/agentic behaviors, especially when it is incompatible with their stated egalitarian values. This test is designed to show people that they might hold associations that they are unaware of and to make people aware of the broad reach of these stereotypes.

SUMMARY

Women are significantly underrepresented in major leadership positions. The barriers women encounter on their leadership journey have been dubbed the *leadership labyrinth*. Removing these barriers will help ensure equal opportunity, access to the greatest talent pool, and diversity, which have been linked to organizational success. There are a number of explanations for the leadership gender gap. One set of explanations focuses on women's lack of *human capital investment* in education, training, and work experience. There is no empirical support for the argument that women are less educated than men are or that they are more likely to quit their jobs or choose the mommy track. There is evidence that women assume significantly more domestic responsibility, which contributes to less work experience and more career interruptions. Additionally, women receive less formal training and have fewer developmental opportunities at work than men.

Another set of explanations for the gender gap focuses on *differences between women and men*. Women are no less effective at leadership, committed to their work, or motivated to attain leadership roles than men. However, women are less likely to self-promote than men are, and they are less likely to initiate negotiation, an important tool all leaders need in order to access the right opportunities and resources in both the professional and domestic spheres. Investigations into leadership style have revealed that women are somewhat more likely to use democratic and transformational styles than men are. Research looking at leadership effectiveness indicates a greater use by women of effective transformational and contingent reward behaviors.

The *prejudice* explanation for the leadership gap is strongly supported. Gender stereotypes of women as communal and men as agentic are particularly damaging to women in leadership. The incongruity between the female gender role and the leadership role leads to prejudice against female leaders, who are evaluated and perceived more negatively than their male counterparts. These biases are particularly detrimental during unstructured decision-making processes that often occur when elite leaders are selected. Gender-based leader stereotypes can threaten women eliciting either a vulnerability or a reactance response. There is evidence that this discrepancy is on the decline as the leader role becomes more androgynous and women become more agentic.

Finally, there are a number of approaches to navigating the labyrinth. Significant organizational reform will make it easier for women to reach top positions—including changes in workplace norms, changes in organizational culture, increases in career development for women, increases in effective mentoring opportunities, and women taking more strategic positions leading to higher leadership roles. Effective negotiations will help decrease the gender gap, especially negotiations regarding role expectations at work and at home. Additionally, the combination of warmth with agentic qualities and in particular the melding of individualized consideration with inspirational motivation can be effective for developing female leaders.

15 Leadership Ethics

This chapter is different from many of the other chapters in this book. Most of the other chapters focus on one unified leadership theory or approach (e.g., trait approach, path–goal theory, or transformational leadership), whereas this chapter is multifaceted and presents a broad set of ethical viewpoints. The chapter is intended not as an "ethical leadership theory," but rather as a guide to some of the ethical issues that arise in leadership situations.

Probably since our cave-dwelling days, human beings have been concerned with the ethics of our leaders. Our history books are replete with descriptions of good kings and bad kings, great empires and evil empires, and strong presidents and weak presidents. But despite a wealth of biographical accounts of great leaders and their morals, very little research has been published on the theoretical foundations of leadership ethics. There have been many studies on business ethics in general since the early 1970s, but these studies have been only tangentially related to leadership ethics. Even in the literature of management, written primarily for practitioners, there are very few books on leadership ethics. This suggests that theoretical formulations in this area are still in their infancy.

One of the earliest writings that specifically focused on leadership ethics appeared as recently as 1996. It was a set of working papers generated from a small group of leadership scholars, brought together by the W. K. Kellogg Foundation. These scholars examined how leadership theory and practice could be used to build a more caring and just society. The ideas of the Kellogg group are now published in a volume titled *Ethics, the Heart of Leadership* (Ciulla, 1998).

Interest in the nature of ethical leadership has continued to grow, particularly because of the many recent scandals in corporate America and the political realm. On the academic front, there has also been a strong interest in exploring the nature of ethical leadership (see Aronson, 2001; Brown & Treviño, 2006; Ciulla, 2001, 2003, 2014; Johnson, 2011, 2018; Kanungo, 2001; Lawton & Páez, 2015; McManus, Ward, & Perry, 2018; Price, 2008; Treviño, Brown, & Hartman, 2003).

Ethics Defined

From the perspective of Western tradition, the development of ethical theory dates back to Plato (427–347 B.C.E.) and Aristotle (384–322 B.C.E.). The word *ethics* has its roots in the Greek word *ethos*, which translates to "customs," "conduct," or "character." Ethics is concerned with the kinds of values and morals an individual or a society finds desirable or appropriate. Furthermore, ethics is concerned with the virtuousness of individuals and their motives. Ethical theory provides a system of rules or principles that guide us in making decisions about what is right or wrong and good or bad in a particular situation. It provides a basis for understanding what it means to be a morally decent human being.

In regard to leadership, ethics is concerned with what leaders do and who leaders are. It has to do with the nature of leaders' behavior, and with their virtuousness. In any decision-making situation, ethical issues are either implicitly or explicitly involved. The choices leaders make and how they respond in a given circumstance are informed and directed by their ethics.

A leader's choices are also influenced by their moral development. For example, in a study of 24 exemplary leaders in journalism, Plaisance (2014) found "an overarching emphasis on notions of care and respect for others, professional duty, concern for harm, and proactive social engagement—all of which characterize higher stages of moral development" (p. 308). The most widely recognized theory advanced to explain how people think about moral issues is *Kohlberg's stages of moral development*. Kohlberg (1984) presented a series of dilemmas (the most famous of which is "the Heinz dilemma") to groups of young children whom he then interviewed about the reasoning behind their choices regarding the dilemmas. From these data he created a classification system of moral reasoning that was divided into six stages: *Stage 1—Obedience and Punishment, Stage 2—Individualism and Exchange, Stage 3—Interpersonal Accord and Conformity, Stage 4—Maintaining the Social Order, Stage 5—Social Contract and Individual Rights*, and *Stage 6—Universal Principles* (Table 15.1). Kohlberg further classified the first two stages as preconventional morality, the second two as conventional morality, and the last two as postconventional morality.

Level 1. Preconventional Morality

When an individual is at the preconventional morality level, they tend to judge the morality of an action by its direct consequences. There are two stages that fall within preconventional morality:

> *Stage 1—Obedience and Punishment*. At this stage, the individual is egocentric and sees morality as external to self. Rules are fixed and handed down by authority. Obeying rules is important because it means avoiding punishment. For example, a child reasons it is bad to steal because the consequence will be to go to jail.

TABLE 15.1 Kohlberg's Stages of Moral Development

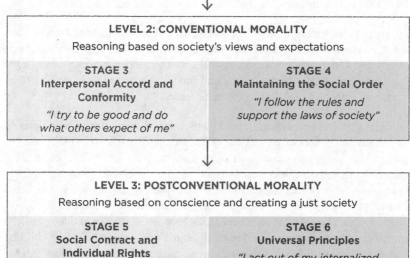

LEVEL 1: PRECONVENTIONAL MORALITY

Reasoning based on self-interest, avoiding punishment, and rewards

STAGE 1	STAGE 2
Obedience and Punishment	Individualism and Exchange
"I follow the rules so I don't get hurt"	*"I will do a favor for you, if you do one for me"*

↓

LEVEL 2: CONVENTIONAL MORALITY

Reasoning based on society's views and expectations

STAGE 3	STAGE 4
Interpersonal Accord and Conformity	Maintaining the Social Order
"I try to be good and do what others expect of me"	*"I follow the rules and support the laws of society"*

↓

LEVEL 3: POSTCONVENTIONAL MORALITY

Reasoning based on conscience and creating a just society

STAGE 5	STAGE 6
Social Contract and Individual Rights	Universal Principles
"I work with others to do what is best for all of us"	*"I act out of my internalized and universal principle of justice"*

Stage 2—Individualism and Exchange. At this stage, the individual makes moral decisions based on self-interest. An action is right if it serves the individual. Everything is relative, so each person is free to do their own thing. People do not identify with the values of the community (Crain, 1985) but are willing to exchange favors. For example, an individual might say, "I'll do a favor for you, if you do a favor for me."

Level 2. Conventional Morality

Those who are at this level judge the morality of actions by comparing them to society's views and expectations. Authority is internalized but not questioned, and reasoning is based on the norms of the group to which the person belongs. Kohlberg identified two stages at the conventional morality level:

Stage 3—Interpersonal Accord and Conformity. At this stage, the individual makes moral choices based on conforming to the expectations of others and trying to behave like a "good" person. It is important to be "nice" and live up to the community standard of niceness. For example, a student says, "I am not going to cheat because that is not what a good student does."

Stage 4—Maintaining the Social Order. At this stage, the individual makes moral decisions in ways that show concern for society as a whole. In order for society to function, it is important that people obey the laws, respect authority, and support the rules of the community. For example, a person does not run a red light in the middle of the night when no other cars are around because it is important to maintain and support the traffic laws of the community.

Level 3. Postconventional Morality

At this level of morality, also known as the principled level, individuals have developed their own personal set of ethics and morals that guide their behavior. Postconventional moralists live by their own ethical principles—principles that typically include such basic human rights as life, liberty, and justice. There are two stages that Kohlberg identified as part of the postconventional morality level:

Stage 5—Social Contract and Individual Rights. At this stage, the individual makes moral decisions based on a social contract and their views on what a good society should be like. A good society supports values such as liberty and life, and fair procedures for changing laws (Crain, 1985), but recognizes that groups have different opinions and values. Societal laws are important, but people need to agree on them. For example, if a boy is dying of cancer and his parents do not have money to pay for his treatment, the state should step in and pay for it.

Stage 6—Universal Principles. At this stage, the individual's moral reasoning is based on internalized universal principles of justice that apply to everyone. Decisions that are made need to respect the viewpoints of all parties involved. People follow their internal rules of fairness, even if they conflict with laws. An example of this stage would be a civil rights activist who believes a commitment to justice requires a willingness to disobey unjust laws.

Kohlberg's model of moral development has been criticized for focusing exclusively on justice values, for being sex-biased since it is derived from an all-male sample, for being culturally biased since it is based on a sample from an individualist culture, and for advocating a postconventional morality where people place their own principles above those of the law or society (Crain, 1985). Regardless of these criticisms, this model is seminal to developing an understanding of what forms the basis for individuals' ethical leadership.

Ethical Theories

For the purposes of studying ethics and leadership, ethical theories can be thought of as falling within two broad domains: theories about leaders' *conduct* and theories about leaders' *character* (Table 15.2). Stated another way, ethical theories when applied to leadership are about both the actions of leaders and who they are as people. Throughout the chapter, our discussions about ethics and leadership will always fall within one of these two domains: conduct or character. Ethical theories that deal with the conduct of leaders are in turn divided into two kinds: theories that stress the *consequences* of leaders' actions and those that emphasize the *duty* or *rules* governing leaders' actions (see Table 15.2). Teleological theories, from the Greek word *telos*, meaning "ends" or "purposes," try to answer questions about right and wrong by focusing on whether a person's conduct will produce desirable consequences. From the teleological perspective, the question "What is right?" is answered by looking at results or outcomes. In effect, the consequences of an individual's actions determine the goodness or badness of a particular behavior.

TABLE 15.2 Domains of Ethical Theories

Conduct	Character
Consequences (teleological theories)	Virtue-based theories
• Ethical egoism	
• Utilitarianism	
Duty (deontological theories)	

In assessing consequences, there are three different approaches to making decisions regarding moral conduct (Figure 15.1): *ethical egoism, utilitarianism,* and *altruism.* Ethical egoism states that a person should act so as to create the greatest good for themselves. A leader with this orientation would take a job or career that they selfishly enjoy (Avolio & Locke, 2002). Self-interest is an ethical stance closely related to transactional leadership theories (Bass & Steidlmeier, 1999). Ethical egoism is common in some business contexts in which a company and its employees make decisions to achieve its goal of maximizing profits. For example, a midlevel, upward-aspiring manager who wants their team to be the best in the company could be described as acting out of ethical egoism.

A second teleological approach, *utilitarianism*, states that we should behave so as to create the greatest good for the greatest number. From this viewpoint, the morally correct action is the action that maximizes social benefits while

FIGURE 15.1 Ethical Theories Based on Self-Interest Versus Interest for Others

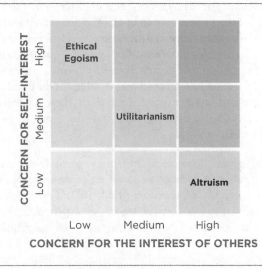

minimizing social costs (Schumann, 2001). When the U.S. government allocates a large part of the federal budget for preventive health care rather than for catastrophic illnesses, it is acting from a utilitarian perspective, putting money where it will have the best result for the largest number of citizens.

Closely related to utilitarianism, and opposite of ethical egoism, is a third teleological approach, *altruism*. Altruism is an approach that suggests that actions are moral if their primary purpose is to promote the best interests of others. From this perspective, a leader may be called on to act in the interests of others, even when it runs contrary to their own self-interests (Bowie, 1991). Authentic transformational leadership (Chapter 8) is based on altruistic principles (Bass & Steidlmeier, 1999; Kanungo & Mendonca, 1996), and altruism is pivotal to exhibiting servant leadership (Chapter 10). The strongest example of altruistic ethics can be found in the work of Mother Teresa, who devoted her life to helping those living in poverty. Quite different from looking at which actions will produce which outcomes, deontological theory is derived from the Greek word *deos*, which means "duty." Whether a given action is ethical rests not only with its consequences (teleological), but also with whether the action itself is good. Telling the truth, keeping promises, being fair, and respecting others are all examples of actions that are inherently good, independent of the consequences. The deontological perspective focuses on the actions of the leader and their moral obligations and responsibilities to do the right thing. A leader's actions are moral if the leader has a moral right to do them, if the actions do not infringe on others' rights, and if the actions further the moral rights of others (Schumann, 2001).

In the late 1990s, the president of the United States, Bill Clinton, was brought before Congress for misrepresenting under oath an affair he had maintained with a White House intern. For his actions, he was impeached by the U.S. House of Representatives, but then was acquitted by the U.S. Senate. At one point during the long ordeal, the president appeared on national television and, in what is now a famous speech, declared his innocence. Because subsequent hearings provided information that suggested that he may have lied during this television speech, many Americans felt President Clinton had violated his duty and responsibility (as a person, leader, and president) to tell the truth. From a deontological perspective, it could be said that he failed his ethical responsibility to do the right thing—to tell the truth.

Whereas teleological and deontological theories approach ethics by looking at the behavior or conduct of a leader, a second set of theories approaches ethics from the viewpoint of a leader's character (Table 15.2). These theories are called virtue-based theories; they focus on who leaders are as people. In this perspective, virtues are rooted in the heart of the individual and in the individual's disposition (Pojman, 1995). Furthermore, it is believed that virtues and moral abilities are not innate but can be acquired and learned through practice. People can be taught by their families and communities to be morally appropriate human beings.

With their origin traced back in the Western tradition to the ancient Greeks and the works of Plato and Aristotle, virtue theories are experiencing a resurgence in popularity. The Greek term associated with these theories is *aretaic*, which means "excellence" or "virtue." Consistent with Aristotle, current advocates of virtue-based theory stress that more attention should be given to the development and training of moral values (Velasquez, 1992). Rather than telling people what to *do*, attention should be directed toward telling people what to *be*, or helping them to become more virtuous.

What, then, are the virtues of an ethical person? There are many, all of which seem to be important. Based on the writings of Aristotle, a moral person demonstrates the virtues of courage, temperance, generosity, self-control, honesty, sociability, modesty, fairness, and justice (Velasquez, 1992). For Aristotle, virtues allowed people to live well in communities. Applying ethics to leadership and management, Velasquez has suggested that managers should develop virtues such as perseverance, public-spiritedness, integrity, truthfulness, fidelity, benevolence, and humility.

In essence, virtue-based ethics is about being and becoming a good, worthy human being. Although people can learn and develop good values, this theory maintains that virtues are present in one's disposition. When practiced over time, from youth to adulthood, good values become habitual, and part of the people themselves. By telling the truth, people become truthful; by giving to those living in poverty, people become benevolent; by being fair to others, people become just. Our virtues are derived from our actions, and our actions manifest our virtues (Frankena, 1973; Pojman, 1995).

Centrality of Ethics to Leadership

As discussed in Chapter 1, leadership is a process whereby the leader influences others to reach a common goal. The *influence* dimension of leadership requires the leader to have an impact on the lives of those being led. To make a change in other people carries with it an enormous ethical burden and responsibility. Because leaders usually have more power and control than followers, they also have more responsibility to be sensitive to how their leadership affects followers' lives.

Whether in group work, organizational pursuits, or community projects, leaders engage followers and utilize them in their efforts to reach common goals. In all these situations, leaders have the ethical responsibility to treat followers with dignity and respect—as human beings with unique identities. This "respect for people" demands that leaders be sensitive to followers' own interests, needs, and conscientious concerns (Beauchamp & Bowie, 1988). In a qualitative study of 17, mostly Swiss, executive ethical leaders, Frisch and Huppenbauer (2014) reported that these ethical leaders cared about other stakeholders, such as customers, suppliers, owners of companies, the natural environment, and society. Although all of us have an ethical responsibility to treat other people as unique human beings, leaders have a special responsibility, because the nature of their leadership puts them in a special position in which they have a greater opportunity to influence others in significant ways.

Ethics is central to leadership, and leaders help to establish and reinforce organizational values. Every leader has a distinct philosophy and point of view. "All leaders have an agenda, a series of beliefs, proposals, values, ideas, and issues that they wish to 'put on the table'" (Gini, 1998, p. 36). The values promoted by the leader have a significant impact on the values exhibited by the organization (see Carlson & Perrewe, 1995; Demirtas, 2015; Eisenbeiss, van Knippenberg, & Fahrbach, 2015; Schminke, Ambrose, & Noel, 1997; Treviño, 1986; Xu, Loi, & Ngo, 2016; Yang, 2014). Because of their influence, leaders play a major role in establishing the ethical climate of their organizations. For example, in a meta-analytic review of 147 articles on ethical leadership, Bedi, Alpaslan, and Green (2016) found that ethical leadership was positively related to followers' perceptions of the leader's fairness and the followers' ethical behavior.

In short, ethics is central to leadership because of the nature of the process of influence, the need to engage followers in accomplishing mutual goals, and the impact leaders have on the organization's values.

The following section provides a discussion of some of the work of prominent leadership scholars who have addressed issues related to ethics and leadership.

Although many additional viewpoints exist, those presented are representative of the predominant thinking in the area of ethics and leadership today.

Heifetz's Perspective on Ethical Leadership

Based on his work as a psychiatrist and his observations and analysis of many world leaders (e.g., President Lyndon Johnson, Mohandas Gandhi, and Margaret Sanger), Ronald Heifetz (1994) has formulated a unique approach to ethical leadership. His approach emphasizes how leaders help followers to confront conflict and to address conflict by effecting changes. Heifetz's perspective is related to ethical leadership because it deals with values: the values of workers and the values of the organizations and communities in which they work. According to Heifetz, leadership involves the use of authority to help followers deal with the conflicting values that emerge in rapidly changing work environments and social cultures. It is an ethical perspective because it addresses the values of workers.

For Heifetz (1994), leaders must use authority to mobilize people to face tough issues. As discussed in the chapter on adaptive leadership (Chapter 11), it is up to the leader to provide a "holding environment" in which there is trust, nurturance, and empathy. In a supportive context, followers can feel safe to confront hard problems. Specifically, leaders use authority to get people to pay attention to the issues, to act as a reality test regarding information, to manage and frame issues, to orchestrate conflicting perspectives, and to facilitate decision making (Heifetz, 1994, p. 113). The leader's duties are to assist the follower in struggling with change and personal growth.

Burns's Perspective on Ethical Leadership

As discussed in Chapter 8, Burns's theory of transformational leadership places a strong emphasis on followers' needs, values, and morals. Transformational leadership involves attempts by leaders to move followers to higher standards of moral responsibility. This emphasis sets transformational leadership apart from most other approaches to leadership because it clearly states that leadership has a moral dimension (see Bass & Steidlmeier, 1999).

Similar to that of Heifetz, Burns's (1978) perspective argues that it is important for leaders to engage themselves with followers and help them in their personal struggles regarding conflicting values. The resulting connection raises the level of morality in both the leader and the follower.

The origins of Burns's position on leadership ethics are rooted in the works of such writers as Abraham Maslow, Milton Rokeach, and Lawrence Kohlberg (Ciulla, 1998). The influence of these writers can be seen in how Burns emphasizes the leader's role in attending to the personal motivations and moral development of the follower. For Burns, it is the responsibility of the leader to help followers assess their own values and needs in order to raise them to a higher level of functioning, to a level that will stress values such as liberty, justice, and equality (Ciulla, 1998).

Burns's position on leadership as a morally uplifting process has not been without its critics. It has raised many questions: How do you choose what a better set of moral values is? Who is to say that some decisions represent higher moral ground than others? If leadership, by definition, entails raising individual moral functioning, does this mean that the leadership of corrupt leaders is not actually leadership? Notwithstanding these very legitimate questions, Burns's perspective is unique in that it makes ethics the central characteristic of the leadership process. His writing has placed ethics at the forefront of scholarly discussions of what leadership means and how leadership should be carried out.

The Dark Side of Leadership

Although Burns (1978) placed ethics at the core of leadership, there still exists a dark side of leadership that exemplifies leadership that is unethical and destructive. It is what we defined in Chapter 8 ("Transformational Leadership") as *pseudotransformational leadership* and discussed in Chapter 13 ("Followership") in regard to *destructive leadership*. The dark side of leadership is the destructive and toxic side of leadership in that a leader uses leadership for personal ends. Lipman-Blumen (2005) suggests that toxic leaders are characterized by destructive behaviors such as leaving their followers worse off than they found them, violating the basic human rights of others, and playing to followers' basest fears. Furthermore, Lipman-Blumen identifies many dysfunctional personal characteristics destructive leaders demonstrate including lack of integrity, insatiable ambition, arrogance, and reckless disregard for their actions. In addition, using two different toxic leadership questionnaires, Singh, Sengupta, and Dev (2017) identified eight factors of perceived toxicity in leaders in Indian organizations. The toxicity factors included managerial incompetency, dark traits, derisive supervision, impervious despotic leadership, dearth of ethics, erratic behavior, narcissism, and self-promoting. The same characteristics and behaviors that distinguish leaders as special can also be used by leaders to produce disastrous outcomes (Conger, 1990). Because researchers have been focused on the positive attributes and outcomes of effective leadership, until recently, there has been little attention paid to the dark side of leadership. Nevertheless, it is important to understand that it exists.

In a meta-analysis of 57 studies of destructive leadership and its outcomes, Schyns and Schilling (2013) found a strong relationship between destructive leadership and negative attitudes in followers toward the leader. Destructive leadership is also negatively related to followers' attitudes toward their jobs and toward their organization as a whole. Furthermore, Schyns and Schilling found it closely related to negative affectivity and to the experience of occupational stress.

FIGURE 15.2 The Toxic Triangle

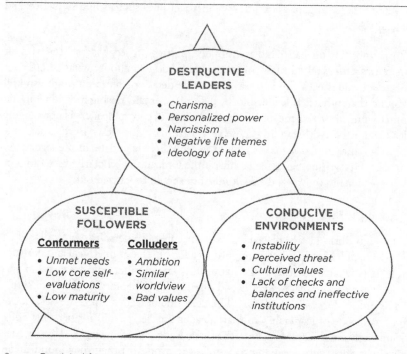

Source: Reprinted from *The Leadership Quarterly, 18,* A. Padilla, R. Hogan & R. B. Kaiser, "The Toxic Triangle: Destructive Leaders, Susceptible Followers, and Conducive Environments," pp. 180, Copyright (2007).

In an attempt to more clearly define destructive leadership, Padilla, Hogan, and Kaiser (2007) developed the concept of a toxic triangle that focuses on the influences of destructive leaders, susceptible followers, and conducive environments (Figure 15.2). As shown in the model, *destructive leaders* are characterized by having charisma and a need to use power and coercion for personal gains. They are also narcissistic and often attention-getting and self-absorbed. Destructive leaders often have negative life stories that can be traced to traumatic childhood events. Perhaps from self-hatred, they often express an ideology of hate in their rhetoric and worldview.

As illustrated in Figure 15.2, destructive leadership also incorporates *susceptible followers* who have been characterized as *conformers* and *colluders. Conformers* go along with destructive leaders to satisfy unmet needs such as emptiness, alienation, or need for community. These followers have low self-esteem and identify with charismatic leaders in an attempt to become more desirable.

Because they are psychologically immature, conformers more easily go along with authority and engage in destructive activity. On the other hand, *colluders* may respond to destructive leaders because they are ambitious, desire status, or see an opportunity to profit. Colluders may also go along because they identify with the leader's beliefs and values, which may be unsocialized such as greed and selfishness.

Finally, the toxic triangle illustrates that destructive leadership includes a *conducive environment*. When the environment is unstable, the leader is often granted more authority to assert radical change. When there is a perceived threat, followers often accept assertive leadership. People are attracted to leaders who will stand up to the threats they feel in the environment. Destructive leaders who express compatible cultural values with followers are more likely to succeed. For example, cultures high on collectiveness would prefer a leader who promotes community and group identity. Destructive leadership will also thrive when the checks and balances of the organization are weak and the rules of the institution are ineffective.

Although research on the dark side of leadership has been limited, it is an area critical to our understanding of leadership that is unethical. Clearly, there is a need for the development of models, theories, and assessment instruments about the process of destructive leadership.

Principles of Ethical Leadership

In this section, we turn to a discussion of five principles of ethical leadership, the origins of which can be traced back to Aristotle. The importance of these principles has been discussed in a variety of disciplines, including biomedical ethics (Beauchamp & Childress, 1994), business ethics (Beauchamp & Bowie, 1988), counseling psychology (Kitchener, 1984), and leadership education (Komives, Lucas, & McMahon, 1998), to name a few. Although not inclusive, these principles provide a foundation for the development of sound ethical leadership: *respect, service, justice, honesty,* and *community* (Figure 15.3).

FIGURE 15.3 Principles of Ethical Leadership

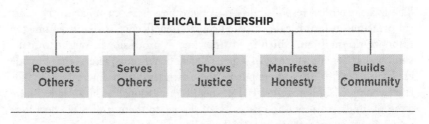

ETHICAL LEADERSHIP

| Respects Others | Serves Others | Shows Justice | Manifests Honesty | Builds Community |

Ethical Leaders Respect Others

Philosopher Immanuel Kant (1724–1804) argued that it is our duty to treat others with respect. To do so means always to treat others as ends in themselves and never as means to ends. As Beauchamp and Bowie (1988, p. 37) pointed out, "Persons must be treated as having their own autonomously established goals and must never be treated purely as the means to another's personal goals." These writers then suggested that treating others as ends rather than as means requires that we treat other people's decisions and values with respect: Failing to do so would signify that we were treating them as a means to our own ends.

Leaders who respect others also allow them to be themselves, with creative wants and desires. They approach other people with a sense of their unconditional worth and valuable individual differences (Kitchener, 1984). Respect includes giving credence to others' ideas and confirming them as human beings. At times, it may require that leaders defer to others. As Burns (1978) suggested, leaders should nurture followers in becoming aware of their own needs, values, and purposes, and assist followers in integrating these with the leader's needs, values, and purposes.

Respect for others is a complex ethic that is similar to but goes deeper than the kind of respect that parents teach little children. Respect means that a leader listens closely to followers, is empathic, and is tolerant of opposing points of view. It means treating followers in ways that confirm their beliefs, attitudes, and values. When a leader exhibits respect to followers, followers can feel competent about their work. In short, leaders who show respect treat others as worthy human beings.

Ethical Leaders Serve Others

Earlier in this chapter, we contrasted two ethical theories, one based on a concern for self (ethical egoism) and another based on the interests of others (ethical altruism). The service principle clearly is an example of altruism. Leaders who serve are altruistic: They place their followers' welfare foremost in their plans. In the workplace, altruistic service behavior can be observed in activities such as mentoring, empowerment behaviors, team building, and citizenship behaviors, to name a few (Kanungo & Mendonca, 1996).

The leader's ethical responsibility to serve others is very similar to the ethical principle in health care of beneficence. Beneficence is derived from the Hippocratic tradition, which holds that health professionals ought to make choices that benefit patients. In a general way, beneficence asserts that providers have a duty to help others pursue their own legitimate interests and goals (Beauchamp & Childress, 1994). Like health professionals, ethical leaders have a responsibility to attend to others, be of service to them, and make decisions pertaining to them that are beneficial and not harmful to their welfare.

In the past, the service principle has received a great deal of emphasis in the leadership literature. It is clearly evident in the writings of Block (1993), Covey (1990), De Pree (1989), Gilligan (1982), and Kouzes and Posner (1995), all of whom maintained that attending to others is the primary building block of moral leadership. Further emphasis on service can be observed in the work of Senge (1990) in his well-recognized writing on learning organizations. Senge contended that one of the important tasks of leaders in learning organizations is to be the steward (servant) of the vision within the organization. Being a steward means clarifying and nurturing a vision that is greater than oneself. This means not being self-centered, but rather integrating one's self or vision with that of others in the organization. Effective leaders see their own personal vision as an important part of something larger than themselves—a part of the organization and the community at large.

The idea of leaders serving others was more deeply explored by Robert Greenleaf (1970, 1977), who developed the *servant leadership* approach. Servant leadership, which is explored in depth in Chapter 10, has strong altruistic ethical overtones in how it emphasizes that leaders should be attentive to the concerns of their followers and should take care of them and nurture them. In addition, Greenleaf argues that the servant leader has a social responsibility to be concerned with the "have-nots" and should strive to remove inequalities and social injustices. Greenleaf places a great deal of emphasis on listening, empathy, and unconditional acceptance of others.

In short, whether it is Greenleaf's notion of waiting on the "have-nots" or Senge's notion of giving oneself to a larger purpose, the idea behind service is contributing to the greater good of others. Recently, the idea of serving the "greater good" has found an unusual following in the business world. In 2009, 20% of the graduating class of the Harvard Business School, considered to be one of the premier schools producing today's business leaders, took an oath pledging that they will act responsibly and ethically, and refrain from advancing their own ambitions at the expense of others. Similarly, Columbia Business School requires all students to pledge to an honor code requiring they adhere to truth, integrity, and respect (Wayne, 2009). In practicing the principle of service, these and other ethical leaders must be willing to be follower centered, must place others' interests foremost in their work, and must act in ways that will benefit others.

Ethical Leaders Are Just

Ethical leaders are concerned about issues of fairness and justice. They make it a top priority to treat all of their followers in an equal manner. Justice demands that leaders place issues of fairness at the center of their decision making. As a rule, no one should receive special treatment or special consideration except when their particular situation demands it. When individuals are treated differently, the grounds for different treatment must be clear and reasonable, and must be based on moral values. For example, many of us can remember being involved with some type of athletic team when we were growing up. The coaches we liked were those we thought were fair with us. No matter what, we did not want the coach to treat anyone differently from the rest. When someone came late to practice with a poor excuse, we wanted that person disciplined just as we would have been disciplined. If a player had a personal problem and needed a break, we wanted the coach to give it, just as we would have been given a break. Without question, the good coaches were those who never had favorites and who made a point of playing everyone on the team. In essence, what we wanted was that our coach be fair and just.

When resources and rewards or punishments are distributed to employees, the leader plays a major role. The rules that are used and how they are applied say a great deal about whether the leader is concerned about justice and how they approach issues of fairness. Rawls (1971) stated that a concern with issues of fairness is necessary for all people who are cooperating together to promote their common interests. It is similar to the ethic of reciprocity, otherwise known as the Golden Rule—"Do unto others as you would have them do unto you"—variations of which have appeared in many different cultures throughout the ages. If we expect fairness from others in how they treat us, then we should treat others fairly in our dealings with them. Issues of fairness become problematic because there is always a limit on goods and resources, and there is often competition for the limited things available. Because of the real or perceived scarcity of resources, conflicts often occur between individuals about fair methods of distribution. It is important for leaders to clearly establish the rules for distributing rewards. The nature of these rules says a lot about the ethical underpinnings of the leader and the organization.

Beauchamp and Bowie (1988) outlined several of the common principles that serve as guides for leaders in distributing the benefits and burdens fairly in an organization (Table 15.3). Although not inclusive, these principles point to the reasoning behind why leaders choose to distribute things as they do in organizations. In a given situation, a leader may use a single principle or a combination of several principles in treating followers.

To illustrate the principles described in Table 15.3, consider the following hypothetical example: You are the owner of a small trucking company that employs 50 drivers. You have just opened a new route, and it promises to be one that pays well and has an ideal schedule. Only one driver can be assigned to the route, but seven drivers have applied for it. Each driver wants an *equal opportunity* to get the route. One of the drivers recently lost his wife to breast cancer and is struggling to care for three young children (*individual need*). Two of the drivers are people of color, and one of them feels strongly that he has a *right* to the job. One of the drivers has logged more driving hours for three consecutive years, and she feels her *effort* makes her the logical candidate for the new route. One of the drivers serves on the National Transportation Safety Board and has a 20-year accident-free

TABLE 15.3 Principles of Distributive Justice

These principles are applied in different situations.

To each person

- An equal share or opportunity
- According to individual need
- According to that person's rights
- According to individual effort
- According to societal contribution
- According to merit or performance

driving record (*societal contribution*). Two drivers have been with the company since its inception, and their *performance* has been meritorious year after year.

As the owner of the company, your challenge is to assign the new route in a fair way. Although many other factors could influence your decision (e.g., seniority, wage rate, or employee health), the principles described in Table 15.3 provide guidelines for deciding who is to get the new route.

Ethical Leaders Are Honest

When we were children, grown-ups often told us we must "never tell a lie." To be good meant we must be truthful. For leaders the lesson is the same: To be a good leader, one must be honest.

The importance of being honest can be understood more clearly when we consider the opposite of honesty: dishonesty (see Jaksa & Pritchard, 1988). Dishonesty is a form of lying, a way of misrepresenting reality. Dishonesty may bring with it many objectionable outcomes; foremost among those outcomes is the distrust it creates. When leaders are not honest, others come to see them as undependable and unreliable. People lose faith in what leaders say and stand for, and their respect for leaders is diminished. As a result, the leader's impact is compromised because others no longer trust and believe in the leader.

When we relate to others, dishonesty also has a negative impact. It puts a strain on how people are connected to each other. When we lie to others, we are in essence saying that we are willing to manipulate the relationship on our own terms. We are saying that we do not trust the other person in the relationship to be able to deal with information we have. In reality, we are putting ourselves ahead of the relationship by saying that we know what is best for the relationship. The long-term effect of this type of behavior is that it weakens relationships.

Even when used with good intentions, dishonesty contributes to the breakdown of relationships.

But being honest is not just about telling the truth. It has to do with being open with others and representing reality as fully and completely as possible. This is not an easy task, however, because there are times when telling the complete truth can be destructive or counterproductive. The challenge for leaders is to strike a balance between being open and candid while monitoring what is appropriate to disclose in a particular situation. Many times, there are organizational constraints that prevent leaders from disclosing information to followers. It is important for leaders to be authentic, but it is also essential that they be sensitive to the attitudes and feelings of others. Honest leadership involves a wide set of behaviors.

Dalla Costa (1998) made the point clearly in his book, *The Ethical Imperative*, that being honest means more than not deceiving. For leaders in organizations, being honest means, "Do not promise what you can't deliver, do not misrepresent, do not hide behind spin-doctored evasions, do not suppress obligations, do not evade accountability, do not accept that the 'survival of the fittest' pressures of business release any of us from the responsibility to respect another's dignity and humanity" (p. 164). In addition, Dalla Costa suggested that it is imperative that organizations recognize and acknowledge the necessity of honesty and reward honest behavior within the organization.

Ethical Leaders Build Community

In Chapter 1, we defined leadership as a process whereby an individual influences a group of individuals to achieve a common goal. This definition has a clear ethical dimension because it refers to a *common* goal. A common goal requires that the leader and followers agree on the direction to be taken by the group. Leaders need to take into account their own and followers' purposes while working toward goals that are suitable for both of them. This factor, concern for others, is the distinctive feature that delineates *authentic* transformational leaders from *pseudo*transformational leaders (Bass & Steidlmeier, 1999) (for more on pseudotransformational leadership see page 187 in Chapter 8). Concern for the common good means that leaders cannot impose their will on others. They need to search for goals that are compatible with everyone.

Burns (1978) placed this idea at the center of his theory on transformational leadership. A transformational leader tries to move the group toward a common good that is beneficial for both the leaders and the followers. In moving toward mutual goals, both the leader and the followers are changed. It is this feature that makes Burns's theory unique. For Burns, leadership has to be grounded in the leader–follower relationship. It cannot be controlled by the leader, such as Hitler's influence in Germany. Hitler coerced people to meet his own agenda and followed goals that did not advance the goodness of humankind.

An ethical leader takes into account the purposes of everyone involved in the group and is attentive to the interests of the community and the culture. Such a leader demonstrates an ethic of caring toward others (Gilligan, 1982) and does not force others or ignore the intentions of others (Bass & Steidlmeier, 1999).

Rost (1991) went a step further and suggested that ethical leadership demands attention to a civic virtue. By this, he meant that leaders and followers need to attend to more than their own mutually determined goals. They need to attend to the *community's* goals and purpose. As Burns (1978, p. 429) wrote, transformational leaders and followers begin to reach out to wider social collectivities and seek to establish higher and broader moral purposes. Similarly, Greenleaf (1970) argued that building community was a main characteristic of servant leadership. All of our individual and group goals are bound up in the common good and public interest. We need to pay attention to how the changes proposed by a leader and followers will affect the larger organization, the community, and society. An ethical leader is concerned with the common good, in the broadest sense. This is underscored by Wilson and McCalman (2017), who argued that leadership for the greater good is the ultimate end toward which ethical leadership ought to be directed.

It is important to note that building community, as well as the other principles of ethical leadership discussed previously (Figure 15.3), vary across cultures. Cultures vary widely in what they view as positive leadership attributes and in what they define as ethical behavior of leaders. As the world becomes more connected and cross-cultural, an understanding of these different cultural perspectives on ethical leadership will be important.

Resick Hanges, Dickson, and Mitchelson, (2006) found that ethical leadership dimensions of character/integrity, altruism, collective motivation, and encouragement were endorsed across all cultures but that the importance of each dimension varied by culture. They also examined the meaning of ethical leadership in six countries and results indicated that cultures agree on the importance of character and integrity. Respondents from the People's Republic of China, Hong Kong, and Germany regarded consideration, respect for others, and collective orientation as crucial to ethical leadership; Ireland, the United States, and Taiwan rated these attributes as less important. The authors concluded that while some country differences exist, there is a general consensus regarding the meaning of ethical leadership (Resick et al., 2011).

STRENGTHS

This chapter discusses a broad set of ideas regarding ethics and leadership. This general field of study has several strengths. First, it provides a body of timely research on ethical issues. There is a high demand for moral leadership in our society today. Beginning with the Richard Nixon administration in the 1970s and continuing through Donald Trump's administration, people have been insisting on higher levels of moral responsibility from their leaders. At a time when there seems to be a vacuum in ethical leadership, this research offers us some direction on how to think about and practice ethical leadership.

Second, this body of research suggests that ethics ought to be considered as an integral part of the broader domain of leadership. Except for servant, transformational, inclusive, and authentic leadership, none of the other leadership theories discussed in this book focuses on the role of ethics in the leadership process. This chapter suggests that leadership is not an amoral phenomenon. Leadership is a process of influencing others; it has a moral dimension that distinguishes it from other types of influence, such as coercion or despotic control. Leadership involves values, including showing respect for followers, being fair to others, and building community. It is not a process that we can demonstrate without showing our values. When we influence, we have an effect on others, which means we need to pay attention to our values and our ethics.

Third, research on ethical leadership clearly demonstrates benefits to the organization. When employees perceive that their leaders are ethical role models, there is less deviance and more cooperation, resulting in higher performance and organizational citizenship (Den Hartog, 2015). Kuenzi, Mayer, and Greenbaum (2019) found that ethical leadership predicts the ethical climate of the organization. The study also found that the ethical climate of an organization explains the relationship between ethical leadership and unethical behavior within work groups. When ethical leaders create ethical climates in organizations, it reinforces the role modeling of ethical behaviors for followers.

In addition, research has demonstrated that followers exhibit ethical norms, positive job attitudes, and constructive ethical behaviors because their leaders serve as role models when they behave ethically (Mayer, Kuenzi, Greenbaum, Bardes, & Salvador, 2009). There appears to be a cascading effect. When leaders are ethical at higher organizational levels, followers emulate their behavior. The cascading effect has been explained by middle-level supervisors' ethical efficacy expectations (the belief in their ability to be ethical) and their expectations of punishments for being unethical (Wang, Xu, & Liu, 2018). However, Thiel, Hardy, Peterson, Welsh, and Bonner (2018) found that the efficacy of ethical leadership is related to the leader's number of followers; leaders with a wider span of control had fewer high-quality relationships and therefore had less influence on the ethical behavior of followers.

Fourth, ethical leadership has been linked to attitudinal, motivational, well-being, and performance-related outcomes; ethical norms and decisions; and ethical behaviors by followers. Ng and Feldman (2015) conducted a meta-analysis of 101 samples published over 15 years (29,620 respondents) and found that ethical leadership showed positive relationships to followers' job attitudes, job performance, and evaluations of their leaders. Further, followers' trust in the leader explained the relationships of ethical leadership with job attitudes and performance. A review of ethical leadership research concluded that it relates positively to satisfaction with the leader, perceived leader effectiveness, followers' job dedication, willingness to report problems to management, well-being, LMX, organizational commitment, and trust and it is negatively related to cynicism (Den Hartog, 2015).

Finally, the measurement of ethical leadership has improved. For example, Brown, Treviño, and Harrison (2005) developed and validated a 10-item measure of ethical leadership (the Ethical Leadership Scale, ELS) that has been employed in subsequent research, and is the most widely used measure (Ng & Feldman, 2015) of ethical leadership.

CRITICISMS

Although the area of ethics and leadership has many strengths, it also has some weaknesses. First, it remains an area of research in an early stage of development, and therefore lacks a strong body of traditional research findings to substantiate it. There is conceptual confusion regarding the nature and definition of ethical leadership (Yukl, Mahsud, Hassan, & Prussia, 2013). Den Hartog (2015) points out that some definitions are based on leader intentions (e.g., "do no harm"), while others describe leader behaviors based on follower perceptions (e.g., "asking what's the right thing to do"). In addition, followers' perceptions of their leaders may be biased. Although many studies have been published on business ethics, these studies have not been directly related to ethical leadership. One exception is the work of Yukl and colleagues (2013), who identified key components of ethical leadership as a result of their efforts to validate an ethical leadership questionnaire, which they developed based on existing measurement instruments that all had limitations. In this work, they suggest the construct domain of ethical leadership includes integrity, honesty, fairness, communication of ethical values, consistency of behavior with espoused values, ethical guidance, and altruism. In general, the dearth of research on leadership ethics makes speculation about the nature of ethical leadership difficult. Until more research studies have been conducted that deal directly with the ethical dimensions of leadership, theoretical formulations about the process will remain tentative.

Another criticism is that, in the past, leadership ethics relied on the writings of just a few people who have penned essays and texts that were strongly influenced by their personal opinions about the nature of leadership ethics and their view of the world. Although these writings, such as Heifetz's and Burns's, have stood the test of time, they have not been tested using traditional quantitative or qualitative research methods. They are primarily descriptive and anecdotal. In recent years, leadership ethics researchers have begun to develop the traditional kind of empirical support that usually accompanies accepted theories of human behavior.

Third, most of the research on ethical leadership has focused primarily on the Western world and Anglo-American countries (Eisenbeiss, 2012; Wilson & McCalman, 2017). There is a need to widen the scope of research on ethical leadership to include European and Asian perspectives because cultures vary widely in how they approach ethical leadership. As the world becomes more connected and cross-cultural, an understanding of these different cultural perspectives on ethical leadership will be important.

Fourth, there are also generational differences in ethical perspectives. From an analysis of the literature, Anderson, Baur, Griffith, and Buckley (2017) suggest that today's generation of workers, millennials, presents unique challenges regarding ethical leadership. First, because millennials are more individualistic than older employees, they are less likely to view the intensity of moral decisions in the same way and less likely to look to their leaders for guidance on making ethical decisions. Second, because millennials see their work as less central to their lives, they are less likely to view ethical dilemmas at work as particularly problematic. Third, because millennials value highly extrinsic rewards, they are less likely to respond to ethical appeals to do the right thing for the organization. In fact, research suggests that these employees may be even more likely to succumb to temptations to be unethical if such behavior is likely to lead to pay-offs (Ethics Resource Center, 2011).

Because ethical perspectives can change quickly, empirical ethical leadership research will struggle to be up-to-date and relevant.

APPLICATION

Although issues of morality and leadership are discussed more often in society today, these discussions have not resulted in a large number of programs in training and development designed to teach ethical leadership. Many new programs are oriented toward helping managers become more effective at work and in life in general, but these programs do not directly target the area of ethics and leadership.

Yet the ethics and leadership research in this chapter can be applied to people at all levels of organizations and in all walks of life. At a very minimum, it is crucial to state that *leadership involves values*, and one cannot be a leader without being aware of and concerned about one's own values. Because leadership has a moral dimension, being a leader demands awareness on our part of the way our ethics defines our leadership.

For example, Moore et al. (2018) combined experiments and field research to demonstrate that ethical leadership reduces followers' tendencies to morally disengage and then engage in deviant behavior. Moral disengagement is thinking that it is acceptable to take credit for someone else's work. The authors cite Pope Francis as an example of how ethical leadership may reduce followers' moral disengagement. During his first year as Pope, instead of kneeling for a symbolic touch of the feet of 12 priests on Holy Thursday, he washed and kissed the feet of 12 imprisoned juveniles. By treating marginalized people in this way, the Pope created a disconnect for followers who talk badly about those who are disenfranchised. He also became a role model for humility for his followers by moving from the Apostolic Palace to a small apartment and replacing the papal Mercedes with a Ford Focus.

Managers and leaders can use the information in research on ethical leadership to better understand themselves and strengthen their own leadership. Ethical theories can remind leaders to ask themselves, "What is the right and fair thing to do?" or "What would a good person do?" Leaders can use the ethical principles described in this research as benchmarks for their own behavior. Do I show respect to others? Do I act with a generous spirit? Do I show honesty and faithfulness to others? Do I serve the community? Finally, we can learn from the overriding theme in this research that the leader–follower relationship is central to ethical leadership. To be an ethical leader, we must be sensitive to the needs of others, treat others in ways that are just, and care for others.

The following section contains three case studies (Cases 15.1, 15.2, and 15.3) in which ethical leadership is needed. Case 15.1 describes a department chair who must choose which student will get a special assignment. Case 15.2 deals with the ethical issues surrounding how a human resource service company established the pricing for its services. Case 15.3 explores the events surrounding U.S. Navy Captain Brett Crozier's firing for sounding the alarm about COVID-19 aboard the aircraft carrier *USS Theodore Roosevelt*. At the end of each case, there are questions that point to the intricacies and complexities of practicing ethical leadership.

Case 15.1 CHOOSING A RESEARCH ASSISTANT

Dr. Angi Dirks is the chair of the state university's organizational psychology department, which has four teaching assistants (TAs). Angi has just found out that she has received a grant for research work over the summer and that it includes money to fund one of the TAs as her research assistant. In Angi's mind, the top two candidates are Roberto and Michelle, who are both available to work over the summer. Roberto, a foreign student from Venezuela, has gotten very high teaching evaluations and is well liked by the faculty. Roberto needs a summer job to help pay for school since it is too expensive for him to return home for the summer to work. Michelle is also an exceptional graduate student; she is married and doesn't necessarily need the extra income, but she is going to pursue a PhD, so the extra experience would be beneficial to her future endeavors.

A third teaching assistant, Carson, commutes to school from a town an hour away, where he is helping to take care of his grandparents. Carson manages to juggle school, teaching, and his home responsibilities well, carrying a 4.0 GPA in his classwork. Angi knows Carson could use the money, but she is afraid that he has too many other responsibilities to take on the research project over the summer.

As Angi weighs which TA to offer the position, a faculty member approaches her about considering the fourth TA, Analisa. It's been a tough year with Analisa as a TA. She has complained numerous times to her faculty mentor and to Angi that the other TAs treat her differently, and she thinks it's racial discrimination. The student newspaper printed a column she wrote about "being a speck of brown in a campus of white," in which she expressed her frustration with the predominantly white faculty's inability to understand the unique perspectives and experiences of minority students. After the column came out, the faculty in the department became wary of working with Analisa, fearing becoming part of the controversy. Their lack of interaction with her made Analisa feel further alienated.

Angi knows that Analisa is a very good researcher and writer, and her skills would be an asset to the project. Analisa's faculty mentor says that giving the position to her would go a long way to "smooth things over" between faculty and Analisa and make Analisa feel included in the department. Analisa knows about the open position and has expressed interest in it to her faculty mentor, but hasn't directly talked to Angi. Angi is afraid that by not giving it to Analisa, she may stir up more accusations of ill treatment while at the same time facing accusations from others that she is giving Analisa preferential treatment.

Questions

1. Of the four options available to Angi, which is the most ethical?

2. Using the principles of distributive justice, who would Angi choose to become the research assistant?

3. From Heifetz's perspective, can Angi use this decision to help her department and faculty face a difficult situation? Should she?

4. Do you agree with Burns's perspective that it is Angi's responsibility to help followers assess their own values and needs in order to raise them to a higher level that will stress values such as liberty, justice, and equality? If so, how can Angi do that through this situation?

Case 15.2 REEXAMINING A PROPOSAL

After working 10 years as the only manager of color in a large printing company, David Jones decided he wanted to set out on his own. Because of his experience and prior connections, David was confident he could survive in the printing business, but he wondered whether he should buy an existing business or start a new one. As part of his planning, David contacted a professional employer organization (PEO), which had a sterling reputation, to obtain an estimate for human resource services for a startup company. The estimate was to include costs for payroll, benefits, worker's compensation, and other traditional human resource services. Because David had not yet started his business, the PEO generated a generic quote applicable to a small company in the printing industry. In addition, because the PEO had nothing tangible to quote, it gave David a quote for human resource services that was unusually high.

In the meantime, David found an existing small company that he liked, and he bought it. Then he contacted the PEO to sign a contract for human resource

(Continued)

services at the previously quoted price. David was ready to take ownership and begin his new venture. He signed the original contract as presented.

After David signed the contract, the PEO reviewed the earlier proposal in light of the actual figures of the company he had purchased. This review raised many concerns for management. Although the goals of the PEO were to provide high-quality service, be competitive in the marketplace, and make a reasonable profit, the quote it had provided David appeared to be much too high. It was not comparable in any way with the other service contracts the PEO had with other companies of similar size and function.

During the review, it became apparent that several concerns had to be addressed. First, the original estimate made the PEO appear as if it was gouging the client. Although the client had signed the original contract, was it fair to charge such a high price for the proposed services? Would charging such high fees mean that the PEO would lose this client or similar clients in the future? Another concern was related to the PEO's support of businesses owned by people of color. For years, the PEO had prided itself on having strong values about affirmative action and fairness in the workplace, but this contract appeared to actually hurt and to be somewhat unfair to a Black client. Finally, the PEO was concerned with the implications of the contract for the salesperson who drew up the proposal for David. Changing the estimated costs in the proposal would have a significant impact on the salesperson's commission, which would negatively affect the morale of others in the PEO's sales area.

After a reexamination of the original proposal, a new contract was drawn up for David's company with lower estimated costs. Though lower than the original proposal, the new contract remained much higher than the average contract in the printing industry. David willingly signed the new contract.

Questions

1. What role should ethics play in the writing of a proposal such as this? Did the PEO do the ethical thing for David? How much money should the PEO have tried to make? What would you have done if you were part of management at the PEO?

2. From a deontological (duty) perspective and a teleological (consequences) perspective, how would you describe the ethics of the PEO?

3. Based on what the PEO did for David, how would you evaluate the PEO on the ethical principles of respect, service, justice, honesty, and community?

4. How would you assess the ethics of the PEO if you were David? If you were among the PEO management? If you were the salesperson? If you were a member of the printing community?

The Cast

Commanding Officer of the USS *Theodore Roosevelt*	Captain Brett Crozier
Commander of Carrier Strike Group (oversees 7 ships including the USS *Theodore Roosevelt*)	Rear Admiral Stuart Baker
Acting U.S. Secretary of the Navy	Thomas Modly
U.S. Secretary of Defense	Mark Esper
The Crew	Sailors and airmen aboard USS *Theodore Roosevelt*

Act 1—The Virus

It was believed to have begun on March 5, 2020, with the Vietnamese port call of the U.S. naval aircraft carrier USS *Theodore Roosevelt*. The port call in Da Nang, only the second visit by an American aircraft carrier to the country since the Vietnam War, was ordered partly as a show of military strength in a region threatened by perceived growing territorialism by China in the South China Sea.

At the time the *Roosevelt* arrived there, Vietnam had 16 reported cases of the highly contagious coronavirus (COVID-19), but they were all in the country's northern region, far from the ship's port of call. Because the *Roosevelt*, commanded by Captain Brett Crozier, a Naval Academy graduate with more than 30 years of service, was too large for the city's docks, the ship anchored offshore and relied on small boats to ferry its sailors to Da Nang, where they spent several days within the city, frequenting its restaurants, shops, and hotels and engaging in community service projects. On the fourth day, several crew members were ordered back to the ship when it was feared they may have been exposed to COVID-19 at a hotel where two British nationals who had tested positive for the virus had also been staying.

The *Roosevelt* then left port and headed out to sea, returning to normal operations with aircraft flying to and from the ship bringing supplies from Japan and the Philippines. Meanwhile, the ship's medical team watched the crew closely for signs of the virus, knowing that symptoms generally appear within the first 14 days after exposure.

On March 24, an announcement came over the ship's loudspeakers: "Set River City 1." This alerted the sailors that the ship had entered into a period of restricted

(Continued)

(Continued)

communications, meaning no internet or phone calls for most everyone onboard. The reason why, the crew soon discovered, was that three sailors aboard the *Roosevelt* had tested positive for COVID-19. Within 24 hours, the number of cases on the ship doubled and each subsequent day rendered new cases (Simkins, 2020).

The *Roosevelt*, a massive 1,000-foot nuclear-powered aircraft carrier, is essentially a small city. It housed almost 5,000 crew members, all living and working in extremely tight quarters. Crew members shared common cafeterias, bathroom facilities, other social areas, and narrow hallways. They worked in close proximity to one another day and night. Even their sleeping quarters were close with bunks often stacked three high.

The sailors who tested positive were all members of the reactor crew, the group responsible for running the core of the ship. They were flown to a Navy hospital in Guam, with the ship following a few days later, docking there to begin testing of the entire crew and engage in professional cleaning of the ship.

Just a few months earlier, the *Diamond Princess*, a cruise ship of 2,600 passengers housed in individual cabins, had eight of its passengers die of the virus while aboard with more than 700 others infected. Captain Crozier knew the *Roosevelt*, with its tight quarters and significantly larger crew, had the potential to be much worse than the *Diamond Princess*; the *Roosevelt*'s doctors were estimating that more than 50 crew members could potentially die from the virus (Gibbons-Neff, Schmitt, Cooper, & Ismay, 2020).

Act 2—The Letter

As the cases aboard the *Roosevelt* rapidly increased, several options were considered with Captain Crozier arguing strongly for evacuating nearly all the sailors from the ship, leaving a skeleton crew of around 500 to perform essential duties and protect the vessel's reactors, bombs, missiles, and war planes. The rest of the crew would be quarantined and tested while the ship was cleaned.

Captain Crozier's commanding officer, Rear Admiral Stuart Baker, disagreed, feeling that less drastic action would still protect the crew and leave the ship in operation. Ultimately, 1,000 of the ship's crew were evacuated to a gymnasium on base where they slept on cots, which quickly resulted in several more confirmed cases.

After continued denials from his superiors and watching the situation escalate each day, on March 30, Captain Crozier laid out his concerns and arguments in a four-page letter titled, *Request for Assistance in Response to COVID-19 Pandemic*. The letter was sent via unclassified email and addressed to Crozier's commanding officer, Rear Admiral Stuart Baker, U.S. Pacific Fleet Commander Admiral John Aquilino, and Naval Air Forces Commander Vice Admiral DeWolfe Miller as well as copied to seven other Navy captains (Simpkins, 2020).

According to the *New York Times*, prior to sending the letter, Captain Crozier shared the email with several of the *Roosevelt's* most senior officers. When they expressed their desire to add their signatures to the letter, Captain Crozier refused, fearing for their careers, knowing the letter might well end his (Cooper, Gibbons-Neff, Schmitt, & Cochrane, 2020).

Pleading for assistance and consideration, Captain Crozier wrote, "This will require a political solution, but it is the right thing to do . . . We are not at war. Sailors do not need to die. If we do not act now, we are failing to properly take care of our most trusted asset — our sailors" (Gafni & Garofoli, 2020). Noting that only a small group of infected crewmen had been removed from the ship and quarantined, and that "the spread of the disease is ongoing and accelerating," Crozier requested "compliant quarantine rooms" be provided on shore in Guam for his entire crew "as soon as possible" (Gafni & Garofoli, 2020).

The letter was leaked to the *San Francisco Chronicle* and the plight of the crewmen on the USS *Theodore Roosevelt* soon became public knowledge in the midst of a worldwide pandemic.

Act 3—Retribution

Infuriated that the letter had been sent to what he considered a wide distribution (though the recipients were all Navy personnel) and consequently became public due to being leaked to the press, acting U.S. secretary of the Navy Thomas Modly fired Captain Crozier on April 2.

Modly, himself a Naval Academy graduate and former Navy helicopter pilot, was the acting secretary positioned to become the permanent Secretary of the Navy. He had replaced Richard Spencer, who had been fired by U.S. president Donald Trump for opposing Trump's support of a Navy Seal who had been charged with war crimes. According to the *New York Times*, Modly, concerned that Captain Crozier's letter would anger Trump, sought the advice of colleagues, including the chief of naval operations and the chair of the joint chiefs of staff, who counseled Modly to first order an investigation (Gibbons-Neff, Schmitt, Cooper, & Ismay, 2020). He did not.

Although Modly acknowledged that there was "no evidence that Captain Crozier leaked the message" to the media (Cooper, Gibbons-Neff, Schmitt, & Cochrane, 2020) he quickly relieved the captain of his duties without a formal investigation and, according to Modly's aides, without pressure from his superiors, U.S. defense secretary Mark Esper or U.S. president Donald Trump. *NavyTimes* would later report that Modly ignored the counsel of his colleagues, "due to the belief that President Donald Trump wanted Crozier fired" (Simkins, 2020).

Modly's immediate superior, Defense Secretary Mark Esper, had previously cautioned his commanders not to make decisions that might contradict Trump's

(Continued)

(Continued)

intended messaging on the growing COVID-19 pandemic. Modly tried to frame the firing of Captain Crozier as a "loss of confidence" rather than retribution by claiming the letter had "raised alarm bells unnecessarily" and that "in sending it out broadly, he [Crozier] did not take care to assure it couldn't be leaked" (Cooper, Gibbons-Neff, Schmitt, & Cochrane, 2020).

As Captain Crozier left his ship, hundreds of sailors and airmen gathered to form a "corridor" for him to openly express their support for the popular and highly respected commander. Videos of this went viral. In response, Modly chartered a Gulf Stream business jet and flew immediately to Guam at a cost of $243,000 where he delivered a scathing, profanity-laced 15-minute reprimand to the *Roosevelt*'s crew over the ship's public address system (Gibbons-Neff, Schmitt, & Ismay, 2020). Modly berated the crew for cheering the captain, calling Crozier "too stupid" and "too naïve" to command a ship and adding that blame for the virus belonged to China. Thirty minutes later, he abruptly left, fielding no questions.

Within 30 minutes of his departure from the *Roosevelt*, social media was widely broadcasting audio recordings of his tirade.

Act 4—R&R: Resignation and Reinstatement?

When Acting Secretary Modly landed back in Washington, D.C., he was immediately directed by Defense Secretary Esper to apologize. Lawmakers and former military officials were calling for Modly's resignation.

The next day, Modly, in quarantine because of his potential exposure to the virus while onboard the *Roosevelt,* tendered his resignation.

Captain Crozier subsequently ended up in quarantine at the naval base in Guam, battling the virus. More than 4,000 of the ship's crew members were also quarantined with more than 800 testing positive for the virus and one crew member dying from it.

But Captain Crozier's plight and that of the USS *Theodore Roosevelt*'s crew had caught the attention of senior military officials and raised awareness and concern for other warships and missions. General John Hyten, chair of the joint chiefs of staff shared, "From my perspective, it's not a good idea to think that the *Teddy Roosevelt* is a one-of-a-kind issue. To think that it will never happen again is not a good way to plan" (Gibbons-Neff, Schmitt, & Ismay, 2020).

The Navy subsequently instituted new health and safety procedures for ships at sea and for those preparing to head out on deployment to prevent future outbreaks, including requiring crew members to wear masks and observe social distancing guidelines. In addition, in preparation for deployment, a ship's crew must be quarantined for 14 days before boarding the ship.

More than 345,000 people signed an online petition to reinstate Captain Crozier. Legislators urged the Pentagon to reconsider. The chair of the House Armed Services Committee and other top subcommittee leaders condemned Crozier's dismissal, stating that "Dismissing a commanding officer for speaking out on issues critical to the safety of those under their command discourages others from raising similar concerns" (Cooper, Gibbons-Neff, Schmitt, & Cochrane, 2020).

Amidst pressure from the public and lawmakers, and after a preliminary inquiry, the Navy's top leadership took the unprecedented step to recommend reinstatement of Captain Crozier as commander of the USS *Theodore Roosevelt*. The final decision on whether Captain Crozier would be reinstated as captain of the USS *Roosevelt* was delayed by acting Navy secretary James E. McPherson (who replaced Thomas Modly) who has called for a broader investigation into the matter (Martinez, 2020). At the time this was written, Crozier remained in the Navy, maintaining his rank, but had been given a temporary duty assignment in San Diego (Ziesulewicz, 2020).

Questions

1. The chapter states that "a leader's choices are also influenced by their moral development." Applying Kohlberg's stages of moral development to this case:

    a. At what stage would you classify Captain Crozier's level of moral reasoning? Why?

    b. At what stage would you classify Acting Navy Secretary Thomas Modly's level of moral reasoning? Why?

    c. What about Rear Admiral Stuart Baker? Why?

    d. What level would you classify Defense Secretary Mark Esper? Why?

2. The chapter outlines three different approaches to assessing consequences—*ethical egoism, utilitarianism,* and *altruism.*

    a. Which of these approaches do you feel most accurately summarizes Captain Brett Crozier's approach? Why?

    b. Which of these do you feel most accurately summarizes Acting Secretary Thomas Modly's approach? Why?

    c. Which approach applies to Rear Admiral Stuart Baker?

3. What elements described in the Toxic Leadership Triangle, were evident in this case? Do you think there are examples of destructive leadership in this case? Explain your answer.

4. The chapter outlines five Principles of Ethical Leadership. Which of these principles applied to Captain Brett Crozier's leadership? Which principles applied to Thomas Modly's leadership?

—Barbara Russell, MBA, BSCS, BBA, Chemeketa Community College

LEADERSHIP INSTRUMENT

It is human to want others to see you as an ethical leader, because being viewed as an unethical leader can carry with it very strong negative connotations. But the social desirability of being judged by others as an ethical leader makes measuring ethical leadership challenging. Self-reported scores of ethical leadership are often biased and skewed in a positive direction.

The Ethical Leadership Style Questionnaire (ELSQ) presented in this chapter is a self-reporting measure of ethical leadership that does not measure whether one is or is not ethical, but rather assesses the leader's style of ethical leadership. The ELSQ is a 45-question instrument that measures how a leader approaches ethical dilemmas. The six ethical styles assessed by the dilemmas are (a) duty ethics (I would do what is right), (b) utilitarianism ethics (I would do what benefits the most people), (c) virtue ethics (I would do what a good person would do), (d) caring ethics (I would do what shows that I care about my close personal relationships), (e) egoism ethics (I would do what benefits me the most), and (f) justice ethics (I would do what is fair). Based on the individual's responses, the ELSQ identifies a leader's primary and secondary ethical leadership styles.

Although the ELSQ is in its initial stages of development, data from two studies (Baehrend, 2016; Chikeleze, 2014) confirmed that when leaders face ethical dilemmas, they have a preference for a particular style of ethical leadership. The ELSQ can be used by leaders as a self-assessment tool to understand their decision-making preferences when confronting ethical dilemmas. Organizations will find it a useful training tool to educate leaders on decision making (Chikeleze & Baehrend, 2017).

Ethical Leadership Style Questionnaire (Short Form)

Purpose: To develop an understanding of your ethical leadership style and understand how your preferred ethical leadership style relates to other ethical leadership styles.

Instructions: Please read the following 10 hypothetical situations in which a leader is confronted with an ethical dilemma. Place yourself in the role of the leader or manager in the situation and indicate with an "X" your most preferred response. Your most preferred response is the response that best describes why you would do what you would do in that particular situation. Choose only one response. There are no right or wrong answers.

Response alternatives explained:

- *I would do what is right:* This option includes following the rules, meeting my responsibilities, fulfilling my obligations, and adhering to organization policy. Rules in this context may be explicit or implicit.

- *I would do what benefits the most people:* This option includes doing what helps the most people overall and what creates the greatest total happiness. It also includes doing the greatest good for the greatest number.

- *I would do what a good person would do:* This option includes exhibiting excellence of character, acting with integrity, and being faithful to one's principles. This option includes employing virtues such as courage, honesty, and loyalty.

- *I would do what shows that I care about my close relationships:* This option includes building and maintaining caring relationships, nurturing relationships, and being responsive to the needs of others. It gives special consideration to those with whom I share a personal bond or commitment.

- *I would do what benefits me the most:* This option includes achieving my goals, being successful in my assigned task, and advancing my career. It also includes doing things that are in my self-interest.

- *I would do what is fair:* This option includes acting with justice, being equitable to others, and treating others fairly. It also includes distributing benefits and burdens to everyone equally.

Situations

1. You are the leader of a manufacturing team and learn that your employees are falsifying product quality results to sell more products. If you report the matter, most of them will lose their jobs, you may lose

(Continued)

(Continued)

yours, and your company will take a significant hit to its reputation. What would you do in this situation?

- ☐ A. I would do what is right.
- ☐ B. I would do what benefits the most people.
- ☐ C. I would do what a good person would do.
- ☐ D. I would do what shows that I care about my relationships.
- ☐ E. I would do what benefits me the most.
- ☐ F. I would do what is fair.

2. You have an employee who has been having performance problems, which is making it hard for your group to meet its work quota. This person was recommended to you as a solid performer. You now believe the person's former manager had problems with the employee and just wanted to get rid of the person. If you give the underperforming employee a good recommendation, leaving out the performance problems, you will have an opportunity to pass the employee off to another group. What would you do in this situation?

- ☐ A. I would do what is right.
- ☐ B. I would do what benefits the most people.
- ☐ C. I would do what a good person would do.
- ☐ D. I would do what shows that I care about my relationships.
- ☐ E. I would do what benefits me the most.
- ☐ F. I would do what is fair.

3. Your team is hard-pressed to complete a critical project. You hear about a job opening that would be much better for one of your key employees' career. If this individual leaves the team, it would put the project in danger. What would you do in this situation?

- ☐ A. I would do what is right.
- ☐ B. I would do what benefits the most people.
- ☐ C. I would do what a good person would do.
- ☐ D. I would do what shows that I care about my relationships.
- ☐ E. I would do what benefits me the most.
- ☐ F. I would do what is fair.

4. An employee of yours has a child with a serious illness and is having trouble fulfilling obligations at work. You learn from your administrative assistant that this employee claimed 40 hours on a time sheet for a week when the employee actually only worked 30 hours. What would you do in this situation?

☐ A. I would do what is right.

☐ B. I would do what benefits the most people.

☐ C. I would do what a good person would do.

☐ D. I would do what shows that I care about my relationships.

☐ E. I would do what benefits me the most.

☐ F. I would do what is fair.

5. You are a manager, and some of your employees can finish their quotas in much less than the allotted time to do so. If upper management becomes aware of this, they will want you to increase the quotas. Some of your employees are unable to meet their current quotas. What would you do in this situation?

☐ A. I would do what is right.

☐ B. I would do what benefits the most people.

☐ C. I would do what a good person would do.

☐ D. I would do what shows that I care about my relationships.

☐ E. I would do what benefits me the most.

☐ F. I would do what is fair.

6. You are an organization's chief financial officer, and you are aware that the chief executive officer and other members of the senior leadership team want to provide exaggerated financial information to keep the company's stock price high. The entire senior management team holds significant stock positions. What would you do in this situation?

☐ A. I would do what is right.

☐ B. I would do what benefits the most people.

☐ C. I would do what a good person would do.

☐ D. I would do what shows that I care about my relationships.

☐ E. I would do what benefits me the most.

☐ F. I would do what is fair.

7. Two new employees have joined your accounting team right out of school. They are regularly found surfing the Internet or texting on their phones. Your accounting work regularly requires overtime at the end of the month to get the financial reports completed. These employees refuse to do any overtime, which shifts work to other team members. The other team members are getting resentful and upset. What would you do in this situation?

☐ A. I would do what is right.

☐ B. I would do what benefits the most people.

(Continued)

(Continued)

- ☐ C. I would do what a good person would do.
- ☐ D. I would do what shows that I care about my relationships.
- ☐ E. I would do what benefits me the most.
- ☐ F. I would do what is fair.

8. You are the director of a neighborhood food cooperative. A member—a single parent with four children—is caught shoplifting $30 in groceries from the co-op. You suspect this person has been stealing for years. You consider pressing charges. What would you do in this situation?
   - ☐ A. I would do what is right.
   - ☐ B. I would do what benefits the most people.
   - ☐ C. I would do what a good person would do.
   - ☐ D. I would do what shows that I care about my relationships.
   - ☐ E. I would do what benefits me the most.
   - ☐ F. I would do what is fair.

9. You have been accused of discriminating against a particular gender in your hiring practices. A new position opens up, and you could hire a candidate of the gender you've been accused of discriminating against over a candidate of another gender, even though the latter candidate has slightly better qualifications. Hiring the former candidate would let you address this accusation and improve your reputation in the company. What would you do in this situation?
   - ☐ A. I would do what is right.
   - ☐ B. I would do what benefits the most people.
   - ☐ C. I would do what a good person would do.
   - ☐ D. I would do what shows that I care about my relationships.
   - ☐ E. I would do what benefits me the most.
   - ☐ F. I would do what is fair.

10. You are a professor. One of your best students buys an essay online and turns it in for a grade. Later in the term, the student begins to feel guilty and confesses to you that the paper was purchased. It is the norm at the university to fail a student guilty of plagiarism. You must decide if you will flunk the student. What would you do in this situation?
    - ☐ A. I would do what is right.
    - ☐ B. I would do what benefits the most people.
    - ☐ C. I would do what a good person would do.
    - ☐ D. I would do what shows that I care about my relationships.

☐ E. I would do what benefits me the most.

☐ F. I would do what is fair.

Scoring

To score the questionnaire, sum the number of times you selected item A, B, C, D, E, or F. The sum of A responses represents your preference for *Duty Ethics*, the sum of B responses represents your preference for *Utilitarian Ethics*, the sum of C responses represents your preference for *Virtue Ethics*, the sum of D responses represents your preference for *Caring Ethics*, the sum of E responses represents your preference for *Egoism Ethics*, and the sum of F responses represents your preference for *Justice Ethics*. Place these sums in the Total Scores section that follows.

A. Duty Ethics: _____

B. Utilitarian Ethics: _____

C. Virtue Ethics: _____

D. Caring Ethics: _____

E. Egoism Ethics: _____

F. Justice Ethics: _____

Scoring Interpretation

The scores you received on this questionnaire provide information about your ethical leadership style; they represent your preferred way of addressing ethical dilemmas. Given a situation with an ethical dilemma, this questionnaire points to what ethical perspective is behind the choices you would make to resolve the dilemma. As you look at your total scores, your highest score represents your primary or dominant ethical leadership style, your second-highest score is the next most important, and so on. If you scored 0 for a category, it means that you put lower priority on that particular ethical approach to guide your decision making when facing ethical dilemmas.

- *If you scored higher on Duty Ethics*, it means you follow the rules and do what you think you are supposed to do when facing ethical dilemmas. You focus on fulfilling your responsibilities and doing what you think is the right thing to do.

- *If you scored higher on Utilitarian Ethics*, it means you try to do what is best for the most people overall when facing ethical dilemmas. You focus on what will create happiness for the largest number of individuals.

- *If you scored higher on Virtue Ethics*, it means that you pull from who you are (your character) when facing ethical dilemmas. You act out of integrity, and you are faithful to your own principles of goodness.

(Continued)

(Continued)

- *If you scored higher on Caring Ethics*, it means that you give attention to your relationships when facing ethical dilemmas. You may give special consideration to those with whom you share a personal bond or commitment.

- *If you scored higher on Egoism Ethics*, it means that you do what is best for yourself when facing ethical dilemmas. You are not afraid to assert your own interests and goals when resolving problems.

- *If you scored higher on Justice Ethics*, it means that you focus on treating others fairly when facing ethical dilemmas. You try to make sure the benefits and burdens of decisions are shared equitably between everyone concerned.

Comparing your scores regarding each of these ethical perspectives can give you a sense of what is important to you when addressing an ethical concern. A low score in any of the categories suggests that you give less priority to that ethical perspective. All of the ethical perspectives have merit, so there is no "best" perspective to maintain.

This questionnaire is intended as a self-assessment exercise. Although each ethical approach is presented as a discrete category, it is possible that one category may overlap with another category. It is also possible that you may have an ethical leadership style that is not fully captured in this questionnaire. Since this questionnaire is an abridged version of an expanded questionnaire, you may wish to take the full questionnaire to gain a more accurate reflection of your ethical approach. It can be taken at **www.leaderdecisionmakingsurvey.com**.

—Abridged and adapted from the Ethical Leadership Style Questionnaire, www.leaderdecisionmakingsurvey.com

SUMMARY

Although there has been an interest in ethics for thousands of years, very little theoretical research exists on the nature of leadership ethics. This chapter has presented an overview of ethical theories as they apply to the leadership process.

Ethical theory provides a set of principles that guide leaders in making decisions about how to act and how to be morally decent. In the Western tradition, ethical theories typically are divided into two kinds: theories about *conduct* and theories about *character*. Theories about conduct emphasize the consequences of leader behavior (teleological approach) or the rules that govern their behavior (deontological approach). Virtue-based theories focus on the character of leaders, and they stress qualities such as courage, honesty, fairness, and fidelity.

Ethics plays a central role in the leadership process. Because leadership involves influence and leaders often have more power than followers, they have an enormous ethical responsibility for how they affect other people. Leaders need to engage followers to accomplish mutual goals; therefore, it is imperative that they treat followers and their ideas with respect and dignity. Leaders also play a major role in establishing the ethical climate in their organization; that role requires leaders to be particularly sensitive to the values and ideals they promote.

Several prominent leadership scholars, including Heifetz, Burns, and Greenleaf, have made unique contributions to our understanding of ethical leadership. The theme common to these authors is an ethic of caring, which pays attention to followers' needs and the importance of leader–follower relationships.

This chapter suggests that sound ethical leadership is rooted in respect, service, justice, honesty, and community. It is the duty of leaders to treat others with *respect*—to listen to them closely and be tolerant of opposing points of view. Ethical leaders *serve* others by being altruistic, placing others' welfare ahead of their own in an effort to contribute to the common good. *Justice* requires that leaders place fairness at the center of their decision making, including the challenging task of being fair to the individual while simultaneously being fair to the common interests of the community. Good leaders are *honest*. They do not lie, nor do they present truth to others in ways that are destructive or counterproductive. Finally, ethical leaders are committed to building *community*, which includes searching for goals that are compatible with the goals of followers and with society as a whole.

Research on ethics and leadership has several strengths. At a time when the public is demanding higher levels of moral responsibility from its leaders, this research provides some direction in how to think about ethical leadership and how to practice it. In addition, this research reminds us that leadership is a moral process. Scholars should include ethics as an integral part of leadership studies and research. Furthermore, ethical leadership has been shown to provide advantages for organizations as well as followers. Last, from a research perspective, this area of research is benefiting from improved measures of ethical leadership.

On the negative side, this research area of ethical leadership is still in an early stage of development. Few studies have been done that directly address the nature of ethical leadership. As a result, the theoretical formulations about the process remain tentative. Second, this area of research relies on the writings of a few individuals whose work has been primarily descriptive and anecdotal. As a result, the development of theory on leadership ethics lacks the traditional empirical support that usually accompanies theories of human behavior. In addition, more research is needed to explain the impact of culture and generational differences in regard to ethical leadership. Despite these weaknesses, the field of ethical leadership is wide open for future research. There remains a strong need for research that can advance our understanding of the role of ethics in the leadership process.

Team Leadership

16

Susan E. Kogler Hill

DESCRIPTION

Work teams are very prevalent in today's organizations. The reliance on teams is due partially to increasingly complex tasks, more globalization, and the flattening of organizational structures. A team is a type of organizational group that is composed of members who are interdependent, who share common goals, and who must coordinate their activities to accomplish these goals. Team members must work collectively to achieve their goals. Examples of organizational teams include senior executive teams, project management teams, task forces, work units, standing committees, quality teams, and improvement teams. Teams can be located in the same place meeting face-to-face, or they can be geographically dispersed "virtual" teams meeting across time and distance via various forms of communication technology. Teams can also be hybrids of face-to-face and virtual teams with some members being co-located and some being dispersed. Exactly what defines an organizational group as a team or not is constantly evolving as organizations confront the many new forms of contemporary collaboration (Wageman, Gardner, & Mortensen, 2012).

The study of organizational teams has focused on strategies for maintaining a competitive advantage. Team-based organizations have faster response capability because of their flatter organizational structures, which rely on teams and new technology to enable communication across time and space (Porter & Beyerlein, 2000). These newer organizational structures have been referred to as "team-based and technology-enabled" (Mankin, Cohen, & Bikson, 1996).

Before the COVID-19 pandemic spread globally and people were forced to work remotely from their homes, relying on videoconferencing for meetings and engagement, a majority of multinational companies were already depending on virtual teams, or teams that are geographically dispersed and rely on technology to interact and collaborate (Muethel, Gehrlein, & Hoegl, 2012). Such teams allow companies to (1) use the best talent across the globe, (2) facilitate collaboration across time and space, and (3) reduce travel costs (Paul, Drake, & Liang,

2016) and, as experienced during the pandemic, allow organizational work to continue when physical locations are shut down or unavailable. The development of social media, video communication technologies, and software applications for meeting management has given virtual teams richer and more realistic communication environments where collaboration is facilitated (Schmidt, 2014; Schouten, van den Hooff, & Feldberg, 2016; Scott, 2013). Despite this, virtual teams face more difficulty with members separated by time, distance, and culture. In virtual teams, face-to-face communication is rare, with decisions and scheduling taking more time. In addition, they often have less trust, more conflict, and more subgroup formation. Breuer, Hüffmeier, and Hertel (2016) found that trust is an important factor when leading virtual teams because trust has been shown to be more important to virtual teams compared to face-to-face teams.

The Center for Creative Leadership worked with 141 virtual teams around the world and found that three key factors influence the effectiveness of virtual teams (Leslie & Hoole, 2018):

1. *Technology*. Effective team leadership uses technology to create connections among team members and make team members feel like they are working face-to-face. The use of videoconferencing (e.g., Zoom) became critical during the COVID-19 pandemic to allow for team success.

2. *Managing distance*. In many cases, virtual teams work across different time zones, and accommodating differing schedules is important. Virtual team leadership must share the burden of early-morning and late-night meetings among team members so that certain members are not always the ones to accommodate the time zone differences. Physical distance is a challenge to the engagement of team members, and team leaders must work to ensure members' commitment to team goals.

3. *Team structure*. Virtual team leadership must carefully consider the members of the team and ensure that those on the team are committed. While this is true for all teams, it is even more critical in a virtual team, since it is easier for team members to "check out." Often, as seen during the COVID-19 pandemic, some people were members of many different virtual teams, which resulted in less effort toward any one team and harmed the overall effectiveness.

Whether traditional or virtual, the organizational team-based structure is an important way for organizations to remain competitive by responding quickly and adapting to constant, rapid changes. Studies of both face-to-face and virtual teams have increasingly become focused on team processes and team outcomes (Ilgen, Hollenbeck, Johnson, & Jundt, 2005; Thomas, Martin, & Riggio, 2013).

Also, researchers focused on the problems work teams confront as well as how to make these work teams more effective (Ilgen, Major, Hollenbeck, & Sego, 1993). Effective organizational teams lead to many desirable outcomes, such as

- greater productivity,

- more effective use of resources,

- better decisions and problem solving,

- better-quality products and services, and

- greater innovation and creativity (Parker, 1990).

However, for teams to be successful, the organizational culture needs to support member involvement. The traditional authority structure of many organizations does not support decision making at lower levels, and this can lead to the failure of many teams. Teamwork is an example of lateral decision making as opposed to the traditional vertical decision making that occurs in the organizational hierarchy based on rank or position in the organization. The dynamic and fluid power shifting in teams has been referred to as *heterarchy* (Aime, Humphrey, DeRue, & Paul, 2014). Such power shifting within teams can lead to positive outcomes as long as team members see these shifting sources of power as legitimate. Teams will have great difficulty in organizational cultures that are not supportive of such collaborative work and decision making. Changing an organizational culture to one that is more supportive of teams is possible, but it takes time and effort (Levi, 2011).

Leadership of teams has also become an important area of study. The ideas of "team leadership" are quite different from leadership within the organizational vertical structure. Many theories of leadership, such as situational (discussed in Chapter 5) and transformational (discussed in Chapter 8), can be applied in the team setting. However, team leadership is a unique setting for leadership, and it is very process oriented. How do teams develop their "critical capabilities"? How do team leaders shift their actions over time to deal with contingencies as they arise? How do leader actions promote task and interpersonal development (Kozlowski, Watola, Jensen, Kim, & Botero, 2009)? Effective team leadership facilitates team success and helps teams to avoid team failure (Stagl, Salas, & Burke, 2007; Stewart & Manz, 1995). Effective leadership processes are the most critical factor in team success (Zaccaro, Rittman, & Marks, 2001, p. 452).

Shared or Distributed Leadership. The complexities of team processes demand the attention and focus of all members of the team. Some teams are autonomous and self-directed with no formal leader. But even those with a formal leader will benefit from shared leadership among team members. Team leadership functions can be performed by the formal team leader and/

or shared by team members. Shared team leadership occurs when members of the team take on leadership behaviors to influence the team and to maximize team effectiveness (Bergman, Rentsch, Small, Davenport, & Bergman, 2012). Shared leadership has been referred to as team leadership capacity, encompassing the leadership repertoire of the entire team (Day, Gronn, & Salas, 2004). Such distributed leadership involves the sharing of influence by team members. Team members step forward when situations warrant, providing the leadership necessary, and then step back to allow others to lead. Such shared leadership has become more and more important in today's organizations to allow faster responses to more complex issues (Morgeson, DeRue, & Karam, 2010; Pearce, Manz, & Sims, 2009; Solansky, 2008).

Shared leadership, while very important, does involve risk and takes some courage for the member who steps forward to provide leadership outside the formal role of team leader (Amos & Klimoski, 2014). Risks aside, teams with shared leadership have less conflict, more consensus, more trust, and more cohesion than teams that do not have shared leadership (Bergman et al., 2012). Shared leadership is even more important for virtual teams. Empowering leadership that shares power with virtual team members promotes both effective collaboration and performance (Drescher & Garbers, 2016; Hill & Bartol, 2016). Virtual teams are simply more effective when there is shared team leadership (Hoch & Kozlowski, 2014; Muethel et al., 2012; Wang, Waldman, & Zhang, 2014). How leaders and members can share the leadership of teams so that these teams can truly become effective and achieve excellence is discussed in this chapter. It introduces a model that provides a mental road map to help the leader or any team member providing leadership diagnose team problems and take appropriate action to correct those problems.

Team Leadership Model

The Hill Model for Team Leadership (Figure 16.1) is based on the functional leadership claim that the leader's job is to monitor the team and then take whatever action is necessary to ensure team effectiveness. The model provides a tool for understanding the very complex phenomenon of team leadership, starting at the top with its initial leadership decisions, moving to leader actions, and finally focusing on the indicators of team effectiveness. In addition, the model suggests specific actions that leaders can perform to improve team effectiveness. Effective team leaders need a wide repertoire of communication skills to monitor and take appropriate action. The model is designed to simplify and clarify the complex nature of team leadership and to provide an easy tool to aid leadership decision making for team leaders and members alike.

Effective team performance begins with how the leader sees the situation that the team is experiencing (the leader's *mental model*). This mental model reflects not only the components of the problem confronting the team, but also the

FIGURE 16.1 The Hill Model for Team Leadership

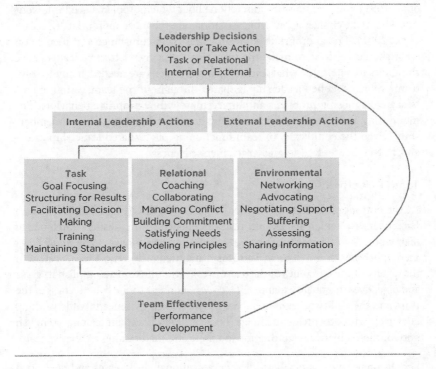

environmental and organizational contingencies that define the larger context of team action. The leader develops a mental conception of what the team problem is and what solutions are possible in this context, given the environmental and organizational constraints and resources (Zaccaro et al., 2001).

To respond appropriately to the problem envisioned in the mental model, a good team leader needs to be behaviorally flexible and have a wide repertoire of actions or skills to meet the team's diverse needs (Barge, 1996). When the leader's behavior matches the complexity of the situation, the leader is behaving with "requisite variety," or the set of behaviors necessary to meet the team's needs (Drecksel, 1991). Effective team leaders are able to construct accurate mental models of the team's problems by observing team functioning, and can take requisite action to solve these problems. Effective team leaders can diagnose correctly and choose the right action.

The leader has special responsibility for functioning in a manner that will help the team achieve effectiveness. Within this perspective, leadership behavior is seen as team-based problem solving, in which the leader attempts to achieve team goals by analyzing the internal and external situation and then selecting and implementing the appropriate behaviors to ensure team effectiveness (Fleishman et al., 1991). Leaders must use discretion about which problems need intervention, and make choices about which solutions are the most appropriate (Zaccaro et al., 2001). The appropriate solution varies by circumstance and focuses on what should be done to make the team more effective. Effective leaders have the ability to determine what leadership interventions are needed, if any, to solve team problems. When leadership is shared throughout the team, various members are diagnosing problems and intervening with appropriate behaviors. The monitoring and selection of behaviors is shared throughout the team membership. Given the complexity of team functioning, such shared leadership can—and, in fact, does—lead to greater team effectiveness.

Team Effectiveness

At the bottom of the Hill Model for Team Leadership (Figure 16.1) is "Team Effectiveness," which focuses on team excellence or the desired outcomes of teamwork. Two critical functions of team effectiveness are *performance* (task accomplishment) and *development* (team maintenance). *Performance* refers to the quality of the outcomes of the team's work. Did the team accomplish its goals and objectives in a quality manner? *Development* refers to the cohesiveness of the team and the ability of team members to satisfy their own needs while working effectively with other team members (Nadler, 1998). Excellent teams accomplish both of these objectives: getting the job done and maintaining a cohesive team.

Scholars have systematically studied organizational work teams and developed standards of effectiveness or criteria of excellence that can be used to assess a team's health (Hackman, 1990, 2002, 2012; Hughes, Ginnett, & Curphy, 1993; Katzenbach & Smith, 2008; LaFasto & Larson, 2001; Larson & LaFasto, 1989; Lencioni, 2005; Zaccaro et al., 2001). Hackman (2012) has posited six enabling conditions that lead to effective team functioning: (1) Is it a real team? (2) Does it have a compelling purpose? (3) Does it have the right people? (4) Are the norms of conduct clear? (5) Is there support from the organizational context? (6) Is there team-focused coaching? Larson and LaFasto (1989) studied successful teams and found that, regardless of the type of team, eight characteristics were consistently associated with team excellence. Table 16.1 demonstrates the similarity of these excellence characteristics to the enabling conditions suggested by Hackman (2012).

It is helpful if team leaders understand the conditions that contribute to or enable team excellence. Such understanding will allow the leaders to benchmark or compare their own or their team's performance to these standards and to determine possible areas of team weakness or ineffectiveness. Assessing how well the team compares to these established indicators of team success provides a valuable source of information to guide the leader to take appropriate actions to improve team success.

Enabling Conditions of Group Effectiveness (Hackman, 2012)	Characteristics of Team Excellence (Larson & LaFasto, 1989)
Compelling purpose	Clear, elevating goal
	Results-driven structure
Right people	Competent team members
Real team	Unified commitment
	Collaborative climate
Clear norms of conduct	Standards of excellence
Supportive organizational context	External support and recognition
Team-focused coaching	Principled leadership

1. *Clear, Elevating Goal.* "A compelling purpose energizes team members, orients them toward their collective objective, and fully engages their talents" (Hackman, 2012, p. 437). Team goals must be very clear so that one can tell whether the performance objective has been realized. Teams sometimes fail because they are given a vague task and then asked to work out the details (Hackman, 1990). In addition, the team goal must be involving or motivating so that the members believe it to be worthwhile and important. Teams often fail because they let something else replace their goal, such as personal agendas or power issues (Larson & LaFasto, 1989). Research data from numerous teams show that effective leaders keep the team focused on the goal (LaFasto & Larson, 2001).

Focusing the team on its goal has been identified as one of the primary responsibilities of good team leaders (Salas, Dinh, & Reyes, 2019). Based on an analysis of a wide range of literature of team leadership and how it is practiced, Salas et al. (2019) argue that at the onset of a team's formation, team leaders have a key opportunity to define team goals and the task interdependence of team members, and this effort can strongly influence the trajectory of the team. Team leaders can do so in several ways, including conducting prebriefings to instill shared affect, cognition, and behavior in team members; emphasizing a common and compelling mission; and engaging team members to work collectively.

2. *Results-Driven Structure.* Teams need to find the best structure for accomplishing their goals. Structural features that lead to effective teamwork

include task design, team composition, and core norms of conduct (Wageman, Fisher, & Hackman, 2009). Top management teams typically deal with power and influence, task forces deal with ideas and plans, customer service teams deal with clients, and production teams deal with technology (Hackman, 1990). Problem resolution teams such as task forces need a structure that emphasizes trust so that all will be willing and able to contribute. Creative teams such as advertising teams need to emphasize autonomy so that all can take risks and be free from undue censorship. Tactical teams such as emergency room teams need to emphasize clarity so that everyone knows what to do and when. In addition, all teams need clear roles for team members, a good communication system, methods of assessing individual performance, and an emphasis on fact-based judgments (Larson & LaFasto, 1989). Appropriate structures enable teams to meet their needs while still accomplishing team goals.

In their effort to answer the question of "what makes a good team leader," Salas et al. (2019) identified *initiating an enabling structure* as a first evidence-based priority. Effective structures are established by team leaders who do five things: (1) compose the group with members having a combination of knowledge, traits, and skills; (2) establish productive norms; (3) identify who is responsible and accountable for what outcomes; (4) designate the team's functions and authority; and (5) instill a sense of ownership among the members.

3. *Competent Team Members.* Teams should be composed of the right number and mix of members to accomplish all the tasks of the team. In addition, members need sufficient information, education, and training to become or remain competent team members (Hackman & Walton, 1986). As a whole, the individual team members need to possess the requisite technical competence to accomplish the team's goals. Members also need to be personally competent in interpersonal and teamwork skills. A common mistake in forming teams is to assume that people who have all the technical skills necessary to solve a problem also have the interpersonal skills necessary to collaborate effectively (Hackman, 1990). Just because someone is a good engineer or doctor does not mean one has the interpersonal skills to function on a team. Team members need certain core competencies that include the ability to do the job and the ability to solve problems. In addition, members need certain teamwork factors such as openness, supportiveness, action orientation, and a positive personal style (LaFasto & Larson, 2001).

4. *Unified Commitment.* A common mistake is to call a work group a team but treat it as a collection of individuals (Hackman, 1990). Teams do not just happen: They are carefully designed and developed. Excellent teams are those that have developed a sense of unity or identification. Such team spirit often can be developed by involving members in all aspects of the process (Larson & LaFasto, 1989).

5. *Collaborative Climate.* The ability of a team to collaborate or work well together is essential to team effectiveness. A collaborative climate is one in which members can stay problem focused, listen to and understand one another, feel free to take risks, and be willing to compensate for one another. To build an atmosphere that fosters collaboration, we need to develop trusting relationships based on honesty, openness, consistency, and respect (Larson & LaFasto, 1989). Integration of individual actions is one of the fundamental characteristics of effective teams. Team members each have their own unique roles that they typically perform to contribute to the team's success. Team failure may result from the members' "collective failure to coordinate and synchronize their individual contributions" (Zaccaro et al., 2001, p. 451). Effective team leaders can facilitate a collaborative climate by managing their own needs to control, by making communication safe, by demanding and rewarding collaborative behavior, and by guiding the team's problem-solving efforts (LaFasto & Larson, 2001).

Similar to building a collaborative climate, Salas et al. (2019) underscore the importance of team leaders fostering a climate where team members experience psychological safety. A climate of safety emerges when team leaders admit their own faults, solicit input and ideas from others, and provide developmental debriefing sessions. In safe environments, team members feel comfortable to be open and express themselves more often because the team leader is supportive and nondefensive when they do. This environment allows team members to also feel more competent about expressing themselves.

6. *Standards of Excellence.* Clear norms of conduct (how we should behave) are important for team functioning (Hackman, 2012). Team members' performance should be regulated so that actions can be coordinated and tasks completed (Hackman & Walton, 1986). It is especially important that the organizational context or the team itself set up standards of excellence so that members will feel pressure to perform at their highest levels. The standards must be clear and concrete, and all team members must be required to perform to standard (Larson & LaFasto, 1989). A team leader can facilitate this process by requiring results—making expectations clear; reviewing results—providing feedback to resolve performance issues; and rewarding results—acknowledging superior performance (LaFasto & Larson, 2001). With such standards in place and monitored, members will be encouraged to perform at their highest levels.

Consistent with establishing standards of excellence, Salas et al.'s (2019) insights on what makes a good team leader suggest that team leaders have to reinforce teamwork with feedback and rewards. Team leaders need to establish clear indicators for individual and group performance and objectively monitor their performance. In addition to rewarding individuals for jobs well done, rewards for excellent performance must be provided at the team level.

7. *External Support and Recognition.* A supportive organizational context includes material resources, rewards for excellent performance, an educational system to develop necessary team skills, and an information system to provide data needed to accomplish the task (Wageman et al., 2009). A common mistake is to give organizational teams challenging assignments but fail to give them organizational support to accomplish these assignments (Hackman, 1990). The leader must identify which type of support is needed and intervene as needed to secure this support (Hackman, 2002). The best goals, team members, and commitment will not mean much if there is no money, equipment, or supplies for accomplishing the goals. Also, organizations often ask employees to work on a difficult team assignment and then do not reward them with raises or bonuses for that performance. Hyatt and Ruddy (1997) found that having systems in place to support teams (clear direction, information, data, resources, rewards, and training) enables the team to become more effective and achieve performance goals. Teams can achieve excellence if they are given the resources needed to do their jobs, are recognized for team accomplishments, and are rewarded for team performance rather than for individual performances (Larson & LaFasto, 1989).

An important, but often overlooked, aspect of reward and recognition is when a team leader supports the growth of team members by providing mentoring and development opportunities. Salas et al. (2019) found that good team leaders support the growth of team members by acting as coaches and helping facilitate their work. Included in this support are debriefings at the outset, at midterm, and in the final stages of the group task efforts. Debriefings provide a chance for team members to dialogue about what they have learned, and this information can improve their performance when facing new challenges. In addition, a good team leader finds and provides team members with opportunities for learning and new skills development.

8. *Principled Leadership.* Effective team leadership has been found to consistently relate to team effectiveness (Zaccaro, Heinen, & Shuffler, 2009). Leadership has been described as the central driver of team effectiveness, influencing the team through four sets of processes: cognitive, motivational, affective, and coordinate (Zaccaro et al., 2001). Cognitively, the leader helps the team understand the problems confronting the team. Motivationally, the leader helps the team become cohesive and capable by setting high performance standards and helping the team to achieve them. Affectively, the leader helps the team handle stressful circumstances by providing clear goals, assignments, and strategies. Coordinately, the leader helps integrate the team's activities by matching members' skills to roles, providing clear performance strategies, monitoring feedback, and adapting to environmental changes.

Effective team leaders are committed to the team's goals and give members autonomy to unleash their talents when possible. Leaders can reduce the effectiveness of their team by being unwilling to confront inadequate performance, diluting the team's ability to perform by having too many priorities, and overestimating the positive aspects of team performance. Leaders can enhance the effectiveness of their team by keeping the team focused on its goals, maintaining a collaborative climate, building confidence among members, demonstrating technical competence, setting priorities, and managing performance (Larson & LaFasto, 1989). It is essential that the leadership of the team be assessed along with the other criteria of team excellence. Such feedback is essential to the health and effectiveness of the team.

The leadership of the team can use these eight characteristics of team excellence (Table 16.1) in a normative fashion to assess the health of the team and to take appropriate action to address any weaknesses. If team leaders assess that one or more of the eight characteristics of team success are not being achieved, then they need to address these weaknesses. Continually assessing the standards of team effectiveness can also provide feedback, enabling leaders to determine whether past actions and interventions had the desired results. To assess team effectiveness, team leaders need to use whatever tools are at their disposal, such as direct observation, surveys, feedback, and performance indicators. The information gained from the analysis of team effectiveness can provide feedback to the leader and guide future leadership decisions. The line on the Hill Model for Team Leadership (Figure 16.1) that connects the "Team Effectiveness" box at the bottom to the "Leadership Decisions" box at the top reflects the ongoing learning process of data gathering, analysis, and decision making. Such feedback loops demonstrate the dynamic and evolving nature of teams (Ilgen et al., 2005). Past leadership decisions and actions are reflected in the team's performance and relational outcomes. In turn, these indicators of team effectiveness shape the future analysis and decisions of the team leadership.

Leadership Decisions

At the top of the Hill Model for Team Leadership (Figure 16.1) are "Leadership Decisions," which include the major decisions the team's leadership needs to make when determining whether and how to intervene to improve team functioning. The first of these decisions is whether it is most appropriate to continue to observe and monitor the team or to intervene in the team's activities and take action. The second decision is to choose whether a task or a relational intervention is needed (i.e., does the team need help in accomplishing its tasks, or does it need help in maintaining relationships?). The final decision is whether to intervene at the internal level (within the team itself) or at the external level (in the team's environment).

Leadership Decision 1: Should I monitor the team or take action? The first decision confronting the team's leadership is whether to keep observing the team or to take action to help the team. McGrath (as cited in Hackman & Walton, 1986) outlined the critical leadership functions of group effectiveness, taking into account the analysis of the situation both internally and externally and whether this analysis indicates that the leader should take an immediate action. Figure 16.2, "McGrath's Critical Leadership Functions," demonstrates these two dimensions of leadership behavior: *monitoring versus taking action* and *internal group issues versus external group issues.* As leaders, we can diagnose, analyze, or forecast problems (monitoring), or we can take immediate action to solve a problem. We can also focus on the problems within the group (internal) or the problems outside the group (external). These two dimensions result in the four types of team leadership functions shown in Figure 16.2.

FIGURE 16.2 McGrath's Critical Leadership Functions

	MONITOR	EXECUTIVE ACTION
INTERNAL	1 Diagnosing Group Deficiencies	2 Taking Remedial Action
EXTERNAL	3 Forecasting Environmental Changes	4 Preventing Deleterious Changes

Source: Based on McGrath's critical leadership functions as cited in "Leading Groups in Organizations," by J. R. Hackman and R. E. Walton, 1986, in P. S. Goodman & Associates (Eds.), *Designing Effective Work Groups* (p. 76). San Francisco, CA: Jossey-Bass.

Quadrants 1 and 2 in Figure 16.2 focus on the internal operations of the team. In Quadrant 1, the leader is diagnosing group deficiencies, and in Quadrant 2, the leader is acting to repair or remedy the observed problems. Quadrants 3 and 4 focus on the external operations of the team. In the third quadrant, the leader is scanning the environment to determine and forecast any external changes that will affect the group. In the fourth quadrant, the leader acts to prevent any negative changes in the environment from hurting the team.

Therefore, the first decision confronting the team's leadership is "Should I continue monitoring these factors, or should I take action based on the information I have already gathered and structured?" To develop an accurate mental model of team functioning, leaders need to monitor both the internal and external environments to gather information, reduce equivocality, provide structure, and overcome barriers. Fleishman et al. (1991) described two phases in this initial process: information search and structuring. First a leader must seek out information to understand the current state of the team's functioning (information search), and then this information must be analyzed, organized, and interpreted so the leader can decide how to act (information structuring). Leaders can also help their information search process by obtaining feedback from team members, networking with others outside the team, conducting team assessment surveys, and evaluating team outcomes. Once information on the team is gathered, the leader needs to structure or interpret this information in order to make action plans. Virtual teams operate under the same group dynamics principles and also need to monitor and intervene as appropriate (Berry, 2011).

All members of the team can engage in monitoring (information search and structuring) and collectively provide distributed or shared leadership to help the team adapt to changing conditions. In fast-paced, rapidly changing situations, the team leader and members might have to work in concert to assess the situation accurately. The official leader of the team might be too busy processing information from the environment to process information internal to the team. The team members can help the leader by staying on top of internal problems. Together, they can form an accurate picture of the team's effectiveness.

In addition to gathering and interpreting information, team leaders must take the right action based on this information. Determining the right action to take is at the very heart of team leadership. It involves selecting from among competing courses of action to facilitate the team's work (Barge, 1996). Leaders differ in their tendencies to take action; they either do so quickly (hasty to act) or delay taking action by analyzing the situation at length (slow to act). While "hasty to act" leaders might prevent problems from getting out of control, they might not make the right intervention if they do not have all the information, and such fast action might undermine the development of shared leadership. "Slow to act" leaders might encourage other team members to emerge as leaders (shared leadership), but the action-taking delay might cause the team's problem to become unmanageable.

The exact timing of a leadership intervention is as important as the specific type of intervention (Wageman et al., 2009). It has been proposed that groups go through developmental stages of forming, storming, norming, performing, and adjourning (Tuckman & Jensen, 2010). Certain behaviors are common and even expected at each of these stages. If, for example, conflict was occurring during the storming stage of team life, the leadership might not intervene at that time but just continue monitoring. Or, the leadership might choose an intervention that advances the team to the next phase of norming. Others have described three phases of group life and the leadership needed during each: (1) motivational coaching (at start), (2) consultative coaching (at midpoint), and (3) educational coaching (at end). The important aspect of timing is that the leader should understand where the team is in its life cycle and provide the type of leadership needed at that time (Hackman, 2012).

Leadership Decision 2: Should I intervene to meet task or relational needs? Returning to the top box in Figure 16.1 ("Leadership Decisions"), the second decision confronting the leader is whether the team needs help in dealing with relational issues or task issues. Since the early study of small groups, the focus has been on two critical leadership functions: task and maintenance. Task leadership functions include getting the job done, making decisions, solving problems, adapting to changes, making plans, and achieving goals. Maintenance functions include developing a positive climate, solving interpersonal problems, satisfying members' needs, and developing cohesion. These two functions have also been referred to in terms of performance and development (i.e., how well the team has accomplished its task and how well the team has developed effective relationships).

Superior team leadership focuses constantly on both task and maintenance functions (Kinlaw, 1998); both types of leadership behaviors (task-focused and person-focused) have been found to be related to perceived team effectiveness (Burke et al., 2006). Task functions are closely intertwined with relational functions. If the team is well maintained and has good interpersonal relationships, then the members will be able to work together effectively and get their job done. If not, they will spend all of their time infighting, sniping, and working at cross-purposes. Similarly, if the team is productive and successful in accomplishing its task, it will be easier to maintain a positive climate and good relations. Conversely, failing teams often take their lack of performance out on each other, and fighting teams often accomplish little.

In virtual teams connected across time and space by electronic media, it is important to focus on both task and relational issues (Han & Beyerlein, 2016). The focus on building team relationships is even more critical for virtual teams than for traditional co-located teams. Virtual team leaders must be able to "read" all the personal and contextual nuances in a world of electronic communications. They must be able to understand the possible causes of silence, misunderstanding, and slights without any of the usual signs to guide them. Leaders must be sensitive to the team process and must pay attention to even small matters that could interfere with the team's success (Pauleen, 2004). Virtual teams place even greater demands on team leaders—50% more time investment—than the more traditional co-located team (Dyer, Dyer, & Dyer, 2007).

Research suggests that leaders of virtual teams should begin the team with face-to-face meetings, if possible, to facilitate trust, comfort, and rapport. In addition, virtual team leaders need to focus on project management and regular, organized team meetings. However, virtual team leaders need to be careful not to be too task focused, and work to develop social relationships among the team. Virtual team leaders also need to keep literate in all new communication technologies and know when to use them for optimal teamwork (Humbley, O'Neill, & Kline, 2009). As the prevalence of virtual teams expands, specific leadership issues and interventions related to these virtual teams are increasingly becoming the focus of study (Berry, 2011; Cordery, Soo, Kirkman, Rosen, & Mathieu, 2009; Zaccaro, Ardison, & Orvis, 2004).

Leadership Decision 3: Should I intervene internally or externally? If a decision was made to take action or intervene, the leader must make the third strategic leadership decision in Figure 16.1 and determine what level of the team process needs leadership attention: internal leadership actions or external leadership actions. Does the leader need to intervene inside of the team, or is the problem external to the team? Effective team leaders analyze and balance the internal and external demands of the team and react appropriately (Barge, 1996).

Is there internal conflict between members of the team? Then perhaps taking an *internal relational action* to maintain the team and improve interpersonal relationships will be most appropriate. Are the team goals unclear? Then perhaps an *internal task intervention* is needed to focus on goals. Is the organizational environment not providing proper support to the team to do its job? Then perhaps an *external environmental intervention* focusing on obtaining external support for the team is the most appropriate intervention.

The current focus of research is on real-life organizational work teams that exist within a larger organizational environment. In addition to balancing the internal task and relational needs of the team, the leader has to help the team adapt to and function effectively in its environment. Most teams focus on the internal problems of the team. But it is increasingly important for teams to also be externally oriented to "reach across boundaries to forge dense networks of connection, both inside and outside the organization," so that they can deal effectively with the fast-changing environment (Ancona, Bresman, & Caldwell, 2009).

Leadership Actions

The middle section of the Hill Model for Team Leadership (Figure 16.1) lists a number of specific leadership actions that can be performed internally ("Task" and "Relational") or externally ("Environmental"). These lists are not exhaustive but are compiled from research on team excellence and team performance discussed earlier in this chapter. For example, teams that have clear goals, clear standards, effective structure, and effective decision making will have higher task performance. Teams that can manage conflict, collaborate well together, and build commitment will have good relationships. Teams that are well connected to and protected from their environment will also be more productive.

It is up to the leader to assess what action, if any, is needed and then intervene with the specific leadership function to meet the demands of the situation. The leader needs the ability to perform these skills and to make a strategic choice as to the most *appropriate function or skill* for the intervention. For example, if team members were arguing, the leader might decide to initiate conflict management. *To be an effective leader, one needs to respond with the action that is required of the situation.* Thus, it is the job of the leader to analyze and mediate the situation to make the best decisions for the good of the team. A detailed knowledge of group dynamics and interpersonal processes is key to effective team leadership.

A team leader also needs to recognize and interpret what is getting in the way of the team's goal accomplishment and then make a strategic choice and respond with the appropriate action (Gouran & Hirokawa, 1996). If a problem is diagnosed as a team performance problem, then the leader needs to determine the appropriate action to solve this task problem (e.g., goal focusing, standard setting, or training). If a problem is diagnosed as a team development problem, then the leader needs to determine the appropriate action to solve this relational problem (e.g., managing conflict or building commitment). If a problem is diagnosed as an environmental problem, then the leader needs to determine the appropriate action to solve this context problem (e.g., networking, advocating, or sharing information).

Internal Task Leadership Actions. The "Task" box in the Hill Model for Team Leadership (Figure 16.1) lists the set of skills or actions that the leader might perform to improve task performance. After monitoring the team's performance, the leader might choose to intervene in one of the following task areas:

- *Goal focusing* (clarifying, gaining agreement)
  For example, if team members seem to be going off in different directions, the leader might intervene to clarify the team's goals or work with members to obtain agreement on goals.

- *Structuring for results* (planning, visioning, organizing, clarifying roles, delegating)
  For example, if the team is stuck in day-to-day affairs and not looking to or building for the future, then the leader might intervene by helping the team vision and plan for the future.

- *Facilitating decision making* (informing, controlling, coordinating, mediating, synthesizing, focusing on issues)
  For example, if team members are not adequately sharing information with each other, the leader might ask questions to seek out the information that is not being shared.

- *Training team members in task skills* (educating, developing)
  For example, if the team members do not have the skills necessary to make well-reasoned decisions, the leader might provide a training seminar in decision making.

- *Maintaining standards of excellence* (assessing team and individual performance, confronting inadequate performance)

For example, if some team members are coming late to meetings or not attending meetings, the leader might take direct action and confront them to address their inadequate performance.

Internal Relational Leadership Actions. The second set of internal leadership actions in Figure 16.1 reflects those that the leader needs to implement to improve team relationships. After monitoring the team's performance, the leader might choose to intervene in one of the following relational areas:

- *Coaching team members in interpersonal skills*
  For example, if team members do not seem to be listening to one another, then the leader might intervene by leading them in a listening exercise.

- *Collaborating* (including, involving)
  For example, if some team members are not taking others' opinions into account, then the leader might intervene to encourage compromise.

- *Managing conflict and power issues* (fighting or avoiding confrontation, questioning ideas, avoiding groupthink)
  For example, if the members are not questioning ideas and are just agreeing with each other in order to move quickly to a decision, then the leader might intervene by providing a discussion on the negative aspects of groupthink (Neck & Manz, 1994).

- *Building commitment and esprit de corps* (being optimistic, innovating, envisioning, socializing, rewarding, recognizing)
  For example, if the team seems to have low morale, the leader could intervene to build commitment and unity by recognizing past team successes.

- *Satisfying individual member needs* (trusting, supporting, advocating)
  For example, if a team member seems stressed due to disrespect from other members, the leader might provide support to the upset member and advocate to the team on this individual's behalf.

- *Modeling ethical and principled practices* (fair, consistent, normative)
  For example, if the team is inconsistent vis-à-vis the in-group members sometimes being treated differently than the out-group members, then the leader might intervene and model a change in behavior to be fair and consistent to all members.

External Environmental Leadership Actions. The "External Leadership Actions" (Figure 16.1) reflect those actions the leader might implement to improve the environmental interface with the team. Real-life teams do not exist in a laboratory—they are subsystems of the larger organizational and societal context. To stay viable, the team needs to monitor this environment closely and determine what actions should be taken to enhance team effectiveness (Barge, 1996; Hyatt & Ruddy, 1997; Zaccaro et al., 2001). If environmental monitoring suggests a leadership intervention, then the leader needs to select from the following functions:

- *Networking and forming alliances in the environment* (gathering information, increasing influence)

  For example, if the team's members are not well known or are not well connected throughout the organization, then the leader might intervene by interacting and forming relationships with powerful and respected individuals in the organization.

- *Advocating and representing the team to the environment*

  For example, if organizational superiors are unaware of the team's successes, the leader might initiate an FYI policy, sending information about all successes upward as they happen. The leader could also initiate a team newsletter that chronicles team efforts to accomplish the same function but to a broader context.

- *Negotiating upward to secure necessary resources, support, and recognition for the team*

  For example, a leader might determine that the team does not have enough clerical support to accomplish its goals. The leader could then negotiate with upper management to provide the needed support or, if failing in this, to persuade upper management to alter the team's goals accordingly.

- *Buffering team members from environmental distractions*

  For example, if the team is overloaded with tasks, then the leader might intervene by keeping unnecessary demands and distractions away from the team members so that they can concentrate on their goals.

- *Assessing environmental indicators of the team's effectiveness* (surveys, evaluations, performance indicators)

  For example, if the leader observes that the members of the team have no way of knowing how well they are doing, the leader can provide data from the environment as to how their performance stacks up with other teams.

- *Sharing relevant environmental information with the team*

  For example, if the team leader reviews the environment and finds that the organization's business is going in a new direction, the leader can share this information with the team to keep members in line with these new directions.

Team leadership is complex; there are no simple recipes for team success. Team leaders must learn to be open and objective in understanding and diagnosing team problems and skillful in selecting the most appropriate actions (or inactions) to help achieve the team's goals. It is important to reemphasize that these critical functions need not be carried out only by the leader. Experienced members in a mature team might share these leadership behaviors. As long as the team's critical needs have been met, the leadership behavior, whether enacted by the leader or by team members, has been effective. *The key assertion of the functional perspective is that the leader is to do whatever is necessary to take care of unmet needs of the team.* If the team members are taking care of most of the needs, then the leader has to do very little.

HOW DOES THE TEAM LEADERSHIP MODEL WORK?

Team leaders and team members can use the model to help them make decisions about the current state of their team and the specific actions they need to take, if any, to improve the team's functioning. The model portrays leadership as a team oversight function in which the leader's role is to do whatever is necessary to help the team achieve effectiveness. The model provides the leader with a cognitive map for identifying team needs, and offers suggestions about how to take appropriate corrective actions. The model helps the leader make sense of the complexity of teams and offers practical suggestions based on theory and research.

In using the model, the team leadership engages in the leader mediation process by deciding which option is most appropriate for the team: monitoring or taking action. If the monitoring reveals that all aspects of the team's functioning are satisfactory, then the leadership should not take any direct actions but continue to monitor the internal and external environments in terms of team performance and development. If monitoring reveals that action is needed, then the leadership decides whether to take an internal-level action or an external-level action or both. Finally, the leadership decides which action is appropriate to meet the needs of the team.

Determining the exact intervention is not as easy as it sounds, however, and it clearly reflects the skills necessary for team leadership. For example, a leader monitoring the internal functioning of the team notices there is infighting for control and power. The leader may see this as an *internal relationship problem* because of the authoritarian and autocratic behavior of one team member. Or perhaps the leader sees it as an *internal task problem* because the structure of the team is not appropriate and the roles and responsibilities of some members are unclear. The leader may also see the problem as an *external environmental problem* because the team is not given sufficient autonomy from the organization; consequently, the members are fighting over what little power and control exist. Or perhaps the leader sees the conflict as temporary given the stage of group development (e.g., storming).

In any case, the leader can decide to keep monitoring the situation and not take any immediate action because of the group's phase of development. Or the leader can decide at which level to intervene and then decide to enact the most appropriate leadership function at that level. The leader can even decide to intervene at all three levels, addressing the authoritarian individual (internal, relational), clarifying team roles (internal, task), and negotiating more team autonomy with those higher up in the organization (external).

The team leadership model aids in team analysis and improvement, much like that of sports teams. In sports, the coach does not stop working just because the team is winning. The coach keeps working to build commitment, develop young players, share expertise, create new methods and strategies, and generally improve team functioning. The effective coach never rests on past successes, but works to improve the team's functioning for the future. After a win or a loss, a football coach will have the team review videos of the game to determine areas of success and failure. Organizational team leaders could learn a great deal from sports team coaches. By comparing their own teams with established standards or criteria of team excellence, leaders can determine the areas of greatest weakness that might need critical intervention.

The Hill Model for Team Leadership has clear implications for the effectiveness of team leadership. The study of team leadership has a number of strengths and weaknesses, which will be reviewed next.

STRENGTHS

One of the strengths of team leadership is that it is designed to focus on the real-life organizational work group and the leadership needed therein. The model places the ongoing work group or team in an environmental context within the organization, industry, or society. In addition, the real-life focus on performance and team effectiveness enables leaders and members to diagnose and correct team problems. A team leader can present the model to the team as a teaching tool. By learning what constitutes excellent teams and applying these criteria to team performance, leaders and members can learn how to better lead teams to the highest levels of excellence. Team leadership focuses on internal and external environments, which encompasses the scope of leadership in teams. Leaders must address dynamics within the team while monitoring the organizational and external environment to assess impacts on the team. Given the inclusion of external leadership, the model can encompass the shift to multi-team systems (MTSs) in organizations. MTSs are needed to solve complex problems that one team cannot address. External team leadership is needed to coordinate overarching goals within MTSs (Shuffler & Carter, 2018).

A second strength of team leadership is that it provides guidelines that help leaders to design and maintain effective teams, especially when performance is below standards. Such an approach is consistent with the emerging theoretical notions of the leader as a medium whose job it is to process the complex information inherent in teamwork (Fisher, 1985). Any model or theory that tries to simplify such a complex process would be inappropriate and inadequate. The team leadership model is not simplistic, and it integrates in a manageable and practical form many complex factors that can help a leader be a good medium or processor of information.

Another strength of the model is that it takes into account the changing role of leaders and followers in organizations (shared leadership). This is consistent with a paradigm shift from top-down, hierarchical leadership toward more horizontal, team processes that has been occurring for the past 20 years (Friedrich, Griffith, & Mumford, 2016). The model does not focus on the position of power of a leader, but instead focuses on the critical functions of leadership as diagnosis and action taking. Any team member can perform the critical leadership functions to assess the current effectiveness of the team and then take appropriate action. This approach is consistent with the current movement in organizations to rethink leadership responsibilities in work teams. The responsibilities or functions of team leadership—such as setting goals, coaching, and rewarding—historically have rested with the team's formal leader, but now, with organizational restructuring, these duties and responsibilities often are distributed across the team. A meta-analysis found that shared leadership in teams is significantly and positively related to team performance (D'Innocenzo, Mathieu, & Kukenberger, 2016).

In addition, this approach to team leadership can help in selection of team leaders and team members. If a leader must be chosen for the team, it might be best to select one who is perceptive, open, objective, analytical, and a good listener who has good diagnostic skills. In addition, it would be wise to select a leader who has a wide repertoire of action-taking skills and is comfortable intervening in the team's processes in many ways, such as with negotiation, conflict resolution, problem solving, goal focusing, and influencing upward. Good leaders not only can diagnose the team's problems, but also can reach into their bag of tricks and pull out the appropriate action or actions. For example, if a leader determines that two members of a team are in conflict with one another, the leader needs to be able to determine the root cause of that conflict and select the most appropriate action (or select nonaction).

CRITICISMS

The Hill Model for Team Leadership (Figure 16.1) is a conceptual framework to assist team-based leadership in its decision making. As such, it lists only some of the many skills that leadership might need to employ in making such decisions. Depending on the type of team or situation, additional skills might be needed that focus more on the environment (Cobb, 2012), coaching and training (Zaccaro et al., 2009), or preplanning and timing (Wageman et al., 2009). A team might need to modify the model to include skills that are particularly relevant to its effectiveness. The model does not include factors that may influence team effectiveness such as individual differences of team leaders and members and aspects of the organizational context such as organizational culture or team size.

Even though the model does not include all possible leadership skills, it is still quite complex. Team leaders need to spend time adjusting to the framework so that it comes naturally to them when decisions are needed. This framework also does not provide on-the-spot answers to specific problems facing the team leader, such as "When is the best time to intervene?" "What do you say to a member who is upset and crying?" or "What specific action do you take to deal with an organizational culture that is not supporting teamwork?" The model only points the leader in the right direction and suggests skills needed to solve these complex problems. The model is not specific on what team leadership skills work best in particular situations. It is more descriptive than prescriptive. The model assumes that the leader is skilled in group process, decision making, interpersonal communication, conflict resolution, and other abilities.

To make matters worse, many teams have shared leadership necessitating that everyone who provides team leadership has a wide range of team-oriented skills. In addition, the roles of leaders and followers can change over time, making it very important for the team leader and team members to possess the requisite leadership skills. In immature teams leaders might need to take on more of the leadership roles, whereas in a mature team the leader might be able to sit back and let the team lead itself. Increasingly, scholars are providing instruction in diagnosing weaknesses in team leadership skills and offering methods for development and improvement (Cobb, 2012; Levi, 2011; Morgeson et al., 2010; Salas, Burke, & Stagl, 2004). Instruction in teamwork and team leadership needs to focus on team diagnosing and action taking so that team leadership skills can be developed throughout the team and be more easily implemented.

Methods for testing and measuring outcomes of team leadership models are not fully refined. Most of the research is based on follower perceptions of team leader behavior, and while these studies provide some guidance, subjective perceptions of team leadership may be biased. Rather than rely on team member ratings, team training should rely on the observation of the team leadership's behaviors as factors in determining team success (Cook, Zill, & Meyer, 2020).

APPLICATION

The primary function of team leadership is to guide the team in accomplishing its goals by monitoring and diagnosing the team and taking the requisite action. There are many ways to apply the team leadership model to increase the effectiveness of organizational teams. The model is useful in helping the leader make decisions: Should I act? If so, how should I do so? For example, if the team is not performing effectively (*team effectiveness*), then the leader can make the first strategic choice by monitoring the situation or acting to improve team functioning. If an action seems warranted, then the leader needs to decide whether the action should be directed inward toward team functioning, outward toward the environment, or both. Once the context for the action is determined, leaders need to choose the most appropriate skill for the situation from their behavioral repertoire. It is important to continue monitoring the results of the intervention and adapting accordingly, depending on these results.

The leader might choose to use an assessment tool such as the Team Excellence and Collaborative Team Leader Questionnaire included in this chapter to help conduct the team's diagnosis and set the steps needed for taking action. Team members are asked to fill out the questionnaire, as is the team leader. The results are fed back to the team members and team leader, allowing them to see the areas of greatest strength and weakness. It is particularly important that both the team leader and team members fill out the questionnaire. Research suggests that team leaders overestimate their effectiveness on these dimensions and often score themselves much higher than do team members (LaFasto & Larson, 2001). By comparing the scores by leaders and by members, the leader along with team members can determine which dimensions of team or leadership effectiveness need improvement. The team and leader can then prepare action plans to correct the highest-priority problems. Such a team assessment approach is very helpful in monitoring and diagnosing team problems. It aids in determining the complex factors affecting team excellence to build a committed team involved in action planning.

Finally, presenting a view from a practical standpoint, Salas, Dinh, and Reyes (2019) reviewed existing research on team leadership and developed key insights that can guide the practice of team leadership. These insights follow the life span of a team from its creation to its sustainment—and reflect many of the components outlined in the Hill Model for Team Leadership (Figure 16.1). These team leadership behaviors reflect the internal functions of task and relational leadership. For example, team leaders create structure and define tasks (task leadership). They also create psychological safety (relational leadership). The external functions discussed in Hill's model are reflected in ensuring that the organization provides rewards to team members as well as the training needed for growth and development of team members.

CASE STUDIES

To improve your understanding of the team leadership model, refer to Cases 16.1, 16.2, and 16.3. For each case, you will be asked to put yourself in the role of team leader and apply the team leadership model in analyzing and offering solutions to the team problems.

Case 16.1 TEAM CRISIS WITHIN THE GATES

Axis Global is a giant oil and gas company that owns nine refineries worldwide and is headquartered in Paris, France. Axis Global's refineries convert crude oil into gasoline, jet fuel, and other products, and each refinery has an information technology (IT) team located "within the refinery gates" that reports to the refinery's management team. Each IT team is responsible for the operation and maintenance of computers and applications that are critical to the safe and efficient operation of its refinery.

In addition to refineries, Axis Global owns and operates oil wells, pipelines, chemical plants, and gas stations across the globe. As a result, some IT operations are standardized across the company, and a centralized team located in Paris makes those decisions for all the IT teams in the company. Recently, the centralized IT organization concluded that IT services company-wide should be outsourced to a third party. Outsourcing means most of the company's IT personnel are no longer employed by Axis Global, and the third party will decide which, if any, of Axis Global's IT employees it will retain, replace, or terminate.

Axis Global has recently notified the Tappan Refinery in Pennsylvania of the global decision to outsource all IT teams. Top executives at the Tappan Refinery are unhappy with the decision because they were not consulted before the decision was made and few details were provided to Tappan's executives on how the outsourcing would be implemented. In addition, these executives are worried that the decision will negatively affect essential tasks performed by Tappan's IT team and result in increased costs. The management at Tappan Refinery is opposed to changing its current IT operations.

Russ Saffold manages IT at the Tappan Refinery and has three members on his team: Alejandro Salis, Samantha Umbia, and Todd Greengold. The IT team is well respected by everyone in the refinery, and their interpersonal relationships are solid. All four team members are officially employees of Axis Global and physically work within the refinery gates at Tappan. Because refineries are frequently bought and sold among oil companies, the refineries prefer to operate as self-contained organizations (i.e., "within the gates"). They have a bunker mentality vis-à-vis the larger organization and often see that relationship between a refinery and the parent organization as "us versus them." Employee loyalty is to the refinery, not to Axis Global.

The outsourcing news creates a crisis within Russ Saffold's IT team. Although Russ will remain an employee of Axis, the other three team members will not. The three team members are now unsure of their futures and find it difficult to focus on their work tasks. Alejandro Salis (age 43) is fairly confident that he will be hired by the outsourcing company as he is the "star" on the team. Samantha Umbia (age 31) fears she will be terminated as she is unable to relocate to the outsourcing company's location. Todd Greengold (age 62) is worried that he will lose his stock options and pension if he is terminated or transferred to the outsourcing company. And the entire team worries about how they will be treated by their new employer. Morale of the team members sinks, and with the likelihood of fewer positions, competition among them begins to emerge. Russ finds himself in the middle of implementing a decision that is unclear, is opposed by his bosses at Tappan Refinery, and is creating personal issues with his staff. He wonders how he will establish a working relationship with the outsourcing company.

Questions

1. Should Russ Saffold intervene to help his team handle this crisis? If so, what type of leadership action should he take? Internal task? Internal relational? External environmental?

2. What leadership actions, if any, should team members take?

3. What should Russ Saffold do (if anything) to mitigate the two opposing positions regarding outsourcing of IT (Axis Global versus Tappan Refinery)?

4. What characteristics of team excellence are currently lacking in this team?

Case 16.2 STARTS WITH A BANG, ENDS WITH A WHIMPER

A faculty member, Kim Green from the Management Department, was asked to chair a major university committee to plan the mission of the university for the next 20 years. Three other senior faculty and seven administrators from across the campus were also asked to serve on this committee. The president of the university, Dr. Sulgrave, gave the committee its charge: What should Northcoast University be like in the year 2020? Dr. Sulgrave told the committee that the work of this task force was of utmost importance to the future of the university, and the charge of this committee should take precedence over all other matters. The task force was allowed to meet in the president's conference room and use the president's assistant. The report of the committee was due in two months.

(Continued)

(Continued)

The task force members felt very good about being selected for such an important team. The team met on a weekly basis for about two hours each time. At first, the members were very interested in the task and participated enthusiastically. They were required to do a great deal of outside research. They came back to the meetings proud to share their research and knowledge. However, after a while the meetings did not go well. The members could not seem to agree on what the charge to the team meant. They argued about what they were supposed to accomplish and resented the time the committee was taking from their regular jobs. Week after week the team met but accomplished nothing. Attendance became a problem, with people skipping several meetings, showing up late, or leaving early. Team members stopped working on their committee assignments. Green didn't want to admit to the university president that the team didn't know what it was doing; instead, she just got more and more frustrated. Meetings became sporadic and eventually stopped altogether. The president was involved in a crisis at the university and seemed to lose interest in the committee. The president never called for the report from the committee, and the report was never completed.

Questions

1. Which characteristics of excellence were lacking in this task force?

2. Which characteristics of excellence were evident in this task force?

3. How would you assess Green as a leader?

4. What actions would you take (internally or externally) if you were the leader of this task force?

Case 16.3   1980 U.S. OLYMPIC HOCKEY TEAM

The 1980 U.S. ice hockey team pulled off one of the greatest upsets in Olympic history, defeating the Soviet Union's team 4–3 before defeating Finland 4–2 to win the gold medal. It was only the second Olympic gold medal for the United States in ice hockey since the sport was introduced to the games in 1920.

Winning the Olympic medal was sweet, but what made this such an upset was the U.S. victory over the Soviet team. The Soviet Union had long dominated Olympic ice hockey, having won seven gold medals since 1956 and not losing an Olympic hockey game since 1968.

There were stark differences between the two teams. Nicknamed the "Red Machine," the Soviet team was made up of professional athletes who had played together for years as the Soviet national team. Despite this being common knowledge, team members had been bogusly designated as students, engineers, or soldiers to maintain the amateur status then required of Olympic athletes. The Soviets were coached by Viktor Tikhonov, a former KGB officer who used a Soviet military style of coaching and leadership that demanded strict obedience and total commitment from all of his players (Shevchenko, 2018). All of the Soviet players lived together for 11 months in a training camp and were not allowed to leave for any reason. The team's total commitment to ice hockey and upholding the Soviet ice hockey tradition was evident in its success, and many saw it as a testimony to the effectiveness of communist leadership and Tikhonov's ability to create effective teams (Lapin, 2015).

Coached by Herb Brooks, the U.S. team was made up of college and amateur hockey players with an average age of 21. Before being tapped to coach the 1980 Olympic team, Brooks was the coach at the University of Minnesota, where he had taken a last-place team and transformed it, amassing one of the most impressive winning records in Division I hockey (175–100–20), including three NCAA championships in 1974, 1976, and 1979. Brooks was no stranger to Olympic hockey, either. Although he had been cut from the 1960 Olympic team days before the games started, Brooks went on to play on eight U.S. national and Olympic teams, including the 1964 and 1968 Olympic teams (Bernstein, 2006).

But Brooks wasn't an automatic choice for the Olympic coaching job; he applied to be the coach in 1978, and after the committee's first choice declined, they met with Brooks. He came prepared with binders outlining his plan for player selection, staffing, conditioning, pre-Olympic scheduling, and his proposed style of play. The last was the most surprising: Brooks wanted to abandon the traditional dump-and-chase, reactive style of North American hockey that had been so successful for his Minnesota teams, and retrain the athletes to play a hybrid style that imitated the Soviets' physical game, phenomenal conditioning, and stickhandling prowess. He got the job (Coffey, 2005).

From the outset, Brooks was determined to find the right players for the team. "My recruiting key—I looked for PEOPLE first, athletes second," he said. "I wanted people with a sound value system as you cannot buy values. You're only as good as your values. I learned early on that you do not put greatness into people . . . but somehow try to pull it out" (Herb Brooks Foundation, n.d.).

Brooks looked for players at the National Sports Festival in Colorado Springs in June 1979. He didn't look for the most talented players, opting for those who could skate hard and fast, who exhibited a work ethic and willingness to embrace his new hybrid style of hockey, and who would fit together as a whole. He punished 68 hopefuls with continuous drills on ice and a 300-question survey to assess their psychological makeup.

Most of the prospects ultimately selected for the team were from Minnesota, Wisconsin, Michigan, and New England—and long-standing regional rivalries often resulted in on-ice brawls during the drills. In order to unify them, Brooks set out to make himself the enemy. "A shared disdain for his ceaselessly demanding

(Continued)

(Continued)

and Machiavellian ways would be the rallying cry, the reason guys would want to go out on the ice and bust their tails, just to show him . . . he kept nearly everyone anxious about their prospects for making the team, almost to the end" (Coffey, 2005, p. 9). As a result, the players commiserated with one another, creating bonds that erased their regional borders.

Brooks knew, however, that the distance and wall he put up between himself and the team would need to be countered by someone with a softer touch. For that he chose Craig Patrick as the team's assistant coach, telling him "I'm going to be tough on them, and you are going to have to be the one who keeps everyone together" (Coffey, 2005, p. 11). Patrick fulfilled his role as a sounding board, advocate, and nurturer for the team's players.

Brooks was relentless, and one of his favorite expressions to use was "prepare to grow through pain" (Brown, 2014; Timetoast, n.d.). As a run-up to the Olympics, the team began a series of exhibition games. After the U.S. team tied in a game against Norway, a team Brooks thought the United States should have easily trounced, he kept his team on the ice making them skate wind sprints the lengths of the rink (infamously called "Herbies"). He kept them at it even after the custodians had shut off lights to the rink and the team physician urged him to stop.

It wasn't just physical stamina that Brooks drilled into his athletes. As Brooks got to know his players, he learned what buttons to push and when to push them for every one of them. He would pick at them, provoke them, verbally berate them, or not talk to them at all.

"Traumatic is the best way to describe playing for him," Goalie Steve Janaszak said, noting that he once went three months without hearing so much as a hello from Brooks (Coffey, 2005, p. 102).

Brooks engaged in mind games with his players, fostering fear into them that they could be cut from the team at any time. Brooks believed that uncertainty made the players more motivated and pushed them to work harder. During the seven months the team played in exhibition games, Brooks would often bring in outside players to audition for spots on the team, making it clear to the current roster of players that they were expendable. In most cases, these mind games triggered renewed determination and skill from his current players. In one case, however, the team fought back.

Mike Eruzione was the team captain, and a unifying force on the team. But during the exhibition games, the usual high scorer was experiencing a scoring slump. Brooks, seeking to cut Eruzione, brought in two outside players to skate with the team as a tryout, which infuriated the team. "They'd been through Brooks's boot camp grind for six months. Eruzione had become a widely admired captain, an emotional lynchpin" (Coffey, 2005, p. 230). With less than three weeks before the Olympics, the team confronted Brooks and told him to stop his revolving door of new players to audition. It was unfair not only to those who were auditioning, but also to those who had been working and sacrificing for months. The players told Brooks that they were a family and the final roster for the Olympic team needed to come from that family. Brooks backed off.

That unity was something Brooks respected and protected. During the Olympics, he angered not only the international press, but Olympic Games organizers, when he refused to make his players available for press interviews after games. While some saw that as Brooks wanting all the attention for himself, the truth was that Brooks had spent months building the spirit and substance of the team and didn't want the players' bonds injured by one or two of the players getting all the media attention (Coffey, 2005, p. 100). He maintained his no-press stance even after the United States' searing Olympic victory over the USSR, when the world's media was clamoring for interviews. But when the team clinched the gold medal against Finland, 3–2, the arena erupted in bedlam with celebration, and the players were swamped by fans, family, and journalists. Brooks was not there, however, to bask in the limelight; right after the final buzzer, he went directly to the team's locker room.

"They were really mentally tough and goal-oriented," said Brooks of his squad. "They came from all different walks of life, many having competed against one another, but they came together and grew to be a real close team. I pushed this team really hard, I mean I really pushed them! But they had the ability to answer the bell . . . The players took to it like ducks to water, and they really had a lot of fun playing it. We were a fast, creative team that played extremely disciplined without the puck. Throughout the Olympics, they had a great resiliency about them. I mean they came from behind six or seven times to win. They just kept on moving and working and digging" (Herb Brooks Foundation, n.d.).

Four months after the Olympic Games, Brooks wrote every player on the team a personal, eight-paragraph letter:

> Under separate cover, you will be receiving a laminated team picture from Craig [Patrick] and myself. This reflects our complete respect we have for you as an athlete and as a person.
>
> I feel respect is the greatest reward in the world of sport. You have earned that from the coaching staff.
>
> Personally, this year was not only my most enjoyable year in coaching, but also my toughest. Toughest because it involved making so many difficult decisions regarding the makeup of our final team.
>
> Because of that, and because I wanted to be as objective as possible, I stayed away from close personal contacts with you. I did not want the U.S. Hockey Community to say that regionalism and/or favoritism entered into my final selections.

(Continued)

(Continued)

This year was a challenge for all of us.

A challenge to:

- *Live and work as a unit.*
- *Play a positive game—a creative way.*
- *Make the most out of our dreams.*

You met those challenges and conquered them. If there was any team I ever wanted to identify with on a personal basis, this was the team. Hopefully that day will come.

Respectfully,

Herb Brooks

—Coach Herb Brooks (1980 US Olympic Hockey team); [Coffey, 2005, p. 263]; Coffey, W. (2005). *The boys of winter: The untold story of a coach, a dream and the 1980 U.S. Olympic hockey team.* New York, NY: Crown.

Herb Brooks died in a car accident in 2003, at the age of 66. Twenty-four years after he brought them together the first time, members of the 1980 U.S. Olympic team came together again at the funeral for their former coach.

In his eulogy, Mike Eruzione likened Brooks "to a father you love deeply but don't always like because he pushed you so hard. 'I firmly believe he loved our hockey team, but we didn't know it,' he said" (Coffey, 2005, p. 3).

Questions

1. What is your reaction to Herb Brooks as a team leader? Do the ends in this case justify the means?

2. Describe how each of the eight characteristics of team excellence applied to Brooks's coaching of the 1980 U.S. Olympic hockey team.

3. The Hill Model for Team Leadership advocates that the leader's job is to monitor the team and take whatever action is necessary to ensure team effectiveness. Describe the actions Brooks took in relation to the internal leadership aspects of the model:

   a. Task (goal focusing, structuring for results, facilitating decisions, training, maintaining standards)

   b. Relational (coaching, collaborating, managing conflict, building commitment, satisfying needs, modeling principles)

4. Hill states that "the leader has special responsibility for functioning in a manner that will help the team achieve effectiveness" While the 1980 U.S. Olympic hockey team was highly successful, do you think it was because of Herb Brooks's leadership? Explain your answer.

LEADERSHIP INSTRUMENT

Larson and LaFasto developed an assessment tool to gauge team effectiveness (a team's health) based on their study of many different types of excellent organizational teams (see Larson & LaFasto, 1989). Their research demonstrated the eight criteria or factors that are consistently associated with team excellence and high performance that were discussed earlier in the chapter. The complete Team Excellence Survey contains more than 40 questions across the eight factors that are used to determine a team's performance level and suggest areas that might need corrective action. The eighth factor on this instrument is *principled leadership*. Subsequent research by LaFasto and Larson led to the development of a 42-item questionnaire focusing on this criterion of leadership. The full Collaborative Team Leader Instrument and a discussion of its reliability and validity can be found in their latest text (LaFasto & Larson, 2001). The questionnaire included here provides a sample of questions from these two surveys so that the reader can see how team and team leadership effectiveness can be evaluated. (Readers who want to assess their own organizational teams are advised to use the complete versions of both surveys.)

The team members are given the questionnaire, and their scores are combined and averaged to obtain a team view; the leader fills out the same questionnaire. The responses from the team leader are then compared with the team members' responses to determine the areas of greatest weakness, if any. Based on these comparisons, the team and its leader can plan the action steps needed to correct and improve the weak areas of team functioning. The action planning is done collaboratively with the leader and team members working together.

The Team Excellence and Collaborative Team Leader assessments are designed as diagnostic tools to help teams sort through any problems and to pinpoint areas for action taking. The Team Excellence and Collaborative Team Leader Questionnaire provided in this chapter combines sample questions from the two instruments developed by LaFasto and Larson. The first seven questions are taken from the Team Excellence Survey, developed by LaFasto and Larson in 1987 (cited in Larson & LaFasto, 1989) to measure a team's health in terms of the criteria of team excellence (goal, structure, team members, commitment, climate, standards, and external support). Leadership is measured by the next six questions, taken from the Collaborative Team Leader Instrument developed by LaFasto and Larson in 1996 (LaFasto & Larson, 2001, pp. 151–154). These six questions assess the effectiveness of the leader in goal focusing, ensuring a collaborative climate, building confidence, demonstrating know-how, setting priorities, and managing performance. All of these team and leadership factors have been found to relate to team effectiveness.

As you fill out the sample questionnaire, think about a team to which you belong or have belonged as a member or as the leader. The items that you score as

1 or 2 (*False* or *More false than true*) are the areas of team weakness from your perspective. To obtain a team assessment, you would compare your scores on this instrument with the scores of the other team members. For example, if almost everyone on the team responds with a 1 or 2 to Item 3 ("Team members possess the essential skills and abilities to accomplish the team's objectives"), then the team leader may need to provide training to increase the competence of team members. Such an instrument that assesses team effectiveness is particularly helpful to the team leader in identifying areas of team or leadership weakness and suggesting solutions for improving team effectiveness.

Team Excellence and Collaborative Team Leader Questionnaire

Purpose: The purpose of this questionnaire is to assess your team's strengths and weaknesses to help your team leader improve you overall effectiveness.

Instructions: This questionnaire contains questions about your team and the leadership within this team. Indicate whether you feel each statement is true or not true of your team. Use the following scale:

Key: 1 = False   2 = More false than true   3 = More true than false   4 = True

1. There is a clearly defined need—a goal to be achieved or   1 2 3 4
    a purpose to be served—that justifies the existence of our
    team. (team: clear, elevating goal)

2. We have an established method for monitoring individual   1 2 3 4
    performance and providing feedback. (team: results-driven
    structure)

3. Team members possess the essential skills and abilities to   1 2 3 4
    accomplish the team's objectives. (team: competent team
    members)

4. Achieving our team goal is a higher priority than any   1 2 3 4
    individual objective. (team: unified commitment)

5. We trust each other sufficiently to accurately share   1 2 3 4
    information, perceptions, and feedback. (team: collaborative
    climate)

6. Our team exerts pressure on itself to improve performance.   1 2 3 4
    (team: standards of excellence)

7. Our team is given the resources it needs to get the job done.   1 2 3 4
    (team: external support and recognition)

8. If it's necessary to adjust the team's goal, our team leader   1 2 3 4
    makes sure we understand why. (leadership: focus on
    the goal)

9. Our team leader creates a safe climate for team members   1 2 3 4
    to openly and supportively discuss any issue related to the
    team's success. (leadership: ensure collaborative climate)

10. Our team leader looks for and acknowledges contributions   1 2 3 4
    by team members. (leadership: build confidence)

11. Our team leader understands the technical issues we must   1 2 3 4
    face in achieving our goal. (leadership: demonstrate
    sufficient technical know-how)

(Continued)

(Continued)

12. Our team leader does not dilute our team's effort with too   1 2 3 4
    many priorities. (leadership: set priorities)

13. Our team leader is willing to confront and resolve issues   1 2 3 4
    associated with inadequate performance by team members.
    (leadership: manage performance)

Sources: Questions 1–7: Adapted from the Team Excellence Survey (copyright 1987 LaFasto and Larson; portions reprinted with permission of Profact). Questions 8–13: Adapted from the Collaborative Team Leader Instrument (copyright 1996 LaFasto and Larson; portions reprinted with permission).

Scoring Interpretation

In addition to such targeted questions on each of the criteria of excellence, the complete surveys ask open-ended questions to allow team members to comment on issues that might not be specifically covered in the directed questions, such as strengths and weaknesses of the team and its leadership, necessary changes, problematic norms, or issues that need to be addressed. The complete version of the survey is given to team members and the team leader, and all are involved in the diagnosis and the resulting action planning. Such a method is clearly consistent with the empowerment movement in organizational teams and helps address the enormous complexity involved in making teams effective.

SUMMARY

The increased importance of organizational teams and the leadership needed for them has produced a growing interest in team leadership theory. The team leadership model provides a framework in which to study the systematic factors that contribute to a team's outcomes or general effectiveness. Within this approach, the critical function of leadership is to help the team accomplish its goals by monitoring and diagnosing the team and taking the requisite action.

A strategic decision model has been developed to reveal the various decisions team leaders must make to improve their team's effectiveness. The model describes these decisions: What type of intervention should be used (monitoring or action taking)? At what level should the intervention be targeted (internal or external)? What leadership function should be implemented to improve team functioning?

Questionnaires filled out by team members and the team leader can aid in diagnosing specific areas of team problems and suggest action steps to be taken by the team.

The strength of this approach is its practical focus on real-life organizational teams and their effectiveness. The model also emphasizes the functions of leadership that can be shared and distributed within the work team. The model offers guidance in selecting leaders and team members with the appropriate diagnostic and action-taking skills. Furthermore, the model is appropriately complex, providing a cognitive model for understanding and improving organizational teams.

On the negative side, this approach is limited in that it does not include all the factors and skills related to team effectiveness. Furthermore, the model does not provide on-the-spot answers to specific problems facing team leaders nor does it address how team leadership skills can be shared throughout the team. Last, methods for testing and measuring the outcomes and effectiveness of team leadership models are not fully refined.

References

CHAPTER 1

Aritz, J., Walker, R., Cardon, P., & Zhang, L. (2017). Discourse of leadership: The power of questions in organizational decision making. *International Journal of Business Communication, 54*(2), 161–181. doi:10.1177/2329488416687054

Bass, B. M. (1985). *Leadership and performance beyond expectations*. New York, NY: Free Press.

Bass, B. M. (2008). *Bass and Stogdill's handbook of leadership: A survey of theory and research* (4th ed.). New York, NY: Free Press.

Bass, B. M., & Riggio, R. E. (2006). *Transformational leadership* (2nd ed.). Mahwah, NJ: Erlbaum.

Bass, B. M., & Steidlmeier, P. (1999). Ethics, character, and authentic transformational leadership. *The Leadership Quarterly, 10*, 181–217.

Bennis, W. G., & Nanus, B. (2007). *Leaders: The strategies for taking charge* (2nd ed.). New York, NY: Harper & Row.

Berger, M. [@Coach_Berger]. (2020, January 30). *An open letter* [Tweet]. Twitter. https://twitter.com/coach_berger?lang=en

Boatner, C. (2020, January 31). College paper goes viral after unpublishing then republishing coach's quote complimenting Hitler. *Student Press Law Center.* https://splc.org/2020/01/college-paper-goes-viral-after-unpublishing-then-republishing-coachs-quote-complimenting-hitler/

Brown, M. E., Treviño, L. K., & Harrison, D. A. (2005). Ethical leadership: A social learning perspective for construct development and testing. *Organizational Behavior and Human Decision Processes, 97*(2), 117–134.

Bryman, A. (1992). *Charisma and leadership in organizations*. London, UK: SAGE.

Bryman, A., Collinson, D., Grint, K., Jackson, G., & Uhl-Bien, M. (Eds.). (2011). *The SAGE handbook of leadership*. London, UK: SAGE.

Burns, J. M. (1978). *Leadership*. New York, NY: Harper & Row.

Burns, J. M. (2003). *Transforming leadership*. New York, NY: Grove Press.

Chiu, C. Y. C., Balkundi, P., & Weinberg, F. J. (2017). When managers become leaders: The role of manager network centralities, social power, and followers' perception of leadership. *The Leadership Quarterly, 28*(2), 334–348.

Ciulla, J. B. (2014). *The ethics of leadership* (3rd ed.). Santa Barbara, CA: Praeger.

Colf, C. (2020, February 14). GVSU to focus on Holocaust education after football coach's Hitler comment. *The Jewish News.* https://thejewishnews.com/2020/02/14/gvsu-to-focus-on-holocaust-education-after-football-coachs-hitler-comment/

Copeland, N. (1942). *Psychology and the soldier*. Harrisburg, PA: Military Service.

Day, D. V., & Antonakis, J. (Eds.). (2012). *The nature of leadership* (2nd ed.). Thousand Oaks, CA: SAGE.

Dinh, J. E., Lord, R. G., Gardner, W. L., Meuser, J. D., Liden, R. C., & Hu, J. (2014). Leadership theory and research in the new millennium: Current theoretical trends and changing perspectives. *The Leadership Quarterly, 25*(1), 36–62.

Ellis, D. G., & Fisher, B. A. (1994). *Small group decision making: Communication and the group process* (4th ed.). New York, NY: McGraw-Hill.

Fairhurst, G. T. (2007). *Discursive leadership: In conversation with leadership psychology.* Thousand Oaks, CA: SAGE.

Fayol, H. (1916). *General and industrial management.* London, UK: Pitman.

Fleishman, E. A., Mumford, M. D., Zaccaro, S. J., Levin, K. Y., Korotkin, A. L., & Hein, M. B. (1991). Taxonomic efforts in the description of leader behavior: A synthesis and functional interpretation. *The Leadership Quarterly, 2*(4), 245–287.

French, J. R., Jr., & Raven, B. H. (1959). The bases of social power. In D. Cartwright (Ed.), *Studies in social power* (pp. 259–269). Ann Arbor, MI: Institute for Social Research.

Fry, L. W. (2003). Toward a theory of spiritual leadership. *The Leadership Quarterly, 14*(6), 693–727.

Gardner, J. W. (1990). *On leadership.* New York, NY: Free Press.

Gardner, W. L., Lowe, K. B., Meuser, J. D., Noghani, F., Gullifor, D. P., & Cogliser, C. C. (2020). The leadership trilogy: A review of the third decade of the leadership quarterly. *The Leadership Quarterly.* Advance online publication. https://doi.org/10.1016/j.leaqua.2019.101379

George, B. (2003). *Authentic leadership: Rediscovering the secrets to creating lasting value.* Warren Bennis signature series. San Francisco, CA: Jossey-Bass.

Graham, J. W. (1991). Servant-leadership in organizations: Inspirational and moral. *The Leadership Quarterly, 2*(2), 105–119.

Heifetz, R. A. (1994). *Leadership without easy answers.* Cambridge, MA: Harvard University Press.

Heller, T., & Van Til, J. (1983). Leadership and followership: Some summary propositions. *Journal of Applied Behavioral Science, 18*, 405–414.

Hemphill, J. K. (1949). *Situational factors in leadership.* Columbus: The Ohio State University, Bureau of Educational Research.

Hickman, G. R. (Ed.). (2016). *Leading organizations: Perspectives for a new era* (3rd ed.). Thousand Oaks, CA: SAGE.

Hogg, M. A. (2001). A social identity theory of leadership. *Personality and Social Psychology Review, 5*, 184–200.

Hollander, E. P. (1992). Leadership, followership, self, and others. *The Leadership Quarterly, 3*(1), 43–54.

Howell, J. M., & Avolio, B. J. (1993). The ethics of charismatic leadership: Submission of liberation? *Academy of Management Executive, 6*(2), 43–54.

Jago, A. G. (1982). Leadership: Perspectives in theory and research. *Management Science, 28*(3), 315–336.

Kellerman, B. (2012). *The end of leadership.* New York, NY: HarperCollins.

Kotter, J. P. (1990). *A force for change: How leadership differs from management.* New York, NY: Free Press.

Krasikova, D. V., Green, S. G., & LeBreton, J. M. (2013). Destructive leadership: A theoretical review, integration, and future research agenda. *Journal of Management, 39*(5), 1308–1338.

McClean, E. J., Martin, S. R., Emich, K. J., & Woodruff, C. T. (2018). The social consequences of voice: An examination of voice type and gender on status and subsequent leader emergence. *Academy of Management Journal, 61*(5), 1869–1891.

Moore, B. V. (1927). The May conference on leadership. *Personnel Journal, 6*, 124–128.

Mumford, M. D. (2006). *Pathways to outstanding leadership: A comparative analysis of charismatic, ideological, and pragmatic leaders.* Mahwah, NJ: Erlbaum.

Nederman, C. (2019, Summer). Niccolò Machiavelli. In Edward N. Zalta (Ed.), *The Stanford encyclopedia of philosophy.* https://plato.stanford.edu/archives/sum2019/entries/machiavelli/

Owens, B. P., & Hekman, D. R. (2012). Modeling how to grow: An inductive examination of humble leader behaviors, contingencies, and outcomes. *Academy of Management Journal, 55*(4), 787–818.

Padilla, A. (2013). *Leadership: Leaders, followers, environments.* Hoboken, NJ: John Wiley & Sons.

Peters, T. J., & Waterman, R. H. (1982). *In search of excellence: Lessons from America's best-run companies.* New York, NY: Warner Books.

Podsakoff, P. M., & Podsakoff, N. P. (2019). Experimental designs in management and leadership research: Strengths, limitations, and recommendations for improving publishability. *The Leadership Quarterly, 30*(1), 11–33.

Posner, B. Z. (2015). An investigation into the leadership practices of volunteer leaders. *Leadership & Organization Development Journal, 36*(7), 885–898.

Raven, B. H. (1965). *Social influence and power.* In I. D. Steiner & M. Fishbein (Eds.), *Current studies in social psychology* (pp. 371–382). New York, NY: Holt, Rinehart, & Winston.

Rost, J. C. (1991). *Leadership for the twenty-first century.* New York, NY: Praeger.

Ruben, B. D., & Gigliotti, R. A. (2017). Communication: Sine qua non of organizational leadership theory and practice. *International Journal of Business Communication, 54*(1), 12–30.

Seeman, M. (1960). *Social status and leadership.* Columbus: The Ohio State University, Bureau of Educational Research.

Shore, L. M., Cleveland, J. N., & Sanchez, D. (2018). Inclusive workplaces: A review and model. *Human Resource Management Review, 28*(2), 176–189.

Simonet, D. V., & Tett, R. P. (2012). Five perspectives on the leadership-management relationship: A competency-based evaluation and integration. *Journal of Leadership & Organizational Studies, 20*(2), 199–213.

Smith, J. A., & Foti, R. J. (1998). A pattern approach to the study of leader emergence. *The Leadership Quarterly, 9*(2), 147–160.

Stogdill, R. M. (1974). *Handbook of leadership: A survey of theory and research.* New York, NY: Free Press.

Tepper, B. J. (2007). Abusive supervision in work organizations: Review, synthesis, and research agenda. *Journal of Management, 33*(3), 261–289.

Voss, K. (2020, January 23). Inside the mind of GVSU's newest offensive coordinator. *Grand Valley Lanthorn.* https://lanthorn.com/73049/sports/inside-the-mind-of-gvsus-newest-offensive-coordinator

Wallner, P. J. (2020, January 30). Grand Valley State coach resigns following his Hitler remarks. *MLive.com.* https://www.mlive.com/sports/grand-rapids/2020/01/grand-valley-state-coach-resigns-for-hitler-remarks.html

Watson, C., & Hoffman, L. R. (2004). The role of task-related behavior in the emergence of leaders. *Group & Organization Management, 29*(6), 659–685.

Zaleznik, A. (1977, May–June). Managers and leaders: Are they different? *Harvard Business Review, 55,* 67–78.

CHAPTER 2

Antonakis, J. (2009). "Emotional intelligence": What does it measure and does it matter for leadership? In G. B. Graen (Ed.), *LMX leadership—game-changing designs: Research-based tools* (Vol. 11, pp. 163–192). Greenwich, CT: Information Age.

Antonakis, J., House, R. J., & Simonton, D. K. (2017). Can super smart leaders suffer from too much of a good thing? The curvilinear effect of intelligence on perceived leadership behavior. *Journal of Applied Psychology, 102*(7), 1003–1021.

Ashkanasy, N. M., Dasborough, M. T., & Ascough, K. W. (2009). Developing leaders: Teaching about emotional intelligence and training in emotional skills. In S. J. Armstrong & C. V. Fukami (Eds.), *The SAGE handbook of management learning, education and development* (pp. 161–183). London, UK: SAGE.

Ashkanasy, N. M., & Daus, C. S. (2002). Emotion in the workplace: The new challenge for managers. *Academy of Management Perspectives, 16*(1), 76–86.

Bass, B. M. (2008). *Bass and Stogdill's handbook of leadership: A survey of theory and research* (4th ed.). New York, NY: Free Press.

Bennis, W. G., & Nanus, B. (2007). *Leaders: The strategies for taking charge* (2nd ed.). New York, NY: Harper & Row.

Blair, C. A., Palmieri, R. E., & Paz-Aparicio, C. (2018). Do Big 5 personality characteristics and narcissism predict engagement in leader development? *Frontiers in Psychology, 9*, 1817.

Boyatzis, R. E. (2019). Emotional intelligence and its measurement. In *Oxford Research Encyclopedia of Business and Management*. DOI: 10.1093/acrefore/9780190224851.013.159

Bryman, A. (1992). *Charisma and leadership in organizations*. London, UK: SAGE.

Buckingham, M., & Clifton, D. (2001). *Now, discover your strengths*. New York, NY: Free Press.

Caruso, D. R., & Wolfe, C. J. (2004). Emotional intelligence and leadership development. In D. V. Day, S. J. Zaccaro, & S. M. Halpin (Eds.), *Leader development for transforming organizations: Growing leaders for tomorrow* (pp. 237–266). Mahwah, NJ: Erlbaum.

Crum, R. (2018, August 17). Worry over Musk's "stability": Tesla stock nosedives after CEO's emotional interview. *Mercury News*. https://www.mercurynews.com/

2018/08/17/elon-musk-cries-laughs-and-calls-past-year-excruciating

Davies, A. (2018, May 3). Elon Musk's attack on Tesla investors could make him a liability. *Wired*. https://www.wired.com/story/elon-musk-tesla-model-3-earnings-call/

Dinh, J., Lord, R., Gardner, W., Meuser, J., Liden, R. C., & Hu, J. (2014). Leadership theory and research in the new millennium: Current theoretical trends and changing perspectives. *The Leadership Quarterly, 25*(1), 36–62.

Dinh, J. E., & Lord, R. G. (2012). Implications of dispositional and process views of traits for individual difference research in leadership. *The Leadership Quarterly, 23*(4), 651–667.

Duckworth, A. L., Peterson, C., Matthews, M. D., & Kelly, D. R. (2007). Grit: Perseverance and passion for long-term goals. *Journal of Personality and Social Psychology, 92*(6), 1087–1101.

Feloni, R. (2014, October 23). Former SpaceX exec explains how Elon Musk taught himself rocket science. *Business Insider*. https://www.businessinsider.com/how-elon-musk-learned-rocket-science-for-spacex-2014-10?r=US&IR=T

Freedman, J. (2014). Case study: Emotional intelligence for people-first leadership at FedEx Express. *Six Seconds*. http://www.6seconds.org/2014/01/14/case-study-emotional-intelligence-people-first-leadership-fedex-express/

French, J. R. P., Jr., & Raven, B. (1962). The bases of social power. In D. Cartwright (Ed.), *Group dynamics: Research and theory* (pp. 259–269). New York, NY: Harper and Row.

Frieder, R., Wang, G., & Oh, I. S. (2018). Linking job-relevant personality traits, transformational leadership, and job performance via perceived meaningfulness at work: A moderated mediation model. *Journal of Applied Psychology, 103*(3), 324–333.

Gardner, H. (1997). *Extraordinary minds: Portraits of exceptional individuals and an examination of our extraordinariness.* New York, NY: Basic Books.

Gelles, D. (2018, August 28). In Elon Musk's world, brakes are for cars, not C.E.O.s. *New York Times.* https://www.nytimes.com/2018/08/28/business/elon-musk-tesla.html

Goldberg, L. R. (1990). An alternative "description of personality": The Big-Five factor structure. *Journal of Personality and Social Psychology, 59,* 1216–1229.

Goleman, D. (1995). *Emotional intelligence.* New York, NY: Bantam.

Goleman, D. (1998). *Working with emotional intelligence.* New York, NY: Bantam.

Goleman, D., & Boyatzis, R. (2017). Emotional intelligence has 12 elements. Which do you need to work on? *Harvard Business Review, 84*(2), 1–5.

Goleman, D., & Nevarez, M. (2018). Boost your emotional intelligence with these three questions. *Harvard Business Review.* https://hbr.org/2018/08/boost-your-emotional-intelligence-with-these-3-questions

Gong, Z., & Jiao, X. (2019). Are effect sizes in emotional intelligence field declining? A meta-meta analysis. *Frontiers in Psychology, 10,* Article 1655.

Jackson, A. E. (2017, June 20). The art (& science) of leadership: Inside the mind of Elon Musk. *Glassdoor.* https://www.glassdoor.com/blog/elon-musk

Jacquart, P., & Antonakis, J. (2015). When does charisma matter for top-level leaders? Effect of attributional ambiguity. *Academy of Management Journal, 58*(4), 1051–1074.

Jago, A. G. (1982). Leadership: Perspectives in theory and research. *Management Science, 28*(3), 315–336.

Judge, T. A., Bono, J. E., Ilies, R., & Gerhardt, M. W. (2002). Personality and leadership:

A qualitative and quantitative review. *Journal of Applied Psychology, 87,* 765–780.

Jung, D., & Sosik, J. J. (2006). Who are the spellbinders? Identifying personal attributes of charismatic leaders. *Journal of Leadership & Organizational Studies, 12,* 12–27.

Kidder, T. (2004). *Mountains beyond mountains: The quest of Dr. Paul Farmer, a man who would cure the world.* New York, NY: Random House.

Killgore, W. D. (2017). *Refinement and validation of a military emotional intelligence training program.* Tucson: University of Arizona. https://apps.dtic.mil/dtic/tr/fulltext/u2/1050120.pdf

Kirkpatrick, S. A., & Locke, E. A. (1991). Leadership: Do traits matter? *The Executive, 5,* 48–60.

Kotsou, I., Mikolajczak, M., Heeren, A., Grégoire, J., & Leys, C. (2019). Improving emotional intelligence: A systematic review of existing work and future challenges. *Emotion Review, 11*(2), 151–165.

Levin, S. (2018, July 16). Elon Musk calls British diver in Thai cave rescue "pedo" in baseless attack. *The Guardian.* https://www.theguardian.com/technology/2018/jul/15/elon-musk-british-diver-thai-cave-rescue-pedo-twitter

Lord, R. G., DeVader, C. L., & Alliger, G. M. (1986). A meta-analysis of the relation between personality traits and leadership perceptions: An application of validity generalization procedures. *Journal of Applied Psychology, 71,* 402–410.

MacKie, D. (2016). *Strength-based leadership coaching in organizations: An evidence-based guide to positive leadership development.* London, UK: Kogan Page.

Mann, R. D. (1959). A review of the relationship between personality and performance in small groups. *Psychological Bulletin, 56,* 241–270.

Marlowe, H. A. (1986). Social intelligence: Evidence for multidimensionality and construct independence. *Journal of Educational Psychology, 78*, 52–58.

Mattingly, V., & Kraiger, K. (2019). Can emotional intelligence be trained? A meta-analytical investigation. *Human Resource Management Review, 29*(2), 140–155.

Mayer, J. D., Caruso, D. R., & Salovey, P. (2000). Selecting a measure of emotional intelligence: The case for ability scales. In R. Bar-On & J. D. A. Parker (Eds.), *The handbook of emotional intelligence* (pp. 320–342). San Francisco, CA: Jossey-Bass.

Mayer, J. D., & Salovey, P. (1995). Emotional intelligence and the construction and regulation of feelings. *Applied & Preventive Psychology, 4*, 197–208.

Mayer, J. D., & Salovey, P. (1997). What is emotional intelligence? In P. Salovey & D. Sluyter (Eds.), *Emotional development and emotional intelligence: Implications for educators* (pp. 3–31). New York, NY: Basic Books.

Mayer, J. D., Salovey, P., & Caruso, D. R. (2000). Models of emotional intelligence. In R. J. Sternberg (Ed.), *Handbook of intelligence* (pp. 396–420). Cambridge, UK: Cambridge University Press.

McCrae, R. R., & Costa, P. T. (1987). Validation of the five-factor model of personality across instruments and observers. *Journal of Personality and Social Psychology, 52*, 81–90.

Mind & Machine. (2017, August 13). Working at SpaceX, building the future of space exploration on MIND & MACHINE [Video file]. https://www.youtube.com/watch?v=N4glvduGG_U

Musk, E. (@ElonMusk). (2018, April 2). About a year ago, I asked Doug to manage both engineering & production. He agreed that Tesla needed eng & prod better aligned, so we don't design cars that are crazy hard to build. Right now, tho, better to divide & conquer, so I'm back

to sleeping at factory. Car biz is hell . . . [Tweet]. https://twitter.com/elonmusk/status/980913157739765761?lang=en

Nadler, D. A., & Tushman, M. L. (2012). What makes for magic leadership? In W. E. Rosenbach & R. L. Taylor (Eds.), *Contemporary issues in leadership* (7th ed., pp. 135–139). Boulder, CO: Westview.

Partners In Health. (2017). *Our work.* https://www.pih.org/programs

Peterson, C. (2006). *A primer in positive psychology.* New York, NY: Oxford University Press.

Peterson, C., & Seligman, M. E. P. (2004). *Character strengths and virtues: A handbook and classification.* New York, NY: Oxford University Press; Washington, DC: American Psychological Association.

Rath, T. (2007). *StrengthsFinder 2.0.* New York, NY: Gallup Press.

Sacket, P. R., & Walmsley, P. T. (2014). Which personality attributes are most important in the workplace? *Perspectives on Psychological Science, 9*(5), 538–551.

Sage, A., & Rodriguez, S. (2018, July 1). Exclusive: Tesla hits Model 3 manufacturing milestone, hours after deadline—factory sources. *Reuters.* https://www.reuters.com/article/us-tesla-model3-exclusive/exclusive-tesla-hits-model-3-manufacturing-milestone-hours-after-deadline-factory-sources-idUSKBN1JR1WX

Sculley, J. (2011, October 10). No bozos. Ever. *Bloomberg Businessweek, 4249*, 27.

Shankman, M. L., & Allen, S. J. (2015). *Emotionally intelligent leadership: A guide for college students* (2nd ed.). San Francisco, CA: Jossey-Bass.

Slaski, M., & Cartwright, S. (2003). Emotional intelligence training and its implications for stress, health and performance. *Stress & Health, 19*(4), 233–239. https://doi.org/10.1002/smi.979

Snow, S. (2015, June 4). Steve Jobs's and Elon Musk's counterintuitive leadership traits. *Fast Company*. https://www.fastcompany.com/3046916/elon-musks-leadership-traits

Sosik, J. J., Chun, J. U., Ete, Z., Arenas, F. J., & Scherer, J. A. (2019). Self-control puts character in action: Examining how leader character strengths and ethical leadership relate to leader outcomes. *Journal of Business Ethics, 160*(3), 765–781.

Sosik, J. J., Gentry, W. A., & Chun, J. U. (2012). The value of virtue in the upper echelons: A multisource examination of executive character strengths and performance. *The Leadership Quarterly, 23*(3), 367–382. https://doi.org/10.1016/j.leaqua.2011.08.010

Space Exploration Technologies Corp. (2020). About SpaceX. SpaceX.com/about

Sternberg, R. J. (Ed.). (2004). *International handbook of intelligence*. New York, NY: Cambridge University Press.

Stogdill, R. M. (1948). Personal factors associated with leadership: A survey of the literature. *Journal of Psychology, 25*, 35–71.

Stogdill, R. M. (1974). *Handbook of leadership: A survey of theory and research*. New York, NY: Free Press.

Stone, B. (2011, October 10). The return. *Bloomberg Businessweek, 4249*, 40.

Zaccaro, S. J. (2002). Organizational leadership and social intelligence. In R. Riggio (Ed.), *Multiple intelligence and leadership* (pp. 29–54). Mahwah, NJ: Erlbaum.

Zaccaro, S. J. (2007). Trait-based perspectives of leadership. *American Psychologist, 62*, 6–16.

Zaccaro, S. J., Green, J. P., Dubrow, S., & Kolze, M. (2018). Leader individual differences, situational parameters, and leadership outcomes: A comprehensive review and integration. *The Leadership Quarterly, 29*(1), 2–43.

Zaccaro, S. J., Kemp, C., & Bader, P. (2004). Leader traits and attributes. In J. Antonakis, A. T. Cianciolo, & R. J.

Sternberg (Eds.), *The nature of leadership* (pp. 101–124). Thousand Oaks, CA: SAGE.

Zaccaro, S. J., Kemp, C., & Bader, P. (2017). Leader traits and attributes. In J. Antonakis, A. T. Cianciolo, & R. J. Sternberg (Eds.), *The nature of leadership* (3rd ed., pp. 29–55). Thousand Oaks, CA: SAGE.

Zaleznik, A. (1977, May–June). Managers and leaders: Are they different? *Harvard Business Review, 55*, 67–78.

CHAPTER 3

Bass, B. M. (2008). *Bass and Stogdill's handbook of leadership: A survey of theory and research* (4th ed.). New York, NY: Free Press.

Connelly, M. S., Gilbert, J. A., Zaccaro, S. J., Threlfall, K. V., Marks, M. A., & Mumford, M. D. (2000). Exploring the relationship of leadership skills and knowledge to leader performance. *The Leadership Quarterly, 11*(1), 65–86.

Gasiorek, J., & Ebesu Hubbard, A. (2017). Perspectives on perspective-taking in communication research. *Review of Communication, 17*(2), 87–105.

Griffith, J. A., Baur, J. E., & Buckley, M. R. (2019). Creating comprehensive leadership pipelines: Applying the real options approach to organizational leadership development. *Human Resource Management Review, 29*(3), 305–315.

Gurdjian, P., Halbeisen, T., & Lane, K. (2014). Why leadership-development programs fail. *McKinsey Quarterly, 1*(1), 121–126.

Katz, R. L. (1955). Skills of an effective administrator. *Harvard Business Review, 33*(1), 33–42.

Kellerman, B. (2012). *The end of leadership*. New York, NY: HarperCollins.

Kerns, C. D. (2015). Motivations to lead: A core leadership dimension. *Journal of Organizational Psychology, 15*(1), 9–23.

Koigi, B. (2019, August 16). Peter Tabichi—the world's best teacher about the role of science in ending poverty. *FairPlanet*. https://www.fairplanet.org/story/peter-tabichi-the-world%E2%80%99s-best-teacher-about-the-role-of-science-in-ending-poverty/

Matara, E., & Njeru, L. (2019, March 31). A teacher who goes above the call of duty. *The Citizen*. https://www.thecitizen.co.tz/magazine/soundliving/1843780-5049978-y7i6dm/index.html

Melia, M., Amy, J., & Fenn, L. (2019, June 10). 3 million US students don't have home internet. *Associated Press News*. https://apnews.com/7f263b8f7d3a43d6be014f860d5e4132

Moorhead, J. (2019, May 29). The secret to unlocking children's potential, by the Kenyan friar named the "world's best teacher." *The Telegraph*. https://www.telegraph.co.uk/family/schooling/secrets-kenyan-friar-became-worlds-best-teacher/

Mumford, M. D., & Connelly, M. S. (1991). Leaders as creators: Leader performance and problem solving in ill-defined domains. *The Leadership Quarterly*, *2*, 289–315.

Mumford, M. D., Hester, K. S., Robledo, I. C., Peterson, D. R., Day, E. A., Hougen, D. F., & Barrett, J. D. (2012). Mental models and creative problem-solving: The relationship of objective and subjective model attributes. *Creativity Research Journal*, *24*(4), 311–330.

Mumford, M. D., Todd, E. M., Higgs, C., & McIntosh, T. (2017). Cognitive skills and leadership performance: The nine critical skills. *The Leadership Quarterly*, *28*(1), 24–39.

Mumford, M. D., Zaccaro, S. J., Connelly, M. S., & Marks, M. A. (2000). Leadership skills: Conclusions and future directions. *The Leadership Quarterly*, *11*(1), 155–170.

Mumford, M. D., Zaccaro, S. J., Harding, F. D., Jacobs, T. O., & Fleishman, E. A. (2000). Leadership skills for a changing world: Solving complex social problems. *The Leadership Quarterly*, *11*(1), 11–35.

Mumford, T. V., Campion, M. A., & Morgeson, F. P. (2007). The leadership skills strataplex: Leadership skill requirements across organizational levels. *The Leadership Quarterly*, *18*, 154–166.

Rose, D. M., & Gordon, R. (2015). Age-related cognitive changes and distributed leadership. *The Journal of Management Development*, *34*(3), 330–339.

Sousa, M. J., & Rocha, Á. (2019). Leadership styles and skills developed through game-based learning. *Journal of Business Research*, *94*, 360–366.

Talking Education. (2019, February 20). The Kenyan teacher who gives his salary to the poor [Video file]. *YouTube*. https://www.youtube.com/watch?v=i41XlsaDc-w

Westfall, C. (2019). Leadership development: Why most programs don't work. *Forbes*. https://www.forbes.com/sites/chriswestfall/2019/06/20/leadership-development-why-most-programs-dont-work/#3e1d233a61de

Wodon, Q. (2019, September 17). An interview with Peter Tabichi, winner of the 2019 Global Teacher Prize. *World Bank*. https://www.worldbank.org/en/topic/education/brief/an-interview-with-peter-tabichi-winner-of-the-2019-global-teacher-prize

World Bank Live. (2019, September 6). The power of teachers in tackling the global learning crisis [Video file]. *YouTube*. https://www.youtube.com/watch?v=k9OAazNAEd8

Yammarino, F. J. (2000). Leadership skills: Introduction and overview. *The Leadership Quarterly*, *11*(1), 5–9.

Zaccaro, S. J., Gilbert, J., Thor, K. K., & Mumford, M. D. (1991). Leadership and social intelligence: Linking social perceptiveness and behavioral flexibility to leader effectiveness. *The Leadership Quarterly*, *2*, 317–331.

Zaccaro, S. J., Mumford, M. D., Connelly, M. S., Marks, M. A., & Gilbert, J. A. (2000). Assessment of leader problem-solving capabilities. *The Leadership Quarterly, 11*(1), 37–64.

Zaki, Y. (2019, March 25). Peter Tabichi: 10 things to know about Kenyan monk-teacher who won $1 million. *Gulf News.* https://gulfnews.com/uae/education/peter-tabichi-10-things-to-know-about-kenyan-monk-teacher-who-won-1-million-1.1553504923391

CHAPTER 4

Andersen, J. A. (2009). Your favourite manager is an organisational disaster. *European Business Review, 21*(1), 5–16.

Begum, R., & Mujtaba, B. G. (2016). Task and relationship orientation of Pakistani managers and working professionals: The interaction effect of demographics in a collective culture. *Public Organization Review, 16*(2), 199–215.

Behrendt, P., Matz, S., & Göritz, A. S. (2017). An integrative model of leadership behavior. *The Leadership Quarterly, 28*(1), 229–244.

Bennett, W. (2020, January 30). Cheer's Morgan Simianer sleeps in her makeup, idolizes Coach Monica—and is back at Navarro. *Vogue.* https://www.vogue.com/article/morgan-simianer-interview-cheer-netflix

Blake, R. R., & McCanse, A. A. (1991). *Leadership dilemmas: Grid solutions.* Houston, TX: Gulf.

Blake, R. R., & Mouton, J. S. (1964). *The Managerial Grid.* Houston, TX: Gulf.

Blake, R. R., & Mouton, J. S. (1978). *The new Managerial Grid.* Houston, TX: Gulf.

Blake, R. R., & Mouton, J. S. (1985). *The Managerial Grid III.* Houston, TX: Gulf.

Bowers, D. G., & Seashore, S. E. (1966). Predicting organizational effectiveness with a four-factor theory of leadership.

Administrative Science Quarterly, 11, 238–263.

Bryman, A. (1992). *Charisma and leadership in organizations.* London, UK: SAGE.

Cai, D. A., Fink, E. L., & Walker, C. B. (2019). Robert R. Blake, with recognition of Jane S. Mouton. *Negotiation and Conflict Management Research.* Advance online publication. https://doi.org/10.1111/ncmr.12151

Cartwright, D., & Zander, A. (1970). *Group dynamics research and theory* (3rd ed.). New York, NY: Tavistock.

Casimir, G., & Ng, Y. N. (2010). Combinative aspects of leadership style and the interaction between leadership behaviors. *Leadership & Organization Development Journal, 31*(6), 501–517.

Church, B. (2020, March 6). The "Queen" of Cheer reveals how Netflix mega-hit changed her life. *CNN.* https://www.cnn.com/2020/03/06/sport/cheer-monica-aldama-netflix-cheerleading-spt-intl/index.html

Dinh, J. E., Lord, R. G., Gardner, W. L., Meuser, J. D., Liden, R. C., & Hu, J. (2014). Leadership theory and research in the new millennium: Current theoretical trends and changing perspectives. *The Leadership Quarterly, 25*(1), 36–62

Engle, R. L., Elahee, M. N., & Tatoglu, E. (2013). Antecedents of problem-solving cross-cultural negotiation style: Some preliminary evidence. *Journal of Applied Management and Entrepreneurship, 18*(2), 83–102.

Greenspan, R. (2020, March 10). *Cheer* shows competitive cheerleading is almost as dangerous as football. So why isn't it officially considered a sport? *Time.* Retrieved from https://time.com/5782136/cheer-netflix-cheerleading-dangers/

Hemphill, J. K., & Coons, A. E. (1957). Development of the Leader Behavior Description Questionnaire. In R. M. Stogdill & A. E. Coons (Eds.), *Leader behavior: Its description and measurement*

(*Research Monograph No. 88*). Columbus: The Ohio State University, Bureau of Business Research.

Iguisi, O. (2014). Indigenous knowledge systems and leadership styles in Nigerian work organisations. *International Journal of Research in Business and Social Science, 3*(4), 1–13.

Judge, T., Piccolo, R., & Ilies, R. (2004). The forgotten ones? The validity of consideration and initiating structure in leadership research. *Journal of Applied Psychology, 89(1)*, 36–51.

Kahn, R. L. (1956). The prediction of productivity. *Journal of Social Issues, 12*, 41–49.

Katz, D., & Kahn, R. L. (1951). Human organization and worker motivation. In L. R. Tripp (Ed.), *Industrial productivity* (pp. 146–171). Madison, WI: Industrial Relations Research Association.

Likert, R. (1961). *New patterns of management*. New York, NY: McGraw-Hill.

Likert, R. (1967). *The human organization: Its management and value*. New York, NY: McGraw-Hill.

Littrell, R. F. (2013). Explicit leader behaviour. *The Journal of Management Development, 32*(6), 567–605.

Martin, M. T., Rowlinson, S., Fellows, R., & Liu, A. M. M. (2012). Empowering the project team: Impact of leadership style and team context. *Team Performance Management, 18*(3), 149–175.

Misumi, J. (1985). *The behavioral science of leadership: An interdisciplinary Japanese research program*. Ann Arbor: University of Michigan Press.

Pellegrini, E. K., & Scandura, T. A. (2008). Paternalistic leadership: A review and agenda for future research. *Journal of Management, 34*(3), 566–593.

Silman, A. (2020, January 21). How *Cheer*'s superstar coach Monica gets it done. *The Cut*. Retrieved from https://www.thecut .com/2020/01/how-cheers-coach-monica-aldama-gets-it-done.html

Stogdill, R. M. (1948). Personal factors associated with leadership: A survey of the literature. *Journal of Psychology, 25*, 35–71.

Stogdill, R. M. (1963). *Manual for the Leader Behavior Description Questionnaire form XII*. Columbus: The Ohio State University, Bureau of Business Research.

Stogdill, R. M. (1974). *Handbook of leadership: A survey of theory and research*. New York, NY: Free Press.

Whiteley, G. (2020, January 8). *Cheer* [TV series]. Boardwalk Pictures, Caviar and One Potato Productions.

Yukl, G. (2003). *Leadership in organizations* (8th ed.). Boston, MA: Pearson.

Yukl, G. (2012). Effective leadership behavior: What we know and what questions need more attention. *Academy of Management Perspectives, 26*(4), 66–85.

Zakin, C., & Weisberg, D. (Producers). (2020, February 4). Skimm'd from the Couch: Coach Monica Aldama [Audio podcast]. https://www.theskimm.com/ money/skimmd-from-the-couch-coach-monica-aldama-3rKxVUjfCIDEm6p3 NGo9SH

CHAPTER 5

Arvidsson, M., Johansson, C. R., Ek, Å., & Akselsson, R. (2007). Situational leadership in air traffic control. *Journal of Air Transportation, 12*(1), 67–86.

Bass, B. M. (2008). *The Bass handbook of leadership: Theory, research, and managerial applications* (4th ed.). New York, NY: Free Press.

Blanchard, K. H. (1985). *SLII®: A situational approach to managing people*. Escondido, CA: Blanchard Training and Development.

Blanchard, K., Zigarmi, D., & Nelson, R. (1993). Situational Leadership® after

25 years: A retrospective. *Journal of Leadership Studies, 1*(1), 22–36.

Blanchard, K., Zigarmi, P., & Zigarmi, D. (1992). *Game plan for leadership and the One Minute Manager.* Escondido, CA: Blanchard Training and Development.

Blanchard, K., Zigarmi, P., & Zigarmi, D. (2013). *Leadership and the One Minute Manager: Increasing effectiveness through Situational Leadership® II.* New York, NY: William Morrow.

Blank, W., Green, S. G., & Weitzel, J. R. (1990). A test of the situational leadership theory. *Personnel Psychology, 43*(3), 579–597.

Bosse, T., Duell, R., Memon, Z. A., Treur, J., & van der Wal, C. N. (2017). Computational model-based design of leadership support based on situational leadership theory. *Simulation, 93*(7), 605–617.

Carew, P., Parisi-Carew, E., & Blanchard, K. H. (1990). *Group development and Situational Leadership II®.* Escondido, CA: Blanchard Training and Development.

Cote, R. (2017). A comparison of leadership theories in an organizational environment. *International Journal of Business Administration, 8*(5), 28–35.

Fernandez, C. F., & Vecchio, R. P. (1997). Situational Leadership theory revisited: A test of an across-jobs perspective. *The Leadership Quarterly, 8*(1), 67–84.

Graeff, C. L. (1983). The Situational Leadership theory: A critical view. *Academy of Management Review, 8,* 285–291.

Graeff, C. L. (1997). Evolution of Situational Leadership theory: A critical review. *The Leadership Quarterly, 8*(2), 153–170.

Hersey, P., & Blanchard, K. H. (1969a). Life-cycle theory of leadership. *Training and Development Journal, 23,* 26–34.

Hersey, P., & Blanchard, K. H. (1969b). *Management of organizational behavior: Utilizing human resources.* Englewood Cliffs, NJ: Prentice Hall.

Hersey, P., & Blanchard, K. H. (1977). *Management of organizational behavior: Utilizing human resources* (3rd ed.). Englewood Cliffs, NJ: Prentice Hall.

Hersey, P., & Blanchard, K. H. (1988). *Management of organizational behavior: Utilizing human resources* (5th ed.). Englewood Cliffs, NJ: Prentice Hall.

Hersey, P., & Blanchard, K. H. (1993). *Management of organizational behavior: Utilizing human resources* (6th ed.). Englewood Cliffs, NJ: Prentice Hall.

Hersey, P., & Blanchard, K. H. (1996). Great ideas revisited: Revisiting the life-cycle theory of leadership. *Training & Development Journal, 50*(1), 42.

Huang, Y. H. (2000). The Personal Influence Model and Gao Guanxi in Taiwan Chinese public relations. *Public Relations Review, 26*(2), 219–236.

Johnson, C. E. (1999). Emerging perspectives in leadership ethics. www .academy.umd.edu/ila/Publications/ Proceedings/1999/cjohnson.pdf

Larsson, J., & Vinberg, S. (2010). Leadership behavior in successful organizations: Universal or situation-dependent? *Total Quality Management & Business Excellence, 21*(3), 317–334.

Lee, Y., Han, A., Byron, T., & Fan, H. (2008). Daoist leadership: Theory and application. In C. Chen & Y. Lee (Eds.), *Leadership and management in China: Philosophies, theories, and practices* (pp. 83–107). Cambridge, UK: Cambridge University Press. doi:10.1017/ CBO9780511753763.005

Meirovich, G., & Gu, J. (2015). Empirical and theoretical validity of Hersey-Blanchard's contingency model: A critical analysis. *Journal of Applied Management and Entrepreneurship, 20*(3), 56–74. http:// dx.doi.org/10.9774/GLEAF.3709.2015 .ju.00006

Min-Huei, C. (2016). How Chinese philosophy applies in today's business world. *International Journal of Arts and Commerce, 5*(3), 102–110. https://www.ijac .org.uk/images/frontImages/gallery/ Vol._5_No._3/12._102-110.pdf

Reddin, W. J. (1967, April). The 3-D management style theory. *Training and Development Journal*, pp. 8–17.

Thompson, G., & Glasø, L. (2015). Situational leadership theory: A test from three perspectives. *Leadership & Organization Development Journal, 36*(5), 527–544.

Thompson, G., & Glasø, L. (2018). Situational leadership theory: A test from a leader-follower congruence approach. *Leadership & Organization Development Journal, 9*(5), 574–591.

Thompson, G., & Vecchio, R. P. (2009). Situational leadership theory: A test of three versions. *The Leadership Quarterly, 20*, 837–848.

Vecchio, R. P. (1987). Situational leadership theory: An examination of a prescriptive theory. *Journal of Applied Psychology, 72*(3), 444–451.

Vecchio, R. P., & Boatwright, K. J. (2002). Preferences for idealized style of supervision. *The Leadership Quarterly, 13*, 327–342.

Vecchio, R. P., Bullis, R. C., & Brazil, D. M. (2006). The utility of situational leadership theory: A replication in a military setting. *Small Group Leadership, 37*, 407–424.

Vroom, V. H., & Yetton, P. W. (1973). *Leadership and decision-making*. Pittsburgh, PA: University of Pittsburgh Press.

Wang, B. (2018, January 1). Chinese leadership: 5 critical differences with the West. *IEDP Developing Leaders*. https:// www.iedp.com/articles/chinese-leadership-5-critical-differences-with-the-west/

Yammarino, F. J., Dionne, S. D., Chun, J. U., & Dansereau, F. (2005). Leadership and levels of analysis: A state-of-the-science review. *The Leadership Quarterly, 16*(6), 879–919.

Yukl, G. A. (1989). *Leadership in organizations* (2nd ed.). Englewood Cliffs, NJ: Prentice Hall.

Yukl, G. A. (1998). *Leadership in organizations* (4th ed.). Upper Saddle River, NJ: Prentice Hall.

Zigarmi, D., & Roberts, T. P. (2017). A test of three basic assumptions of Situational Leadership® II model and their implications for HRD practitioners. *European Journal of Training and Development, 41*(3), 241–260.

CHAPTER 6

Ambrogi, M. (2013, April 28). New coach, no scholarship: "I'm sorry, we don't want you," is first thing Indy-area recruit told. *Indianapolis Star*, p. C1.

Asamani, J. A., Naab, F., & Ansah Ofei, A. M. (2016). Leadership styles in nursing management: Implications for staff outcomes. *Journal of Health Sciences, 6*(1), 23–36.

Bess, J. L., & Goldman, P. (2001). Leadership ambiguity in universities and K–12 schools and the limits of contemporary leadership theory. *The Leadership Quarterly, 12*, 419–450.

Cote, R. (2017). A comparison of leadership theories in an organizational environment. *International Journal of Business Administration, 8*(28), 1923–4007. http://doi.org/10.5430/ijba.v8n5p28

Drew, D. (2013, May 15). WMU football coach P. J. Fleck explains his "Row the Boat" mantra and hopes it will define the program and his tenure. *MLive.com*. https://www.mlive.com/broncos/2013/05/ wmu_football_coach_pj_fleck_ex.html

Eagly, A. H., & Johnson, B. T. (1990). Gender and leadership style: A meta-analysis. *Psychological Bulletin, 108*, 233–256.

Eagly, A. H., Makhijani, M. G., & Klonsky, B. G. (1992). Gender and the evaluation of leaders: A meta-analysis. *Psychological Bulletin, 111,* 3–22.

Evans, M. G. (1970). The effects of supervisory behavior on the path-goal relationship. *Organizational Behavior and Human Performance, 5,* 277–298.

Evans, M. G. (1996). R. J. House's "A path-goal theory of leader effectiveness." *The Leadership Quarterly, 7*(3), 305–309.

Fulk, J., & Wendler, E. R. (1982). Dimensionality of leader-subordinate interactions: A path-goal investigation. *Organizational Behavior and Human Performance, 30,* 241–264.

Giambalvo, E. (2019, November 5). Skeptical of P.J. Fleck and his slogans? So were others, but 8–0 Minnesota believes. *Washington Post.* https://www .washingtonpost.com/sports/2019/11/05/ skeptical-pj-fleck-his-slogans-so-were-others-minnesota-believes/

Greder, A. (2017, November 17). What is the "spiritual" part of P.J. Fleck's Gophers football makeover? *St. Paul Pioneer Press.* https://www.grandforksherald.com/sports/ 4361595-what-spiritual-part-pj-flecks-gophers-football-makeover

Halpin, A. W., & Winer, B. J. (1957). A factorial study of the leader behavior descriptions. In R. M. Stogdill & A. E. Coons (Eds.), *Leader behavior: Its description and measurement* (pp. 39–51). Columbus: The Ohio State University, Bureau of Business Research, Monograph No. 88.

Heilman, M. E., Wallen, A. S., Fuchs, D., & Tamkins, M. M. (2004). Penalties for success: Reactions to women who succeed at male gender-typed tasks. *Journal of Applied Psychology, 89,* 416–427.

Hemphill, J. K., & Coons, A. E. (1957). Development of the Leader Behavior Description Questionnaire. In R. M. Stogdill & A. E. Coons (Eds.), *Leader behavior: Its description and measurement* (pp. 6–38). Columbus: The Ohio State University, Bureau of Business Research, Monograph No. 88.

Hersey, P., & Blanchard, K. H. (1969). Life cycle theory of leadership. *Training & Development Journal, 23*(5), 26–34.

House, R. J. (1971). A path-goal theory of leader effectiveness. *Administrative Science Quarterly, 16,* 321–328.

House, R. J. (1977). A 1976 theory of charismatic leadership. In J. G. Hunt & L. L. Larson (Eds.), *Leadership: The cutting edge* (pp. 189–207). Carbondale: Southern Illinois University Press.

House, R. J. (1996). Path-goal theory of leadership: Lessons, legacy, and a reformulated theory. *The Leadership Quarterly, 7*(3), 323–352.

House, R. J., & Dessler, G. (1974). The path-goal theory of leadership: Some post hoc and a priori tests. In J. Hunt & L. Larson (Eds.), *Contingency approaches in leadership* (pp. 29–55). Carbondale: Southern Illinois University Press.

House, R. J., & Mitchell, R. R. (1974). Path-goal theory of leadership. *Journal of Contemporary Business, 3,* 81–97.

Indvik, J. (1985). *A path-goal theory investigation of superior-subordinate relationships.* Unpublished doctoral dissertation, University of Wisconsin–Madison.

Indvik, J. (1986). Path-goal theory of leadership: A meta-analysis. In *Proceedings of the Academy of Management Meeting* (pp. 189–192). Briarcliff Manor, NY: Academy of Management.

Indvik, J. (1988). *A more complete testing of path-goal theory.* Paper presented at the Academy of Management, Anaheim, CA.

Jermier, J. M. (1996). The path-goal theory of leadership: A subtextual analysis. *The Leadership Quarterly, 7*(3), 311–316.

Kanfer, R., Frese, M., & Johnson, R. E. (2017). Motivation related to work: A century of progress. *The Journal of Applied Psychology, 102*(3), 338–355.

Markgraff, P. (2018). PJ Fleck on coaching your culture. *AFCA Insider.*

https://insider.afca.com/pj-fleck-coaching-culture/

Mattingly, B. (2017a). Into the fire [Television series episode]. In *Sports Talk with Bo Mattingly* and JM Associates (Executive Producers), *Being P.J. Fleck*. Bristol, CT: ESPN.

Mattingly, B. (2017b). Sleeping giant [Television series episode]. In *Sports Talk with Bo Mattingly* and JM Associates (Executive Producers), *Being P.J. Fleck*. Bristol, Connecticut: ESPN.

Mendez, M. J., & Busenbark, J. R. (2015). Shared leadership and gender: All members are equal . . . but some more than others. *Leadership & Organization Development Journal, 36*(1), 17–34.

Nichols, B. (2016, December 31). Whether with dances or costumes, P.J. Fleck always found ways to motivate Western Michigan all the way to Cotton Bowl. *Dallas News*.

Nothaft, P. (2017, October 12). Former WMU coach P.J. Fleck using past success, failures in Minnesota rebuild. *MLive.com*. https://www.mlive.com/sports/2017/10/former_wmu_coach_pj_fleck_usin.html

Rittenberg, A. (2019, November 8). How P.J. Fleck rebuilt Minnesota football using batting doughnuts, "The Dig" and the Nekton mentality. *ESPN*. https://www.espn.com/college-football/story/_/id/28028337/how-pj-fleck-rebuilt-minnesota-football-using-batting-doughnuts-dig-nekton-mentality

Rosette, A. S., Koval, C. Z., Ma, A., & Livingston, R. (2016). Race matters for women leaders: Intersectional effects on agentic deficiencies and penalties. *The Leadership Quarterly, 27*(3), 429–445.

Schriesheim, C. A., Castro, S. L., Zhou, X., & DeChurch, L. A. (2006). An investigation of path-goal and transformational leadership theory predictions at the individual level of analysis. *The Leadership Quarterly, 17*, 21–38.

Schriesheim, C. A., & Kerr, S. (1977). Theories and measures of leadership: A critical appraisal. In J. G. Hunt & L. L. Larson (Eds.), *Leadership: The cutting edge* (pp. 9–45). Carbondale: Southern Illinois University Press.

Schriesheim, C. A., & Neider, L. L. (1996). Path-goal leadership theory: The long and winding road. *The Leadership Quarterly, 7*(3), 317–321.

Schriesheim, J. R., & Schriesheim, C. A. (1980). A test of the path-goal theory of leadership and some suggested directions for future research. *Personnel Psychology, 33*, 349–370.

Stinson, J. E., & Johnson, R. W. (1975). The path-goal theory of leadership: A partial test and suggested refinement. *Academy of Management Journal, 18*, 242–252.

Stogdill, R. M. (1963). *Manual for the Leader Behavior Description Questionnaire form XII*. Columbus: The Ohio State University, Bureau of Business Research.

Stumpf, S. A., Tymon, W. G., Ehr, R. J., & vanDam, N. H. M. (2016). Leading to intrinsically reward professionals for sustained engagement. *Leadership & Organization Development Journal, 37*(4), 467–486.

Turner, J. R., Baker, R., & Kellner, F. (2018). Theoretical literature review: Tracing the life cycle of a theory and its verified and falsified statements. *Human Resource Development Review, 17*(1), 34–61.

Vroom, V. H. (1964). *Work and motivation*. New York, NY: McGraw-Hill.

Wofford, J. C., & Liska, L. Z. (1993). Path-goal theories of leadership: A meta-analysis. *Journal of Management, 19*(4), 857–876.

CHAPTER 7

Anand, S., Hu, J., Liden, R. C., & Vidyarthi, P. R. (2011). Leader–member exchange: Recent research findings and prospects for the future. In A. Bryman, D. Collinson, K. Grint, G. Jackson, &

B. Uhl-Bien (Eds.), *The SAGE handbook of leadership* (pp. 311–325). London, UK: SAGE.

Atwater, L., & Carmeli, A. (2009). Leader–member exchange, feelings of energy, and involvement in creative work. *The Leadership Quarterly, 20,* 264–275.

Bakar, H. A., & Sheer, V. C. (2013). The mediating role of perceived cooperative communication in the relationship between interpersonal exchange relationships and perceived group cohesion. *Management Communication Quarterly, 27,* 443–465.

Bernerth, J. B., Armenakis, A. A., Feild, H. S., Giles, W. F., & Walker, H. J. (2007). Leader–member social exchange (LMSX): Development and validation of a scale. *Journal of Organizational Behavior, 28,* 979–1003.

Buch, R., Kuvaas, B., Dysvik, A., & Schyns, B. (2014). If and when social and economic leader–member exchange relationships predict follower work effort. *Leadership & Organization Development Journal, 35*(8), 725–739.

Catmull, E. (2008, September). How Pixar fosters collective creativity. *Harvard Business Review.* https://hbr.org/2008/09/how-pixar-fosters-collective-creativity

Cropanzano, R., Dasborough, M. T., & Weiss, H. M. (2017). Affective events and the development of leader–member exchange. *Academy of Management Review, 42*(2), 233–258.

Dansereau, F., Graen, G. B., & Haga, W. (1975). A vertical dyad linkage approach to leadership in formal organizations. *Organizational Behavior and Human Performance, 13,* 46–78.

Fairhurst, G., & Uhl-Bien, M. (2012). Organizational discourse analysis (ODA): Examining leadership as a relational process. *The Leadership Quarterly, 23*(6), 1043–1062.

Gerstner, C. R., & Day, D. V. (1997). Meta-analytic review of leader–member exchange theory: Correlates and construct issues. *Journal of Applied Psychology, 82,* 827–844.

Gottfredson, R. K., & Aguinis, H. (2017). Leadership behaviors and follower performance: Deductive and inductive examination of theoretical rationales and underlying mechanisms. *Journal of Organizational Behavior, 38*(4), 558–591.

Gottfredson, R. K., Wright, S. L., & Heaphy, E. D. (2020). A critique of the Leader–Member Exchange construct: Back to square one. *The Leadership Quarterly.* Advance online publication. https://doi.org/10.1016/j.leaqua.2020.101385

Graen, G. B. (1976). Role-making processes within complex organizations. In M. D. Dunnette (Ed.), *Handbook of industrial and organizational psychology* (pp. 1202–1245). Chicago, IL: Rand McNally.

Graen, G. B., & Cashman, J. (1975). *A role-making model of leadership in formal organizations: A developmental approach.* In J. G. Hunt & L. L. Larson (Eds.), *Leadership frontiers* (pp. 143–166). Kent, OH: Kent State University Press.

Graen, G. B., & Scandura, T. A. (1987). Toward a psychology of dyadic organizing. In B. Staw & L. L. Cumming (Eds.), *Research in organizational behavior* (Vol. 9, pp. 175–208). Greenwich, CT: JAI.

Graen, G. B., & Uhl-Bien, M. (1991). The transformation of professionals into self-managing and partially self-designing contributions: Toward a theory of leadership making. *Journal of Management Systems, 3*(3), 33–48.

Graen, G. B., & Uhl-Bien, M. (1995). Relationship-based approach to leadership: Development of leader–member exchange (LMX) theory of leadership over 25 years: Applying a multi-level, multi-domain perspective. *The Leadership Quarterly, 6*(2), 219–247.

Harris, K. J., Wheeler, A. R., & Kacmar, K. M. (2009). Leader–member exchange and empowerment: Direct and interactive effects on job satisfaction, turnover intentions, and performance. *The Leadership Quarterly, 20,* 371–382.

Harter, N., & Evanecky, D. (2002). Fairness in leader–member exchange theory: Do we all belong on the inside? *Leadership Review, 2*(2), 1–7.

Herman, H. M. Tse, & Troth, A. C. (2013). Perceptions and emotional experiences in differential supervisor-subordinate relationships. *Leadership & Organization Development Journal, 34*(3), 271–283.

Hill, L. (2014, September). How to manage for collective creativity [Video file]. *TEDxCambridge.* https://www.ted.com/talks/linda_hill_how_to_manage_for_collective_creativity

Hill, N. S., Kang, J. H., & Seo, M. (2014). The interactive effect of leader–member exchange and electronic communication on employee psychological empowerment and work outcomes. *The Leadership Quarterly, 25*(4), 772–783.

Ilies, R., Nahrgang, J. D., & Morgeson, F. P. (2007). Leader–member exchange and citizenship behaviors: A meta-analysis. *Journal of Applied Psychology, 92*(1), 269–277.

Katz, D. (1964). Motivational basis of organizational behavior. *Behavioral Science, 9,* 131–146.

Kelley, K. M. (2014). Leaders' narrative sensemaking during LMX role negotiations: Explaining how leaders make sense of who to trust and when. *The Leadership Quarterly, 25*(3), 433–448.

Lee, A., Thomas, G., Martin, R., Guillaume, Y., & Marstand, A. F. (2019). Beyond relationship quality: The role of leader–member exchange importance in leader–follower dyads. *Journal of Occupational and Organizational Psychology, 92*(4), 736–763.

Liao, Z., Liu, W., Li, X., & Song, Z. (2019). Give and take: An episodic perspective on leader–member exchange. *Journal of Applied Psychology, 104*(1), 34–51.

Liden, R. C., & Maslyn, J. M. (1998). Multidimensionality of leader–member exchange: An empirical assessment through scale development. *Journal of Management, 24,* 43–72.

Liden, R. C., Wayne, S. J., & Stilwell, D. (1993). A longitudinal study on the early development of leader–member exchange. *Journal of Applied Psychology, 78,* 662–674.

Madlock, P. E., & Booth-Butterfield, M. (2012). The influence of relational maintenance strategies among coworkers. *Journal of Business Communication, 49,* 21–47.

Malik, M., Wan, D., Ahmad, M. I., Naseem, M. A., & Rehman, R. ur. (2015). The role of LMX in employees' job motivation, satisfaction, empowerment, stress and turnover: Cross country analysis. *Journal of Applied Business Research (JABR), 31*(5), 1897–2000.

Martin, R., Guillaume, Y., Thomas, G., Lee, A., & Epitropaki, O. (2016). Leader–member exchange (LMX) and performance: A meta-analytic review. *Personnel Psychology, 69*(1), 67–121.

Maslyn, J. M., Schyns, B., & Farmer, S. M. (2017). Attachment style and leader–member exchange. *Leadership and Organization Development Journal, 38*(3), 450–462.

Matta, F. K., & Van Dyne, L. (2020). Understanding the disparate behavioral consequences of LMX differentiation: The role of social comparison emotions. *Academy of Management Review, 45*(1), 154–180.

McClane, W. E. (1991). Implications of member role differentiation: Analysis of a key concept in the LMX model of leadership. *Group & Organization Studies, 16*(1), 102–113.

Nahrgang, J. D., Morgeson, R. P., & Ilies, R. (2009). The development of leader–member exchanges: Exploring how personality and performance influence leader and member relationships over time. *Organizational Behavior and Human Decision Processes, 108*, 256–266.

Omilion-Hodges, L. M., & Baker, C. R. (2017). Communicating leader–member relationship quality: The development of leader communication exchange scales to measure relationship building and maintenance through the exchange of communication-based goods. *International Journal of Business Communication, 54*(2), 115–145.

Omilion-Hodges, L. M., Ptacek, J. K., & Zerilli, D. H. (2015). A comprehensive review and communication research agenda of the contextualized workgroup: The evolution and future of leader–member exchange, coworker exchange, and team-member exchange. In E. L. Cohen (Ed.), *Communication yearbook* (Vol. 40, pp. 343–377). New York, NY: Routledge.

Organ, D. W. (1988). *Organizational citizenship behavior: The good soldier syndrome.* Lexington, MA: Lexington Books.

Randolph-Seng, B., Cogliser, C. C., Randolph, A. F., Scandura, T. A., Miller, C. D., & Smith-Genthôs, R. (2016). Diversity in leadership: Race in leader–member exchanges. *Leadership & Organization Development Journal, 37*(6), 750–773.

Rockstuhl, T., Dulebohn, J. H., Ang, S., & Shore, L. M. (2012). Leader–member exchange (LMX) and culture: A meta-analysis of correlates of LMX across 23 countries. *Journal of Applied Psychology, 97*(6), 1097.

Scandura, T. A. (1999). Rethinking leader–member exchange: An organizational justice perspective. *The Leadership Quarterly, 10*(1), 25–40.

Schriesheim, C. A., Castro, S. L., & Cogliser, C. C. (1999). Leader–member exchange (LMX) research: A comprehensive review of theory, measurement, and data-analytic practices. *The Leadership Quarterly, 10*, 63–113.

Schriesheim, C. A., Castro, S. L., Zhou, X., & Yammarino, F. J. (2001). The folly of theorizing "A" but testing "B": A selective level-of-analysis review of the field and a detailed leader–member exchange illustration. *The Leadership Quarterly, 12*, 515–551.

Sheer, V. C. (2014). "Exchange lost" in leader–member exchange theory and research: A critique and a reconceptualization. *Leadership, 11*, 1–17.

Sparrowe, R. T., & Liden, R. C. (2005). Two routes to influence: Integrating leader–member exchange and social network perspectives. *Administrative Science Quarterly, 50*(4), 505–535.

Uhl-Bien, M., Maslyn, J., & Ospina, S. (2012). The nature of relational leadership: A multitheoretical lens on leadership relationships and processes. In D. V. Day & J. Antonakis (Eds.), *The nature of leadership* (2nd ed., pp. 289–330). Thousand Oaks, CA: SAGE.

Volmer, J., Spurk, D., & Niessen, C. (2012). Leader–member exchange (LMX), job autonomy, and creative work involvement. *The Leadership Quarterly, 23*(3), 456–465.

Xu, A. J., Loi, R., Cai, Z., & Liden, R. C. (2019). Reversing the lens: How followers influence leader–member exchange quality. *Journal of Occupational and Organizational Psychology, 92*(3), 475–497.

Yukl, G. (1994). *Leadership in organizations* (3rd ed.). Englewood Cliffs, NJ: Prentice Hall.

CHAPTER 8

Andersen, J. A. (2015). Barking up the wrong tree: On the fallacies of the transformational leadership theory. *Leadership & Organization Development Journal, 36*(6), 765–777.

Anderson, H. J., Baur, J. E., Griffith, J. A., & Buckley, M. R. (2017). What works for you may not work for (Gen)me: Limitations of present leadership theories for the new generation. *The Leadership Quarterly, 28*(1), 245–260.

Antonakis, J. (2012). Transformational and charismatic leadership. In D. V. Day & J. Antonakis (Eds.), *The nature of leadership* (2nd ed., pp. 256–288). Thousand Oaks, CA: SAGE.

Antonakis, J., Avolio, B. J., & Sivasubramaniam, N. (2003). Context and leadership: An examination of the nine-factor full-range leadership theory using the Multifactor Leadership Questionnaire. *The Leadership Quarterly, 14*(3), 261–295.

Antonakis, J., & House, R. J. (2014). Instrumental leadership: Measurement and extension of transformational transactional leadership theory. *The Leadership Quarterly, 25*(4), 746–771.

Arthur, C. A., & Hardy, L. (2014). Transformational leadership: A quasi-experimental study. *Leadership & Organization Development Journal, 35*(1), 38–53.

Avolio, B. J. (1999). *Full leadership development: Building the vital forces in organizations.* Thousand Oaks, CA: SAGE.

Avolio, B. J., & Gibbons, T. C. (1988). Developing transformational leaders: A life span approach. In J. A. Conger, R. N. Kanungo, & Associates (Eds.), *Charismatic leadership: The elusive factor in organizational effectiveness* (pp. 276–308). San Francisco, CA: Jossey-Bass.

Bailey, J., & Axelrod, R. H. (2001). Leadership lessons from Mount Rushmore: An interview with James MacGregor Burns. *The Leadership Quarterly, 12*, 113–127.

Bass, B. M. (1985). *Leadership and performance beyond expectations.* New York, NY: Free Press.

Bass, B. M. (1990). From transactional to transformational leadership: Learning to share the vision. *Organizational Dynamics, 18*, 19–31.

Bass, B. M. (1997). Does the transactional–transformational leadership paradigm transcend organizational and national boundaries? *American Psychologist, 52*(2), 130–139.

Bass, B. M. (1998). The ethics of transformational leadership. In J. Ciulla (Ed.), *Ethics: The heart of leadership* (pp. 169–192). Westport, CT: Praeger.

Bass, B. M., & Avolio, B. J. (1990a). The implications of transactional and transformational leadership for individual, team, and organizational development. *Research in Organizational Change and Development, 4*, 231–272.

Bass, B. M., & Avolio, B. J. (1990b). *Multifactor Leadership Questionnaire.* Palo Alto, CA: Consulting Psychologists Press.

Bass, B. M., & Avolio, B. J. (1993). Transformational leadership: A response to critiques. In M. M. Chemers & R. Ayman (Eds.), *Leadership theory and research: Perspectives and directions* (pp. 49–80). San Diego, CA: Academic Press.

Bass, B. M., & Avolio, B. J. (1994). *Improving organizational effectiveness through transformational leadership.* Thousand Oaks, CA: SAGE.

Bass, B. M., & Avolio, B. J. (1995). *Multifactor Leadership Questionnaire for research.* Menlo Park, CA: Mind Garden.

Bass, B. M., & Riggio, R. E. (2006). *Transformational leadership* (2nd ed.). Mahwah, NJ: Erlbaum.

Bass, B. M., & Steidlmeier, P. (1999). Ethics, character, and authentic transformational leadership. *The Leadership Quarterly, 10*, 181–217.

Bennis, W. G., & Nanus, B. (1985). *Leaders: The strategies for taking charge.* New York, NY: Harper & Row.

Bennis, W. G., & Nanus, B. (2007). *Leaders: The strategies for taking charge* (2nd ed.). New York, NY: Harper & Row.

Boehm, S. A., Dwertmann, D. J. G., Bruch, H., & Shamir, B. (2015). The missing link? Investigating organizational identity strength and transformational leadership climate as mechanisms that connect CEO charisma with firm performance. *The Leadership Quarterly, 26*(2), 156–171.

Brandt, T., & Laiho, M. (2013). Gender and personality in transformational leadership context. *Leadership & Organization Development Journal, 34*(1), 44–66.

Bryman, A. (1992). *Charisma and leadership in organizations.* London, UK: SAGE.

Burns, J. M. (1978). *Leadership.* New York, NY: Harper & Row.

Caza, A., & Posner, B. Z. (2019). How and when does grit influence leaders' behavior? *Leadership & Organization Development Journal, 40*(1), 124–134.

Chibanda, D. (2017a, June 15). How a community-based approach to mental health is making strides in Zimbabwe. *The Conversation.* https://theconversation.com/how-a-community-based-approach-to-mental-health-is-making-strides-in-zimbabwe-79312

Chibanda, D. (2017b, May 16). The grandmothers who save lives. *Los Angeles Times.* https://www.latimes.com/world/global-development/la-fg-global-dixon-chibanda-oped-20170516-story.html

Chibanda, D. (2017c). Why I train grandmothers to treat depression [Video file]. *TEDWomen2017.* https://www.ted.com/talks/dixon_chibanda_why_i_train_grandmothers_to_treat_depression

Christie, A., Barling, J., & Turner, N. (2011). Pseudo-transformational leadership: Model specification and outcomes. *Journal of Applied Social Psychology, 44*(12), 2943–2984.

Conger, J. A. (1999). Charismatic and transformational leadership in organizations: An insider's perspective on these developing streams of research. *The Leadership Quarterly, 10*(2), 145–179.

Conger, J. A., & Kanungo, R. N. (1998). *Charismatic leadership in organizations.* Thousand Oaks, CA: SAGE.

Credé, M., Jong, J., & Harms, P. (2019). The generalizability of transformational leadership across cultures: A meta-analysis. *Journal of Managerial Psychology, 34*(3), 139–155.

Dinh, J. E., Lord, R. G., Gardner, W. L., Meuser, J. D., Liden, R. C., & Hu, J. (2014). Leadership theory and research in the new millennium: Current theoretical trends and changing perspectives. *The Leadership Quarterly, 25*(1), 36–62.

Dong, Y., Bartol, K. M., Zhang, Z.-X., & Li, C. (2017). Enhancing employee creativity via individual skill development and team knowledge sharing: Influences of dual-focused transformational leadership. *Journal of Organizational Behavior, 38*, 439–458.

Gilbert, S., Horsman, P., & Kelloway, E. K. (2016). The motivation for transformational leadership scale. *Leadership & Organization Development Journal, 37*(2), 158–180.

Hamstra, M. R., Van Yperen, N. W., Wisse, B., & Sassenberg, K. (2014). Transformational and transactional leadership and followers' achievement goals. *Journal of Business and Psychology, 29*(3), 413–425.

Hinkin, T. R., & Schriesheim, C. A. (2008). A theoretical and empirical examination of the transactional and non-leadership dimensions of the Multifactor Leadership Questionnaire (MLQ). *The Leadership Quarterly, 19*, 501–513.

House, R. J. (1976). A 1976 theory of charismatic leadership. In J. G. Hunt & L. L. Larson (Eds.), *Leadership: The cutting edge* (pp. 189–207). Carbondale: Southern Illinois University Press.

Howell, J. M., & Avolio, B. J. (1993). The ethics of charismatic leadership: Submission or liberation? *Academy of Management Executive, 6*(2), 43–54.

Hunt, J. G., & Conger, J. A. (1999). From where we sit: An assessment of transformational and charismatic leadership research. *The Leadership Quarterly, 10*(3), 335–343.

Jung, D. I., Chow, C., & Wu, A. (2003). The role of transformational leadership in enhancing organizational innovation: Hypotheses and some preliminary findings. *The Leadership Quarterly, 14*(4–5), 525–544.

Kirkman, B. L., Chen, G., Farh, J., Chen, Z. X., & Lowe, K. B. (2009). Individual power distance orientation and follower reactions to transformational leaders: A cross-level, cross-cultural examination. *Academy of Management Journal, 52*, 744–764.

Knippenberg, D. van, & Sitkin, S. B. (2013). A critical assessment of charismatic–transformational leadership research: Back to the drawing board? *The Academy of Management Annals, 7*(1), 1–60.

Kouzes, J. M., & Posner, B. Z. (2002). *The leadership challenge* (3rd ed.). San Francisco, CA: Jossey-Bass.

Kouzes, J. M., & Posner, B. Z. (2017a). *The leadership challenge: How to get extraordinary things done in organizations* (6th ed.). San Francisco, CA: Jossey-Bass.

Kouzes, J., & Posner, B. (2017b). Who you are isn't who you will be. *Leader to Leader, 83*, 30–34.

Kuhnert, K. W. (1994). Transforming leadership: Developing people through delegation. In B. M. Bass & B. J. Avolio (Eds.), *Improving organizational effectiveness through transformational leadership* (pp. 10–25). Thousand Oaks, CA: SAGE.

Kuhnert, K. W., & Lewis, P. (1987). Transactional and transformational leadership: A constructive/developmental analysis. *Academy of Management Review, 12*(4), 648–657.

Landay, K., Harms, P. D., & Credé, M. (2019). Shall we serve the dark lords? A meta-analytic review of psychopathy and leadership. *Journal of Applied Psychology, 104*(1), 183–196.

Lovelace, J. B., Neely, B. H., Allen, J. B., & Hunter, S. T. (2019). Charismatic, ideological, & pragmatic (CIP) model of leadership: A critical review and agenda for future research. *The Leadership Quarterly, 30*(1), 96–110.

Lowe, K. B., & Gardner, W. L. (2001). Ten years of *The Leadership Quarterly*: Contributions and challenges for the future. *The Leadership Quarterly, 11*(4), 459–514.

Lowe, K. B., Kroeck, K. G., & Sivasubramaniam, N. (1996). Effectiveness correlates of transformational and transactional leadership: A meta-analytic review of the MLQ literature. *The Leadership Quarterly, 7*(3), 385–425.

Mason, C., Griffin, M., & Parker, S. (2014). Transformational leadership development: Connecting psychological and behavioral change. *Leadership & Organization Development Journal, 35*(3), 174–194.

Mohammed, Y. G., Fernando, M., & Caputi, P. (2013). Transformational leadership and work engagement. *Leadership & Organization Development Journal, 34*(6), 532–550.

Nemanich, L. A., & Keller, R. T. (2007). Transformational leadership in an acquisition: A field study of employees. *The Leadership Quarterly, 18*, 49–68.

Ng, E. S., Schweitzer, L., & Lyons, S. T. (2010). New generation, great expectations: A field study of the millennial generation. *Journal of Business and Psychology, 25*, 281–292.

Nicholls, J. (1988). Transforming leadership in organisations: Bringing meta "visioning" into the macro leadership role. *European Management Journal, 6*(3), 269–276.

Notgrass, D. (2014). The relationship between followers' perceived quality of relationship and preferred leadership style. *Leadership & Organization Development Journal, 35*(7), 605–621.

Nuwer, R. (2018, October 16). How a bench and a team of grandmothers can tackle depression. *BBC.* https://www.bbc

.com/future/article/20181015-how-one-bench-and-a-team-of-grandmothers-can-beat-depression

Posner, B. Z. (2016). Investigating the reliability and validity of the Leadership Practices Inventory®. *Administrative Sciences, 6*(4), 17. doi:10.3390/admsci6040017

Puni, A., Mohammed, I., & Asamoah, E. (2018). Transformational leadership and job satisfaction: The moderating effect of contingent reward. *Leadership & Organization Development Journal, 39*(4), 522–537.

Rowold, J., & Heinitz, K. (2007). Transformational and charismatic leadership: Assessing the convergent, divergent and criterion validity of the MLQ and the CKS. *The Leadership Quarterly, 18*, 121–133.

Shamir, B., House, R. J., & Arthur, M. B. (1993). The motivational effects of charismatic leadership: A self-concept based theory. *Organization Science, 4*(4), 577–594.

Sosik, J. J., & Jung, D. I. (2010). *Full range leadership development: Pathways for people, profit, and planet.* New York, NY: Psychology Press.

Tejeda, M. J., Scandura, T. A., & Pillai, R. (2001). The MLQ revisited: Psychometric properties and recommendations. *The Leadership Quarterly, 12*, 31–52.

Tengblad, S. (2012). *The work of managers: Towards a practice theory of management.* Oxford, UK: Oxford University Press.

Tims, M., Bakker, A. B., & Xanthopoulou, D. (2011). Do transformational leaders enhance their followers' daily work engagement? *The Leadership Quarterly, 22*, 121–131.

Tourish, D. (2013). *The dark side of transformational leadership: A critical perspective.* New York, NY: Routledge.

Tracey, J. B., & Hinkin, T. R. (1998). Transformational leadership or

effective managerial practices? *Group & Organization Management, 23*(3), 220–236.

Weber, M. (1947). *The theory of social and economic organizations* (T. Parsons, trans.). New York, NY: Free Press.

World Health Organization. (2018). Dixon Chibanda: Grandmothers help to scale up mental health care. *Bulletin of the World Health Organization, 96*(6), 376–377.

Yammarino, F. J. (1993). Transforming leadership studies: Bernard Bass' leadership and performance beyond expectations. *The Leadership Quarterly, 4*(3), 379–382.

Yang, I. (2015). Positive effects of laissez-faire leadership: Conceptual exploration. *The Journal of Management Development, 34*(10), 1246–1261.

Yukl, G. A. (1999). An evaluation of conceptual weaknesses in transformational and charismatic leadership theories. *The Leadership Quarterly, 10*(2), 285–305.

Zhu, W., Avolio, B. J., Riggio, R. E., & Sosik, J. J. (2011). The effect of authentic transformational leadership on follower and group ethics. *The Leadership Quarterly, 22*, 801–817.

CHAPTER 9

Alvesson, M., & Einola, K. (2019). Warning for excessive positivity: Authentic leadership and other traps in leadership studies. *The Leadership Quarterly, 30*(4), 383–395.

Anderson, H. J., Baur, J. E., Griffith, J. A., & Buckley, M. R. (2017). What works for you may not work for (Gen)me: Limitations of present leadership theories for the new generation. *The Leadership Quarterly, 28*(1), 245–260.

Avolio, B. J., & Gardner, W. L. (2005). Authentic leadership development: Getting to the root of positive forms of leadership. *The Leadership Quarterly, 16*, 315–338.

Avolio, B. J., Walumbwa, F. O., & Weber, T. J. (2009). Leadership: Current theories, research, and future directions. *Annual Review of Psychology, 60*, 421–449.

Avolio, B. J., & Wernsing, T. S. (2008). Practicing authentic leadership. *Positive psychology: Exploring the best in people, 4*, 147–165.

Avolio, B. J., Wernsing, T., & Gardner, W. L. (2018). Revisiting the development and validation of the authentic leadership questionnaire: Analytical clarifications. *Journal of Management, 44*(2), 399–411.

Azanza, G., Moriano, J. A., Molero, F., & Lévy Mangin, J. (2015). The effects of authentic leadership on turnover intention. *Leadership & Organization Development Journal, 36*(8), 955–971.

Bandura, A. (1997). *Self-efficacy: The exercise of control*. New York, NY: Freeman.

Bass, B. M. (1990). *Handbook of leadership*. New York, NY: Free Press.

Bass, B. M., & Steidlmeier, P. (1999). Ethics, character, and authentic transformational leadership. *The Leadership Quarterly, 10*, 181–217.

Brown, B. (2010). The power of vulnerability [Video file]. *TED*. https://www.ted.com/talks/brene_brown_the_power_of_vulnerability

Brown, B. (2012). Listening to shame [Video file]. *TED*. https://www.ted.com/talks/brene_brown_listening_to_shame

Brown, B. (2017). *Braving the wilderness: The quest for true belonging and the courage to stand alone*. New York, NY: Random House.

Brown, B. (2019a). Official bio. *Brené Brown*. https://Brenebrown.com/media-kit/

Brown, B. (2019b). Research. *Brené Brown*. https://Brenebrown.com/the-research/

Brown, B. (2019c, May 1). Let's rumble [Blog post]. *Brené Brown*. https://Brenebrown.com/blog/2019/05/01/lets-rumble/

Burns, J. M. (1978). *Leadership*. New York, NY: Harper & Row.

Cameron, K. S., Dutton, J. E., & Quinn, R. E. (2003). Foundations of positive organizational scholarship. In K. S. Cameron, J. E. Dutton, & R. E. Quinn (Eds.), *Positive organizational scholarship* (pp. 3–13). San Francisco, CA: Berrett-Koehler.

Chan, A. (2005). Authentic leadership measurement and development: Challenges and suggestions. In W. L. Gardner, B. J. Avolio, & F. O. Walumbwa (Eds.), *Authentic leadership theory and practice: Origins, effects, and development* (pp. 227–251). Oxford, UK: Elsevier Science.

Cianci, A. M., Hannah, S. T., Roberts, R. P., & Tsakumis, G. T. (2014). The effects of authentic leadership on followers' ethical decision-making in the face of temptation: An experimental study. *The Leadership Quarterly, 25*, 581–594.

Cooper, C., Scandura, T. A., & Schriesheim, C. A. (2005). Looking forward but learning from our past: Potential challenges to developing authentic leadership theory and authentic leaders. *The Leadership Quarterly, 116*, 474–495.

Covey, S. R. (1990). *Principle-centered leadership*. New York, NY: Fireside.

Dalton, K. (2002). *Theodore Roosevelt: A strenuous life*. New York, NY: Knopf.

Eagly, A. H. (2005). Achieving relational authenticity in leadership: Does gender matter? *The Leadership Quarterly, 16*, 459–474.

Efros, D., Findlay, D., & Mussman, J. (Producers), & Restrepo, S. (Director). (2019). Brené Brown: The call to courage [Video file]. *Netflix*. https://www.netflix.com/title/81010166

Fry, L. W., & Whittington, J. L. (2005). In search of authenticity: Spiritual leadership theory as a source for future theory, research, and practice on authentic leadership. In W. Gardner, B. J. Avolio, & F. O. Walumbwa (Eds.), *Authentic leadership theory and practice: Origins, effects, and development* (pp. 183–202). Oxford, UK: Elsevier Science.

Gardner, W. L., Avolio, B. J., Luthans, F., May, D. R., & Walumbwa, F. O. (2005). "Can you see the real me?" A self-based model of authentic leader and follower development. *The Leadership Quarterly, 16*, 343–372.

Gardner, W. L., Avolio, B. J., & Walumbwa, F. O. (2005a). *Authentic leadership theory and practice: Origins, effects and development* (Monographs in leadership and management, vol. 3). Bingley, UK: Emerald Group.

Gardner, W. L., Avolio, B. J., & Walumbwa, F. O. (2005b). Authentic leadership development: Emergent trends and future directions. In W. L. Gardner, B. J. Avolio, & F. O. Walumbwa (Eds.), *Authentic leadership theory and practice: Origins, effects, and development* (pp. 387–406). Oxford, UK: Elsevier Science.

Gatling, A., Kang, H. J. A., & Kim, J. S. (2016). The effects of authentic leadership and organizational commitment on turnover intention. *Leadership & Organization Development Journal, 37*(2), 181–199.

George, B. (2003). *Authentic leadership: Rediscovering the secrets to creating lasting value.* San Francisco, CA: Jossey-Bass.

George, B., & Sims, P. (2007). *True north: Discover your authentic leadership.* San Francisco, CA: Jossey-Bass.

Gill, C., & Caza, A. (2018). An investigation of authentic leadership's individual and group influences on follower responses. *Journal of Management, 44*(2), 530–554.

Helgesen, S. (1981). *Wildcatters: A story of Texans, oil, and money.* New York, NY: Doubleday.

Helgesen, S. (1990). *The female advantage: Women's ways of leadership.* New York, NY: Doubleday.

Hirst, G., Walumbwa, F., Aryee, S., Butarbutar, I., & Chen, C. J. H. (2016). A multi-level investigation of authentic leadership as an antecedent of helping behavior. *Journal of Business Ethics, 139*(3), 485–499.

Hoch, J. E., Bommer, W. H., Dulebohn, J. H., & Wu, D. (2018). Do ethical, authentic, and servant leadership explain variance above and beyond transformational leadership? A meta-analysis. *Journal of Management, 44*(2), 501–529.

Howard Schultz: Starbucks' first mate. (2008, October 10). *Entrepreneur.* Retrieved from https://www.entrepreneur.com/article/197692

Howell, J. M., & Avolio, B. J. (1993). The ethics of charismatic leadership: Submission or liberation? *Academy of Management Executive, 6*(2), 43–54.

Hu, Y., Wu, X., Zong, Z., Xiao, Y., Maguire, P., Qu, F., Wei, J., & Wang, D. (2018). Authentic leadership and proactive behavior: The role of psychological capital and compassion at work. *Frontiers in Psychology, 9*, 2470. https://doi.org/10.3389/fpsyg.2018.02470

Ilies, R., Morgeson, F. P., & Nahrgang, J. D. (2005). Authentic leadership and eudaemonic well-being: Understanding leader-follower outcomes. *The Leadership Quarterly, 16*, 373–394.

Kernis, M. H. (2003). Toward a conceptualization of optimal self-esteem. *Psychological Inquiry, 14*, 1–26.

Kumar, A. (2014). Authentic leadership and psychological ownership: Investigation of interrelations. *Leadership & Organization Development Journal, 35*(4), 266–285.

Lemoine, G. J., Hartnell, C. A., & Leroy, H. (2019). Taking stock of moral approaches to leadership: An integrative review of ethical, authentic, and servant leadership. *Academy of Management Annals, 13*(1), 148–187.

Leroy, H., Anseel, F., Gardner, W., & Sels, L. (2015). Authentic leadership, authentic followership, basic need satisfaction, and work role performance: A cross-level study. *Journal of Management, 41*(6), 1677–1697.

Luthans, F., & Avolio, B. J. (2003). Authentic leadership development. In K. S. Cameron, J. E. Dutton, & R. E. Quinn (Eds.), *Positive organizational scholarship* (pp. 241–258). San Francisco, CA: Berrett-Koehler.

Lyubovnikova, J., Legood, A., Turner, N., & Mamakouka, A. (2017). How authentic leadership influences team performance: The mediating role of team reflexivity. *Journal of Business Ethics, 141*(1), 59–70.

Miao, C., Humphrey, R., & Qian, S. (2018). Emotional intelligence and authentic leadership: A meta-analysis. *Leadership and Organization Development Journal, 39*(5), 679–690.

Mintz, S. (2015, September 9). Is Donald Trump an authentic leader? *Ethics Sage.* http://www.ethicssage.com/2015/09/is-donald-trump-an-authentic-leader-.html

Peus, C., Wescher, J. S., Streicher, B., Braun, S., & Frey, S. (2012). Authentic leadership: An empirical test of its antecedents, consequences, and mediating mechanisms. *Journal of Business Ethics, 107*(3), 331–348.

Rego, A., Sousa, F., Marques, C., & Pina e Cunha, M. (2012). Authentic leadership promoting employees' psychological capital and creativity. *Journal of Business Research, 65*(3), 429–437.

Rego, A., Sousa, F., Marques, C., & Pina e Cunha, M. (2014). Hope and positive affect mediating the authentic leadership and creativity relationship. *Journal of Business Research, 67*(2), 200–210.

Semedo, A. S. D., Coelho, A. F. M., & Ribeiro, N. M. P. (2016). Effects of authentic leadership, affective commitment and job resourcefulness on employees' creativity and individual performance. *Leadership & Organization Development Journal, 37*(8), 1038–1055.

Shamir, B., & Eilam, G. (2005). "What's your story?" A life-stories approach to authentic leadership development. *The Leadership Quarterly, 16*, 395–417.

Sidani, Y. M., & Rowe, W. G. (2018). A reconceptualization of authentic leadership: Leader legitimation via follower-centered assessment of the moral dimension. *The Leadership Quarterly, 29*(6), 623–636.

Stander, F. W., Beer, L. T. de, & Stander, M. W. (2015). Authentic leadership as a source of optimism, trust in the organisation and work engagement in the public health care sector. *SA Journal of Human Resource Management, 13*(1), 1–12.

Steffens, N. K., Mols, F., Haslam, S. A., & Okimoto, T. G. (2016). True to what we stand for: Championing collective interests as a path to authentic leadership. *The Leadership Quarterly, 27*(5), 726–744.

Sutcliffe, K. M., & Vogus, T. J. (2003). Organizing for resilience. In K. S. Cameron, J. E. Dutton, & R. E. Quinn (Eds.), *Positive organizational scholarship* (pp. 94–110). San Francisco, CA: Berrett-Koehler.

TED. (n.d.). The most popular talks of all time [Video file]. https://www.ted.com/playlists/171/the_most_popular_talks_of_all

Terry Fox Foundation. (2017). http://www.terryfox.org/

Walumbwa, F. O., Avolio, B. J., Gardner, W. L., Wernsing, T. S., & Peterson, S. J. (2008). Authentic leadership: Development and validation of a theory-based measure. *Journal of Management, 34*(1), 89–126.

Wang, H., Sui, Y., Luthans, F., Wang, D., & Wu, Y. (2014). Impact of authentic leadership on performance: Role of followers' positive psychological capital and relational processes. *Journal of Organizational Behavior, 35*, 5–21.

Wei, F., Li, Y., Zhang, Y., & Liu, S. (2018). The interactive effect of authentic leadership and leader competency on followers' job performance: The mediating role of work engagement. *Journal of Business Ethics, 153*(3), 763–773.

Winfrey, O. (2013, March 17). Dr. Brené Brown's vulnerability breakdown [Television series episode]. In O. Winfrey (Producer), *SuperSoul Sunday*. West Hollywood, CA: Oprah Winfrey Network (OWN).

Xu, B., Zhao, S., Li, C., & Lin, C. (2017). Authentic leadership and employee creativity: Testing the multilevel mediation model. *Leadership & Organization Development Journal, 38*(3), 482–498.

Yavuz, M. (2020). Transformational leadership and authentic leadership as practical implications of positive organizational psychology. In E. Baykal (Ed.), *Handbook of research on positive organizational behavior for improved workplace performance* (pp. 122–139). Hershey, PA: IGI Global.

CHAPTER 10

Alverà, M. (2017). The surprising ingredient that makes businesses work better [Video file]. *TED@BCG Milan.* https://www.ted.com/talks/marco_Alvera_the_surprising_ingredient_that_makes_businesses_work_better

Bande, B., Fernández-Ferrín, P., Varela-Neira, C., & Otero-Neira, C. (2016). Exploring the relationship among servant leadership, intrinsic motivation and performance in an industrial sales setting. *The Journal of Business & Industrial Marketing, 31*(2), 219–231.

Bao, Y., Li, C., & Zhao, H. (2018). Servant leadership and engagement: A dual mediation model. *Journal of Managerial Psychology, 33*(6), 406–417.

Barbuto, J. E., Jr., Gottfredson, R. K., & Searle, T. P. (2014). An examination of emotional intelligence as an antecedent of servant leadership. *Journal of Leadership & Organizational Studies, 21*(3), 315.

Barbuto, J. E., Jr., & Wheeler, D. W. (2006). Scale development and construct clarification of servant leadership. *Group and Organizational Management, 31*, 300–326.

Bauer, T. N., Perrot, S., Liden, R. C., & Erdogan, B. (2019). Understanding the consequences of newcomer proactive behaviors: The moderating contextual role of servant leadership. *Journal of Vocational Behavior, 112*, 356–368.

Beck, C. D. (2014). Antecedents of servant leadership: A mixed methods study. *Journal of Leadership & Organizational Studies, 21*(3), 299.

Bennis, W. (2002). Become a tomorrow leader. In L. C. Spears & M. Lawrence (Eds.), *Focus on leadership: Servant-leadership for the twenty-first century* (pp. 101–110). New York, NY: Wiley.

Blanchard, K., & Hodges, P. (2003). *The servant leader: Transforming your hearts, heads, hands, and habits.* Nashville, TN: Thomas Nelson.

Chen, Z., Zhu, J., & Zhou, M. (2015). How does a servant leader fuel the service fire? A multilevel model of servant leadership, individual self identity, group competition climate, and customer service performance. *Journal of Applied Psychology, 100*(2), 511–521.

Chiniara, M., & Bentein, K. (2016). Linking servant leadership to individual performance: Differentiating the mediating role of autonomy, competence and relatedness need satisfaction. *The Leadership Quarterly, 27*(1), 124.

Coetzer, M. F., Bussin, M., & Geldenhuys, M. (2017). The functions of a servant leader. *Administrative Sciences, 7*(1), 5. http://dx.doi.org/10.3390/admsci7010005

Covey, S. R. (2002). Foreword. In R. K. Greenleaf (Ed.), *Servant leadership: A journey into the nature of legitimate power and greatness* (pp. 1–14). New York, NY: Paulist Press.

Dennis, R. S., & Bocarnea, M. (2005). Development of the servant leadership assessment instrument. *Leadership & Organization Development Journal, 26,* 600–615.

DePree, M. (2002). Servant-leadership: Three things necessary. In L. C. Spears & M. Lawrence (Eds.), *Focus on leadership: Servant-leadership for the twenty-first century* (pp. 27–34). New York, NY: Wiley.

Ehrhart, M. G. (2004). Leadership and procedural justice climate as antecedents of unit-level organizational citizenship behavior. *Personnel Psychology, 57,* 61–94.

Elliott, S. (2018, June 7). View from the top: An interview with Marco Alverà, Snam CEO [Video file]. *S&P Global Platts.* https://www.bing.com/videos/search?q=marco+Alverà&&&view=detail&mid=A610E9158A05C05711AAA610E9158A05C05711AA&&FORM=VDRVRV

Eva, N., Robin, M., Sendjaya, S., van Dierendonck, D., & Liden, R. C. (2019). Servant leadership: A systematic review and call for future research. *The Leadership Quarterly, 30*(1), 111–132.

Gandolfi, F., & Stone, S. (2018). Leadership, leadership styles, and servant leadership. *Journal of Management Research, 18*(4), 261–269.

Gergen, D. (2006, June 11). Bad news for bullies. *U.S. News and World Report, 140,* 54.

Graham, J. W. (1991). Servant leadership in organizations: Inspirational and moral. *The Leadership Quarterly, 2,* 105–119.

Greenleaf, R. K. (1970). *The servant as leader.* Westfield, IN: Greenleaf Center for Servant Leadership.

Greenleaf, R. K. (1972). *The institution as servant.* Westfield, IN: Greenleaf Center for Servant Leadership.

Greenleaf, R. K. (1977). *Servant leadership: A journey into the nature of legitimate power and greatness.* New York, NY: Paulist Press.

Hale, J. R., & Fields, D. L. (2007). Exploring servant leadership across cultures: A study of followers in Ghana and the USA. *Leadership, 3,* 397–417.

Hesse, H. (1956). *The journey to the East.* London, UK: P. Owen.

Hoch, J. E., Bommer, W. H., Dulebohn, J. H., & Wu, D. (2018). Do ethical, authentic, and servant leadership explain variance above and beyond transformational leadership? A meta-analysis. *Journal of Management, 44*(2), 501–529.

Hu, J., & Liden, R. C. (2011). Antecedents of team potency and team effectiveness: An examination of goal and process clarity and servant leadership. *Journal of Applied Psychology, 96*(4), 851–862.

Hunter, E. M., Neubert, M., Perry, S. J., Witt, L. A., Penney, L. M., & Weinberger, E. (2013). Servant leaders inspire servant followers: Antecedent and outcomes for employees and the organization. *The Leadership Quarterly, 24*(2), 316–331.

Kidder, T. (2003). *Mountains beyond mountains: The quest of Dr. Paul Farmer, a man who would cure the world.* New York, NY: Random House.

Knowledge@Wharton. (2008, July 9). *Southwest Airlines' Colleen Barrett flies high on fuel hedging and "servant leadership."* http://knowledge.wharton.upenn.edu/article.cfm?articleid=2006

Laub, J. A. (1999). Assessing the servant organization: Development of the servant organizational leadership assessment (SOLA) instrument. *Dissertation Abstracts International, 60*(2), 308. (UMI No. 9921922)

Lemoine, G. J., Hartnell, C. A., & Leroy, H. (2019). Taking stock of moral approaches to leadership: An integrative review of ethical, authentic, and servant leadership. *Academy of Management Annals, 13*(1), 148–187.

Liden, R. C., Panaccio, A., Hu, J., & Meuser, J. D. (2014). Servant leadership:

Antecedents, consequences, and contextual moderators. In D. V. Day (Ed.), *The Oxford handbook of leadership and organizations* (pp. 357–379). Oxford, UK: Oxford University Press.

Liden, R. C., Wayne, S. J., Meuser, J. D., Hu, J., Wu, J., & Liao, C. (2015). Servant leadership: Validation of a short form of the SL-28. *The Leadership Quarterly, 26*(2), 254–269.

Liden, R. C., Wayne, S. J., Zhao, H., & Henderson, D. (2008). Servant leadership: Development of a multidimensional measure and multi-level assessment. *The Leadership Quarterly, 19*, 161–177.

Meuser, J. D., Liden, R. C., Wayne, S. J., & Henderson, D. J. (2011, August). *Is servant leadership always a good thing? The moderating influence of servant leadership prototype.* Paper presented at the meeting of the Academy of Management, San Antonio, TX.

Neubert, M. J., Kacmar, K. M., Carlson, D. S., Chonko, L. B., & Roberts, J. A. (2008). Regulatory focus as a mediator of the influence of initiating structure and servant leadership on employee behavior. *Journal of Applied Psychology, 93*, 1220–1233.

Newman, A., Schwarz, G., Cooper, B., & Sendjaya, S. (2017). How servant leadership influences organizational citizenship behavior: The roles of LMX, empowerment, and proactive personality. *Journal of Business Ethics, 145*(1), 49–62.

Otero-Neira, C., Varela-Neira, C., & Bande, B. (2016). Supervisory servant leadership and employee's work role performance. *Leadership & Organization Development Journal, 37*(7), 860–881.

Ozyilmaz, A., & Cicek, S. S. (2015). How does servant leadership affect employee attitudes, behaviors, and psychological climates in a for-profit organizational context? *Journal of Management and Organization, 27*(3), 263–290. http://dx.doi.org/10.1017/jmo.2014.80

Page, D., & Wong, P. (2000). A conceptual framework for measuring servant-leadership. In S. Adjibolosoo (Ed.), *The human factor in shaping the course of history and development* (pp. 69–110). Lanham, MD: University Press of America.

Partners In Health. (2011). *History.* http://www.pih.org/pages/partners-in-health-history.html

Partners In Health. (2013). *2013 annual report.* http://www.pih.org/pages/2013-annual-report

Patterson, K. A. (2003). *Servant leadership: A theoretical model* (Doctoral dissertation, Regent University, ATT 30882719).

Ronen, Z. (2018, May 9). On the power of fairness in generating employee motivation. *Ze'ev Ronen–Business Excellence.* https://business-excellence.co.il/en/my-blog/634-fairness-motivation

Russell, R. F., & Stone, A. G. (2002). A review of servant-leadership attributes: Developing a practical model. *Leadership & Organization Development Journal, 23*, 145–157.

Schaubroeck, J., Lam, S. S. K., & Peng, A. C. (2011). Cognition-based and affect-based trust as mediators of leader behavior influences on team performance. *Journal of Applied Psychology, 96*(4), 863–871.

Sendjaya, S., & Sarros, J. C. (2002). Servant leadership: Its origin, development, and application in organizations. *Journal of Leadership & Organizational Studies, 9*(2), 57–64.

Sendjaya, S., Sarros, J. C., & Santora, J. C. (2008). Defining and measuring servant leadership behaviour in organizations. *Journal of Management Studies, 45*(2), 402–424.

Senge, P. M. (2002). Afterword. In R. K. Greenleaf (Ed.), *Servant leadership: A journey into the nature of legitimate power and greatness* (pp. 343–360). New York, NY: Paulist Press.

Sousa, M., & van Dierendonck, D. (2017). Servant leadership and the effect of the interaction between humility, action, and hierarchical power on follower engagement. *Journal of Business Ethics, 141*(1), 13–25.

Spears, L. C. (2002). Tracing the past, present, and future of servant-leadership. In L. C. Spears & M. Lawrence (Eds.), *Focus on leadership: Servant-leadership for the 21st century* (pp. 1–16). New York, NY: Wiley.

Spears, L. C. (2010). Servant leadership and Robert K. Greenleaf's legacy. In D. van Dierendonck & K. Patterson (Eds.), *Servant leadership: Developments in theory and research* (pp. 11–24). New York, NY: Palgrave Macmillan.

UniBocconi. (2019, September 20). Executive chat with Marco Alverà, CEO of Snam [Video file]. https://www.bing .com/videos/search?q=marco+Alverà&&v iew=detail&mid=438956C3E9633D3365 77438956C3E9633D336577&&FORM= VDRVRV

van Dierendonck, D. (2011). Servant leadership: A review and synthesis. *Journal of Management, 37*(4), 1228–1261.

van Dierendonck, D., & Nuijten, I. (2011). The servant leadership survey: Development and validation of a multidimensional measure. *Journal of Business and Psychology, 26*, 249–267.

Walumbwa, F. O., Hartnell, C. A., & Oke, A. (2010). Servant leadership, procedural justice climate, service climate, employee attitudes, and organizational citizenship behavior: A cross-level investigation. *Journal of Applied Psychology, 95*, 517–529.

Wang, M. M., Kwan, H. K., & Zhou, A. Q. (2017). Effects of servant leadership on work-family balance in China. *Asia Pacific Journal of Human Resources, 55*(4): 387–407.

Wheatley, M. (2002). The work of the servant leader. In L. C. Spears & M. Lawrence (Eds.), *Focus on leadership: Servant-leadership for the twenty-first century* (pp. 349–362). New York, NY: Wiley.

Whittington, J. L. (2017). Creating a positive organization through servant leadership. In C. J. Davis (Ed.), *Servant leadership and followership* (pp. 51–79). New York, NY: Palgrave Macmillan, Cham.

Williams, W. A., Randolph-Seng, B., Hayek, M., Haden, S. P., & Atinc, G. (2017). Servant leadership and followership creativity: The influence of workplace spirituality and political skill. *Leadership & Organization Development Journal, 38*(2), 178–193.

Winston, B., & Fields, D. (2015). Seeking and measuring the essential behaviors of servant leadership. *Leadership & Organization Development Journal, 36*(4), 413–434.

Wong, P. T. P., & Davey, D. (2007). *Best practices in servant leadership.* Paper presented at the Servant Leadership Research Roundtable, Regent University, Virginia Beach, VA.

Wu, J., Liden, R. C., Liao, C., & Wayne, S. J. (2020, April 9). Does manager servant leadership lead to follower serving behaviors? It depends on follower self-interest. *Journal of Applied Psychology.* Advance online publication. http://dx.doi .org/10.1037/apl0000500

CHAPTER 11

Adams, J. A., Bailey, D. E., Jr., Anderson, R. A., & Galanos, A. N. (2013). Adaptive leadership: A novel approach for family decision making. *Journal of Palliative Medicine, 16*(3), 326–329.

Adams, J. A., Bailey, D. E., Jr., Anderson, R. A., & Thygeson, M. (2013). Finding your way through EOL challenges in the ICU using adaptive leadership behaviours: A qualitative descriptive case study. *Intensive and Critical Care Nursing, 29*, 329–336.

Audette, B. (2019a, November 11). Town struggles with Marlboro closure

plan. *Battleboro Reformer.* https://www
.reformer.com/stories/town-struggles-with-
marlboro-college-closure-plan,589942

Audette, B. (2019b, December 16).
Marlboro board chairman defends
decision. *Bennington Banner.* https://www
.benningtonbanner.com/stories/marlboro-
board-chairman-defends-merger-
decision,592654

Audette, B. (2020, January 17). Marlboro
College alum, former administrator
laments "missed opportunity." *Berkshire
Eagle.* https://www.berkshireeagle.com/
stories/marlboro-college-alum-former-
administrator-laments-missed-
opportunity,595009?

Benzie, H. J., Pryce, A., & Smith, K.
(2017). The wicked problem of embedding
academic literacies: Exploring rhizomatic
ways of working through an adaptive
leadership approach. *Higher Education
Research & Development, 36*(2), 227–240.

Corazzini, K., Twersky, J., White, H. K.,
Buhr, G. T., McConnell, E. S., Weiner, M.,
& Colón-Emeric, C. S. (2014).
Implementing culture change in nursing
homes: An adaptive leadership framework.
The Gerontologist, 55(4), 616–627.

DeRue, D. S. (2011). Adaptive leadership
theory: Leading and following as a
complex adaptive process. *Research in
Organizational Behavior, 31*, 125–150.

Eubank, D., Geffken, D., Orzano, J., &
Ricci, R. (2012, September). Teaching
adaptive leadership to family medicine
residents: What? Why? How? *Families,
Systems & Health, 30*(3), 241–252.

Gilbert, N. L. (2013). *The challenges
of starting and leading a charter school:
Examining the risks, the resistance, and
the role of adaptive leadership—An
autoethnography* (Dissertation, University of
Pennsylvania, AAI3562369).

Halpert, M., & Rosenfeld, E. (2014, May 21).
Depressed, but not ashamed. *New York Times.*
http://www.nytimes.com/2014/05/22/
opinion/depressed-but-not-ashamed.html

Harlow, T. (2019, December 12). Declining
enrollment prompts staff, budget cuts
at Bethel University. *Star Tribune.*
http://www.startribune.com/declining-
enrollment-prompts-staff-budget-cuts-at-
bethel-university/566126311

Heifetz, R. A. (1994). *Leadership without
easy answers.* Cambridge, MA: Belknap
Press.

Heifetz, R. A., Grashow, A., & Linsky, M.
(2009). *The practice of adaptive leadership:
Tools and tactics for changing your
organization and the world.* Boston, MA:
Harvard Business School Press.

Heifetz, R. A., & Laurie, D. L. (1997).
The work of leadership. *Harvard Business
Review, 7*(1), 124–134.

Heifetz, R. A., & Linsky, M. (2002).
*Leadership on the line: Staying alive through
the dangers of leading.* Boston, MA: Harvard
Business School Press.

Heifetz, R. A., Sinder, R., Jones, A.,
Hodge, L., & Rowley, K. (1991). Teaching
and assessing leadership courses: Part one.
Phi Kappa Phi Journal (Winter), 21–25.

Hess, A. (2019, December 13). The cost
of college increased by more than 25%
in the last 10 years—here's why. *CNBC.*
https://www.cnbc.com/2019/12/13/
cost-of-college-increased-by-more-than-
25percent-in-the-last-10-years.html

Hlalele, D., Manicom, D., Preece, J., &
Tsotetsi, C. T. (2015). Strategies and
outcomes of involving university students
in community engagement: An adaptive
leadership perspective. *JHEA/RESA,
13*(1&2), 169–193.

Jaschik, S. (2019, January 24). Another small
college will close. *Inside HigherEd.* https://
www.insidehighered.com/news/2019/01/24/
green-mountain-latest-small-college-close.

Klau, M., & Hufnagel, J. (2016).
Strengthening communities through
adaptive leadership: A case study of
the Kansas Leadership Center and the
Bangladesh Youth Leadership Center.
In *Creative social change: Leadership for a*

healthy world (pp. 279–294). Bingley, UK: Emerald Group.

Lapierre, L. M., & Carsten, M. K. (2014). *Followership: What is it and why do people follow?* Bingley, UK: Emerald Group.

Marlboro College. (2019). What's next for Marlboro: Work continues on options for Marlboro's future. *Marlboro College News.* https://www.marlboro.edu/community/news/what-is-next-for-marlboro/updates/?id=14

Marlboro College Board of Trustees. (2019). What's next for Marlboro: Open letter from Marlboro College Board of Trustees. *Marlboro College News.* https://www.marlboro.edu/community/news/what-is-next-for-marlboro/updates/?id=42&fbclid=IwAR2-mlBBVo0BOmPoGGXLdgdi5SyZkNPzi24gZUY9ue7-ulqGyVZsZ1pukq4

Marques-Quinteiro, P., Ramos-Villagrasa, P., Passos, A. M., & Curral, L. (2015). Measuring adaptive performance in individuals and teams. *Team Performance Management, 21*(7–8), 339–360.

Modell, A. H. (1976). The "holding environment" and the therapeutic action of psychoanalysis. *Journal of the American Psychoanalytic Association, 24*(2), 285–307.

Mugisha, S., & Berg, S. V. (2017). Adaptive leadership in water utility operations: The case of Uganda. *Sustainable Water Resources Management,* 1–9.

Nadworny, E., & Larkin, M. (2019, December 16). Fewer students are going to college. Here's why that matters. *Morning Edition.* https://www.npr.org/2019/12/16/787909495/fewer-students-are-going-to-college-heres-why-that-matters

National Public Radio. (2014, May 24). Students struggle with depression—and with telling the story (S. Simon, interviewer). *Weekend Edition Saturday.* http://www.npr.org/2014/05/24/315445104/students-struggle-with-depression-and-with-telling-the-story

Nelson, T., & Squires, V. (2017). Addressing complex challenges through adaptive leadership: A promising approach to collaborative problem solving. *Journal of Leadership Education, 16*(4), 111–123.

Preece, J. (2016). Negotiating service learning through community engagement: Adaptive leadership, knowledge, dialogue and power. *Education as Change, 20*(1), 104–125.

Ramalingam, B., Wild, L., & Ferrari, M. (2020). Adaptive leadership in the coronavirus response. *Coronavirus Briefing Note.* https://www.odi.org/sites/odi.org.uk/files/resource-documents/032020_pogo_coronavirus_adaptation.pdf

Rosenhead, J., Franco, L. A., Grint, K., & Friedland, B. (2019). Complexity theory and leadership practice: A review, a critique, and some recommendations. *The Leadership Quarterly, 30*(5), 101–304.

Shapiro, S. (2018, June 18). A Middlebury professor surveys student attitudes about free speech (opinion). *Inside Higher Ed.* https://www.insidehighered.com/views/2018/06/18/middlebury-professor-surveys-student-attitudes-about-free-speech-opinion

Sunderman, H. M., Headrick, J., & McCain, K. D. (in press). Addressing complex issues and crises in higher education with an adaptive leadership framework. *Change: The Magazine of Higher Learning.*

Thygeson, M., Morrissey, L., & Ulstad, V. (2010). Adaptive leadership and the practice of medicine: A complexity-based approach to reframing the doctor-patient relationship. *Journal of Evaluation in Clinical Practice, 16,* 1009–1015.

Tourish, D. (2019). Is complexity leadership theory complex enough? A critical appraisal, some modifications and suggestions for further research. *Organization Studies, 40*(2), 219–238.

Uhl-Bien, M., & Arena, M. (2017). Complexity leadership. *Organizational Dynamics, 1*(46), 9–20.

Uhl-Bien, M., & Arena, M. (2018). Leadership for organizational adaptability: A theoretical synthesis and integrative framework. *The Leadership Quarterly, 29*(1), 89–104.

Uhl-Bien, M., Marion, R., & McKelvey, B. (2007). Complexity leadership theory: Shifting leadership from the industrial age to the knowledge era. *The Leadership Quarterly, 18*, 298–318.

Winnicott, D. W. (1965). *The maturational processes and the facilitating environment: studies in the theory of emotional development.* London, UK: Hogarth Press.

Zahneis, M. (2019, November 18). A college prepares to close its doors as students and alumni mourn—and scheme. *The Chronicle of Higher Education.* https://www.chronicle.com/article/A-College-Prepares-to-Close/247567

CHAPTER 12

Arnett, D. B., & Wittmann, C. M. (2014). Improving marketing success: The role of tacit knowledge exchange between sales and marketing. *Journal of Business Research, 67*(3), 324–331.

Booysen, L. (2014). The development of inclusive leadership practice and processes. In B. M. Ferdman & B. Deane (Eds.), *Diversity at work: The practice of inclusion* (pp. 296–329). San Francisco, CA: Jossey-Bass.

Brewer, M. B. (1991). The social self: On being the same and different at the same time. *Personality & Social Psychology Bulletin, 17,* 475–482.

Carmeli, A., Reiter-Palmon, R., & Ziv, E. (2010). Inclusive leadership and employee involvement in creative tasks in the workplace: The mediating role of psychological safety. *Creativity Research Journal, 22,* 250–260.

Carter, D. R., Cullen-Lester, K. L., Jones, J. M., Gerbasi, A., Chrobot-Mason, D., & Nae, E. Y. (2020, February). Functional leadership in interteam contexts: Understanding "what" in the context of why? where? when? and who? *The Leadership Quarterly, 31*(1), 101378.

Choi, S. B., Tran, T. B. H., & Kang, S.-W. (2017). Inclusive leadership and employee well-being: The mediating role of person-job fit. *Journal of Happiness Studies, 18,* 1877–1901.

Choi, S. B., Tran, T. B. H., & Park, B. I. (2015). Inclusive leadership and work engagement: Mediating roles of affective organizational commitment and creativity. *Social Behavior and Personality, 43,* 931–944.

Chrobot-Mason, D., Ruderman, M., & Nishii, L. (2013). Leadership in a diverse workplace. In Q. Roberson's (Ed.), *Oxford handbook of diversity* (pp. 315–340). New York, NY: Oxford University Press.

Chung, B. G., Ehrhart, K. H., Shore, L. M., Randel, A. E., Dean, M. A., & Kedharnath, U. (2020). Work group inclusion: Test a scale and model. *Group and Organization Management, 45*(1), 75–102.

Church, A. H., Rotolo, C. T., Shull, A. C., & Tuller, M. D. (2014). Inclusive organizational development. In B. M. Ferdman & B. Deane (Eds.), *Diversity at work: The practice of inclusion* (pp. 287–288). San Francisco, CA: Jossey-Bass.

Corsaro, D., Ramos, C., Henneberg, S. C., & Naudé, P. (2012). The impact of network configurations on value constellations in business markets: The case of an innovation network. *Industrial Marketing Management, 41*(1), 54–67.

Cox, T. H., Jr., & Blake, S. (1991). Managing cultural diversity: Implications for organizational competitiveness. *The Executive, 5*(3), 45.

Dass, P., & Parker, B. (1999). Strategies for managing human resource diversity. *Academy of Management Executive, 13,* 68–80.

Davidson, M. N., & Ferdman, B. M. (2002, April). Inclusion: What can I and my organization do about it? *The Industrial-Organizational Psychologist, 39,* 80–85.

Edmondson, A. (1996). Learning from mistakes is easier said than done: Group and organizational influences on the detection and correction of human error. *Journal of Applied Behavioral Science, 32,* 5–32.

Edmondson, A. (1999). Psychological safety and learning behavior in work teams. *Administrative Science Quarterly, 44,* 350–383.

Edmondson, A. (2003). Speaking up in the operating room: How team leaders promote learning in interdisciplinary action teams. *Journal of Management Studies, 40,* 1419–1452.

Edmondson, A. (2004). Psychological safety, trust, and learning in organizations: A group-level lens. In R. M. Kramer & K. S. Cook (Eds.), *Trust and distrust in organizations: Dilemmas and approaches* (pp. 239–272). New York, NY: Russell Sage.

Ely, R. J., & Thomas, D. A. (2001). Cultural diversity at work: The effects of diversity perspectives on work group processes and outcomes. *Administrative Science Quarterly, 46,* 229–273.

Ernst, C., & Chrobot-Mason, D. (2010). *Boundary spanning leadership: Six practices for solving problems, driving innovation, and transforming organizations.* New York, NY: McGraw-Hill Professional.

Ferdman, B. M. (1992). *The dynamics of ethnic diversity in organizations: Toward integrative models.* In K. Kelley (Ed.), *Advances in psychology: Issues, theory, and research in industrial/organizational psychology* (pp. 339–384). Amsterdam, Netherlands: North-Holland.

Ferdman, B. M. (2014). The practice of inclusion in diverse organizations: Toward a systemic and inclusive framework. In B. M. Ferdman & B. Deane (Eds.), *Diversity at work: The practice of inclusion* (pp. 3–54). San Francisco, CA: Jossey-Bass.

Ferdman, B. M., & Davidson, M. N. (2002). A matter of differences—Inclusion: What can I and my organization do about it? *The Industrial-Organizational Psychologist, 39,* 80–85.

Ferdman, B. M., & Morgan Roberts, L. (2014). Creating inclusion for oneself: Knowing, accepting, and expressing one's whole self at work. In B. M. Ferdman & B. Deane (Eds.), *Diversity at work: The practice of inclusion* (pp. 93–127). San Francisco, CA: Jossey-Bass.

Greenwald, A. G., McGhee, D. E., & Schwartz, J. L. K. (1998). Measuring individual differences in implicit cognition: The Implicit Association Test. *Journal of Personality and Social Psychology, 74,* 1464–1480.

Hays-Thomas, R. (2017). *Managing workplace diversity and inclusion: A psychological perspective.* New York, NY: Routledge.

Hirak, R., Peng, A. C., Carmeli, A., & Schaubroeck, J. M. (2012). Linking leader inclusiveness to work unit performance: The importance of psychological safety and learning from failures. *The Leadership Quarterly, 23,* 107–117.

Hollander, E. P. (2009). *Inclusive leadership: The essential leader-follower relationship.* New York, NY: Routledge.

Ibarra, H. (1993). Personal networks of women and minorities in management: A conceptual framework. *Academy of Management Review, 18,* 56–87.

Ivancevich, J. M., & Gilbert, J. A. (2000). Diversity management: Time for a new approach. *Public Personnel Management, 29,* 75–92.

Javed, B., Naqvi, S. M. M. R., Khan, A. K., Arjoon, S., & Tayyeb, H. H. (2017). Impact of inclusive leadership on innovative work behavior: The role of psychological safety. *Journal of Management and Organization, 25,* 117–136.

Johnston, W. B., & Packer, A. H. (1987). *Workforce 2000: Work and workers for the*

21st century. Indianapolis, IN: Hudson Institute.

Kalev, A., Kelly, E., & Dobbin, F. (2006). Best practices or best guesses? Assessing the efficacy of corporate affirmative action and diversity policies. *American Sociological Review, 71,* 589–617.

Kossek, E. E., & Zonia, S. C. (1993). Assessing diversity climate: A field study of reactions to employer efforts to promote diversity. *Journal of Organizational Behavior, 14,* 61–81.

Levashina, J., Hartwell, C. J., Morgeson, F. P., & Campion, M. A. (2014). The structured employment interview: Narrative and quantitative review of the research literature. *Personnel Psychology, 67*(1), 241–293.

Linnehan, F., & Konrad, A. M. (1999). Diluting diversity: Implications for intergroup inequality in organizations. *Journal of Management Inquiry, 8*(4), 399–414. doi:10.1177/105649269984009

McIntosh, P. (1988). *White privilege and male privilege: A personal account of coming to see correspondence through work in women's studies.* Working Paper No. 189. Wellesley, MA: Wellesley Centers for Women.

Miles, R. E., Snow, C. C., Fjeldstad, O. D., Miles, G., & Lettl, C. (2010). Designing organizations to meet 21st-century opportunities and challenges. *Organizational Dynamics, 39,* 93–103.

Mitchell, R., Boyle, B., Parker, V., Giles, M., Chiang, V., & Joyce, P. (2015). Managing inclusiveness and diversity in teams: How leader inclusiveness affects performance through status and team identity. *Human Resource Management, 54,* 217–239.

Mor Barak, M. E., & Cherin, D. A. (1998). A tool to expand organizational understanding of workforce diversity: Exploring a measure of inclusion-exclusion. *Administration in Social Work, 22,* 47–64.

Mor Barak, M. E., Cherin, D. A., & Berkman, S. (1998). Organizational and personal dimensions of diversity climate: Ethnic and gender differences in employee perceptions. *Journal of Applied Behavioral Science, 34,* 82–104.

Nembhard, I. M., & Edmondson, A. C. (2006). Making it safe: The effects of leader inclusiveness and professional status on psychological safety and improvement efforts in health care teams. *Journal of Organizational Behavior, 27,* 942–966.

Nishii, L. H. (2013). The benefits of climate for inclusion for gender-diverse groups. *Academy of Management Journal, 50,* 1754–1774.

Nishii, L. H., & Mayer, D. M. (2009). Do inclusive leaders help to reduce turnover in diverse groups? The moderating role of leader-member exchange in the diversity to turnover relationship. *Journal of Applied Psychology, 94,* 1412–1426.

Nkomo, S. M., & Ariss, A. A. (2014). The historical origins of ethnic (white) privilege in US organizations. *Journal of Managerial Psychology, 29*(4), 389–404.

Northouse, P. G. (2018). *Introduction to leadership: Concepts and practice* (4th ed.). Thousand Oaks, CA: SAGE.

Offermann, L. R., Basford, T. E., Graebner, R., Jaffer, S., De Graaf, S. B., & Kaminsky, S. E. (2014). See no evil: Color blindness and perceptions of subtle racial discrimination in the workplace. *Cultural Diversity and Ethnic Minority Psychology, 20*(4), 499–507.

Pettigrew, T. F., & Martin, J. (1989). Organizational inclusion of minority groups: A social psychological analysis. In J. P. Van Oudenhoven & T. M. Willemsen (Eds.), *Ethnic minorities: Social psychological perspectives* (pp. 169–200). Berwyn, PA: Swets North America.

Qi, L., Liu, B., Wei, X., & Hu, Y. (2019). Impact of inclusive leadership on innovative behavior: Perceived innovative support as a mediator. *PLoS ONE, 14*, 1–14.

Randel, A. E., Dean, M., Ehrhart, K. H., Chung, B., & Shore, L. (2016). Leader inclusiveness, psychological diversity climate, and helping behaviors. *Journal of Managerial Psychology, 31*, 216–234.

Randel, A. E., Galvin, B. M., Shore, L. M., Ehrhart, K. H., Chung, B. G., Dean, M. A., & Kedharnath, U. (2018). Inclusive leadership: Realizing positive outcomes through belongingness and being valued for uniqueness. *Human Resource Management Review, 28*, 190–203.

Roberson, Q. M. (2006). Disentangling the meanings of diversity and inclusion in organizations. *Group & Organization Management, 31*, 212–236.

Roberson, Q. M., King, E. B., & Hebl, M. (2020). Designing more effective practices to address workplace inequality. *Behavioral Science and Policy, 6*(1), 39–49.

Roberson, Q. M., Ryan, A. M., & Ragins, B. R. (2017). The evolution and future of diversity at work. *Journal of Applied Psychology, 102*(3), 483–499.

Schutz, W. (1958). *FIRO: A three-dimensional theory of interpersonal behavior.* New York, NY: Rinehart.

Shore, L. M., Randel, A. E., Chung, B. G., Dean, M. A., Ehrhart, K. H., & Singh, G. (2011). Inclusion and diversity in work groups: A review and model for future research. *Journal of Management, 37*, 1262–1289.

Strauss, J. P., & Connerley, M. L. (2003). Demographics, personality, contact, and university-diverse orientation: An exploratory examination. *Human Resource Management, 42*(2), 159–174.

Thomas, D. A., & Ely, R. J. (1996, September–October). Making differences matter: A new paradigm for managing diversity. *Harvard Business Review*, pp. 79–90.

Tyler, T. R., & Lind, E. A. (1992). A relational model of authority in groups. In

M. P. Zanna (Ed.), *Advances in experimental social psychology* (Vol. 25, pp. 115–191). New York, NY: Academic Press.

Uhl-Bien, M. (2006). Relationship leadership theory: Exploring the social processes of leadership and organizing. *Leadership Quarterly, 17*, 654–676.

van Knippenberg, D., Homan, A. C., & van Ginkel, W. P. (2013). Diversity cognition and climates. In Q. Roberson (Ed.), *Oxford Handbook of Diversity* (pp. 220–238). New York, NY: Oxford University Press.

Van Velsor, E., McCauley, C. D., & Ruderman, M. N. (2010). *The Center for Creative Leadership handbook of leadership development* (3rd ed.). San Francisco, CA: Jossey-Bass.

Wasserman, I. C. (2014). Strengthening interpersonal awareness and fostering relational eloquence. In B. M. Ferdman & B. Deane (Eds.), *Diversity at work: The practice of inclusion* (pp. 128–154). San Francisco, CA: Jossey-Bass.

Yang, Y., & Konrad, A. M. (2011). Understanding diversity management practices: Implications of institutional theory and resource-based theory. *Group and Organization Management, 36*, 6–38.

Ye, Q., Wang, D., & Li, X. (2018). Promoting employees' learning from errors by inclusive leadership: Do mood and gender matter? *Baltic Journal of Management, 13*, 125–142.

CHAPTER 13

Alipour, K. K., Mohammed, S., & Martinez, P. N. (2017). Incorporating temporality into implicit leadership and followership theories: Exploring inconsistencies between time-based expectations and actual behaviors. *The Leadership Quarterly, 28*(2), 300–316.

Bastardoz, N., & Van Vugt, M. (2019). The nature of followership: Evolutionary analysis and review. *The Leadership Quarterly, 30*(1), 81–95.

Benson, A. J., Hardy, J., & Eys, M. (2016). Contextualizing leaders' interpretations of proactive followership. *Journal of Organizational Behavior, 37*(7), 949–966.

Braun, S., Kark, R., & Wisse, B. (2018). Fifty shades of grey: Exploring the dark sides of leadership and followership. *Frontiers in Psychology, 9,* 1877.

Brown, D. J. (2013). *The boys in the boat: Nine Americans and their epic quest for gold at the 1936 Berlin Olympics.* New York, NY: Penguin.

Cain, S. (2012). *Quiet: The power of introverts in a world that can't stop talking.* New York, NY: Crown.

Cain, S. (2017, March 24). Not leadership material? Good. The world needs followers. The glorification of leadership skills, especially in college admissions, has emptied leadership of its meaning. *New York Times.* https://www.nytimes.com/2017/03/24/opinion/sunday/not-leadership-material-good-the-world-needs-followers.html

Carsten, M. K., Harms, P., & Uhl-Bien, M. (2014). Exploring historical perspectives of followership: The need for an expanded view of followers and the follower role. In L. M Lapierre & R. K. Carsten (Eds.), *Followership: What is it and why do people follow?* (pp. 3–26). Bingley, UK: Emerald Group.

Carsten, M. K., Uhl-Bien, M., & Huang, L. (2018). Leader perceptions and motivation as outcomes of followership role orientation and behavior. *Leadership, 14*(6), 731–756.

Carsten, M. K., Uhl-Bien, M., West, B. J., Patera, J. L., & McGregor, R. (2010). Exploring social constructions of followership: A qualitative study. *The Leadership Quarterly, 21,* 543–562.

Chaleff, I. (1995). *The courageous follower: Standing up to and for our leaders.* San Francisco, CA: Berrett-Koehler.

Chaleff, I. (2008). Creating new ways of following. In R. E. Riggio, I. Chaleff, & J. Lipman-Blumen (Eds.), *The art of followership: How great followers create great leaders and organizations* (pp. 67–87). San Francisco, CA: Jossey-Bass.

Chaleff, I. (2009). *The courageous follower: Standing up to and for our leaders* (3rd ed.). San Francisco, CA: Berrett-Koehler.

Crossman, B., & Crossman, J. (2011). Conceptualising followership: A review of the literature. *Leadership, 7*(4), 481–497.

DeRue, S., & Ashford, S. (2010). Who will lead and who will follow? A social process of leadership identity construction in organizations. *Academy of Management Review, 35*(4), 627–647.

de Zilwa, D. (2014) A new conceptual framework for authentic followership. In L. Lapierre & M. Carsten (Eds.), *Followership: What is it, and why do people follow?* (pp. 47–72). Bingley, UK: Emerald Group.

Epitropaki, O., Kark, R., Mainemelis, C., & Lord, R. G. (2017). Leadership and followership identity processes: A multilevel review. *The Leadership Quarterly, 28*(1), 104–129.

Fairhurst, G. T., & Uhl-Bien, M. (2012). Organizational discourse analysis (ODA): Examining leadership as a relational process. *The Leadership Quarterly, 23*(6), 1043–1062.

Follett, M. P. (1949). *The essentials of leadership.* London, UK: Management Publications Trust.

Foti, R. J., Hansbrough, T. K., Epitropaki, O., & Coyle, P. T. (2017). Dynamic viewpoints on implicit leadership and followership theories: Approaches, findings, and future directions. *The Leadership Quarterly, 28*(2), 261–267.

Hughes, R. L., Ginnett, R. C., & Curphy, G. J. (2014). *Leadership: Enhancing the lessons of experience* (8th ed.). New York, NY: McGraw-Hill.

Keller, J. (2012, July 12). How the Penn State report implicates top officials. *The Chronicle of Higher Education.* http://www.chronicle.com/article/How-the-Penn-State-Report/132837

Kellerman, B. (2008). *Followership: How followers are creating change and changing leaders.* Boston, MA: Harvard Business Press.

Kelley, R. E. (1988). In praise of followers. *Harvard Business Review,* 66(6), 141–148.

Kelley, R. E. (1992). *The power of followership.* New York, NY: Doubleday Business.

Kelley, R. E. (2008). Rethinking followership. In R. E. Riggio, I. Chaleff, & J. Lipman-Blumen (Eds.), *The art of followership: How great followers create great leaders and organizations* (pp. 5–16). San Francisco, CA: Jossey-Bass.

Lapierre, L. M., & Carsten, R. K. (Eds.). (2014). *Followership: What is it and why do people follow?* Bingley, UK: Emerald Group.

Lipman-Blumen, J. (2005). *The allure of toxic leaders: Why we follow destructive bosses and corrupt politicians—and how we can survive them.* New York, NY: Oxford University Press.

Lord, R., & Maher, K. J. (1991). *Leadership and information processing: Linking perceptions and performance.* Boston, MA: Unwin-Everyman.

Mahler, J. (2011, November 8). Grand experiment meets an inglorious end. *New York Times,* B12.

Meindl, J. R. (1990). On leadership: An alternative to the conventional wisdom. In B. M. Staw & L. L. Cummings (Eds.), *Research in organizational behavior* (Vol. 12, pp. 159–203). Greenwich, CT: JAI Press.

Meindl, J. R. (1995). The romance of leadership as a follower-centric theory: A social constructionist approach. *The Leadership Quarterly,* 6(3), 329–341.

Pietraszewski, D. (2019). The evolution of leadership: Leadership and followership as a solution to the problem of creating and executing successful coordination and cooperation enterprises. *The Leadership Quarterly.* doi:10.1016/j.leaqua.2019.05.006.

Popper, M. (2014). Why do people follow? In L. M. Lapierre & R. K. Carsten (Eds.), *Followership: What is it and why do people follow?* (pp. 109–120). Bingley, UK: Emerald Group.

Riggio, R. E., Chaleff, I., & Lipman-Blumen, J. (Eds.). (2008). *The art of followership: How great followers create great leaders and organizations.* San Francisco, CA: Jossey-Bass.

Schutz, W. C. (1958). *FIRO: A three dimensional theory of interpersonal behavior.* New York, NY: Holt, Rinehart & Winston.

Schyns, B., Wisse, B., & Sanders, S. (2019). Shady strategic behavior: Recognizing strategic followership of Dark Triad followers. *Academy of Management Perspectives,* 33(2), 234–249.

Shamir, B. (2007). From passive recipients to active co-producers: Followers' roles in the leadership process. In B. Shamir, R. Pillai, M. Bligh, & M. Uhl-Bien (Eds.), *Follower-centered perspectives on leadership: A tribute to the memory of James R. Meindl* (pp. ix–xxxix). Charlotte, NC: Information Age.

Sy, T. (2010). What do you think of followers? Examining the content, structure, and consequences of implicit followership theories. *Organizational Behavior and Human Decision Processes,* 113, 73–84.

Tajfel, H., & Turner, J. C. (1986). The social identity theory of intergroup behavior. In S. Worchel & W. G. Austin (Eds.), *Psychology of intergroup relations* (pp. 7–24). Chicago, IL: Nelson-Hall.

Uhl-Bien, M., Riggio, R. E., Lowe, K. B., & Carsten, M. K. (2014). Followership theory: A review and research agenda. *The Leadership Quarterly,* 25, 83–104.

Wolverton, B. (2012, July 12). Penn State's culture of reverence led to "total disregard" for children's safety. *The Chronicle of Higher Education.* http://www.chronicle.com/article/Penn-States-Culture-of/132853

Yelsma, P. (1999). Small group problem solving as academic service-learning. In D. Droge & B. O. Murphy (Eds.), *Voices of democracy, concepts and models for service-learning in communication studies,* American Association for Higher Education/NCA Press, pp. 87–96.

Zaleznik, A. (1965, May/June). The dynamics of subordinacy. *Harvard Business Review.*

CHAPTER 14

Adams, R. B., & Funk, P. (2012). Beyond the glass ceiling: Does gender matter? *Management Science, 58,* 219–235.

Amanatullah, E. T., & Tinsley, C. H. (2013a). Ask and ye shall receive? How gender and status moderate negotiation success. *Negotiation and Conflict Management Research, 6,* 253–272.

Amanatullah, E. T., & Tinsley, C. H. (2013b). Punishing female negotiators for asserting too much . . . or not enough: Exploring why advocacy moderates backlash against assertive female negotiators. *Organizational Behavior and Human Decision Processes, 120,* 110–122.

American Bar Association. (2019, April). *Commission on women in the profession: A current glance at women in the law.* https://www.americanbar.org/content/dam/aba/administrative/women/current_glance_2019.pdf

Andrews, P. H. (1992). Sex and gender differences in group communication: Impact on the facilitation process. *Small Group Research, 23,* 74–94.

Atkinson, N. (2018, July 10). *Jacinda Ardern: Biography.* New Zealand History. https://nzhistory.govt.nz/people/jacinda-ardern

Ayman, R., Korabik, K., & Morris, S. (2009). Is transformational leadership always perceived as effective? Male subordinates' devaluation of female transformational leaders. *Journal of Applied Social Psychology, 39,* 852–879.

Babcock, L., & Laschever, S. (2003). *Women don't ask: Negotiation and the gender divide.* Princeton, NJ: Princeton University Press.

Bass, B. M. (1985). Leadership: Good, better, best. *Organizational Dynamics, 13,* 26–40.

Belkin, L. (2003, October 26). The opt-out revolution. *The New York Times,* p. 42.

Belkin, L. (2008, June 15). When mom and dad share it all. *The New York Times.* http://www.nytimes.com/2008/06/15/magazine/15parenting-t.html?ref=jobs&pagewanted=all

Bell, E., & Nkomo, S. (2001). *Our separate ways: Black and white women and the struggle for professional identity.* Boston, MA: Harvard Business School Press.

Bergeron, D. M., Block, C. J., & Echtenkamp, B. A. (2006). Disabling the able: Stereotype threat and women's work performance. *Human Performance, 19,* 133–158.

Bernardi, R. A., Bosco, S. M., & Columb, V. L. (2009). Does female representation on boards of directors associate with the "Most Ethical Companies" list? *Corporate Reputation Review, 12,* 270–280.

Bielby, D. D., & Bielby, W. T. (1988). She works hard for the money: Household responsibilities and the allocation of work effort. *American Journal of Sociology, 93,* 1031–1059.

Blank, R., & Slipp, S. (1994). *Voices of diversity.* New York, NY: AMACOM.

Book, E. W. (2000). *Why the best man for the job is a woman.* New York, NY: HarperCollins.

Borowski, N. (2019, March 21). 4 things to know about Jacinda Ardern, New Zealand's

prime minister. *USA Today*. https://www
.usatoday.com/story/news/world/2019/
03/21/new-zealand-prime-minister-
jacinda-ardern-leads-after-mosque-
killings-christchurch/3231942002/

Boulouta, I. (2012). Hidden connections:
The link between board gender diversity
and corporate social performance. *Journal of
Business Ethics, 113*, 185–197.

Bowles, H. R., Babcock, L., & Lai, L.
(2007). Social incentives for gender
differences in the propensity to initiate
negotiations: Sometimes it does hurt to
ask. *Organizational Behavior and Human
Decision Processes, 103*, 84–103.

Bowles, H. R., & McGinn, K. L. (2005).
Claiming authority: Negotiating challenges
for women leaders. In D. M. Messick &
R. M. Kramer (Eds.), *The psychology of
leadership: New perspectives and research*
(pp. 191–208). Mahwah, NJ: Erlbaum.

Burgess, D., & Borgida, E. (1999).
Who women are, who women should
be: Descriptive and prescriptive gender
stereotyping in sex discrimination.
Psychology, Public Policy, & Law, 5, 665–692.

Burns, J. M. (1978). *Leadership*. New York,
NY: Plenum.

Carli, L. L. (2001). Gender and social
influence. *Journal of Social Issues, 57*,
725–741.

Catalyst. (2004). *The bottom line: Connecting
corporate performance and gender diversity*.
New York, NY: Author.

Catalyst. (2020, January 15). *Pyramid:
Women in S&P 500 companies*.
https://www.catalyst.org/research/
women-in-sp-500-companies/

Cave, D. (2020, May 23). Jacinda Ardern
sold a drastic lockdown with straight
talk and mom jokes. *The New York Times*.
https://www.nytimes.com/2020/05/23/
world/asia/jacinda-ardern-coronavirus-
new-zealand.html

Center for American Women and
Politics. (2020a). *Women in elective

office 2020*. https://cawp.rutgers.edu/
women-elective-office-2020

Center for American Women and
Politics. (2020b). *Women of color in elective
office 2020*. https://cawp.rutgers.edu/
women-color-elective-office-2020

Chandler, A. (2020). 10 things we can
learn from the way Jacinda Ardern
communicates. *Business Chicks*. https://
businesschicks.com/jacinda-ardern/

Chemers, M. M. (1997). *An integrative
theory of leadership*. Mahwah, NJ: Erlbaum.

Chemers, M. M., & Murphy, S. E. (1995).
Leadership and diversity in groups and
organizations. In M. M. Chemers, S.
Oskamp, & M. A. Constanzo (Eds.),
*Diversity in organizations: New perspectives
for a changing workplace* (pp. 157–190).
Thousand Oaks, CA: SAGE.

Cohen, P., & Hsu, T. (2020, June 3).
Pandemic could scar a generation of working
mothers. *The New York Times*. https://www
.nytimes.com/2020/06/03/business/
economy/coronavirus-working-women.html

Cook, A., & Glass, C. (2015). Diversity
begets diversity? The effects of board
composition on the appointment and
success of women CEOs. *Social Science
Research, 53*, 137–147.

Cook, A., & Glass, C. (2016). Do women
advance equity? The effect of gender
leadership composition on LGBT-friendly
policies in American firms. *Human
Relations, 69*(7), 1431–1456.

Cook, A., Ingersoll, A. R., & Glass, C.
(2019). Gender gaps at the top: Does board
composition affect executive compensation?
Human Relations, 72, 1292–1314.

Cooper, C. L., & Lewis, S. (1999). Gender
and the changing nature of work. In G. N.
Powell (Ed.), *Handbook of gender and work*
(pp. 37–46). Thousand Oaks, CA: SAGE.

Couric, K. (2008, June 11). *Katie
Couric's notebook: Sexism and politics*. CBS
News. http://www.cbsnews.com/news/
katie-courics-notebook-sexism-and-politics/

Craig, L. (2006). Does father care mean fathers share? A comparison of how mothers and fathers in intact families spend time with children. *Gender and Society, 20,* 259–281.

Dasgupta, N., & Asgari, S. (2004). Seeing is believing: Exposure to counterstereotypic women leaders and its effect on automatic gender stereotyping. *Journal of Experimental Social Psychology, 40,* 642–658.

Davies, P. G., Spencer, S. J., & Steele, C. M. (2005). Clearing the air: Identity safety moderates the effects of stereotype threat on women's leadership aspirations. *Journal of Personality and Social Psychology, 88,* 276–287.

Deaux, K., & Kite, M. (1993). Gender stereotypes. In F. L. Denmark & M. Paludi (Eds.), *Psychology of women: A handbook of theory and issues* (pp. 107–139). Westport, CT: Greenwood.

Dobbins, G. H., & Platz, S. J. (1986). Sex differences in leadership: How real are they? *Academy of Management Review, 11,* 118–127.

Dodge, K. A., Gilroy, F. D., & Fenzel, L. M. (1995). Requisite management characteristics revisited: Two decades later. *Journal of Social Behavior and Personality, 10,* 253–264.

Eagly, A. H. (2013). Women as leaders: Leadership style versus leaders' values and attitudes. In *Gender and work: Challenging conventional wisdom.* Boston, MA: Harvard Business School. http://www.hbs.edu/faculty/conferences/2013-w50-research-symposium/Documents/eagly.pdf

Eagly, A. H. (2016). When passionate advocates meet research on diversity, does the honest broker stand a chance? *Journal of Social Issues, 72,* 199–222.

Eagly, A. H., & Carli, L. L. (2003). The female leadership advantage: An evaluation of the evidence. *The Leadership Quarterly, 14,* 807–834.

Eagly, A. H., & Carli, L. L. (2004). Women and men as leaders. In J. Antonakis,

R. J. Sternberg, & A. T. Cianciolo (Eds.), *The nature of leadership* (pp. 279–301). Thousand Oaks, CA: SAGE.

Eagly, A. H., & Carli, L. L. (2007). *Through the labyrinth: The truth about how women become leaders.* Boston, MA: Harvard Business School Press.

Eagly, A. H., Johannesen-Schmidt, M. C., & van Engen, M. (2003). Transformational, transactional, and laissez-faire leadership styles: A meta-analysis comparing women and men. *Psychological Bulletin, 129,* 569–591.

Eagly, A. H., & Johnson, B. T. (1990). Gender and leadership style: A meta-analysis. *Psychological Bulletin, 108,* 233–256.

Eagly, A. H., & Karau, S. J. (1991). Gender and the emergence of leaders: A meta-analysis. *Journal of Personality and Social Psychology, 60,* 685–710.

Eagly, A. H., & Karau, S. J. (2002). Role congruity theory of prejudice toward female leaders. *Psychological Review, 109,* 573–598.

Eagly, A. H., Karau, S. J., & Makhijani, M. G. (1995). Gender and the effectiveness of leaders: A meta-analysis. *Psychological Bulletin, 117,* 125–145.

Eagly, A. H., Makhijani, M., & Klonsky, B. (1992). Gender and the evaluation of leaders: A meta-analysis. *Psychological Bulletin, 111,* 3–22.

Eagly, A. H., & Wood, W. (2013). The nature–nurture debates: 25 years of challenges in understanding the psychology of gender. *Perspectives on Psychological Science, 8,* 340–357.

Ensher, E. A., & Murphy, S. E. (2005). *Power mentoring: How successful mentors and protégés get the most out of their relationships.* San Francisco, CA: Jossey-Bass.

Fiske, S. (1998). Stereotyping, prejudice, and discrimination. In D. T. Gilbert, S. T. Fiske, & G. Lindzey (Eds.), *The handbook of social psychology* (4th ed., Vol. 2, pp. 982–1026). Boston, MA: McGraw-Hill.

Fiske, S., Bersoff, D. N., Borgida, E., Deaux, K., & Heilman, M. E. (1991). Social science research on trial: Use of sex stereotyping research in *Price Waterhouse v. Hopkins. American Psychologist, 46,* 1049–1060.

Fletcher, J. K. (2001). *Disappearing acts: Gender, power, and relational practice at work.* Boston, MA: MIT Press.

Forsyth, D. R. (2010). *Group dynamics* (5th ed.). Belmont, CA: Wadsworth.

Friedman, U. (2020, April 19). New Zealand's prime minister may be the most effective leader on the planet. *The Atlantic.* https://www.theatlantic.com/politics/archive/2020/04/jacinda-ardern-new-zealand-leadership-coronavirus/610237/

Galinsky, E., Aumann, K., & Bond, J. (2008). *Times are changing: Gender and generation at work and at home.* http://familiesandwork.org/site/research/reports/Times_Are_Changing.pdf

Glass, C., & Cook, A. (2018). Do women leaders promote positive change? Analyzing the effect of gender on business practices and diversity initiatives. *Human Resource Management, 57,* 823–837.

Glick, P., & Fiske, S. T. (1999). Sexism and other "isms": Independence, status, and the ambivalent content of stereotypes. In W. B. Swann Jr. & J. H. Langlois (Eds.), *Sexism and stereotypes in modern society: The gender science of Janet Taylor Spence* (pp. 193–221). Washington, DC: American Psychological Association.

Goldin, C., & Rouse, C. (2000). Orchestrating impartiality: The impact of "blind" auditions on female musicians. *American Economic Review, 90,* 715–741.

Goodwin, R. D., Dodson, S. J., Chen, J. M., & Diekmann, K. A. (2020). Gender, sense of power, and desire to lead: Why women don't "lean in" to apply to leadership groups that are majority-male. *Psychology of Women Quarterly.* Advance online publication.

Greenwald, A. G., McGhee, D. E., & Schwartz, J. L. K. (1998). Measuring individual differences in implicit cognition: The implicit association test. *Journal of Personality and Social Psychology, 74,* 1464–1480.

Gurin, P. (1985). Women's gender consciousness. *Public Opinion Quarterly, 49,* 143–163.

Hall, D. T. (1972). A model of coping with role conflict: The role behavior of college-educated women. *Administrative Science Quarterly, 17,* 471–486.

Hamilton, D. L., Stroessner, S. J., & Driscoll, D. M. (1994). Social cognition and the study of stereotyping. In P. G. Devine, D. L. Hamilton, & T. M. Ostrom (Eds.), *Social cognition: Impact on social psychology* (pp. 291–321). New York, NY: Academic Press.

Heilman, M. E. (2001). Description and prescription: How gender stereotypes prevent women's ascent up the organizational ladder. *Journal of Social Issues, 57,* 657–674.

Helgesen, S. (1990). *The female advantage: Women's ways of leadership.* New York, NY: Doubleday.

Hess, A. (2019, November, 11). *Applications to business schools are down—but women are making modest gains.* CNBC. https://www.cnbc.com/2019/11/11/business-school-applications-are-down-but-women-are-making-gains.html

Hewlett, S. A. (2002). *Creating a life: Professional women and the quest for children.* New York, NY: Talk Miramax.

Hjelmgaard, K. (2019, March 19). Jacinda Ardern leads New Zealand in aftermath of killings police say could have been worse. *USA Today.* https://www.usatoday.com/story/news/world/2019/03/19/new-zealand-jacinda-ardern-wins-praise-handling-mosque-shootings-prime-minister/3209576002/

Hollander, S. (2018, October 1). Jacinda Ardern's juggling act. *The New Yorker.*

https://www.newyorker.com/magazine/2018/10/08/jacinda-arderns-juggling-act

Hoyt, C. L. (2010). Women, men, and leadership: Exploring the gender gap at the top. *Social and Personality Psychology Compass*, *4*, 484–498.

Hoyt, C. L., Allison, S. T., Barnowski, A., & Sultan, A. (2020). Lay theories of heroism and leadership: The role of gender, communion, and agency. *Social Psychology*. Advance online publication.

Hoyt, C., & Blascovich, J. (2007). Leadership efficacy and women leaders' responses to stereotype activation. *Group Processes and Intergroup Relations*, *10*, 595–616.

Hoyt, C., & Blascovich, J. (2010). The role of self-efficacy and stereotype activation on cardiovascular, behavioral and self-report responses in the leadership domain. *The Leadership Quarterly*, *21*, 89–103.

Hoyt, C. L., & Chemers, M. M. (2008). Social stigma and leadership: A long climb up a slippery ladder. In C. L. Hoyt, G. R. Goethals, & D. R. Forsyth (Eds.), *Leadership at the crossroads: Leadership and psychology* (Vol. 1, pp. 165–180). Westport, CT: Praeger.

Hoyt, C., Johnson, S., Murphy, S., & Skinnell, K. (2010). The impact of blatant stereotype activation and group sex-composition on female leaders. *The Leadership Quarterly*, *21*, 716–732.

Hoyt, C. L., & Simon, S. (2016). The role of social dominance orientation and patriotism in the evaluation of racial minority and female leaders. *Journal of Applied Social Psychology*, *46*, 518–528.

Hymowitz, C., & Schellhardt, T. D. (1986, March 24). The glass ceiling: Why women can't seem to break the invisible barrier that blocks them from the top jobs. *The Wall Street Journal*, pp. D1, D4–D5.

Inter-Parliamentary Union. (2020). *Monthly ranking of women in national parliaments*. https://data.ipu.org/women-ranking?month=6&year=2020

Jacobson, M. B., & Effertz, J. (1974). Sex roles and leadership perceptions of the leaders and the led. *Organizational Behavior and Human Performance*, *12*, 383–396.

Jones, A. (2017, October 19). Jacinda Ardern: "Stardust" ousts experience in New Zealand. *BBC News*. https://www.bbc.com/news/world-asia-41226232

Kaiser, R. B., & Wallace, W. T. (2016). Gender bias and substantive differences in ratings of leadership behavior: Toward a new narrative. *Consulting Psychology Journal: Practice and Research*, *68*, 72–98.

Kanter, R. (1977). *Men and women of the corporation*. New York, NY: Basic Books.

Kelly, J. (2020, January, 13). Women now hold more jobs than men in the U.S. workforce. *Forbes*. https://www.forbes.com/sites/jackkelly/2020/01/13/women-now-hold-more-jobs-than-men/#17a487528f8a

Knoke, D., & Ishio, Y. (1998). The gender gap in company job training. *Work and Occupations*, *25*, 141–167.

Koenig, A. M., Eagly, A. H., Mitchell, A. A., & Ristikari, T. (2011). Are leader stereotypes masculine? A meta-analysis of three research paradigms. *Psychological Bulletin*, *137*, 616–642.

Konrad, A. M., Ritchie, J. E., Jr., Lieb, P., & Corrigall, E. (2000). Sex differences and similarities in job attribute preferences: A meta-analysis. *Psychological Bulletin*, *126*, 593–641.

Kray, L., Reb, J., Galinsky, A., & Thompson, L. (2004). Stereotype reactance at the bargaining table: The effect of stereotype activation and power on claiming and creating value. *Personality and Social Psychology Bulletin*, *30*, 399–411.

Kray, L. J., Thompson, L., & Galinsky, A. (2001). Battle of the sexes: Gender stereotype confirmation and reactance in negotiations. *Journal of Personality & Social Psychology, 80,* 942–958.

Kunda, Z., & Spencer, S. J. (2003). When do stereotypes come to mind and when do they color judgment? A goal-based theory of stereotype activation and application. *Psychological Bulletin, 129,* 522–544.

Livingston, R. W., Rosette, A. S., & Washington, E. F. (2012). Can an agentic Black woman get ahead? The impact of race and interpersonal dominance on perceptions of female leaders. *Psychological Science, 23,* 354–358.

Maume, D. J., Jr. (1999). Glass ceilings and glass escalators. *Work & Occupations, 26,* 483.

Miller, T., & Del Carmen Triana, M. (2009). Demographic diversity in the boardroom: Mediators of the board diversity-firm performance relationship. *Journal of Management Studies, 46,* 755–786.

Morgenroth, T., Kirby, T. A., Ryan, M. K., & Sudkämper, A. (2020). The who, when, and why of the glass cliff phenomenon: A meta-analysis of appointments to precarious leadership positions. *Psychological Bulletin.* Advance online publication.

Morrison, A., & Von Glinow, M. A. (1990). Women and minorities in management. *American Psychologist, 45,* 200–208.

Mulcahy, M., & Linehan, C. (2014). Females and precarious board positions: Further evidence of the glass cliff. *British Journal of Management, 25,* 425–438.

National Association of Women Business Owners. (2020). *Women business owner statistics.* https://www.nawbo.org/resources/women-business-owner-statistics

National Center for Education Statistics. (2018). Table 318.30. Bachelor's, master's, and doctor's degrees conferred by degree-granting institutions, by sex of student and discipline division: 2017–18. In *Digest of education statistics.* https://

nces.ed.gov/programs/digest/d19/tables/dt19_318.30.asp

New Zealand History. (n.d.). *Jacinda Ardern biography.* https://nzhistory.govt.nz/people/jacinda-ardern

Nielsen, S., & Huse, M. (2010). The contribution of women on boards of directors: Going beyond the surface. *Corporate Governance—An International Review, 18,* 136–148.

Nieva, V. E., & Gutek, B. A. (1981). *Women and work: A psychological perspective.* New York, NY: Praeger.

Ohlott, P. J., Ruderman, M. N., & McCauley, C. D. (1994). Gender differences in managers' developmental job experiences. *Academy of Management Journal, 37,* 46–67.

Pailhe, A., & Solaz, A. (2006). Time with children: Do fathers and mothers replace each other when one parent is unemployed? *European Journal of Population, 24,* 211–236.

Powell, G. N. (1990). One more time: Do female and male managers differ? *Academy of Management Executive, 4,* 68–75.

Powell, G. N., & Graves, L. M. (2003). *Women and men in management* (3rd ed.). Thousand Oaks, CA: SAGE.

Purdie-Vaughns, V., & Eibach, R. P. (2008). Intersectional invisibility: The distinctive advantages and disadvantages of multiple subordinate-group identities. *Sex Roles, 59*(5–6), 377–391.

Ragins, B. R., Townsend, B., & Mattis, M. (1998). Gender gap in the executive suite: CEOs and female executives report on breaking the glass ceiling. *Academy of Management Executive, 12,* 28–42.

Rosener, J. (1995). *America's competitive secret: Utilizing women as a management strategy.* New York, NY: Oxford University Press.

Rosette, A. S., Koval, C. Z., Ma, A., & Livingston, R. (2016). Race matters for women leaders: Intersectional effects on agentic deficiencies and penalties. *The Leadership Quarterly, 27*, 429–445.

Rosette, A. S., & Livingston, R. W. (2012). Failure is not an option for Black women: Effects of organizational performance on leaders with single versus dual-subordinate identities. *Journal of Experimental Social Psychology, 48*, 1162–1167.

Rudman, L. A. (1998). Self-promotion as a risk factor for women: The costs and benefits of counter-stereotypical impression management. *Journal of Personality and Social Psychology, 74*, 629–645.

Rudman, L. A., & Glick, P. (2001). Prescriptive gender stereotypes and backlash toward agentic women. *Journal of Social Issues, 57*, 743–762.

Ryan, M. K., & Haslam, S. A. (2005). The glass cliff: Evidence that women are over-represented in precarious leadership positions. *British Journal of Management, 16*, 81–90.

Ryan, M. K., Haslam, S. A., Hersby, M. D., & Bongiorno, R. (2011). Think crisis–think female: The glass cliff and contextual variation in the think manager–think male stereotype. *Journal of Applied Psychology, 96*, 470–484.

Ryan, M. K., Haslam, S. A., & Postmes, T. (2007). Reactions to the glass cliff: Gender differences in the explanations for the precariousness of women's leadership positions. *Journal of Organizational Change Management, 20*, 182–197.

Sandberg, S. (2013). *Lean in: Women, work, and the will to lead.* New York, NY: Knopf.

Schein, V. E. (2001). A global look at psychological barriers to women's progress in management. *Journal of Social Issues, 57*, 675–688.

Schwartz, M. (2019, April 10). *New Zealand passes law banning most semi-automatic weapons.* NPR. https://www.npr.org/2019/04/10/711820023/new-zealand-passes-law-banning-most-semi-automatic-weapons

Schwartz, S. H., & Rubel, T. (2005). Sex differences in value priorities: Cross-cultural and multimethod studies. *Journal of Personality and Social Psychology, 89*, 1010–1028.

Sekaquaptewa, D., & Thompson, M. (2003). Solo status, stereotype threat, and performance expectancies: Their effects on women's performance. *Journal of Experimental Social Psychology, 39*, 68–74.

Sergent, K., & Stajkovic, A. D. (2020). Women's leadership is associated with fewer deaths during the COVID-19 crisis: Quantitative and qualitative analyses of United States governors. *Journal of Applied Psychology, 105*, 771–783.

Simon, S., & Hoyt, C. L. (2013). Exploring the effect of media images on women's leadership self-perceptions and aspirations. *Group Processes & Intergroup Relations, 16*, 232–245.

Small, D. A., Gelfand, M., Babcock, L., & Gettman, H. (2007). Who goes to the bargaining table? The influence of gender and framing on the initiation of negotiation. *Journal of Personality and Social Psychology, 93*, 600–613.

Smith, A., & Stewart, A. J. (1983). Approaches to studying racism and sexism in Black women's lives. *Journal of Social Issues, 39*, 1–15.

Stangor, C., Lynch, L., Duan, C., & Glass, B. (1992). Categorization of individuals on the basis of multiple social features. *Journal of Personality and Social Psychology, 62*, 207–218.

Thoits, P. A. (1992). Identity structures and psychological well-being: Gender and marital status comparisons. *Social Psychology Quarterly, 55*, 236–256.

Tsui, A. S., & Gutek, B. A. (1984). A role set analysis of gender differences in performance, affective relationship, and career success of industrial middle managers. *Academy of Management Journal, 27*, 619–635.

Twenge, J. M. (2001). Change in women's assertiveness in response to status and roles: A cross-temporal meta-analysis, 1931–1993. *Journal of Personality and Social Psychology, 81*, 133–145.

van Engen, M. L., van der Leeden, R., & Willemsen, T. M. (2001). Gender, context and leadership styles: A field study. *Journal of Occupational and Organizational Psychology, 74*, 581–598.

van Engen, M. L., & Willemsen, T. M. (2004). Sex and leadership styles: A meta-analysis of research published in the 1990s. *Psychological Reports, 94*, 3–18.

Vinkenburg, C. J., van Engen, M. L., Eagly, A. H., & Johannesen-Schmidt, M. C. (2011). An exploration of stereotypical beliefs about leadership styles: Is transformational leadership a route to women's promotion? *The Leadership Quarterly, 22*, 10–21.

Wallenfeldt, J. (2020). Jacinda Adern. *Brittanica*. https://www.britannica.com/biography/Jacinda-Ardern/

Warner, J., Ellman, N., & Boesch, D. (2018, November, 20). *The women's leadership gap*. Center for American Progress. https://www.americanprogress.org/issues/women/reports/2018/11/20/461273/womens-leadership-gap-2/

Williams, C. L. (1992). The glass escalator: Hidden advantages for men in the "female" professions. *Social Problems, 39*, 253–267.

Williams, C. L. (1995). *Still a man's world: Men who do "women's work."* Berkeley: University of California Press.

Williams, J. (2010). *Reshaping the work-family debate: Why men and class matter*. Cambridge, MA: Harvard University Press.

Williams, R. J. (2003). Women on corporate boards of directors and their influence on corporate philanthropy. *Journal of Business Ethics, 42*, 1–10.

Wirth, L. (2001). *Breaking through the glass ceiling: Women in management*. Geneva, Switzerland: International Labour Office.

Woolley, A. W., Chabris, C. F., Pentland, A., Hashmi, N., & Malone, T. M. (2010). Evidence for a collective intelligence factor in the performance of human groups. *Science, 330*, 686–688.

Zenger, J., & Folkman, J. (2012, March 15). Are women better leaders than men? *Harvard Business Review*. https://hbr.org/2012/03/a-study-in-leadership-women-do

Zenger, J., & Folkman, J. (2019, June 25). Research: Women score higher than men in most leadership skills. *Harvard Business Review*. https://hbr.org/2019/06/research-women-score-higher-than-men-in-most-leadership-skills

CHAPTER 15

Anderson, H. J., Baur, J. E., Griffith, J. A., & Buckley, M. R. (2017). What works for you may not work for (Gen)me: Limitations of present leadership theories for the new generation. *The Leadership Quarterly, 28*(1), 245–260.

Aronson, E. (2001). Integrating leadership styles and ethical perspectives. *Canadian Journal of Administrative Sciences, 18*(4), 244–256.

Avolio, B. J., & Locke, E. E. (2002). Contrasting different philosophies of leader motivation: Altruism versus egoism. *The Leadership Quarterly, 13*, 169–191.

Baehrend, W. R., Jr. (2016). Refinement of the Ethical Leadership Style Questionnaire. Lisle, IL: Benedictine University. (Pro Quest Number 10255065)

Bass, B. M., & Steidlmeier, P. (1999). Ethics, character, and authentic transformational leadership behavior. *The Leadership Quarterly, 10*(2), 181–217.

Beauchamp, T. L., & Bowie, N. E. (1988). *Ethical theory and business* (3rd ed.). Englewood Cliffs, NJ: Prentice Hall.

Beauchamp, T. L., & Childress, J. F. (1994). *Principles of biomedical ethics* (4th ed.). New York, NY: Oxford University Press.

Bedi, A., Alpaslan, C. M., & Green, S. (2016). A meta-analytic review of ethical leadership outcomes and moderators. *Journal of Business Ethics, 139*(3), 517–536.

Block, P. (1993). *Stewardship: Choosing service over self-interest.* San Francisco, CA: Berrett-Koehler.

Bowie, N. E. (1991). Challenging the egoistic paradigm. *Business Ethics Quarterly, 1*(1), 1–21.

Brown, M. E., & Treviño, L. K. (2006). Ethical leadership: A review and future directions. *The Leadership Quarterly, 17*, 595–616.

Brown, M. E., Treviño, L. K., & Harrison, D. A. (2005). Ethical leadership: A social learning perspective for construct development and testing. *Organizational Behavior and Human Decision Processes, 97*(2), 117–134.

Burns, J. M. (1978). *Leadership.* New York, NY: Harper & Row.

Carlson, D. S., & Perrewe, P. L. (1995). Institutionalization of organizational ethics through transformational leadership. *Journal of Business Ethics, 14*(10), 829–838.

Chikeleze, M. C. (2014). Validation of the Ethical Leadership Style Questionnaire (ELSQ) (Doctoral dissertation). Lisle, IL: Benedictine University. Retrieved from ProQuest Dissertations and Theses database. (Order No. 3584797)

Chikeleze, M. C., & Baehrend, W. R. (2017). Ethical leadership style and its impact on decision-making. *Journal of Leadership Studies, 11*(2), 45–47. doi:10.1002/jls.21523

Ciulla, J. B. (1998). *Ethics, the heart of leadership.* Westport, CT: Greenwood.

Ciulla, J. B. (2001). Carving leaders from the warped wood of humanity. *Canadian Journal of Administrative Sciences, 18*(4), 313–319.

Ciulla, J. B. (2003). *The ethics of leadership.* Belmont, CA: Wadsworth/Thomson Learning.

Ciulla, J. B. (2014). *Ethics, the heart of leadership* (3rd ed.). Santa Barbara, CA: Praeger.

Conger, J. (1990). The dark side of leadership. *Organizational Dynamics, 19*, 44–55.

Cooper, H., Gibbons-Neff, T., Schmitt, E., & Cochrane, E. (2020, April 2). Navy Removes Captain of Aircraft Carrier Stricken by Coronavirus. *New York Times* (Online).

Covey, S. R. (1990). *Principle-centered leadership.* New York, NY: Fireside.

Crain, W. C. (1985). Kohlberg's stages of moral development. In W. C. Crain (Ed.), *Theories of development: Concepts and applications* (pp. 118–136). New York, NY: Prentice Hall.

Dalla Costa, J. (1998). *The ethical imperative: Why moral leadership is good business.* Reading, MA: Addison-Wesley.

Demirtas, O. (2015). Ethical leadership influence at organizations: Evidence from the field. *Journal of Business Ethics, 126*(2), 273–284.

Den Hartog, D. N. (2015). Ethical leadership. *Annual Review of Organizational Psychology and Organizational Behavior, 2*(1), 409-434.

De Pree, M. (1989). *Leadership is an art.* New York, NY: Doubleday.

Eisenbeiss, S. A. (2012). Re-thinking ethical leadership: An interdisciplinary integrative approach. *The Leadership Quarterly, 23*(5), 791–808.

Eisenbeiss, S. A., van Knippenberg, D., & Fahrbach, C. M. (2015). Doing well by doing good? Analyzing the relationship between CEO ethical leadership and firm performance. *Journal of Business Ethics, 128*(3), 635–651.

Ethics Resource Center. (2011). Generational differences in workplace ethics: A supplemental report of the 2011 National Business Ethics Survey. Retrieved

from http://www.ethics.org/research/
eci-research/nbes

Frankena, W. (1973). *Ethics* (2nd ed.).
Englewood Cliffs, NJ: Prentice Hall.

Frisch, C., & Huppenbauer, M. (2014).
New insights into ethical leadership:
A qualitative investigation of the
experiences of executive ethical leaders.
Journal of Business Ethics, 123(1), 23–43.

Gafni, M. & Garofoli, J. (2020, March 31).
Exclusive: Captain of aircraft carrier with
growing coronavirus outbreak pleads for
help from Navy. *San Francisco Chronicle.*
https://www.sfchronicle.com/bayarea/
article/Exclusive-Captain-of-aircraft-
carrier-with-15167883.php

Gibbons-Neff, T., Schmitt, E., Cooper, H.,
& Ismay, J. (2020, April 12). There will be
losses: How a captain's plea exposed a rift
in the military. *New York Times* (Online).

Gilligan, C. (1982). *In a different voice:
Psychological theory and women's development.*
Cambridge, MA: Harvard University
Press.

Gini, A. (1998). Moral leadership and
business ethics. In J. B. Ciulla (Ed.), *Ethics,
the heart of leadership* (pp. 27–46). Westport,
CT: Greenwood.

Greenleaf, R. K. (1970). *The servant as
leader.* Newton Centre, MA: Robert K.
Greenleaf Center.

Greenleaf, R. K. (1977). *Servant leadership:
A journey into the nature of legitimate power
and greatness.* New York, NY: Paulist.

Heifetz, R. A. (1994). *Leadership without
easy answers.* Cambridge, MA: Harvard
University Press.

Hoch, J. E., Bommer, W. H., Dulebohn, J. H.,
& Wu, D. (2018). Do ethical, authentic,
and servant leadership explain variance
above and beyond transformational
leadership? A meta-analysis. *Journal of
Management, 44*(2), 501–529.

Jaksa, J. A., & Pritchard, M. S. (1988).
Communication ethics: Methods of analysis.
Belmont, CA: Wadsworth.

Johnson, C. R. (2011). *Meeting the ethical
challenges of leadership* (4th ed.). Thousand
Oaks, CA: SAGE.

Johnson, C. R. (2018). *Meeting the ethical
challenges of leadership* (6th ed.). Thousand
Oaks, CA: SAGE.

Kanungo, R. N. (2001). Ethical values of
transactional and transformational leaders.
*Canadian Journal of Administrative Sciences,
18*(4), 257–265.

Kanungo, R. N., & Mendonca, M. (1996).
Ethical dimensions of leadership. Thousand
Oaks, CA: SAGE.

Kitchener, K. S. (1984). Intuition,
critical evaluation, and ethical principles:
The foundation for ethical decisions
in counseling psychology. *Counseling
Psychologist, 12*(3), 43–55.

Kohlberg, L. (1984). *Essays on moral
development, Vol. 2: The psychology of
moral development.* New York, NY:
Harper & Row.

Komives, S. R., Lucas, N., & McMahon,
T. R. (1998). *Exploring leadership: For college
students who want to make a difference.* San
Francisco, CA: Jossey-Bass.

Kouzes, J. M., & Posner, B. Z. (1995). *The
leadership challenge: How to keep getting
extraordinary things done in organizations*
(2nd ed.). San Francisco, CA: Jossey-Bass.

Kuenzi, M., Mayer, D. M., & Greenbaum,
R. L. (2019). Creating an ethical
organizational environment: The
relationship between ethical leadership,
ethical organizational climate, and
unethical behavior. *Personnel Psychology,
73*(1), 43–71.

Lawton, A. & Páez, I. (2015). Developing a
framework for ethical leadership. *Journal of
Business Ethics, 130*(3), 639–649.

Lipman-Blumen, J. (2005). *The allure
of toxic leaders.* New York, NY: Oxford
University Press.

Martinez, L. (2020, April 29). Navy
delays Crozier decision, launches broader
investigation into carrier COVID-19

outbreak. *ABC News.* https://abcnews.go
.com/Politics/navy-delays-crozier-decision-
launches-broader-investigation-carrier/
story?id=70404055

Mayer, D. M., Kuenzi, M., Greenbaum,
R. L., Bardes, M., & Salvador, R. (2009).
How low does ethical leadership flow?
Test of a trickle-down model.
*Organizational Behavior & Human
Decision Processes, 108,* 1–13.

McManus, R. M., Ward, S. J., & Perry,
A. K. (2018). *Ethical leadership: A primer.*
Northampton, MA: Elgar.

Moore, C., Mayer, D. M., Chiang, F. F. T.,
Crossley, C., Karlesky, M. J., & Birtch,
T. A. (2019). Leaders matter morally:
The role of ethical leadership in shaping
employee moral cognition and misconduct.
The Journal of Applied Psychology, 104(1),
123–145.

Ng, T. W., & Feldman, D. C. (2015).
Ethical leadership: Meta-analytic evidence
of criterion-related and incremental
validity. *Journal of Applied Psychology,
100*(3), 948–965.

Padilla, A., Hogan, R., & Kaiser, R. B.
(2007). The toxic triangle: Destructive
leaders, susceptible followers, and
conducive environments. *The Leadership
Quarterly, 18,* 176–194.

Plaisance, P. L. (2014). Virtue in media:
The moral psychology of U.S. exemplars
in news and public relationships.
*Journalism and Mass Media Quarterly,
91*(2), 308–325.

Pojman, L. P. (1995). *Ethical theory:
Classical and contemporary readings* (2nd
ed.). Belmont, CA: Wadsworth.

Price, T. (2008). *Leadership ethics: An
introduction.* New York, NY: Cambridge
University Press.

Rawls, J. (1971). *A theory of justice.* Boston,
MA: Harvard University Press.

Resick, C. J., Hanges, P. J., Dickson, M. W.,
& Mitchelson, J. K. (2006). A cross-cultural
examination of the endorsement of ethical

leadership. *Journal of Business Ethics, 63,*
345–359.

Resick C. J., Martin, G. S., Keating, M. A.,
Dickson, M. W., Kwan, H. K., & Peng, C.
(2011). What ethical leadership means
to me: Asian, American, and European
perspectives. *Journal of Business Ethics,
101*(3), 435–457.

Rost, J. C. (1991). *Leadership for the
twenty-first century.* New York, NY:
Praeger.

Schminke, M., Ambrose, M. L., & Noel,
T. W. (1997). The effect of ethical
frameworks on perceptions of
organizational justice. *Academy of
Management Journal, 40*(5), 1190–1207.

Schumann, P. L. (2001). A moral
principles framework for human resource
management ethics. *Human Resource
Management Review, 11,* 93–111.

Schyns, B., & Schilling, J. (2013). How bad
are the effects of bad leaders? A meta-
analysis of destructive leadership and its
outcomes. *The Leadership Quarterly, 24,*
138–158.

Senge, P. M. (1990). *The fifth discipline: The
art and practice of the learning organization.*
New York, NY: Doubleday.

Simkins, J. D. (2020, April 16). "Regardless
of the impact to my career"—Crozier's email
revealed, Navy won't rule out reinstatement.
Navy Times. https://www.navytimes.com/
news/your-navy/2020/04/16/regardless-of-
the-impact-to-my-career-croziers-email-
revealed-navy-wont-rule-out-reinstatement/

Singh, N., Sengupta, S., & Dev, S.
(2017). Toxicity in leadership: Exploring
its dimensions in the Indian context.
*International Journal of Management
Practice, 10*(2), 109.

Thiel, C. E., Hardy, J. H., Peterson, D. R.,
Welsh, D., & Bonner, J. M. (2018).
Too many sheep in the flock? Span of
control attenuates the influence of ethical
leadership. *Journal of Applied Psychology,
103*(12), 1324–1334.

Treviño, L. K. (1986). Ethical decision making in organizations: A person–situation interactionist model. *Academy of Management Review, 11*(3), 601–617.

Treviño, L. K., Brown, M., & Hartman, L. P. (2003). A qualitative investigation of perceived executive ethical leadership: Perceptions from inside and outside the executive suite. *Human Relations, 56*(1), 5–37.

Velasquez, M. G. (1992). *Business ethics: Concepts and cases* (3rd ed.). Englewood Cliffs, NJ: Prentice Hall.

Wang, Z., Xu, H., & Liu, Y. (2018). How does ethical leadership trickle down? Test of an integrative dual-process model. *Journal of Business Ethics, 153*(3), 691–705.

Wayne, L. (2009, May 29). A promise to be ethical in an era of immorality. *The New York Times.* Retrieved from http://www.nytimes.com/2009/05/30/business/30oath.html

Wilson, S., & McCalman, J. (2017). Re-imagining ethical leadership as leadership for the greater good. *European Management Journal, 35*(2), 151–154.

Xu, A. J., Loi, R., & Ngo, H. (2016). Ethical leadership behavior and employee justice perceptions: The mediating role of trust in organization. *Journal of Business Ethics, 134*(3), 493–504.

Yang, C. (2014). Does ethical leadership lead to happy workers? A study on the impact of ethical leadership, subjective well-being, and life happiness in the Chinese culture. *Journal of Business Ethics, 123*(3), 513–525.

Yukl, G., Mahsud, R., Hassan, S., & Prussia, G. E. (2013). An improved measure of ethical leadership. *Journal of Leadership & Organizational Studies, 20*(1), 38.

Ziesulewicz, G. (2020, May 5). Fired Theodore Roosevelt commander Brett Crozier reassigned to San Diego. *NavyTimes.* https://www.navytimes.com/news/your-navy/2020/05/05/fired-tr-commander-reassigned-to-san-diego/

CHAPTER 16

Aime, F., Humphrey, S., DeRue, D. S., & Paul, J. B. (2014). The riddle of heterarchy: Power transitions in cross-functional teams. *Academy of Management Journal, 57*(2), 327–352.

Amos, B., & Klimoski, R. J. (2014). Courage: Making teamwork work well. *Group & Organizational Management, 39*(1), 110–128.

Ancona, D., Bresman, H., & Caldwell, D. (2009). The X-factor: Six steps to leading high-performing X-teams. *Organizational Dynamics, 38*(3), 217–224.

Barge, J. K. (1996). Leadership skills and the dialectics of leadership in group decision making. In R. Y. Hirokawa & M. S. Poole (Eds.), *Communication and group decision making* (2nd ed., pp. 301–342). Thousand Oaks, CA: SAGE.

Bergman, J. Z., Rentsch, J. R., Small, E. E., Davenport, S. W., & Bergman, S. M. (2012). The shared leadership process in decision-making teams. *The Journal of Social Psychology, 152*(1), 17–42.

Bernstein, R. (2006). *America's coach: Life lessons and wisdom for gold medal success: A biographical journey of the late hockey icon Herb Brooks.* New Brighton, MN: Bernstein Books.

Berry, G. R. (2011). Enhancing effectiveness on virtual teams: Understanding why traditional team skills are insufficient. *Journal of Business Communication, 48*(2), 186–206.

Breuer, C., Hüffmeier, J., & Hertel, G. (2016). Does trust matter more in virtual teams? A meta-analysis of trust and team effectiveness considering virtuality and documentation as moderators. *Journal of Applied Psychology, 101*(8), 1151–1177.

Brown, J. (2014). *"Miracle" players recall Herb Brooks as gruff, great.* NHL. https://www.nhl.com/news/miracle-players-recall-herb-brooks-as-gruff-great/c-704235

Burke, C. S., Stagl, K. C., Klein, C., Goodwin, G. F., Salas, E., & Halpin, S. M. (2006). What type of leadership behaviors are functional in teams? A meta-analysis. *The Leadership Quarterly, 17*, 288–307.

Cobb, A. T. (2012). *Leading project teams: The basics of project management and team leadership* (2nd ed.). Thousand Oaks, CA: SAGE.

Coffey, W. (2005). *The boys of winter: The untold story of a coach, a dream and the 1980 U.S. Olympic hockey team.* New York, NY: Crown.

Cook, A. S., Zill, A., & Meyer, B. (2020, April). Observing leadership as behavior in teams and herds—An ethological approach to shared leadership research. *The Leadership Quarterly, 31*(2), 101296. https://doi.org/10.1016/j.leaqua.2019.05.003

Cordery, J., Soo, C., Kirkman, B., Rosen, B., & Mathieu, J. (2009). Leading parallel global virtual teams: Lessons from Alcoa. *Organizational Dynamics, 38*(3), 204–216.

Day, D. V., Gronn, P., & Salas, E. (2004). Leadership capacity in teams. *The Leadership Quarterly, 15*, 857–880.

D'Innocenzo, L., Mathieu, J. E., & Kukenberger, M. R. (2016). A meta-analysis of different forms of shared leadership–team performance relations. *Journal of Management, 42*(7), 1964–1991.

Drecksel, G. L. (1991). Leadership research: Some issues. *Communication Yearbook, 14*, 535–546.

Drescher, G., & Garbers, Y. (2016). Shared leadership and commonality: A policy-capturing study. *The Leadership Quarterly, 27*, 200–217.

Dyer, W. G., Dyer, W. G., Jr., & Dyer, J. H. (2007). *Team building: Proven strategies for improving team performance* (4th ed.). San Francisco, CA: Jossey-Bass.

Fisher, B. A. (1985, May). Leadership as medium: Treating complexity in group communication research. *Small Group Behavior, 16*(2), 167–196.

Fleishman, E. A., Mumford, M. D., Zaccaro, S. J., Levin, K. Y., Korotkin, A. L., & Hein, M. B. (1991). Taxonomic efforts in the description of leader behavior: A synthesis and functional interpretation. *The Leadership Quarterly, 2*(4), 245–287.

Friedrich, T. L., Griffith, J. A., & Mumford, M. D. (2016). Collective leadership behaviors: Evaluating the leader, team network, and problem situation characteristics that influence their use. *The Leadership Quarterly, 27*(2), 312–333.

Gouran, D. S., & Hirokawa, R. Y. (1996). Functional theory and communication in decision-making and problem-solving groups: An expanded view. In R. Y. Hirokawa & M. D. Poole (Eds.), *Communication and group decision making* (2nd ed., pp. 55–80). Thousand Oaks, CA: SAGE.

Hackman, J. R. (1990). Work teams in organizations: An orienting framework. In J. R. Hackman (Ed.), *Groups that work (and those that don't): Creating conditions for effective teamwork* (pp. 1–14). San Francisco, CA: Jossey-Bass.

Hackman, J. R. (2002). *Leading teams: Setting the stage for great performances.* Boston, MA: Harvard Business School Press.

Hackman, J. R. (2012). From causes to conditions in group research. *Journal of Organizational Behavior, 33*, 428–444.

Hackman, J. R., & Walton, R. E. (1986). Leading groups in organizations. In P. S. Goodman & Associates (Eds.), *Designing effective work groups* (pp. 72–119). San Francisco, CA: Jossey-Bass.

Han, S. J., & Beyerlein, M. (2016). Framing the effects of multinational cultural diversity on virtual team processes. *Small Group Research, 47*(4), 351–383.

Herb Brooks Foundation. (n.d.). *About Coach Brooks.* https://www.herbbrooksfoundation.com/coachbrooks

Hill, N. S., & Bartol, K. M. (2016). Empowering leadership and effective collaboration in geographically dispersed teams. *Personnel Psychology, 69*, 159–198.

Hoch, J. E., & Kozlowski, W. J. (2014). Leading virtual teams: Hierarchical leadership, structural supports, and shared team leadership. *Journal of Applied Psychology, 99*(3), 390–403.

Hughes, R. L., Ginnett, R. C., & Curphy, G. J. (1993). *Leadership: Enhancing the lessons of experience.* Homewood, IL: Irwin.

Humbley, L. A., O'Neill, T. A., & Kline, T. J. B. (2009). Virtual team leadership: Perspectives for the field. In N. Kock (Ed.), *Virtual team leadership and collaborative engineering advancements: Contemporary issues and implications* (pp. 84–104). Hershey, NY: Information Science Reference.

Hyatt, D. E., & Ruddy, T. M. (1997). An examination of the relationship between work group characteristics and performance: Once more into the breach. *Personnel Psychology, 50*, 553–585.

Ilgen, D. R., Hollenbeck, J. R., Johnson, M., & Jundt, D. (2005). Teams in organizations: From input–process–output models to IMOI models. *Annual Review of Psychology, 56*, 517–543.

Ilgen, D. R., Major, D. A., Hollenbeck, J. R., & Sego, D. J. (1993). Team research in the 1990s. In M. M. Chemers & R. Ayman (Eds.), *Leadership theory and research: Perspectives and directions* (pp. 245–270). San Diego, CA: Academic Press.

Katzenbach, J. R., & Smith, D. K. (2008). *The discipline of teams.* Boston, MA: Harvard Business Press.

Kinlaw, D. C. (1998). *Superior teams: What they are and how to develop them.* Hampshire, UK: Grove.

Kozlowski, S. W. J., Watola, D. J., Jensen, J. M., Kim, B. H., & Botero, I. C. (2009). Developing adaptive teams: A theory of dynamic team leadership. In E. Salas, G. F. Goodwin, & C. S. Burke (Eds.), *Team effectiveness in complex organizations:*

Cross-disciplinary perspectives and approaches (pp. 113–155). New York, NY: Taylor & Francis Group.

LaFasto, F. M. J., & Larson, C. E. (1987). *Team Excellence Survey.* Denver, CO: Author.

LaFasto, F. M. J., & Larson, C. E. (1996). *Collaborative Team Leader Instrument.* Denver, CO: Author.

LaFasto, F. M. J., & Larson, C. E. (2001). *When teams work best: 6,000 team members and leaders tell what it takes to succeed.* Thousand Oaks, CA: SAGE.

Lapin, A. (2015, January 22). *The tale of the hockey players for whom 1980 was no miracle on ice.* NPR. https://www.npr.org/2015/01/22/378609166/the-tale-of-the-hockey-players-for-whom-1980-was-no-miracle-on-ice

Larson, C. E., & LaFasto, F. M. J. (1989). *Teamwork: What must go right/what can go wrong.* Newbury Park, CA: SAGE.

Lencioni, P. (2005). *Overcoming the five dysfunctions of a team: A field guide for leaders, managers, and facilitators.* San Francisco, CA: Jossey-Bass.

Leslie, J., & Hoole, E. (2018). *Leading virtual teams.* Center for Creative Leadership. https://www.ccl.org/articles/white-papers/how-to-lead-virtual-teams/

Levi, D. (2011). *Group dynamics for teams.* Thousand Oaks, CA: SAGE.

Mankin, D., Cohen, S. G., & Bikson, T. K. (1996). *Teams and technology.* Boston, MA: Harvard Business School Press.

Morgeson, F. P., DeRue, D. S., & Karam, E. P. (2010). Leadership in teams: A functional approach to understanding leadership structures and processes. *Journal of Management, 36*(1), 5–39.

Muethel, M., Gehrlein, S., & Hoegl, M. (2012). Socio-demographic factors and shared leadership behaviors in dispersed teams: Implications for human resource management. *Human Resource Management, 51*(4), 525–548.

Nadler, D. A. (1998). Executive team effectiveness: Teamwork at the top. In D. A. Nadler & J. L. Spencer (Eds.), *Executive teams* (pp. 21–39). San Francisco, CA: Jossey-Bass.

Neck, C. P., & Manz, C. C. (1994). From groupthink to teamthink: Toward the creation of constructive thought patterns in self-managing work teams. *Human Relations, 47*(8), 929–952.

Parker, G. M. (1990). *Team players and teamwork.* San Francisco, CA: Jossey-Bass.

Paul, R., Drake, J. R., & Liang, H. (2016). Global virtual team performance: The effect of coordination effectiveness, trust, and team cohesion. *IEEE Transactions on Professional Communication, 59*(3), 186–202.

Pauleen, D. J. (2004). An inductively derived model of leader-initiated relationship building with virtual team members. *Journal of Management Information Systems, 20*(3), 227–256.

Pearce, C. L., Manz, C. C., & Sims, H. P. (2009). Where do we go from here? Is shared leadership the key to team success? *Organizational Dynamics, 38*(3), 234–238.

Porter, G., & Beyerlein, M. (2000). Historic roots of team theory and practice. In M. M. Beyerlein (Ed.), *Work teams: Past, present and future* (pp. 3–24). Dordrecht, Netherlands: Kluwer.

Salas, E., Burke, C. S., & Stagl, D. C. (2004). Developing teams and team leaders: Strategies and principles. In D. V. Day, S. J. Zaccaro, & S. M. Halpin (Eds.), *Leader development for transforming organizations: Growing leaders for tomorrow* (pp. 325–355). Mahwah, NJ: Erlbaum.

Salas, E., Dinh, J., & Reyes, D. (2019). What makes a good team leader? *The Journal of Character & Leadership Development, 6*(1), 88–100.

Schmidt, G. B. (2014). Virtual leadership: An important leadership context. *Industrial and Organizational Psychology, 7*(2), 182–187.

Schouten, A. P., van den Hooff, B., & Feldberg, F. (2016). Virtual teamwork. *Communication Research, 43*(2), 180–210.

Scott, M. E. (2013). "Communicate through the roof": A case study analysis of the communicative rules and resources of an effective global virtual team. *Communication Quarterly, 61*(3), 301–318.

Shevchenko, N. (2018, May 2). *The fearsome Red Machine: The meteoric rise and dramatic decline of Soviet hockey.* Russia Beyond. https://www.rbth.com/history/328171-rise-and-fall-soviet-hockey

Shuffler, M. L., & Carter, D. R. (2018). Teamwork situated in multiteam systems: Key lessons learned and future opportunities. *American Psychologist, 73*(4), 390–406.

Solansky, S. T. (2008). Leadership style and team processes in self-managed teams. *Journal of Leadership and Organizational Studies, 14*(4), 332–341.

Stagl, K. C., Salas, E., & Burke, C. S. (2007). Best practices in team leadership: What team leaders do to facilitate team effectiveness. In J. A. Conger & R. E. Riggio (Eds.), *The practice of leadership: Developing the next generation of leaders* (pp. 172–197). San Francisco, CA: Jossey-Bass.

Stewart, G. L., & Manz, C. C. (1995). Leadership for self-managing work teams: A typology and integrative model. *Human Relations, 48*(7), 747–770.

Thomas, G., Martin, R., & Riggio, R. E. (2013). Leading groups: Leadership as a group process. *Group Processes and Intergroup Relations, 16*(1), 3–16.

Timetoast. (n.d.). *1980 USA hockey team wins gold.* https://www.timetoast.com/timelines/1980-usa-olympic-hockey-team-wins-gold

Tuckman, B. W., & Jensen, M. A. C. (2010). Stages of small-group development revisited. *Group Facilitation: A Research and Applications Journal, 10*, 43–48.

Wageman, R., Fisher, C. M., & Hackman, J. R. (2009). Leading teams when the time is right: Finding the best moments to act. *Organizational Dynamics, 38*(3), 192–203.

Wageman, R., Gardner, H., & Mortensen, M. (2012). The changing ecology of teams: New directions for teams research. *Journal of Organizational Behavior, 33*, 301–315.

Wang, D., Waldman, D. A., & Zhang, Z. (2014). A meta-analysis of shared leadership and team effectiveness. *Journal of Applied Psychology, 99*(2), 181–198.

Zaccaro, S. J., Ardison, S. D., & Orvis, K. L. (2004). Leadership in virtual teams. In D. V. Day, S. J. Zaccaro, & S. M. Halpin (Eds.), *Leader development for transforming organizations: Growing leaders for tomorrow* (pp. 267–292). Mahwah, NJ: Erlbaum.

Zaccaro, S. J., Heinen, B., & Shuffler, M. (2009). Team leadership and team effectiveness. In E. Salas, G. F. Goodwin, & C. S. Burke (Eds.), *Team effectiveness in complex organizations: Cross-disciplinary perspectives and approaches* (pp. 83–111). New York, NY: Taylor & Francis Group.

Zaccaro, S. J., Rittman, A. L., & Marks, M. A. (2001). Team leadership. *The Leadership Quarterly, 12*, 451–483.

Author Index

Subject Index

LMX-MDM, 171
mature partnership phase,
163–164
overview, 157–158
quality of, 160–162
stranger phase, 162–163
VDL theory, 158–160, 169
working of, 166–167
Leadership (Burns), 15, 186
Leadership (Hughes, Ginnett
& Curphy), 374
Leadership Behavior
Questionnaire, 104–106
Leadership Grid, 87–90,
89 (figure), 96, 104
Leadership Practices
Inventory (LPI), 201
Leadership styles
authority–compliance
management, 88
coaching, 110
country-club
management, 88
delegating, 111
development level of
followers and, 113
high directive–high
supportive, 110
high directive–low
supportive, 110
high–high style, 95
high supportive–low
directive, 110
impoverished
management, 88
low supportive–low
directive, 111
middle-of-the-road
management, 89
supporting, 110
team management, 90
Leadership Trait
Questionnaire (LTQ),
51–53
*Leadership Without Easy
Answers* (Heifetz),
285, 304
Legitimate power, 11 (table)
Listening attribute, 255
LMX-7, 171, 180–182
LMX theory. *See* Leader–
member exchange
(LMX) theory

Long, J., 365
Low supportive–low
directive leadership
style, 111
LPI. *See* Leadership Practices
Inventory (LPI)
LTQ. *See* Leadership Trait
Questionnaire (LTQ)

Machiavelli, N., 14
Management
authority–compliance, 88
country-club, 88
exception, by, 196
functions of, 17 (figure)
impoverished, 88
leadership and, 16–18
middle-of-the-road, 89
skills, 58 (figure)
team, 90
Managerial Grid, 87–90,
94, 96
Mandela, N., 14, 193, 224
Marin, S., 394
Marlboro College,
312–314
Marshall, B., 341–344
Martin, R., 379–381
Martinez, R., 113–114
Maslow, A., 430
Maternalism, 90, 90 (figure)
Mayer-Salovey-Caruso
Emotional Intelligence
Test (MSCEIT), 38
McQueary, M., 384–385
Meaning, strengths about,
37 (table)
Measurement. *See*
Assessment
Merkel, A., 394
Metrocity Striders Track
Club (MSTC), 120
Metts, K., 45–46
Middle-of-the-road
management, 89,
89 (figure)
Milošević, S., 369
Minnesota Multiphasic
Personality Inventory, 51
MLQ. *See* Multifactor
Leadership
Questionnaire (MLQ)
Moral conduct, 426

Moral development, stages
of, 423, 424 (table)
conventional morality,
424–425
postconventional
morality, 425
preconventional morality,
423–424
Morality, leadership and,
13–16
Moral process, leadership as,
15–16
Moral reasoning, 230
Mother Teresa, 14,
265–266, 427
Motivation, 61–62, 132–133
expectancy theory of,
133–134, 141, 143
inspirational, 193
MSCEIT. *See* Mayer-
Salovey-Caruso
Emotional Intelligence
Test (MSCEIT)
Multifactor Leadership
Questionnaire (MLQ),
197, 206
Multi-team systems
(MTSs), 480
Musk, E., 47–50
Myers-Briggs Type
Indicator, 51

Nelson, P., 46–47
Neuroticism, 35 (table)
Neutral process, leadership
as, 14–15
"New Leadership"
paradigm, 185
Nixon, R., 439
Noncoercive influence, 4 (box)
Norms, 295

Obama, B., 28
O'Brien, M., 310
Ohio State behavior study,
85–86
Openness, 35 (table)
Opportunism, 90–91,
91 (figure)
Optimal distinctiveness
theory, 325
Optimism, 229
Out-group, 159–160

Made in the USA
Monee, IL
30 August 2021

76921228R00331